T0347378

Disciplinary Approaches to Aging

General Editor

Donna Lind Infeld, Ph. D.
George Washington Univesity

A ROUTLEDGE SERIES

Contents of the Collection

Disciplinary Approaches to Aging

Volume 4
Anthropology of Aging

Edited with introductions by

Donna Lind Infeld, Ph. D.
George Washington University

 Routledge
Taylor & Francis Group

NEW YORK AND LONDON

First published by Garland Publishing, Inc.

This edition published 2013 by Routledge

Routledge   Routledge
711 Third Avenue   2 Park Square, Milton Park
New York   Abingdon
NY 10017   Oxon, OX14 4RN

Routledge is an imprint of the Taylor & Francis Group, an informa business

10 9 8 7 6 5 4 3 2 1

Library of Congress Cataloging-in-Publication Data

Disciplinary approaches toward aging / edited with introductions by Donna Lind Infeld.
     p. cm.
     Includes bibliographical references.
     Contents: v. 1. Biology of aging—v. 2. Psychology of aging—v. 3. Sociology of aging—v. 4. Anthropology of aging—v. 5. Economics of aging—v. 6. Politics, policy, aging.
ISBN 0-415-93895-3 (set : alk paper)—ISBN 0-415-93896-1 (vol. 1 : alk. paper) — ISBN 0-415-93897-X (vol. 2 : alk. paper)—ISBN 0-415-93898-8 (vol. 3 : alk. paper)—ISBN 0-415-93899-6 (vol. 4 : alk. paper)—ISBN 0-415-93900-3 (vol. 5 : alk. paper)—ISBN 0-415-93901-1 (vol. 6 : alk. paper)
     1. Gerontology. 2. Aged. 3. Aging. I. Infeld, Donna Lind.
HQ1061.D557 2002
305.26—dc21   2002020627

SET ISBN 9780415938952
POD ISBN 9780415870665
     Vol1 9780415938969
     Vol2 9780415938976
     Vol3 9780415938983
     Vol4 9780415938990
     Vol5 9780415939003
     Vol6 9780415939010

Contents

Medical Anthropology

Biological and Physical Anthropology

Series Introduction

Life expectancy around the world has been increasing dramatically over the last several decades. Global average life expectancy has now reached 66 years (U.N. 2000). This trend has resulted in a large, and still growing, elderly population. There are currently well over 550 million people in the world who are over age 60, and this number is expected to approach 1.2 billion by 2025 (AoA 1998).

Increasing longevity is a result of numerous factors. Chief among them are improved nutrition and sanitation, higher levels of healthy behaviors (e.g., reduced smoking), and improved medical care. Underlying these changes at the population level are higher levels of education, income, and knowledge about health, trends that are continuing to spread throughout the world.

However, this lengthening life expectancy and increasing size of the older population is not occurring evenly. In more developed regions of the world, including Europe, Northern America, Australia/New Zealand and Japan, the 14 percent of the population that was 65 or older in 2000 is expected to increase to 19 percent by 2020 (U.N. 2001). Life expectancy in the United States, now 76.9 years, is almost 30 years longer than it was in 1900 (AoA 2001). The age group 65 and over makes up over 12 percent U.S. of the population and is expected to increase to 20 percent by 2030 (Ibid). One way I like to represent this proportion to students is to compare it to the current 17.6 percent of the population of Florida that is age 65 and older. In other words, there will be a greater proportion of older people throughout the United States than currently live in Florida. If you have ever visited Florida, you will understand why this is hard to comprehend.

In less developed regions of the world, including Africa, Asia (excluding Japan), Latin America, the Caribbean, Melanesia, Micronesia and Polynesia, the growth rate of the elderly population is even greater than it is in more developed regions. The projected increase of people over age 60 is from 5 percent in 2000 to over 7 percent by 2020 (ibid.). This is increase of two percentage points represents a faster rate of growth than that occurring in the more developed parts of the world.

In addition to the growth of the older population, the older population itself is getting older. The oldest old population (age 80 and older) is growing at an even faster rate than the young-old (age 60–79), with an increase of the 60 and older age group worldwide from 11 percent to 19 percent projected for 2050 (U.N. 2000).

These numbers are so large and changing so rapidly that the consequences to societies and to individuals' lives are almost impossible to comprehend. Gerontology, the study of aging, is the field that attempts to undertake this daunting task. Further extension of the life span, and more importantly adding quality to the added years, will be based on our knowledge of the multi-faceted components of aging. These components include new levels of understanding and intervention in the normal processes of aging (biology), mood, morale, and life-satisfaction (psychology), productive and rewarding roles in retirement and widowhood (sociology), cultural norms and supports for aging members of communities (anthropology), distribution of resources, particularly income opportunities for retired persons (economics) and the ability to shape public policy to assure equity of access to public resources (political science). These challenges are at the core of the disciplines that contribute to the field of gerontology.

GERONTOLOGY

The term gerontology is based on the Greek word *geron*, which means old men. It is the field that involves the study of the many dimensions of aging. It is a relatively young field. The Gerontological Society of America, the primary American organization devoted to promoting the scientific study of aging, was founded in 1945, and the behavioral and social sciences section was established in 1956 (www.geron.org/history.htm). Since the 1960s, the study of aging has grown dramatically and there has been extensive theoretical development and growing research applying a wide range of disciplinary approaches to examining the phenomenon of aging.

Gerontology is a multidisciplinary field. Numerous disciplines are interested in and make unique contributions to understanding aging. What is less clear is the extent to which gerontology can be considered interdisciplinary, that is reflecting integration among disciplines in the study of aging. While some studies have interdisciplinary research questions and methods, most research on age-related topics continues to be either disciplinary or multidisciplinary. In other words, research is generally grounded in a single discipline or else involves a team of researchers exploring a range of discipline-based issues. However, in some cases it achieves significant integration of theoretical concepts and approaches within an individual study.

I come from a multidisciplinary gerontological background. My aging career started with support from the Administration on Aging as an undergraduate trainee at Portland State University. My degree was in Psychology with a minor in Sociology. My doctoral work at the Florence Heller

Graduate School for Advanced Studies of Social Welfare at Brandeis University continued this multidisciplinary approach involving coursework in economics and political science as well as continued work in gerontology.

In the twenty-five years since completing my formal education, my professional positions have involved teaching aging courses to students in the applied fields of health services management and policy, public health, and public administration. As a result of this education and these academic settings, I view my background as strong on breadth and short on depth in the basic disciplines that contribute to understanding aging. This lack of depth was a motivating factor for creating this anthology. In preparing for classes in my gerontology overview course I found myself trying to stay up to date with the latest disciplinary work in numerous fields. It was my goal to produce a set of publications to help faculty members and other professionals in the field of aging to keep abreast of these developments.

DEVELOPMENT OF THE ANTHOLOGY

The series is designed to provide an integrated set of foundational articles from the primary disciplines interested in the study of aging. Each volume includes articles that provide an historical overview of theoretical perspectives in that discipline. Each volume also explores major concepts and issues within the discipline, highlights recent research findings, and provides directions for future research

I decided to organize this anthology along traditional disciplinary lines for two reasons. First, most academic training in gerontology continues to be organized along disciplinary lines. Thus, disciplinary-based readings can be more easily integrated into courses and training. Second, despite the inter/multidisciplinary nature of much research in aging, most theoretical developments continue to emerge from disciplinary homes.

University courses and textbooks about aging can be found in all major academic disciplines. According to the Association for Gerontology in Higher Education, there are more than 500 campuses in the United States that offer aging courses in more than 30 disciplines and fields of study (www.aghe.org/natdbase.htm). For example, The University of Southern California, arguably among the most extensive gerontology programs in the United States, offers 37 undergraduate and 35 graduate courses thorough its Leonard Davis School of Gerontology. Disciplines represented include biology, physiology, psychology, sociology, demography, policy, and ethics (www.usc.edu/dept/gero/ldsg/index.htm).

In addition to these traditional disciplinary approaches, numerous professional fields offer courses related to aging, many of which are grounded on disciplinary theories and applied research. Training in fields such as social work, nursing, counseling, recreation therapy, and health care administration depend on the multi-disciplinary literature on aging. Further, international attention to aging is expanding rapidly. As a result there is broad and growing demand for accessible and coherent gerontological literature.

This six-volume anthology on Disciplinary Approaches to Aging is designed to help respond to the need for more gerontological literature. The volumes include 1) Biology, 2) Psychology, 3) Anthropology, 4) Sociology, 5) Economics, and 6) Political Science. The series draws from a wide array of published sources from the United States and around the world. While most articles were selected from academic journals, a broad range of sources was reviewed including professional publications, book chapters, web sites and government reports and documents.

The process of searching for articles was complex and varied across the disciplines. The criteria I used in making selections were:

Overview or review articles rather than reports of single research studies

My goal was to provide articles that would bring readers up to date with current developments in each discipline. Review articles were easier to identify in biology because several medical literature databases provide a search option for them. In each of the other disciplines I had to look through hundreds of abstracts and articles to identify those that provide a broad overview of the topic or field.

Recent publication

Almost all of the articles were published within the last five years, with the large majority less than two years old. Recent publication supports the anthology's objective of focusing on *current* developments in each discipline.

Broadest possible array of authors and publications

In several disciplines I could have produced a whole volume from articles published in a single journal or written by a single author. However, my objective was to represent the widest possible range of publications that address issues of aging. Therefore, no authors or publications have more than one article in any volume of the anthology.

Inclusion of publications from around the world

Priority was given to articles that contribute to the understanding of current *international* theoretical and research developments contributing to disciplinary approaches to aging as part of the effort to represent the breadth of the field.

With these criteria in mind, I applied multiple search engines and databases, focusing first on the academic and professional journals they catalogue. I started with broad terms (e.g., anthropology and aging/old age/aged/elderly) but also searched a range of subtopics (culture, ethnography, etc.). For some of the volumes there was ample material identified using these steps. Next I had to make difficult choices, again using the criteria identified above. For several volumes the initial search processes did not provide adequate coverage of work in the discipline. I then turned to other sources such as the web and book chapters to round out the coverage.

Despite these efforts, I know that there are some gaps in the selections included here. When I was overwhelmed with the choices and decisions, I tried to keep in mind the overall goal of creating a resource for faculty and other professionals to use to provide the basis for developing and updating lectures in a wide range of aging-related courses. To supplement the readings, a list of additional references is provided in each volume to direct readers to additional resources and recent examples of research conducted in that field.

The multi-disciplinary nature of aging research and theory presented a particular challenge when sorting and organizing the articles into discipline-specific volumes. Not only do many major research studies include, for example, psychological as well as sociological and economic data, but concepts often cut across disciplinary lines as well. Concepts such as norms and roles, whose homes are in sociology, are also prevalent in psychological and anthropological research. Further, it was not always easy to decide where to place an article when a sociologist was publishing in an anthropological journal or visa versa. And, of course, research in social psychology belongs in both sociology and psychology. The most significant area of overlap was between economics and political science, more specifically, public policy. In fact much of the economic research on aging could have been just as appropriately considered to be public policy research. Despite these challenges, I feel the resulting compilation meets the goal of being a collection of articles that captures the major issues, concepts, and research directions of each disciplinary field.

As I struggled with making the many decisions involved in producing this anthology, it became painfully clear that knowledge simply does not fit into neat and distinct boxes. Thanks to Mark Georgiev, Associate Editor at Routledge, who reminded me that there is no perfect anthology. Without his support, encouragement, and prompting this project would not have been completed. My thanks also go to Lauren Block who tried to make the product as perfect as possible. Her help was invaluable throughout every step. Thanks also to Marcel and Amanda for their never-ending love and support. In the end, producing *Disciplinary Approaches to Aging* was an education for me and I hope it will be a useful resource for my colleagues around the world.

Donna Lind Infeld, Ph.D.

REFERENCES

Administration on Aging (November 9, 1998). International Activities of the Administration on Aging. Retrieved March 4, 2002 from *http://www.aoa.gov/Factsheets/international.html.*

Administration on Aging (December 21, 2001). A Profile of Older Americans: 2001. Retrieved March 4, 2002, from *http://www.aoa.gov/aoa/STATS/profile/profile.pdf.*

Association for Gerontology in Higher Education. Retrieved April 1, 2002, from *http://www.aghe.org/natdbase.thm.*

Gerontological Society of America. Retrieved April 1, 2002, from *http://www.geron.org/history.htm.*

United Nations/Division for Social Policy Development, (May 24, 2000). The Aging of the World Population. Retrieved March 4, 2002, from *http://www.un.org/esa/socdev/ageing/agewpop.htm.*

United Nations, Population Division (2001). Population Division of the Department of Economic and Social Affairs of the United Nations Secretariat, World Population Prospects: The 2000 Revision. Retrieved March 4, 2002, from *http://esa.un.org/unpp/index.asp?Panel=3*

University of Southern California. Leonard Davis School of Gerontology. Retrieved April 2, 2002, from *http://usc.edu/dept/gero/ldsg/index.htm.*

Volume Introduction

The word anthropology comes from the Greek words *anthropos* (human being) and *logia* (science). Thus it is the scientific study of humankind. Some argue that sociology, psychology, and other social sciences also entail the scientific study of humankind. However, unlike other social sciences, which focus narrowly on one segment of human behavior, anthropology covers the broad array of human and social behaviors from our earliest beginnings. "Of all the sciences—such as biology, psychology, and sociology—only anthropology attempts to study the entire human condition over time and space." (Smithsonian Institution 2002). Thus, anthropology looks at the full range, from physical to social behaviors, of humans throughout history and across cultures.

There are several branches within the discipline of anthropology. These include social or cultural anthropology (including, for example cultural ecology and cultural materialism, feminist anthropology, cognitive anthropology, applied anthropology, psychological anthropology, medical anthropology, urban anthropology, and anthropology of religion), linguistic anthropology, physical or biological anthropology, and archeology. Each of these branches can involve studying an individual group or culture or comparing multiple groups or cultures to contrast different approaches to specific human behaviors of interest. This comparative approach is fundamental to explorations in cultural anthropology

Ethnography, the dominant methodological approach in cultural anthropology, involves field studies designed to provide holistic, contextual, and comparative data upon which to build and evaluate theory.

In some social sciences, it common for research to introduce an intervention designed to change behaviors, outcomes, or improve social conditions. With the exception of "applied anthropology," the goal of this discipline is to understand the behaviors rather than to manipulate them. As a result, anthropology can be seen more of an observational social science, accepting things as they are.

I must admit that anthropology was the biggest 'stretch' for me, having the least formal education in this discipline compared to the others included in this anthology. However, I felt it was important to include it to help give anthropology the attention that it deserves in the study of aging. As a result of my limited background, I had the most difficulty getting a clear focus on this discipline. Therefore, I was comforted to read the following statement: "Anthropology is, at once, both easy to define but difficult to describe; its subject matter is both exotic and commonplace; its focus both sweeping and microscopic" (University of Louisville 2002).

As I searched for theories to use as organizing themes in this volume, I found philosophical theories, such as relativism and functionalism, social/biological theories such as evolution, and economic theories such as Marxism. Even the definition used by the British journal *Anthropological Theory* did not help me identify uniquely anthropological theories that might inform the study of aging. That journal publishes articles "engaging with a variety of theoretical debates in areas including: Marxism, feminism, political philosophy, historical sociology, hermeneutics, critical theory, philosophy of science, cultural studies, and psychoanalysis" (Anthropological Theory 2002). In other words, I found that anthropology is so broad that it incorporates theories from a range of other disciplines, rather than having a narrower set of its own.

Key concepts in anthropology are clearer and easier to define than its theories. For example, one concept of central importance is culture. Broadly viewed, culture incorporates all characteristics of a particularly form or group of human life. More narrowly, it focuses on a system of values of a particularly human group. Clearly aging, old age, and the status of the elderly are all affected by the norms and values of the culture in which they occur. Therefore, it is not surprising that, "An increasing share of anthropological research is focusing on concepts of age (Fry 1999). This sub-field is referred to as geroanthropology.

ANTHROPOLOGY AND AGING

Anthropology comes into clearest focus when looking at specific research. For example, Project AGE (Keith et al. 1994) provided a major contribution to our understanding of aging and culture. For ten years, a team of anthropologists conducted cross-cultural comparisons in seven sites in Botswana, Ireland, Hong Kong, and the United States. The study focused on age as a structural feature as society and on the life experiences of older persons by examining well-being, life course, political economy, and health and functionality. Specifically, the research questions explored were:

> What is defined as a good life for older people, and by older people, in different social and cultural settings?
>
> How are older people's lives affected by broad characteristics of their social environment?
>
> How are the influences of these social characteristics mediated by cultural norms and values?

How are the implications of health or functionality shaped by attributes of the social and cultural context? (1994, xvii)

These questions continue to be explored in research presented in the articles in this anthology. As a foundation, the volume begins with two overview chapters that provide a general understanding of the scope and tools used in geroanthropology. The first, "The Anthropological Perspective," by Ellen Rhoads Holmes and Lowell D. Holmes, based on their study of aging in Samoa, examines anthropology as a discipline. Christine L. Fry (1999), one of the researchers involved in Project AGE, is the author of the second overview chapter entitled, "Anthropological Theories of Age and Aging." Written for the "Handbook of Theories of Aging" (Bengston and Schaie (1999), it explores anthropologies applications to gerontology. The final two articles in this section focus on two current issues of debate, D'Andrade's ideational definition of culture (2001) and Cohen's critical view of geroanthropology (1994).

The next section explores cultural meanings of age, aging, and the role of the elderly, starting with premodern times (Warren 1998). The collection of articles on cross-cultural aging reflects the true breadth and range identified with the study of anthropology. Areas studied include Ghana (Van der Geest 2001), rural Nepal (Goldstein and Beall 1981), Malaysia (Merriam 2000), China (Eckholm 2000), and other parts of Asia (Sung 2000, Yamaori 1997). Specific cultures of focus include Ismaili Canadians (Dossa 1994), American Indians (Baldridge 2001). Finally, a comparative study looks at aging in Israel and England (Hazan 1990).

Anthropology draws on a wide range of sources of "data" for its examination of humankind and culture. The next section, Cultural Aging reflected in Art and Literature, includes an analysis of aging in the Chinese novel (Levy 1999) and in Tuareg popular performances (Rasmussen 2000). These articles focus on the role of anthropology in examining human values and how they are passed from generation to generation within a culture.

Other sections of this volume include articles from the fields of medical anthropology, biological and physical anthropology, and archaeology. The array of articles presented help to define the scope of anthropology's reach; from exploring an anthropological perspective of dementia (Pollit 1996) to an exploration of archeological material to delve into human aging in ancient times (Telmon 1996, Whittaker 1992).

It is my hope that the articles in this volume will shed light on the breadth of anthropological contributions to our understanding of human aging.

REFERENCES

Anthropological Theory. Accessed on April 6, 2002 at *http://www.sagepub.co.uk/journals/details/j0280.html*.

Keith, J., C.L. Fry, A.P. Glascock, C. Ikles, J. Dickerson-Putman, H.C. Harpending, P. Draper (1994). *The Aging Experience: Diversity and Commonality across Cultures*. Thousand Oaks: Sage.

Smithsonian Institution. Department of Anthropology. What is Anthropology? Accessed April 6, 2002 at
http://www.nmnh.si.edu/anthro/whatisan.htm.

University of Louisville. What is Anthropology? Accessed March 4, 2002 at *http://www.louisville.edu/a-s/anthro/whatis.htm*.

Additional References

Ajrouch, K. J., Antonucci, T. C., & Janevic, M. R. (2001). Social Networks among Blacks and Whites: The Interaction between Race and Age. *J. Gerontology. B. Psychological Science and Social Science* 56(2), S112–480.

Bledsoe, C. H., F. Banja. (2002). Contingent *Lives: Fertility, Time, and Aging in West Africa*. The Lewis Henry Morgan Lectures, 1999. Chicago: University of Chicago Press.

Chambre, S. (1993). Volunteerism by elders: past trends and future prospects. *Gerontologist*, 33(2), 221–480.

Cohen, L. (1998). *No Aging in India: Alzheimer's, the Bad Family, and Other Modern Things*. Berkeley: University of California Press.

Crawford, M. H. (Ed.) (2000). *Different Seasons: Biological Aging in Midwestern Mennonites, United States*. Lawrence, Kansas: University of Kansas.

Crews, D. E. and R. M. Garruto. (1994). *Biological Anthropology and Aging: Perspectives on Human Variation over the Life Span*. Oxford: Oxford University Press.

Foner, N. (1994). Nursing home aides: saints or monsters? *Gerontologist*, 34(2), 245–480.

Gignac, M. A. M., Cott, C., & Badley, E. M. (2000). Adaptation to Chronic Illness and Disability and Its Relationship to Perceptions of Independence and Dependence. *J. Gerontology. B. Psychology and Social Science*, 55(6), P362–480.

Grigsby, J. (1996). The meaning of heterogeneity: an introduction. *Gerontologist*, 36(2), 145–480.

Gullette, M.M. (1997). *Declining to Decline: Cultural Combat and the Politics of the Midlife*. Charlottesville, VA: University Press of Virginia.

Hays, J. C., Meador, K. G., Branch, P. S., & George, L. K. (2001). The Spiritual History Scale in Four Dimensions (SHS-4): Validity and Reliability. *Gerontologist*, 41(2), 239–480.

Hjertstedt, J., Burns, E. A., Fleming, R., Raff, H., Rudman, I., Duthie, E. H., & Wilson, C. R. (2001). Mandibular and Palatal Tori, Bone Mineral Density, and Salivary Cortisol in Community-Dwelling Elderly Men and Women. *J. Gerontology. A Biol. Sci. Med. Sci.,* 56(11), M731–480.

Ikles, C., Keith, J., Dickerson-Putman, J., Draper, P., Fry, C. Glascock, A., Harpending, H. (1992). Perceptions of the adult life course: A cross-cultural analysis. *Ageing and Society* 12(1), 48–84.

Jendrek, M. (1994). Grandparents who parent their grandchildren: circumstances and decisions. *Gerontologist,* 34(2), 206–480.

Johnson, C., & Troll, L. (1994). Constraints and facilitators to friendships in late late life. *Gerontologist,* 34(1), 79–480.

Judge, D. S., & Carey, J. R. (2000). Postreproductive Life Predicted by Primate Patterns. *J. Gerontology. A Biol. Sci. Med. Sci.,* 55(4), B201–480.

Keith, J., Fry, C. L., Glascock, A. P., Ikels, C., Dickerson-Putman, J. Harpending, H.D., Draper, P. (1994). The Aging Experience: Diversity and commonality across cultures. Thousand Oaks, CA: Sage Publications.

Kurimoto, E. and S. Simonse (Eds.) (1998). *Conflict, Age and Power in North East Africa: Age Systems in Transition.* Athens, OH: Ohio University Press.

Lynott, P., & Roberts, R. (1997). The developmental stake hypothesis and changing perceptions of intergenerational relations, 1971–1985. *Gerontologist,* 37(3), 394–480.

McConatha, D., McConatha, J., & Dermigny, R. (1994). The use of interactive computer services to enhance the quality of life for long-term care residents. *Gerontologist,* 34(4), 553–480.

McMullin, J. A., & Marshall, V. W. (2001). Ageism, Age Relations, and Garment Industry Work in Montreal. *Gerontologist,* 41(1), 111–480.

Mitchell, J., Mathews, H. F., Hunt, L. M., Cobb, K. H., & Watson, R. W. (2001). Mismanaging Prescription Medications among Rural Elders: The Effects of Socioeconomic Status, Health Status, and Medication Profile Indicators. *Gerontologist,* 41(3), 348–480.

Molloy, D. W., Russo, R., Pedlar, D., & Bedard, M. (2000). Implementation of Advance Directives among Community-Dwelling Veterans. *Gerontologist,* 40(2), 213–480.

Pearsall, M. and S. Sontag. (1997). *The Other Within Us: Feminist Explorations of Women and Aging.* NY: Hapercollins.

Shawler, C., Rowles, G. D., & High, D. M. (2001). Analysis of Key Decision-Making Incidents in the Life of a Nursing Home Resident. *Gerontologist,* 41(5), 612–480.

Stuart, M., & Weinrich, M. (2001). Home- and Community-Based Long-Term Care: Lessons from Denmark. *Gerontologist,* 41(4), 474–480.

Rasmussen, S. J. (1997). *The Poetics and Politics of Tuareg Aging: Life Course and Personal Destiny in* Niger. Dekalb, IL: Northern Illinois University Press.

Rubinstein, R. L., J. Keith, D. Shenk, D. Wieland. (1990). *Anthropology and Aging: Comprehensive Reviews*. NY: Kluwer Academic Publishers.

Wallace, J. (1992). Reconsidering the life review: the social construction of talk about the past. *Gerontologist,* 32(1), 120–480.

Wilmoth, J. M. (2001). Living Arrangements among Older Immigrants in the United States. *Gerontologist,* 41(2), 228–480.

Woodward, K. M. (Ed.) (1999). *Figuring Age: Women, Bodies, Generations.* Theories of Contemporary Culture Volume 23. Bloomington, IN: Indiana University Press.

15

Anthropological Theories of Age and Aging

Christine L. Fry

A nthropological theories have their roots in an intellectual tradition that is distinctive from the other social sciences. Nineteenth-century thinkers such as Edward B. Tylor and Lewis Henry Morgan documented a natural universal history of humankind and the laws of evolution. We now see these theories as antique curiosities and points of departure. Largely through the research agendas of Franz Boas (Stocking, 1996), who has been called the father of American anthropology, and the work of Bronislaw Malinowski and Radcliffe-Brown in Great Britain, the foundations for contemporary anthropological thought were created (Goody, 1995; Stocking, 1995). Anthropology, like other disciplines, has its share of schisms and "isms," resulting in diverse perspectives.

Despite diversity in paradigms and a marked increase in specialization during the last half of the 20th century, anthropological research and theory generally embrace three tenets. First is a perspective that includes the entire globe. This means attempting to apply anthropological theory to the entirety of the human experience and explain variance. Second, anthropological theory is rooted in the comparative method. Ethnographic descriptions of specific cultures and contexts provide comparative data for theory-building and evaluation on a global or regional basis (referred to as ethnology). Third, anthropological theory is holistic. Because the comparative method requires comparable data, anthropologists emphasize the context in which the data are found. This usually means an entire context, which can include ecology,

1

social life, culture or meaning, and human variation and historical context as revealed by written records or archaeological reconstructions.

In this chapter we examine how the distinctive disciplinary perspective of anthropology has contributed to our theorizing about age and aging. First, we discuss anthropological theories of aging and old age. Second, because age is a temporal phenomenon, we review the nature of time and the distinctive ways in which humans use maturational differences. Third, we turn to the question of cultural variation in models of the life course. Fourth, we consider the strengths and promises of anthropological theories of age and aging. In conclusion, the possibilities of unified theories of age, aging, and the aged are appraised.

AGE IN ANTHROPOLOGICAL THEORIES

Once anthropologists began describing specific cultures, age became a part of anthropological theory. It was never very prominent, usually imbedded in discussions of kinship or the typical life cycle, with a focus of domestic groups. A major exception is the problem of age organization as a fairly esoteric problem in social anthropology, focused in the ethnography of Africa and of Native Americans on the Great Plains. In the few societies involved, males are formally ordered into classes by age. For social scientists interested in age and social organization, these cultures provided tantalizing models from simple societies, which could serve as heuristic contrasts for age in complex industrial societies. (See below, under "Age Class Systems" for discussion.)

Old age came late for anthropology. In fact it was the sociologist Leo Simmons who was the first to explore the accumulating ethnographic data organized into the Human Relations Area Files. In *The Role of the Aged in Primitive Society,* Simmons (1945) employed data from 71 nonindustrialized societies to statistically examine the status and treatment of the old from records of 19th-century ethnographers, missionaries, and colonists. His independent variables are ecological, economic, social, and political organization and religious beliefs. Although no singular hypothesis concerning better or worse treatment of older people in simpler societies emerged, Simmons's data documented the complexity and variability of the issues. Among the surprises were that some people lived a very long time (the superaged) in small-scale societies with little technology. Promoting their security was continued involvement in subsistence activities, personal services, and contributions to civil and religious life.

Nearly two decades later, Margaret Clark and Barbara Anderson (1967) used a culture and personality framework to examine mental illness and wellness in late life. In their volume *Culture and Aging* (1967), they assess

2

the hypothesized relationship between cultural values and mental health. Adherence to American values involving independence and rugged individualism is maladaptive in late life. Changed value orientations, with different expectations, promote successful aging and mental health.

Perhaps the most explicit theory on aging was formulated by sociologist Donald Cowgill and anthropologist Lowell Holmes on aging and modernization. In *Aging and Modernization,* Cowgill and Holmes (1972) propose a quasi-evolutionary theory linking marginalization of older people to modernization (see also Cowgill, 1986). Explicit hypotheses involve independent variables of productive technology, health technology, urbanization, and education with the dependent variable, status of older people. Precisely because of its explicit hypothesis, this theory has received considerable debate and revision. In spite of difficulties with modernization and aging, this theory has done more than any other to remind us of the diversity of cultures in which humans live and grow old. It also reminds us of the cultural evolutionary changes that have occurred in the past 12,000 years. Modernization is too narrow a process to capture the broader picture of cultural evolution. Modernization refers to 20th-century economic and political changes and has shifted to a model of world systems. An evolutionary framework is desirable in conceptualizing.the costs and benefits of increased scale, technology, intensification, and political centralization and their effects on peoples lives.

If the first four decades of anthropological theory and age are noted for the paucity of research, the last two decades are noteworthy for their abundance. An entire volume, *Age and Anthropological Theory* (Kertzer & Keith, 1984), invited anthropologists to theorize about age from evolutionary, social, and cultural perspectives. Anthropologists have investigated the contexts in which older adults are living, ranging from age-homogeneous retirement communities to inner cities and rural communities. Ethnographic research has explored special populations, including ethnic groups and older people with disabilities. Cross-cultural research continues, as seen in Project AGE (Keith et al., 1994). There have been many reviews of this research (see Albert & Cattel, 1994; Climo, 1992; Fry, 1996; Keith, 1990; Sokolovsky, 1997), and it cannot be covered in detail in this essay.

In generalizing from this third generation of anthropological work in aging, several themes are apparent. These are discussed below.

1. *Complexity.* As Leo Simmons (1945) discovered a half-century ago, aging is complicated. It is next to impossible to confirm a linkage between variables such as the social status of older people or even well-being of older people and an evolutionary transformation (simple to global or nonindustrial to industrial capitalism) or specific economic cores (foraging, domestication, peasantry or industry). The reason for this is that aging is experienced

3

in a *cultural* context. Because culture is adaptive, it presents multiple paths in decision making and reflection. In other words, there are multiple ways to get from here to there. If one thing does not work, humans will use their culture and knowledge to figure out a way that will work.

2. *Diversity.* There are many different ways of being human, and there are even more ways of being an older human. The diversity of aging experiences is one of the major discoveries in gerontological research. This diversity has been confirmed time and time again in cross-cultural and intracultural research on older people.

3. *Context specificity.* Living, aging, and growing old are experienced in specific contexts. What happens in one social context is not necessarily transferrable across cultures. For instance, in defining functionality, vision is likely to be a critical ability. For all primates, sight is a primary sense. Yet different contexts will place distinct demands on abilities. In contexts where management of daily life is predicated on literacy and recreation consists of reading, television, or driving a recreational vehicle, loss of sight is tragic. But where literacy is minimal and the environment familiar, reduction in vision may not be as catastrophic.

4. *Culture and understanding.* To understand age is to interpret phenomena of change over time and the rhythms of the normal life course. Interpretation of these changes involves culture. Everyone uses culture, and its multiple perspectives are to be expected. Culture is also at the foundation of evaluation. What is the best for people? For older people? When it comes to questions about social policy, we have learned to ask, Whose culture is it? For instance, if we had listened to the wisdom of Lewis Mumford (1956), who argued for the integration of older people, age-segregated retirement communities would never have been built. When anthropologists looked into life in these age-segregated settings, they found viable communities, not the projected geriatric ghettos.

Thus, in looking toward anthropological theories of aging, we must first look at time and how humans have culturally incorporated temporal phenomena in understanding age and aging.

THE CHALLENGE OF TIME

Time actually is not a challenge. Time just happens, as a property of the universe in which we live. Discontinuities and continuities in experience give the sensation of periodicity and duration of time. Because of the organization of the solar system, every living thing experiences the periodicity associated with the rotation of our small planet, Earth—night and day—

plus seasonality caused by the axis of the rotation and Earth's elliptical orbit around the sun. The challenge of time rests in how humans incorporate the experience culturally and thus interpret the phenomenon (Gell 1992).

Because culture is not completely arbitrary, we are in for no surprises. Virtually every culture organizes time by days, months, and years. Lunar months leave a few extra days that are worked into the calendar, similar to February 29 in a leap year. Calendrics, in fact, are very ancient for our species, dating to the Upper Paleolithic of Europe some 20,000 years ago, in the Magdalenian Period. The passage of time is noted ritually in fertility festivals and other rites, such as first fruits and harvesttime.

Although calendars calibrate time and schedule human events in time, they do not translate into age and aging. Indeed, age is that which happens in time from birth to the present or to death. To measure age calendrically, the calendar has to be transformed. Most cultural calendars reckon time in a relative fashion. Time is anchored in the present, which is forever changing. Events are seen as relative to each other—that is, earlier or later, before or after. People are seen as junior or senior, younger or older than one another. For age to be measured, three things have to happen to a calendar. First, the units of time must be rationalized into explicitly bounded segments. Second, and most important, time has to become absolute and fixed. The calendar has to be anchored at a specific point in time. Third, time so rationalized is seen as independent of any social order and thus politically neutral; that is, time and its prognostication are not dust in the hands of the priests but seen as an element in the universe.

Time as currently reckoned by the Christian calendar is based on the Gregorian calendar, which, in 1582, revised the Julian calendar. Our units are millennia, centuries, decades, years, months, days, hours, minutes, seconds. Time is anchored in the year 0 and the supposed birth of Christ (actually missing the event by 30 or so years). From 0 on the A.D. side, count forward to the present; on the B.C. side, count backward. Time is transcendent for societies, dating history; for individuals, it fixes their births on a day and a year. Without these conventions, age expressed chronologically would be a conceptual impossibility. Why were absolute time and chronological age invented? How has age been incorporated into specific models of the life course?

Chronological time is dominant for Euro-American culture and cultures incorporated into the 19th- and 20th-century industrial order. It is so central that an aging individual's confusion on questions dealing with present year, date, or hour can result in recommendations to institutionalize, as seen on Mini-Mental Status tests. In a broader time frame, long after an individual's biography has faded from memory the dates on the tombstone attest to that person's presence in time. It is not surprising that when observers from Europe and North America encountered peoples of smaller-scale cultures,

5

they were blinded by their own temporal orientation. Smaller-scale cultures, using relative time, were misrepresented by ethnographers. Chronological age per se did not exist; but relative age, as expressed in kinship (generational differences) and in maturational stages, were translated into terms that could be understood by Euro-Americans. Age grades, often with chronological markers, were used to organize descriptions of domestic life. Even the chronological ages of informants are translated from relative time by creating local event calendars and birth orders.

If gerontology is as "chronocentric" as it seems to be, then we should critically reexamine our theories of age and social organization. Indeed, during the 1960s and 1970s, one of the major debates in social gerontology centered on chronological age, which became less useful than functional age (Austin & Loeb, 1982). The argument was that age based in functionality is more sensitive to an individual's abilities and needs. Yet when we turn to the conceptual building blocks of what theories we have, we find they are all cast in a chronometric framework. Here I am thinking of such concepts as age strata, cohorts, age grades, life stages, social clocks, on/off time, age norms, young old/old old, and even *the* life course. When we hedge our bets by pointing to variability and heterogeneity in searching for pattern, we are left with temporal order. Chronology may conceptually be appropriate for the contexts being modeled, but chronology is but one alternative. Hence time—its use and meaning—is best seen as a variable.

To begin a reexamination of age and culture for the 21st century, I see two necessary starting points. First, we need to examine maturational differences and how they are incorporated into a social order. Second, we must clarify variability as to how differences in maturity are modeled by human cultures in transforming maturation into ideas about age and aging.

SOCIETIES AND MATURATIONAL DIFFERENCES

Maturational differences are selected because we want to minimize our chronocentric view of age by looking at differences in the way maturity is used socially. The question I pose is, what possible advantages are offered to a social group by encoding and defining normative behavior for individuals who differ by maturity? We should answer this question on a pan-human basis, regardless of how time and its conceptualization creates variability.

To discover how maturational differences are used, we must look at humans in comparison with nonhumans for the most telling contrast. Social hierarchy is a common organizing principle for all social groups. For both nonhuman and the simplest of human societies, hierarchy is based on differential maturation. In chimpanzee societies, males organize themselves into a dominance hierarchy based on physical strength and abilities to manipulate and threaten others. Alpha males are those in their physical prime or allied with males who are in their prime and who will support their cause. The rewards are sex and privileges of power (de Waal, 1989; Heltne & Marquardt, 1989).

But here a marked contrast must be noted. *No human society invests power in young males*. The maturation and strength of young male individuals are superseded, culturally, by strong controls regarding generation and kinship. The young are, indeed, often excluded from full adulthood (namely, parenthood) until they are socially mature and ready to replace the senior generation in social leadership. In small-scale human societies, generational differences usually work to the advantages of seniority. From an evolutionary perspective, the reasons lie in the fact that humans are cultural, whereas chimpanzees are protocultural. Humans have the abilities, through language and culture, to encode experience and to share knowledge with each other. Senior members have more experience with diverse situations and potential novelty and therefore can provide solutions that enhance group survival.

In larger-scale societies, hierarchy and stratification are based more on material accumulation by senior generations, with resulting power differentials to the disadvantage of the young. Maturational differences are by no means neutral in the quest for wealth and influence, but these favor some, although not all, older adults. In short, in cultural evolution, *generational differences* have become an important axis of social life that is more important than the physical changes associated with maturation or the decrements associated with aging.

CULTURAL MODELS OF THE LIFE COURSE

If generations are a point of departure from nonhuman populations to the development of culture and human society, then generation should be a starting point for any anthropological theory of age. Each human culture can be seen as a "theory" about how things work or as a model for living. Through the transmission of knowledge, norms, and expectations, each culture provides guidelines for generational relations, for age, and for the life course. Although much has been written about the life course, theoretically our efforts have been tentative at best.

Anthropologists use the life course as a paradigm or heuristic device to organize our research. However, we haven't given the life course the benefit of theory to classify and clarify variation on a cross-cultural basis. Using generational and cultural comparisons as our starting point, I suggest that there are three major types of cultural models or theories of the life course: (1) generational systems, (2) age class systems, and (3) staged life courses.

7

GENERATIONAL SYSTEMS

Generations have been discussed and recommended as fruitful beginnings in thinking about the life course (see Bengtson & Cutler, 1976; Fortes, 1984; Kertzer, 1982). Generations are based on relative time: junior and senior. Generations have very little to do with chronological time. We are reminded of this when a cousin shows up who is old enough to be an uncle or when a stepmother is young enough to be a sister. Generational time places a person—or an "ego" in anthropological terminology—in a web of relationships by seniority. First there are seniors: parents and a class of people related to parents by generation. Second, there are juniors: children and other classes of people such as nieces and nephews. Third, there equals, who are ranked by birth order (siblings and cousins). The principles can be extended up through ascending generations and down through descending generations. Relative time and the work of kinship (reproduction) places each person in a fixed web of relationships. The language of generations is kinship. Every human society has generational principles that organize all or a part of social life. For small-scale, band, and tribal societies, generations and generational placement are primary mechanisms for organizing the life course.

Age Class Systems

Age class systems have long been an interesting problem in social anthropology and have offered inspiration for theorizing about the life course. S. N. Eisenstadt (1956) introduced the phenomenon to sociological thinking about age in *From Generation to Generation* with an explicit functional theory. Later Leonard Cain (1964), in a seminal article, saw parallels for age grading, age norms, and the life course in industrial societies. Even age stratification theory drew on ethnographic cases for illustration of simpler societies (Foner & Kertzer, 1978, Kertzer, 1978, 1989). As fascinating as age classes are for models of the life course, they are not helpful as models of the life course in complex societies (Spencer, 1990). Something very different appears to be at work in these societies.

One of the first challenges in understanding age classes is their variability (see Bernardi [1985] for a classification and alternative theories). In spite of variability, the defining feature of age classes is that males are ordered hierarchically by something that would appear to be age. The appearance of age is most likely the chronocentrisim of observers, who translate the relative age into chronological terms. Thus, the literature is full of the ages of initiates and ages of transition, which are not relevant to the actors. Males are grouped by generation and pass through life together as their class ascends generationally or as their class makes the transition into the next senior

8

class. Each class is ranked, junior or senior. Women are rarely organized into age classes.

A number of theories have been proposed to explain this, ranging from mobilization of labor to population regulation. However, when we realize that generations are the foundation of age classes, it becomes clear that age class systems are a special case of generational systems. A minimal rule is that a son must belong to a different class from that of his father. In minimizing conflict between father and son, who may be competing for the same resources, age class systems have used generations to organize the political structure of the broader community. Age classes thus are kinship and generation projected onto the larger social fabric (Fortes, 1984).

Staged Life Courses

Even more has been said about the conceptual and theoretical development of the life course perspective (see Dannefer & Uhlenberg, chapter 17 in this volume, for a review). In addition to the often cited principles (Bengtson & Allen, 1993) underlying the idea of progressions and sequences of behaviors, the life course in complex societies is (1) based on a combination of generational and chronological age and (2) understood as staged or divisible into a variable number of age grades.

Chronological age as a marker of behavior had to be invented and needed a good reason to be created. We often look to the record keeping of churches and the emergence of vital statistics and demography in Europe as the origin of chronological age as a measuring point. The Romans were among the first to use age as a defining term, for conscription into their military forces. Chronological age is clearly associated with state-level societies. Age defined chronologically becomes the basis for universalistic (in contrast to particularistic) norms in regulating a large population. Age defines the responsibilities of citizenship. With capitalism and industry, age has further been used to define adulthood and labor force participation. Legal norms prevent children from working and force them into educational institutions. Legal norms define when one can enter into adult activities—voting, military service, marriage, driving, drinking, and so on. Legal norms also define if and when one is pensionable and expected to retire from the labor force.

Legal norms gauge the life course and calibrate a social clock of role entrances and exits. At minimum there is a stage of preparation, a stage of participation, and a stage of retirement. Preparatory stages are ones of enculturation and skill acquisition for an adult life of work and a career in the labor market. What begins at home, with nurturance by parents, is completed in formal educational institutions, with finely age-graded classes defined by chronological age. Children are launched into adulthood once they have completed their schooling and have attained the chronological age defined by the legal norms of adult privilege. Especially relevant are the norms concerning age of work and age of marriage as thresholds into the stage of adult participation. Retirement from participation in the labor force is similarly guided by chronological legal norms, most notably the age of eligibility for state social security programs or pensions. In the nation-states of the industrialized world the pensionable age has arbitrarily been set at 65, with some flexibility upward or downward and exceptions for specific occupations.

Legal norms defined by the state create an understanding of life as something that is staged. Beyond the basics of preparation, participation, and retirement we find considerable variability in how the life course is refined into smaller and more defined stages. For instance, Americans, Irish, and Hong Kong Chinese, when asked to divide adulthood (participation and retirement) into age groups, saw from 1 or 2 divisions up to 10, with an average of 5 (Keith et al. 1994; see also chapter 6 by Fry). In spite of the variability in number of divisions, they represent periods life that are graded by age. Passage through the stages is ordered by chronological expectations on work, marriage, family cycles, and especially the participation of children in schools.

Visions of a postmodern life course (Featherstone & Hepworth, 1991) and an age-irrelevant society (Neugarten, 1982) have been depicted as an ideal toward which gerontology should work. Family, work, and retirement could be significantly reconfigured and redistributed across the life course (Riley, Kahn, & Foner, 1994); yet the American age norms, first investigated by Neugarten (1982), display considerable stability from the 1960s to the 1990s (Settersten & Hagestad, 1996a; 1996b). The staged life course is an institution of regulation and rationalization of the labor force (Kohli, 1986, Mayer & Muller, 1986). Where adulthood is organized by labor force participation, life courses are staged. Where participation in labor markets is marginal to sporadic, generational principles organize life.

In our Project AGE, research communities in western Ireland and Africa did not see life as divisible into age-graded stages. Wage labor in these communities did not organize adult life. Even in marginalized minority groups, generational age, not chronological norms, are more important. Among African Americans an "age of wisdom" defines successful older women. Attaining wisdom is through parenting one's own children, grandchildren, and foster children (Peterson, 1997).

AGE, VARIABLES, AND THEORIES

Age and aging are clearly temporal phenomena at the core of gerontology and theories about becoming old. But on second thought, is age really a variable? The answer is yes and no. On the negative side, age is time, and time is not a variable. Time is a property of the universe. Time never caused anything. It is what happens in time that is of importance to theories of aging. Indeed, most research on aging in biology, psychology, and the social sciences has focused on what happens in time. Bodies are transformed and societies respond to individuals who are very young and those who have been here a long time. Age becomes a variable only insofar as it is culturally conceptualized and incorporated into social life. Age also becomes a variable when a society becomes aware of its own demographics and begins to worry. As suggested above, generational time and chronological time are two ways of conceptualizing age.

If aging is what happens in time, then theories have to be focused on specific issues for a hypothesis to be generated and evaluated. A central challenge for gerontology is that so much happens in time that it is difficult to establish a paradigm to order our theories and integrate our knowledge. Aging transcends disciplinary specializations. One alternative in organizing what we know about aging is to recognize a disciplinary division of labor and try to cross boundaries in maintaining a "big picture" view of aging. That is the approach taken by academic gerontology as reflected in this volume. Another option is an applied approach to practical difficulties in old age, using relevant but fragmentary theories from appropriate disciplines. Either way, we end up with the atheoretical gerontology described by Bengtson and his colleagues (Bengtson, Burgess, & Parrott, 1997; Bengtson, Parrott, & Burgess, 1996). Perhaps a unifying paradigm is not possible or even desirable for gerontology, simply because it is so complex and multidimensional.

One of the purposes of theory is to organize what we know. Anthropology offers some distinct advantages in its emphasis on holism, comparison, and global perspective. Although anthropology as a discipline embraces all aspects of humans, biological and cultural in all times and places, my suggestions are decidedly cultural. In over a century of anthropological thought, culture remains central to our understanding of human experiences. Culture can be seen as a theory about how things work. Each society, each social group, has worked out a collective folk theory about the world, people, and relationships. As people pass through time and their social world, they forever are learning their culture and organizing their lives and groups in the process. Age and aging are a part of those theories.

The holism, comparison, and globalism of anthropological theory enhance our efforts to construct theory about age and aging. Most positive is the recognition of diversity. It is in diversity that we find the variables comprising hypothesis and theories about cultural phenomena. A challenge to the construction of theories about aging is finding the classification of diversity that is theoretically productive but at the same time does not oversimplify and stereotype. Anthropologists have dealt with this issue either in

11

terms of regional studies or by a theoretical organization of cultural types. How we approach diversity for theories of aging is something that must be theoretically driven.

For gerontology, anthropological theories offer an enticing promise. Aging is universal. All human beings experience temporal change from birth to death. In spite of the ubiquity of age and time, how these are experienced is subject to cultural interpretation. Each culture is localized knowledge anchored in specific circumstances and relationships. A significant challenge for a theory of aging is to disentangle what is universal from what is specific and locally defined. Anthropological theories have been developed for rather basic issues of human existence, such as kinship and economic organization. For investigating problems of aging, these efforts are maturing with much promise.

AGE, AGING, AGED

Age, aging, and *aged* are three words frequently used in gerontological discourse. Sometimes they are used interchangeably; sometimes they are used to argue for theoretical advances. Certainly, gerontology began with a focus on the old—the aged. Soon we recognized that the end of life had a beginning and a connection with what goes before—aging. Finally, we called for a theory of age. Age, aging, and aged are neither interchangeable nor mark theoretical advancement. As we work toward a more sophisticated body of knowledge in gerontology, we must recognize that age, aging, and the aged are indeed three windows into the phenomena we study.

Age

Theories about age are theories about cultural and social phenomena. How are time and age conceptualized? How is age used in the regulation of social life? How does age enter into the manipulation and negotiation of daily living? As we have argued above, the connections between time and the life course are variable on a cross-cultural and perhaps on an intracultural basis. Generations, age classes, and staged life courses based on chronological norms are at least three ways in which age is understood. Each conceptualization has its causes and consequences for the people who define their lives through the respective cultural models.

Aging

Theories about aging are theories about living. These theories are organized around a life span perspective and life courses. Because so much happens in

12

living, the list of potential research topics and theories would appear to be vast. These include questions about aging and changes in health and functionality, changes in participation in the division of labor, changes in family roles, and changes in cultural values and safety nets—all subjects for anthropological theories of aging.

For example, kinship, like age, is a universal. Families are age-heterogeneous groupings in which and through which people live all or important parts of their lives. Like aging, families change through time as the cast of characters matures, passing through adulthood and age. Domestic groups pass through a cycle of formation (marriage), expansion (children), and contraction (marriage of children). Although universal, the relationships between parents and children as they pass together through life courses and domestic cycles are by no means identical across cultures.

In small-scale egalitarian societies, parents and children remain interdependent all of their lives. Families are groups of people who have learned to work together and support their membership. Kin and the work they do comprise the safety net. Parents can expect to and do command children in the interest of their kin unit. In contrast, families in large-scale capitalist societies are only a part of the safety net. Wage labor and market economies have reduced the role of families in production. Essential goods and services may be purchased in the marketplace. Relationships between parents and children are transformed from those based on economic interdependence to those of companionship, friendship, and intimacy. Children are nurtured as individuals, to be launched into a life course (Fry, 1995). A middle-class ideal is that children will continue to develop and grow independent of parental guidance. The failed "launch" and the resultant "domestic interdependence" are by no means desirable.

Aged

Theories about the aged are theories of old age. Without the focus on late life, gerontology as we know it would disappear. This focus on late life is the culmination of age and aging. It is the realization that lives, life chances, and the consequences of how age is understood are all culturally constructed. Here our theories are most important, because they have real consequences for people who are aged. Historically, with industrialization and urbanization, old age has been defined as a problematic state. Old age is seen not only as a medical and economic problem but also as a social problem, especially in terms of social support and caregiving. As defined, however, predicaments associated with the aged have potentials for improvement.

Our theories about the aged become relevant for social policy, legislation, and political action. In politics and policy there are winners and losers. Thus, any theory about old age must account for the diversity in the cultural

13

contexts in which older adults who are classified as problematic are actually experiencing their old age. The reasons are straightforward: (1) Is what we see as problematic really a problem? (2) Are there any strengths in the context that can be improved or supported? (3) Are there any weaknesses that can be reduced? (4) Because old age is the culmination of aging, is there any way of preventing the future old from experiencing what is seen as problematic?

Over a half-century ago, Leo Simmons (1945), in the first systematic cross-cultural analysis of the problems of aging and the aged, documented a host of complex issues and no simplistic theories. Time is not complex; time is elementary. Age, aging, and the aged are a complicated part of the human experience because they are subject to cultural interpretations.

Culture is always perplexing. As a design for living, culture is central to the way humans comprehend, negotiate, and manipulate their natural and social worlds. Culture is not a property of the universe like space or time. Consequently, we should expect complexity and diversity. Although theoretical unification and parsimony are scientific goals, culture and what happens in time may not be amenable.

Any theory explaining the puzzles of age, aging, or the aged is likely to be multifaceted and eclectic. At the same time, if we are ever to arrive at scientific explanations of age, aging, and the aged, theory is *the* essential ingredient. Explicit theory is a tool that enables us to separate cultural inventions from more general explanations. Explicit hypotheses relating study variables in a specific way not only clarify our thinking about phenomena but lead to the appropriate methods for evaluation of the relationships. The cost of relying on implicit theory is to potentially perpetuate "home-grown" cultural models as scientific generalizations.

REFERENCES

Albert, S. M., & Cattell, M. G. (1994). *Old age in global perspective: Cross-cultural and cross-national views.* New York: G. K. Hall.

Austin, C., & Loeb, M. (1982). Why age is relevant in social policy and practice. In B. Neugarten (Ed.), *Age or need? Public policies for older people* (pp. 263–288). Beverly Hills, CA: Sage Publications.

Bengtson, V. L., & Allen, K. R. (1993). The life course perspective applied to families over time. In P. Boss, W. Doherty, R. LaRossa, W. Schumm, & S. Steinmetz (Eds.), *Sourcebook of family theories and methods: A contextual approach* (pp. 469–498). New York: Plenum Press.

Bengtson, V. L., Burgess, E. O., & Parrott, T. M. (1997). Theory, explanation, and a third generation of theoretical development in social gerontology. *Journals of Gerontology: Social Sciences, 52B*(2), S72–S88.

Bengtson, V. L., & Cutler, N. E. (1976). Generations and inter-generational relations: Perspectives on age groups and social change. In R. Binstock & E. Shanas (Eds.),

The handbook of aging and the social sciences (pp. 130–159). New York: Van Nostrand Reinhold.

Bengtson, V. L., Parrott, T. M., & Burgess, E. O. (1996). Progress and pitfalls in gerontological theorizing. *Gerontologist, 36*, 768–772.

Bernardi, B. (1985). *Age class systems: Social institutions and politics based on age.* Cambridge, U.K.: Cambridge University Press.

Cain, L. D., Jr. (1964). Life course and social structure. In R. L. Faris (Ed.), *Handbook of modern sociology* (pp. 272–309). Chicago: Rand McNally.

Clark, M. M., & Anderson, B. (1967). *Culture and aging: An anthropological study of older Americans.* Springfield, IL: Charles C. Thomas.

Climo, J. J. (1992). The role of anthropology in gerontology: Theory. *Journal of Aging Studies, 6*(1), 41–56.

Cowgill, D. O. (1986). *Aging around the world.* Belmont, CA: Wadwsorth.

Cowgill, D. O., & Holmes, L. D. (Eds.). (1972). *Aging and modernization.* New York: Appleton-Century-Crofts.

de Waal, F. (1989). *Chimpanzee politics: Power and sex among apes.* Baltimore: Johns Hopkins University Press.

Eisenstadt, S. N. (1956). *From generation to generation: Age groups and social structure.* New York: Free Press.

Featherstone, M., & Hepworth, M. (1991). The mask of ageing and the postmodern life course. In M. Featherstone, M. Hepworth, & B. S. Turner (Eds.), *The body: Social process and cultural theory* (pp. 371–389). Thousand Oaks, CA: Sage Publications.

Foner, A., & Kertzer, D. I. (1978). Transitions over the life course: Lessons from age-set societies. *American Journal of Sociology, 83*, 1081–1104.

Fortes, M. (1984). Age, generation and social structure. In D. I. Kertzer & J. Keith (Eds.), *Age and anthropological theory.* (pp. 99–122). Ithaca, NY: Cornell University Press.

Fry, C. L. (1996). Age, aging and culture. In R. H. Binstock & L. K. George (Eds.), *Handbook of aging and the social sciences* (4th ed., pp. 118–136). San Diego, CA: Academic Press.

Fry, C. L. (1995). Kinship and individuation: Cross-cultural perspectives on intergenerational relations. In V. L. Bengtson, K. W. Schaie & L. M. Burton (Eds.), *Adult intergenerational relations: Effects of societal change* (pp. 126–156). New York: Springer Publishing Co.

Gell, A. (1992). *The anthropology of time: Cultural constructions of temporal constructions of temporal maps and images.* Providence, RI: Berg Publishers.

Goody, J. (1995). *The expansive moment: Anthropology in Britain and Africa, 1918–1970.* Cambridge, U.K.: Cambridge University Press.

Heltne, P. G., & Marquardt, L. A. (Eds.). (1989). *Understanding chimpanzees.* Cambridge, MA: Harvard University Press.

Keith, J. (1990). Age in social and cultural context: Anthropological perspectives. In R. H. Binstock & L. K. George (Eds.), *Handbook of aging and the social sciences* (3rd ed., pp. 91–111). San Diego, CA: Academic Press.

Keith, J., Fry, C. L., Glascock, A. P., Ikels, C., Dickerson-Putman, J., Harpending, H. C, & Draper, P. (1994). *The aging experience: Diversity and commonality across cultures.* Thousand Oaks, CA : Sage Publications.

15

Kertzer, D. I. (1978). Theoretical developments in the study of age-group systems. *American Ethnologist, 5,* 368–374.

Kertzer, D. I. (1982). Generation and age in cross-cultural perspective. In M. W. Riley, R. P. Abeles, & M. S. Teitelbaum (Eds.), *Aging from birth to death: Sociotemporal perspectives* (pp. 27–50). Boulder, CO: Westview Press.

Kertzer, D. I. (1989). Age structuring in comparative and historical perspective. In D. I. Kertzer & K. W. Schaie (Eds.), *Age structuring in comparative perspective* (pp. 3–20). Hillsdale, NJ: Lawrence Erlbaum Associates.

Kertzer, D. I., & Keith, J. (Eds.) (1984). *Age and anthropological theory.* Ithaca, NY: Cornell University Press.

Kohli, M. (1986). Social organization and subjective construction of the life course. In A. B. Sorensen, F. E. Weinert, & L. R. Sherrod (Eds.), *Human development and subjective construction of the life course: Multidisciplinary perspectives.* (pp. 271–292). Hillsdale, NJ: Lawrence Erlbaum Associates.

Mayer, K. U., & Muller, W. (1986). The state and the structure of the life course. In A. B. Sorensen, F. E. Weinert, & L. R. Sherrod (Eds.), *Human development and subjective construction of the life course: Multidisciplinary perspectives* (pp. 217–246). Hillsdale, NJ: Lawrence Erlbaum Associates.

Mumford, L. (1956). For older people: Not segregation, but integration. *Architectural Record, 119,* 191–194.

Neugarten, B. L. (Ed.) (1982). *Age or need? Public policies for older people.* Beverly Hills, CA: Sage Publications.

Peterson, J. W. (1997). Age of wisdom: Elderly Black women in family and church. In J. Sokolovsky (Ed.), *The cultural context of aging: Worldwide perspectives* (2nd ed., pp. 276–292). Westport, CT: Bergin & Garvey.

Riley, M. W., Kahn, R. L., & Foner, A. (Eds.). (1994). *Age and structural lag: Society's failure to provide meaningful opportunities in work, family and leisure.* New York: John Wiley & Sons.

Settersten, R. A., Jr., & Hagestad, G. O. (1996a). What's the latest? Cultural age deadlines for family transitions. *Gerontologist, 36,* 178–188.

Settersten, R. A., Jr., & Hagestad, G. O. (1996b). What's the latest? 2. Cultural age deadlines for educational and work transitions. *Gerontologist, 36,* 602–613.

Simmons, L. W. (1945). *The role of the aged in primitive society.* New Haven, CT: Yale University Press.

Sokolovsky, J. (Ed.). (1997). *The cultural context of aging: Worldwide perspectives* (2nd ed.). Westport, CT: Bergin & Garvey.

Spencer, P. (1990). The riddled course: Theories of age and its transformations. In P. Spencer (Ed.), *Anthropology and the riddle of the sphinx: Paradoxes of change in the life course* (pp. 1–34). London: Routledge.

Stocking, G. W., Jr. (1995). *After Tylor: British social anthropology, 1888–1951.* Madison: University of Wisconsin Press.

Stocking, G. W., Jr. (1996). *Volksgeist as method and ethic: Essays on Boasian ethnography and the German anthropological tradition.* Madison: University of Wisconsin Press.

16

1

⊡ The Anthropological
Perspective

The authors of this volume are anthropologists—cultural
anthropologists—who, because of their training and scientific interests, look at the contemporary world in all its cultural complexity and variety and attempt to understand and interpret human behavior.
A book on gerontology written by anthropologists may seem unusual,
because most gerontologists are sociologists, psychologists, or social
workers. Anthropologists have long been interested in the aged, but
unfortunately mostly as sources of information on a non-Western culture
as it was when they were young or before contact with white people and
Western civilization. When Franz Boas (the father of American anthropology) sent out his Columbia University graduate students (Margaret
Mead, Alfred Kroeber, Ruth Benedict, Melville Herskovits, and others)
with instructions to seek out the elders first as major sources of cultural
information, it apparently never occurred to him or his students that they
might also ask what life was like for the elderly. Many anthropologists

are doing that today, and anthropology is bringing new information and a new way of looking at aging to the science of gerontology.

The Discipline of Anthropology

Anthropology is the study of human beings—total human beings. No other science or humanistic discipline examines the human animal as thoroughly. Anthropology addresses itself to the study of the physical makeup of humans, to their social and cultural behavior in the contemporary world as well as in historic and prehistoric days. It is the science concerned with the evolutionary development of humans as animals, with their patterns of group interaction, and with the nature of their cultural traditions in industrialized as well as tribal and peasant societies.

Anthropology maintains a broad, holistic approach to the study of humankind but, like other social scientists, anthropologists tend to specialize. The anthropological fraternity includes physical anthropologists, archaeologists, linguists, and social/cultural anthropologists. Physical anthropologists study people as members of the animal kingdom, recognizing that they are vertebrates, mammals, primates, and, finally, because of their superior brains and culture-building capacities, *hominids* or human beings. Physical anthropologists concern themselves with human evolution, demography, population genetics, and human variation (race), and they are valuable contributors to knowledge in such gerontological and geriatric areas as morbidity, mortality, health, longevity, and the genetic basis of aging. Given that there are both hereditary and environmental components to aging, these scholars can be expected to contribute heavily to gerontological science.

Archaeologists also contribute to our knowledge of aging, particularly in the area of longevity. While archaeologists are generally concerned with reconstructing the lifestyles of past cultures through excavation and analysis of artifacts such as weapons, tools, and ceremonial objects, those with interests in paleodemography calculate age at death from human skeletons, figure mortality rates, and construct survivorship curves and life tables. Excellent examples of such studies are those by Mann (1968) and McKinley (1971), who studied average age at death of South and East African populations of australopithecines (19.8 years), as well as by Acsadi and Nemeskeri (1970), who determined from

18

skeletal material in Asia that *Homo erectus* had a maximum life span of 60-70 years and an average age at death of 37-48 years of those who had reached adulthood. Lovejoy and others (1977) analyzed 1,327 articulated skeletons of Native Americans in an ossuary (communal burial ground) at Libben site in northern Ohio. Evaluating age at death through skeletal maturation and dental condition over a period from A.D. 800 to 1100, the researchers determined that life expectancy for this hunting and fishing population was approximately 20 years and the maximum life span was approximately 55+.

Anthropological linguists also have a potential role in gerontology. These scholars specialize in language analysis, with interests ranging from the history of language development to the study of language structure and semantics and to the use of language as a reflection of class, ethnic, or sex differences within a society. The branch of linguistics known as *sociolinguistics* has demonstrated that our language reflects American racism and sexism, and it is now recognizing ageism in our patterns of communication.

According to Herbert Covey (1988), the terms used to refer to older people not only have changed over time but there has been a proliferation of negative terms since the late nineteenth century, reflecting change in the status of the aged. Some words that had a neutral or positive meaning are now viewed more negatively. For example, *old* has generally referred to a stage of life, but when used in expressions like *old maid* or *old geezer*, it becomes negative. Many older people now object to being called "old" at all (Covey, 1988). In a survey of adults that studied preferred labels for the aged, persons age 65 and over found *senior citizen* the most acceptable term (Barbato & Feezel, 1987). It is interesting to note that this positive label is not a recent development; *senior* denoted a person deserving of respect in the 1300s and *senior citizen* is also an early reference. *Senile*, which in the 1600s was a general reference to old age, has become much more negative, implying mental and physical impairment. Even some words typically used for grandparents have had negative connotations at times. For old women, *granny* has referred to a gossip and later implied stupidity. *Gramps* has frequently been used in a negative sense for old men since the 1800s. The use of *hag* for an old woman has a long history and has undergone a dramatic change in meaning. Its earliest meaning was "holy one," but since 1225 it has carried connotations of evil, ugliness, and even witchcraft. While there is an abundance of negative terms for old men, historical evidence of language usage suggests old women have experienced more negativism and do so beginning at earlier ages than men (Covey, 1988).

Social anthropologists (who specialize in studies of social structure and social interaction) and cultural anthropologists (who study cultural traditions and systems) consider the many societies of our planet to be multiple experiments in human adaptation and survival in a wide variety of physical environments. The customs evolved by the societies represent their *cultures*, or systems of traditional behavior. One of the traditions that all societies have evolved concerns how the process of growing old is to be handled by the society and by the aging person. The ways aging is approached are infinitely varied around the world.

Anthropologists not only specialize in specific subjects, but most of them also specialize in a particular part of the world. Although some choose to remain at home and study their own people, a considerable number take a special interest in the peoples of the Pacific, Africa, Asia, Europe, or the Middle East. Some may be American Indian specialists. Because anthropology is dedicated to studying all peoples in all times and to documenting their infinitely varied configurations of customs, anthropologists often feel they must live among foreign peoples—often for extended periods of time. They investigate the value systems, worldviews, and cultural norms of people in far-off lands because they wish to test hypotheses about the nature of human beings in a worldwide laboratory.

Ethnographers are cultural anthropologists who engage in field studies, and *ethnography* is the term used to describe the empirical, fact-finding activities carried out by anthropologists in the field. As Michael Agar (1980) succinctly describes it, ethnography "always involves long-term association with some group, to some extent in their own territory, with the purpose of learning from them their ways of doing things and viewing reality" (p. 6). *Participant observation*, a time-honored method by which ethnographic data are acquired by anthropologists, is explained by Hortense Powdermaker (1966) as follows:

> To understand a strange society, the anthropologist has traditionally immersed himself in it, learning, as far as possible, to think, see, feel, and sometimes act as a member of its culture and at the same time as a trained anthropologist from another culture. This is the heart of the participant observation method—involvement and detachment. (p. 9)

20

This approach basically amounts to sharing the way of life, participating as much as appropriate, and keeping one's eyes and ears open to patterns of behavior and value assumptions of the people under study.

A great deal may be learned about a cultural situation from observation alone, but when the researcher carefully augments it with interviewing, observation becomes even more valuable. Observations may prompt questions or topics for interview, and they can also be useful in verifying interview data. A particular social event, for example, can be described in great detail from observation alone, but the meanings, symbolism, and function of the event will be best understood through interviews with participants themselves. Participation in a people's way of life is also an excellent way to establish rapport and gain the trust of those being studied, but more than that, through participation the researcher begins to understand their day-to-day routine, their pleasures, and their problems, and the resultant description of the culture will be to a large extent from their point of view. Of course, the participant observer never really becomes a part of the group being studied, and he or she will be more respected for being a nonjudgmental, sympathetic representative of his or her own culture.

In conducting our own research on aging in Samoa, we spent many months living in the islands. During this time we went into homes to interview older people and younger family members living with them. This approach allowed us to observe not only the circumstances in which families lived but also the nature of interaction between young and old. We also became involved in a broad range of activities and institutions that are part of life in the islands. We visited the hospital and talked with some of the staff, spent time in classrooms of elementary and high schools and the community college, attended church in several villages, were able to observe weddings and celebrate holidays with Samoan friends. We shopped in the local stores and the farmers' market, ate in restaurants, stood in line at the bank and the post office, and traveled on the local busses and interisland boats and airlines. In short, we experienced firsthand many of the conditions and some of the frustrations that Samoans experience, and in doing so we gained a better understanding of the context in which Samoans live and grow old. And later on, when we extended our research to Samoan migrants living in California, this knowledge of their native culture was invaluable for assessing the challenges and adjustments they faced in a new environment. These experiences are the essence of the participant-observation method of gathering ethnographic data.

Ethnography, then, is literally the science of describing cultural phenomena. Accurate documentation of human ways of life is considered of vital importance in this social science, but it is also considered important to carry the fact-finding activity one step further to the level of *ethnology*, which is a theorizing activity where cultural descriptions (ethnographies) are compared and generalizations then made about human nature.

Fully understanding the nature and cause of the problems and adjustments in regard to aging in a given society (let us say our own) is important, but it is also important to gain the wider perspective that embraces all societies in all times and in all places. Worldwide comparisons allow us to bring our own culture into sharper focus, and they may suggest new solutions to common problems or new adjustments to meet unique needs.

Not only does the broad scope of anthropology establish it as a useful discipline in studying gerontological phenomena but its unique perspective is also valuable. That perspective may be described as being (a) comparative, (b) holistic, (c) concerned with *emic* and *etic* viewpoints, (d) relativistic, (e) case-study oriented, and (f) committed to process or dynamic analysis.

Before we can deal with the nature of these various approaches, we must realize that these are all ways of analyzing culture, and that culture is a major concept of reference in anthropological analysis. *Culture* is defined as the shared patterns of values and behavior that are characteristic of a society, because they are passed on from generation to generation through symbolic communication. Once transmitted through teaching and learning, culture shapes the lives of individuals and gives form and stability to societal behavior.

Although aging is a biological phenomenon, our attitudes toward the aged and our own aging, the treatment our aged receive, the evaluation of the importance of the aged, and the roles considered appropriate for the old are more a matter of cultural tradition than of physiology. As Gregory Bateson (1950) put it:

Man lives by propositions whose truth depends upon his believing them. If he believes that the old are no good, weak, stubborn, whatever terms of abuse he likes to attach to them, then to a great extent that will become true of the old in the population where that is believed, and the old themselves will believe it and will reinforce the general belief that it is so. (p. 52)

Culture lies at the heart of all anthropological thought and investigation, and the cultural perspective represents an important factor of insight for gerontology. With the exception of certain aspects of longevity covered in Chapter 2, this book will be focused on the sociocultural aspects of aging.

Comparative Analysis

Anthropology was once known as the science that studied "primitive" or "nonliterate" peoples. However, in these waning years of the twentieth century, cultural change in the form of industrialization, urbanization, mass communication, and Westernization has made it increasingly difficult to find such preindustrial peoples. But anthropology does not require the existence of these populations to be a relevant social science discipline. More and more anthropologists are turning to their own culture or to subcultures within it for their studies, and simple isolated, preindustrial societies no longer dominate the interest and subject matter of anthropology. The science does continue to be comparative and cross cultural, however. Not only are *synchronic* studies (those comparing many cultures) important, but so are *diachronic* ones (where single societies are described at various time periods).

In *The Counterfeiters*, André Gide (1931) describes a particular species of fish that, because of its unique biological makeup, must swim at a particular depth in the ocean. It has never been able to descend to the bottom nor has it ever been able to rise to the surface. Such a fish, suggests Gide, has no insight into the nature of its watery environment because it has experienced neither sand nor air. Human beings who know only their own culture are in danger of this kind of provincialism. If one has never experienced another culture—through residence or reading—then there is a good chance that person does not fully understand the significance of what is happening in his or her own society.

Comparative analysis is frequently used in anthropology to determine whether a particular form of behavior—such as competitiveness, pugnacity, mother love, or acquisitiveness—is cultural behavior (and therefore learned) or whether it is a product of the human biological heritage (and therefore passed on genetically). In 1961 Cumming and Henry proposed that it was "natural" and beneficial for elders to disengage socially and economically. Because such disengagement was presented as "natural," anthropologists might expect to find the phenomenon in all cultures. They have not. In fact, they found that disengagement was quite common in Western industrial societies but relatively uncommon elsewhere.

Cross-cultural comparison has been tremendously helpful in investigating the concept of human longevity. Although the relative importance of nature and nurture are difficult to determine precisely, comparison of dietary differences, variations in work and play patterns, and differences in supportive social structures and respect patterns in various societies shed important light on some of the cultural influences on longevity.

In general, anthropology, because of its comparative emphasis, has much to offer in the study of aging. In addition to the question of disengagement and longevity, anthropology can enlighten us about many other issues as well: What defines a person as old? Is retirement a universal characteristic of old age? What roles are available to the elderly? How does family type affect the welfare of older persons? What can cross-cultural research teach us about the alternative approaches to long-term care within the family and in institutions? What are the determinants of status of the aged? Are the elderly the losers when cultural change occurs? Is it possible that elderly residents of a high-rise apartment building and those who travel about in recreational vehicles can be considered communities? Have people in certain areas of the world learned the secret to extreme longevity? These are just a few of the questions that comparative research on aging has examined and are among the topics that will be considered in subsequent chapters of this book.

Holistic Perspective

Anthropologists think of culture as a configuration of interrelated traits, complexes, and patterns, and they believe that one aspect of culture cannot be effectively studied without taking the totality into consideration. As Ruth Benedict (1934) so aptly phrased it: "All the miscellaneous behavior directed toward getting a living, mating, warring and worshipping the gods, is made over into consistent patterns in accordance with unconscious canons of choice that develop within the culture" (p. 48). Because life is really merely a series of events and people interacting, we must realize that to categorize human behavior as "economic," "political," or "religious" is to arbitrarily divide up human behavior for the convenience of study. Distortions occur when facts are taken out of context, and there has been a long history of faulty thinking that has resulted from this practice. Racial, economic, biological, and other forms of determinism are reductionist, oversimplified forms of analysis that have stressed one causal factor to the exclusion or under-emphasis of others. Comparative and holistic analysis has proved to be a valuable weapon against this kind of reasoning.

Although anthropology recognizes a great advantage in specialization, it is more interested in the total configuration of culture—in its organic wholeness—than in documenting every minute detail of every facet of human life. If forced to do so, the anthropologist will sacrifice detail for a comprehension of form.

Not only have anthropologists stressed the interrelationship of all aspects of culture, they have also emphasized the biocultural totality of human experience. Human behavior is partly a response to physical or animal needs and partly a following of established traditions. Although humanity is one biologically, there are almost as many kinds of culture as there are societies. To consider one factor without the other is to distort human nature. People require a given amount of nutriment to survive, but whether they receive it in two meals a day or five or in the form of raw fish or sauerbraten is a cultural matter.

Emic-Etic Perspectives

Any cultural situation can be viewed from the *inside* and from the *outside*. Anthropologists believe that much can be gained by attempting to see the culture as its participants see it. This approach, sometimes called *ethnoscience*, attempts to discover "folk" or local categories of thought and reality. This insiders' window on the world is referred to as the *emic* perspective, and this term comes from the word *phonemic*, which refers to the combination of meaningful sounds unique to a particular language. Therefore *emic* is not a universal reference to language but a specific reference to a particular language. The *etic* approach (deriving from the word *phonetic*), on the other hand, is the scientific perspective that the well-trained anthropologist brings to the analysis. This constitutes his or her cross-cultural frame of reference and is an objective and controlled procedure for weighing and sifting facts and theoretical viewpoints. Its approach to human behavior is a general, outsiders' approach, just as *phonetics* is the term for the science of all human speech production.

The best way to distinguish between *emic* and *etic* perspectives is to imagine the difference in perceptions of a worshipper and an art historian who are both observing a great stained-glass cathedral window. The window no doubt represents something very different, very personal, and very meaningful for the worshipper, who would include the window in his total complex of worship. The window might move him spiritually as well as artistically. The art historian, on the other hand, might be moved by the window's beauty but not by its connections with worship. He would analyze it coldly and objectively in terms of other great cathedral windows and in terms of established scholarly criteria for judging such architectural or artistic features.

Relativistic Perspective

Because of anthropology's insistence on a cross-cultural perspective and because several generations of anthropologists have lived among their foreign subjects and have come to respect them and see the wisdom of their lifeways, anthropology has come to be dominated by a kind of philosophical stance known as *cultural relativism*. Cultural relativism is both a *methodological* tool that ensures objective data collection and a *philosophical* and *theoretical* principle that calls for open-mindedness in accepting cultural diversity. It emphasizes the idea that no single culture can claim to have a monopoly on the "right" or "natural" way of doing things. From this standpoint, anthropologists who study gerontology believe that the meaning of old age and the effectiveness of solutions to the problems of old age can only be understood and evaluated in terms of the cultural context in which the aged reside. Although the common biological heritage of human beings and the inevitability of senescence create elements of common experience, anthropologists are extremely cautious about declaring that the customs in one society are more acceptable or more honorable than those in other societies. Who is to say that locking the elderly up in nursing homes is more humane than allowing them to wander off on the ice flow and freeze to death as Eskimo elders are sometimes permitted to do? Cultural behavior that may imply low status for the aged in one society may mean something entirely different in another.

Cultural relativism also warns that cultural institutions within one society may not easily transfer to another. Proof of this was observed by the authors in American Samoa, where a nutrition program for the aged was attempted. To begin with, Samoa is not a society that has a history of volunteerism, a major factor in such programs elsewhere. In Samoa, *families* serve the elderly—not neighbors or strangers who volunteer. Thus, when the government's planning began, Samoans suggested that food or money be distributed among families who would then make sure that their elderly got proper nourishment. American government officials (mostly funding agency personnel) objected to this on the grounds that other family members would perhaps get the food intended for the elderly. After long consideration, the government officials decided that the food should be cooked in the kitchens of the 26 consolidated elementary schools where food was already being prepared by kitchen personnel for government-subsidized hot meals for the schoolchildren. The elderly could simply go to the school for lunch. This solution created another problem because it did not take into consideration appropriate age status and role behavior, particularly in respect to titled chiefs, who maintained that it was beneath their dignity to go to school and line up like children just for a midday meal. Also, the usual time for Samoans to eat is not noon but at 10 a.m. and 7 p.m. A later attempt involved having restaurants provide meals for elders, again with little success.

In 1988, more than a decade after initial implementation of the nutrition program, older persons were being issued vouchers for $30 per month to use for food items at participating stores. These businesses were subject to penalties if they allowed purchase of nonfood items with a voucher. These approaches over the years have continued to highlight the conflict between foreign program guidelines and culturally acceptable behavior. In essence, an American program designed to assist elders who may benefit from meals and social interaction because many live alone does not translate easily into a culture "where the elderly live with and are adequately fed by their families" (Borthwick, 1977, p. 250). In Samoa, as in Micronesia where Borthwick did research, if an elder is in need of food, then the entire family is probably at risk.

Cultural relativism is a difficult concept to apply, because all peoples in all places tend to be *ethnocentric*, which means that they believe that their own values, customs, and attitudes are superior to those of people in other societies. Although respect for one's own cultural system and loyalty to one's own group is necessary and worthwhile, social scientists in particular must realize that there are many effective and efficient ways of doing things, and no one way of life is either "natural" or necessarily best. In fact, no technique of qualitatively evaluating cultures has ever been discovered.

Case-Study Approach

Anthropologists typically study small groups or communities through intensive long-term involvement as detailed earlier. In anthropological studies of aging and the aged, while the results of research in a retirement residence, a nursing home, a caregivers' support group, an ethnic neighborhood, or a small community are recognized as not necessarily representative of all such groups, each example would be a case study that can be compared with other similar studies to establish generalizations and theories about various phenomena. The title of the largest and most popular series of ethnographic monographs used in college courses, *Case Studies in Cultural Anthropology*,[1] is an indication of the fact that anthropologists consider their monographs cultural case studies.

Anthropology's use of the case-study method is similar in some respects to that found in the field of social work. Just as social workers go into homes to observe and document the lifestyle of individual families in their caseloads, so anthropologists go to communities or other cultures to investigate the circumstances of the peoples they wish to understand.

The holistic approach is characteristic of case studies, and in their book on case-study method, the Committee on the Family (1970) maintained that, in studying the family, four determinants of family functioning must be considered. They are (a) the cultural, (b) the interpersonal, (c) the psychological, and (d) the biological. This manual for social workers elaborates on the determinants:

> The cultural area includes the profile of value orientations associated with cultural affiliation of the family and the belief systems that pattern all role activities, including domestic roles, as well as the structure of the nuclear and extended family. The interpersonal area is composed of overt, day-to-day interactions between family members in maintenance of their role relations—their communications, alliances, and coalitions; expressions of feeling; ways of reaching decisions; methods of child rearing and control; handling of illness, finances, education, religion, recreation and losses through death or separation. The intrapsychic processes of individual members, including their unconscious cognitions, emotions, defenses, and object relations, comprise the psychological area. The biological area embraces the physical constitution of family members, including their age and sex, the state of their physical health, and the patterning of biological functions in nutrition, sleep, excretion, and motility. (Committee on the Family, 1970, pp. 258-259)

The above prescription for a case study for social workers could easily, with minor changes, serve as a guide for anthropologists studying cultures or cultural situations. Like social workers, anthropologists are not always sure what they will find, what aspects of the situation they will be required to document, or exactly what methods they will have to use in collecting their data. But they know without doubt that there will be some difficulties in establishing rapport, in comprehending the value systems of their subjects, and in understanding the complexities and subtleties of communication. Participant observation has proven effective in meeting these challenges.

Process Analysis

Anthropology's interest in change and process is perhaps older than any of its other interests. Beginning with speculations about the principle of cultural evolution before anthropology was even an established scholarly discipline, anthropologists have, for more than 200 years, attempted to understand the reasons for and ramifications of change under such headings as evolution, revolution, innovation, discovery, acculturation, diffusion, and modernization. Anthropologists interested in gerontology have been particularly concerned with modernization influences in developing countries and the effect that they have on status and roles of the elderly. The general assumption has been that the influence of Western industrial cultures will destroy the traditional values and agencies of support and recognition for the aged and that the status and authority of the aged will be reduced, despite a general increase in the number of elderly. Because change is an ongoing process in all societies, we will note the impact of cultural change on the elderly throughout this book and also in the chapter devoted to the issue.

We begin our exploration of aging in other cultures by drawing upon knowledge from physical anthropology to investigate human longevity, an evolutionary perspective on the hominid life span and senescence, the demographic transition occurring throughout the world, and, finally, the validity of claims of unusually long average life spans in enclaves long heralded as Shangri-las. We then discuss the work of anthropologists and other social scientists in regard to the status and role of the elderly, a topic that has dominated the interest of gerontologists since Leo Simmons wrote his classic volume, *The Role of the Aged in Primitive Society*, in 1945. This will be followed by cross-cultural considerations of the nature of the life cycle (including such topics as retirement and death), the structure and function of family, and the concept of community and how the nature of community affects senior citizens.

Because we believe that it is of vital importance to study human phenomena in cultural context, Chapter 6 will focus on what it means to grow old in a hunting society, that of the Eskimos, in a simple agricultural society, that of the Samoans, and, finally, in a modern industrial society—the United States. A chapter on ethnic and minority aging concentrates on subcultures in the United States, explaining how cultural tradition shapes the needs and roles of seniors. The chapter on applying anthropology also deals with cultural differences as they affect health and long-term care of the aged in America. Our final concern is with change, especially modernization and accompanying demographic change, and its effect on the status and well-being of the elderly. With a theoretical foundation established in regard to the many facets and factors of change and its ramifications, we will close with a prophetic chapter, "The Future of Aging in America," and a hope that our book will help our readers move into the next century with confidence, comprehension, and anticipation for their own golden years.

SUMMARY

From this brief treatment of the nature of anthropology, its interests, and its potential for gerontological research, we can see that anthropology's concern for cultural, biological, and historical dimensions of humankind makes it unique among the sciences that deal with aging. Even though anthropology has only recently developed its interest in aging and the aged, its somewhat different approach can profitably supplement the work of sociologists, psychologists, social workers, and biologists. Because it concerns itself with all peoples everywhere in the world today and at all times in history and prehistory, anthropology is specially equipped to deal with universal problems of aging and, through its comparative data, is able to shed valuable light on the relative adequacy or shortcomings of solutions to gerontological problems in America. Anthropologists consider the many societies of the world as so many experiments in human adjustment and survival in a variety of physical, ideological, and sociological environments. It is appropriate that they include in their study each society's adjustment to the process of growing old and societal accommodation to this phenomenon. A famous American anthropologist, Clyde Kluckhohn (1949), once suggested that "anthropology provides a mirror for man wherein he may see himself in all his infinite variety" (p. 11). This is anthropology's most important contribution to gerontology.

Growing out of anthropology's insistence on cross-cultural comparison is a philosophical attitude toward other cultures that greatly affects both its methodological approach and its theoretical conceptualizations. That philosophical position is known as *cultural relativism*, and it basically represents an open-mindedness in accepting cultural diversity around the world. Cultural relativism demands that no one culture be held up as offering the "right," "moral," "natural," or "superior" solutions to growing old or dealing with old people. Furthermore, moral or scientific judgments based on experience with but a single culture are

31

suspected of being unfair and invalid. Anthropological gerontologists believe that problems or understandings relating to old age must be analyzed only in terms of the cultural context in which they occur. The relativist approach also warns that cultural institutions cannot easily be transplanted from one culture to another. One society's solutions to their aging problems could prove disastrous to another society with different basic values and institutions.

NOTE

1. This series was edited by George and Louise Spindler and published by Holt, Rinehart & Winston, 1960-1961; it is currently published by Harcourt Brace Company.

A Cognitivist's View of the Units Debate in Cultural Anthropology

Roy D'Andrade
University of California, San Diego

This article explores some of the implications of the current ideational definition of culture. If culture consists of shared ideas, then the findings of cognitive psychology concerning the limits of short-term memory necessarily constrain the size and complexity of cultural units. Wierzbicka's universal linguistic primes *or* primitives *would then be the atomic units of culture. Although this approach has much to recommend it, problems remain concerning the relation of cultural ideas to their physical manifestations in artifacts and actions, and a classification of the kinds of relations cultural ideas have to their physical manifestations is presented. Finally, the notion that the collection of cultural items held by the members of a society form any kind of entity is critiqued, and the argument is made that there is just one common culture for all humans.*

There is a long-standing debate about whether it is possible to define basic units of culture. If it is possible, what are the basic units? Are beliefs about ghosts, for example, the same kind of thing as an initiation ceremony? Beliefs about ghosts are ideas that people

Author's Note: *This article was originally prepared for "Themes, Memes, and Other Schemes: What Are the Units of Culture?" (Garry Chick, organizer), 27th Annual Meeting of the Society for Cross-Cultural Research, February 1999, Santa Fe, NM.*

Cross-Cultural Research, Vol. 35 No. 2, May 2001 242-257

34

have, but initiation ceremonies are not ideas, they are a system of observable activities. Are both ideas and activities units of culture? What about physical objects—are they culture too? Any decision about the nature of units of culture first requires a definition of culture.

For the past 40 years, there has been general consensus in anthropology about the definition of culture (see Chick, 1997, for a discussion of types of cultural definitions). Following Parsons, Geertz (1973), Schneider (1968), Swartz (1991), Spiro (1987), and others presented persuasive arguments for defining culture as symbol and meaning. Ward Goodenough's (1957) definition of a society's culture as "whatever it is one has to know or believe in order to operate in a manner acceptable to its members" (p. 168) has also been very influential. In this modern paradigm, culture becomes purely mental—ideas and beliefs and knowledge and meanings. The ideas and knowledge needed to put on an initiation ceremony are culture, but the actual activities of the initiation ceremony are not culture and neither are the masks and ritual paraphernalia.

In one sense, this is a trivial change. One just does a bit of rewording—instead of saying "culture consists of shared ideas, shared activities, and artifacts," one says "culture consists of shared ideas about the world in general, ideas about how to perform certain activities, and ideas about how to make and use certain things." However, in another sense, a profound change has taken place; culture is now a purely mental phenomenon and hence a psychological phenomenon and hence constrained by the psychological processes of cognition and learning.

COGNITIVE CULTURAL UNITS

If we define culture as a kind of mental phenomenon—something cognitive—what follows? A central idea in the study of cognition is that humans have two kinds of memory systems, short-term or working memory and long-term memory. It is well-known that short-term or working memory is very limited. The number of items one can be aware of and hold in working memory is very small, approximately five to seven things (five according to George Mandler, 1985; seven according to George Miller, 1956). Long-term memory, on the other hand, can contain many hundreds of thousands of items (Dudai, 1997; Landauer, 1986).

The tiny size of working memory creates a severe bottleneck in human information processing. The external world at any moment contains many million potential chunks of information, information that human beings could learn and make use of. But for this information to become part of long-term memory, it must pass through a tiny space of about five items of working memory and be held there for a second or so. As a result, only a very small part of the information about the world ever gets remembered.

One might think that this bottleneck would constrain human intelligence quite severely, leaving humans with the sort of intellect exhibited by earthworms and snails. With such a tiny working memory, how can humans be so smart? A desktop computer's working memory holds a hundred million bytes of information—which means a desktop computer's working memory is approximately 10 million times larger than a human's working memory. And desktop computers are not very smart. How is it that people, despite their tiny working memories, have such impressive intellects?

How humans manage to be smart is undoubtedly the result of a number of things, including multiple parallel processing systems and distributed brain activation. Perhaps the most relevant process is *chunking*. The phenomenon of chunking is easy to demonstrate. For a classroom demonstration, an instructor prepares sheets of paper with large letters printed on them. The instructor holds up a sheet for a few seconds and then asks the students to write down the letters they saw on the sheet. Given only three letters on a sheet—for example, *X*, *Q*, and *B*—recall is excellent and students find the task easy. As the number of letters rises to six or so, students find the task more difficult but still possible. Above six or seven letters, the task becomes too difficult, and only five or six letters are remembered.

To illustrate the phenomenon of chunking, one of the sheets shown to the participants contains a set of scrambled letters (e.g., *R K Q O F U C B X N W O I*), which, if unscrambled, make simple words (e.g., *QUICK BROWN FOX*). Shown the sheet with the scrambled letters, recall is poor. But shown the sheet with the letters grouped into simple words, recall of all the letters is easy and accurate. What has happened is that the letters have obviously been chunked or packaged into larger units (words), and once packaged, only a small number of items need to be retained in working memory because recall of the words makes possible recall of the letters that make up the words. Without chunking, humans

36

would be unable to talk or make complex designs or objects. Any kind of complexity—in planning, reasoning, or categorizing—would be very difficult because complexity requires the mental manipulation of multiple items, and to manipulate more than a small number items, one must be able to chunk and then unpack items.

Less discussed in psychology are the sources of the chunks that make humans so smart. Some chunks are learned through simple experience. For example, the patterns that make up faces, trees, rocks, and so on are learned by observation, not just by humans but by most vertebrates. However, for humans, many chunks or patterns are culturally learned. Houses, furniture, cars, clothing, and so on—the artifacts of culture—are hierarchically complex arrangements of items. If these artifacts were not present to learn about, we would not be able to conceive of them. The development of these artifacts is the result of thousands of years of trial and error. Humans also live in a world of meaning artifacts. The speech sounds and written marks of language are meaning artifacts, physical stuff the child must learn to decode and encode.

What are the implications of this perspective for the problem of units? First, given the ideational definition culture, the basic units of culture are by definition cognitive processes. Although full consensus is lacking on exactly which cognitive processes are most basic, there is considerable agreement that the human cognitive system operates to produce an experiential world of objects. This basic cognitive proclivity is directly reflected in language. Langacker and others in the field of cognitive linguistics argued that the basic and universal sense of a noun is, as we were once told, of something being a thing. Langacker (1987) said,

> Counter to received wisdom, I claim that the basic grammatical categories such as noun, verb, adjective, and adverb are semantically definable. . . . A noun, for example, is a symbolic structure whose semantic pole instantiates the schema [THING]; or to phrase it more simple, a noun designates a *thing*. In a similar fashion, a verb is said to designate a process, whereas adjectives and adverbs designate different kinds of *atemporal relations*. (p. 189)

Humans have an impressive ability to entify almost anything, ranging from the perceptual objects that our visual system naturally isolates, such as trees and babies, to reifications of abstract relationships, such as equality.

An equally basic part of cognition is *predication*, the conceptualization of things participating in processes. In its simple sense, predication is the assertion that something is doing/having/being something, for example, "The dog barks." Langacker (1987) presented a detailed account of predication in his *Foundations of Cognitive Grammar*. Predication is important because humans do not just live in a world of objects; they live in a world in which objects are somewhere, have certain properties, and do something. From this perspective, noun-verb combinations are the basic molecules of thought.

Given an ideational definition, intersubjectively shared objects and the perceptual features of these objects constitute the basic building blocks or units of culture. These objects are then chunked into larger units through the process of predication. This claim follows from the cognitive perspective described earlier but does not necessarily help in creating a useful taxonomy of cultural things. However, the claim does have clear methodological implications. Thus, as Romney and Moore (2001 [this issue]) point out in their article in this collection, powerful techniques have been developed for the discovery of the nature and organization of cultural features characterizing the objects of a domain, and a variety of ethnographic questions can be answered using these techniques.

Over the past 25 years, a strong case has been made by Anna Wierzbicka that a small number of universal concepts are found as lexical items in all languages (Wierzbicka, 1972, 1992). Wierzbicka argued that these words are conceptual *primes* or *primitives* that form the basic units from which all other concepts are constructed. Wierzbicka's goal is to construct a simple, clear, universal semantic metalanguage, a language made up of the ordinary little words that everyone knows. Wierzbicka's universal metalanguage offers a potential means to ground all complex concepts in ordinary language and translate concepts from one language to another without loss or distortion in meaning. The idea of developing a universal metalanguage has often been proposed by philosophers and linguists. Wierzbicka's work is the most thorough and complete working out of this agenda to date. As Goddard (1998) said in his text on semantics about Wierzbicka's work,

> The main "discovery method" which has led to the current NSM [Natural Semantic Metalanguage] inventory has been experimentation (trial and error) with trying to define a wide variety of expressions. All the proposed primitive have proved themselves, on the one

38

TABLE 1
Proposed Natural Semantic Metalanguage (NSM)
Semantic Primitives (after Wierzbicka, 1996)

Substantives: I, YOU, SOMEONE, PEOPLE/PERSON, SOMETHING/THING
Mental predicates: THINK, KNOW, WANT, FEEL, SEE, HEAR
Speech: SAY, WORD
Actions, events, and movement: DO, HAPPEN, MOVE
Existence: THERE IS
Life: LIVE, DIE
Determiners: THIS, THE SAME, OTHER
Quantifiers: ONE, TWO, SOME, ALL, MANY/MUCH
Evaluators: GOOD, BAD
Descriptors: BIG, SMALL
Time: WHEN/TIME, NOW, BEFORE, AFTER, A LONG TIME, A SHORT TIME,
FOR SOME TIME
Space: WHERE/PLACE, HERE, ABOVE, BELOW, FAR, NEAR, SIDE, INSIDE
Interclausal linkers: BECAUSE, IF
Clause operators: NOT, MAYBE
Metapredicate: CAN
Intensifier, augmentor: VERY, MORE
Taxonomy, partonomy: KIND OF, PART OF
Similarity: LIKE

hand, to be very useful and versatile in framing explications, and, on the other hand, to be themselves resistant to (non-circular) explication. Ultimately, the only way to show that something is NOT an indefinable element is to succeed in defining it. It is never possible, strictly speaking, to prove absolutely that something is indefinable. The best we can say is that various attempts are made and seen to fail—as in the case of elements like I, YOU, SOMEONE, SOMETHING, THIS—to the claim to indefinability becomes stronger and stronger. (p. 59)

The current inventory (taken from Goddard, 1998) is presented in Table 1.

As an aside, an interesting use of Wierzbicka's natural semantic metalanguage is to construct clear definitions for technical terms in the social sciences. For example, using Wierzbicka's metalanguage, Goddard (1998) critiqued writers who present definitions that are more complex semantically than the original term to be defined. I have found attempting to translate social science theoretical terms into Wierzbicka's universals to be a sobering experience.

39

To give an example of Wierzbicka's (1992) use of NSM, consider her analysis of the difference between the English word *disgust* and the approximate French translation *dégoût*:

> *disgust*
> X thinks something like this:
> I now know: this person did something bad
> people shouldn't do things like this
> when one thinks about it, one can't not feel something bad
> because of this, X feels something bad
> X feels like someone who thinks something like this:
> I have something bad in my mouth
> I don't want this
> *dégoût*
> X thinks something like this: this is bad
> because of this, X feels something bad
> X feels like someone who thinks this:
> I have something bad in my mouth
> I don't want this
>
> The differences in the definitions reflect the fact that "dégoût" is associated more closely and directly with eating than "disgust," while "disgust" involves feelings caused by bad and ugly human actions. Thus "disgust" is more moral and judgmental than "dégoût."
> (pp. 125-129)

Wierzbicka has been remarkably effective in illuminating and specifying cultural differences in meaning between near equivalent words in different languages. Her inventory of prime terms has empirical claims to universality. Although there are obvious problems with regard to polysemy—consider all the different senses of *know* found in any good English dictionary—such difficulties do not seem unsolvable. The Natural Semantic Metalanguage project will, I think, be refined and elaborated with ever-increasing amounts of data and will continue to grow in value as a technique of semantic analysis.

If one defines culture as shared ideas/meanings/knowledge/understandings, then these shared ideas must either be composed of undefinable prime terms or they must be composed of chunks made up of prime terms. To the extent that Wierzbicka has succeeded in finding a universal metalanguage, all cultural ideas/meanings/knowledge/understandings are definable within this metalanguage. This inventory also needs to include the features of the terms and the syntax by which these terms can be put into sentences/propositions/beliefs.

Wierzbicka's universal terms are analogous to the atoms of the physical world (unfortunately, use of this analogy seems to annoy many anthropologists). Of the enormous number of combinations of these terms that make up the sentences that correspond to the possible ideas/meanings/knowledge/understandings of a person, some are cultural—that is, are intersubjectively shared by collectives within a society. Just as more than a hundred kinds of atoms can combine into more than 20 million kinds of molecules, so the 50 or more universal concepts can combine into hundreds of thousands of ideas. This puts the anthropologist who knows and is able to use the Natural Semantic Metalanguage in the same position as the chemist who knows about atoms—most of the actual things in the world are molecules, and it is their properties that one wants to investigate. Knowledge about atoms is helpful to the chemist only because it helps in understanding the nature of the molecules. Thus, knowing the basic units does not answer questions about how to classify the many things that ethnographers see and write about. A few simple elements can be chunked or combined into a huge variety of complex things. Gatewood's (2001 [this issue]) problem of how to classify bows still remains. How to build a bow and how to use a bow can be described in using a few basic universal concepts, but that fact does not solve the problem of how to construct a taxonomy of bows. A major difficulty involves the fact that most cultural items can be packed into larger and larger cultural chunks or broken down into smaller and smaller cultural chunks. The problem then becomes one of picking the right level or size chunks—that is, the level of detail that will facilitate analysis and comparison.

PROBLEMS WITH THE DEFINITION
OF CULTURE AS PURE IDEA

In my view, it is a mistake to treat culture as consisting of nothing but ideas, meanings, understandings, and so on. Definitions, to be useful, should "carve nature at the joints." But cultural ideas/meanings/knowledge/understandings are always fused to physical manifestations. Just as language needs both meaning and sound, so culture needs both ideas and physical manifestations. It would be odd if linguists decided to define language as just meanings and to treat the sounds of speech as something else entirely.

Unfortunately, anthropologists have done exactly this with respect to the definition of culture.

To make matters even more confusing, anthropologists and other social scientists tend to use many technical terms that are ambiguous with respect to whether they include both ideas and physical manifestations. Thus the term *discourse* is ambiguous with respect to whether it refers just to the actual talk that people produce, just to the ideas that are expressed in the talk, or to both. Standard terms such as *role, norm, structure,* and *symbol* also have this dual character; rarely is it clear whether the person using the term wants to include both the physical and mental or wants to refer to only one of these. The advantage of such ambiguity is that it avoids taking either an idealist or materialist position. The disadvantage is that it leaves unanalyzed the relations between cultural ideas and the physical manifestations of these ideas.

There are a number of ways in which cultural ideas are fused to physical events. First, there is the relation of the physical symbol to the meaning of the symbol. Ideas, to be communicated, need a medium—pantomime, speech, writing, or whatever—and conventional meanings need conventional physical forms or physical symbols. Second, there is the fusion between cultural ideas and physical artifacts that instantiates those ideas. Chairs and tables are examples. There is the idea of what a chair is, the ideas needed to build a chair, and the ideas about the use of chairs; all of these fuse the connection between this type of physical thing and mental processes.

Third, there is the kind of complex fusion that exists between a dollar bill and the idea of *money.* John Searle (1995) called money, marriage, names, and rights *culturally constructed objects.* The dollar bill counts as money or wealth, although it is paper and wealth is not. A dollar bill is not a symbol for money in the way the word *hamburger* is a symbol for a hamburger. A dollar bill counts as money, but the word *hamburger* does not count as food (one can use a dollar bill for money but one cannot use the word *hamburger* for a hamburger). Whereas many culturally constructed objects have direct physical instatiations (dollar bills, coins, signatures, voting ballots, etc.), many other culturally constructed objects are manifest only indirectly. One's right to free speech, for example, is manifested by actions such as standing on a soapbox and denouncing the government and no one from the government being able to do anything legally to stop it. This is indeed a complex contingency but a contingency between ideas and kinds of physical events nonetheless.

Fourth, cultural ideas can be conventionally externalized in a society. For example, Western cultural ideas about love are conventionally externalized in numerous sayings, jokes, stories, movies, songs, paintings, and so on. Each of these externalizations involves the physical expression of the cultural idea. Finally, cultural ideas can also be institutionalized in roles; for example, the cultural concept of *grades* is institutionalized in the role of the student who must obtain a certain grade to pass a course, and gender-related ideas are institutionalized in gender roles in a great variety of ways.

In summary, each of the cognitive molecules that make up the shared learnings of a society is in variable ways fused to physical events: as the physical sign of a symbol, as an artifact, as a culturally constructed object, as a conventional externalization, and to role behavior through institutionalization. Defining culture as just shared ideation leaves out the fact that cultural ideas are always fused to a variety of physical manifestations through which they are learned, communicated, and enacted. With respect to the problems of identifying cultural units, the fusion of cultural ideas to physical events creates complexities, as Gatewood's (2001) discussion of problems of form, function, and meaning with respect to the Sun Dance illustrates. However, such complexities do not affect the possibility of using cognitive molecules (or *schemas*, as I would term them) as the basis for identifying and classifying cultural items. Form, function, and meaning are each composed of cognitive molecules with physical fusions, and the Sun Dance variations are just that—variations in the cognitive molecules and their physical fusions that make up different macromolecules in different Plains tribes.

CULTURE AS A UNIT

Although one can argue that there are real cultural units in the sense that the ideational aspect of culture must be composed of whatever conceptual primes there are, one cannot argue from either facts or first principles that cultures are units, at least not in the usual sense of the word *unit*—something that has some degree of *real thingness*.

43

Culture is not an entity, but it is a collection. For example, the items now on my desk can be considered a collection of items, and I can say "This collection of things on my desk—*it* is growing," as if *it* were a thing. Similarly, one can say that the collection of cultural items active in the minds of the people of Bali form a collection of sorts and therefore constitute a *thing*. But the collection of things on my desk doesn't really make much of a thing because the items on my desk aren't in immediate contact with each other, aren't made of the similar stuff, don't have much of a common fate, don't strongly resist dispersion, and don't interact strongly. Basically, the collection as whole has no causal properties. These criteria for *entitativity* are Donald Campbell's (1958) and are presented in more detail in Gatewood's (2001) article. In my opinion, the situation with respect to the entitativity of the collection of cultural items found in the minds of people living on Bali is not much better than that for the things on my desk, Geertz's (as presented in Shweder & LeVine, 1984) opinion on the matter notwithstanding.

There are three strong arguments against thinking of a culture as an entity. The first is defining a culture as the total collection of cultural items held by the members of a society—the items held by members of any one society are almost always held by members of many other societies. Try, for example, to think of a truly unique cultural item found in only one society in the world. It is not impossible, but it is difficult. Different cultures—that is, the collection of cultural items held by members of different societies—are not very different. Cultures are recombinations of a limited stock of cultural items. I take this to be an established empirical fact, amply documented by many hundreds of ethnographies.

True, the particular combination of cultural items found on Bali is unique, but this kind of uniqueness is without consequence unless one can show that this collection has special causal properties that it would not have if it were not exactly this particular combination. No one has been able to demonstrate—or even argue convincingly—that complex collections as total entities have special causal properties.

Second, the particular combination of cultural items found for any one society is usually in a state of change. Diffusion, innovation, drift, and other processes are at work, making the claim that there is one collection of items that can characterize a given society for any substantial time period hard to maintain. Of course, there are always items that are relatively permanent, and one could arbitrarily call the collection of items that haven't changed recently "the culture of society X," but this is not a very satisfactory way to construct a definition.

Third, in 30 years of investigation in cognitive anthropology, I have rarely found much conceptual interrelatedness across cultural domains (D'Andrade, 1995). Within domains, on the other hand, there is often a good deal of cognitive connectivity. But American ideas about how to use soupspoons are not cognitively related to American ideas about the washability of cotton or the theorems related to the square root of −1 or how to be a good friend. And so it goes for most items—they are cognitively connected only to items in the same domain and unrelated cognitively to the huge number of items residing in other domains. Of course, again there is the option of defining "the culture of society X" as just those items that one believes are most strongly related to each other, but again, this seems like a poor way of constructing a definition.

The real point here is that it doesn't matter that one can't define the *it* that makes up culture because culture isn't really an *it* at all. The total collection of cultural items is a fact but not a thing. Each of the items is a thing, and these things are real—they have physical existence in human brains, and they have causal powers. Do not think of culture as a thing that does something. *It* doesn't—it, as a collection, has no causal powers. So it doesn't matter if one can't enumerate the entire collection or that the collection changes rapidly. Cultural items matter; culture as a total entity doesn't.

CULTURAL UNITY

I would argue that in a real sense there is only one culture—the culture of humankind—and that societal differences with respect to cultural items are small. The argument here is not that of psychic unity but cultural unity. The basic assertion is that there is a common basic culture that all humans learn that involves similar shared understandings about people and the world. There are interesting elaborations of this basic culture, but these elaborations are tightly constrained by a common psychobiological heritage (psychic unity comes in here) shared by all humans (Spiro, 1987). I agree with Gatewood (2001), who said, "Lowie (1936) had it right more than 50 years ago when he wrote, 'There is only one cultural reality that is not artificial, to wit: the culture of all humanity at all periods and in all places (p. 305) " (p. 228).

Although I do not think that cultures are entities, and although I believe there is just one basic culture for all humanity, I also believe that small differences in individual cultural items have great causal effects. Consider a society that is exactly like other societies in most ways except that rather than having the typical understanding that one should fight one's enemies and kill them if necessary, its members have the understanding that one should whenever possible kill everyone who is not a member of one's own society. The change in propositional content is not great, but the effects of that change would be, especially on visiting strangers.

Perhaps it is for reasons such as this that we humans have learned to be very sensitive to small cultural differences and to be very wary when we encounter unusual ways of acting or thinking. The sense of being in a totally different universe when one encounters small cultural differences can be very powerful. For example, tourists from San Diego who go to Tijuana encounter minor differences in the way buildings and roads are constructed along with certain differences in smells and dress. It is interesting that many tourists say they feel they are in a totally exotic and alien world. For them, it all seems different. Perhaps this strong human sensitivity to small cultural differences has led anthropologists to experience the culture they have studied as if it were almost totally different than anything else.

One problem with arguments about similarity and difference is that it is hard to establish the relevant population of features or items. For example, how different are a horse and a camel? It depends on the set of features one selects. One can pick a set of features such that no camel would share any feature with a horse. Or, one could select a set of features such that every feature is shared by both. How different one thinks horses and camels are depends on the selection of items through which they are compared. Similarly, the degree of difference between the collections of cultural items held by different societies depends on how we select and define items. If we select items such as getting food, having families, interacting with spirits, using fire, and so on, then all cultures are going to be very similar. If we select items such as having an emperor who spends a lot of time gardening, not believing in human physiological paternity, having a flag with 50 white stars on it, and so on, then very few societies will be similar. However, if cognitive molecules of culture are treated as real things, then constraints are placed on how items of culture are selected and defined. Items of culture must correspond to the items that exist in the shared short-term memories of the people of a society. This fixes the population of items and makes possible meaningful statements about similarity and difference.

Perhaps it would be helpful to mention the kinds of experience that have led me to argue that societies do not differ greatly in their collections of cultural items. As a graduate student, I was a research assistant for John Whiting, and among other things, I worked in the HRAF files, coding the presence or absence of various culture traits. Together with William Stephens (Stephens & D'Andrade, 1961), I worked on the coding of kin avoidances. In reading the ethnographic literature, the first impression was that with respect to kin avoidances, societies differed greatly. However, after analyzing the usual items that make up avoidances (e.g., "not being permitted to be alone together," "not being permitted to use the other person's name," "not being permitted to sleep in the same bed," "not being permitted to touch," etc.), it became clear that most of these items are found in various relationships in almost every society. Furthermore, it also became clear that there is considerable patterning of avoidance items; avoidance items form Guttman scales using both between- and within-society data. Finally, it also became clear that there is a high degree of patterning across societies in which relatives are avoided and which are not. Of course, there is variation across societies, but the degree of variation is more accurately described as the elaboration of underlying universal patterns than as a world of large differences.

It is important to be clear about such matters. Although the collections of cultural items held by different societies may be broadly similar, there are differences, and these differences can have huge effects on everything from the psychological health of a people to the number of fish in the sea. Culture is not a structure in any meaningful sense, but it is a complex and pervasive network of causally active items, as Malinowski argued.

What then is the difference between a cultural structure and a cultural causal system? A cultural structure is a set of culture elements that are cognitively related to each other. Examples are the taxonomic structure of plant terms in many languages, componential paradigms of kin terms, Levi-Straussian analyses of myths, the grammars of languages, story grammars, and a variety of cultural models. A cultural system, in contrast, consists of a number of cultural elements that are causally related such that every item in the structure can be connected along a long or short pathway of causal links to every other element. Thus, modern

47

automobiles need computer chips in the engines to regulate the flow of gas and air, the production of computer chips is a result of the invention of the transistor, which is causally related the development of research laboratories, which require huge capital investments, and so on. The ramifications of the causal networks connecting cultural elements are so great that almost any cultural element can be plausibly related to another in 5 to 10 causal steps. Much of the confusion about the entitativity of culture may be due to confusing the widespread systematicity of culture with the very limited structuring of culture.

SUMMARY

The items of culture are complex cognitive molecules or schemas, chunked out of universal cognitive atoms. They are cognitively particulate, fused to a variety of physical manifestations, variably distributed within societies, widely shared across societies, and variably internalized psychologically. Because they are internalized in human minds, they have causal powers. As a result of the fact that cognitive atoms can be chunked into many different kinds of cognitive molecules of varying size and complexity, it is sometimes difficult to classify cultural items. But as an empirical matter, cross-cultural research has been able to establish strong functional, geographic, and historical correlations by doing exactly this.

References

Campbell, D. T. (1958). Common fate, similarity, and other measures of the status of aggregates of persons as social entities. *Behavioral Science, 3,* 14-25.

Chick, G. (1997). Cultural complexity: The concept and its measurement. *Cross-Cultural Research, 31,* 275-307.

D'Andrade, R. G. (1995). *The development of cognitive anthropology.* Cambridge, UK: Cambridge University Press.

Dudai, Y. (1997). How big is human memory, or on being just useful enough. *Learning and Memory, 3,* 341-365.

Gatewood, J. B. (2001). Reflections on the nature of cultural distributions and the units of culture problem. *Cross-Cultural Research, 35,* 227-241.

Geertz, C. (1973). *The interpretation of cultures.* New York: Basic Books.

Goddard, C. (1998). *Semantic analysis.* Oxford, UK: Oxford University Press.

Goodenough, W. (1957). *Cultural anthropology and linguistics. Language and linguistics 9.* Washington, DC: Georgetown University.

Landauer, T. K. (1986). How much do people remember? Some estimates of the quantity of learned information in long-term memory. *Cognitive Science, 10,* 477-493.

Langacker, R. (1987). *Foundations of cognitive grammar.* Stanford, CA: Stanford University Press.

Mandler, G. (1985). *Cognitive psychology: An essay in cognitive science.* Hillsdale, NJ: Lawrence Erlbaum.

Miller, G. (1956). The magical number seven, plus or minus two: Some limits on our capacity for processing information. *Psychological Review, 63,* 2.

Romney, A. K., & Moore, C. C. (2001). Systemic culture patterns as basic units of cultural transmission and evolution. *Cross-Cultural Research, 35,* 154-178.

Schneider, D. (1968). *American kinship: A cultural account.* Englewood Cliffs, NJ: Prentice Hall.

Searle, J. R. (1995). *The construction of social reality.* New York: Free Press.

Shweder, R. A., & LeVine, R. (1984). *Culture theory: Essays on minds, self, and emotion.* Cambridge, UK: Cambridge University Press.

Spiro, M. (1987). *Culture and human nature: Theoretical papers of Melford E. Spiro.* Chicago: University of Chicago Press.

Stephens, W. B., & D'Andrade, R. G. (1961). Kin avoidance. In W. B. Stephens (Ed.), *Oedipus complex, cross-cultural evidence* (pp. 124-150). New York: Free Press.

Swartz, M. (1991). *The way the world is: Cultural processes and social relations among the Mombasa Swahili.* Berkeley: University of California Press.

Wierzbicka, A. (1972). *Semantic primitives.* New York: Athaneum.

Wierzbicka, A. (1992). *Semantics, culture, and cognition.* Oxford, UK: Oxford University Press.

Wierzbicka, A. (1996). *Semantics, primes and universals.* Oxford, UK: Oxford University Press.

Roy D'Andrade is professor of anthropology at the University of California, San Diego. He received his Ph.D. from Harvard University in 1962. His major interests are in cognitive anthropology, quantitative methods, theory, and American culture. He is the author of The Development of Cognitive Anthropology *(Cambridge University Press, 1995) and is a member of the National Academy of Sciences.*

Annu. Rev. Anthropol. 1994. 23:137–58

OLD AGE: Cultural and Critical Perspectives

Lawrence Cohen

Department of Anthropology, University of California, Berkeley, California 94720

KEY WORDS: old age, gerontology, generation, critical gerontology, aging

INTRODUCTION

Despite numerous review articles and programmatic essays surveying the social and cultural anthropology of old age (2, 13, 14, 41, 47, 53, 55, 79, 82, 99, 102, 103), a theme in many of them is the relative paucity of anthropological attention to the topic. In 1967 Clark made the classic observation that "if one is to judge from typical anthropological accounts, the span of years between the achievement of adult status and one's funerary rites is either an ethnographic vacuum or a vast monotonous plateau of invariable behavior" (13). Clark's criticism, opening anthropology's future while closing its past to old age, was soon routinized into a requisite lament preceding many essays on the anthropology of aging (79).

This gerontological lament did not, however, correlate with the writing of actual monographs. In 1980, after thirteen years and much productive research by many scholars, Fry could still begin her edited anthology by noting that "anthropology has a long history of being interested in age, but not in aging or the aged" (41). Similarly, in 1981 Amoss & Harrell offered an anthology to "help to remedy a massive neglect of old age by the discipline of anthropology" (2); and in 1984 Keith & Kertzer began their introduction to another anthology by again drawing attention to the need in anthropology to "pay more systematic attention to the role of age in human societies and cultural sys-

51

tems." What was at stake for the authors was perhaps summed up in the first sentence: "This book admittedly aims to proselytize" (58).

An abundance of writing about an apparent lack of writing presents an interesting contradiction, and it forces us to rethink what this writing—all these reviews that by their own accounts survey and signify an absence—might then be about. Why, it might be asked, were so many reviews and assessments produced that share the sense that there isn't much to review? In dwelling on the contradictions and paradoxes of this emergent discourse of geroanthropology[1] (84), I want to offer a heretical reading of its narrative claims of a salvatory future against a blighted past. Heresy seems to me a necessary response to the language of mission and conversion ubiquitous to the field, Kertzer & Keith's will to proselytize. Yet if the review article is itself somewhat of an instantiating genre within geroanthropology, legitimating in its frequent reiteration this enforced youth with its Golden Future and Leaden Past, then any new review must tread carefully if it would claim to do otherwise. Rather than reiterate the few oases in the imagined desert [classically, the work of Simmons (100)] or chronicle the important achievements of the new geroanthropology—which have been carefully documented in the review literature cited above—I want to frame another past and another present, both to focus on the kind of questions geroanthropology has not tended to ask and to reread the ethnographic vacuum taken by now as an unquestioned part of geroanthropological prehistory.

This review makes no claim to be a comprehensive review of all significant ethnographically or cross-culturally defined work in gerontology. The several published bibliographies of old age, anthropology, and ethnicity indicate that such work numbers in the thousands of articles, books, and films (40, 97). It eschews reproducing the standard categories of cross-cultural gerontology, such as life history, life span and life course, age stratification, grandparenthood, modernization and disengagement theories and challenges to them, caregiving, chronicity, and most recently, critical gerontology. Each of these perspectives and debates engages important questions, but their separation as independent areas of inquiry with reliable and clear-cut methodologies and boundaries may have more to do with the funding structure of much American gerontological work and its relationship to biomedical authority than with their stated objects. To borrow a phrase of Strathern, what is of concern here is the methodological rhetoric involved in "the manufacture of a subdiscipline" (108).

---

[1]
  Several disciplinary labels have appeared to describe the subdiscipline. *The anthropology of aging* is perhaps the most common, but it is less about aging from birth to death than about old age, and the euphemism is significant. *Gerontology and anthropology* is also common, perhaps because it leaves open whether the disciplinary commitment of the researcher is primarily to one or the other field or to both. I use *geroanthropology* because it is, quite blessedly, the shortest.

This second point is best illustrated by example. One of the characteristics of geroanthropology is its rapid alchemy of theoretical perspective into scientistic and pseudo-operationalizable jargon. Even Luborsky & Sankar's critical geroanthropological essay (68), which parallels some of the concerns of this review, ironically conjoins a critical sociology of science to a far less critical mystification of the authors' method. Luborsky & Sankar claim to utilize Frankfort School sociology to apply "critical theory" to gerontological research agendas. As anthropologists, they are concerned specifically with adding "culture" to what has become known as the Critical Gerontology perspective (3, 75). But their discussion of critical theory is vague and limited to the assertion that "scientific and philosophical constructs are enmeshed in and serve to recreate the wider socio-historical settings." The term *critical* is taken as a monolithic and unambiguous signifier of method. The text's referent is ultimately not the Continental tradition that it invokes yet never engages, but rather a simulacrum of that tradition used to mark subdisciplinary boundaries.

Luborsky & Sankar move immediately from the invocation of critique to the naturalization of their approach as CG (Critical Geronotology) and CG Studies. Culture, when added to CG, generates extended CG. Along with a scientific-sounding nomenclature, an operationalizable method is offered, promising "the systematic pursuit of a set of clearly articulated questions" through a quantifiable set of components. Over and over, the language of hard science and real results is proffered: the considerable irony and rapidity of this move from critical stance to positivist rhetoric goes unnoticed.

A related concern raised by the authors' invocation of critical theory is the seldom articulated relationship between sociological and anthropological theory in gerontological social science. The authors' appeal to a sociological framework for a critical theory and their mechanistic use of culture as something one can insert into an analysis recapitulate the institutional history of professional gerontology and its embeddedness in ideologies of applied sociology and social work. With such a dearth of anthropological theory in gerontological settings, the term *anthropology* becomes less an epistemological than a professional marker, and the term *culture*—elsewhere an increasingly treacherous foundation for the anthropologist's practice—is proudly displayed as disciplinary icon.

The Luborsky & Sankar essay is state-of-the-art gerontological anthropology. I cite it at the beginning of this review to stress what is at stake in the debate I hope to engender. In short: Where is contemporary anthropological theory in the contemporary anthropology of old age? Why is it represented but seldom engaged? Is a genuinely critical gerontology possible within the parameters of the subfield? If we are to avoid, paraphrasing Clark, either a theoretical vacuum or a vast monotonous plateau of invariable "culture," how must we renegotiate a history?

THE EPISTEMOLOGY OF GEROANTHROPOLOGY

In the 1980s, disciplinary lament slowly shifted to cries of victory: American geroanthropological narratives of mission among the unbelievers gave way to those of successful conversion. In 1981, Nydegger contrasted the dearth of work in the anthropological past with an emerging shift: "...interest is accelerating. Anthropological gerontology is shaping itself into a distinct speciality" (82). By 1990 Sokolovsky confirmed the strength of an "important new specialty" and offered several more names for it: comparative sociogerontology, ethnogerontology, and the anthropology of aging (102). Professional structures emerged: a coterie of leaders, including many of the editors of the anthologies cited above; an organization, the Association of Anthropology and Gerontology (AAGE); and a journal, the *Journal of Cross-Cultural Gerontology*. Group rituals and narratives appeared, for example, centered around the scramble to attend the often conflicting meetings of the Gerontological Society of America (GSA) and the American Anthropological Association (AAA). By 1992, Keith (54) could declare triumphantly, at the GSA meetings in Washington, DC, that the battle for the inclusion and serious consideration of old age within anthropology had been won. But the language of unending mission still dominated her remarks, through its inversion. Now that gerontology has conquered anthropology, Keith suggested, the new task is the spreading of the anthropological gospel within gerontology. No rest for the faithful.

There are two possible approaches to the pervasiveness of this explicit and apparently unceasing language of conversion in geroanthropology. One is a hermeneutic of generosity reading it as the necessary accompaniment of a paradigm shift in a passively but pervasively ageist discipline. The other is a hermeneutic of suspicion taking the sheer quantity and force of this language seriously in asking what else might be at stake for the architects of discourse, particularly in terms of their relationship to old persons, the disciplinary object.

Both approaches are necessary. Ageist language and potentially dehumanizing assumptions continue to influence anthropological work, often in very subtle ways. A recent anthology of feminist anthropology begins in the editor's acknowledgements with a reminder of gendered difference in the extraprofessional pressures placed upon academics: "This project was uniquely arduous, in part for a gendered reason. Most of the contributors (and I) are women in 'sandwich generation' positions...my thanks to contributors who made valiant efforts in hard times" (25). The authors' dilemma as women taking care of teenagers and elderly parents is quite real, and is inarguably gendered. But the sandwich generation as a construction of a middle aged and middle class authorial voice draws its irony not from the expected burden of college-aged children but from the other source of pressure—the inherently difficult and here dangerously naturalized burden of older parents. The elaboration of middle-aged experience as a series of arduous and valiant efforts assumes an unquestioned sense of the burdensomeness of old people. Links and bridges to women older than the volume's contributors are effectively denied in this reduction of older persons to nameless pressures. That the reference is situated within a text otherwise carefully attentive to the politics of difference and their representation suggests the continued invisibility of the representational politics of generation and old age in anthropological writing.

Yet the example of feminist anthropology is instructive in a second sense. Whereas this field is constituted in terms of questions of women both as authors and as subjects of anthropological discourse, geroanthropology is not primarily or even partially a movement generated by old anthropologists. Old persons remain distinctly the Other. Given the extent of geroanthropology's construction as an unrepentant heterology, I adopt the latter hermeneutic, of suspicion, in reviewing its claims to knowledge. Specifically, I challenge both geroanthropology's paradigmatic novelty and its anti-ageist self-construction, drawing on the critical approaches Luborsky & Sankar describe and in particular on Estes' now classic analyses (27–30).

Estes chronicles the paradox of gerontology as a growing service industry that dedicates itself to preserving and protecting the independence and normality of old persons yet requires their dependence and marginality to survive. I have elsewhere built upon her analysis in a critique of international gerontology (16). Estes' *The Aging Enterprise* is about the "programs, organizations, bureaucracies, interest groups, trade associations, providers, industries, and professionals that serve the aged in one capacity or another" (27). Both the book and Estes' follow-up article a decade and a half later (29) focus on the relationship between old age as service industry and the articulation of policy. In extending the critique to the sociology of knowledge, I foreground an anthropological concern with local epistemologies.

Like critical gerontology, Estes' own practice is an ironic site of gerontology as aging enterprise. "The Aging Enterprise Revisited" was delivered as the 1992 Kent Lecture at the GSA meetings in Washington, DC, the same meetings where Keith renewed the call to mission. In front of several thousand gerontologists, the aging enterprise incarnate, Estes invoked Maggie Kuhn and the Gray Panthers and other signifiers of an activist gerontology articulated by and for older persons. But the gap between the vision of the Gray Panthers and the constitution of the gerontological audience, who through Estes' powerful speech could erase all generational difference and envision themselves as fellow travelers, mirrored the gap between critical theory and CG studies: again, politics as representation.

Geroanthropology, like gerontology as a whole, fails to articulate an internal politics or hermeneutics of generational difference, and disguises this difference through the language of conversion and the trope of anger that underlies it ("no one here cares about old age") and through the language of exploration ("old age is *terra incognita*, awaiting our discovery"). The language of conversion is ubiquitous in gerontological and geriatric writing. For the World Assembly on Aging in Vienna in 1982, the United States Department of State (110) produced a document summarizing the history of American gerontology, which from the outset is framed as a missionary speciality. Thus the report notes that in the 1950s an "Inter-University Council on Social Gerontology [met to] further professional training" through "two month-long indoctrination programs for 75 college and university faculty members who had developed an interest in aging."

By a trope of anger, I mean that writing in gerontology and geriatrics frequently takes the narrative form: "Old people are neglected. No one appears to realize this unpleasant fact. I [the author] do; I hope to convince you. Together we can make old age a good age." Nascher, the New York physician who coined the term *geriatrics* in 1909, in later life offered a classic conversion narrative (quoted in 109) explaining his founding of the field. Early in his medical training in the 1880s, Nascher was struck by the frequency with which physicians used the rationale of "it's just old age" to avoid disentangling the complex medical problems of elderly patients. Nascher retells the birth of geriatrics as an epiphany: visiting a slum workhouse with mostly elderly inhabitants, young Nascher and his medical preceptor are accosted by an old woman complaining of her pain. "It's just old age," Nascher is told. Suddenly he realizes that it is not just old age, but rather disease. In the declaration of old age's normality and the refusal of others to see, Nascher has the vision of geriatrics. He composes a monumental text, *Geriatrics* (81), drawing on contemporary debate on the line between the normal and the pathological in medicine (9, 10) both to assert the normality of old age and to declare that in old age, the distinction between normal and pathological is lost. The contradiction in this foundational text continues to suffuse geriatric and gerontological practice and theory. A discipline is articulated to demonstrate the normality of old age by segregating its study and treatment from that of young and middle adulthood.

De Beauvoir's 1970 *La Vieillesse (The Coming of Age)* (24) is rooted in this trope of anger, as are other classic works of the 1970s. The titles of Butler's *Why Survive? Being Old in America* (8), Curtin's *Nobody Ever Died of Old Age: In Praise of Old People, In Outrage at their Loneliness* (22), and in anthropology, Kayser-Jones' *Old, Alone, and Neglected: Care of the Aged in the United States and Scotland* (52) convey a sense of old age as a state of misery and offer gerontology and politically engaged fieldwork as responses. The generational location of the author is seldom taken as relevant to these politics, save when, like young Nascher, youth sees through the denials of middle age to the truths of the old. De Beauvoir (24) likewise concludes: "The young man dreads this machine that is about to seize hold of him, and sometimes he tries to defend himself by throwing half-bricks; the old man, rejected by it, exhausted and naked, has nothing left but his eyes to weep with. Between youth and age there turns the machine."

The language of exploration similarly maintains a distinction between the young or ageless author and the old subject. Kaufman begins her important study, *The Ageless Self: Sources of Meaning in Late Life* (51), with an appeal to demographic urgency—"how to cope with an aging population"—and follows with an appeal to exploring "meaning" in old age:

> The research upon which this book is based grew out of my awareness of this gap [between the added years of life and our knowledge of how best to spend them], the uncharted territory in which we find ourselves both as aging individuals and as an aging nation. In order to improve the quality of life experience for those in their later years, we must understand what it means to be old.... For only by first knowing how the elderly view themselves, their lives, and the nature of old age can we hope to fashion a meaningful present and future for them and for those who follow (p. 4).

Katz (50) has called attention to such uses of alarmist demography, and from the beginning old age is framed in a split fashion in *The Ageless Self,* as the aged Other presenting a threat and the aging Self who is threatened. The latter is the explorer, adrift in "uncharted territory," the heart of darkness of old age where we encounter the natives in classic anthropological fashion: "for only by first knowing how the elderly view themselves, their lives, and the nature of old age can we hope to fashion a meaningful present and future for them and for those who follow." We fashion for them, and what is exchanged in this colonial encounter is meaning. We lack it, and search among them for "what it means to be old"; then we extract this meaning like Indian cotton to Manchester mills and refashion it, for both them and, ultimately, us. Meaning circulates within the exploratory text much as politics circulate within the gerontological polemic.

THE TROPE OF AMBIGUITY

There is a third form of circulating argument in gerontology and geroanthropology, which I call a trope of ambiguity. For Minois, ambiguity is a phenomenological universal of old age, a time both of maximal experience and of maximal debility, simultaneously vaunted and evaded. Minois looks for and finds this ambiguity "throughout the whole of history" (74:18); the fairly exhaustive text proceeds from period to period over millennia, evaluating whether old age was more gerontophobic or gerontophilic in each.

Minois' history deals in the murky currency of "attitudes" toward old age; history for him is a cyclical narrative of their oscillation. The book is a response both to aging and modernization theory accounts that posit a law of the diminishing status of old persons with industrialization (20, 21) and to revisionist accounts that place the decline prior (32) or subsequent (1) to industrialization or that challenge the possibility of a decline (62, 88). Minois suggests that the image of old age has always shifted around the fundamental ambiguity at its core.

Cole's *The Journey of Life: A Cultural History of Aging in America* provides a far more nuanced history (18), yet the ambiguity of aging remains the central insight offered. For Cole, ambiguity is not the slightly ironic fact that it appears to be for Minois, but a lost truth about aging that "postmodern culture" can help us recover:

> We need to revive existentially nourishing views of aging that address its paradoxical nature. Aging, like illness and death, reveals the most fundamental conflict of the human condition: the tension between infinite ambitions, dreams, and desires on the one hand, and vulnerable, limited, decaying physical existence on the other—the tragic and ineradicable conflict between spirit and body. This paradox cannot be eradicated by the wonders of modern medicine or by positive attitudes toward growing old. Hence the wisdom of traditions that consider old age both a blessing and a curse (p. 239).

Cole here notes the ironic ageism of gerontological ideology in its denial of old age as a time of inevitable suffering, but he is specific in placing the blame far earlier, with the Victorians. *The Journey of Life* is ultimately an appeal to an awkwardly romanticized and thinly contextualized Puritan ideology. Cole closes by invoking a Lyotardian postmodernism as metaphor for a return to an invented tradition of gerontological ambiguity.

Cole's argument, that "the wisdom of traditions" successfully negotiates the ambiguity of old age by accepting it, is a key theme of Myerhoff's classic ethnography *Number Our Days* (77) and the genre it spawned. Myerhoff's brilliantly constructed work on Jewish members of a senior center in Venice Beach, Los Angeles, came more than any other to define the potential for an anthropology of old age, as Kaminsky (49) and others have noted. Myerhoff utilized Turner's processual and performative analyses of social systems and developed a sophisticated interpretive methodology, transforming the ethnography of communal and institutional old age in the United States from the more static and skeletal accounts that preceded her work (44, 46, 48).

Like the aging and modernization literature of the 1960s and 1970s, with its normative focus on whether old age is better now or then, here or there (83), Myerhoff's work centers on sets of fundamentally moral oppositions: success or failure, joy or pain, independence or dependency, and continuity or disruption. But whereas in the aging and modernization paradigm the central question is in which society or period is old age better, for Myerhoff the poignancy of old age lies in its comprehending both poles of each of these oppositional frames. The power of the work lies in its reconstruction of informants' lives as momentous struggles for dignity, survival, autonomy, continuity, and joy within such an oppositional universe. Like the Huichol Indians on pilgrimage in Myerhoff's earlier work, the old people of Venice Beach are liminal figures, here not the ritually created liminality of the pilgrimage but the existential condition of old age. Ritual, in the senior center, is articulated by the elders to maintain a sense of continuity and *communitas,* binding together the oppositions that frame their old age against a dissolution into meaninglessness. Culture—the center's rituals, the heretic Shmuel's wisdom, the fashioning of everyday life—manages ambiguity.

A danger in this approach is its use of culture and ritual as inherently holistic. Myerhoff's romanticization of Yiddishkeit as authentic culture healing the Eriksonian crises of late life has been taken to task by Kaminsky in an introduction (49) to his edited collection of Myerhoff's essays (78). Kaminsky points out Myerhoff's deemphasis of the class location and the cohort experience of the Venice Beach elders in the labor movement, her insistence on culture as a totalizing construct, and her unacknowledged reworking of the biographies of the book's *dramatis personae* to achieve her desired effects. The closing of analysis to other axes of social difference and the emphasis on culture as a response to existential ambiguity are not limited to Myerhoff but characterize the genre of institutional and community studies that build on her text. Kugelmass chronicles the life of a synagogue and its elderly members in the South Bronx (59); like Myerhoff's work, his ethnography offers a powerful narrative of survival and a testimony to the healing miracles of ritual and myth. Shield examines "daily life in an American nursing home," using a similar focus on liminality and culture (98). The nursing home Shield studies is the inverse of Myerhoff's senior center, a total institution represented as lacking ritual and culture and thus lacking the possibility of a response to generational and institutional ambiguity. Each of these ethnographies examines complex questions of class and racial boundaries and the relation of everyday experience to the state and the aging enterprise; but in each, Turnerian tools of liminality, ritual process, and social drama are used to construct what Vesperi criticizes as an "ethnographic present" (111) in which the everyday relevance of the macrosocial world is sidelined to give way to the morality play of old age, in triumph and in pathos.

The liminality of old age may often be more rooted in generational politics than existential conditions; the trope of ambiguity tends to obscure this difference. Vesperi's study of old age, local communities, and the state in St. Petersburg, Florida (111) marks a radical break from the trope. *City of Green Benches* weaves together macrosocial issues—national advertising campaigns, local and state business interests, representations by gerontologists—with a complex ethnography that resists situating old persons within a single institution, includes gerontological professionals as ethnographic subjects, and draws on the lifelong and ongoing construction of race and class in the constitution of old age. Culture and ritual do not serve as the totalizing constructs that they do in the Myerhoff genre of ethnography; local knowledge is often distorted within the politics of social interaction. Like other anthropologists of aging who focus on class (6, 15, 48, 104, 105), Vesperi relies primarily on interactionist—sociological and social psychological—frameworks of analysis, but here they are thickened through a more sophisticated use of ethnographic and macrosocial data.

Neither interactionist nor Turnerian studies attempt an integration of their respective foci on class and culture; concurrent and subsequent debates on practice theory, on *habitus*, and on hegemony, ideology, and culture seem far removed from most geroanthropological concerns. The subdiscipline crystallizes around an academic aging enterprise and its associated incitements to speak of old age in moral, oppositional terms: it is as much about a fantasized uncharted territory of Old Age as about the everyday lives of older persons. Through the mobilization of anger and ambiguity, a disciplinary ethos emerges that envisions itself as mission practice against an empty past and writes itself through a mix of applied sociology and romanticized narrative. To reintroduce anthropological theory into and to write against the geroanthropological enterprise, it may be time to reappropriate an anthropological past.

FRAZER AND THE SYMBOLIC CONSTRUCTION OF GENERATION

A cultural anthropology of old age might begin its genealogy with Frazer's repudiated classic, *The Golden Bough* (39), organized around the figure of the hunted, killed, and regenerated king or god. Frazer is read in at least three ways; I suggest a fourth. Within anthropology's own narrative of its emergence into cultural particularism, Frazer is represented as the archetypical armchair anthropologist brandishing a theory of primitive error, here that of sympathetic magic. A Freudian appropriation takes the deep meaning of the violence as Oedipal conflict, and neglects Frazer's focus on magic as socially constituted reality. A reading that draws on Joseph Conrad centers on the social (particularly the colonial and gendered) constitution of the text's regicidal violence but downplays the generational specificity of *The Golden Bough.*

The reduction of Frazer to a theory of primitive error is premature. Like Robertson Smith (101), Frazer grapples with Christianity and prefigures a much later celebration of anthropology as cultural critique (70). The implicit and ultimate referent of the dying god is Christ, and the scope of sympathetic irrationality implicitly encompasses contemporary European civilization. Errors of sympathetic magic for Frazer raise the question of the social construction of reality for both primitives and moderns. Magic, which in this extended sense encompasses most of civilization, is what a subsequent anthropology would call the symbolic. In asking how generations magically reconstitute themselves, Frazer is concerned primarily with the symbolic reproduction of the body in time.

Kings and human representatives of the divine are put to death, Frazer argues in his introduction to the third volume of the work, "to arrest the forces of decomposition in nature by retrenching with ruthless hand the first ominous symptoms of decay" (39:v–vi). Sickness and particularly old age are signs of enfeeblement and of death, and are perceived as challenges to the body not only of the individual but of the community and the state. The continuity of the social body is challenged by the potential degeneration of each successive generation. Symbolically, continuity is maintained by preventing the degeneration of charismatic authority vested in the king or god, through the circulation of charisma in a series of youthful bodies. Generations must replicate themselves: "no amount of care and precaution will prevent the man-god from growing old and feeble" (p. 9). Aging is a challenge not only to individual lives but to the possibility of social meaning, to culture. The hegemonic location of dominant bodies in society is achieved by and through their identification with the social body; Frazer recognizes aging in later life as a challenge to the seamless constitution of the hegemonic.

At stake is not only the particular interests of age groups—a reduction of Frazer by Radcliffe-Brown, maintained in most subsequent work on generation—but the very possibility of hegemony in itself. Thus the patriarchal body in decline central to the text presents a problem in signification: it forces the question of the continuity of the Symbolic—in Lacanian terms the Law of the Father—in a world full of ruptures in lived experience, a world where fathers and mothers and other embodiments of the hegemonic grow old and die. By reading a violent act at the core of culture, Frazer does not just open the way for psychodynamic hearts of darkness, but grounds a symbolic theory of generational difference and particularly of the construction of old age within a crisis of meaning. *The Golden Bough* concerns itself at length not only with questions of the politics of debility (When do societies mark the powerful body as senescent?) and of the means of destruction (How do societies disassociate the individual from the social body?), but with the semiotics of exchange (How is a new body seamlessly enabled to become the social body?).

Frazer's emphasis on the integrity of violence and culture differentiates the position of intergenerational conflict in *The Golden Bough* from the less meaning-centered and more social structural analyses of generational conflict of Radcliffe-Brown and his successors, of the French structural Marxists, of the theorists of the domestic cycle, and of the age stratification theorists in sociology and their anthropological proponents. Central for Frazer is the relationship between debility and the impossibility of magical, or symbolic, representation, reframing Clark's question of why anthropology has erased the period between marriage and funerary rites. Instead, we are pushed to asked what is it about local constructions of middle and late adulthood that may or may not resist certain modes of representation. Geroanthropology, born of the bureaucratic construction of old age and its particular moral imperative, cannot see crises of meaning in such absences. It must, endlessly, produce the requisite old body to be simultaneously romanticized and fixed, like the realist aesthetic of the old bodies that each month adorn the cover of *The Gerontologist.*

Work on generation from Radcliffe-Brown through the domestic cycle literature fails to take up the symbolic dimension of Frazer's work; yet, this literature is still more relevant to a contemporary anthropology of old age than geroanthropology is sometimes willing to consider. Radcliffe-Brown's famous essays on joking relationships present a second moment in a provisional genealogy (90, 91). Like de Beauvoir, Radcliffe-Brown shifts a two-generational model of the politics of aging, the old being replaced by their children, into a three-generational model, the old and young in conjunctive joking alliance with each other and in an asymmetric disciplinary relationship with the intermediate generation. Intergenerational joking relationships, for Radcliffe-Brown, are again structural responses to the predicament of social and cultural reproduction: "The social tradition is handed down from one generation to the next. For the tradition to be maintained it must have authority behind it. The authority is therefore normally recognized as possessed by members of the preceding generation and it is they who exercise discipline." In contrast, "grandparents and their grandchildren are grouped together in the social structure in opposition to their children and parents. An important clue to the understanding of the subject is the fact that in the flow of social life through time, in which men are born, become mature and die, the grandchildren replace their grandparents" (90).

The Frazerian concern with symbolic action has given way to a functionalism that foreshadows future gerontological analysis. Yet Radcliffe-Brown merits closer attention. Social reproduction is twofold: parents hand down tradition to children; grandparents are replaced by grandchildren. Two processes are detailed: an assymetrical and contractual gifting of culture and a symmetrical and informal circulation of bodies and roles. Both are explained, in the contemporary fashion of the discipline, as responses to the problem of social reproduction. The old attempt to discipline and are marginalized by their children, like Frazer's dying king. For the successive generation of grandchildren, however, grandparents are not a threatening body of decrepitude but a source of support and alliance and meaning in their own agonal struggles with parents. Multiple threats and threatening bodies emerge, as do multiple constructions of old age, middle age, and youth. The political landscape of generational analysis thickens, if not its symbolic terrain.

Two avenues of contemporary geroanthropological interest draw upon these responses to questions of social reproduction: the study of formalized age groups and age stratification theory. The first of these subfields never became central to geroanthropological self-construction. Rooted in a sense of its connectedness to social anthropology and resistant to the incitement to name and isolate old age central to the subdiscipline, age set research shares few of the epistemological concerns detailed above. The field therefore does not share geroanthropology's amnesic tendencies but constructs a genealogy for itself. In Bernardi's literature review (5), "the first interpretive scheme for the cultural and social significance of age" is Schurtz's (96) 1902 *Alterklasses und Männerbünde*. For Schurtz, men's age-specific groups are formed as secret societies to wrest societal control from the primeval matriarchy. Bernardi passes on quickly to Webster's 1932 study of postpubertal male institutions (112) and the work of Radcliffe-Brown (89), Lowie (66), and Evans-Pritchard (31), but despite Schurtz's specific emphasis on the destruction of the matriarchy, he offers an early argument for the close relationship of the politics of gender and generation, an idea later elaborated by Meillassoux (73).

There are two types of traditional anthropological work on age sets or age classes: 1. monographs concerned with their particularities as social institutions and 2. those concerned with the integrated analysis of age sets and other forms of age grades and age stratification. The former include classic ethnographies—e.g. Spencer's work on gerontocracy among the Samburu (106), Wilson's work on Nyakyusa age-villages (113), Maybury-Lewis' study of Shavante age sets (71), and Legesse's (63) work on the Boran *gada*—as well as attempts like Bernardi's to construct broader theories and typologies of age sets (4, 56, 67, 72, 107). The latter, like Radcliffe-Brown, see formal age sets and age grades on a continuum of social organization, and take as their focus either the totality of the system or the dynamics between age groups. Systemic approaches stress either functional or symbolic integrity. Eisenstadt offers a Parsonian typology of age groups (26). Maybury-Lewis, in a comparison of Brazilian and African age group systems, develops a meaning-centered alternative that sees the essence of age group structure not in the utility of its social functions but in age as both ideology and principal of organization (72). He suggests applying a meaning-centered analysis of age as category not only to the East African ethnography but to studies of age set, grade, and generation worldwide. The Frazerian concern with the symbolic construction of age groups is revived, though not Frazer's emphasis on the violence—symbolic or enacted—of intergroup relations and thus his concern with the breakdown of signification.

Rey (92–94) raises the question of age groups as social classes in a structural Marxist framework, a point contested by Meillassoux in a well-known debate (73). Meillassoux's argument again centers on social reproduction: within the domestic mode of production, junior men become senior men and "recover the product of their productive agricultural labour" (p. 79), but the cycling of male bodies through systems of age stratification only intensifies sex stratification. Meillassoux develops the theme enunciated far earlier by Schurtz through a lineal rather than affinal interpretation of Levi-Strauss' celebrated figure of the circulation of women. Male intergenerational struggle becomes patriarchal *entente cordiale*.

Geroanthropological readings of these literatures misrepresent them as theoretically impoverished, maintaining the sense of mission. N. Foner's (34) anthropological interpretation of Riley's (95) and A. Foner's (33) age stratification theory begins with the requisite denial of a past: "there has been no systematic attempt in anthropology to build a model of age inequality—or for that matter, of age and aging" (34:xi). The French structural Marxists are begrudgingly mentioned but soon dismissed: "But the French...are so worried about whether or not elder-junior distinctions are class divisions that they overlook many critical features of inequalities between old and young"; thus, they ignore issues beyond male gerontocracy, such as the prevalence of disadvantaged and exploited elders and age inequalities between older and younger women.

Age stratification theory as adapted by N. Foner addresses these critical concerns. But the dismissal of an anthropological past is premature. Meillassoux does not closely examine age inequalities between women, but he does link the possibility of age inequalities between men to sexual stratification more generally, refusing to separate analyses of age from sexual inequality (73); the point is central to his critique of Rey. Foner ignores it, constructing a straw man in Meillassoux and offering in his stead a functionalist account (34:253–254), which neglects the economic questions he poses and articulates an adoptive lineage through American sociological theory. Foner's text is important in its consideration of gender-specific age inequalities, but it does not take up Maybury-Lewis' challenge to develop a symbolic anthropology of age (72). Nor is the work of Fortes (101), Goody (43), and Mandelbaum (69) on domestic cycles and the processual analysis of age stratification, offering another critical moment in the construction of a geroanthropological lineage, seen as relevant. Foner offers a neofunctionalist and highly tautological account of gerontocratic and gerontophobic roles of old women and old men, ultimately making few theoretical advances except for an iterated reminder that nonindustrial societies are often gerontophobic and not just gerontocratic: the invocation, again, of ambiguity.

Like other theorists of generation and the domestic cycle, Fortes (38) covers related terrain without the amnesia, noting that "the way [age and aging] are incorporated into tribal forms of social structure or invested with cultural value and significance is a topic of central relevance for anthropological theory." His review of a lifetime of his and others' work is read inversely by Kertzer & Keith as "an important first step." Fortes summarizes much work in West Africa and elsewhere on the processual relationship between biological, social, and cultural aging with a set of observations: 1. Intergenerational relations are characterized both by the continuity and the struggle inherent in generational reproduction. Fortes defines the latter in Oedipal terms. 2. Aging is an individual process positioned "between two poles of social structure," the domestic and juridical domains. Thus, the "recognition and consideration of chronological age as opposed to maturation and generation depend on the differentiation between the politicojural and the domestic domains of social life."

But the politicojural and the domestic—anthropological categories often rooted in colonial constructions of public and private domains—are not made objects of inquiry in themselves. Their respective logics are constructed through a universalizing sociological rationality. The symbolic, for Fortes, remains external to processual dynamics, as an "investment" of the interplay of biological (individual) and social (domestic and civic) structures with meaning. Radcliffe-Brown's legacy in Fortes is marked (35, 36); Frazer's legacy is limited to an acknowledgment of the struggle between generations, but here read solely in Oedipal terms. Age, generation, and time present social structural challenges rather than crises in meaning; intergenerational conflict is splayed between social and intrapsychic causes. The first step imagined by Kertzer & Keith, though demonstrating geroanthropology's rootedness in British structural functionalism, sidesteps most interpretive and symbolic disciplinary concerns, let alone the possibility of a poststructural inquiry.

AGING RELOCATED: PHENOMENOLOGIES, RATIONALITIES, AND HERMENEUTICS

A critical gerontology, of which this essay forms a part, is an inadequate response to geroanthropological amnesia if, like the Luborsky & Sankar review, it does little more than validate recent paradigms. I suggest three directions in which anthropologists have critically engaged the study of old age beyond current subdisciplinary isolation: a phenomenological focus on experience, embodiment, and identity; a critical focus on the rationalities and hegemonies through which aging is experienced and represented; and an interpretive focus on examining the relevance of the ethnographer's age to the forms of knowledge produced.

Phenomenologies

In *The Ageless Self,* Kaufman (51) challenges the professional search for the meaning of old age, suggesting that her old informants do not perceive being old as central to the experienced self. According to Kaufman, in looking for meaning in old age by assuming that old age is at the core of the meaningful, gerontologists often reify a political and bureaucratic identity as phenomenological universal. Against the moralism of the usual tropes of anger and ambiguity, Kaufman refuses to paint her subjects as *a priori* caricatures of wrenching pathos or gritty survivorship, and the result is a far subtler ethnographic texture. Kaufman's introduction is cited above as emblematic of the failure of geroanthropological authors to locate themselves generationally within a sustained hermeneutic; and yet against the language of mission inciting us to name Old Age, Kaufman problematizes the easy availability of the term as meaningful ethnographic construct.

The limits of Kaufman's project mark directions for further work building on her insights. The old persons in *The Ageless Self* experience the assaults of bodily aging as distinct from their sense of continuity in self; against an aging body and externally imposed labeling, individuals report experiencing an ageless self. In taking these reports of continuity as lived experience, Kaufman may neglect political and psychodynamic questions of denial and resistance in interpreting her subjects' construction of self against body. The text does not locate the specifics of cultural and more particularly class histories upon which the Cartesian embodiment of its subjects is predicated. The possibility that the experience of the body—and thus of the relationship between an aging body and an aging self—may be differentially constituted across class and cultural and other axes of social difference needs to be explored in the move toward a political phenomenology of age.

Rationalities

Work that links the study of old age to a critical focus on ideologies, nationalisms, modernities, and gender constructions, in various settings is emerging (16, 17, 61, 64, 65). In the Netherlands and in India, a group of South Asian scholars working under the auspices of the Indo-Dutch Programme for Alternatives in Development (IDPAD) have placed questions of modernity, postcoloniality, and the application of the social theory of Elias, Foucault, and Bakhtin at the center of a gerontological project (11, 12, 23, 87). The IDPAD is one of the few attempts to reverse the flow of anthropological knowledge production as well as to decenter international gerontology's Euro-American bias.

Much of this emergent work is characterized by attention to the complexities of symbolic structure and cultural politics. In *Encounters with Aging: Mythologies of Menopause in Japan and North America,* Lock (65) traces the replication of hegemonic constructions of the aging person within research and clinical practice, focusing on menopause and gendered aging. The text combines personal narrative, quantitative and comparative data, a critical but serious attention to biomedical discourse, and a historicized discussion of the politics of menopausal knowledge. Japanese scholarly literature on aging is engaged closely, against the usual Eurocentricism. Like Plath's (86) set of life histories of older Japanese, the cultural specificity of aging is closely examined, but here the invocation of cultural difference does not obscure the political dimensions of signification.

Lamb's (61) study of aging in a Bengali village engages multiple debates in the anthropology of South Asia on the nature of interpersonal transactions and the construction of persons and genders. Old age is central to the text, yet as in Kaufman's and Lock's work it resists becoming an end in itself. Processual attention to generation is central to Lamb's analysis, as in the work of Fortes, but the structural logics of practice are not presumed to be precultural but are rooted in local constructions of action and substance. Yet even as the experience of age is carefully located within the Bengali construction of the person, this construction is located within the phenomenology of aging. Lamb challenges static conceptions of personhood by tracing across the life cycle the meanings of and challenges to being a person in a Bengali village. The lesson of geroanthropology—that age is critical to the study of culture—is acknowledged without subdisciplinary impoverishment.

Modernity and the postcolony have become critical foci in some of this work in a different sense than in the aging and modernization literature of the 1970s. Questions of the constitution of the old person as subject are foregrounded through emphases on feminist theory, critical medical anthropology, and Gramsci. Cohen (17) situates Indian debates on senility within a universe of discourse in which the old body becomes a powerful sign both of the state and of imagined core values in Indian culture and their perceived disappearance. The politicization of the old body is juxtaposed with the experience of old persons across class and gender. Attention to local phenomenologies and hegemonies articulating the experience of the aging body is combined with a focus on the impact of shifting religious and state ideologies.

In Chatterji's work (11), the subjectivity of the older person is framed in terms of institutional practice in the context of the ongoing medicalization of old age. The old age home as a total institution is not just an impediment to personal integration as in Shield's work and the trope of anger literature but becomes the site of new forms of subjectivity. For example, Chatterji discusses the file self, the old person known through medical and professional records that increasingly determine the socially meaningful organization of his or her subjective experience. Like Lamb, Chatterji looks at the construction of the person in time, but here the construction of time itself is at stake. Like Ostör (85), who suggests that geroanthropology needs to locate not only age and generation but time in local practice and knowledge, Chatterji offers a subtle analysis of the construction of temporality within the intersecting forms of rationality of the multiply located institution. The file self of the medicalized old body presents the problem of a cyborg anthropology, after Haraway (45), the need to examine the constitution of aging within the implosion of ever more encompassing technologies, markets, and media representations.

Hermeneutics

Interpretive inquiries in which the age of the anthropologist is critical to the construction of gerontological knowledge are few. Myerhoff (77) was perhaps the first to explore the hermeneutics specific to generational difference, from arguably teaching herself to walk like an older woman to inserting herself centrally into her ethnography long before such a move became fashionable. Kaminsky (49) has pointed out the limits to Myerhoff's self-location, but his concern is less with the specific interpretive politics of generational difference than with more general questions of ethnographic representation.

The concerned younger gerontologist as angry spokesperson for the disenfranchised elderly is a stock character in gerontological writing, but such reflexivity—echoing Nascher's epiphany in the New York poorhouse—seldom extends to an interrogation of ethnographic practice. Two works that open up the interpretive politics of old age are by anthropologists writing not as old age professionals but as older persons. Colson (19) muses on the shifts in what anthropologists take as ethnographically relevant both as they age and as the persons with with whom they work and from whom they learn age. As Moore (76) and Lamb articulate in their work, a processual attention to individual and group practice over the course of a lifetime is critical to the analysis of social or symbolic structures at any moment in time. Colson applies a similar insight to the life of the anthropologist herself.

At age 78 the anthropologist Laird found herself ensconced in a Phoenix nursing home with no means, as she puts it, of escape. *Limbo* is her chronicle of the better part of a year at the pseudonymous Golden Mesa nursing home, written with often painful clarity and irony: "Recently a friend sent me a newspaper clipping telling of a senile patient in a Southern California nursing home who was found drowned in a therapy pool, still strapped in her wheelchair. Such an event would have been impossible at Golden Mesa; it had no therapy pool" (60:1). Anger here is powerful but nuanced. Laird's institutionalization is presented at the intersection of personal, kin, institutional, and state realities. The violence conveyed in the opening anecdote about the therapy pool is not, in her account of everyday life at Golden Mesa, the story of gross abandonment and abuse but rather of the ongoing banality, infantilization, and denial of personhood within the institution through the most minute, and damning, of gestures. Central to this denial, for Laird, is the grouping together of residents by physical functioning rather than social and cognitive awareness: the false mirror of demented roommates and hallmates. Ambiguity, the shifting meaning of old age, here as simultaneously wise and demented, is constructed, Laird suggests, through the social spaces mandating the institution. *Limbo* resists the easy romance of gerontological narratives of old age pathos and triumph. Laird had great difficulty finding a publisher; Buffington-Jennings (7) notes in an epilogue to the book that one prospective editor had written: "Maybe I'm a monster, but it doesn't move me."

The politics of catharsis in the construction of geroanthropological narratives are particularly critical. The unquestioned importance of the aging enterprise ("we must know") and more generally reified differences between generations as interpretive communities ("they can't understand") are at stake in geroanthropology's resistance to taking seriously the hermeneutics and politics of its appropriation of old persons' experience as a fundamental dimension of practice. The bulk of gerontological practice remains the transformation of critical agendas into routinized scientistic jargon abetting the biomedicalization of and control over old persons. Without a sustained effort at change, the concerns of the field will remain in subdisciplinary limbo.

ACKNOWLEDGMENTS

I am indebted to my mentors in gerontological activism and critique, Jerry Avorn, at Harvard Medical School, and Edith Stein, formerly of Action for Boston Community Development. Discussions with my students in a 1992 seminar on Old Age and Anthropological Theory at the University of California, Berkeley, were very helpful, particularly with Cheryl Theis. So were talks with Sarah Lamb, Robert LeVine, Elizabeth Colson, Sharon Kaufman, and Andrew Achenbaum. Veena Das started me thinking about the importance of Frazer to a theory of signification and time. It has been my good fortune to be affiliated with anthropologists at the University of California, San Francisco, where much work on geroanthropology is being pursued.

Literature Cited

1. Achenbaum WA. 1978. *Old Age in the New Land: The American Experience Since* *1790*. Baltimore: Johns Hopkins Univ. Press

2. Amoss PT, Harrell S. 1981. Introduction: an anthropological perspective on aging. In *Other Ways of Growing Old: Anthropological Perspectives*, ed. PT Amoss, S Harrell, pp. 1–24. Stanford, CA: Stanford Univ. Press

3. Baars J. 1991. The challenge of critical gerontology: the problem of social constitution. *J. Aging Stud.* 5:219–43

4. Baxter PTW, Almagor U, eds. 1978. *Age, Generation and Time: Some Features of East African Age Organisations.* London: Hurst

5. Bernardi B. 1984. *Age Class Systems: Social Institutions and Polities Based on Age.* Transl. DI Kertzer, 1985. Cambridge: Cambridge Univ. Press (From Italian)

6. Bohannan P. 1981. Food of old people in center-city hotels. See Ref. 42, pp. 185–200

7. Buffington-Jennings A. 1979. Epilogue: before and after limbo. See Ref. 60, pp. 171–78

8. Butler RN. 1975. *Why Survive? Being Old in America.* San Francisco: Harper & Row

9. Canguilhem G. 1978. *The Normal and the Pathological.* Transl. CR Fawcett, RS Cohen. Dordrecht: Reidel (From French)

10. Charcot JM. 1874. *Leçons Cliniques sur les Maladies des Vieillards et les Maladies Chroniques.* Paris: Delahaye. 2nd ed.

11. Chatterji R. 1989. *The organisation of the self under dementia.* Presented at Symp. Soc. Aging Comp. Perspect., New Delhi

12. Chattoo S. 1989. *The absence of geriatrics: the self that can be retrieved.* Presented at Symp. Soc. Aging Comp. Perspect., New Delhi

13. Clark M. 1967. The anthropology of aging, a new area for studies of culture and personality. *Gerontologist* 7(1):55–64

14. Climo J. 1992. The role of anthropology in gerontology—theory. *J. Aging Stud.* 6(1): 41–55

15. Cohen CI, Sokolovsky J. 1989. *Old Men of the Bowery: Strategies for Survival Among the Homeless.* New York: Guilford

16. Cohen L. 1992. No aging in India: the uses of gerontology. *Cult. Med. Psychiatr.* 16: 123–61

17. Cohen L. 1995. *No Aging in India: Alzheimer's, Bad Families, and Other Modern Things.* Berkeley: Univ. Calif. Press. In press

18. Cole TR. 1992. *The Journey of Life: A Cultural History of Aging in America.* Cambridge: Cambridge Univ. Press

19. Colson E. 1984. The reordering of experience: anthropological involvement with time. *J. Anthropol. Res.* 40(1):1–13

20. Cowgill DO. 1974. Aging and modernization: a revision of the theory. In *Late Life*, ed. J Gubrium, pp. 123–46. Springfield, IL: Thomas

21. Cowgill DO, Holmes LD, eds. 1972. *Aging and Modernization.* New York: Appleton-Century-Crofts

22. Curtin SR. 1972. *Nobody Ever Died of Old Age: In Praise of Old People, In Outrage at their Loneliness.* Boston: Little, Brown

23. Dattachowdhury S. 1989. *The home in the city: privacy, space and the person in a home for the aged.* Presented at Symp. Soc. Aging Comp. Perspect., New Delhi

24. De Beauvoir S. 1970. *The Coming of Age.* Transl. P O'Brien, 1972. New York: Putnam (From French)

25. di Leonardo M. 1991. Acknowledgements. In *Gender at the Crossroads of Knowledge: Feminist Anthropology in the Postmodern Era*, ed. M di Leonardo, pp. xi–xii. Berkeley: Univ. Calif. Press

26. Eisenstadt SN. 1956. *From Generation to Generation: Age Groups and Social Structure.* Glencoe, IL: Free Press

27. Estes C. 1979. *The Aging Enterprise.* San Francisco: Jossey-Bass

28. Estes C. 1986. The politics of ageing in America. *Ageing Soc.* 6:121–34

29. Estes C. 1993. The aging enterprise revisited. *Gerontologist* 33:292–98

30. Estes C, Binney E. 1989. The biomedicalization of aging: dangers and dilemmas. *Gerontologist* 29:587–96

31. Evans-Pritchard EE. 1940. *The Nuer, A Description of the Modes of Livelihood and Political Institutions of a Nilotic People.* Oxford: Clarendon

32. Fischer DH. 1977. *Growing Old in America.* New York: Oxford Univ. Press

33. Foner A. 1974. Age stratification and age conflict in political life. *Am. Soc. Rev.* 39: 187–96

34. Foner N. 1984. *Ages in Conflict: A Cross-Cultural Perspective on Inequality Between Old and Young.* New York: Columbia Univ. Press

35. Fortes M. 1949. Time and social structure: an Ashanti case study. See Ref. 37, pp. 1–32

36. Fortes M. 1955. Radcliffe-Brown's contributions to the study of social organization. See Ref. 37, pp. 260–78

37. Fortes, M. 1970. *Time and Social Structure and Other Essays.* London: Athlone

38. Fortes M. 1984. Age, generation, and social structure. See Ref. 57, pp. 99–122

39. Frazer JG. 1935. *The Golden Bough: A Study in Magic and Religion.* London: Macmillan. 3rd ed.

40. Frisch CF, Setzer RG. 1982. *Bibliography/Filmography: Ethnicity and Aging.* Salt Lake City: Univ. Utah Gerontol. Prog.

41. Fry CL. 1980. Toward an anthropology of aging. In *Aging in Culture and Society*, ed. CL Fry, pp. 1–20. South Hadley, MA: Bergin & Garvey

42. Fry CL, ed. 1981. *Dimensions: Aging, Culture, and Health.* New York: Bergin

43. Goody J. 1962. The fission of domestic

groups among the Lodagaba. In *The Developmental Cycle in Domestic Groups*, ed. J Goody, pp. 53–91. Cambridge: Cambridge Univ. Press

44. Gubrium JE. 1975. *Living and Dying at Murray Manor.* New York: St. Martin's

45. Haraway DJ. 1991. *Simians, Cyborgs, and Women: The Reinvention of Nature.* New York: Routledge

46. Hochschild AR. 1973. *The Unexpected Community: Portrait of an Old Age Subculture.* Englewood Cliffs, NJ: Prentice-Hall

47. Holmes L. 1976. From Simmons to the seventies: trends in anthropological gerontology. *Int. J. Aging Hum. Dev.* 7:211–20

48. Johnson SK. 1971. *Idle Haven: Community Building Among the Working-class Retired.* Berkeley: Univ. Calif. Press

49. Kaminsky M. 1992. Introduction. See Ref. 78, pp. 1–97

50. Katz S. 1992. Alarmist demography: power, knowledge, and the elderly population. *Int. J. Aging Stud.* 6:203–25

51. Kaufman SR. 1986. *The Ageless Self: Sources of Meaning in Late Life.* Madison: Univ. Wisc. Press

52. Kayser-Jones JS. 1981. *Old, Alone, and Neglected: Care of the Aged in the United States and Scotland.* Berkeley: Univ. Calif. Press

53. Keith J. 1980. "The best is yet to be": toward an anthropology of age. *Annu. Rev. Anthropol.* 9:339–64

54. Keith J. 1992. *An anthropological perspective on method and substance of gerontology in the 21st century.* Presented at Annu. Meet. Gerontol. Soc. Am., Washington, DC

55. Keith J, Kertzer DI. 1984. Introduction. See Ref. 57, pp. 19–61

56. Kertzer D. 1978. Theoretical developments in the study of age-group systems. *Am. Ethnol.* 5:368–74

57. Kertzer D, Keith J, eds. 1984. *Age & Anthropological Theory.* Ithaca, NY: Cornell Univ. Press

58. Kertzer D, Keith J. 1984. Preface. See Ref. 57, pp. 13–15

59. Kugelmass J. 1986. *The Miracle of Intervale Avenue: The Story of a Jewish Congregation in the South Bronx.* New York: Schocken

60. Laird C. 1979. *Limbo.* Novato, CA: Chandler & Sharp

61. Lamb S. 1993. *Growing in the net of Maya: persons, gender and life processes in a Bengali society.* PhD thesis. Univ. Chicago. 440 pp.

62. Laslett P. 1985. Societal development and aging. In *Handbook of Aging and the Social Sciences*, ed. RH Binstock, E Shanas, pp. 199–230. New York: Van Nostrand Reinhold. 2nd ed.

63. Legesse A. 1973. *Gada—Three Approaches to the Study of African Society.* New York: Free Press

64. Lock M. 1993. Ideology, female midlife, and the greying of Japan. *J. Jpn. Stud.* 19(1):43–78

65. Lock M. 1993. *Encounters with Aging: Mythologies of Menopause in Japan and North America.* Berkeley: Univ. Calif. Press

66. Lowie R. 1920. *Primitive Society.* New York: Liveright & Boni

67. Lowie R. 1930. Age societies. In *The Encyclopedia of the Social Sciences*, ed. ERA Seligman, 1:482–83. New York: Macmillan

68. Luborsky MR, Sankar A. 1993. Expanding the critical gerontology perspective: cultural dimensions—introduction. *Gerontologist* 33:440–44

69. Mandelbaum D. 1970. *Society in India.* Berkeley: Univ. Calif. Press

70. Marcus GE, Fischer MMJ. 1986. *Anthropology as Cultural Critique: An Experimental Moment in the Human Sciences.* Chicago: Univ. Chicago Press

71. Maybury-Lewis D. 1967. *Akwe-Shavante Society.* Oxford: Clarendon

72. Maybury-Lewis D. 1984. Age and kinship: a structural view. See Ref. 57, pp. 123–40

73. Meillassoux C. 1975. *Maidens, Meal, and Money: Capitalism and the Domestic Community.* Transl. Cambridge Univ. Press, 1981. Cambridge: Cambridge Univ. Press (From French)

74. Minois G. 1987. *History of Old Age: From Antiquity to the Renaissance.* Transl. SH Tenison, 1989. Chicago: Univ. Chicago Press (From French)

75. Moody HR. 1988. Toward a critical gerontology. In *Emergent Theories of Aging*, ed. JE Birren, VL Bengston, pp. 19–40. New York: Springer

76. Moore SF. 1978. Old age in a life-term social arena: some Chagga of Kilimanjaro in 1974. See Ref. 80, pp. 23–76

77. Myerhoff B. 1978. *Number Our Days.* New York: Simon & Schuster

78. Myerhoff B. 1992. *Remembered Lives: The Work of Ritual, Storytelling, and Growing Older*, ed. M Kaminsky. Ann Arbor: Univ. Mich. Press

79. Myerhoff B. 1970. Aging and the aged in other cultures: an anthropological perspective. See Ref. 78, pp. 101–26

80. Myerhoff BG, Simic A, eds. 1978. *Life's Career—Aging: Cultural Variations on Growing Old.* Beverly Hills, CA: Sage

81. Nascher IL. 1914. *Geriatrics: The Diseases of the Old Age and Their Treatment.* Philadelphia: Blakiston's

82. Nydegger CN. 1981. Gerontology and anthropology: challenge and opportunity. See Ref. 42, pp. 293–302

83. Nydegger CN. 1983. Family ties of the

aged in cross-cultural perspective. *Gerontologist* 23:26–32

84. Nydegger CN. 1983. Introduction. *Res. Aging* 5(4):451–53
85. Ostör A. 1984. Chronology, category, and ritual. See Ref. 57, pp. 281–304
86. Plath DW. 1980. *Long Engagements: Maturity in Modern Japan.* Stanford, CA: Stanford Univ. Press
87. Pradhan R. 1989. *Family, inheritance and the care of the aged: contractual relations and the axiom of kinship amity.* Presented at Symp. Soc. Aging Comp. Perspect., New Delhi
88. Quadagno J. 1982. *Aging in Early Industrial Society: Work, Family, and Social Policy in Nineteenth-Century England.* New York: Academic
89. Radcliffe-Brown AR. 1929. Age-organisation—terminology. *Man* 29:21
90. Radcliffe-Brown AR. 1940. On joking relationships. *Africa* 13:195–210
91. Radcliffe-Brown AR. 1949. A further note on joking relationships. *Africa* 19:133–40
92. Rey PP. 1971. *Colonialisme, Néo-Colonialisme et Transition au Capitalisme.* Paris: Maspero
93. Rey PP. 1975. L'esclavage lignager chez les Tsangui, Punu et les Kuni du Congo-Brazzaville. In *L'Esclavage en Afrique précoloniale,* ed. C Meillassoux, pp. 509–20. Paris: Maspero
94. Rey PP. 1979. Class contradiction in lineage societies. *Crit. Anthropol.* 4:41–60
95. Riley MW. 1971. Social gerontology and the age stratification of society. *Gerontologist* 11:79–87
96. Schurtz H. 1902. *Alterklasses und Männerbünde.* Berlin: Reimer
97. Schweitzer MM. 1991. *Anthropology of Aging: A Partially Annotated Bibliography.* New York: Greenwood Press
98. Shield RR. 1988. *Uneasy Endings: Daily Life in an American Nursing Home.* Ithaca, NY: Cornell Univ. Press

99. Simic A. 1978. Introduction: aging and the aged in cultural perspective. See Ref. 80, pp. 9–22
100. Simmons L. 1945. *The Role of the Aged in Primitive Society.* New Haven, CT: Yale Univ. Press
101. Smith WR. 1885. *Kinship and Marriage in Early Arabia.* Cambridge: Cambridge Univ. Press
102. Sokolovsky J. 1990. Introduction. In *The Cultural Context of Aging: Worldwide Perspectives,* ed. J Sokolovsky, pp. 1–11. New York: Bergin & Garvey
103. Sokolovsky J. 1993. Images of aging: a cross-cultural perspective. *In Generations* 17(2):51–54
104. Sokolovsky J, Cohen CI. 1978. The cultural meaning of personal networks for the inner-city elderly. *Urban Anthropol.* 7:323–43
105. Sokolovsky J, Cohen CI. 1981. Being old in the inner city: support systems of the SRO aged. See Ref. 42, pp. 163–84
106. Spencer P. 1965. *The Samburu: A Study of Gerontocracy in a Nomadic Tribe.* Berkeley: Univ. Calif. Press
107. Stewart FH. 1977. *Fundamentals of Age-Group Systems.* New York: Academic
108. Strathern M. 1981. Culture in a netbag: the manufacture of a subdiscipline in anthropology. *Man* 16:665–88
109. Thewlis MW. 1941. *The Care of the Aged (Geriatrics).* St. Louis: Mosby. 3rd ed.
110. United States Department of State. 1982. *U.S. National Report on Aging for the United Nations World Assembly on Aging.* Washington, DC: US Dept. State
111. Vesperi MD. 1985. *City of Green Benches: Growing Old in a New Downtown.* Ithaca, NY: Cornell Univ. Press
112. Webster H. 1908. *Primitive Secret Societies: A Study in Early Politics and Religion.* New York: Macmillan
113. Wilson M. 1951. *Good Company: A Study of Nyakyusa Age-Villages.* London: Oxford Univ. Press

Aging and Identity in Premodern Times

CAROL A. B. WARREN
University of Kansas

In premodern as in modern (and postmodern) times in the West, the social and personal identity of the aging and aged is mediated through the decay of the gendered and biomedicalized body. The social identity of the premodern aged was marked by ambivalence: images of the wise, spiritual, or useful elder contrasting with that of the spiteful, fearful, and ugly aged person. Both social place and personal identity were shaped, for aging men, by war, work, and sexual potency, and for aging women, by the reproductive, domestic, and cosmetic body. The movement toward collective identity in modern times is not likely to change Western cultural ambivalence toward the aging self, since aging, unlike gender, race, or sexual orientation, represents and is represented by physical decline.

My purpose in this article is to explore the relationship between aging and identity in premodern Western culture, in the context of the gendered, biomedical body.[1] I propose that the body forms the link between the aging process and the social place of the elderly—and thus their social and personal identity—in both premodern and modern Western culture. While highlighting continuities in the relationship between aging, the body, and identity, I also touch briefly upon change: the shift in the meaning of identity from difference to sameness, in a postmodern context of identity politics and social movements.

During the twentieth century, the connotations of the term "identity" have changed considerably, indeed even reversed in meaning. Early in the century, according to the *New English Dictionary on Historical Principles* (Murray et al. 1933:19), "identity" or "idemptitie" referred to "absolute or essential sameness, oneness," a word with late Latin roots ("identitas" c. 425 CE). Identity was a person's essential sameness over time and circumstances—continuity—and differentness from others: "The sameness of a person or thing at all times or in all circum-

RESEARCH ON AGING, Vol. 20 No. 1, January 1998 11-35
© 1998 Sage Publications, Inc.

11

stances; the condition or fact that a person or thing is itself and not something else; individuality, personality." John Locke and Washington Irving capture aspects of this sense of identity: "Consciousness always accompanies thinking . . . in this alone consists personal identity"; "He doubted his own identity and whether he was himself or another man" (Murray et al. 1933:19).

This definition of identity is similar to the "self" juxtaposed to "society" in the symbolic interactionism of the Chicago school of sociology. The symbolic interactionists of the early twentieth century proposed that the identity or self was not freestanding, but was shaped by and formative of society; the personal was at the same time profoundly social. But the 1960s (seen by some as heralding the beginning of the postmodern) shifted the meaning of identity and of the self intertwined with society to a different kind of relationship between individual and others. Society seemed, or became, no longer one entity but many, fragmentary, a mosaic of enclaves, communities, groups of all types and stripes.

In the third edition of the *American Heritage Dictionary of the American Language* (1996:896), it is sameness to others that is the core of identity's meaning, not differentness or uniqueness. The definitions in 1996 include "2. The set of behavioral or personal characteristics by which an individual is recognizable as a member of a group;[2] 3. The quality or condition of being the same as something else."[3] Identity, rather than expressing uniqueness of self and difference from others, has become sameness of self to others, linked most commonly to race, nation or ethnicity, gender, or sexual preference, and expressed within a nexus of organization or lifestyle. Continuity remains a core part of the definition: Those of a particular gender, race, or sexual orientation are commonly supposed to remain so.

Both the old and the new reference points of identity have salience for the aging and aged, in different ways.[4] Identity as sameness in consciousness and through time, experienced as linked with society (the symbolic interactionist's self) is problematic for aged persons as they experience changes and differences in their bodies, social roles, and selves. This self, or personal identity, is linked to the social order through social place. And, as I argue in this article, the body (height, skin, size, hair, face, gender, beauty) is the marker of change in social and personal identity; the converse of social and personal continuity.

74

Identity as sameness to others, as identification with a collectivity, is also problematic for the aged. During the twentieth century, but especially from the 1960s onward, the symbolic interactionist's dialectic of self/society was replaced with one of individual/collectivity, as blacks, women, and gays entered the arena of identity politics separate from the general body politic. Affirmative action, the National Organization for Women, and gay rights merged social movement activism, formal organization, and identity. Although the aged and aging in the twentieth century also have their formal organizations, social movements, from the American Association of Retired Persons (AARP) to Older Women's Leagues (OWLs), and anti-age discrimination legislation, this does not necessarily translate into identity politics or personal identity. While elderly people may "exhibit the behaviors and characteristics that make them identifiable as part of a group," a considerable amount of nutritional, exercise, cosmetic, and even surgical work may have gone into the task of evading that identification. Although we all know we are growing old, many of us (despite our willingness to use AARP discounts) want to try to conceal our aging from others, and perhaps even ourselves. And aging is the numerative and bodily sign of the universal process of decline; aging, unlike gender, class, race, or sexual preference, does not distinguish one from another.

It is one of the myths of modern aging that elders in premodern times were revered, seen as wise, and accorded an important identity and role, and that the industrial revolution swept away the social sources of their wisdom and place. The identity politics of the modern-to-postmodern era seemed to hold out a new, alternative source of place and role for elders, as it had for minorities, women, and gays.[5] But I will argue the reverse. Given bodily decay as the fulcrum of the aging process in Western culture (and any other culture we might know), the sameness of identity is always challenged by the aging body. And, furthermore, this same process of bodily decay makes it unlikely that the aged will find personal identity within postmodern social movements. I argue in this article that the aging process has given rise to an enduring ambivalence about the aged in Western culture from premodern into modern and postmodern times and that the identity of the aged was, and is, linked both to the betrayal of the body and to the resulting cultural ambivalence about the aged.

The Representation of Old Age

This article is part of a larger project that seeks to explore premodern aging in Western culture.[6] There are many ways of carving up eras for the purpose of describing the history of aging and gerontological inquiry; following Freeman (1979), I refer to the premodern as the eighteenth century and earlier, giving way to the modern in the early nineteenth century. Freeman sees the modern era of gerontology as marked by the work of J. M. Charcot (mentor of Sigmund Freud). To Freeman, Charcot in an 1874 publication "initiated the modern era of gerontology. . . . [He] brought an end to the classical period and introduced the modern era" (p. 81). The modern era of method and measurement began with the physiologic-statistical studies performed by Quetelet and others in the nineteenth century (Freeman 1979).[7]

Freeman (1979) notes, from the perspective of social gerontology, that "the literature on aging has undergone a process of assemblage from remote times" by "gerontologists of centuries ago" (p. 80).[8] I use both primary and secondary sources from this assemblage, including twentieth century histories of aging (for example, Richardson, 1933; Freeman, 1979; Minois, 1989; Demaitre, 1990). The primary sources I use are mainly medical, prescriptive treatises with moral and religious (sometimes satirical) overtones, either written originally in English or translated into English (from Greek, Latin, and other languages).[9] For ancient times, the primary sources are the treatises (in translation) of Greek and Roman physicians such as the Hippocratics (c. 400 BCE) and Galen (1-2 CE). For medieval times, the sources (some translated and some later texts written in English) are sparse for the fourth to eleventh century (the dark ages) but are of increasing volume with the drawing-near of the Renaissance and into the Enlightenment.

It is a truism that narratives are written in particular social contexts for particular audiences and thus do not mirror the realities of everyday life. Wortley points out, for example, that epigrams, which were sometimes inscribed on tombstones, were "full of references to the fading of beauty and the approach of death" (Wortley 1996d:3). Proverbs represented "what is commonly said," including what was commonly said of the aging. But despite the limitations of narratives, and despite the vast differences in the social contexts of ancient Greece and postmodern America, many premodern proverbs echo precisely what is commonly said of the aging today; from ancient Greece: "Life is a bubble"; "Old folks are children twice over"; "the evening of life"; "one foot in Charon's ferry"; "Hitch a smaller cart to an aging horse"; "An old ship will not sail the open sea"; "Hard work best earns a dinner for old age"; "Even of the autumn of the beautiful is beautiful"; "it is too late to accustom an old dog to the leash" (Wortley 1996b).

REPRESENTING SURVIVAL INTO OLD AGE

The work of Freeman and others (Talmadge 1990; Russell 1990) challenges one of the myths of modern sociology: that the aging did not survive before the late industrial era with enough frequency to shape social policies, roles, and politics. But as the historical record indicates, survival into old age was quite variable across time and locale during ancient and medieval times. The ages given on 2,022 grave inscriptions for ancient Greece indicate that 10.40 percent lived to age 61 or beyond and 1.49 percent to between ages 86 and 110 (Richardson 1933:232).[10] The numbers of aged (over 60) in the West from Roman to medieval times varied by geographic locale within Europe from 0 percent to 25 percent (Russell 1990:221).

Throughout most of Western history, according to Minois (1989), more males than females survived into old age due to problems surrounding childbirth. Russell (1990:126) proposes that the comparative longevity of medieval men and women "depends upon their age group," with women who reached forty likely to live longer than men who reached forty. In premodern narratives, women were spoken of as living longer than men, with various reasons offered. A thirteenth century summary of Aristotle's *de Longitudine* explained longevity as the consequence of "sexual abstinence, abundance of flesh, being a woman, a warm and moist climate" (Lewry 1990:26). Francis Bacon wrote that overexercising hinders longevity, "which is one cause why women live longer than men, because they stir less" (1903:127).

Class, citizenship, and occupation were also related to survival into old age in premodern times. David (1991:12) estimates that around the middle of the third century BCE among Spartan citizens—who were all males and who represented the highest status in Spartan society—perhaps 15% were sixty or older. In medieval Europe, according to

Russell, the "simplicity of food and action" of monks gave them a longer life span than that of the laity (1990:126). Elderly statesmen, knights, monks, and rich men were more likely to be the object of attentive caretaking than the surviving poor, although charity for paupers also occurred (Minois 1989).

Richardson (1933) for ancient Greece and Demaitre (1990) for medieval times both point out that many of those who wrote texts, including texts on old age and longevity (and whose texts survived), lived long lives, although the actual age claimed often varies from one source to another. Richardson gives the following ages for the ancient philosophers at their deaths: Aristotle, sixty-three; Plato, eighty-one; Socrates, seventy (1933:215-21). Cohausen, writing in the eighteenth century, refers to the great age of "antediluvian patriarchy" when people lived upward of 300 years. In later times, when the earth's density increased consequent to the Flood, this life span was reduced—but still the important men lived to be over 100. Cohausen tells us of the famous aged: Attila the Hun, 124; Piastus King of Poland, 120; Hippocrates, 104; Ascelepiades, 150; Galen, 104; Sophocles, 130 (1771:16). Easton (1799) describes the circumstances of 1,712 people who lived for 100 or more years. Cornaro, who was born in 1464, wrote four discourses on aging at age 83, 86, 91, and 95, finally dying at the age of 103 (Cornaro 1903). [11] Demaitre says of the twenty-odd male writers on longevity who lived between 1200 and 1600, "the average lifespan was an astonishing sixty-seven years" (1990:22).

The Aging Self: Social Place and the Betrayal of the Body

Unlike the concept of identity, concepts of aging and the aged have remained remarkably consistent throughout the centuries, since Plato, Aristotle, and the Hippocratic writers sought the meaning of growing old. Although there is a general myth of great change in the cultural meaning and evaluation of old age and the aged during the late twentieth century, premodern as well as modern, writings on old age are concerned with the problematic social place of elders in the social order and with the relationship of gender to the aging process. And the aging of the body is at the center of this discourse.

Both modern and premodern theories (and experiences) of aging rest upon the body. It is in the body that aging takes place and is taken notice of by the social order—in the graying of the hair, the appearance of wrinkles, the battle of flesh with gravity, and (for women) the cessation of menstruation. The embodiment of aging ensures that Western cultural interpretations are writ upon the gendered body.

For many premodern writers on aging, the body was the betrayer of personal identity: that which changed sameness of flesh, circumstances, and consciousness into an altered self. These writers turned to the classical conceptions of the body and its place in the universe to try to explain, and in some cases to deny, reverse, or chase away, the sense of personal decline and loss of self associated with growing old. They wrote of the humors of the body, longevity, and the stages of "man,"[12] themes that echo modern concern with the biomedicine of old age, the importance of balance and moderation in diet and lifestyle, and the stages of human development.

THE HUMORS OF THE BODY

The biomedical theory of the humors, institutionalized by the Hippocratic writers and disseminated through the writings of Galen and other Greek, Roman, and Arab physicians, linked the human body to the cosmos through the body's fluids.[13] The four elements in the universe were air (hot and moist), earth (cold and dry), fire (hot and dry), and water (cold and moist). The corresponding humors were blood, black bile, yellow bile, and phlegm; the corresponding temperaments or complexions were sanguine, melancholic, choleric, and phlegmatic (Minois 1989:7).[14] Health, illness, gender, and the stages of life were characterized by various combinations of dryness/wetness and heat/coldness. In some versions of the Galenic system, the child was damp and hot, the young man hot and dry, the grown man dry and cold, and the elder cold, dry, and damp (dry in the wrong places such as the skin, damp in the wrong places such as the lungs; Wortley 1996a; Demaitre 1990:8-9). The primary cause of old age was the drying out of the body accompanied in advanced old age by an influx of the adust, or melancholic and phlegmatic humors (Lewry 1990:32).

Human fate, and the aging process, was dominated by the relationship between these bodily humors and their interlinked astral influences at the time of birth, together with heredity. Gabriele Zerbi, author of a fifteenth century handbook on old age homes and the biomedical treatment of old age, noted the complexity of the relationship between the humoral body, its constitution, and the stars:

> Aristotle says that the time and life of each man has its number and . . . it is determined . . . by the revolutions of the heavens . . . the extension of life, the period and limit of each living creature are determined by the kind of complexion which is contained in that individual. ([1489] 1988:72-3)

> As Averroes says, there may be two men of similar complexion directed equally by the same regimen; one, however, will reach the optimum length of life according to nature, while the other will incur death on account of the evil humors which are generated in him. Averroes says that the cause of this situation is a bad preparation fixed in his complexion which creates his ill even if we do not know just what this preparation is. ([1489] 1988:46)

Despite this seeming fixity of the body's fate, it was also responsive to the "airs, waters, places" of the environment, and to nutritional and other bodily habits. For Cornaro the long-lived Venetian, as for so many medieval to Renaissance writers on old age:

> Our birth is subject to the revolutions of the heavens, which have great power over it, especially with regard to good and bad constitutions. . . . And there is no doubt that man can, by means of art, free himself from the control of the heavens. (1903:78)

Especially from the thirteenth century onward there was considerable interest in longevity, in particular, achieving a life span of 100 years or more. Medieval Christian and Jewish scholars sought to explain both why there had been a shortening of the lifespan since the time of the patriarchs and why some individuals lived longer than others. As Bacon (1638) noted, "Before the Flood, as the sacred Scriptures declare, men lived an hundred years." Each generation from the flood onward had been foreshortened, from Sem aged 600 to Abraham at 175 to Plato at 81. Like modern environmentalists, medieval writers attributed damage to the atmosphere (Talmadge 1990) or changes in the earth's density and gravitational field (Cohausen 1771:16) to the biblical flood.

Yet even after the flood, some people lived longer than others. In addition to the natural process of decay were the unnatural consequences of intemperate behavior, which cut short the life span. During the eighteenth century, Leonard Lessius was among many scholars who lamented "The Profusion of Luxury and Intemperance into which this Age has fallen," the consequence of which was poor diet and damaged nerves and muscles. Thus mistreated, "Bodies at long run become full of crude and Vicious Humours," which "increase . . . [and] at last turn to Putrefaction and grow malignant," clogging up the muscles and nerves and obstructing the animal spirits, the "Spring of life . . . Power of Sense and Motion" (1743: Preface, 18).

MODERATION AND MEDICINE

Premodern narratives of aging did not, however, portray complete helplessness in the face of biomedical change. Both youth and age were exhorted, throughout the centuries, to attend to dietary and lifestyle "moderation" and (humoral) "balance" in order to avoid the worse ravages of old age. One well-known handbook on aging, Arnaldus of Villa Nova's (1290), is said by his translator Jonas Drummond to have gone through 240 editions between 1475 and 1846. In this thirteenth century tract, Villa Nova recommends "moderation inn all things" for old people, together with a set of hygienic principles that included living in ventilated houses, washing out the mouth after each meal, and drinking chicken broth (1290:8).

These exhortations to moderation were based on enduring biomedical principles of the humors as the source of the effects of aging. To dispel old age, for Villa Nova, it was necessary to "reduce the existing humor and removing those things which produce it," for example, the brain vapors that caused white hair (1290:39). More than 200 years later, Cornaro wrote that temperance "united, equalized and disposed all my humors so well" (1526:53). Two hundred and fifty years after Cornaro, Cohausen proposed to transmit vital humors from the young to the old; the "sucked in" breath of healthy young people would "carry the medicine" of vital humors into the body of the aged (1771:107-8).

Some premodern authors, while working within the biomedical theory of the humors and Hippocratic notions of balance and moderation, promoted the view of old age as a disease. Seneca, says Wortley, wrote that "old age is the sickness for which there is no cure, echoing an ancient equation of age with disease" (1996c:12-3). Many centuries later, in his introduction to his translation of Roger Bacon's thirteenth century *The Cure of Old Age and the Preservation of Youth*, Browne wrote that "Old Age . . . is itself a Disease" ([1240] 1653:A3). Maimonides (1135-1204) "advised older people to see a physician regularly . . . and . . . avoid excesses of all types" (Freeman 1979:27). The contemporary focus on lifestyle moderation, and the medicaliza-tion of old age, are not new but ancient phenomena.

But, as with modern authors, premodern writers on longevity had different positions on the advisability of the aged's resorting to phy-sicians, and to stronger medicines than broth, to treat old age. Many warned their readers sternly away from physicians, pharmacists, and their nostrums. James Easton, in 1799, wrote that "it is not the rich and great, but those who depend on medicine, who become old" (p. xi). The continuing moistness—thus youthfulness—of old people depended on

Not Galen's skill, or Aesculapian rules
The pride of learning or the boast of fools;
But Tempr'ance, Exercise, and all the train
Of sober virtues, chace disease and pain. (p. x)[15]

Others took a different tack, proposing physicians and medicine for the care of the aged. Old people, according to Roger Bacon in the thirteenth century, should take "Amber Gryse . . . the medicine which is cast out of the sea," for old age, since it consumes "the Phlegmatic and Melancholick Moister" ([c. 1240] 1653:143). Browne, Bacon's translator, opposed the idea that "we" only need a physician when we are actually sick; rather, he claimed we need to routinely check with physicians to monitor our everyday bodily states (1653:A3). He declared his belief in the possibility of immortality, but modestly disclosed that he could not provide the key, only a "Reprieve" from old age by "Temperance and Medicine" (1653:A4).

In a 1771 satire on "Hermippus Revivivus," an Englishman in the Roman Empire said to have lived somewhere between 115 and 155 years. Cohausen set the natural term of life at between 300 and 500 years. He quoted approvingly Bacon's thirteenth century admonition to take to the art of physicians to cure old age and proposed that since "old age is the only disease to which we are subject by nature . . . it is very possible men may be much longer defended than they usually are by the help of art" (p. 13). Dying at under 100 years of age was a sign of "a want of skill, of care, or of attention" (p. 14) and not a natural process. After all, the revered ancients sought medicines to treat old age: as Sir Francis Bacon noted, "The ancients seemed not to despair of attaining the skill, by means of medicines, to put off old age, and to prolong life" (1903:127). And Zerbi, in the late fifteenth century proposed the *Gerontocomia* or old age home, with the gerontocomos (administrator) in charge, for the medical, psychological, and social treatment of aged men.[16]

THE STAGES OF "MAN"

Human development was predicated upon changes in the balance of the humors over time: the "stages of 'man.'" For the ancient Greeks, and in the chain of medical narratives built upon their writings, growing old was a process of the drying up of the humors and, like ash from a dying fire, blowing away. Throughout premodern times, philosophers and physicians proposed various numbers of stages and different age boundaries for human development. Metaphors of old age in the Greek tradition were often seasonal and rural, with the process of aging compared to the approach of winter, and old people portrayed as animals: the conniving fox, the crafty and long-lived crow, or the nasty, bad-tempered dog (Wortley 1996a).

The Hippocratic writers proposed four stages of man, linked to other sets of four within the physical world, not only the humors but also the seasons, the elements, and the primary qualities (Siraisi 1990:110). A common tetradic version, from the Galenic writings into the middle ages, is that of pueritia, adolescentia, iuventus (or juventus), and senectus (Wortley 1996a:6-7). Richardson notes that Aristotle divided life into the three stages of youth, the prime of life, and old age, while Solon proposed ten stages of 7 years each (1933:2). In the sixteenth century, Andreas Laurentius divided the life cycle into "infancie, Adolescencie, Manhood . . . and Old Age." Much given to subdivisions, Laurentius divided old age into the first (green, from fifty), second (from seventy), and third stages, characterized, respectively, by wisdom, drying out, and decrepitude ([1599] 1938:173-4).

What was, and is, common to these stage theories (beyond the notion of stages itself, which seems to have permanently captured the Western imagination) is the idea of developmental alteration of the individual from his or her fixed identity as a person, Jane or Joe, into a shared identity of the aged—changes associated with the humoral body. One set of age-changes is common to both men and women and consists of such implacable signs as wrinkling skin, graying hair, and the effects of time and gravity upon muscle tone. Another set pertains to the senses: the memory loss, deafness, blindness, and other sensory afflictions of some old age and more advanced old age. A third is gendered and sexual: the differential effect of time upon reproductive systems, with almost no women but many men able to beget children after the turning of the half-century. And, since selves are social, these bodily, sexual, and gendered changes had, and have, social and moral implications. Old people in both modern and premodern Western culture are taught that they are in a particular stage of life with particular bodily changes to be experienced and expected, and they are also taught the social and moral meanings of those changes; meanings that impinge upon the aging self.

The Meanings of Old Age

The general social place of the elder, today and in the past, is derived from a premodern Western morality of the body, predicting changes in behavior and character consequent upon bodily changes. Those social meanings that flow from the aging body might best be summarized as ambivalent and ambiguous, thus giving to aging selves some perhaps quite mixed messages. This ambivalence originates at least from the time of Plato and Aristotle, with their contrasting perspectives on old age: the myth of the universally revered elder in premodern Europe is just that, a myth. While there were throughout ancient and medieval times strands of thought that revered elders, there were as many strands of thought that despised not only the passage of time but those affected by it. A web of disparate perspectives on the meaning of growing old can be found in Greek, Roman, patristic, and medieval

Christian and Jewish texts into the Enlightenment. And from those meanings—negative, positive, and ambiguous—flowed expectations concerning interactions with the elderly by others, and hence their social place.

In his translation of the *Anthology* of John Stobaeus 1 (c.500 CE), Wortley notes three sayings about old age:

> That old age is not a bad thing . . . That old age is regrettable . . . That old age is a grave matter, worthy of all reverence [in which] the intellect is brought to perfection. (1996e:6)

He adds:

> It is pleasant to think that these three parts balanced each other out, but fifty-four citations are produced to say that old age is regrettable against only thirty-one to say it is not, and a mere eight in favor of the third proposition. (1996e:6)

On the side of the regrettable, Sir Francis Bacon quotes a young man of his acquaintance, who described the elderly as

> dry skinn'd and impudent, hard bowell'd, and unmercifull; bleare ey'd, and envious; downlooking, and stooping . . . trembling limbs, wavering, and unconstant, crooked finger'd, greedy and covetous, knee trembling, and fearefull, wrinkled and crafty. (1638:279-20)

In ancient to patristic Greek aphorisms, epigrams, and other writings on old age, the negative traits associated with the elderly include their lessened mental capacities and bodily strength and being fearful, angry, overly talkative, miserly, and (for a few misguided elders) trying to act youthful. From these characteristics flowed social consequences. Elders who tried to act young were to be made to feel ashamed of themselves. Fearful, angry, gossipy, or miserly elders could expect to be mocked or avoided by the young and duped by unscrupulous persons taking advantage of their ineptitude (Wortley 1996a).

The positive qualities attributed to the elderly by premodern writers included wisdom, education and being learned, spirituality, discipline, moderation, and self-control. Among the ancient Greeks, "Erinna paints a charming picture of old ladies with silver hair, gifted with golden thoughts." Aristotle "calls attention to the fact that while a youth may be a geometrician or a mathematician that does not make him prudent . . . for prudence can come only from experience. Elder men restrain the insurgents in political strife" (Richardson 1933:17-8). These are the good, useful, moral elders of Western mythology.

The idea of the wise elder weaves through the web of premodern ambivalence about age, taking various shapes, and coalescing in the social role of elder orator, teacher, caretaker, or chaperone for the young (Richardson 1933; Wortley 1996c). The spiritual elder is the ideal elder of the medieval Christian church, someone whose bodily decay is matched by compensatory—and much more valuable— spiritual growth (Wortley 1990). The mid to late medieval wise elder, perhaps himself engaged in writing about longevity, exemplified the virtues of moderation, balance, and self-control in the bodily arenas of eating, drinking, and sexuality (Demaitre 1990). Somewhere in between these opposites of virtue and vice is the shrewd old person, compensating for her or his lack of physical strength by manipulation and cunning. In Aesop's *Fables*, the fable of the "Elderly Lion and the Fox" begins, "An elderly lion no longer capable of hunting to feed himself would have to do it by using his wits." But as another Aesopian fable reminds us, wits, like the body, also decline for some in old age: "An elder out of his wits is good for nothing, like an old garment" (Wortley 1996a:15-7, 38).

GENDER, AGING, AND IDENTITY

The premodern social place of the elderly was framed by clear-cut gender roles. In ancient Greece, the male citizen was a warrior, politician, worker, defined by his ability to fight, participate, and labor. The lessened strength associated with old age rendered many aged men unfit for battle, political participation, or labor, and thus they were, in a sense, no longer men. Ironically, that same lack of strength and social place forced some elderly men, despite their weakness, to toil at hard manual labor.

The place of women in ancient Greece was all domesticity or sexuality. Wives were for the domestic hearth and reproduction, courtesans for sexuality and entertainment, and a few older women for nursing and chaperoning duties (Richardson 1933). Aside from the nurses and chaperones, the central identity of women in ancient times was related to reproduction, men, children, and sexuality. As women aged, they gradually or rapidly lost these parameters of the self to the ravages of time and the body.

Although many special qualities (setting them apart from the young, and from their younger selves) were attributed to all old people of whichever gender, other kinds were associated particularly with either women or men. Richardson describes the ancient Greeks' depictions of amorous men intolerant of the young, and contrary women:

> Old men, although they devote their time to amorous pursuits . . . express antipathy towards the love affairs of the young. Old women are frequently very contrary. The old women in Aristophanes are regularly drunken, morose, and shrewish. (1933:29)

The different social place accorded aging women and men in premodern times was based upon humoral notions of reproduction and sexuality. Blood, including menstrual blood, occupied a central place in humoral theory and in ancient reproductive, nutritional, medical, and psychological schema. For the ancients, menstrual blood was toxic, and the function of menstruation was to eliminate poisonous humors. Thus, "once menstruation ceased," the old woman "grew into a repository of poison" (Rawcliffe 1995:175). A medieval poem warns young men: "With women aged fleshly have na ta do" (quoted in Nitecki 1990:111). Although sex with young women was an antidote to old age for men, marriage between old women and young men was fatal to the man:

> To see a woman advanced in age grow not only brisk and lively, but strong and healthy, by marrying a young husband? She drinks his breath, exhales his spirits, extracts his moisture, and invigorates herself, while the poor man, suffering from the impure contagion of her breath and vapours, and from the malignity of this ill-chosen union, sinks very quickly into an apparent weakness—and falls at last into what the common people call a galloping consumption. Strange! that the death of a young man should result from his marriage with an old woman, and that the taking of a young wife should repair the waste, and prolong the life, of an old man. Yet so it is. (Cohausen 1771:1089-9)

Men's place in premodern society was in battle, at work, and as the procreator of the next generation. Although the general place of old men during battles was with the women and children on top of the city walls, there were counterexamples of brave aged warriors, for example, "The soldiers of Eumenes, who had served under Philip and Alexander, and not a man younger than sixty" (Richardson 1933:37-9). And although some physicians such as Zerbi (1489) warned that "Sex should simply be avoided by old men" (p. 173), old men who were able to function (especially with younger partners) were likely to be objects of admiration rather than derision. Thomas Parr, an Englishman who was reputed to have been born in 1483 and lived until 1635, was saluted in a long poem both for his first marriage at 80 and (disguised as reprimand) his adultery at 105.

The changes in the body, social place, and identity that occurred in premodern times for men and women prompted a search for the preservation or prolongation of youth beyond the possibilities of moderation or medicine. One form of this search was occult or magical: the quest for immortality and the fountain of youth. Others were somewhat more practical: the search for ways of modifying or eliminating the symptoms of old age and the attempt to preserve appearances through cosmetics. The ambivalent, sometimes savage literature on aging and the cosmetic preservation of youth is directed mainly at women.

WOMEN AND THE COSMETIC PRESERVATION OF YOUTH

If the bodily changes attendant upon old age cannot be held back or even reversed by moderation or medicine, they might possibly be disguised. While moderation was recommended for everyone, and medicine for men who could afford it, the cosmetic preservation of youth was the premodern provenance of women—as it is the modern. While there are indeed references to men dyeing their hair and trying to appear younger, these references are far less fierce than those that describe women's use of hair dye and cosmetics. As Richardson comments:

It appears that the Greek women, in an effort to appear youthful as long as possible, sometimes used a substance resembling white lead to

render the wrinkles less conspicuous, and sometimes had their eye-
brows polled [sic] and painted. There is some evidence that they dyed
their hair and wore false hair. (1933:11)

Although women were seen (once having survived childbirth) as
living longer than men, they were also seen as aging faster than men.
As Signer (1990) notes with reference to aging in medieval Jewish
texts, "Women reach old age when they no longer have the power of
procreation; men display age through a loss of physical agility and
mental acumen" (p. 43). The reproductive body is the inferior body:
Despite its greater longevity, the female body "groweth old alwaies
sooner than the male" because of her "weakness" and habitual "idle-
nes" (Laurentius [1599] 1938:38). Thus the preservation of youth
formed a rather different challenge for women than for men: the
challenge of a beautiful face and body.

As today, women who preserved their youthful beauty without
apparent resort to cosmetics (who did not look their age) were valor-
ized, while those who looked their age were objects of contempt—and
if they tried to disguise their age and failed, they were doubly so. In
an epigram from Meleager around the first to second century CE:

Timo . . . your back is bent like a yard-arm lowered, and your grey
fore-stays are slack, and your relaxed breasts are like flapping sails,
and the belly of your ship is wrinkled by the tossing of the waves, and
below she is full of bilge-water and her joints are shaky. Unhappy he
who has to sail still alive across the lake of Acheron on this old
coffin-galley. (Wortley 1996d:5)

And, also courtesy of Wortley, in a narrative by Antiphilus of Byzan-
tium from the first century CE:

Even if you smooth the skin of your many-trenched cheeks and blacken
with coal your lidless eyes and dye your white hair black and hang
round your temples curly ringlets crisped by fire this is useless and
ridiculous. (Wortley 1966d:7)

Ancient writings focus upon the general tendencies of women's and
men's aging, for women to lose their beauty and sex appeal and men
to become weak, but they also provide counterexamples. Some few
women remain sexually attractive despite aging—more so than the

young—and some men retain their ability to fight and lead others into battle. In the *Patmos Florilegium*:

> Charito [who] has completed sixty years but still the mass of her dark hair is as it was, and still upheld by no encircling band those marble cones of her bosom stand firm. Still her skin without a wrinkle distils ambrosia, distils fascination and ten thousand graces. Ye lovers who shrink not from fierce desire, come hither, unmindful of her decades. (Wortley 1996d:10)

Richardson (1933:12) quotes "A late writer [who] sings the praises of a certain Melite who, though on the threshold of old age, has not lost the grace of youth." She adds, however, that "It can readily be observed that this conception of old age had a very small place in the Greek mind."

These are the cultural scripts of aging in premodern Western culture. Old age is a stage, or set of stages, characterized by bodily changes, biomedicalized, and read as decline. Old age, therefore, means a changing social and moral place in the world—a change in social role and social self. The social and moral meanings of these changes are, in Western culture, a mixed message, interweaving images of decline, inutility, and decay with those of wisdom, grace, and proximity to deities and the afterlife. For women, the message is less mixed, with a fixed point of insistence that in the final stages of life, old age must be accepted gracefully and not cosmetically, since a sexualized aging woman is a creature of absurdity.

Aging and Personal Identity

What then of the aging self living within these bodily and social boundaries? The betrayal of the body is universal, shaping the experience of aging across time and space. And, as we have seen, the Western cultural ambivalence about the aging self also shapes the elder's place in society and her or his reflected personal identity.[17]

Returning to the theme of identity as lack of change due to changing circumstances, time, or other vicissitudes, it is clear that the experience of aging is the antithesis of identity as continuity over time. The bodily and social changes that attend old age often cause the elder to wonder, to paraphrase Washington Irving, if I am myself, or another man; myself, or another woman? In his discussion of the sayings about old age in John Stobeaus's anthology, about 500 CE, Wortley notes that "generally speaking the complaints made about old age seem to be by people who are speaking in the first person or from personal experience." He cites the aged Sophocles as saying, "All the evils occur in high old age: the mind departed . . . uselessness for work, vain anxieties" (1996f; np). But Sophocles's response to his own aging is only one of the ambivalent threads of personal identity in premodern times: focusing on decline. The other thread, based on a humoral conception of moderation (and perhaps medicine), is that of continuity in old age despite the betrayals of the body.

Cornaro's various sixteenth century treatises on aging, temperance, and moderation are typical of the more optimistic personal literature on aging. In a style and tone befitting a modern self-help manual, Cornaro describes his youthful bad habits, drinking, and obesity—and his subsequent determination to live a life of balance and moderation in all things. Once this moral and humoral state was reached—although old age and death could not be eliminated, neither ill health nor dissatisfaction was inevitable—no mind departed, uselessness for work, or vain anxieties for Cornaro and other writers on personal longevity. At age eighty-one he wrote:

> I am continually in health, and am so nimble that I can easily get on horseback without the advantage of the ground, and sometimes I go up high stairs and hills on foot. Then I am ever cheerful, merry and well contented, free from all troubles and troublesome thoughts. . . . Neither is this my pleasure made less by the decaying dulness of my senses, which are all in their perfect vigor. ([1562] 1898:42-5)

Those who wrote of the betrayal of the body focused both on general decline and on the particular decline of the sexual powers. What we hear in the text is the male voice describing the aging sexual body of both male and female: We do not hear much directly from women in ancient and medieval times about the impact of menopause and aging upon personal identity, we hear only what men said about this. Erasmus, in the sixteenth century, mocks the sexuality of old women:

> Yet it is even more fun to see the old women who can scarcely carry their weight of years and look like corpses that seem to have risen from

the dead. They still go around . . . on heat, "longing for a mate." . . .
They're forever smearing their faces with make-up and taking tweezers
to their pubic hairs . . . trying to rouse failing desire. . . . absolute
foolishness. (Quoted in Minois 1989:255-6)

From men we hear directly of their failing sexual power, their failing
selves. The aging Maximianus wrote, circa 550 CE, of his impotence
with a Greek cabaret performer (Elegy V) and of his general weakness
(Elegy 1):

'Pecker,' the busy provider of festive days,
Once the delight of my heart, and a treasure to me,
What dirge can I moan for you, drowned in your tears. . . .
Unhappy as though from a funeral I arise:
Although my member is dead I shall live in my art.
([c. 550] 1988: 335-6)

Jealous old age, reluctant to hasten my end,
Why come a laggard in this my worn-out body?
Set free my wretched life from such a prison. . . .
Now hearing is less, taste less, my very eyes
Grow dim; I barely know the things I touch,
No smell is sweet, no pleasure now is grateful,
Devoid of feeling, who's sure that he survives?
([c. 550] 1988:319-22)

POSTMODERN AGING AND THE POLITICS OF IDENTITY

The postmodern politics of collective identity are missing from this
discussion of the premodern; although the elites of the Greek city-
states might appreciate the nationalist basis of collective identity, the
significance of sexual preference and other postmodern identity markers would probably elude them. And throughout recorded Western
history, age has, by and large, been a thing to lament and chase away
rather than one to celebrate, amplify, and ideologize.[18]

There are some partial exceptions in the historical record, most
notably the recorded occurrence of gerontocracies in ancient societies,
particularly Sparta (see David 1991). Where old people—old men—
hold economic and/or political power, a basis exists for a politics of
age identity. Much has been made in postmodern America of the

increasing economic and political clout of the aging population as the baby boomers pass out of their first half century. It is possible that during this demographic process, a new Sparta may emerge, a class of ruling elders self-consciously and socially an elite.

But it is unlikely that the developmental betrayal of the body can be overcome by the political and the social, that biomedical (humoral, hormonal) decline will be conquered by advances in medicine (eternal, youthful life as sought by the alchemists), or that it will cease to matter as an aspect of gendered social roles (with the consequent disappearance of the cosmetic search for youthfulness). Neither a political-economic nor a social-constructionist position can negate the biomedical body at the center of the aging process, whether humoral or hormonal in its dominating fluids, nor the social consequences that flow therefrom. Even in gerontocratic Sparta, "geriatric traits [were not] . . . an aesthetic ideal . . . they could at times even there be associated with ugliness, infirmity, and morbidity" (David 1991:73). The celebratory politics of identity, of Chicanas, gays, or Lithuanians, are unlikely sources of a new collective identity for the aged in postmodern society.

Aging and identity in premodern times turns out to have much in common with aging and identity in modernity and postmodernity. The social place of the individual alters with the passage of time—the stages of aging—and with it the social self. At the center of this process is the body and its betrayals: the graying, wrinkling, sagging, weakening, and their gendered meanings. Men are distanced from phallic and public power, women from their desirability to men—each from the center of their social (if not always personal) identity. Men and women fight back, men with amorous conquests and trophy wives, women with cosmetics—sometimes the reverse. Balance and moderation in diet, exercise, and drink are recommended by experts and sages. Old age is biomedicalized, its symptoms treated (if someone can afford these measures) by physicians and nursing home attendants. The old person's identity is fixed upon the body by its changes and by the experts on longevity who surround the process of aging in Western society.

Social policies of old age in modern society risk absurdity to the precise extent that they become or remain ahistorical or antidevelopmental. To ignore the long history of aging as change and decay, the betrayal of the body, and the ambivalence of the young and old toward aging and the elderly is to fly in the face of the wisdom of generations past and those to come. Aging is not gender, race, religion, or sexual orientation: it belongs to all, not some of us, and it brings with it a long, enduring cultural and personal ambivalence.

NOTES

1. Grateful thanks to J. Wortley for his marvelous translations of Greek works on aging and for his teachings on the history of aging. Thanks also to those Kansas colleagues who read and commented on drafts of this and related papers: Tracy X. Karner, Joane Nagel, Susan Case, and the anonymous reviewers of *Research on Aging*.

2. The first definition relates to concepts or things not persons, although it does reference the relationship between collectivities and things: "1. The collective aspect of the set of characteristics by which a thing is definitively recognizable or known: *if the broadcast group is the financial guts of the company; the news division is its public identity*" (1996:896).

3. In definitions 1 and 4, however, the sense of identity as continuity over time remains. This notion of continuity fits our cultural notions of identity in relation to ethnicity or sexual preference but is the reverse of the developmental, in which bodily (and thus social and self) change is inevitable.

4. Like any other word or concept, "identity" has many situated meanings-in-use as well as dictionary definitions. I chose the dictionary definitions I use here because they seemed to me to resonate well with meanings-in-use in nineteenth and twentieth century representations of aging and identity. There is also a vast sociological literature on identity, the symbolic interactionists' engagement with self and society, upon which I build; this literature is indeed too vast to be cited here.

5. This possibility seemed to peak with the formation of Gray Power organizations parallel to Black Power; unlike Black Power and similar movements, Gray Power did not expand into a full-blown identity politics for the aged.

6. This article, and the larger project, are both sketches of a much vaster terrain of primary and secondary sources, intended to begin rather than end debate on the changing, and changeless, aspects of the aging process in Western history.

7. By the "classical era" preceding the clinical gaze, Freeman means an approach to aging, and a geriatric or gerontological expertise, characterized by immersion in the classical Greek and Roman philosophers and physicians, and the Asiatic and Arab traditions that preceded and superseded them. This era, in the view of Freeman and other historians of aging, stretched from the beginning of written history into the seventeenth and eighteenth centuries and was characterized authorially by aging men writing about old age (during modern times the voices of younger and female "experts" were added to this chorus).

8. Another view is that gerontology is of recent origin; Green, for example, notes that "The biologist Metchnikoff coined the term in 1903 but the field did not emerge for about another 50 years" (1993:38). As Demaitre (1990:3-4) notes, the scarce and scattered nature on premodern social life makes "the danger of oversimplification . . . only one" of the "pitfalls" of studying aging in ancient times. Anachronistic use of terms such as "gerontology" is another. My take on the anachronistic use of the term "gerontology" is this: If I read of the attempt to develop *expert knowledge* of something socially named and conceptualized (*aging, the aged*), and the training of experts to handle those named (the *gerontocomos and his assistants*; hence the

importance of Zerbi's 1489 work), I am willing, with Freeman (1979) to conceptualize a premodern "gerontology."

9. Primary sources in English are identified with one asterisk (*) in the references, translations with two asterisks (**). The remaining citations are secondary sources.

10. Grave inscriptions are not necessarily a reliable source of data in age since various kinds of "rounding" could have taken place, particularly close to the age of 100. Richardson (1933:234) notes that the Greeks tended to round off numbers in units of 5.

11. Obviously these data and commentaries on aging and the aged in premodern times cannot be taken as reflections of "fact" but, rather, as rough estimates and/or as legends. Cornaro also wrote a treatise on temperance and sobriety, republished in 1898; this translation (see the bibliography) gives his birth to death dates as 1475-1566.

12. Although some gerontological literature asserts (or laments) that biomedicalization of old age is a modern phenomenon, it is clear that to the extent that the theory of the humors is biomedical (which the reader can judge), the biomedical conception of old age is indeed an ancient one.

13. Much ancient Western medical and philosophical writing was mislaid during the Christian Dark Ages in Europe but was preserved in Arabic translations. During the Renaissance, these translations were retranslated into Latin for an educated European audience. Aristotle's natural philosophy—which dealt with aging—was, for example, put back into the curriculum of the Universities of Paris and Oxford during the 1240s and 1250s (Lewry 1990:24).

14. I refer to the theory of the humors as biomedical based upon the contemporary definition of biomedicine as "clinical medicine dealing with the relationship of body chemistry and function" (Webster's Desk Dictionary 1983:89). Both ancient humoral and modern hormonal theories, among others, come within the border of the biomedical.

15. Here, with "chace" for our "chase" and in other quotes I have preserved the spelling and usage that occur in the primary document.

16. The men whose residential treatment was proposed by Zerbi were clearly wealthy, given the nature of some of the treatments (gold, gems). But there are mentions in various texts of old age homes for other categories of persons during medieval and renaissance times, for example, old monks, old nuns, or paupers (Minois 1989).

17. Of course the historical record is only an infinitesimal fraction of the lived experience of humans, and a representation of lived experience at that. Given the great chain of being, we would expect far fewer women to have written about their experiences and proportionately less of what they wrote to have survived. Still, there is a lot of evidence out there.

18. Some of the themes noted in this essay also appear in non-Western cultures. Freeman (1979) claims that in the Han Dynasty in China c. 2500-2600 BCE, "the expressions of the aging process were seen as a disease" (p. 18-9). In Egypt, Imhotep ("Father of medicine and spiritual predecessor of Hippocrates") wrote on "Transforming an old Man into a Youth" (p. 20).

REFERENCES

The American Heritage Dictionary of the English Language. 1996. 3rd ed. Boston: Houghton Mifflin.

Arnaldus of Villa Nova. 1290. The Conservation of Youth and Defense of Age. Translated by Dr. Jonas Drummond. No publication information.**

Bacon, Francis. [1638] 1977. The Historie of Life and Death. London: Okes. Arno Press Facsimile ed., New York.*

Bacon, Roger. [c. 1240] 1653. *The Cure of Old Age and Preservation of Youth*. Translated by Richard Browne. No publication information.*

Bacon, Sir Francis. 1903. "Extracts Selected and Arranged From Lord Bacon's 'History of Life and Death' Etc." Pp. 117-30 in *The Art of Living Long*, edited by Louis Cornaro. Milwaukee: William F. Butler.*

Browne, Richard. 1653. "Introduction and Translation" to Roger Bacon's *The Cure of Old Age and Preservation of Youth. No publication information.*

Cohausen, J. D. 1771. *Hermippus Redivivus*. 3d ed. London.*

Cornaro, Louis (Luigi). 1903. *The Art of Living Long*. Milwaukee:William F. Butler.**

Cornaro, Ludovico (Luigi). [1562] 1898. *A Treatise on Temperance and Sobriety*. Translated by George Herbert. Reprint, Cleveland: Helman-Taylor Co.**

David, Ephraim. 1991. *Old Age in Sparta*. Amsterdam: Adolf M. Hakkert.

Demaitre, Luke. 1990. "The Care and Extension of Old Age in Medieval Medicine." Pp. 3-22 in *Aging and the Aged in Mediaeval Europe*, edited by Michael M. Sheehan. Toronto, Canada: Pontifical Institute of Medieval Studies.

Easton, James. 1799. *Human Longevity*. Salisbury: James Easton.*

Freeman, Joseph T. 1979. *Aging: Its History and Literature*. New York: Human Sciences Press.

Green, Bryan S. 1993. *Gerontology and the Construction of Old Age*. New York: Aldine de Gruyter.

Laurentius, Andreas. [1599] 1938. *A Discourse on the Preservation of the Sight: Of Melancholicke Diseases; of Rheumes, and of Old Age*. Translated by Richard Surphlet. Shakespeare Association Facsimile No. 5, Oxford University Press.*

Lessius, Leonard. 1743. *Treatise on Health and Long Life*. London: Charles Hitch.*

Lewry, P. Osmund. 1990. "Study of Aging in the Arts Faculties of the Universities of Paris and Oxford." Pp. 23-38 in *Aging and the Aged in Medieval Europe*, edited by Michael M. Sheehan. Toronto, Canada: Pontifical Institute of Medieval Studies.

Maximianus. [c.550 CE] 1988. *Elegies on Old Age and Love*. Translated by L. R. Lind. Philadelphia: American Philosophical Society.**

Minois, Georges. 1989. *History of Old Age: From Antiquity to the Renaissance*. Chicago: University of Chicago Press.

Murray, James A. H., Henry Bradley, William A. Craigie, and C. T. Onions. 1933. *A New English Dictionary on Historical Principles*. Oxford: Clarendon.

Nitecki, Alicia K. 1990. "Figures of Old Age in Fourteenth-Century English Literature." Pp. 107-16 in *Aging and the Aged in Medieval Europe*, edited by Michael Sheehan. Toronto, Canada: Pontifical Institute of Medieval Studies.

Rawcliffe, Carole. 1995. *Medicine and Society in Later Medieval Life*. United Kingdom: Alan Sutton.

Richardson, B. E. 1933. *Old Age Among the Ancient Greeks*. New York: AMS Press.

Russell, Josiah C. 1990. "How Many of the Population were Aged?" Pp. 119-27 in *Aging and the Aged in Medieval Europe*, edited by Michael M. Sheehan. Toronto, Canada: Pontifical Institute of Medieval Studies.

Signer, Michael. 1990. "Honour the Hoary Head: The Aged in the Medieval European Jewish Community." Pp. 39-48 in *Aging and the Aged in Medieval Europe*, edited by Michael M. Sheehan. Toronto, Canada: Pontifical Institute of Medieval Studies.

Siraisi, Nancy G. 1990. *Medieval and Early Renaissance Medicine: An Introduction to Knowledge and Practice*. Chicago: University of Chicago Press.

Talmadge, Frank. 1990. "So Teach Us to Number Our Days: A Theology of Longevity in Jewish Exigetical Literature." Pp. 49-62 in *Aging and the Aged in Medieval Europe*, edited by Michael M. Sheehan. Toronto, Canada: Pontifical Institute of Medieval Studies.

Webster's Desk Dictionary of the English Language. 1983. New York: Chain Sales Marketing.

Wortley, John. 1990. "Aging and the Desert Fathers: The Process Reversed." Pp. 63-74 in *Aging and the Aged in Medieval Europe*, edited by Michael M. Sheehan. Toronto, Canada: Pontifical Institute for Medieval Studies.

————. 1996a. "Aging and the Aged in Aesopic Fables." University of Manitoba, Canada. Unpublished manuscript.

————. 1996b. "Aging and the Aged in Classical Proverbs." University of Manitoba, Canada. Unpublished manuscript.

————. 1996c. "Aging and the Aged in 'The Greek Anthology.' " University of Manitoba, Canada. Unpublished manuscript.

————. 1996d. "Aging in the *Patmos Florilegium*." University of Manitoba, Canada. Unpublished manuscript.

————. 1996e. "Old Age According to John Stobaeus 1." University of Manitoba, Canada. Unpublished manuscript.

————. 1996f. "Old Age According to Stobaeus 11." University of Manitoba, Canada. Unpublished manuscript.

Zerbi, Gabriele. [1489] 1988. *The Gerentocomia: On the Care of the Aged.* Translated by R. L. Lind. Philadelphia: American Philosophical Society.**

Carol A. B. Warren is professor of sociology at the University of Kansas. Her research and teaching interests include gender and psychiatry, social control, and ethnographic and historical methods. Her work on aging includes a study of involuntary and voluntary electroconvulsive therapy among elderly mental patients in the 1970s to 1980s, and historical essays on gender and aging. She has written a number of scholarly monographs, including Madwives: Schizophrenic Women in the 1950s *(Rutgers University Press) and, most recently,* The Body Electric: Gender, Electricity and Psychiatry From Ancient Times to the Second Millenium. *She is working on a book tentatively titled* Eyes: Seeing and the Social Order.

Evolving, Aging, and Making Culture[*]

by A. F. Robertson

University of California, Santa Barbara, USA

In a recent polemic, Leda Cosmides and John Tooby offer new proposals to bridge the gulf between biological and cultural explanations of human behaviour. By focussing on the evolved architecture of the human mind, they seek specific psychological mechanisms by which genes may influence human social institutions. A major challenge for this approach is how to trace precisely which psychological endowments, formed by the Pleistocene age, have shaped which aspect of our contemporary cultures. Here it is suggested that the temporal framework of individual human lives may provide one means of establishing clearer connections between brain structure and social institutions. For biologists this will involve extending conventional views of human ontogeny to include the phases of aging and death, which have been so important for the genesis of culture. This image of the lifespan may in turn help anthropologists come to terms with the physical bases of intergenerational transfers on which the perpetuation of culture depends.

In the lengthy introductory chapter to their collection (edited, with J. H. Barkow, 1992) on *The Adapted Mind: Evolutionary Psychology and the Generation of Culture*, John Tooby and Leda Cosmides offer a succinct and provocative statement of the powers of evolutionary theory in social science. The piece is imperiously polemic, but the style is cogent and accessible, buoyed up with witty illustration. The authors' aim is to bring culture into "the scientifically analyzable landscape of causation" (Tooby & Cosmides 1992 [hereafter "T&C"]: 20) by regarding it as a product of cognition, which is in turn based on mechanisms of the evolved human mind. These ambitions will place Tooby and Cosmides's work definitively beyond the pale for many contemporary social and cultural anthropologists. However, it would be a pity if such a spirited essay were to fall victim so easily to the dogmatism

Ethnos, vol. 59:1-2 (1994)
© Scandinavian University Press

which afflicts our discipline. I seek here to identify a level at which some progress may be made towards bridging what remains a formidable analytical gap.

While insisting that they, too, are bridge-builders, Tooby and Cosmides mount a vigorous assault not simply on contemporary cultural studies, but on a "Standard Social Science" which they characterise as isolated (from science) and thus intellectually debilitated. Their proposed "Integrated Causal Model" proceeds from the assumption that the "human mind consists of a set of evolved information-processing mechanisms instantiated in the human nervous system", which have evolved "in ancestral environments". Many of these are "functionally specialized to produce behavior which solves particular adaptive problems, such as mate selection, language acquisition, family relations, and cooperation". The functional specificity of these information-processing mechanisms depends on the mind being "richly structured in a content-specific way". As such they "generate some of the particular content of human culture, including certain behaviors, artifacts, and linguistically transmitted representations". This "cultural content" may then be "adopted or modified by psychological mechanisms situated in other members of the population"—which "sets up epidemiological and historical population-level processes", which are "located in particular ecological, economic, demographic and intergroup social contexts or environments" (T&C:24).

Any attempt to argue a relationship between biology and culture confronts formidable dogmatic obstacles, most clearly evoked in Marshall Sahlins' indictment (1976) of E.O.Wilson's *Sociobiology*.[1] Sahlins insisted that this new, heretical sub-discipline afforded no purchase on culture, the symbolic apparatus which distinguishes humans from other beings. "Men interact in the terms of a system of meanings, attributed to persons and the objects of their existence, but precisely as these attributes are symbolic they cannot be discovered in the intrinsic properties of the things to which they refer". Thus, for Sahlins, culture is the obstacle to, rather than a plausible object of, biological explanations of society: "the sociobiological reasoning from evolutionary phylogeny to social morphology is interrupted by culture" (Sahlins 1976:11–12). Students of culture need take little interest in human biology, beyond recognising that it places "a set of natural limits on human functioning" and "puts at the disposition of culture a set of means for the construction of a symbolic order" (Sahlins 1976:66).

Centrally concerned with defining this "set of means", Tooby and Cosmides are uncontrite about their intrusion into the cultural domain. They would regard the "Durkheimian notion of the independent existence and persistence of the social fact" not simply as "a lapse into mysticism" (Sahlins 1976:5), but as intellectually isolationist and probably tautological—a determination to explain culture only with reference to culture. In the prevailing mood of relativism in anthropology, Tooby and Cosmides' insistence that "The research program we and others are advocating is one of integration and consistency, not of psychological or biological reductionism" (T&C:114–5), will be read simply as a hegemonic claim—the imperial thrust of scientistic "truth" against all others.[2] The indignant response from the scientist— "show us a more efficient means of organizing knowledge"— is directly at odds with the postmodern quest for "de-centered" discourses. Nor will the plea that "valid scientific knowledge—whether from the same or different fields —should be mutually consistent" (T&C:22) cut much ice.

Relativists will not be appeased by assertions of modern science's unrivalled predictive powers, or its methodologies for refutation. Nor will they be comforted by the starkly universalistic terms in which Tooby and Cosmides lay "culture" out on their dissecting table: "We will use *culture* to refer to any mental, behavioral, or material commonalities shared across individuals, from those that are shared by an entire species down to the limiting case of those shared only by a dyad, regardless of why these commonalities exist" (T&C:117). Culture in this formulation exists not "out there", disembodied in social space, but within human brains: it is "the manufactured product of evolved psychological mechanisms situated in individuals living in groups". It is "richly variable because it is generated by an incredibly intricate, contingent set of functional programs that use and process information from the world, including information which is provided both intentionally and unintentionally by other human beings" (T&C:24). Culture is formed by people making inferences about each other's behaviour, on the basis of "domain specific, evolved psychological mechanisms" (T&C:119). The idiom for explicating evolutionary functions is essentially the communications machine. While cybernetics provides the processual metaphor, engineering and architecture provide the structural metaphors.

From the basic isomorphism of human brains emerges the hypothesis of a "single human metaculture". This *fons et origo* of cultural detail is ontologically awkward. It is a massive deductive hypothesis, attributing the minutiae of daily life to fundamental causes, the scientific proof of which can only be fragmentary and instantiated. Tooby and Cosmides would wish to avoid naive evolutionist assumptions that everything is attributable to adaptive fitness, and explicable by ex-post reasoning to genetic cause. They accordingly qualify the unifying postulate by insisting on genetic/environmental *codetermination*: "*everything*, from the most delicate nuance of Richard Strauss's last performance of Beethoven's Fifth Symphony to the presence of calcium salts in his bones at birth, is totally and to exactly the same extent genetically and environmentally codetermined. 'Biology' cannot be segregated off into some traits and not others". However, insisting on omnipresence does not in itself advance the explanatory power of biology. A more discriminatory argument about codetermination emerges towards the end of their essay: acknowledging that social institutions are shaped not only by "psychological mechanisms" but also by "populational processes", Tooby and Cosmides strive to disengage "metaculture" from a medley of other sorts of "culture" with which it interacts: the "epidemio-logical", and the "evoked", "reconstructed", or "adopted" (T&C:118).

If the theory is actually making the more modest proposal that some aspects of culture are attributable to the evolved architecture of the human mind, then it must be able to discriminate which aspects are *not* so attributable (e.g.those "caused by social learning or transmission" [T&C:116]) and why.[3] The best Tooby and Cos-mides can do is warn that "social scientists should be extremely uneasy about positing an improbably complex structure in the system with the capacity to serve nonbiological functional ends, unless that capacity is a by-product of functionality that evolved to serve adaptive ends" (T&C:110).

It is easy to see why Durkheim, so concerned to discriminate social from psychological facts, should have become the *bête noire* of biosocial scientists like Tooby and Cosmides. But until they can specify more clearly the limits of their ex-planation, it seems prudent to respect Durkheim's warning that while a generalisable human nature may make culture possible, it can not explain it. While admitting that culture may, through human interaction, have its own logics or internal consistencies, Tooby and Cosmides' approach directly opposes any notion that culture has a men-tality of its own—that, as some anthropologists like to imagine, it has the auto-nomous capacity to "think", or reform itself. Recognition that culture can in some sense be "out there" interacting with individual human minds, can not displace the basic premise that the human mind is the ultimate analytical locus of culture:

> ... human superindividual interactions depend intimately on the representations and other regulatory elements present in the head of every individual involved and, therefore, on the systems of computation inside each head. These govern what is selected from "out there," how this is represented, what procedures act on the representations, and what behaviors result that others can then observe and interact with in a population dynamic fashion (T&C:47).

Tooby and Cosmides insist that "the component parts of the population are individual humans, so any social dynamics must be anchored in models of the human psychological architecture" (T&C:47). The grail for evolutionary psychology, therefore, is for an "artificer" in the human mind, "the content-determining pro-cesses that manufacture individual cultures and social systems" (T&C:46). For sociobiologists interested in nothing more than how mentalities established in the infant brain determine adult reproductive strategy, the artificer will reveal itself in body chemistry. However, explanations of culture as ambitious as those envisaged by Tooby and Cosmides may be obliged to admit other sorts of artificer which, by their very nature, may be less amenable to "hard science".

Tooby and Cosmides's endeavour evokes an arboreal image: reaching towards the branches and twigs of culture while cleaving to the biological stem from which they grow. If "Standard Social Scientists" seem obstinately oblivious of this trunk on which their evidence and arguments depend, the inability to find reliable purchase among the upper branches impedes the biologists' ascent into the cultural foliage. Although they are well enough aware that the peculiar reproductive success of human beings has depended on transcendent social processes which they themselves have created through time, there is very little room in Darwinian hypotheses for the notion that culture can have played any role in forming our physical selves.[4]

I would argue that any attempt to reconcile biological and cultural process must proceed from some clearer distinctions within the dimension of time. Tooby and Cosmides' hypotheses raise, but do not adequately resolve, potent questions about how the temporalities of evolution, human history, and the mundane rhythms of our individual lives are interconnected. The fundamental temporal discontinuity in their argument is between the pace of human evolution and of human history. Our current mental architecture is that of Pleistocene man.[5] Codetermination processes are locked into that primeval epoch: "the development of increasing cultural varia-tion throughout the Pleistocene was made possible by the evolution of psychological specializations that exploited the regularities of human metaculture in order to learn the variable features of culture" (T&C:93). Tooby and Cosmides warn that there is no use looking for adaptive functional explanations for structures which have had no time to evolve and which have not been dealing with "long standing adaptive problems": for example, "designs that serve the larger social good, or that complexly manipulate symbolic codes to spin webs of meaning, or that cause one to maximize monetary profit" (T&C:110).

Central to Tooby and Cosmides' approach is the insistence that we are not simply empty vessels waiting to be filled up with cultural specificities; our brains are hard-wired to inform us not simply *how* to think, but *what* to think about such fundamental matters as learning to speak, or competing for a mate. But again we must ask how we are to discriminate between elements of culture which are shaped by our Pleistocene brains, and those which are not. In precisely what sense, and to what extent, might we be hard-wired to operate a nuclear power-plant? Like other biosocial scientists, Tooby and Cosmides scrutinise the formation of the infant mind and the contemporary relics of our distant hunter-gatherer past for clues. They conclude, for example, that these distant cousin/ancestors' dependence on sharing rather than monopolising information is a predisposition for the contagion of cultural values on which we have latterly depended (T&C:120).

In the light of Tooby and Cosmides' agenda, the phylogenetic limitations on the explanation of cultural development come as something of a disappointment.

The physiological bases of our mental dispositions evolved too long ago to afford a plausible account of the diversity and mutability of cultures today. This helps to explain why anthropologists have slipped the biological anchor, and pursued the explanation of culture *sui generis*, retaining (in Tooby and Cosmides's eyes) only the vaguest commitment to scientific principles. With cultural variation as the prime object of explanation, the generalities of human nature lose much of their interest. For sociobiologists, on the other hand, cultural *variation* has little relevance beyond providing the means for sorting out what is and what is not universally human, or "metacultural".[6]

In these analytical schemes the individual mind is reduced, at one extreme, to a cluster of innate drives, and at the other, to an instrument of external symbolic systems. While human agency is indispensable to all such arguments, they seem to have lost sight of the living, breathing, human individuals who, in the brief hiatus between birth and death, apply their physical and mental capacities to the task of preserving species and culture—as well as themselves. The central bio-social fact of human individuality, so easily ignored, is that it is a process, not a state. The intergenerational sequence of birth, maturation, procreation and death may be regarded as a biosocial "artificer", a mediating process of physical and mental growth and decline which animates, and in return is accorded meaning by, social institutions. To make progress beyond the bio-cultural impasse we must accordingly find a means of inserting this agency of human lives between the rival temporal schemes of evolution and history.[7]

One detail about the physical development of human beings over the last few thousand years has drawn the attention of cultural anthropologists: increasing longevity.[8] In his introduction to a recent collection of anthropological essays on aging (*The Riddle of the Sphinx*) Paul Spencer notes that a major distinction between us and the other primates has been the increasing chances of survival into what we would now call "middle age". This has brought a shift "from physical supremacy of young adults—an ability to contest in direct encounters—to the moral supremacy of their elders" (Spencer 1990:6). Cultural development, he argues, is a concomitant of the extension of the lifespan. "Rudimentary families" of primates become the extended kin system of mankind, with a parallel moralising of intergenerational relations. The shift from "internecine destructiveness" to savvied alliance-building is "a problem which forms the basis of political science": a distinction between "short-term physical solutions that would favour some younger men in their prime and long-term diplomatic solutions for young and old alike". It is the social strategies of aging—with gerontocracy its apogee—which subvert Darwin's image of virile brute strength running the herd; among the Samburu in East Africa studied by Spencer, it is the aging polygynist who prevails (Spencer 1990:6).

Ethnos, vol. 59:1-2 (1994)

A chapter by Holy in the same collection of essays elaborates the ways in which old people depend on cultural values to secure themselves in old age. Apropos the Berti of the Sudan, Holy remarks that while "much of their culture can be seen as geared towards the interest of the old rather than of the young", the young, as prospective elders, are self-interestedly complicit in "making culture", because they are influenced by "their perception of their own position in the future". Normative frameworks sustain the transaction of self interest *in the long term*: "it is appropriate to do something at a certain stage in the life course to ensure a desirable outcome at some future stage in one's life course" (Holy 1990:180, 181). Among the Berti this intergenerational logic of culture bears directly on the social organisation of reproduction, especially the construction of "good marriages"—ideally those which, like cousin marriage, reinforce kin solidarities. In arranging these, parents seek access to future services, especially from a resident grandchild, which in turn depend on remaining on good terms with in-laws.

Securing our personal survival in old age gives us a direct interest in the construction and perpetuation of normative systems. Economic development provides the political key: the appropriation of nature through farming which helped to extend the human lifespan also laid the foundations of intergenerational power. Property is the basis of extended kinship formations; latterly and on a grander scale, it became the basis of social classes, but primordially it was the key to security in age. In this perspective it is pre-eminently the threat of physical dependence in age which attaches men to mother-child family units, although the will to retain patriarchal control depends more on external power relations among men themselves than on gender solidarities within the household. In this and other respects the rubric of the human life course has been important for speculation about the development of relations between the sexes. Gender is not a fixed disposition, a moment, but a developmental sequence, the meanings of which have as much to do with events after puberty as before. Its qualities unfold in progressions from maiden to matriarch to dependent widow, and are accordingly imprinted on culture.

While longevity seems a promising topic for discussion between cultural anthropologists and biologists, on this occasion it is the latter who appear stand-offish. The trouble is that aging is an ontogenetic detail of little interest to Darwinian scientists, not simply because it became prominent so recently in our evolutionary history, but because aging itself appears to have no adaptive function. If cultural anthropologists are much exercised by the relationship between cultural continuity and the physical replacement of people by death and birth, the Darwinian scientist has little interest in what happens to the human organism after the transmission of genes into offspring has been accomplished.[9] From a biological perspective, "longevity" is essentially extended *senescence*, a process which "begins" in the period of adult maturity and is by definition a concomitant of declining (sexual) reproductive capacity.[10]

Analysis of the biological bases of human societies has fixed on the preforma-
tion of the adult mind: evolutionary psychologists are seeking evidence for generalised intuitive ontologies by focussing on the very early sequences of somatic
development. Tooby and Cosmides' quest for content-specific features of our mental architecture likewise depends on experimental psychological techniques, the
apparent purpose of which is to distinguish general innate structures from cul-
turally-specific effects of child-rearing. These tactics produce objects of analysis
which remain psychic abstractions (fear, aggression, territoriality, altruism, the propensity to communicate, etc.) whose effects at the level of conventional social interaction are formidably difficult to validate empirically.[11] The shift from gene to
human population is too abrupt, the artificers too vague or inert, to come to terms
with the overlapping human lifespans in which cultures develop and institutions are
consolidated.[12] Unpacking the mental apparatus of the child does not bring us adequately to terms with the increasingly dense social intercourse as adulthood progresses, nor does it help us discriminate between such things as the capacity to learn
language and to use it suasively.[13] Biosocial science makes very little systematic use
of the framework of ontogeny, the development of the individual organism.[14]
Tooby and Cosmides acknowledge its relevance to their argument, but tell us little
about how links between human evolution and social institutions might be construed within this particular temporal framework.[15] They note that the functionally
evolved, content-specific human mental architecture is not "manifest" *in toto* in
the newborn, but operates like a time-release capsule during the life course:

> Not all features of evolved human design are or can be present at any one time in any
> one individual. Thus the genetically universal may be developmentally expressed as
> different maturational designs in the infant, the child, the adolescent, and the adult;
> in females and males; or in individuals who encounter different circumstances
> (T&C:82).

Biological endowments are not just predispositions which are established in the
infant mind, they pervade social organisation by way of entire lifespans. Sociobiologists have been crucially interested in certain reproductive activities and their
consequences, like mate and kin selection, but it seems that a programmatic interpretation of the full range of life course events would reveal more clearly how mental endowments and social institutions converge. Such an approach could engage
fruitfully with analytical interest in the temporal framework of the life course now
well established among sociologists, economists and historians.[16] A very promising
attempt at collaboration is the collection of essays on *Parenting Across the Life Span*,
edited by Lancaster and others (1987).[17]

The opportunities for further enquiry seem abundant. The propensity to make
coalitions, for example, is a favourite biosocial topic, but has very different social

expressions, for men and for women, in the transition from childhood to old age, and imprints itself in very different ways on normative structures: the rules of a street gang and of the Daughters of the American Revolution are constituted by some important biological differences. Again, it may be possible to specify how the acquisition, selection, and attrition of memories relate to the formation and transmission of knowledge, and hence to ways in which power is acquired and relinquished. More specific biosocial attention to aging is of considerable topical interest, given the dramatic changes in the demographic structure of our populations. For example, attention has been drawn to the relatively recent increase in prospects for grandparenthood, which qualifies maternal and paternal instincts in interesting ways.[18] A salient question is whether any "late-emerging" cultural propensities can be identified—mechanisms which were incipient in our Pleistocene state of mind, but which have only found expression as extended senescence made them realisable.

Such investigations might help us close the gap between assumptions about the biologically-contained selfishness of genes and the socially-contained selfishness of people; between human phylogeny on the one hand, and social history on the other.[19] The origins of culture may be traced in the very early development of our physical constitution and in our most fleeting and mundane transactions—and in a range of temporal levels in between. This is, to put it mildly, a daunting analytical conspectus, which the division of academic labour has done nothing to encourage. Basic vocabulary is appropriated and sequestered at the cost of coherent scholarly communication. A fundamental instance is the key word "reproduction", whose metaphorisation in the social sciences and humanities has become grossly convoluted and distanced from its basic physical meaning.[20] Specialised usage is valid only to the extent that it enhances communication. Anthropology, with its traditional "four fields" of study,[21] may still afford the broadest perspective on biological and social analysis, and on time past and time present, but this has always been threatened by subdisciplinary dogmatism. Although Tooby and Cosmides rightly complain that disciplinary proprieties have frustrated attempts to restore coherence to our arguments about the human condition, there is still reason to doubt that "science" provides a comprehensive explanatory rubric. Instead of pursuing grand unification theories we may have to content ourselves with finding convergent points of interest between one sort of argument and another, such as the human lifespan in its intergenerational context.

NOTES

* I am very grateful to John Tooby, Donald Brown, Donald Symons, and the anonymous reviewer for *Ethnos*, for helpful comments on this essay.

1. It should be noted that arguments against the extension of evolutionary biology to cul-

ture have been made by biologists themselves. See for example Brandon (1991).

2. Critics will catalogue the suasive vocabulary of scientism in Tooby and Cosmides' essay, for example: "explanatory power" (T&C:19), "reliable and deeply satisfying" (T&C: 19), "elegant" (T&C:19, 51), "compelling" (T&C:51), "economically organized" (T&C:75), "core logic" (T&C:52), and "superlative 'engineering'" (T&C:59).

3. Sahlins (1976:65) notes the ontological weakness of a theory which can only account for some small percentage of social life. See also E. O. Wilson's foreword to Caplan (ed. 1978: xiii): "Contemporary general sociobiology might at best explain a tiny fraction of human behavior in a novel manner". The urgent question remains—which fraction, and why that particular fraction?

4. For tentative efforts to argue gene-culture coevolution, see for example Durham (1978; 1991); Lumsden & Gushurst (1991).

5. See, for example, Kitahara's speculation (1991) on the tragic consequences of the gap between our 35,000-year-old adaptation, and the complexity of the world in which we now live.

6. On the logical problems of using cultural diversity as an index for psychic universality, especially if a subsequent purpose is to ascertain the extent to which a generalised human nature expresses itself in cultural diversity, see Rosenberg (1980:179).

7. I have explored this more fully in Robertson (in press).

8. The pioneering text was undoubtedly Simmons (1945).

9. The classic notions of ontogeny certainly do not extend comfortably to morbidity. Von Haekel's famous dictum to the effect that ontogeny recapitulates phylogeny would imply a dreadful prognostication for the species.

10. For a biological discussion of senescence see especially Stini (1991); also Hamilton (1964), and Kirkwood & Holliday (1979). In a notable contribution, Williams (1957) explained senescence as a quirk of pleiotropy - a sort of gene-on-the-rebound. Increasing attention to geriatric issues in modern human populations has revived the interest of some geneticists in the scheduling of death and its function in clearing the way for replacement organisms.

11. This is strikingly evident in biological propositions about the adult activities of mate and kin selection, which remain very contentious. See for example Sahlins (1976); Reynolds and Kellet (1991). Again, Rosenberg (1980:185) comments on sociobiological efforts to account for the phenomenon of altruism within the rubric of inclusive fitness; more plausible explanations can be found at the level of cultural norm rather than natural selection.

12. The credibility gap is notorious: see, for example, Betzig's account of the behavior of chiefs in a western Pacific island (1988), and Green's speculations on a biocultural analysis of revolution (1991); and see Symons' cautionary remarks (1989; 1992) about the need for precise specification of "artificers" in biosocial argument.

13. See for example Smillie (1991).

14. For a commentary see Oyama (1985), and Featherman & Lerner (1985); and see Brown (1991:112-3).

15. In a recent review emphasising the positive contribution of Cosmides and Tooby, Ridley remarks that "If the distinction between genes in natural selection and in individual development were better understood, most of the sociobiology controversy would

collapse. But I have detected little progress in the past decade" (1993:7).

16. See especially Elder (1985); Haines (1985); Rossi (1985); Hareven (1986).
17. Siblingship is amenable to similar treatment: see for example the essays edited by Lamb & Sutton-Smith (1982), and Fortes's psycho-social discussion of 'The First Born' (1974).
18. See Anderson (1985).
19. For a detailed exploration of the relationships between evolutionary theory and social history, and proposals for a synthesis, see Ingold (1986).
20. See Robertson (1991:155-6).
21. Archaeology, linguistics, cultural or social anthropology, and physical or biological anthropology.

REFERENCES

ANDERSON, M. 1985. The emergence of the modern life cycle in Britain. *Social History*, 10:69-87.

BETZIG, L. 1988. Redistribution: equity or exploitation? In *Human Reproductive Behavior: a Darwinian Perspective*, edited by L. Betzig, M. Borgerhoff Mulder & P. Turke. Cambridge: Cambridge University Press, pp. 49-63.

BINSTOCK, R. H. & L. K. GEORGE. (eds.). 1990. *Handbook of Aging and the Social Sciences* (Third edition). New York: Academic Press.

BRANDON, ROBERT. 1991. Phenotypic plasticity, cultural transmission, and human sociobiology. In *Sociobiology and Epistemology*, edited by James H. Fetzer. Dordrecht: D. Reidel Publishing Co., pp. 57-73.

BROWN, D. E. 1991. *Human Universals*. New York: McGraw Hill.

CAPLAN, A. L. (ed.). 1978. *The Sociobiology Debate: Readings on Ethical and Scientific Issues*. New York: Harper Row.

DURHAM, W. H. 1978. Toward a coevolutionary theory of human biology and culture. In *The Sociobiology Debate*, edited by Arthur L. Caplan. New York: Harper Row, pp 428-448.

—1991. *Coevolution: Genes Culture and Human Diversity*. Stanford: Stanford University Press.

DURKHEIM, E. 1953. On the process of change in social values. In *Sociology and Philosophy*, by E. Durkheim. Glencoe: The Free Press.

ELDER, G.H. (ed.) 1985. *Life Course Dynamics: Trajectories and Transitions 1968-1980*. Ithaca: Cornell University Press.

FEATHERMAN, D. L. & R. M. LERNER. 1985. Ontogenesis and sociogenesis: problematics for theory and research about development and socialization across the lifespan. *American Sociological Review*, 50:659-676.

FINCH, & MASON, J. 1990. Filial obligations and kin support for elderly people. *Ageing and Society*, 10:151-175.

FORTES, M. 1974. The first born. *Journal of Child Psychology and Psychiatry*, 15:81-104.

FRY, D. P. 1987. What human sociobiology has to offer economic anthropology and vice versa. *Journal of Social and Biological Structures*, 10:37-51.

GREEN, P. A. 1991. A Biocultural Analysis of Revolution. *Journal of Social and Biological Structures*, 14:435-454.

Ethnos, vol. 59:1-2 (1994)

HAINES, M. R. 1985. The life cycle, savings, and demographic adaptation: Some historical evidence for the United States and Europe. In *Gender and the Life Course*, edited by Alice S.Rossi, New York: Aldine, pp. 43–63.

HAMILTON, W. D. 1964. The moulding of senescence by natural selection. *Journal of Theoretical Biology*, 12:12–45.

HAREVEN, T. K. 1986. Historical changes in the social construction of the life course. *Human Development*, 29:171–180.

HERRMANN-PILLATH, C. 1991. A Darwinian framework for the economic analysis of institutional change in history. *Journal of Social and Biological Structures*, 14:127–148.

HOLY, L. 1990. Strategies for old age among the Berti of the Sudan. In *Anthropology and the Riddle of the Sphinx: Paradoxes of Change in the Life Course*, edited by Paul Spencer. London: Routledge, pp. 167–182.

INGOLD,TIM. 1986. *Evolution and Social Life*. Cambridge: Cambridge University Press.

—1990. An anthropologist looks at biology. *Man* (N.S.) 25:208–229.

KIRKWOOD, T. B. L. & R. HOLLIDAY. 1979. The evolution of aging and longevity. *Proceedings of the Royal Society*, 205:531–546.

KITAHARA, M. 1991. *The Tragedy of Evolution: The Human Animal Confronts Modern Society*. New York: Praeger.

LAMB, M. E. & SUTTON-SMITH, B. (eds.). 1982. *Sibling Relationships: Their Nature and Significance across the Life Span*. Hillsdale, N. J.: Erlbaum.

LANCASTER, J. B., J. ALTMANN, A. S. ROSSI, & L. R. SHERROD (eds). 1987. *Parenting across the Life Span: Biosocial Dimensions*. New York: Aldine de Gruyter.

LUMSDEN, C. J. & A. C. GUSHURST. 1991. Gene-culture coevolution: Humankind in the making. In *Sociobiology and Epistemology*, edited by James H. Fetzer. Dordrecht: D. Reidel Publishing Co., pp. 3–28.

OYAMA, SUSAN. 1985. *The Ontogeny of Information: Developmental Systems and Evolution*. Cambridge: Cambridge University Press.

REYNOLDS, V. & J. KELLETT. (eds). 1991. *Mating and Marriage*. Oxford: Oxford University Press.

RIDLEY, MARK 1993. The rite of the genes. *The Times Literary Supplement*, No. 4711:7–8.

ROBERTSON, A. F. 1991. *Beyond the Family: The Social Organization of Human Reproduction*. Berkeley & Los Angeles: University of California Press.

— in press: Time and the modern family: Reproduction and the making of history. In *Nowhere: Space Time and Modernity*, edited by R. Friedland & D. Boden. Berkeley & Los Angeles: University of California Press.

ROSENBERG, A. 1980. *Sociobiology and the Preemption of Social Science*. Baltimore: Johns Hopkins University Press.

ROSSI, A. S. (ed.). 1985. *Gender and the Life Course*. New York: Aldine.

SAHLINS, M. 1976. *The Use and Abuse of Biology: An Anthropological Critique of Sociobiology*. Ann Arbor: The University of Michigan Press.

SAMUEL, G. 1990. *Mind, Body and Culture: Anthropology and the Biological Interface*. Cambridge: Cambridge University Press.

SIMMONS, L. W. 1945. *The Role of the Aged in Primitive Society*. New Haven: Yale University Press.

SMILLIE, D. 1991. Sociobiology and human culture. In *Sociobiology and Epistemology*, edited by James H. Fetzer. Dordrecht: D. Reidel Publishing Co., pp. 75–95.

SPENCER, P. 1990. The riddled course: Theories of age and its transformations. In *Anthropology and the Riddle of the Sphinx: Paradoxes of Change in the Life Course*, edited by Paul Spencer. London: Routledge, pp. 1–34.

STINI, WILLIAM A. 1991. The biology of human aging. In *Applications of Biological Anthropology to Human Affairs*, edited by C. G. N. Mascie-Taylor & G. W. Lasker. Cambridge: Cambridge University Press, pp. 207–236.

SYMONS, D. 1989. A critique of Darwinian anthropology. *Ethnology and Sociobiology*, 10: 131–144.

—1992. On the use and misuse of Darwinism in the study of human behavior. In *The Adapted Mind: Evolutionary Psychology and the Generation of Culture*, edited by J. H. Barkow, L. Cosmides & J. Tooby. New York: Oxford University Press, pp. 137–159.

TOOBY, J. & COSMIDES, L. 1992. The psychological foundations of culture. In *The Adapted Mind: Evolutionary Psychology and the Generation of Culture*, edited by J. H. Barkow, L. Cosmides & J. Tooby. New York: Oxford University Press, pp. 19–136.

WILLIAMS, G.C. 1957. Pleiotropy, natural selection, and the evolution of senescence. *Evolution*, 11:398–411.

WILSON, E.O. 1975. *Sociobiology: The New Synthesis*. Cambridge (Mass.): The Belknap Press of Harvard University.

111

INT'L. J. AGING AND HUMAN DEVELOPMENT, Vol. 48(4) 347-351, 1999

AFTERWORD

QUESTIONS FOR FUTURE STUDIES: SOCIAL RELATIONSHIPS IN OLD AGE

LILLIAN E. TROLL
Professor Emerita, Rutgers University;
Adjunct Professor, University of California San Francisco

It is impressive, not to mention refreshing, to see four careful, weighty studies on social relationships that are not primarily concerned with caregiving. The fact that they are both longitudinal and cross-cultural makes them even more impressive and highlights general issues in the area of social relationships as well as more specific issues of aging. Four issues seem to me to be notable: 1) kinds of relationships, 2) continuity of relationships, 3) functions of relationships, and 4) cultural differences. I will consider each in turn.

KINDS OF RELATIONSHIPS

I have been impressed in recent years with a difference between one-to-one specific connections between individuals and generic connectedness to systems. Specific individual connections would be dyadic and of varying degrees of closeness or attachment, exemplified by interactions and relationships between a parent and child, a husband and wife, or two friends. Generic connections, relationships, or interactions could be exemplified by embeddedness in family systems, communities, or social networks. Both kinds, incidentally, could be with kin or not. The word "connections" suggests a passive mode, "interactions" a more active one.

Of the four articles in this issue, Dorothy Fields' refers to person-to-person relationships, and the Israeli and Swedish studies more to generic ones, family systems or friendship networks. The Netherlands study includes both specific and generic; it focuses on individual interactions with children but primarily considers their generic aspects—children as a system, if you will. An interesting incidental question occurs to me. Does the constriction of social relationships to those that are most emotionally satisfying, observed by Laura Carstensen (1993) in her studies of aging, apply to specific relationships, to generic ones, or to both? Do active interactions change to passive connections, whether specific or generic?

And what about those people who are neither interactive nor embedded? We know little about lifelong isolates. At one time I concluded (Troll, 1972, for example) that isolates were as content as lifelong relaters, in fact that it might be better to have never had loved ones than to have had them and lost them. Now I wonder whether this would be true more in younger years than in old age. Do the "family deprived" whom I found in such distress among the San Francisco oldest-old (Troll, 1994) include people who had done well earlier in life as isolates until they required more—more attention as well as more help? To answer this question, of course, we need longitudinal studies of greater length.

CONTINUITY VS. CHANGE

Since the four studies included here asked different questions, it is not surprising that their findings are not completely alike. Cheryl McCamish-Svensson and her colleagues wanted to know about continuity of relationships and found that their Swedish subjects showed continuity in family relations but decline in friendships, as have most American studies. Broese van Groenou and Knipscheer wanted to know whether Dutch children would respond to increased need for help by their old parents and found that indeed there was such a change. Adrian Walter-Ginzburg and her colleagues wanted to know what Israelis felt about who came to their aid and found that those who moved to an institution or lost a confidant felt that they had lost emotional support even though not instrumental support. Dorothy Field wanted to know whether there were changes in friendship patterns on the part of California respondents as they move from young-old to old-old age and found more continuity than might be expected from other studies, particularly among the women. Sheldon Tobin, who writes about the importance of preservation of the self (Tobin, 1991), would be pleased at this amount of continuity.

Given that old people are survivors and that many of their former friends and relatives are likely to be gone—dead or moved away or no longer mobile or competent to carry on relationships—what are their options for finding new friends or other relatives as replacements or substitutions? Is there a reservoir of potential relationships from which to draw, as Shanas (1979) originally reported? Furthermore, is there continuity or change in criteria for an intimate, for who is desirable or for what is desirable? Are those people who were formerly important now less important? Must old people make do with whom they can get, as the white San Franciscans seemed to be doing when they enlarged their definitions of who was a friend (Johnson & Troll, 1994).

The issue of replacement or substitution has been salient since the beginning of the field of family and aging, but Johnson and Barer (1997) did not find evidence for such substitution in their research. If the (white) oldest-old had no children available, nieces or nephews or grandchildren did not usually take over, and this was also true for the Israelis of European origin. On the other hand, the San Francisco black oldest old and the Israelis of African or Asian origin both drew from wider pools. In the case of the Israelis, the pool was still within the family but the African Americans, as noted, drew from nonkin sources. Dorothy Field's respondents maintained close friendships, although it is true that the men seemed less interested in close friendships than they once had been. The Israelis of European origin shifted from people who provided emotional support to those who could or would give instrumental support.

Laura Carstensen (1993) asks a related question: on what basis do old people select those who are important to them? She hypothesizes a principle of "socio-emotional selectivity" that is similar to the principle of "selective optimization" suggested by Baltes and Baltes (1990). As strength, health, and energy diminish, one narrows one's emotional involvements to the most meaningful. Dorothy Field's data seem to support this principle in terms of intimacy of friendships, and the Israeli data suggest a similar process.

Some of us have recently begun asking questions about the nature of emotion in close relationships (Magai & McFadden, 1996; Troll & Fingerman, 1996). By emotions do we mean positive versus negative affect? Is the mother-daughter dyad so prominent in old age because it is the most affectionate? Is it the most intense? The most tolerant? The most long-suffering? Do we mean strength of affect instead of valence of affect, positive and negative? What do we do about conflictful relations? I look forward to more studies that shift from an emphasis on helping and caring in relationships to feelings involved. The *Handbook of Emotion and Aging* edited by Carol Magai and Susan McFadden, cited above, has made a giant step in this direction.

FUNCTION

Many respondents in the San Francisco study of the oldest-old (Johnson & Barer, 1997) preferred to hire caregivers or to get help from impersonal sources rather than from their intimates. If there is a choice, do old people prefer to separate instrumental from emotional support? We often assume that "loved ones" like children and spouses are the preferred ones for giving care and that these "loved ones" in turn get special pleasure in turning from previous kinds of relationships to caretaking. But is that so? Svenssen and her colleagues point to the continued frequent contact and satisfaction with families in spite of abundant instrumental help given by governmental services in Sweden. This question is

115

not raised in the Dutch study and considered only indirectly in the Israeli one, while Field found that only men, not women, changed in the function they wanted from friends as they got older.

Or one could ask questions about definitions of relationships. A few years ago, Colleen Johnson and I (Johnson & Troll, 1994) found that one way some very old respondents in San Francisco dealt with losses of friends was to redefine, to loosen up their requirement for whom they would consider friends. Once friends probably meant intimate companions. Now they included the woman passed in the hall or the deliverer of meals on wheels. Dorothy Field also found a possible change in the nature of friendship. Do some old people need friends more than others and so rope in candidates for the role whom other old people would not consider? What, further, is the process of transmutation from being a child to being a caretaker? From being a parent to being a needer of care? From being a spouse to being a nurse?

CULTURE

It is not surprising to find a good deal of similarity in family values, social relationships, and processes of aging among the Europeans of Sweden, Holland, Germany, and the Israelis of European background. Further, these populations remind me of the white San Franciscan oldest-old studied by Colleen Johnson and her colleagues (Johnson & Barer, 1997). All these cultures stand in contrast to the non-European Israelis and several other cultures studied by Johnson (in press): aging Hawaiian Japanese, San Francisco oldest-old blacks, and individualistic whites of Marin County, California.

The highly traditional Japanese-Americans in Hawaii (Johnson, 1973) are prime exemplars of family embeddedness, and they place family over individuals. In this way they resemble the Israelis of Asian and African origin. They also value their older family members highly; we are not sure this is as true of the Asian and African Israelis. The oldest-old white people in San Francisco and those in the Netherlands, Sweden, and Israel can still count on their children, particularly their daughters, to provide instrumental care when needed and affection and interest, at least until they become too much of a burden. Are there cultural differences in what happens then? Who sees nursing homes as a viable end route, and who does not? On the other hand, perhaps related to their low birth and survival rates, the Bay Area African Americans show a different pattern, in which fictional kin such as "church children" or "play children" often serve as substitute providers of both instrumental and expressive support (Johnson & Barer, 1990). In many cases, these relationships seem to be closer than those with biological kin.

As for culture, some wider questions might relate to differences in expectations about who should be included in social networks, about the boundaries for friendships or families, or about whose job it is to take care of the old, women vs. men, daughters vs. sons, daughters-in-law vs. daughters, etc.? Not only do we have more to learn, but we can no doubt expect profound changes in all these issues as cultures over the world change in the coming years.

REFERENCES

Baltes, P., & Baltes, M. M. (1990). Psychological perspectives on successful aging: The model of selective optimization with compensation. In P. Baltes & M. M. Baltes (Eds.), *Successful aging: Perspectives from the behavioral sciences* (pp. 1-34). New York: Cambridge University.

Carstensen, L. L. (1993). Motivation for social contact across the life span: A theory of socioemotional selectivity. In J. E. Jacobs (Ed.), *Nebraska symposium on motivation: Developmental perspectives on motivation* (pp. 209-254). Lincoln: University of Nebraska.

Johnson, C. L. (1973). Alternatives to alienation: A Japanese-American example. In F. A. Johnson (Ed.), *Alienation: Context, term, meaning*. New York: Springer.

Johnson, C. L. (in press). Perspectives on American kinship in the late 1990s. K. Allen & M. Fine (Eds.), *Handbook of family diversity*. New York: Greenwood Press.

Johnson, C. L., & Barer, B. (1990). Families and social networks among older inner-city blacks. *The Gerontologist, 30*, 726-733.

Johnson, C. L., & Barer, B. (1997). *Life beyond 85 years: The aura of survivorship*. New York: Springer.

Johnson, C. L., & Troll, L. (1994). Constraints and facilitators to friendships in late late life. *The Gerontologist, 34*, 79-87.

Magai, C., & McFadden, S. H. (1996). *Handbook of emotion: Adult development and aging*. New York: Academic Press.

Shanas, E. (1979). The family as a social support system in old age. *The Gerontologist, 19*, 169-174.

Tobin, S. S. (1991). *Personhood in advanced old age: Implications for practice*. New York: Springer.

Troll, L. E. (1972). *Continuations: Adult development and aging*. Monterey, CA: Brooks/Cole.

Troll, L. E. (1994). Family-embedded vs. family-deprived oldest-old: A study of contrasts. *International Journal of Aging and Human Development, 38*, 51-64.

Troll, L. E., & Fingerman, K. (1996). Connections between parents and their adult children. In C. Magai and S. H. McFadden (Eds.), *Handbook of emotion: Adult development and aging* (pp. 185-211). New York: Academic Press.

Direct reprint requests to:

Lillian Troll
1001 Shoreline Drive #302
Alameda, CA 94501

THE SOCIAL CONSTRUCTION OF FRAILTY:
An Anthropological Perspective

SHARON R. KAUFMAN*

University of California

ABSTRACT: *This article proposes to broaden the discussion of frailty beyond instrumental definitions by exploring its socio-cultural sources and dimensions in American culture. It is based on an ongoing study of increased dependence among community-living elderly over the age of 80. The primary research goal was to investigate ways in which frailty is defined, framed, and understood by older persons, their family members, and their health care providers in the context of a multidisciplinary geriatric assessment service. I argue that frailty is socially produced in response to cultural discourses about surveillance and individualism. I suggest that frailty be conceived as an adaptational process that emerges and is fully articulated during the health care encounter.*

This article is an anthropological exploration of the process of increasing frailty in advanced old age. It pays particular attention to the responses of health professionals, old people, and their families as they variously attempt to understand, accept, manage and combat frailty within the context of the American health care system. It argues that frailty is socially produced in response to powerful discourses about surveillance and individualism in American culture. And it suggests that the scientific framework for understanding frailty be broadened from instrumental to socio-cultural dimensions.

As a cultural anthropologist mapping the terrain of frailty, debility, and increasing dependence in late life, I am interested in two conflicting conceptual frameworks currently applied in American health care delivery especially (but not exclusively) to older persons. The first framework, most commonly termed *medicalization* by social scientists and other observers of health care delivery, refers to a process in which

Direct all correspondence to: Sharon R. Kaufman, Social and Behavioral Sciences, School of Nursing and Medical Anthropology Program, School of Medicine, University of California, San Francisco, CA 94143-0612.

JOURNAL OF AGING STUDIES, Volume 8, Number 1, pages 45-58
Copyright © 1994 by JAI Press Inc.
All rights of reproduction in any form reserved.
ISSN: 0890-4065.

personal and social problems and behaviors come to be viewed as diseases or medical problems that the medical and allied health professions have a mandate to "treat." Scholars have described how medicine has permeated many behavioral aspects of life, as social deviance, behavioral eccentricities, or moral problems are transformed into medical concerns, or as ordinary life processes (especially birth and death) are reinterpreted as events requiring medical intervention (Arluke and Peterson 1981; Conrad and Schneider 1980; Zola 1972). The elderly are particularly vulnerable to medical management since old age is equated with illness in the public view (Estes 1979; Sankar 1984): old people and their families, in increasing numbers, perceive the health care system to be the locus of expertise and resolution as they attempt to solve and cope with the problems created by debility in late life. The personal, social, and political consequences for older persons—and indeed, for society—of exposing more and more areas of life to the clinical "gaze"[1] and medical intervention are only beginning to be explored (Estes and Binney 1989; Miller et al. 1992).

The second conceptual framework, called here the autonomy paradigm, represents the widespread application of philosophical principles of ethics to clinical decision-making (Beauchamp and Childress 1989; Pellegrino and Thomasma 1981; Veatch 1981). Bioethics as a field of practice emerged from debates during the 1960s about moral and legal implications of human experimentation. The bioethics enterprise places supreme value on the patient's or client's autonomy, self-determination, and right to choose as primary considerations in any medical treatment (Fox 1990; Rothman 1990). A variety of scholars have drawn attention to the predominance of individualism in Western, especially American bioethical theory and practice (Clark 1991; Marshall 1992; Thomasma 1984). They note how individualism has framed and dominated debate about resolving moral dilemmas in medicine and has, until very recently, excluded or muted consideration of other values such as community, interdependence, and mutual obligation in medical decision-making.

Over the past two decades, the field of bioethics has focused much of its problem-solving attention on the use of life sustaining technology, most specifically, when and why to withhold or withdraw such technology. Fueled by the publicity of the Karen Quinlan (1976) and Nancy Cruzan (1990) cases, bioethicists have brought questions and dilemmas of the patient's and family's role in decisions about quality of life and termination of life to the attention of the wider public. Those debates, taken together with the recent federally mandated Patient Self-Determination Act (1991), have honed the awareness of many older people and their families to issues of individual rights, responsibility and choice in the context of medical care.

The medicalization and autonomy paradigms coexist as powerful but *contradictory* ways of understanding the old body and relationships among the person/patient, family, health care system, and society. Those paradigms frame conflicting methods of approaching and understanding aging and the dependencies it produces. On the one hand, aging is assumed (both in Western popular culture and in a great deal of the gerontological literature [Tornstam 1992]) to be demarcated largely and most importantly by physiological change for the worse.[2] Biomedical science is revered and people want the medical profession to intervene in their distress with the goal of thwarting, monitoring, or managing decline. On the other hand, the cultural ideals of personal autonomy and freedom from institutional constraint and domination compete for expression in medical decision-making. People clamor for options, choice, and the right to refuse in their desire to be informed consumers of health care. They—we— want to passively sit back and let the doctor "fix" the problem *at the same time* as we want to retain full control over our lives.

The coexistence of these paradigms presents a baffling situation to American society regarding the creation and implementation of appropriate health care policy for the extremely aged, and it promotes frequently insoluable tension for frail elderly individuals and their families when they encounter the health care and related social service systems. For the very old become the field on which the discourse on autonomy and freedom of choice competes with the discourse on intervention, surveillance, safety, and risk. Dialogues surrounding diagnosis, treatment, managment and care of very old persons invoke the language of these two discourses as persons turned patients, families, and health professionals all struggle to solve the problems created by increasing debility.

In the lives of very old Americans particularly, the ideal of autonomy, understood as unequivocal self-reliance, is pitted against the ever-growing threat of dependence— on family, community, and the health care system. Aging is conceived as a battle between the discrete and opposing forces of independence and dependence: one can remain in one's own home, relinquishing more and more roles and abilities, until a catastrophe, usually a health care crisis, makes one rely on others for the fulfillment of basic needs and eventually forces one to a nursing home. In a recent assessment of autonomy in long-term care, George Agich notes how abstract ideals of autonomy are counterproductive and that an adversarial approach to independence/dependence prevents us, as a society, from developing adequate models of care and choice. He states:

> "Long-term care of all sorts, including home care services, is required precisely because individuals experience to some degree an actual loss of functions that we associate with a full sense of developed adult autonomy. They lose various abilities to act in the world and so require more than usual amounts and kinds of support and care from others. Our society displays profound ambivalence about this situation in that we seem to want these individuals to deny their need for care—in short, we want to support their individual right to noninterference even at great personal cost—and yet we recognize that individuals who cannot care for themselves and who place undue burdens on family members require specialized professional care" (1990, p. 14).

A growing population of very old individuals exposes society to the many varieties of aging—physiological, psychological, emotional, behavioral, etc.—and reveals the need for new visions of long term care which actualize the values of interdependence, community, and cooperation. Yet we are slow, as a society, to emerge from our bipolar and simplistic views of assessing aging. Demographic changes make it imperative that we reconsider the primacy of individualism in shaping attitudes about and thus policy for the very old.

In studying the phenomenon of frailty and exploring its social construction, I am interested in ways in which the competition between paradigms finds its voice and is played out. Based on years of research with frail and chronically ill old people, I suggest that though the conflict may find solutions in individual cases, it has not been resolved culturally. I further suggest that the existence of these contradictory paradigms is one source—perhaps the source—of the "problem" of frailty in old age in American society.

METHODS AND RATIONALE: WHAT IS FRAILTY?

In an ongoing study of growing dependence among a sample of 100 community-living elderly over the age of 80,[3] the investigators wanted to know what frailty looks like in advanced old age. How is it defined, framed, and understood? What mechanisms are employed by older persons, family members, and health care providers to cope with it and solve the variety of problems it creates? To explore these questions, we sought out individuals who were perceived by family members, friends, or health professionals to be "at risk," that is, whose health had recently changed for the worse and engendered their need for greater medical care, social support, and/or supervision so that they could remain in the community. Becker reports on persons living in the community and in long-term care institutions who do not have cognitive impairments (described by Becker in "The Oldest Old: Autonomy in the Face of Frailty").

In 1992 and 1993, I observed a multidisciplinary geriatric assessment team (including physician, nurse, social worker, psychologist and podiatrist) discuss the cases of forty-three individuals over the age of 80 whose health statuses had recently declined. Of those cases, I observed twenty-five family conferences with the team and was able to subsequently interview ten elderly persons or family members. Cases described below are drawn from this portion of the study.

Two patterns emerged among the forty-three cases regarding why the assessment was sought. Half of the clients were brought to the service, usually by family members, because they had experienced a rapid decline in functional status—either mental, physical, or both—following an acute-care hospitalization, fall, or other acute medical incident in the preceding six months. The family wanted to know what was wrong and how the older person could be returned to the status quo. The other half were brought to the multidisciplinary team because a family member or other person was experiencing new difficulty in caring for or managing the life of a debilitated person, or simply could no longer cope with the growing strain and responsibility for caring for another person's body, home, finances, and safety.

Functional status among the very old was not consistent across the forty-three cases. Some of the old people were driving cars, managing expenses, and controlling their daily schedules at the time they were brought to the assessment service. Others were significantly demented and/or wheelchair-bound and homebound when their families sought the team's advice.

Frailty is one of those complex terms—like independence, life satisfaction, and continuity—that trouble gerontologists with multiple and slippery meanings. The American Heritage Dictionary defines frailty as (1) physically weak or delicate, and (2) not strong or substantial (1992, p. 720). In gerontology, frailty is usually defined in opposition to independence. In their study of frailty and the perception of choice among a sample of old people who live alone, Rubinstein, Kilbride, and Nagy employ an open, qualitative definition: "having one or more health or functioning decrements that seriously affect the person's ability to carry out the expected and usual activities of daily living" (1992, p. 4).

Knight and Walker (1985) note the lack of precision in definitions of frailty and the fact that concepts of independence, dependence, and "at risk for institutionalization" are always intertwined. Their research indicates that frailty can be measured by a variety of criteria such as medical disorders producing functional disability, memory deficits, other mental disorders, behavior dangerous to self or others, behavior deemed socially inappropriate, and support system breakdown. Other studies of frailty do not necessarily employ those or similar criteria in their analyses. In a study to identify persons at risk for institutionalization, Shapiro and Tate (1985, 1988) considered 28 potential risk factors, and found that having any one of them (such as age over 85, living alone, living in retirement housing, ADL problem, mental impairment) was not enough to create risk for institutionalization.

While attempts to measure frailty by objective parameters have their place in gerontology and may be useful to health care providers and policy analysts, those instrumental definitions restrict discussion to the elderly's "need" for services or to assessment of their losses. My goal is to open up the discussion of frailty to its socio-cultural dimensions and explore how it is socially produced through the interaction of older individuals, their caregivers, and their health providers. Frailty is conceived here both as a *quality* whose source is the competing paradigms discussed above and as a dynamic *adaptational process* on the part of elderly persons, families, and health care personnel. As both quality and process, frailty is open to multiple interpretations. It comes into focus at the moment when any combination of an old person's symptoms and behaviors is construed to tip the balance towards *a problem* of more dependence than independence with regard to functional ability and social role performance. Frailty thus conceived forces the individuals who encounter it to reconsider and renegotiate the meanings of autonomy and freedom, risk and responsibility, choice and surveillance, and interdependence in their own lives.

In confronting and then reformulating these concepts, the very old and their families are cultural pioneers, enabling us to consider the idea that both the medicalization and autonomy paradigms and the discourses they produce are misplaced arguments for the realities of frailty in our aging society. The phenomenon of day-to-day frailty shows us that while surveillance of health conditions and risk behaviors may provide a "solution" to concerns about safety, it is no solution to the highly idiosyncratic desire for emotional well-being in late life. Similarly, individualism in its various guises is becoming impractical as our population ages, becomes more vulnerable, and cries out for interdependence and flexibility in addressing the tasks of day-to-day existence. The very old and their families, in responding to frailty, are in fact forcing us to think about interdependence in ways that do not as yet exist in the wider culture.

I wish to make it clear that I am interested in *existential* and *experiential* expressions of and responses to frailty, rather than instrumental definitions. Such responses and expressions are explored below, in this, the first stage of our research on this topic. In looking at experiential dimensions of frailty in the context of competing paradigms, I am concerned with what happens when the old and vulnerable *person* becomes a *patient*. While there is a growing literature on the need for physicians and other health professionals to treat patients as persons, to approach them in their biopsychosocial wholeness and thus to blur the boundaries between person and patient (Cassell 1991; Engel 1977; Kleinman 1988), here my focus is the construction of frailty through the ascription of the patient role.

THE PROCESS OF FRAILTY

Frailty is proposed when someone conceives there to be a *lived problem* with a very old person. (See Note #2.) Either the old person has a medical condition that has not been diagnosed or resolved, or has a condition that seems to be growing worse or spreading to other bodily systems or areas of the person's life, or a concerned family member can no longer cope with caring for the old person and thus begins to think of symptoms or behaviors as a problem. Unless the caregiver or older person are highly educated or are health professionals themselves, the lived problem, as subjectively experienced, is not usually understood in terms of discrete categories of biomedical knowledge. Thus the family member comes to the health provider with the complaint that his parent "seems to be more forgetful and isn't sleeping lately," or "has lost a lot of weight and stopped walking," or "can't concentrate on his card game anymore."

The old person becomes a patient at the time of contact with the health care system. In that transformation, the lived problem is fractured into component parts which are viewed through a biomedical and social service lens. Thus *frailty becomes more fully articulated* within the discourse of surveillance, safety, and care. A list of discrete diagnoses is made and treatments are created. In some cases, a negotiation process takes place among health provider(s), caregiver, and patient over whether to or how to implement treatment plans. The treatments are conceived as potential or partial solutions both to bodily ailments caused by medical conditions and to the more messy and unbounded dilemmas of social existence caused by inappropriate, irrational, or unsafe behaviors. The solutions, created within the limits of existing medical and social service structures in a particular community, become the scientific *and* moral "facts" of the case. The solutions are frequently claimed as ways to preserve, as completely as possible, the autonomy of the patient in spite of his or her functional limitations. Self-determination is conceived then as valuable, but appropriate only when it is enacted within the structure and rationale of social service and health care intervention. The cases presented below illustrate this process of frailty construction.

I wish to point out that I do not interpret the process of constructing frailty as a clear-cut dichotomy between health care provider ideology about surveillance and risk reduction on the one hand, and patient and family beliefs about autonomy on the other. It is not that simple. Rather, I argue that practitioners, patients, and families *share*, though to different degrees and in different ways, the contradictory understandings about autonomy and intervention described above. Real and satisfactory solutions to problems of frailty are elusive *because* the competing discourses are so deeply embedded in the thinking of all participants in the health care encounter. The case studies below are evidence of how both discourses are used by the participants and how resolution to the conflict between them is so difficult to realize.

STORIES OF FRAILTY

Three cases address a series of questions pertinent to this exploration of frailty: What behaviors or symptoms are perceived to place elderly persons at risk? Who considers them at risk, and how do they try to intervene? What problems, in fact, are they trying to solve? Can we discern some cultural assumptions about the patient's or the family's expectations about participation in the health care system? The following case examples illustrate common problems of people in late life that bewilder, trouble, and sadden families and that are seen regularly by health care providers. Anyone who has observed or worked with very old people in the context of health care delivery will recognize these stories.

Case #1

Mrs. A, an 80 year old woman, was brought to the assessment service by her friend and neighbor of 15 years, M, who was concerned about her increasing inability to remember appointments, pay bills, prepare food for herself, and maintain her personal hygiene. The friend had noticed that Mrs. A's memory was deteriorating and she was worried about Mrs. A's ability to continue living alone safely. Several weeks before the assessment, the friend had discovered Mrs. A on the floor of her apartment, where she had fallen two days before, unable to arise unassisted. Mrs. A reported other falls in the past year as well to the assessment team.

According to the friend, Mrs. A's electricity and telephone service had been discontinued in the past year because she had not paid her bills. Mrs. A had also inadvertently run up a $900 bill at the corner grocery store which was still unpaid. Because she had severe arthritis in her knees and trouble walking, Mrs. A only left her apartment, a task that requiring climbing 20 steps, once every two weeks to get groceries. The friend noticed that Mrs. A was eating mainly snacks and canned food and realized that Mrs. A needed some household assistance. M began visiting her more often and helping her with grocery shopping, cleaning, and paying bills. She also prepared a meal each time she visited. Mrs. A had a brother, niece and daughter who visited her infrequently. According to M, they did not know the extent of Mrs. A's disabilities. Mrs. A's social life revolved around an organization that provided, in her words, "foster home care to animals." At the time of the assessment, she was caring for nine cats, three birds, and one dog. Aside from M, members of the animal organization were her only regular, though infrequent, social contact. According to M, Mrs. A's apartment was appallingly dirty, she was incontinent, especially at night, and she needed assistance caring for her animals. She also informed the team that Mrs. A was feisty, resiliant, and resented any interference with her life or her affairs.

Two years prior to the assessment I observed, a community agency case manager had attempted to provide a variety of services to Mrs. A including house cleaning, meal delivery, participation at an adult day health center, and a money management program. Mrs. A rejected all the services offered because she was afraid that anyone who entered her life would have some authority over it and would take her animals away.

Mrs. A was not able to give a detailed medical or social history to the team physician during the assessment because of her memory deficits and she relied on M to answer questions for her. She had not seen a physician for four years, claiming that she did not really need to and that she would have great difficulty getting to a doctor's office in any case. Following the examinations by physician, neuropsychologist, podiatrist and nurse and the meeting with the social worker, the assessment team concluded that Mrs. A was obese, incontinent, visually impaired, had degenerative joint disease, a history of hypertension, anemia, significant gait and balance instability, and severe memory and concentration problems that pointed to progressive dementia. The team nurse, who visited Mrs. A at home to assess her physical and mental capabilities in her own environment, wrote in her report:

"Inside the house there are two bird cages with birds in the front living room. The cages are dirty and the water for the birds has a strong stench. The dining area and kitchen are inhabited by at least nine cats. The room off the dining area is full of old clothes, mail, books, and appliances. Mrs. A is a pleasant woman who is dressed appropriately. When asked if she could locate several phone numbers, including her daughter's phone number and address, she was unable to do so. She has fair grooming and hygiene, although there is an odor of urine on her clothes and about the house...She is borderline functional in her ability to care for herself. The house shows a great need of assistance."

The team wrote in their report that Mrs. A's physical and cognitive condition had deteriorated to the point where she needed "daily intervention" "in an attempt to support her living independently." They agreed that she would be safe in her apartment, temporarily, only if the following conditions were met: (1) her apartment be professionally cleaned; (2) she accept a Medicaid-paid aide to provide personal assistance, hygiene, food preparation, and cleaning on a daily basis, five hours a day, five to seven days per week; (3) she have prepared meals delivered to her; (4) she have a money manager; (5) she reduce the number of pets; (6) she attend an adult day health care center twice a week to have her physical health monitored, have a meal, and receive physical therapy because her walking was so unstable.

These criteria for her health, well-being, and safety were discussed during the follow-up conference with Mrs. A and her friend. M was informed by the team that even with all such services in place, Mrs. A's mental condition would worsen and that she would be able to remain in her own apartment for another year at most. Mrs. A was congenial during the conference but left without giving her consent for or acceptance of any of the services suggested. Nevertheless, both the team social worker and the agency case manager who had attempted to provide services years before told me they would try to arrange for those services so she would be as safe and healthy as possible at home.

Case #2

The daughter of an 84 year old woman, Mrs. B, requested an evaluation of her mother's condition in the hope that she could leave the skilled nursing wing of a residential care facility where she had resided for four months and return to her independent apartment in the same facility. Mrs. B had been placed in the hospital-like skilled nursing wing by facility personnel following several months of frequent fainting episodes and difficulty in maintaining her balance while walking. Her physical problem had been accompanied by a state of mental confusion and disorientation. The staff at the facility felt that Mrs. B's overall medical condition needed to be watched closely and that she was not safe in an apartment on her own.

Prior to her placement in skilled nursing, Mrs. B had a series of health assistants living with her in a compromise attempt by facility personnel to monitor her condition daily while she remained in her own home. Mrs. B hated their presence and discharged each one, stating that they restricted her right to make choices for herself. She said,

"I can accept the feebleness of my body but cannot deal with restrictions over my ability to make my own decisions."

The assessment evaluation was sought because although Mrs. B's mental and physical condition had seemed to stabilize, that is, she no longer fainted or fell and was not confused, there were conflicting opinions regarding whether Mrs. B continued to be at risk for further falls or other problems. At the time of her evaluation, Mrs. B could not walk unaided. She was diagnosed by the team as having severe memory deficits, difficulty with visual and motor skills, depression, gait and balance instability, chronic alcohol use, allergic dermatitis, normal pressure hydrocephalus, and spinal stenosis. The staff at the facility felt she had not made enough "progress" to return to her apartment. The daughter was unsure about her mother's health yet wanted to be an advocate for her mother who was angry and frustrated about her loss of freedom and privacy. Mrs. B claimed the skilled nursing wing rules and regulations were too restrictive for her, were making her depressed, and were ruining her life.

Following the assessment, Mrs. B was informed by the team's physician and social worker that "she was in a sticky situation: between independent and assisted living." She was told that if she wanted to return to her own apartment, she "must bend a little with the health aides and not fire them." She was advised that she could return to her apartment only if she had a health aide present eight hours per day, a call button installed, saw a neurologist about her gait, and appointed someone to take care of her finances. Psychotherapy for her depression was recommended as was the purchase of a medic-alert identification bracelet. The team social worker wrote in Mrs. B's chart, "She is adamant about returning to her apartment but is not realistic about the support services necessary to minimize her risk and maintain her independence."

Case #3

Mrs. C, an 81 year old woman, was referred to the assessment service by a community agency social worker who served as her case manager and with whom she met weekly for grief counseling. Two of her siblings and a close friend had died in the past two years. Mrs. C, who had lived alone for 40 years, had hired a live-in companion three months previously because she was becoming increasingly aware of problems with her memory and her ability to live safely alone. The companion had worked for Mrs. C years before, helping Mrs. C raise her children after her husband died. Mrs. C trusted this woman a great deal. Mrs. C told the team that she was "frightened" of her memory losses and living alone. Two months before the assessment, Mrs. C had been referred to a psychiatrist for evaluation of her increasing memory loss, insomnia, and depression. According to the assessment physician, that evaluation revealed no remarkable findings. She was referred to the muldisciplinary assessment team in the hope of a clear-cut diagnosis: dementia or depression. Mrs. C's three children concurred with the need for the assessment.

Mrs. C was fully functional at the time of the assessment and lived a largely independent life, cooking, shopping, exercising, and attending college-level evening classes that were of interest to her. She had willingly and with considerable relief turned over the responsibility for managing the household finances to her live-in companion and to one of her children. The companion payed the bills and cleaned the house in addition to providing Mrs. C with emotional support.

Mrs. C's only initial complaint to the assessment team was that she had been having difficulty sleeping for the past two years. She told the team, "I feel flaky. I can't think." Since she had recently started to complain about it daily, her companion and children were worried about the result of sleep deprivation on her. As she met with team members, a constellation of other problems emerged as well. Her personal physician had prescribed various sleeping medications for her, but she threw them all away, stating that they left her "feeling punchy." Instead of the prescribed medication, she drank a glass of Scotch at night as an aid to sleep. She also drank during the day, a habit she had been enjoying on a daily basis for forty years. Her children expressed the concern that her alcohol intake, recently increased sometimes to the point of intoxication, was interfering with her sleep. They wanted her to stop drinking altogether. Her children were also concerned about the fact that she smoked in bed.

In addition, Mrs. C and her companion had not been living amiably. They had been arguing about the household and, according to the companion, about Mrs. C's increasingly belligerent, agitated behavior. Mrs. C said she would do anything to prevent the companion from moving out of the house, but their disagreements were escalating, causing Mrs. C's children to become alarmed.

The assessment team physician assured Mrs. C and her children that she did not have Alzheimer's disease. They concurred however that she did have some memory impairment and that she was clinically depressed. The physician then informed Mrs. C that her alcohol use was contributing to her sleep disorder, depression, and memory loss, and he talked at some length about how the body is affected adversely by prolonged alcohol use. The physician said that the team could suggest methods for stopping her alcohol dependency (by joining a 12-step therapeutic program), resolving her sleep disorder (by participating in a sleep disorder clinic), and working on her depression caused by loss (more intensive grief counseling/psychotherapy/support groups). He noted that the team could only advise her; she would have to follow through with their suggestions and referrals. He advised her to stop smoking. He also noted that she would have to resolve the interactional problems with the companion on her own and suggested that it might be wise to consider getting a new companion. The social worker summed up the closing family conference by saying to Mrs. C, "If you do these things, we think your quality of life will be better. That's the goal here."

DISCUSSION: FINDING SOLUTIONS FOR LIVED EXPERIENCE

The transformation from lived problem to diagnosis, then to treatment plan, then to rules about what ought to be done, and finally to negotiated compliance is the form the social construction of frailty takes in the context of health care. At least three features of frailty's social construction emerge from these cases. First, we learn how subjective experience is interpreted in a medical/social service idiom. Though old persons come willingly enough to such services (Epstein et al. 1987), they do not come with the expectation that behaviors, habits, and patterns of a lifetime will be scrutinized along with the symptoms they choose to identify and present as troublesome.

Lived experience is transformed during the medical encounter into a problem list that encompasses personal and social behaviors as well as physiological disorders. It is important to note that the problem list is created through the interaction of older person, family or friend, and health care personnel. No one party is solely responsible for the transformation. Thus Mrs. A, who never sought medical services but was brought to the team by her concerned friend, was diagnosed by the friend and the team as having a dirty house, unpaid bills, too many pets, and not enough cooked food in addition to having medical diseases. Mrs. B's problem was identified by her daughter and herself as wanting to return to her own apartment. Mrs. C's diagnosis included grief and insomnia which she reported, as well as smoking, alcohol use, and communication difficulties with her companion which emerged as family members spoke with the health care team.

Multidisciplinary health care teams can assess a range of difficulties beyond the biomedical, and in fact can assess the "whole" person, a skill considered essential for good geriatric care (Kane 1988). But not only is the problem list frequently more pervasive than patients or families could conceive alone, the proposed solutions are in some cases more invasive than they imagined, requiring active, unsolicited behavior modification. For some persons, such as Mrs. A, treatment plans suggesting behavioral change are not viewed as solutions. They are viewed instead as unwanted meddling. Others, like Mrs. B and Mrs. C, see the point of proposed treatments, but balk at infringement on their privacy and personal routines. Ironically, failure to comply with health care team proposals does indeed put persons at risk for institutionalization, the greatest threat to autonomy in American culture.

All participants in this encounter—old persons, family, and health care providers—face an extremely difficult question: How can the health care system "fix" problems that reflect the lived experience of a lifetime? One cultural assumption shared by all participants is that the health care system can, and indeed should, contribute to the resolution of such problems. For frailty, as other conditions, is informed by the belief in the power of the American health care system to restore, manage, and order (Kaufman 1988a; Miller et al. 1992).

Yet proposals to resolve the problems frailty produces through major or multiple behavioral changes in late life contribute to a sense of impending identity loss for many old people. We have found that very old people, even those with some forms of mental impairment, weigh that potential loss against the potential cessation or reduction of the problems defined by others during the medical encounter (Kaufman 1988b; Becker 1993) That process, in and of itself, can be wrenching for old people and their families. As a result, older persons may feel trapped by solutions proposed to them. And health care providers, who invest much energy and many hours in devising the most appropriate way to keep people out of institutions and in their own homes, may be frustrated when clients reject their proposals.

Second, we see that health care providers, and sometimes family as well, invoke the language of surveillance and risk reduction as *the key* to maintaining personal autonomy and independence. They try to resolve the lived problem by adapting surveillance strategies to the idiosyncratic forms of autonomy embodied by very old persons. Through the strategy of risk reduction, health care providers and caregivers attempt to resolve the conflict between competing discourses by incorporating one into the other. Thus Mrs. A will have to reduce the number of pets she cares for, receive a meal service, attend an adult day health center, and have her body and environment cleaned by a housekeeper/personal assistant *so that* she can remain "independent" in her own home.

Mrs. B needs to be watched eight hours a day *in order to* reside in her apartment alone. Mrs. C should stop smoking, drinking, and arguing with her companion *so that* she can achieve piece of mind.

Persons turned patients, for whom subjective experience is not a problem list, frequently do not view health care proposals as solutions: Mrs. A only sees such life management as a threat to her ability to shelter animals. Mrs. B refuses to be watched all day and is not concerned about her instability and tendency to fall. Mrs. C does not view alcohol as contributing to her problems and views its cessation as a "deprivation." Family members can be torn as they acknowledge the appropriateness of both the patient's and the health team's viewpoints, a situation that is extremely unsettling and frustrating for them and for the ensuing decisions that must be made.

Third, in all these cases we see how "rules" become "facts" (Arney and Bergin 1984, p. 5). The lived experience of the old person *becomes* the problem list; surveillance *is* the key to autonomy. Patient or case management, with its institutionally created rules and regulations, has stepped in to fill an apparent void. The extended family, with its mandate to care and its knowledge about what is right, appropriate, and natural for its old and debilitated members, has vanished as an institution for many groups in American society. Furthermore, there are no explicitly shared standards or values regarding the nature of intervention in frail lives. The structure of health care delivery and social services, as well as the knowledge its providers share and the ideologies they invoke, create the facts, the only informational context that patients and families have as a basis for decision-making and coping with frailty. The health care context provides the method for addressing frailty. At the present time, no other institutions in American culture provide alternatives.

CONCLUSION

By broadening the discussion of frailty beyond instrumental definitions, I have tried to explore the relationship between experiential and socio-cultural sources of that phenomenon. I do so in an attempt to enlarge gerontology's scope and purpose, in the spirit of "bursting its borders" as Lars Tornstam suggests (1992, p. 323). I agree with Jay Gubrium, that the formulation of research questions itself has empirical consequences (1992, p. 582). In this case, what we ask about frailty frames its definition: It can be understood as a state of being that can be operationalized and measured instrumentally, as a parameter of risk for institutionalization, as a socially constructed problem, and as a quality and adaptational process, one that forces us to reconsider the meaning of independence and dependence in advanced old age.

ACKNOWLEDGMENTS I am indebted to my research partner, Gay Becker, for her continual support. Though the ideas expressed in this paper are my own, they emerge from our long collaboration. I wish to thank Barbara Koenig for her specific suggestions which are incorporated here.

NOTES

1.   A term employed by Foucault (1975) and explored in great detail by Arney and Bergin (1984). It refers to the development of an informed, purposeful look at the patient and disease. As notions

of disease have expanded in recent history, so too has the clinical gaze expanded to encompass "man within a hierarchy of systems" (Arney and Bergin 1984, pp. 78-79).

2.   This is how aging is largely perceived in the United States and other Western industrialized countries. But neither aging nor frailty are biological givens or objective facts meant to be revealed by health care professionals. Rather, they are socially constructed categories of meaning. For example, Lock (1984) notes that in Japan, where old people go to physicians quite often, the clinical gaze is focused only on the biological body. The social distress of old people is rendered invisible and is ignored. Cohen (1992) suggests that old age and debility in India are not viewed as states of being that require attention, medical or otherwise, because they are not interpreted as a social threat (p. 144). Thus old age is not medicalized at all and "geriatrics" is not meaningful or relevant.

3.   National Institute on Aging Research Award, # AG09176, "From Independence to Dependence among the Oldest Old," (1991-1994). Gay Becker, Ph.D., Principal Investigator and Sharon R. Kaufman, Ph.D., Co-Principal Investigator.

REFERENCES

Agich, G.J. 1990. "Reassessing Autonomy in Long-Term Care." *Hastings Center Report* (November/December): 12-17.

American Heritage Dictionary, 3rd edition. 1992. New York: Houghton Mifflin Company.

Arluke, A. and J. Peterson. 1981. "Accidental Medicalization of Old Age and Its Social Control Implications." Pp. 217-284 in *Dimensions: Aging, Culture and Health*, edited by C. Fry. New York: Praeger.

Arney, W.R. and B.J. Bergen. 1984. *Medicine and the Management of Living*. Chicago: University of Chicago Press.

Beauchamp, T.L. and J.F. Childress. 1989. *Principles of Biomedical Ethics*, 3rd edition. New York: Oxford University Press.

Becker, G. 1993. "Continuity After a Stroke: Implications of Life Course Disruption in Old Age." *The Gerontologist* 33:148-158.

Cassell, E.J. 1991. *The Nature of Suffering*. New York: Oxford University Press.

Clark, P.G. 1991. "Ethical Dimensions of Quality of Life in Aging." *The Gerontologist* 31:631-639.

Cohen, L. 1992. "No Aging In India: The Uses of Gerontology." *Culture, Medicine and Psychiatry* 16:123-161.

Conrad, P. and J.W. Schneider. 1980. *Deviance and Medicalization: From Badness to Sickness*. St. Louis: Mosby.

Engel, G. 1977. "The Need for a New Medical Model: A Challenge for Biomedicine." *Science* 196:129-136.

Epstein, A.M., J.A. Hall, R. Besdine, E. Cumella, Jr., M. Feldstein, B.J. McNeil, and J. W. Rowe. 1987. "The Emergence of Geriatric Assessment Units." *Annals of Internal Medicine* 106:299-303.

Estes, C.L. 1979. *The Aging Enterprise*. San Francisco: Jossey-Bass.

Estes, C.L. and E.A. Binney. 1989. "The Biomedicalization of Aging: Dangers and Dilemmas." *The Gerontologist* 29:587-596.

Foucault, M. 1975. *The Birth of the Clinic*. New York: Vintage Books.

Fox, R.C. 1990. "The Evolution of American Bioethics: A Sociological Perspective." Pp. 201-220 in *Social Science Perspectives on Medical Ethics*, edited by G. Weisz. Philadelphia: University of Pennsylvania Press.

Gubrium, J.F. 1992. "Qualitative Research Comes of Age in Gerontology." *The Gerontologist* 32:581-582.

Kane, R.A. 1988. "Beyond Caring: The Challenge to Geriatrics." *Journal of the American Geriatrics Society* 36:467-472.

Kaufman, S.R. 1988a. "Toward a Phenomenology of Boundaries in Medicine: Chronic Illness Experience in the Case of Stroke." *Medical Anthropology Quarterly* 2:338-354.

————. 1988b. "Stroke Rehabilitation and the Negotiation of Identity," Pp. 82-103 in *Qualitative Gerontology*, edited by S. Reinharz and G. Rowles.

Kleinman, A. 1988. *The Illness Narratives*. New York: Basic Books.

Knight, B. and D.L. Walker. 1985. "Toward a Definition of Alternatives to Institutionalization for the Frail Elderly." *The Gerontologist* 25:358-363.

Lock, M. 1984. "Licorice in Leviathan: The Medicalization of Care for the Japanese Elderly." *Culture, Medicine and Psychiatry* 8:121-139.

Marshall, P.A. 1992. "Anthropology and Bioethics." *Medical Anthropology Quarterly* 6:49-73.

Miller, B., M. Glasser, and S. Rubin. 1992. "A Paradox of Medicalization: Physicians, Families and Alzheimer's Disease." *Journal of Aging Studies* 6:135-148.

Pellegrino, E.D. and D.C. Thomasma. 1981. *A Philosophical Basis of Medical Practice*. New York: Oxford University Press.

Rothman, D.J. 1990. "Human Experimentation and the origins of Bioethics in the United States." Pp. 185-200 in *Social Science Perspectives on Medical Ethics*, edited by G. Weisz. Philadelphia: University of Pennsylvania Press.

Rubinstein, R.L., J.C. Kilbride, and S. Nagy. 1992. *Elders Living Alone: Frailty and the Perception of Choice*. New York: Aldine de Gruyter.

Sankar, A. 1984. "It's Just Old Age." Pp. 250-280 in *Age and Anthropological Theory*, edited by D. Kertzer and J. Keith. Ithaca, NY: Cornell University Press.

Shapiro, E. and R. Tate. 1985. "Predictors of Long-Term Care Facility Use Among the Elderly." *Canadian Journal on Aging* 4:11-19.

————. 1988. "Who is Really at Risk of Institutionalization?" *The Gerontologist* 28:237-245.

Thomasma, D.C. 1984. "Freedom, Dependency, and the Care of the Very Old." *Journal of the American Geriatrics Society* 32:906-914.

Tornstam, L. 1992. "The Quo Vadis of Gerontology: On the Scientific Paradigm of Gerontology." *The Gerontologist* 32:318-326.

Veatch, R.M. 1981. *A Theory of Medical Ethics*. New York: Basic Books.

Zola, I.K. 1972. "Medicine as an Institution of Social Control." *Sociological Review* 20:487-504.

THE "SCHEMING HAG" AND THE "DEAR OLD THING":

THE ANTHROPOLOGY OF AGING WOMEN

Linda Cool and Justine McCabe

There is indeed no one entity we can call the "aged." This is due to sociocultural as well as sexual variation. In this first article of its kind, anthropologists Cool and McCabe cross-culturally explore late adulthood from the female perspective. In doing so they attempt to go beyond the simplistic view of older women as either malevolent "scheming hags" or kingly "dear old things." They contrast the U.S. themes of the depressed middle-aged or older woman and the leveling of sex-role differences with the themes of growing dominance and power and role reversal of older women in many nonindustrial societies. Using their research experience in two Mediterranean societies known for their ideal of female subordination, the authors illustrate the paths by which women gain power and satisfaction in later life.

One of the most salient features in the research now available on human aging is that there is no *one* entity that can be termed the "aged." Yet, in spite of a call for its recognition (Maddox, 1969b: 7-8), the issue of the heterogeneity of experiences and interests among older people has been largely preempted by an apparent desire to focus on homogeneity in the aging process. As a case in point, although there are obvious and universally recognized differences in the biological endowment and in the social, cultural, and psychological experiences of men and women, surprisingly little attention has been devoted to the question of whether and/or how women and men differ in the aging process. In fact, the attention that has been focused on the condition of older women has tended to center on two stereotypes that appear at opposite ends of a power/weakness continuum. On the one hand, many societies (and the anthropologists who study them) represent older women as scheming manipulators of personal and magical powers--powers over which they may not have full control. At the opposite extreme lie the representations of older women as smiling, kindly grandmothers whose main interest in life is amusing and spoiling grandchildren. In actuality, the experiences of older women may lie somewhere between these extremes, and, as for most people, the differences that do appear among them are the result of psychological, social, and cultural variables. Often the particular representation of a society's older women is as much a cultural myth and even a creation of the anthropologist's expectations as it is a depiction of a "social reality."

The implicit challenge to anthropology in the area of gerontology is to question existing theories of aging by putting them to the cross-cultural test and to formulate cross-cultural models of aging as a universal phenomenon which transcends the immediate sociopolitical situations of industrialized nations. As Shanas et al. have observed, we must seek both to ask and answer "...the basic question: can a hypothesis about social behavior be considered proved by a study carried out within a single culture?" (1968: 7). This present work attempts to review, integrate, and evaluate the theories and data that do exist concerning female and male responses to aging. More importantly, this chapter provides, by means of detailed examples, a useful method of analyzing the aging process of men and women in the hope that new interest and dialogues may be kindled in this area.

WOMEN AND AGING: THE COMPARATIVE APPROACH

Prior to the 1960s, Leo Simmons's (1945) monograph was the only anthropological work devoted to the subject of aging (Clark, 1973: 79). As one facet of his study, Simmons compared sex-role related differences in the aging experience. He concluded by denying the existence of any "feminine patriarchy" in later life, at least in terms of *formal* office holding. In fact, only two of the societies which Simmons examined yielded examples of women (young or old) who held office. Based on such findings concerning formal office holding by women, Simmons dismisses women's ability to exercise control functions in society. However, in pursuing this argument, he overlooks very important areas of potential control and dominance for women, namely informal networks and *de facto* power: gossip groups which control others' actions by their negative and public commentary, self-help groups, communications networks for the sharing of information, and private dominance in the households.

In a later attempt to estimate the extent of possible matriarchy among older women, Gold (1960) questioned 24 anthropologists about their observations of age variations in the sex-role patterns of the various cultures they had studied: 13 reported a matriarchal shift; 11 reported no change; no one reported an increase in dominance among older men. Gold only partly concurs with Summonses earlier generalizations:

> *Like him, I find that matrilineality coincides with old women being dominant over old men. there is also some support of his finding that women tend to be dominant over old men in hunting-gathering societies, since two of the three examples in my sample [of 24] manifest the pattern (Blackfoot and Mohave versus the Pilaga).... The peasant communities (and urban middle class America), with their strong emphasis on ideal male supremacy but actual patter of old women dominating old men, conflict with his observation that where there is settled agriculture, old men tend to be dominant; if the people are peasants, the old women get the upper hand. (1960: II)*

In a more recent attempt to study sex-role differences in aging by means of a large-scale, cross-cultural comparison, Bart (1969) selected 30 societies representing the eight culture areas of the world from data contained in the Human Relations Area Files. From these societies, she gathered information on the presence of "six post-child-rearing roles available to women" (1969: 2): grandmother, mother or mother-in-law, economic producer, participator in government, performer of religious or magical rites, and daughter of aged parents. Working from the belief that in American society women lose one of their most important identity-giving roles (namely mother) which results in a "mutilated self" (Rose, 1962), Bart sought to document the relationship between changes in status and the availability of important roles. In general, she found that when society has a multiplicity of roles available for older women their status "...not only does not drop necessarily at this stage of the life cycle, but in most cases also rises..." (1969: 15). According to Bart, only two of the six roles she examined are *not* associated with higher status for women, namely economic producer ("...it cannot be concluded that the mere presence of an economic role will keep women's status from declining" [Bart, 1969: 4]) and daughter of aged parents (a role found only rarely.

One obvious problem with studies of this kind involves definitions. For example, Bart says that she did not include housekeeping and food preparation as economic producer roles for they are so common. But, might not a woman's *control* and leadership in these activities in the context of her household or family be considered such a producer role, or at least provide the woman with a positive self-image? In a similar vein, Summonses, Gold, and Bart all include consideration of some formal aspect of control (Bart talks of "participator in government" and Summonses of "formal office holding") and conclude that women (of any age) rarely are allowed to fill such roles. Rather than focusing on *public* control through formalized offices, it seems that studies ought to deal with areas where women in a variety of cultures do seem to have some power: informal networks, the domestic situation, and personal attributes. These, of course, are difficult to recognize and code in nomothetic studies.

Finally, like so much of this nomothetic research, Bart's work has illuminated certain structural features of society which seem to be associated with a particular aspect of life. But she is unable to prove a causal relationship or deal effectively with individual manipulations of these structural features. For example, Bart has suggested that a woman's status does not remain static throughout the life cycle. However, she cannot illustrate *how* a woman undergoes such status variations. Is the change abrupt or gradual, is the woman able to control the timing of the status change or is she at the mercy of external forces? Even though Bart does examine six societies in more detail, the reader is not particularly enlightened in the dynamics of *how* and *why* the status changes come about. The remainder of this article will attempt to resolve these questions by examining structural and cultural factors which influence the female response to aging in a variety of cultures.

THE PARADOX OF THE AGING AMERICAN WOMAN

Studies carried out in the United States have not only failed to provide clear-cut answers to questions concerning gender differences in the aging process, but have produced confusing and often contradictory results. This becomes evident in the kinds of portraits painted of older women by a variety of researchers.

The Ignored Older Woman

Some studies characterize older American women as members of a minority group who see themselves as a social problem: a group of people who have been excluded from full participation in society, accorded an inferior position within it, and denied access to power and authority (Bell, 1970; Lopata, 1971; Palmore, 1971; Sommers, 1974; Sontag, 1972). In this perspective, women seem particularly disadvantaged as they age since the roles that are allowed them in American society either are never accorded real power or are rendered obsolete by time, for example childbearer or sex object. Older women's lack of power and status is reflected in their invisibility in American society and their absence as subjects in research endeavors. Lewis and Butler (1972) have pointed out that even the women's liberation movement has largely ignored the problems of older women by focusing on issues of special concern to younger women such as abortion and day care facilities. In all fairness, however, it must be stated that the social sciences are not the only area to render women invisible. Nancy Sheehan (1976: 59), for example, notes that most historical studies of women are written by men who seem to be bent on preserving the status quo and that "...while histories of men are written concerning their relationship to the environment, histories of women are written concerning their relationship to men."

The Depressed Older Woman

An indication of the difficulties that American women face in growing older is reflected in the incidence of middle-age depression among women. Although American folk wisdom (and often science) attributes such depression to biological changes occurring during "the change of life," Bart found no cross-cultural correlation between the biological fact of the menopause and depression: "Depressions in middle-aged women are due to their lack of important roles and subsequent loss of self-esteem rather than hormonal changes of menopause" (1972: 139). the roles that women are allowed to play in America (wife and mother) are such that a woman's sense of worth comes not from

135

her own accomplishments but from the lives of others, namely her husband and children. As these people change or depart, a woman must be able to change her self-concept or face debilitating psychological stress.

Other social scientists (e.g., Davis, 1979; Dowty, 1971; Flint, 1975; Neugarten and Kraines, 1965; Neugarten et al., 1963; Silverman, 1967; Vatuk, 1975) have also attempted to distinguish culturally determined responses to menopause from those biological imperatives shared by women in all societies. Like Bart, Flint (1975, 1976) links a woman's status from midlife on to the attitudes and symptoms that characterize menopause. In contrast to the experiences of American postmenopausal women, Flint describes the situation of Indian Rajput women for whom menopause marks the end of *purdah* and the beginning of a freedom and power previously unknown to them:

> When these women were asked if they had any problems associated with the menopause, a most unusual response was forthcoming. Few women were found who had other than menstrual cycle changes--there were no depression migraines, no incapacitations, nor any of the classical symptoms associated with what we call the "menopausal syndrome." Furthermore, these women informed the author that they were eagerly looking forward to achieving this event in their lives, if they had not yet achieved it, and if they had already reached the menopause, they were also most positive about this fact. (Flint, 1976: 48)

In general, the aforementioned studies have all suggested that high or unchanging female status in middle age will be related to a positive attitude toward and/or the absence of difficulty with menopause. In contrast, Davis (1979) emphasizes the emic perceptions of menopause and the *total* biosocial self of the Anglican women she interviewed in a Newfoundland fishing village. These women were found to have a very high status and positive self-image *throughout* adulthood. Furthermore, this high status persisted in the face of the negative physical symptoms and attitudes that the *majority* of women experienced in menopause. Davis (1979: 7) explains this by three factors: (1) that bodily, psychological, and sociocultural processes are not compartmentalized, (2) that menopause is viewed as a normal process, and (3) that the major symptoms of menopause are not considered unique to midlife or cessation of the menses. Within the anthropological literature on the menopause, Davis's study is unique in its treatment of the menopause as one more biosocial phenomenon--no more or less significant--within the context of *all* biosocial events of the culture in question:

> Newfoundland women do not distinguish among biological, psychological, and social realms of experience. The folk notions of nerves and blood act in the conceptual integration of these realms throughout adult life. They have a folk system which explains what is happening to their minds and bodies at menopause and provides a female support system for those who experience difficulty. This effective support system reflects the continual high status of Newfoundland women which is characterized by extensive social networks, open communication channels, and a varied range of meaningful activities. (Davis, 1979: 13-14)

What about the Men?

While Bart and Davis have approached the study of menopause differently, both researchers' data suggest a similar theory to explain some depression among middle-aged men. Typically, those older American men who suffer depression, according to Bart (1972: 142), have immersed themselves in their jobs just as the "feminine" women have immersed themselves in their children and husbands. And, like the women whose children leave home, these men face depression upon retirement when all the public "props" to their self-esteem are removed. The severity (and disastrous consequences) of such depression is evidenced by the fact that in the urban American setting men die earlier than their female counterparts and also are more likely to commit suicide (Gutmann, 1980: 442). Similarly, Davis (1979: 5) indicates that because of the relentlessly strenuous physical life endured by the Newfoundland fishermen she observed, many of these men at middle age must relinquish the high status role of fisherman for the alien one of a land-based worker, supported by disability or unemployment insurance or work at the local fish plant. Thus it appears that in this case too, without the "props" to his self-esteem, and threatened by a loss of status, the middle-aged Newfoundland man--not the woman--is apt to become depressed.

The Older Woman as a Success Story

One general attitude fostered by some gerontological literature (see especially Cumming, 1964) in comparing female and male reactions to the aging process is that personal adjustment to later stages of the life cycle is somehow easier for women than for men because of the women's "smoother life cycle." The argument here is that from girlhood to death, a woman's key roles (wife and mother) remain essentially unchanged, while men suffer the sudden and complete loss of their core roles (worker and provider) when they reach retirement age. Although this situation is particularly dramatic · in industrialized nations like the United States which have artificially created mandatory retirement ages, Cumming's implication is that women universally face fewer age-related social and personal adjustment problems than do their male counterparts because of this "smooth," continuous social development.

While apparently agreeing with Cumming that women are more successful at adjusting to age changes, Kline (1975) suggests that this success may be due *not* to social role continuity (the "smooth" life cycle), but rather to women's socialization to repeated role loss and to their ensuing adaptability to role change. Thus, according to this argument, women experience fewer adjustment problems as they grow older because they are more accustomed to dealing with status and role variations, of which aging is merely one more example.

Age, the Great Leveler of Sex-Role Differences

The research of Lipman (1961) and Cameron (1967, 1968) among aging populations in the United States generally provides a different outlook on the experience of aging. their studies suggest that old age is in fact a greater leveler of sex-role differences, for men and women become increasingly more alike as they grow older. Specifically, Lipman (1961: 271) finds that the retirement of the husband contributes to the apparent egalitarian character of the observed marriages, and that, consequently, such marriages appear to be happier. According to Lipman, this egalitarian state is fostered by the sharing of household tasks, which are no longer defined as the wife's duties, and by the emphasis on the expressive aspects of marriage, such as love, companionship, and affection. These trends lead Lipman to conclude that in such happy, older marriages, "...apparently role differentiation by sex is reduced with increased age and retirement" (1961: 271).

In a similar vein, Cameron's data indicate that the *interests* of the aged may be typed as feminine, while their basic personality is more typically masculine than that of a comparison group of young people (1968: 64). Although his data actually seem to support the concept that older men and women have convergent interests, Cameron interprets this tendency as a reflection of socioeconomic status rather than old age per se:

> *...accessibility to and success in various kinds of endeavors also determine interests. The lower SES and general physical weakening of the aged often preclude participating in the relatively expensive and vigorous masculine activities. One often has to be content with what one can do, and what one does is generally what one professes to desire. (1968: 65)*

Unfortunately, Cameron provides no examples of these "expensive and vigorous" interests.

Sex Role Reversal in Old Age--The Dominant Older Woman

The research of Cumming and Henry (1961), Kerckhoff (1966), Lowenthal et al. (1975), Neugarten (1968), and Neugarten and Gutmann (1968) contrasts with the position of Lipman. For example, Lowenthal et al. find that middle-aged and older women become more dominant in the family, and Kerckhoff (1966: 179-80) believes that he has found data indicating

> *...a greater sensitivity to interpersonal relationships in the conjugal unit on the part of the husband and a greater concern with the practical activities of daily living on the part of the wife. If such an interpretation is acceptable, it would indicate a kind of role reversal from the presumed model of husband-wife relationship in our society which calls for the husband to emphasize an instrumental orientation and the wife to have more of an expressive orientation.*

In attempting to make a comparison with non-American populations, one finds a relative dearth of cross-cultural gerontological literature with regard to gender differences in aging. for example, this possible "role reversal" among aging American men and women has been only alluded to in studies of other cultures.[1] In one of the more detailed comparisons, Kardiner et al. (1945: 65) describe the older Comanche women:

> *Women, with few exceptions, had no power before the menopause. After the menopause a woman could acquire power as readily as a man. It was common for a medicine man to have his wife assist him, teaching her everything that was required for curing, except rituals for the actual transfer of power. Immediately after the menopause, the husband gave power to her.... After the menopause, the distinction between the sexes, as far as medicine power went, was largely disregarded.... As she grows older her security becomes greater.... In comparison with the male, therefore, the woman starts with initial disadvantage, but she has greater mobility as she gets older.*

Similarly, Borgese (1964) and Gutmann (1974, 1977) note that over the life cycle women who had earlier been subordinate to men with regard to authority (Rosaldo, 1974), become quite dominant and powerful vis-a-vis men. In Gutmann's terms, men begin with active mastery of their biosocial environment and move toward passive mastery (characterized by dependence and passivity) with increasing age and lessening physical capabilities. Women, on the other hand, move from passive mastery (cultural deference to and resulting personal dependence on fathers and husbands) to active mastery of their social environments in later life. Gutmann argues that such inner subjective shifts together with their overt behavioral indicators are universal for men and women.

The Older Woman as Witch

A traditional context in which older women are seen as dominant and aggressive within the anthropological literature is the recurrent theme of the older woman as witch or sorcerer (for example, Evans-Pritchard, 1937; Fortes, 1962; Fuller, 1961; Harper, 1969; Kluckhohn, 1967; LeVine, 1963; and Nadel, 1952). In these cases, even implicit recognition by men of the power of senescent women can often be made only by ascribing evil motivations to their hegemony. Fuller (1961: 51) confirms this in her description of the Lebanese villagers she studied: "Men sense this invisible power of women. To older women, in particular, is attributed the power of witchcraft or of the evil eye, both signs of an uncanny force."

One possible explanation for this malevolent characterization of older women is a correlation suggested by Douglas (1966: 120):

> ...where the social system recognizes positions of authority, those holding such positions are endowed with explicit spiritual power, controlled, conscioous, external, and approved--powers to bless or curse. Where the social system requires people to hold dangerously ambigious roles, these persons are credited with uncontrolled, unconscious, dangerous, disapproved powers--such as witchcraft and evil eye.

Nadel's work among the Nupe of Northern Nigeria appears to support this viewpoint: older Nupe women occupy an ambiguous position in their society. They are female and therefore normatively inferior to men; yet, they resemble the male cultural ideal by possessing power (albeit *de facto* power). In other words, in these situations, because women are, in men's eyes, usurping what is "rightfully" male (i.e., the exercise of power), men "punish" older women by accusing them of witchcraft and other acts of malevolence.

> The general picture is that of a sharp sex-antagonism, which assigns the evil intentions to the female, and to the male, a benevolent and ideally decisive--if somewhat utopian role.... Men are never blamed or accused of witchcraft, and the main collective weapon against witchcraft lies in the activities of a male secret society which, by threats and torture, "cleanses" the villages of witchcraft.... In the majority of cases the alleged witch is a woman, usually an older and domineering female, who would attack a younger man who somehow fell under her dominance.... the men, though on the utopian or fantasy plane the masters of the female witchcraft, are, on the plane of "real" incidents and fears, its main victims.

A second possible explanation is that this pervasive ascription of evil motivation to older women is related to their actual powerlessness and low status position. This reasoning is pursued by Harper (1969) in his study of the belief system of the Havik Brahmins of South India. In this situation, Harper (1969: 81) proposes that the dangerous nature attributed to Havik widows may be the result of guilt on the part of those who occupy high status positions (men) toward those who formally lack power and prestige and occupy the lowest positions (widows) in this social system.

Despite their explicitly inferior and powerless status, Havik women are, in fact, rather powerful, at least in a negative sense: They influence and affect the lives and behavior of others--especially men. In keeping with Hvik men's attitudes toward all women, it is possible that widows, who are mainly older females, are feared simply because they are believed to possess the ultimately powerful weapon--death through witchcraft. However, Harper's explanation of guilt on the part of high status Havik men could be made even more compelling. At present, it merely emphasizes projections of

139

recent resentment of Havik widows, and their *currently* intolerable status; instead, this explanation could be extended to attribute males' fears to projections of *long-hidden*, accumulated anger which men could expect these mainly older women to feel and express in response to a lifelong inferior position.

CULTURE AND WOMEN'S STATUS

An increasingly significant source of data with regard to women's power in society is found in anthropological studies of women's status. This growing body of literature (e.g., Collier, 1974; Friedl, 1975; Lamphere, 1974; Murphy and Murphy, 1974; Quinn, 1977; Wolf, 1972) indicates that female solidarity, flexibility, and a keen perception of male-female relationships characterize women with age, and enable them to adapt with increasing success to situations normally controlled by men. One emphasis of this literature is that, although the power of women--old and young--increases most dramatically in informal, domestic setttings, its expression is felt throughout the societies in question.

For example, Wolf (1972: 40) describes the influence that older Taiwanese women have on men's behavior in a family of which they are never a member but to which they are essential:

> *Taiwanese women can and do make use of their collective power to lose face for their menfolk in order to influence decisions that ostensibly are not theirs to make. Although young women may have little or no influence over their husbands and would not dare express an unsolicited opinion...to their fathers-in-law, older women who have raised their sons properly retain considerable influence over their sons' actions, even in activities exclusive to men.... When a man behaves in a way that they consider wrong, they talk about it--not only among themselves, but to their sons and husbands.*

By banding together in informal gossip and work groups, these Taiwanese women have gained a great deal of power to effect changes and maintain some independence in their lives--an ability unavailable to a lone woman living in the "foreign" territory of her husband's particlan. Without such an informal control mechanism, the Taiwanese woman would be as powerless and unsupported as the stereotyped image predicts.

We could continue to cite references to the increasing power of senescent women in many dissimilar societies. However, it becomes increasingly clear that two themes regarding gender differences in adaptation to aging that have been reported in research carried out in the United States are not apparent in the literature concerning the aging experience in other cultures. The first is the theme of the older woman becoming depressed with increasing age, and the second concerns age as the great leveler of sex-role differences. This latter theme emphasizes the male loss of power to being him down to the level of women, while much of the cross-cultural literature emphasizes the increased status of older women. This is not to say that these themes are "wrong." These situations may hold in the United States because of specific social and cultural features which must be determined. Whatever their cultural souces, these adaptations to the aging process are not a universal or biological fact of life to be faced by all older men and women.

Two conclusions appear from the cross-cultural evidence cited so far: (1) Women in many disparate societies become increasingly dominant and powerful as they age, and (2) with such a transition in female power and status, there may be a concomitant decline in the power and dominance of the older men in these societies. The remainder of this article will focus on a detailed analysis on two distinct cultures in an effort to determine the bases of self-perceived success in adjustment to growing older among men and women. In particular, we will focus on two of the adaptive strategies employed by women which were delineated earlier: (1) the self-assessed success of older women as based on the continuity of the core role throughout life *or* on their socialization throughout the life cycle to role changes, and (2) the question of the increasing dominance (both in terms of personality and social roles) of older women.

AGING WOMEN IN MEDITERRANEAN SOCIETY

Following the anthropological principle that researchers can best discover the operation of a variable when its functions are observed in extreme cases, the ethnographic foci in the following analyses are two locales within the Mediterranean culture area: (1) the Niolo, a mountainous region composed of five autonomous villages in the center of the island of Corsica, and (2) Bayt al-'asir, a modernizing peasant community of about 600 people in southern Lebanon. These are "extreme" environments compared to the urban United States in several ways. First, the informants presented in the following analyses live in small towns where the traditional economy is based on transhumant pastoralism (the Niolo) or wage laboring with small-scale agriculture (Bayt al-'asir). In addition, both these locales are firmly entrenched in the Mediterranean culture area where one of the defining cultural characteristics is a seemingly obsessive (at least to Western eyes) concern with female modesty and submission, for male and familial honor is embodied in the chastity of kinswomen, especially wives. In this manner, it appears that these societies offer valuable cross-cultural checks on the general validity of some of the findings concerning the adaptive success and growing domination of women as they age.

In both societies, women perceive themselves (and are also considered by the men) to be aging successfully and to be better off than their male counterparts in old age. For example, aged Niolan men say that women adapt better to old age "because they have less desire to get out" and "because they are less independent." Older women are of the same opinion, but for different reasons: "Men find it harder to grow old well because they are not accustomed to resignation." The anthropologists' data agree with their informants' perception of the women's relative success in aging. However, in analyzing the perception of greater life satisfaction on the part of their female informants, Cool and McCabe tend to focus on different factors. Cool emphasizes the *individual* manipulations of a Niolan woman as she undergoes socialization to role change and personal adaptability in her move from timid bride to domineering older mother-in-law. McCabe stresses that this life-satisfying situation for older Lebanese women is the result of an accumulation of several cultural factors which are differentially emphasized at various points in the life cycle. With increasing age, Lebanese women become relatively more competent and confident in their roles than do men. There is a sense of *control* in their lives, which is absent in those of men.

THE NIOLO

Successful aging depends on the developmental cycle of the traditional Niolan household. It demands that a woman learn to adapt to changing roles and statuses[2]. Such socialization begins early for Niolan girls, for they learn the basic skills while helping their mother and sisters. The ideal was for all daughters to marry; but financial limitations of all but the wealthiest families sometimes prevented this realization. In the past, even the unmarried daughter who remained at home had important roles to perform: she first helped her parents and later her brother (the heir) and his wife. As a "blood" relative of the patricentric family, she had an important standing even though she would never be a "housewife," and often she developed a close, confidante relationship with her sister-in-law as the two women worked to increase the reputation of the household.

In the Niolo, a bride is expected to be fully capable of running a household upon marriage. This is the case even if the new couple is to live patrilocally. For upon arriving in her new home, the first person the young bride meets is her mother-in-law, the woman under whose authority she will live and work for the next several years. In this sort of patricentric household, the young woman must work hard to establish herself in her new household and to win even grudging approval from the mother-in-law who is convinced that no one can care for her beloved son as well as his own mother.

A period of expansion in the developmental cycle of the household arrives with the pregnancy and birth of the young wife's first child. Although she continues in her submission to her mother-in-law's authority, the young mother finally is recognized as having personal value other than that of "another worker." In the role of mother, the young woman creates emotional bonds and achieves positive status in her husband's household. From her, the infant receives the emotional ties and support of which the young wife must herself feel deprives, especially when her husband is away with the animals. In this regard, some old women mentioned that the most important part of their lives was giving birth to a son and then raising him so that they would be assured of affection and care in their old age.

The peak stage (arriving eight to ten years after the marriage) for the Niolan household begins when the young wife has several children, for she begins to prove her own ability as a housewife and domestic decision maker. Her husband begins to appreciate her more as a partner, and the complementarity of teh roles of wife and husband become clearer in the young couple's intense activity to support a nuclear family and a household. When she has reached 35 and has had five, six, or more children, her family may continue to expand but the older children have reached an age and a developmental stage where they can make useful contributions to the group. And in spite of the fact that this is the busiest period of her life, the housewife might have attained some peace. For by now, the mother-in-law, although still the priveleged head housewife, begins to entrust her younger counterpart with more responsibilities in the household's management.

When the wife is aged 45 to 50 years, her first child usually leaves the home to emigrate or prepares to marry. Although the household still includes children, the wife's childbearing years are over and the remaining children are her youngest and last. Gerontologists predict that this shrinking circle stage is the most difficult for urban women: The urban housewife loses prestige as she ceases to perform the housewife role at its peak. The Niolan housewife, however, does not seem to experience this letdown as she herself acquires a new status and role, that of mother-in-law, as she welcomes her own son's wife into *her* household.

Finally, when most of the children are either married or away from home, the Niolan wife faces the likely prospect of widowhood. In spite of the loss of her role as wife, she continues as mother, grandmother, and organizer of the home. Child care which was once just another burden among other tasks becomes a pleasure since grandchildren need only be loved, not trained. Although her knowledge of house and children may be common to younger women, her advice in an emergency can be vital. Such advice includes the ability to diagnose illness as to whether it was caused by the evil eye and to effect cures. Although younger women may also perform this role (*signadore*), older women are more sought after since they have more experience and, probably, more successful cures about which they can boast. An older woman's knowledge of the community and its inhabitants is unique, and she often is skilled in problem solving. In this manner, the elder female in the Niolo is in a position not only to maintain her prestige, but to actually improve her status as well.

Thus we have traced the developmental cycle of the housewife from the timid, subservient bride to the respected and confident head of the domestic unit. The basic role concept remained the same. However, the woman constantly underwent modifications in the characteristics of each assigned role. These variations occurred as the woman entered different stages of the life cycle and correspondingly changed her definitions of her roles. Having reached old age, the housewife can look at her children and her home with a sense of pride in accomplishment. Women are not the submissive, powerless creatures which are often portrayed in the Mediterranean. Rather they are manipulators of people, events, and the rules themselves.

What about the life cycle of Niolan men? The young man selected as his father's heir is under the older man's domination. The young man acquires the role of father upon the birth of his first child, but his relationship to his children is remote due to his frequent and prolonged absences from the home while caring for the animals. In fact, the most commonly given description of a traditional Niolan father emphasizes his rigidity and distance ":The mother is the person the child loves. The father has little significance. He commands the children, but he is less important to them than the mother. (62-year-old man)."

In time, a man's failing health requires him to delegate more and more responsibility to his son, and the old man must watch his role as the household's chief provider disappear. Some old men are able to assume the respected roles of advisor, arbitrator, or adjudicator in their later years. But, for the most part, the old men seem to be left with ephemeral authority as they tell their sons how best to manage the household's affairs. In changing from the aggressor to the negotiator, the aging Niolan male begins to show behavior that is less stereotypically masculine while his wife assumes more and more control within her own domain.

In analyzing such age-based changes in roles, Cottrell (1942) suggested that an individual will make an easy adjustment to a role change to the extent that he has undergone anticipatory preparation for the role. Kline attempted to pursue this viewpoint with regard to aging American women:

> *Women have had considerable experience in adjusting to age-linked changes (children leaving home, menopause) and have therefore become accustomed to change and impermanence. Thus, women are not as devastated as men are likely to be when old age, another impermanance, separates them from the productive, involved...world of middle age. (Kline, 1975: 490)*

From the analysis of the life cycle of a Niolan housewife, it appears that Niolan women do undergo role changes throughout the life cycle to a greter extent than do their male counterparts. It is suggested that this is one reason for the apparent privileges of women in successful aging.

BAYT AL-'ASIR, LEBANON

By the time a woman in Bayt al-'asir has reached her sixth decade of life, her ever increasing air of confidence has emerged with a rather bold and assertive countenance. Earler, as a middle-aged woman, for instance, it is likely that she had already become a controller of her household budget and appropriator of its funds; these responsibilities were earned through deference paid, services rendered, and the manipulation of her various cultural assets (e.g., her sexuality, kinsmen, and children). However, as an even older woman, she fills her influential position with increasingly less dependence upon and consultation with her husband.

Thus, it is this older woman--not her husband--whom grown and dependent children and kin approach with requests for new clothing or other material (and emotional) needs. Indeed, where a younger, middle-aged woman would still *ask* her husband for money when the local peddler came around, the (healthy) woman approaching old age would often *tell* her husband to give her the money or use funds which she herself has put aside.[3]

The manifestation of the power of female sexuality changes as a woman ages: Before menopause, she influences male honor largely by her own sexual behavior; after menopause, she influences younger women's status and reputations (and male honor) by what she chooses to say about them in the community. Older village women have the credibility in the eyes of both men and women and can effectively pass judgment on another woman's virtue; moreover, their advice, and especially their approval, are sought by their sons and other young men who are contemplating marriage. To vital older women, respect and a kind of homage accrue: from younger women, an empathetic recognition for their having weathered a hard life, raised children, and contended (usually successfully) with a normatively second-class, powerless status; from men, (especially sons) there is a gratitude and emotional dependency, and some recognition of the wise, prophetic, and mediating qualities of older women who are at the center of the community's daily social, culturel, economic, and political activities.

The first half of the life cycle of these Lebanese women is largely characterized by nurturance and attendance to the needs of others--husbands and children--rather than to personal needs and wants. As young wives and mothers, these women are so occupied with raising their children and maintaining their households that they virtually have no free time to devote to "frivolities" such as their own pleasure or interests. Although women of all ages extolled the virtues of "country" living, they wistfully spoke of the easier life of urban women or those depticted in Western television. By contrast, young husbands spent little time around their homes, coming and going with their male friends during nonworking hours.

With increasing age, village women realize that their strength, satisfaction, security, and invluence ultimately derive from the very source of their hardships and struggle: marriage and motherhood. Nonetheless, some women express resentment and frustration at having to remain at home with so much work while their menfolk are able to move about--like children--unfettered by teh demands of housework, children, etc. However, as the children mature and become independent and helpful, village women, too, have more time for themselves. Young and older women espouse the prevalent attitude of "better late than never" found among women in late middle age.

Accordingly, the psychological aging of the women of Bayt al-'asir is characterized by the Arab "masculine" qualities of self-assertiveness and confidence, at least partially replacing the "feminine" traits of self-denial and passivity. They not only approach equality with men, but appear also to surpass them at least with regard to the personal satisfaction of life task achievement (i.e., as mothers and homemakers).

Able older women in this community begin to be conspicuously more mobile, even going visiting or on errands out of the village. For example, some of the numerous visits by older women to the doctor in another community are regarded as "legitimate" desires for personal attention and/or somply for going on an outing. A village woman at this stage of life is even more candid in telling others that she does or does not like something that affects her personally, whether it is a kind of food, her child's spouse, or visitors. One 62-year-old matron rather eloquently expressed her perceptions of growing old: "As I grow older, I have more confidence in myself, more faith in only my ability to make myself happy. I find that there is a greater sensitivity and listening to my feelings, thoughts, and even to my body."

Also, societal norms (i.e., with regard to modesty) have a decidedly lesser influence on old women's behavior, although they may still pay them lip service where *other* women are concerned. Moreover, because an old woman is not longer able to bear children or menstruate, she is perceived as having moved from the realm of women and nature (to which "femaleness" is likened) toward that of men and culture, an analogy which Ortner (1974) has duly elaborated. It is the perception of this symbolic shift that at least partly permits the often audaciously bawdy and otherwise inappropriate behavior of older women to occur without societal sanctions.

This bawdy, sometimes brash behavior of old women was amply illustrated during the research period. For example, one summer day, McCabe was standing near her village home speaking with an elderly neighbor, Zayna, a very vivacious grandmother of 72 years, in the presence of a few young, unmarried women and men. The conversation touched on several topics, including her opinions on the scandalous type of clothing young women were wearing (a subject she raised). In so speaking, Zayna unabashedly hoisted her skirt a considerable distance above her knees to expose her bloomerlike underpants, all the while disapproving the skimpy panties she knew the young girls were wearing. The onlookers' obvious embarrassment did not seem to disturb her in the slightest; she eventually pulled her skirt down and acted as if nothing extraordinary had happened. McCabe later asked the young people whether such behavior was considered shameful. They stammered a bit and said yes, it was, but that it really did not matter because "...she is an old woman."

In sum, an older woman's public behavior and attitude acquires the stereotypically Arab masculine dimensions of self-indulgence and assertiveness. According to McCabe's observations, an older woman spends more time visiting her cronies for the sake of socialization and not just under the guise of doing work with them or going on an errand. She is more likely to get around to preparing her husband's meals or fulfilling his requests when or if she feels like it, rather than automatically kowtowing to him as before.

Simultaneously, a man of the same age acquires the stereotypically Arab feminine dimensions of passivity and patience. As his job retirement approaches, he begins to gravitate toward home more and more, sitting there alone or with a few friends. According to older village women, these men just seem to get tired of cavorting and always trying to have fun. In his home--his wife's domain--an older man's feminine side is most evident. McCabe observed older women telling their husbands to do this or that. The old men complied and obviously did not care enough about the issue to disagree, preferring instead to avoid any potentially hostile situation. In the face of his often vivacious, but sometimes irascible wife, an older man stays out of her way or tries to mollify her in an argument-- just as she often did as a younger woman.

Therefore, over the lifetime of these Lebanese women, there ocurs a transition from a feminine influence that is implicit, covert, and marked by subterfuge, to one that is increasingly overt, and recognized by at least those in an older woman's immediate environment. Essentially this transition involves a change from *de facto* to *de jure* control; that is, feminine power in older women acquires an aspect of authority. By contrast, the power enjoyed by men in this society is *de jure*; they have authority over women. However, due to certain psychosocioeconomic components, this masculine power is tenuous. As men age, the fragile nature of the foundations of their authority is increasingly exposed and eroded.

In conclusion, among the several ways by which these life cycle changes in the hegemony and concomitant life satisfaction of women and men occur in this society are the following:

1. There is little incongruity between the ideal and real life task of a Lebanese village woman. In one form or another, *mothering* (of children and even husbands) is still the role not only idealized by society and a woman herself, but also the one actually attained by her. By contrast, for a Lebanese man there is considerably less consonance between what his society expects him to be, and what it actually allows him to be. Generally, the men of this community are not wealthy, important, or powerful in the public marketplace--the sphere to which they have been assigned by society. Consequently, by middle age, men perceive themselves as unsuccessful, women perceive them as unsuccessful, and men perceive women's perceptions of them as unsuccessful. Hence, they become increasingly impotent vis-a-vis the successful and confident older women.

2. Female solidarity and support are great sources of comfort and power for women individually and as a group. By contrast, the divisiveness of men and their perception of one another as competitors and exploiters of one another's kinswomen allow them to become increasingly isolated as individuals in their later years.

3. Finally, the locus and source of female power and satisfaction over time are a woman's home and her children. With increasing age, she becomes the focal point of the lives of her husband, her children, and their own young families. The support of children for their mother, even in opposition to their father, cannot be overemphasized. Moreover, this locus of power (the home) for a village woman in the first half of her life continues to be such in the latter half. Her expertise and confidence in the performance of her life tasks are manifest in the same place over time. By contrast, the working life of a man in this wage-laboring community is characterized by absence from village, family, and other men. When he retires, a village man retires to his wife's domain of influence and expertise. Also, he is without benefit of the equality-enhancing symbols of the skills and seniority he may have acquired in his own work place--one which is still separate from where he will live out his old age.

CONCLUSION

Based on the cross-cultural evidence presented here, it does appear that women, especially in the later life cycle stages, are not the powerless, submissive creatures that have often been portrayed in the literature. Rather, some sources of power are available to women in all societies, and women's ability to manipulate their own lives and the lives of others around them increases with the passage of years. This emphasis on women as capable, energetic members (and sometimes the recognized leaders) of society has typically been overlooked. Most studies focus on *de jure* power (or authority, the publicly recognized right to exercise control) which is typically a male domain. Therefore, most cultural descriptions fail to examine the full range of social interactions in a society, focusing mainly on the more active, public, and dominant relationships. As Hammond and Jablow point out, "...descriptions of curing concentrate on the medicine man, not the patient; accounts of government focus on rulers, not the ruled; we are told a gret deal about parental behavior to children and little of children's responses" (1976: 132). When anthropologists turn their attention to *de facto* power and control that is exercised in the private rather than the public sphere, the strengths of women begin to appear. Thus, we find today that cross-cultural analyses of sex roles such as Rosaldo and Lamphere's *Woman, Culture, and Society* (1974) and Schlegel's *Sexual Stratification* (1977), to name but two, are pointing to the relative power of women.

This article has focused on a cross-cultural analysis of women's greater adaptability and success in growing old and has indicated the sources of this success: women's socialization to continued changes in their roles and self-concept, their increasing expertise and confidence in their domain (the home), their move from covert use of power (in their manipulations of their children's affection) to overt and recognized control in the eyes of the larger community, and the strength and comfort they draw from female solidarity. Such an emphasis seems particularly compelling because the detailed ethnographic examples are drawn from the Mediterranean, an area of the world commonly thought to represent one of the extreme cases of the domination of men and the subordination of women. The message is clear. There is no biological imperative for a submissive (or powerful) female role. Women, like men, are products (and producers) of the particular culture in which they are socialized and live out their lives.

NOTES

1. As just a few examples from the anthropological literature, see Fortes, 1962 (Tallensi of Kenya); LeVine, 1963 (Gusii of Kenya); Nadel, 1952 (Nupe); Spencer, 1965 (Samburu); Leonard, 1967 (Mexican-Americans); and Yap, 1962 (Chinese).

2. The stages of the life cycle of the Niolan housewife are adapted from the stages developed for an American housewife by Lopata (1966: 5-22).

3. With regard to the latter, McCabe discovered that from a younger age, some village women in the constant struggle for economic security and independence had found one way to put money aside. Having paid for the article or service, they would then tell their husbands that it cost twice as much as it actually did, and they then would pocket half of the amount for themselves.

CULTURAL CONSTRUCTIONS OF AGE AND AGING

"AGE":
A Problematic Concept for Women

Hilda L. Smith

Devoting a special issue of the *Journal of Women's History* to age as a concept of analysis for women's past is problematic for a number of reasons. Descriptions of aging as a process—maturing through various stages of life from birth to death—have not traditionally occurred in histories of women. Nor have historians delineated how the process applies to women's lives in histories of childhood or old age. Scholars of women's history have overcome such voids by establishing new sets of categories or definitions that relate explicitly to women's experiences. Those analyzing women's contributions to the history of art have emphasized such alternative media and skills as quilting or the use of multiple and unorthodox materials; those focusing on women in science have stressed women's private experimentation at home, the role of chemistry in cooking, and the duty of housewives in earlier periods to provide medical treatment for families and neighbors; and those focusing on politics have examined women's "gossip circles" and neighborhood organizing. These have been studied even when men's informal and family connections were most important to their success and when a female monarch and female advisors existed as clear examples of women's political standing. In short, scholars have studied a range of topics in a framework of gender stereotypes (both for women and men) outside the contributions women have made to mainstream "male" institutions.

But these efforts have often left us in a situation where men stand for the species norm while women represent a specialized form of human being. To avoid such a problem we must treat age as a significant marker, but one that has taken its meaning from the distinct lived experiences of women and men. Can we, therefore, redefine categories as broad and as central to the nature of being human as aging to make them conform to women's distinct history? Or must we treat them as problematic and inappropriate to use without clarifying how gender is embedded within them?

To make this theoretical point more clearly, I link it to the concerns I have with feminist attempts to extirpate sexist language from everyday and academic use. While I understand the motivation behind such efforts,

© 2001 JOURNAL OF WOMEN'S HISTORY, VOL. 12 NO. 4 (WINTER)

I still believe that it often does more harm than good simply to add "she" or "women" to an account when the reality, or author's intent, clearly excludes them. If an author used "people" or "person" to mean men or man, then it is more effective to reveal such usage by placing "man" in brackets, or a masculine pronoun following the falsely inclusive term. This makes clear the author's intent, rather than inserting "he or she" or "men and women" when a historical phenomenon (or commentary on that phenomenon) clearly excluded women. One must first acknowledge exclusion to change it, not simply alter language or definitions to create new categories or narratives that place women within existing frameworks.

My own research is on how the false universal operated in England from 1640 to 1832, but I believe my findings affect our understanding of gender definitions well beyond the early modern period or English national boundaries. My main argument is that women have been most effectively excluded from the nation (and central qualities of being human) not so much through explicit exclusion, and certainly not based on the characteristics attached to femininity and masculinity, but more so through language that has assumed inclusion while being encased in exemplary material and historical context that reveals they were never included at all. The use of such words as "all" (which was consistently used to mean "all men") to exclude women has been much more effective than employing explicit phraseology. At the heart of this falsely universal inclusion has been the concept of a process of aging that was implicitly based on a male maturation process which claimed to be representative of the normal development of both men and women. The men who wrote political, philosophical, and educational treatises, which were based on this false universal, not surprisingly, never explicitly defined this process as being limited to men. We must read such descriptions carefully and weigh what was gained and lost when such terms as aging were falsely or mistakenly employed as gender neutral categories.

In this essay, I outline some of these problematic conceptions of aging and gender in early-twentieth-century American and European efforts to establish the parameters of psychological inquiry and treatment. As we will see, modern psychological concepts of age had their roots in the early modern period. Yet not all contemporaries embraced the sexist theories of such psychologists as G. Stanley Hall and Sigmund Freud, which perpetuated the tradition of the false universal. M. Carey Thomas, president of Bryn Mawr College and leading feminist among U.S. educators between 1890 and 1930, foreshadowed many of my own criticisms of these theories. In arguing for the important role the introduction of women's colleges had played in society's assessment of women's capacities, Thomas drew a striking comparison between Jules Michelet (the nineteenth-century French Romantic historian who linked women's distinct and weaker qualities to an abundance of blood) and Hall's *Adolescence* (1904).[1]

> I can well remember one endless scorching summer's day [in 1874] when sitting in a hammock under the trees with a French dictionary, blinded by tears more burning than the July sun, I translated the most indecent book I have ever read, Michelet's famous—were it not now forgotten, I should be able to say infamous—book on woman, *La femme*. Altho during these thirty years [that had since passed] I had read in every language every book on women that I could obtain, I had never chanced again upon a book that seemed to me so to degrade me in my womanhood as the seventh and seventeenth chapters on women and women's education, of President [G.] Stanley Hall's *Adolescence*.[2]

Today, Hall, when he is remembered at all, is considered one of the fathers of modern psychology and the founder of adolescent psychology. This was hardly how Thomas saw Hall, president of Clark University from 1888 to 1920. Thomas, who took any slight to women's intellectual abilities seriously and with great offense, particularly disliked the Michelet-like qualities of Hall's work, which she termed "sickening sentimentality and horrible over-sexuality." Moreover, Hall had added new elements: "pseudo-scientific" language and assumptions.[3]

G. Stanley Hall and Sigmund Freud on Age

Hall titled chapter 7 of his study "Periodicity." In it he claimed that women's menstrual cycle was grounded in the biology and habits of higher primates. He situated his findings within the Social Darwinist paradigm that assessed the onset of menarche in relation to racial and cultural characteristics while framing such distinctions within falsely universal male pronoun use. American women's early menstruation (age fourteen versus fifteen and one-half for Europeans) was not based on race or climate, but rather on "nerves" and cultural differences. Analyzing the work of gynecologist George J. Engelmann, Hall included the following assessment: "The native American is more precocious than the American born of foreign parents, and only one year behind his average for southern climate. . . . This is due chiefly to mentality and nerve stimulation, which also hastens the development of the red and black races. Here, too, he finds the difference between the development of girls of the refined and those of the laboring classes to average less than half a year."[4] Chapter 7 continued with Hall's narrative of how menstruation was set within the framework of sociobiology, a narrative that was especially troubling to

Thomas (and many like her), who believed that women should be defined by something other than their supposed sexual characteristics. Hall combined the summary and analysis of physiological and anthropological studies of menstruation with more informal (one could almost say playful) comments on the reactions of individual women who had come to accept their sexual nature. For example: "During the first few days she is introverted to strange sensations which ideally are not painful, but deliciously and sometimes almost ecstatically charming. The volume of her emotional life is greatest, as is its depth and range. Then, actually though unconsciously, if entirely healthful, she is more attractive to man; . . . She feels her womanhood and glories in it like a goddess. . . . The flow itself has been a pleasure and the end of it is a slight shock. The instinct to conceal is a part of female coyness, which is directed only toward others, and she is most of all reserved toward any chosen one."[5]

In titling chapters 16 and 17 of *Adolescence*, Hall again employed the false universal to his discussions of aging. Chapter 16, "Intellectual Development and Education," focused almost exclusively on boys and used their lives as the defining framework for his analysis; chapter 17 simply addressed "Adolescent Girls and Their Education." While the former focused on broad stages of educational development, the latter was situated within sexual difference and repeated nineteenth-century American educator and doctor Edward Clarke's often-repeated concerns about the supposed threat posed to women's health by serious study. Hall devoted two different sections to the reportedly low birthrate among female college graduates, and the political nature of his writing is clear even in the abstract of sections offered at the beginning of the chapter: "Dangers of aping man-made education and of complacency—Arrest in the first stages of a movement just begun—Training for spinsterhood and self-support *versus* for maternity—Hints and general outlines of a higher education for girls based on their nature and needs and not on convention or the demands of feminists."[6]

Because his views blended so well with Hall's, it seems fitting, and hardly accidental, that Freud came to lecture at Clark University during Hall's tenure. While Freud's views on women's distinct sexuality, and their sense of inferiority toward men supposedly exemplified through "penis envy" and a "masculinity complex," are commonly recognized, not so well-known are his gendered distinctions in aging, which were tied also to his broader understanding of female inferiority. Freud argued that a thirty-year-old man was a different creature than a woman of the same age; he still had a life full of options ahead of him, but her domestic role had al-ready established her singular destiny.[7] In a letter attacking philosopher John Stuart Mill for his "'ridiculous'" views that found "'the suppression of women an analogy to that of negroes,'" Freud delineated his belief that women had little chance of maturing to a complex adult life compared to their male counterparts. "'I believe that all reforming action in law and education would break down in front of the fact that, long before the age at which a man can earn a position in society, Nature has determined woman's destiny through beauty, charm, and sweetness.... The position of women will surely be what it is: in youth an adored darling and in mature years a loved wife.'"⁸ Such views from men like Hall and Freud who established much of the intellectual parameters of modern psychology make it difficult to treat aging as a concept distinct from these sexually limited and biased views. Although their conceptions of what age has meant for men dictated the term's abstract or dictionary definition, this false universal has never held the same meanings for women. The roots of this false universal were laid nearly four centuries ago and have persisted until the present day.⁹

Concepts of Early Modern Aging

An emergent concept of individualism during the early modern period was central to the formation of aging as a male-restricted process. As the modern individual took on the qualities of independent adulthood, those qualities became associated only with male lives. They were situated within a falsely universal assumption that male maturation lay at the heart of learning, social relationships, economic standing, and political membership. Men were portrayed both as individuals and as exemplars of the qualities that broadly characterized human existence. Women were discussed in much more specialized ways: either in terms of their "natural" sexual functions, relationships, and domestic roles, or as exceptions in public, economic, or political roles. Although the English queen was the most powerful political figure in the nation, she did not symbolize women's political power (or generic political authority) while members of Parliament or magistrates illustrated men's general political standing. Yet the king both symbolized male political authority and mutually reinforced the standing of the father as head of the family, while the father in turn embodied the patriarchal authority on which the king's, as well as his own, leadership was grounded. There was never a discussion of the nature, training, and adult goals of two distinct sexes; rather, writings on early modern maturation were consistently grounded in a conflation of man and human in a large range of works directed to sons, apprentices, and students, combined with a smaller body of work that supported specialized training for daughters, female servants, and girls.

William Shakespeare illustrated this process of maturation in *As You*

Like It when he shifted his well-known portrayal of the world as a stage to the seven ages of man in a manner that conflated the identities of both sexes with the qualities of just one.[10] The passage be-gan with language that made it seem as if women were included, but Shakespeare quickly shifted to a single man as representative of human aging:

All the world's a stage,
And all the men and women, merely players;
They have their exits and their entrances,
And one man in his time plays many parts
His acts being seven ages (2.7.139–43).

Shakespeare not only used such terms as "schoolboy" and "soldier," which would have designated stages relevant only to men's lives, but he also modified gender-neutral terms to ensure that they referred only to males. The categories infant, lover, and pantaloon possessed no gender-restricted qualities, but Shakespeare incorporated such distinctions in his description of the aging process: the lover directed his attention to his "mistress" and the pantaloon lost his "big manly voice." The seven ages of man was a common medieval trope that was used until recently.[11] For instance, a 1964 text on child psychology, *The Seven Ages of Man*, noted that its title came from the famous line from Shakespeare's comedy *As You Like It.* [12] And the commentary on the comedy is instructive because scholars have paid considerable attention to the class limitations of Shakespeare's stages of life without commenting on its gender exclusion.[13]

Early modern training (whether in grammar schools and universities for the more privileged or through apprenticeships for those less so) was tied to a sense that intellectual growth came with physical maturity and that aging occurred only among men. Thus the maturing process and its ultimate product, the adult man, was imbued with qualities that women presumably lacked. *A Handkercher for Parents' Wet Eyes* (1630), a work mourning the death of a young man who was no longer a child but had not yet reached manhood, expressed such ideas. The author described an individual who died in the midst of acquiring the qualities of maturity that made adult men such admirable representatives of the human species: "arrived halfe way to the Solstice of his Age; Strong, active, well-shaped, well-graced, faire demeanoured, studious, of an honest and vertuous disposition, yeelding not onely the blossomes but the fruits of a good education."[14] Not even the best women were seen as holding, or able to attain, such qualities. These universal standards, which people understood as essential to defending the nation, sustaining its traditions, and understanding its intellectual principles and values, passed down from generation to generation through family, school, courts, and councils and were founded upon a male maturation process that was consistently characterized in falsely universal language.

In grappling with the manner in which men's aging process underlay a false universal of human experience in early modern Britain, one must grasp the essential link between the processes of male maturation, education, and citizenship. While not exploring the gender distinctions of early modern works, French historian Philippe Ariès, in his classic *Centuries of Childhood* (1962), pointed out the two most important facts underpinning this discussion. First, the early modern period was a crucial transition period during which the way children became adults changed; and, second, this transition was almost entirely restricted to men. Ariès made clear that "boys were the first specialized children," who experienced discrete stages of growth that corresponded with their attendance at public schools, and which were indicated by such changes in clothing as the transition from short to long pants.[15] Similarly, Ruth Kelso, in *The Doctrine for the Lady of the Renaissance* (1956), noted, when speaking of humanist education and the expanding educational opportunities of grammar schools and universities during the early modern period in England: "the free, bright world into which we step when it is a question of education for boys vanishes on consideration of girls, and we move in an atmosphere of doubt, timidity, fear, and niggardly concession."[16]

The falsely universal language and gender-restricted realities of mid-seventeenth-century education reform plans and general guides for appropriate education for children continually interchanged the terms "children," "scholars," and "boys" as if they had identical meanings, and "men" and "parents" as if they signified the same individuals. Often based on Puritan teaching, there was an underlying assumption in each of these works (and numerous others of a similar nature) that all children grew up to be men. Such writers offered suggestions for the best educational, moral, and political training to accompany a child's progression, in Puritan educator Hezekiah Woodward's language, as he "goeth along from infancy to Childhood, thence to youth, and so on till he brings his childe to a growne, yea, an old man, full of dayes."[17] John Milton promoted the relationship of scholars to men of lower social standing, and offered generous and positive assessments of the latter's place in English society. His schools sought to produce "brave men and worthy patriots" who would "scorn all their childish and ill-taught qualities."[18] While Milton did not mention mothers specifically (or women generally), one might assume that he believed some of male pupils' prior "childish" learning came from women as mothers and nurses.

In 1649, John Dury offered an important proposal for Puritan educational reform that he termed an "Advancement of Universal Learning."

Such expanded learning, he argued, was essential in a reformed common-wealth, and Dury stressed the importance of the teacher in molding citi-zens of this new society. "The School-Master in a well-ordered Common-wealth, is no lesse considerable than either the Minister or the Magistrate," he intoned.[19] While Dury gave girls a small role in this expansion of edu-cation beyond the privileged classes, he allowed women no place in the planning of such education. He stressed that "The Association should be only of free Persons; therefore we shall not consent to joyn with any (spe-cially with women) but such as are free to dispose of themselves."[20] Not only could women not become citizens, or individuals with political rights and responsibilities, but the gendered nature of Puritan educational re-form also prevented their education on the same terms as their brothers' and assumed that they should not speak independently for themselves or others. Male maturation was a closed circle; only those who had standing could enter it, and being within it prepared them for future independence.

Age, as I hope this brief essay has demonstrated, from its integra-tion into ideas underpinning the formation of the modern individual that emerged during the seventeenth century in England to its place in the concepts which formed a basis for modern psychology at the beginning of the twentieth century, has been consistently and perniciously tied to personal characteristics and stages of life deemed relevant only for men. Women's supposedly distinct qualities have denied them standing as in-dividuals and disallowed them from possessing the range of adult quali-ties attached to being human. We must consider the gendered distinctions attached to broad categories such as age and aging, and not employ them in ways that reify and reaffirm harmful and inaccurate differences between women and men.

NOTES

[1]G. Stanley Hall, *Adolescence, Its Psychology and Its Relation to Physiology, Anthropology, Sociology, Sex, Crime, Religion, and Education* (New York: D. Appleton, 1904).

[2]*The Educated Woman in America: Selected Writings of Catherine Beecher, Mar-garet Fuller, and M. Carey Thomas,* ed. Barbara M. Cross (New York: Teachers Col-lege Press, 1965), 159–60. On Michelet, see Jules Michelet, *Woman (La Femme), From the French of M. J. Michelet,* trans. J. W. Palmer (New York: Carleton, 1867). For a discussion of Michelet's importance as a historian, see Arthur Mitzman, *Michelet, Historian: Rebirth and Romanticism in Nineteenth-Century France* (New Haven, Conn.: Yale University Press, 1990); and for the most complete analysis of the impor-tance of blood to his views about women, see Thérèse Moreau, *Le sang de l'histoire: Michelet, l'historie at l'idée de la femme au xix⁴ siècle* (Paris: Flammarion, 1982).

[3]*Educated Woman in America,* 160.

⁴Hall, *Adolescence*, 1:478.

⁵Ibid., 1:492–93. Gail Bederman has offered a sophisticated analysis of Hall's contribution to the debates over manliness at the turn of the twentieth century and the ways in which they were racialized and tied to Darwinian values of civilization. See Gail Bederman, *Manliness and Civilization: A Cultural History of Gender and Race in the United States, 1880–1917* (Chicago: University of Chicago Press, 1995).

⁶Hall, *Adolescence*, 2:561. The arguments made here are so familiar as to need little elaboration, but it is important that the man who is revered as the founder of adolescent psychology held such restricted views of young girls. After outlining the limited numbers of births among the "best" Americans, Hall extended his analysis to a framework that in many ways aped Freud's *Civilization and Its Discontents*: "Excessive intellectualism insidiously instils the same aversion to 'brute maternity' as does luxury, overindulgence, or excessive devotion to society. Just as man must fight the battles of competition, and be ready to lay down his life for his country, so woman needs a heroism of her own to face the pain, danger, and work of bearing and rearing children, and whatever lowers the tone of her body, nerves, or *morale* so that she seeks to escape this function, merits the same kind of opprobrium which society metes out to the exempts who can not or who will not fight to save their country in time of need" (ibid., 2:609). See also Sigmund Freud, *Civilization and Its Discontents*, trans. James Strachey (New York: W. W. Norton, 1961), esp. 50.

⁷This discussion appeared in Freud's most famous statement on women, the essay "Femininity," in Sigmund Freud, *New Introductory Lectures on Psycho-Analysis and Other Works, Vol. XXII (1932–36) of the Standard Edition of the Complete Psychological Works of Sigmund Freud*, trans. James Strachey (London: Hogarth Press and the Institute of Psycho-Analysis, 1964), no. 33. While the entire essay is instructive for those unfamiliar with the explicit misogyny of Freud's works, perhaps most telling is his disempowerment of women in three select statements. For example, Freud argued that "the accomplishment of the aim of biology has been entrusted to the aggressiveness of men and has been made to some extent independent of women's consent" (131). Similarly, in a discussion of age, a man of thirty is "a youthful, somewhat unformed individual, whom we expect to make powerful use of the possibilities ... opened ... by analysis. A woman of the same, age, however, often frightens us by her psychical rigidity and unchangeability. ... There are no paths open to further development; ... as though, indeed, the difficult development to femininity had exhausted the possibilities of the person concerned" (134–35). Finally, in the concluding paragraph, it is hard not to be struck by the use of the word "may." "It is true that that [sexual function] influence extends very far; but we do not overlook the fact that an individual woman may be a human being in other respects as well" (135).

⁸Freud, quoted in Ernest Jones, *The Life and Work of Sigmund Freud: The Formative Years and the Great Discoveries, 1856–1900*, vol. 1 (New York: Basic Books, 1953), 1:176–77.

⁹I elaborate this argument further in Hilda L. Smith, *"All Men and Both Sexes": Gender and the False Universal in England, 1640–1832* (Pennsylvania State University Press, forthcoming).

[10]*A New Variorum Edition of Shakespeare: As You Like It*, ed. Richard Knowles, with a survey of criticism by Evelyn Joseph Mattern (New York: Modern Language Association of America, 1977), 139–43. Not only were the seven ages of man restricted to men—infant, school boy, lover, soldier, justice, pantaloon, and old age—but the qualities determining their nature and transition from one to the next were also clearly gendered.

[11]A useful overview of the concept of the ages of man during the medieval period can be found in John Anthony Burrow, *The Ages of Man: A Study in Medieval Writing and Thought* (Oxford: Clarendon Press, 1986), 1. The introduction to his work began: "As people grow up and grow old, they change. Individuals change in different ways, but there are held to be certain established norms in this matter" (3). Burrow, along with his predecessors, mingled man and a man, people and a person as if they had overlapping meanings.

[12]Robert R. Sears and S. Shirley Feldman, eds., *The Seven Ages of Man* (Los Altos, Calif.: W. Kaufmann, 1964), vi.

[13]*As You Like It*, 10. The latest Variorum edition of *As You Like It* made clear the antecedents for the idea that human life may be divided into stages and included various authors' concerns over the inclusiveness and accuracy of Shakespeare's stages. Questions were raised about why there were no toys for infancy and "no playmates in boyhood; no hawking or jousting in youth," but no one questioned the conflation of "human life" with male maturation. See ibid., 131–34.

[14]J. C., *A Handkercher for Parents' Wet Eyes* (London: Printed by E[liz] A[llde] for M. Sparkes, 1630), 3.

[15]Philippe Ariès, *Centuries of Childhood: A Social History of Family Life*, trans. Robert Baldick (New York: Vintage, 1962), 58.

[16]Ruth Kelso, *The Doctrine for the Lady of the Renaissance* (1956; reprint, Urbana: University of Illinois Press, 1978), 58–77, quotation on 48.

[17]Hezekiah Woodward, *A Childes Patrimony Laid Out Upon the Good Culture of Tilling over His Whole Man* (London: J. Legatt, 1640). In his work on old age, *Senescence: The Last Half of Life* (New York: D. Appleton, 1922), Hall devoted more space to anecdotal materials about aging in individual women, but still established norms for old age, and proper actions to be taken by those entering senescence, in the framework of men's lives. For example, "If the man who has lived solely for sport is ill prepared to meet old age, he who has lived solely for business is still less so. He has had no time to cultivate his more human tastes but has developed his potentialities in only one direction and when superannuation comes his soul is bankrupt" (137).

[18]John Milton, *Of Education, To Master Samuel Hartlib* (London: Thomas Underhill, 1641), 3–5.

[19]John Dury, *The Reformed School* (London: Printed by R. D. for Richard Wodnothe, 1649), 3–5.

[20]Ibid., 14.

Proc. Natl. Acad. Sci. USA
Vol. 95, pp. 1336–1339, February 1998
Anthropology

Grandmothering, menopause, and the evolution of human life histories

K. HAWKES*†, J. F. O'CONNELL*, N. G. BLURTON JONES‡, H. ALVAREZ*, AND E. L. CHARNOV§

Departments of *Anthropology and §Biology, University of Utah, Salt Lake City, UT 84112; and ‡Departments of Psychiatry and Anthropology and the Graduate School of Education, University of California, Los Angeles, CA 90024

Communicated by Sarah Blaffer Hrdy, University of California, Davis, CA, November 18, 1997 (received for review July 24, 1997)

ABSTRACT   Long postmenopausal lifespans distinguish humans from all other primates. This pattern may have evolved with mother–child food sharing, a practice that allowed aging females to enhance their daughters' fertility, thereby increasing selection against senescence. Combined with Charnov's dimensionless assembly rules for mammalian life histories, this hypothesis also accounts for our late maturity, small size at weaning, and high fertility. It has implications for past human habitat choice and social organization and for ideas about the importance of extended learning and paternal provisioning in human evolution.

Mother–child food sharing occurs among many primates (1), but only human mothers provide a substantial fraction of their weaned children's diets. This allows mothers to use resources that they themselves can gather at high rates but that their children cannot. Among some hunter–gatherers, for example, deeply buried tubers are year-round staples (2, 3). Young children cannot extract them efficiently (4, 5), but their mothers do so well enough to earn a surplus that can support more than one child. Postmenopausal women earn the same high rates (2). With no young children of their own, they help feed their daughters' and nieces' offspring. This help is especially important for the nutritional welfare of weaned children when their mothers forage less at the arrival of a newborn (3).

This division of labor suggests a solution to the riddle of menopause in humans. Other apes live no longer than ~50 years (6). That is, they become frail with age so that all physiological systems, including fertility, fail in tandem. This threshold defines maximum lifespan, a parameter that can be used to estimate other life history averages (7, 8) (see note 1 to Table 1). In humans, maximum lifespan is nearly 100 years, but fertility in women universally ends in approximately half that time, well in advance of other aspects of physiological frailty (9). The question is how natural selection came to favor this distinctly human "postreproductive" component of life history.

Many have assumed that the answer lies in Williams' (10) suggestion that early termination of fertility would likely evolve when extended maternal care became crucial to offspring survival. Aging mothers who stopped being fertile and devoted their reproductive effort to insuring the survival of children already born would leave more descendants than those who continued risky pregnancies with babies unlikely to survive the mother's death.

The "stopping early" hypothesis continues to stimulate useful work (11–15), but there are good reasons to be skeptical of it. Other primates among whom extended maternal care is vital fail to show the predicted early end to fertility. In chimpanzees, for example, available data indicate low survival

probabilities for late-borns (16–17), yet a substantial fraction of aging females still continue to produce them (18). In fact, human reproduction does not end early in comparison with other apes. Our reproductive spans are at least as long as those of chimpanzees. The striking difference between us and the other great apes lies in the low adult mortalities that give us long average lifespans after menopause. This characteristic is not restricted to populations in which age-specific mortalities have declined recently with scientific medical advances. Age structure among hunter–gatherers with no access to Western pharmaceuticals shows distinctively low adult mortalities compared with other apes (12, 19). Schultz's (20) often reprinted figure makes the point (Fig. 1) (see also ref. 11). Postmenopausal longevity, not early termination of fertility, appears to be the derived characteristic of our species.

There are two evolutionary explanations for aging: mutation–selection balance and inter-temporal tradeoffs in reproductive effort (reviewed in ref. 21). Because the risks of mortality accumulate over time, there are fewer individuals in older cohorts for selection to affect. So the force of selection declines with age (22). Mutation–selection balance is reached when the force of selection is no greater than the mutation rate. Deleterious effects on adaptive performance thus accumulate at later ages. Inter-temporal tradeoffs lead to senescence because genes have multiple effects. The same genes can affect fitness in different ways at different stages in an individual's life history. Genes that have positive effects at younger ages may be favored even though they have negative effects later in life. Those that have positive effects late in life will be disfavored if they have negative early effects. Senescence results from this antagonistic pleiotropy (10).

Grandmothering could slow aging by either means. It would strengthen selection against late-acting deleterious mutations by increasing the contribution to descendant gene pools of longer-lived females through the increased reproductive success of their daughters. It would also change the tradeoffs between opposing effects expressed at different ages. Slower senescence generally comes at the cost of reduced fertility at younger ages (23). If ape adult mortalities are in equilibrium on this tradeoff, then apes age early by human standards because mutations that would increase adaptive performance at later ages are continually removed by the reductions those mutations impose on fertility earlier in life. Regular mother–child food sharing could perturb that equilibrium by increasing the payoffs for late somatic performance as vigorous senior women earned more descendants by feeding grandchildren. Increased "somatic effort" that slowed aging would come at the cost of lower "reproductive effort" at younger ages. But the contributions of senior females would increase the reproductive success of childbearers more than enough to offset the reduced expenditure of the childbearers themselves. Continued childbearing, on the other hand, which would conflict with grandmothering, would be no more favored than in other ape

---

Abbreviation: CM, Charnov's model.
†To whom reprint requests should be addressed.

Table 1. Average values for selected life history variables

1	Average adult lifespan, $1/M^*$	Age at maturity[†]	Age at weaning[‡]	α[§]	αM	Ratio of weaning weight to adult weight,[¶] δ	Daughters per year,[ǁ] b	αb
Orangutans	17.9	14.3	6.0	8.3	0.46	0.28	0.063	0.52
Gorillas	13.9	9.3	3.0	6.3	0.45	0.21	0.126	0.79
Chimpanzees	17.9	13.0	4.8	8.2	0.46	0.27	0.087	0.70
Humans	32.9	17.3	2.8	14.5	0.44	0.21	0.142	2.05

*If mortality is Gompertz, maximum lifespan increases with the double logrithm of sample size, making it nearly independent of sample size for samples on the order of 10^3 or more (8). Maximum lifespan (T_{max}) can then be used to estimate average adult mortality (M), the inverse of which is average adult life span, by the method described in Charnov (see legend to figure 5.6, ref. 24) that we follow here: $1/M = 0.47T_{max} - 0.1$. Values for orangutans: Leighton *et al.* (29); gorillas: Stewart *et al.* (30); chimpanzees: Nishida *et al.* (31). The human value is estimated from Howell's (19) oldest observed !Kung individual, age 88, and Hill and Hurtado's (12) oldest observed (forest-living) Ache individual, age 77.

[†]Age at first birth minus gestation. Orangutans: Leighton *et al.* (29); gorillas: Stewart *et al.* (30); chimpanzees: the mean of the means from Wallis (32) for Gombe, Nishida *et al.* (31) for Mahale, and Sugiyama (33) for Bossou; humans: the mean of the mode for !Kung in Howell (19) and Ache in Hill and Hurtado (12).

[‡]Orangutans: Galdikas and Wood (34); gorillas: Stewart *et al.* (30); chimpanzees: the mean of the estimate from Goodall (16) for Gombe and from Nishida *et al.* (31) for Mahale; humans: the mean of the median for !Kung in Howell (19) and Ache in Hill and Hurtado (12).

[§]Defined as the period of independent growth, from weaning to maturity.

[¶]Data from Lee *et al.* (35) for the great apes. Maternal size for orangutans is estimated to be 40 kg, for gorillas 93 kg, and for chimpanzees 40 kg. In that data set, δ for humans is 0.16 with maternal size at 55 kg (the upper end of the range for modern foragers who are generally smaller than either contemporary nonforagers or pre-Mesolithic moderns). We use the mean of the !Kung (19) (who are at the lower end of the size range for modern foragers) and the Ache (12) (who are at the upper end) to represent humans.

[ǁ]Great ape data from Galdikas and Wood (34), who reappraise birth spacing in all species in the same way. We use medians calculated therein (for closed intervals) plus 2 months to approximate the mean interval, then divide by 2 to get the rate in daughters. Galdikas and Wood use the Gainj, a population of horticulturalists in highland Papua New Guinea, to represent humans for which $b = 0.132$. We use the mean of the !Kung (19) and the Ache (12).

species. Aging in all aspects of physiology, except fertility, would be slowed as a result.

Charnov's (7, 24, 25) dimensionless approach to life histories provides a framework for developing and testing this argu-

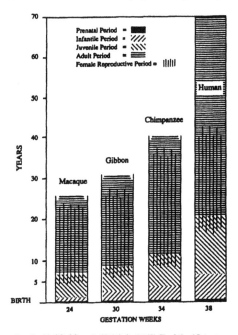

FIG. 1. Modified from A. H. Schultz (1969) *The Life of Primates* (20), page 149.

ment. His "assembly rules" for mammalian life histories seem quite robust. The general fit of empirical patterns to predictions [since confirmed on other, larger data sets (26)] suggests that Charnov's model (CM) identifies key tradeoffs that shape mammalian life histories. Several extensions of the basic model (24, 27) are discussed elsewhere but do not play a role in the comparisons made here.

In CM, growth is comprised of two periods: (*i*) conception to independence (weaning) and (*ii*) independence to maturity. At maturity, production previously allocated to growth is redirected to offspring. Growth rates are approximately an allometric function of body mass (W) and a characteristic "production coefficient" (A); individual production rates take the form $dW/dt = AW^c$, where the exponent c is ≈ 0.75. Adult size at maturity ($W\alpha$) and production available for offspring both vary directly with A, which is characteristically low in primates compared with other mammals (28) and even lower in humans (12).

CM assumes that, given adult mortalities, selection sets α (the period of independent growth) according to the tradeoff between the benefits of growing longer vs. reproducing sooner. Because production is a function of maternal size, it generally increases with age of maturity. Time available to use those gains depends on the instantaneous adult mortality rate (M). As that rate falls (and average adult lifespans increase), selection favors delayed maturity to reap the benefits of larger size. α and M thus vary widely but inversely. Their product (αM) is approximately invariant.

If human longevity has been extended by grandmothering, then age at maturity should be delayed accordingly. Humans reach maturity at a relatively late age compared with other large bodied primates (Table 1). CM extracts previously unappreciated information from the difference. αM for humans is similar to that of other apes, implying that α is adjusted to whole lifespan. The extreme delay in maturity for humans, another characteristic human feature evident in the Schultz diagram (Fig. 1), indicates that gains from growing longer before reproducing pay off throughout adulthood, including both childbearing and grandmothering years.

CM finds that, for a large sample of mammals (and for primates separately), the ratio of size at independence to adult size ($W_0/W\alpha = \delta$) is approximately constant (see figure 5.4 in

161

ref. 24). Weaning size scales approximately isometrically with adult size whereas the production allometry is less steep. Thus, the size of weanlings increases more rapidly with maternal size than does the production the mother can put into them. Consequently, annual fecundity (b) declines as age at maturity (α) increases. Larger mothers produce larger but fewer babies; αb is another approximate invariant.

If the grandmothering hypothesis is correct, childbearing women should produce babies faster than otherwise expected because of grandmothers' contribution to production. Grandmothers might affect the growth of infants in two ways: (*i*) by feeding nursing mothers and infants, thus accelerating the growth of infants, who then reach size of independence more quickly and (*ii*) by supplying food to weanlings, thus allowing infants to be weaned earlier. Here, we consider only the second alternative. If humans wean infants early, δ should be relatively low. Values in Table 1 show it to be as low as any of the great apes.

Grandmother's contribution must increase daughters' annual fecundity. Table 1 includes estimates of b for four modern hominoid species. As expected, interbirth intervals are shortest (b is highest) for humans. Because b scales inversely with α, the αb value is of special interest. αb for humans is at least double that of the other great apes. The grandmother hypothesis predicts just such a result. αb should be high because it incorporates the production of both mothers and grandmothers. The production of the whole lifespan is concentrated in the childbearing years.

Combined with CM, the grandmother hypothesis can account for long lifespans after menopause, late age at maturity, early weaning, and high fertility. Other hypotheses have been offered to account for each of these distinctive features of human life history individually (36, 37), but all could be systematic adjustments on the primate pattern that follow from grandmothering. Longstanding ideas about human evolution can be profitably reviewed in this light.

The notion that childhood has been extended to allow the development of larger brains and the learning required of competent human adults has long been a central tenet of paleoanthropology, even though a broad perspective on life history variation does not favor it (38). It is adult lifespans that predict age at maturity, not only in mammals but in other classes of vertebrates as well (24). Very late ages of maturity for body size occur in many species with small brains and limited learning. Among nonhuman primates, juvenile periods are much longer than needed to learn the ecological skills of adulthood (39). Studies of modern hunter–gatherers indicate wide variation in the ages at which children begin to forage, even in broadly similar ecological circumstances (40). There is no indication that large differences in time spent "practicing" affect adult performance (41). If longer lifespans favor later maturity as the advantages for growing longer before reproducing outweigh the cost of delay, then that "waiting time" can be allocated in ways that enhance the child's fitness. Among primates like us, these could include substantial learning. This argument draws the causal arrow from long childhood to learning, not the other way around (39).

In emphasizing the provisioning role of women, the grandmother hypothesis also runs counter to the idea that long childhoods and relatively high fertility evolved as results of men's big game hunting (37, 42). Elsewhere we have challenged this argument on two grounds, one pointing to the relative unreliability of big game hunting as a means of supporting mates and offspring (43, 44), the other to the likelihood that men have more to gain from mating than from parenting effort (45, 46). The grandmother hypothesis not only avoids problematic assumptions about men's foraging goals but in addition shows several distinctive aspects of human life history to be systematic variations on the primate pattern.

Inferences about community organization among ancestral hominids also are challenged. Apparent similarities in local group composition between humans and the other African apes, especially chimpanzees, have supported arguments about likely patterns of natal dispersal among ancestral hominids. At maturity, other African ape females, unlike females in most monkey species, usually leave the social unit of their birth to join another (47). Among humans, postmarital residence is usually patrilocal (48). The bias toward female natal dispersal in living hominoids suggested that the pattern might characterize past members of the African ape clade as well, including all hominids (47, 49–51).

The grandmother hypothesis directs attention to likely ecological pressures for variation. The use of high return resources that young juveniles cannot handle favors mothers and daughters remaining together. As daughters grow, they acquire the strength and skill needed to help feed their younger siblings (5, 41). When daughters mature, the assistance of aging mothers continues to enhance the benefits of proximity (3).

Cross-cultural tabulations show that there is variation in the expected direction; patrilocality is less frequent among non-equestrian, nonfishing-dependent hunter–gatherers than in the *Ethnographic Atlas* sample as a whole (56% vs. 71%) (52, 53). Among hunter—gatherers, the tendency toward matrilocality increases with women's relative contribution to subsistence and (separately) with increased dependence on gathering (48).

Although modern humans might be expected to display more variation in social organization with local ecology than nonhuman primates, other apes also show variation both within and among populations. Chimpanzee females often migrate at maturity but not always (16, 54). In one community, paternity tests showed that more than half of the infants sampled were not fathered by resident males (55), revising estimates of inbreeding costs to any nondispersing females and also raising questions about the frequency of female dispersal in that population. Sometimes it is males that disperse (56). In captivity, male chimpanzees readily construct and manipulate alliances with unrelated strangers (57), suggesting an evolutionary history that favored those capacities.

Senior females could affect the fertility of their sons' mates through food sharing as well as that of their daughters. But the grandmother hypothesis, combined with the assembly rules of CM and the variation in ape life histories highlighted here, favors co-residence between older mothers and their daughters. Coincident foraging patterns between mother and maturing daughter, with increasing benefits to older daughters helping junior siblings, would guide this transition. Moreover, any effects on the production of descendants through a son's mate would be diluted by uncertain paternity.

The important question of male life histories is left unexplained here. Increased selection against senescence in women would surely have correlated effects on men, but selection pressures on male life histories would necessarily differ (an issue discussed further in ref. 3, pp. 573–574).

We expect routine mother–child provisioning to have been favored initially under ecological conditions that promoted access to resources yielding high return rates to adults but not to young juveniles. This pattern would allow expansion into previously unoccupied habitats and relax density-dependent effects on juvenile mortality (7, 12, 24), thereby stimulating sharp increases in local population densities. Both effects should be evident archaeologically. The life history changes initiated by grandmothering should be marked by evidence for later age at maturity and increased postmenopausal lifespan.

Available archaeological and paleontological data suggest at least three possible dates for the evolution of this distinctively human set of behavioral and life history traits. The initial appearance of *Homo erectus* (more narrowly *ergaster*) 1.8 million years ago (58) is associated with delayed maturity relative to earlier hominids (59) and wide dispersal into previously unoccupied habitats outside Africa (60). Early archaic *sapiens* [≤600,000 years ago (61)] spread to higher latitudes (62) and may have been first to show the specific pattern of delayed maturity typical of modern humans (63). Alternatively, the modern pattern may not have appeared until ~50,000 years ago, coincident with the dispersal of anatomically modern *sapiens*, who may have enjoyed unprecedented ecological and competitive success because they had what other, earlier hominids lacked (64): long postmenopausal lifespans and the associated population dynamics underwritten by grandmothers.

We thank C. van Schaik, D. Sellen, R. Foley, and J. Fleagle for useful advice and Ursula Hanly for redrafting the figure.

1. Feistner, A. T. C. & McGrew, W. C. (1989) in *Perspectives in Primate Biology*, eds. Seth, P. K. & Seth, S. (Today and Tomorrow's Printers and Publishers, New Dehli, India), Vol. 3, pp. 21–36.
2. Hawkes, K., O'Connell, J. F. & Blurton Jones, N. G. (1989) in *Comparative Socioecology of Mammals and Man*, eds. Standen, V. & Foley, R. (Blackwell, London), pp. 341–366.
3. Hawkes, K., O'Connell, J. F. & Blurton Jones, N. G. (1997) *Curr. Anthropol.* 38, 551–577.
4. Blurton Jones, N. G., Hawkes, K. & O'Connell, J. F. (1989) in *Comparative Socioecology of Mammals and Man*, eds. Standen, V. & Foley, R. (Blackwell, London), pp. 365–390.
5. Hawkes, K., O'Connell, J. F. & Blurton Jones, N. G. (1995) *Curr. Anthropol.* 36, 688–700.
6. Harvey, P., Martin, R. & Clutton Brock, T. H. (1987) in *Primate Societies*, eds. Smuts, B., Cheney, D., Seyfarth, R., Wrangham, R. & Struhsaker, T. (Univ. of Chicago, Chicago), pp. 181–196.
7. Charnov, E. L. (1991) *Proc. Natl. Acad. Sci. USA* 88, 1134–1137.
8. Beverton, R. J. H. & Holt, S. J. (1959) in *CIBA Foundation Colloquia in Aging. V. The Lifespan of Animals* (Churchill, London), pp. 142–177.
9. Pavelka, M. & Fedigan, L. (1991) *Yearbook Physical Anthropol.* 34, 13–38.
10. Williams, G. (1957) *Evolution* 11, 398–411.
11. Hill, K. & Hurtado, A. M. (1991) *Hum. Nat.* 2, 313–350.
12. Hill, K. & Hurtado, A. M. (1996) *Ache Life History: The Ecology and Demography of a Foraging People* (Aldine de Gruyter, Hawthorne, NY).
13. Rogers, A. (1993) *Evol. Ecol.* 7, 406–420.
14. Peccei, J. S. (1995) *Ethol. Sociobiol.* 16, 425–449.
15. Turke, P. W. (1997) *Evol. Hum. Behav.* 18, 3–14.
16. Goodall, J. (1986) *The Chimpanzees of Gombe: Patterns of Behavior* (Harvard Univ. Press, Cambridge, MA).
17. Goodall, J. (1989) in *Understanding Chimpanzees*, eds. Heltne, P. & Marquardt, L. (Harvard Univ. Press, Cambridge, MA), pp. 2–21.
18. Caro, T. M., Sellen, D. W., Parish, A., Frank, R., Brown, D. M., Voland, E. & Borgerhoff Mulder, M. (1995) *Int. J. Prim* 16, 205–220.
19. Howell, N. (1979) *Demography of the Dobe !Kung* (Academic, New York).
20. Schultz, A. H. (1969) *The Life of Primates.* (Universe Books, New York).
21. Partridge, L. & Barton, N. H. (1993) *Nature (London)* 362, 305–311.
22. Medawar, P. B. (1952) *An Unsolved Problem of Biology* (H. K. Lewis, London).
23. Kirkwood, T. B. L. & Rose, M. R. (1991) *Phil. Trans. R. Soc. London B* 332, 15–34.
24. Charnov, E. L. (1993) *Life History Invariants: Some Explorations of Symmetry in Evolutionary Ecology* (Oxford Univ. Press, Oxford).
25. Charnov, E. L. & Berrigan, D. (1991) *Phil. Trans. R. Soc. London B* 33, 241–248.
26. Purvis, A. & Harvey, P. H. (1995) *J. Zool.* 237, 259–283.
27. Kozlowski, J. & Weiner, J. (1997) *Am. Nat.* 149, 352–380.
28. Charnov, E. L. & Berrigan, D. (1993) *Evol. Anthropol.* 1, 191–194.
29. Leighton, M., Seal, U. S., Soemarna, K., Ajisasmito, Wijaya, M., Mitra Setia, T., Shapiro, G., Perkins, L., Traylor-Holzer, K. & Tilson, R. (1995) in *The Neglected Ape*, eds. Nadler, R. D., Galdikas, B. F. M., Sheeran, L. K. & Rosen, N. (Plenum, New York), pp. 97–107.
30. Stewart, K. J., Harcourt, A. H. & Watts, D. P. (1988) in *Natural Human Fertility: Social and Biological Determinants*, eds. Diggory, P., Potts, M. & Teper, S. (MacMillian, New York), pp. 22–38.
31. Nishida, T., Takasaki, H. & Takahata, Y. (1990) in *The Chimpanzees of the Mahale Mountains: Sexual and Life History Strategies*, ed. Nishida, T. (Univ. Tokyo Press, Tokyo), pp. 63–97.
32. Wallis, J. (1997) *J. Reprod. Fertil.* 109, 297–307.
33. Sugiyama, Y. (1994) *Am. J. Primatol.* 32, 311–318.
34. Galdikas, B. & Wood, J. (1990) *Am. J. Phys. Anthropol.* 83, 185–191.
35. Lee, P. C., Majluf, P. & Gordon, I. J. (1991) *J. Zool.* 225, 99–114.
36. Smith, H. & Tomkins, R. L. (1995) *Annu. Rev. Anthropol.* 24, 257–279.
37. Hill, K. (1993) *Evol. Anthropol.* 2, 78–88.
38. Austad, S. N. & Fischer, K. E. (1992) *Am. J. Prim.* 28, 251–261.
39. Janson, C. & van Schaik, C. (1993) in *Juvenile Primates: Life History, Development, and Behavior*, eds. Pereira, M. & Fairbanks, L. (Oxford Univ. Press, Oxford), pp. 57–76.
40. Blurton Jones, N. G., Hawkes, K. & Draper, P. (1994) *J. Anthropol. Res.* 50, 217–248.
41. Blurton Jones, N. G., Hawkes, K. & O'Connell, J. F. (1997) in *Uniting Psychology and Biology: Integrative Perspectives on Human Development*, eds. Segal, N., Weisfeld, G. E. & Weisfeld, C. C. (American Psychological Association, Washington, D. C.), pp. 279–313.
42. Washburn, S. & Lancaster, C. (1968) in *Man the Hunter*, eds. Lee, R. & DeVore, I. (Aldine, Chicago), pp. 293–303.
43. Hawkes, K. (1990) in *Risk and Uncertainty In Tribal and Peasant Economies*, ed. Cashdan, E. (Westview Press, Boulder, CO), pp. 145–166.
44. Hawkes, K., O'Connell, J. F. & Blurton Jones, N. G. (1991) *Phil. Trans. R. Soc. London B* 334, 243–251.
45. Hawkes, K. (1993) *Curr. Anthropol.* 34, 341–361.
46. Hawkes, K., Rogers, A. R. & Charnov, E. L. (1995) *Evol. Ecol.* 9, 662–677.
47. Wrangham, R. W. (1987) in *The Evolution of Human Behavior: Primate Models*, ed. Kinzey, W. (SUNY Press, Albany, NY), pp. 51–71.
48. Ember, C. (1978) *Ethnology* 17, 439–448.
49. Foley, R. & P. Lee (1989) *Science* 243, 901–906.
50. Ghiglieri, M. (1987) *J. Hum. Evol.* 16, 319–358.
51. Rodseth, L., Wrangham, R., Harrigan, A. & Smuts, B. (1991) *Curr. Anthropol.* 32, 221–254.
52. Ember, C. (1975) *Behav. Sci. Res.* 3, 199–227.
53. Murdock, G. P. (1967) *The Ethnographic Atlas* (Univ. Pittsburg Press, Pittsburg).
54. Pusey, A., Williams, J. & Goodall, J. (1997) *Science* 277, 828–831.
55. Gagneux, P., Woodruff, D. S. & Boesch, C. (1997) *Nature (London)* 387, 358–359.
56. Sugiyama, Y. & Koman, J. (1979) *Primates* 20, 323–339.
57. de Waal, F. (1982) *Chimpanzee Politics: Power and Sex Among the Apes* (Harper and Row, New York).
58. Feibel, C. S., Brown, F. H. & MacDougal, I. (1989) *Am. J. Phys. Anthropol.* 78, 595–622.
59. Walker, A. & R. Leakey (1993) *The Nariokotome Homo erectus Skeleton*, (Harvard Univ. Press, Cambridge, MA).
60. Swisher, C. C., Curtis, G. H., Jacob, T., Getty, A. G., Suprijo, A. & Widiasmoro (1994) *Science* 263, 1118–1121.
61. Clark, J. D., Asfaw, B., Assefa, G., Harris, J. W. K., Kurashina, H., Walter, R. C., White, T. D. & Williams, M. A. J. (1994) *Nature (London)* 307, 423–428.
62. Klein, R. G. (1989) *The Human Career: Human Biological and Cultural Origins*, (Univ. Chicago Press, Chicago).
63. Tompkins, R. L. (1996) *Am. J. Phys. Anthropol.* 99, 103–116.
64. Trinkaus, E. & Tompkins, R. L. (1990) in *Primate Life History and Evolution, Monographs in Primatology 14*, ed. DeRousseau, C. J. (Wiley-Liss, New York), pp. 153–180.

Modernization and Aging in the Third and Fourth World: Views from the Rural Hinterland in Nepal

MELVYN C. GOLDSTEIN and CYNTHIA M. BEALL

Introduction

THE NUMBER OF AGED PEOPLE in Third World countries is increasing dramatically. In 1970, 190 million people on this planet were 65 years old or more. Fifty-five percent (105 million) resided in developed countries (DCs) and 45% (85 million) in less developed countries (LDCs). By the year 2000, as a result of continued population growth and improvements in health care, this proportion will change. There will then be about 396 million persons 65 years of age or older (a nearly 200% increase), of whom 166 million (42%) will reside in DCs and 230 million (58%) in LDCs. Moreover, by 2000, in the short span of 30 years, South Asia and East Asia will account for about one-fourth (100 million) of the world's aged, and as many elderly people will live there as now exist in the entire developed world (Hauser 1976). This pattern of population increase will affect Nepal as well. Based on current growth rates, by the year 2000, Nepal will contain over 1 million persons aged 65 or over out of a total population of about 18 million.

The prevalent view is that aging in rural, traditional societies is not a problem since the aged in such societies are viewed as possessing high status. The aged are said to become problematic only as modernization disrupts family and community supports and the esteem and respect characteristic of traditional societies. This widely held viewpoint is exemplified by the theory of modernization and aging proposed by Cowgill and Holmes (1972) and Cowgill (1974). This theory defines modernization and its consequences for the elderly in the following terms:

Modernization is the transformation of a total society from a relatively rural way of life based on animate power, limited technology, relatively undifferentiated institutions, parochial and traditional outlook and values, toward a predominately urban way of life based on inanimate sources of power, highly developed scientific technology, highly differentiated institutions matched by segmented individual roles, and a cosmopolitan outlook which emphasizes efficiency and progress. [Cowgill 1974:127]

Melvyn C. Goldstein is Professor and Chairman and Cynthia M. Beall is Assistant Professor, Department of Anthropology, Case Western Reserve University, Cleveland, Ohio. This paper is based on research supported by funding from a Case Western Reserve University Biomedical Research Fund award. We thank the people of Pemagyang and Norbugyang for their hospitality and cooperation.

... the introduction of modern health technology, modern economic technology, urbanization and rising levels of education . . . tend to have a depressing effect on the status of the aged in society (140) . . . the theory holds that with increasing modernization the status of older people declines. [ibid.:124]

This theory predicts that poor, preindustrial countries like Nepal need concern themselves little with problems of the elderly. Ninety-six percent of Nepal's population are rural agriculturalists, and the impact of health, education, and urbanization has been small, particularly in the hills and mountains where most of the population lives. Economic production and distribution in the hills is still based entirely on animal and human muscle power, and there are virtually no roads. Nepal is classified as a part of the Fourth World, the group of poorest and least developed nations among the LDCs. Thus, despite the increases in the number of elderly projected for a country such as Nepal, given the absence of modernization there, it would be reasonable to assume that the elderly will be absorbed in the traditional manner.

We suggest that this view of the process of aging and the state of the aged in Third and Fourth World countries is questionable and requires clarification. First, it is not clear precisely what is meant by "high status." Cowgill and Holmes (1972) do not define the concept explicitly, although they use it mainly to refer to high prestige and social standing. As we shall indicate below, the high-prestige component of "status" is only one of several important factors that must be considered if we are to understand the manner in which the elderly live cross-culturally. Second, the contemporary world is so intertwined that changes in the areas adjoining the backward and rural areas of Third and Fourth World countries like Nepal can have important effects on the situation and status of the elderly in these rural areas. The indirect impact of modernization and change on the situation of the elderly can be substantial even in the most remote and unmodernized areas. Third, this viewpoint assumes a high status for the elderly in traditional societies, an assumption that is not documented and that may be a misleading overgeneralization.

Although there is an amazing paucity of empirical data on the state of the elderly in traditional societies, Simmons (1945) discusses preindustrial societies in which the status of the elderly does not appear to be particularly high. Moreover, significant intracultural differences such as class, ethni-

Human Organization, Vol. 40, No. 1, 1981
Copyright © 1981 by the Society for Applied Anthropology
0018-7259/81/040048-08$1.30/1

ity, and caste are present in traditional peasant societies. Bengtson et al. (1975:689) also have critiqued the
modernization and aging theory discussed above as suffering "from a romanticized or naive portrayal of eldership
in pre-industrial societies." While this appraisal has merit, the
data they present in support of it may be inappropriate. Bengtson et al. cite Harlan's (1968) article on aging in India. In this
paper, Harlan attacks the idea that the status of the elderly was
or is higher in preindustrial societies than in urban-industrial
areas and that the contemporary problems of the aged are consequences of urbanism and industrialism. He argues that while
each of the villages he mentioned is a "pre-industrial agricultural community, little affected by urbanization," the elderly
occupy precarious positions (ibid.:475). He describes Burail,
the key village in his study, as follows:

The village is on a low hill near the center of its partially irrigated
fields. It has no electricity, telephone, or sanitary system; water for
household use is obtained by rope and bucket from deep wells. A
rough dirt road leads out to an asphalt road one-half mile away, and
hence to the fringes of the city at a distance of two miles more. [470]

Although Harlan suggests that there is little reason to think
that the situation in Burail was different when he studied it
than it was several generations earlier, the India he studied is
hardly a traditional preindustrial society. India makes its own
airplanes, automobiles, textiles, televisions, etc.; has a nationwide system of air, rail, and road communication; and has
governmental programs throughout the country, especially in
the area he studied. Furthermore, Burail's location a few
kilometers from a major city makes it untypical of even rural
India villages. We suggest, therefore, that Harlan's data may
well exemplify not "traditional" society as he and Bengtson
argue, but a type of village society that has remained rural and
nonmodernized by the normal indices of modernization, yet
has been seriously affected by modernization around it.

We suggest also that many, or most, areas such as these
would be better termed "impacted" communities, i.e., communities that have been indirectly affected by modernization
and the world economic system. Thus, the status of the elderly
in traditional societies is confused by the common, but unfounded, equation of the poor, backward rural communities
of the Third and Fourth World with traditional societies.
Absence of overt indices of modernization does not imply
absence of impact.

In this paper we will explore this indirect impact of change
on the status of the elderly in one of the world's most traditional and nonmodernized societies, the Hindu Kingdom of
Nepal. It will focus specifically on a community of Sherpas living in the rugged mountain terrain of central Nepal.

The Sherpas of Nepal

Sherpa society presents an excellent setting to examine aging
and modernization. Sherpas are the Tibetan-speaking, Buddhist population of mountaineering and trekking fame who in-
habit northern areas in east and central Nepal. Sherpas trace
their ancestry to Tibetan groups that emigrated about 450
years ago from eastern Tibet to the Solu-Khumbu region of
eastern Nepal. The Sherpas of Helambu, in turn, claim descent
from Solu-Khumbu.

Helambu, or Yelmu, as it is known in Tibetan, is an area

situated about two days' walk northeast of Kathmandu, the
capital of Nepal. It contains Sherpa villages at the higher eleva-
tions (1829-2896 m) and Tamang and Brahman-Chetri villages
at the lower altitudes. This pilot study was conducted over a
six-week period during July through August, 1979, in the con-
tiguous villages of Norbugyang and Pemagyang (both pseud-
onyms) situated at an altitude of about 2621 m. These two
villages together consisted of 75 households of Sherpas containing 373 persons, of whom 257 were in residence at the time
of the study.

This area seemed appropriate for several reasons. First, it
was rural and agricultural. Second, despite this, it has been
suggested (Fürer-Haimendorf 1979; Ortner 1978) that elderly
Sherpas hold low status. Third, like all Tibetans, they have a
precise and universally known age-reckoning system which is
directly translatable into Western calendar years.

In this area agriculture is still the basic subsistence strategy
and cultivation is done by hand in the traditional way. The
area has no roads, telephones, or electricity, although a piped
water system to several public taps has been recently established. There are no Western-type health facilities, and the
presence of a Nepali-language primary school is a recent
phenomenon. Diet is also traditional and the use of manufactured goods is rare. While very important changes—which
will be discussed below—have occurred in Helambu over the
past few decades, anyone walking through these villages would
consider them traditional and preindustrial. Helambu is not
modernized or even modernizing in any of the usual meanings
of the concept as used earlier by Cowgill (1974). The elderly,
therefore, should have "high status" according to Cowgill and
Holmes.

Two ethnologists who studied Sherpa society in Solu-
Khumbu, however, have suggested that the status of the elderly there is low. Ortner (1978), for example, writes that a basic
conflict in Sherpa society pits parents against their children,
and that parents when they become old are left propertyless
and abandoned. She sees this as one of the "great tragic
themes of Sherpa culture" (ibid.:47):

In real life, as one gets old and one's children marry away; as one's
property disperses bit by bit with each of their marriages; as one's
physical powers, including one's sexuality, wanes; and as the social
structural realities of lay life are such that in fact one is not taken care
of by one's children but is left to fend for one's self. . . . [ibid.:52]

Fürer-Haimendorf (1979:87) writes that "an occasional
casualness towards aged parents, though by no means frequent, mars to some extent the otherwise pleasant picture of
Sherpa family life."

The Concept of "Status"

Before discussing this apparent contradiction, the meaning
of "status of the elderly" must be clarified. The term "status"
has not been defined precisely but rather has been used in-
tuitively and can often connote whatever the reader wants. If
status is taken to mean only, or primarily, prestige and social
standing, the concept has minimal utility for the comparative
study of aging and the elderly. In this sense, status is only one
component of the total *situation* of the elderly. If, however,
high status (prestige) is taken ipso facto to imply health,
wealth, and happiness, then the concept is incorrect. We sug-

gest that in addition to prestige (social status), eight dimensions are of equal or greater importance:

1. Biological status (e.g., biological function and biological capacity including physical fitness)
2. Health status (morbidity and mortality)
3. Activity status (i.e., the work and activities actually performed by the elderly)
4. Authority status (power and authority exercised in the community and family)
5. Economic status (the resources and wealth controlled by the elderly)
6. Household status (the type of household situation in which the elderly reside)
7. Psychological status (the degree to which the elderly are satisfied with their personal situation)
8. Ritual status (role played in ritual life)

Each of these aspects of the "status" of the elderly can be operationalized and measured by various means. Each can also vary independently of the others, e.g., physical fitness and activity levels may rank high but economic status may be low, or social status may be high but psychological status may be low. This tentative framework also allows for intrasocietal as well as intersocietal comparisons for each dimension, as well as for eliciting the relationships between these dimensions within a single society.

Another consideration is the widely held belief that the social and psychological status of the elderly is correlated with their ability to perform productive tasks. Cowgill and Holmes (1972:10) have articulated this, stating that "certainly we must expect that the status of the aged will be highest in those societies in which they are able to continue to perform useful and valued functions." Similarly, Osako (n.d.:13), in a bibliographic article on modernization and aging, summarizes the work of Simmons (1945), Cowgill and Holmes (1972), and DeBeauvoir (1972) as follows:

All three volumes stress the importance of distinguishing able-bodied aged and decrepit aged who have stopped being productive. Fortunate able-bodied elderly enjoy power and prestige, but the best that the decrepit can hope for in any society is pity and benign neglect. Many of them suffer from outright contempt and neglect and even abandonment in extreme cases.

Leaf (1973) has also emphasized the importance of activity and work for physical fitness, longevity, and psychological well-being.

Like the "modernization and aging" theory, we suggest that this, too, is potentially misleading. The Sherpa data will indicate clearly that there is no necessary correlation between physical fitness, productive activity, personal satisfaction, and happiness.

The Research: Aged Sherpas

The pilot study in Helambu focused on 37 persons over the age of 50: 12 were in their 50s; 11 in their 60s; 11 in their 70s; and 3 in their 80s. Of these, 60% of the individuals over 60 and 73% of those over 70 lived alone or with a spouse. Thirty-one percent of those over 60, and 33% of those over 70 lived alone. This sample includes 86% of the persons 60 years or older.

One of the first things we noticed about the overall situation of the elderly was the large number of elderly people living

alone. Eleven households (15%) consisted of one elderly person, and in seven of these, the lone elderly person was over 70 years of age. Another six (8%) households consisted of an old couple living alone.

The large number of elderly persons living alone or with an elderly spouse was surprising, given the almost universally accepted belief that the elderly in traditional societies reside with their children, who take care of them as they age and become dependent. Our study revealed that not only were a substantial proportion of the elderly living alone, they appeared physically fit, active, and self-reliant. Almost all were engaged in heavy work, either agricultural fieldwork or carrying heavy loads. None of the elderly living alone had servants, and each cooked, cleaned, and worked for himself or herself. All but one owned land in the village.

A fundamental shortcoming in the literature on cross-cultural aging is the lack of attention given to actual behavior. The focus in anthropology and sociology has been on the emic perspective; on what informants say and think about aging, on the cognitive and normative systems rather than on what the elderly actually do. It is likely, therefore, that the stereotypical view of the hale, hearty, and happy elderly in traditional societies is an artifact of "ideal" culture, and that empirical investigation of actual social and economic behavior could yield results very different than commonly supposed. Therefore, in our pilot study we tried to investigate and measure what the elderly do.

We conducted an activity-work survey of 30 different elderly persons aged 50 and over, using recall interviews on 15 different days during the peak agricultural season, yielding a total of 69 person-days of activity. The subjects in this survey were asked to enumerate all their activities and meals for the previous day, and this was supplemented with spot-check direct observation. Since Western time concepts are not well developed in this society, and since very few persons had (and could use) watches, the time dimension was organized according to the Sherpas' own division of daily time. They discussed their activities with reference to the four daily meals. For example, they would normally state that they had worked in the fields from the second meal (about 10 a.m.) to the third meal (about 3 p.m.). The time spent performing activities such as field work was estimated based on the average length of time (as we measured it) between these culturally delimited meal times. Categorizing work and activity into five general types yielded the following activity-level ranking:

1. Heavy work
   a. Agricultural field labor
      (Agricultural field labor during the period of observation consisted almost entirely of digging up potatoes. Sherpas use an iron hoe with an inwardly curved blade to do this. The handle is about .6 m long and the blade about 5 cm × .3 m. To use this implement, the worker must bend over almost horizontally from the waist and dig in that position.)
   b. Carrying loads
      (This involved either a basket of potatoes, leaves, or fertilizer; a brass jug of water; or a load of firewood or grass. The lightest load we spot-measured was 14.4 kg and the heaviest was 34.7 kg.)
2. Moderate work
   (This consisted of herding, milking animals, feeding

animals, cutting loads of grass (but not carrying it back), carrying meals to the field for workers, and collecting mushrooms in the forest.)

3. Household work
(This involves a variety of tasks such as cooking, cleaning, washing clothes, drying potatoes, cleaning the stable, etc.)

4. Wage labor
(Two types were observed: government-office work (one person) and construction-carpentry work.)

5. Craft labor
(Making wooden bins, weaving mats, sewing, etc.)

This ranking illustrates the heavy work performed by the elderly subjects. Ninety-one percent of the person-days worked by men and 87% of those worked by women including heavy labor, defined as at least one instance of either carrying a heavy load or field work. The data show also that there is no significant difference between the heavy labor patterns of the elderly 50 years of age and those 70 and 80 years of age. These findings indicate that elderly persons 70 years and over are as likely to do field work and carry loads as those 50 years of age. When agricultural work was performed, the average number of hours worked was 4.1 hours a day for males and 3.6 hours a day for females.

Although stress tests and formal health surveys have not yet been conducted, a number of factors indicate that these elderly possess good health status and physical fitness. Systolic and diastolic blood pressure did not increase significantly with age and the average blood pressure for men over 60 was 114/77, and for females over 60 it was 125/86. Virtually none of the elderly had Heberden's or Bouchard's nodes,[1] and all had full movement of their fingers. There was only one case of partial blindness (the 87-year-old man mentioned below) and no deafness or overt senility at all. The elderly communicated clearly and had no apparent thought or memory disorders. Only one male was too ill to perform heavy labor during the period we observed; he was hypertensive and appeared to have recently suffered a heart attack.

A typical day in the life of the eldest male in the village is illustrative of the vitality and self-reliance the elderly generally exhibit. Dorje Jakri is 87 years old. He had three sons and two daughters, but all three sons have died. His wife died three years ago at the age of 80, and he now lives alone, although his adult grandsons (son's sons and their families) also live in the village. He does all his housework and cooking, gets his own water and firewood, and works in his fields although he has let out most of the land he owns on a lease basis. On the day we interviewed him, he indicated that on the previous day he had performed the following activities.

He got up late when others in the village were already up and about. He walked to the water tap near his house and got a full jug of water (about 15.8 kg) which he carried back to his household. Then he made a fire, boiled water, and churned a pot of Tibetan-style tea (tea with salt and butter). He reheated the previous night's leftovers (rice and potatoes) and ate that with the tea as his first meal. After this he went to one of his fields to dig potatoes. He carried back a load of about 14.4 kg and commented that he thinks he misses a lot of the potatoes since he is virtually blind in his left eye. He then walked back to his field carrying a load of manure which he spread on the field in preparation for planting radishes. Then he returned

home and spread out the potatoes he had carried back earlier on the porch to dry. After this he walked to the water tap, washed his hands and feet, returned home, and again made a fire. He cooked a pot of potatoes and ate them with salt and hot chili for his second meal. He also had one cup of locally distilled liquor (rakshi) with the meal. After washing the pots he again went to the field this time to plant radishes. He worked at this for three or four hours and then returned to his home where he repacked the potatoes he had left out earlier and carried them into the house. It was about 4 p.m. by then. He drank another cup of liquor and ate the leftovers from his second meal. He didn't go back to the fields to work any more and stayed home for the remainder of the day and cooked dinner in the evening.

Despite their high level of economically productive activity, their relative physical fitness, and their ownership of agricultural land, many elderly Helambu Sherpas overtly expressed unhappiness with their lot. Several spontaneously volunteered that they wished they were dead, and others commented that their children had abandoned them and that the young in general did not care about the elderly. Almost all of those living alone drank home-brew liquor daily and a few consumed three or more cups per day.

These negative feelings existed even though being elderly was not considered a low social status. On the contrary, Tibetan and Buddhist culture confers high social status on the elderly. Ideally, it is a time when the trials and tribulations of obtaining subsistence shift to one's children and a process of disengagement is begun that culminates in death and rebirth. Tibetan norms and values hold that one's parents in particular, and the elderly in general, should be respected.[2]

While the positive cultural ideal regarding the elderly is never completely realized with respect to individual elderly in specific Tibetan populations, the Sherpas of Helambu (and apparently Solu-Khumbu) seem to deviate markedly in that so many of the elderly persons over 60 either lived alone or with a spouse, even though in most instances they had children or grandchildren living in the village. Other Tibetan societies for which data exist do not exhibit this pattern. In Limi, a remote Tibetan-speaking area in northwest Nepal, studied by Goldstein (1975, 1976, 1978), only one elderly male lived alone in the village of Tsang; all others (except one old Tibetan refugee) lived with children or close relatives in extended families. The elderly, moreover, were treated with respect and held authority and social status. In Dhinga, another Tibetan area three days south of Limi, none lived alone. Ross (personal communication) reports that the 21 persons over 60 years of age (8% of the total population) reside in 13 households, of which 10 include married children with their spouses and children, 2 contain unmarried children, and one female has no household, residing with her employers. In Kyilung, a Ladakhi village studied by Goldstein in 1980, which has recently begun to undergo significant socioeconomic changes, 69% of the 77 elderly Buddhist persons over 60 lived with sons, 9% with daughters, 13% as old couples, 3% alone, and 6% with other relatives.

Several possible explanations exist for this apparent contradiction. First, it is possible that Sherpas are not typical examples of Tibetan culture and the current status of the elderly may be merely a reflection of their different traditional value and normative system. Second, important changes may have occurred in the recent past that have affected Sherpa society and culture and altered traditional patterns. This is consonant with the Cowgill and Holmes theory in the sense that it holds that things were better for the elderly in traditional society, but at the same time is at variance with it since Nepal and the Helambu Sherpas are not "modernized" by any definition of the concept.

The data argue that the latter alternative is the major causal factor, i.e., that major changes that have influenced Solu-Khumbu and Helambu are transforming traditional Sherpa social organization and the norms and values associated with it. The psychological and emotional malaise expressed by many Sherpas stems precisely from a discrepancy between traditional expectations and the actual social reality with which the elderly must now cope. What are these changes?

The Indirect Impact of Modernization among Sherpas

Nepal was closed to foreign travelers until 1951 and to mountaineers until 1953. Nevertheless, important changes had already begun to have an impact on the social and economic life of the Sherpa area of Solu-Khumbu 50 years earlier. The first Sherpas used in mountaineering as high-altitude porters were recruited in Darjeeling, India in 1909 (Miller 1965:245), and it is clear that a number of Sherpas had already emigrated to Darjeeling by that year. Miller (ibid.) cites a figure of 3,450 Sherpas resident in Darjeeling district in 1901, 5,295 in 1941, and 8,998 in 1951. Furer-Haimendorf (1979:4) has estimated that by 1947 there were about 7,000 Sherpas in Darjeeling district.

The main impetus for this migration appears to have been the wage-labor opportunities offered by portering on mountain-climbing expeditions and trekking parties, recruitment for which centered in Darjeeling until Nepal opened in 1953.

How Sherpas came to settle at Darjeeling is not known in detail, but it would seem that at first it was the prospect of trade which drew Sherpas to Darjeeling and Kalimpong and that the association with mountaineering enterprises occurred at a time when they had already established themselves in the Darjeeling District. The first of these settlers belonged perhaps to the wave of emigrants from Solu who were responsible for the establishment of Sherpa communities in the Nepalese districts of Bhojpur and Dhankuta as well as in the region immediately east of the Nepal-Darjeeling border. But once the news of the earnings of expedition porters spread to Khumbu, many enterprising young men, some alone and some accompanied by their wives, went to seek their fortunes in Darjeeling. There are few families in Khumbu which cannot name one kinsman or another settled in Darjeeling and when I started to compile genealogies and family histories, I was told of the men and women living there. [Furer-Haimendorf 1975:85]

The impact of these new economic opportunities and the associated out-migration have been devastating for traditional Sherpa family structure. Furer-Haimendorf and Ortner have both commented on the prevalence and centrality of nuclear families among the Sherpas of Khumbu and Solu. Ortner, in fact, argues that the independent nuclear family is the fundamental atom of Sherpa social structure and sees this dominance of the nuclear family over the extended family as a major factor producing the plight of the elderly. However, she

sees this not as an outcome of indirect modernization, but as a traditional pattern. We suggest otherwise.

Both Furer-Haimendorf and Ortner have indicated that extended family types are also present, and their statements indicate that they are the cultural ideal for parents. Fraternal polyandry (two or more brothers jointly sharing a wife), for example, is a family type found throughout most of Tibet. According to Furer-Haimendorf (1979:68), it still comprised 8% of the marriages in Khumbu in 1957. Furer-Haimendorf, moreover, writes that Sherpas considered fraternal polyandry a "time-honored and highly respectable device enacted to prevent fragmentation of property and foster the solidarity of brothers . . ." (ibid.). Fraternal polyandry accomplishes this because males in Sherpa and Tibetan society have demand rights to a share of the family's arable land. By marrying polyandrously, they leave this right in abeyance and avoid splitting the family estate. Goldstein (1971, 1975, 1976, 1978) has discussed in detail the motivations underlying brothers' decisions to remain together (marry polyandrously) or marry monogamously, and a key factor is whether brothers perceive that they can supplement their inherited land by other economic activities so that they can attain a comfortable style of life within a reasonable time. Traditionally this was difficult in Tibetan and Sherpa society, but the changes that began six or seven decades ago in Darjeeling appear to have presented just such an opportunity. Furer-Haimendorf comments on the lucrativeness of the new economic resources.

To poor but energetic and adventurous young men, expedition work offered unique possibilities. Previously, a Sherpa without land or capital could not hope to attain more than modest prosperity even in a lifetime's hard work. . . . But a successful high-altitude porter could in a single season earn sufficient cash to engage in some modest trade deals or buy his first plot of land. . . . A further complaint by villagers against expedition porters was that many of the younger men used their earnings largely for themselves though they continued to live in a household maintained by the efforts of their brothers who worked on the family's land without having any personal cash income. [1975:86–87]

The growing importance of cash earnings and the corresponding diminishment of the Sherpas' interest in preserving a family's land holdings and herds undivided seems to have affected their attitude toward polyandry. [1979:99]

This new income, first in Darjeeling and later in Nepal, has played a major role in eliminating fraternal polyandry in Khumbu as a form of marriage and family.

The disintegration of the fraternal polyandrous family in Khumbu, however, is not synonymous with the elimination of the extended family. In Tibet, and among Sherpas, the traditional pattern was for at least one son to remain with his parents in their natal home. This remaining son is expected to marry patrilocally, and to care for the parents as they age. When his parents die, he inherits the family name and status and, in addition to his own share of land, inherits their share of land together with the house and other movable possessions. In most Tibetan groups it is the eldest son who remains in the natal homestead, but among Sherpas it appears to be the youngest son. Furer-Haimendorf, Ortner, and Lang and Lang (1971) have all commented on this pattern:

The inheritance rule is such that the youngest son will receive the parental house. He is theoretically obliged to feed and care for the parents out of this last share of their estate. [Ortner:46]

Thus a significant percentage of households in a Sherpa village are composed of three generations. [Ortner:20]

It is the youngest son remaining in the parents' house on whom a father depends for continued support, and such a youngest son is therefore usually most closely attached to his father. [Furer-Haimendorf 1979:86]

Traditionally, therefore, it was the expectation of parents in Solu-Khumbu that they would be living with at least one of their children in their later years, and that they would control a share of arable land until they died.

The history of change in Helambu is not nearly as well known as that in Solu-Khumbu. In fact, little is known about the ethnology of Helambu. Fraternal polyandry appears not to have been traditionally present, but extended families with the youngest son were and are still the ideal.

Helambu is near Kathmandu, and even before the recent construction of the Kathmandu-Lhasa motor road which shortened the traditional three-day walk to Kathmandu by one-to-two days, Helambu was primarily oriented to Kathmandu and not Tibet. This, in conjunction with the greater distance from Darjeeling and the lower altitude at which they reside, are perhaps some of the reasons why Helambu Sherpas were never significantly involved in the mountaineering trade. It appears that substantial emigration from Helambu began much later than in Solu-Khumbu, probably only during World War II. The last 20 years, however, have seen large-scale, long-term outmigration, primarily to India. The modernization of the Indian economic system and the creation and maintenance of an extensive communication/transportation infrastructure via a vast network of roads underlie the migration of Helambu Sherpas, as it is in India's booming mountain-road and office construction industry that most of the Helambu Sherpas are employed. The obvious geopolitical significance of India's northern mountain regions has resulted in a major Indian effort to modernize and integrate politically and economically those areas with the rest of the country. It is this modernization in India that has indirectly affected the remote and backward Sherpa area in the Nepal Himalayas. As was the case in the early period of migration in Solu-Khumbu (Miller 1964), parents in Helambu tried (and still try) to keep their sons and daughters from migrating to Kathmandu and India. But the draw of income, new skills, and excitement, and the avoidance of what young people say is the tedium and harshness of farming, have drawn away substantial numbers from Helambu. Thirty-one percent of the villagers of Pemagyang and Norbugyang are living outside the village on a long-term basis. In the younger age categories this was even higher, with 36% of those between 30 and 40 and 35% of those between 20 and 30 living in India or Kathmandu.

Whatever the causes of this migration, it has produced a tremendous disruption in the Sherpa family system, both in Solu-Khumbu and in Helambu. In Helambu, youngest sons who would otherwise have remained with their parents in extended stem families leave, and even though they often plan someday to return permanently, the likelihood that the traditional extended-family ideal of the elderly can be attained has been seriously diminished. The independence experienced living abroad makes return to a subordinate position in an extended family difficult, and these sons often ask that their share of the land be legally transferred to them while they are living abroad thus depriving the elderly of the double share

that they normally would have held. High mortality among Sherpas has probably exacerbated this situation. Speaking of the Darjeeling Sherpas in 1957, Furer-Haimendorf (1975:85) writes:

Living in quarters little better than the old-fashioned coolie lines of tea gardens, and exposed to contact with the crowds of an Indian bazaar, many Sherpas fell victim to tuberculosis, venereal diseases and other infectious ailments. In the healthy climate and comparative isolation of their mountain homes they had developed no immunity against diseases common in Indian towns. . . .

It is reasonable to suggest that more younger sons die in India than would have died had they remained in Helambu, and demographic research with other traditional Tibetan populations (Goldstein, in press) suggests that once infancy has been survived there is little mortality risk until old age.

The situation with regard to the elderly living alone in Helambu, therefore, does not reflect the traditional cultural pattern. Elderly Sherpas were living alone not because of traditional values and norms but because they had to. Massive emigration has precluded the realization of the extended family since the sons who should be living with the parents are either residing in India, have died untimely deaths there, or have experienced independence and do not wish to live under the direct authority and financial management of their parents. This does not mean that the younger generation no longer cares for or respects their parents. Sons and daughters living abroad send occasional gifts, and the elderly living alone all indicated that elder sons and daughters living in the village or nearby would care for them if they got sick.

Examination of the elderly living alone and as couples reveals, however, that many of them have living children. Of 17 households, 2 had no children (1 of the households was a nun) and for 2 there is no information. Of the remaining 13 households, 9 have living sons and the other 4 have living daughters. In many cases there were also married grandchildren and/or siblings in the village. This raises an important question. Since family life is valued, in cases where the youngest son is living in India or has died, why then don't the elderly live with their other sons, or with an adult daughter or a married grandchild? The extensive out-migration reported for Helambu cannot, in and of itself, explain the presence of so many elderly folk living alone bitter and unhappy about their "abandonment."

The answer to this question lies in the Sherpa's own definition of dependency. Since dependency and aging are discussed in a separate paper (Beall and Goldstein, in press), we will only mention here that dependency can be conceptualized etically as well as emically. Etically, it is a continuum concept, indicating the degree to which the elderly receive goods and services from others. Emically, from the point of view of the actors, very different types of goods, services, situations, etc., may be categorized as dependency in different societies. The Sherpa example illustrates this.

As elder sons in Helambu marry and separate from their parental household, they receive a share of the land and set up independent nuclear households that are considered jurally distinct from their natal ones. Furer-Haimendorf (1979:86) comments on this for Khumbu Sherpas:

Elder sons and married daughters may visit the parents off and on and bring gifts of food and beer on feast days, but only in exceptional circumstances will they work for their parents without receiving the usual wage.

If, after all the elder sons separate, the youngest son migrates to India or dies, the elderly couple is left alone. At this point, however, it is considered culturally inappropriate for the elderly to move in with other children even if invited. To do so would be to abdicate their independence and demean their self-esteem. It would mean leaving their own house and turning over their fields to their son (and daughter-in-law). It would mean becoming a powerless appendage to the *son's household*. As in our own society, while "crisis dependency" (Clark 1972) is acceptable, long-term dependency has a strong pejorative connotation. When the indirect impact of modernization produced substantial numbers of old folk in just such a situation, they chose to live alone, despite the fact that they do not want to live that way and are lonely and unhappy with their fate. They are bitter about the recent changes that have caused this transformation but have themselves been unable to ignore or redefine their cultural definition of dependency to accommodate the new situation. The cultural expectations and aspirations of the elderly in Helambu are incongruent with the new reality in which they are immersed. The consequence of this is the anomalous situation of elderly who are hale, healthy, productive, and economically not wanting, but psychologically and emotionally maladapted.

It is interesting to note, however, that certain aspects of the cultural system do appear to be changing. In response to our queries, many of the elderly indicated that they thought small families were better than large families. Their rationale for this was that since one cannot count on children to "look after parents" when they are old (i.e., let parents live with them), the less sons a person has, the more land the parent retains when old, and the more security he or she has.[3] It is not surprising that there was general feeling among the old and young that family planning and sterilization were good things. Nonetheless, with respect to their household situation, so long as they are able to function independently, this was the option they grudgingly preferred.

Conclusion

This paper has illustrated the way in which modernization can indirectly influence the social, economic, and cultural life of rural, agricultural areas in Third and Fourth World countries. It demonstrates the manner in which changes in India offered new economic opportunities and life styles and, via out-migration, indirectly weakened the extended family system in Helambu, a rural farming area in the hills of Nepal. This, in turn has seriously affected the situation of the elderly, a large proportion of whom now reside alone. The paper points up, therefore, the growing problem that the increasing number of elderly persons in Asia represent. It cannot be assumed, as the aging-and-modernization theory does, that traditional rural community patterns will accommodate these elderly. Contrary to the commonly held view, the future of the elderly in such areas is anything but rosy.

In this paper we also question another widely held viewpoint concerning the elderly, namely, the view that physical activity, productive work, and life in rugged mountain environments produce elderly who are physically fit, free from debilitating

chronic diseases, and emotionally and psychologically well adjusted to the process of aging. The Helambu data show that emotional and psychological adjustment is not necessarily linked to these factors.

NOTES

[1] Heberden's and Bouchard's nodes are two forms of osteoarthritis, the frequency of which increases with age in U.S. populations. Heberden's nodes are bony prominences at the margins of distal interphalangal joints, and Bouchard's nodes are bony swellings of the proximal, interphalangal joints.

[2] Ortner, however, argues that Tibetan religious literature such as Milarepa's songs portrays the elderly as abused and that this reflects traditional values and behavior. We disagree. This view confuses Buddhist philosophic theory with the "little tradition" and actual village life. Buddhism views life as inherently characterized by misery. Love, marriage, family, children, and the very process of life with its myriad attachments inevitably result in misery. Use of the abandonment of the elderly as an example of this fundamental Buddhist principle is not necessarily representative of real patterns of behavior. It is a symbolic rather than statistical statement. To read it as an empirical statement flies in the face of Tibetans' own verbalized statements and is not supported by other studies of Tibetan communities.

[3] More land for the elderly does not necessitate more work for them, as this land can be leased to others who do the work and share the yield, or neighboring Tamang can be hired to do field work.

REFERENCES CITED

Beall, Cynthia, and Melvyn C. Goldstein
  in press Work, Aging and Dependency in a Sherpa Population in Nepal. *In* Biocultural Perspectives on Aging. Cynthia Beall, ed. Social Science and Medicine.
Bengtson, Vern L., James J. Bowd, D. Smith, and A. Inkeles
  1975 Modernization, Modernity, and Perceptions of Aging: A Cross-cultural Study. Journal of Gerontology 30(6):688-95.
Clark, Margaret
  1972 Cultural Values and Dependency in Later Life. *In* Donald Cowgill and L. Holmes, eds. Pp. 263-74. Aging and Modernization. New York: Appleton-Century-Crofts.
Cowgill, Donald O.
  1974 Aging and Modernization: A Revision of the Theory. *In* Late Life-Communities and Environmental Policy. Jaber Gubrium, ed. Pp. 123-45. Springfield: Charles C Thomas.
Cowgill, Donald O., and L. D. Holmes, eds.
  1972 Aging and Modernization. New York: Appleton-Century-Crofts.
DeBeauvoir, Simone
  1972 The Coming of Age. New York: Putnam.
Furer-Haimendorf, Christoph von
  1975 Himalayan Traders. London: John Murray Publishers.
  1979 The Sherpas of Nepal. New Delhi: Sterling.
Goldstein, Melvyn C.
  1971 Stratification, Polyandry and Family Structure in Tibet. Southwestern Journal of Anthropology 27:64-74.
  1975 Development Report on Limit Panchayat, Humla District, Karnali Zone. Contributions to Nepalese Studies 2(2):89-101.
  1976 Fraternal Polyandry and Fertility in a High Himalayan Valley in Northwest Nepal. Human Ecology 4:223-33.
  1978 Pahari and Tibetan Polyandry Revisited. Ethnology 17: 325-37.
  In press New Perspectives on Tibetan Fertility and Population Decline. American Ethnologist.

Harlan, William H.
1968 Social Status of the Aged in Three Indian Villages. *In* Middle Age and Aging. Bernice L. Neugarten, ed. Pp. 469–78. Chicago: University of Chicago Press.

Hauser, Philip M.
1976 Aging and World-Wide Population Change. *In* Handbook of Aging and the Social Sciences. Robert H. Binstock and E. Shanas, eds. Pp. 58–86. New York: Van Nostrand Reinhold.

Lang, S. D. R., and A. Lang
1971 The Kunde Hospital and a Demographic Survey of the Upper Khumbu, Nepal. The New Zealand Medical Journal 74:1–8.

Leaf, Alexander
1973 Unusual Longevity: The Common Denominators. Hospital Practice 8:75–86.

Miller, Robert
1965 High Altitude Mountaineering, Cash Economy, and the Sherpa. Human Organization 24(3):244–49.

Ortner, Sherry
1978 Sherpas Through Their Rituals. Cambridge: Cambridge University Press.

Osako, Masako
n.d. Social Participation of Rural Elderly in Developing Nations—With Special Emphasis on Their Roles in Family, Community and Economy. Manuscript.

Simmons, Leo W.
1945 The Role of the Aged in Primitive Society. New Haven: Yale University Press.

PARIN A. DOSSA

CRITICAL ANTHROPOLOGY AND LIFE STORIES: CASE STUDY OF ELDERLY ISMAILI CANADIANS

ABSTRACT. This paper explores the potential of life story approach in the new wave of ethnographic writing. The latter, also referred to as critical anthropology, has come under intense scrutiny as its expressed goal of giving space to the voices of subjects of research continues to remain discretely confined to the ethnographic text. This paper suggests that the life story approach can expand the scope of new ethnography through its explicit recognition of the ongoing dialogue between narrators (research subjects) and the ethnographer. Using the case study of Canadian elderly Ismaili Muslims, this paper shows how the worlds of the latter and the author converge on the common ground of a search for mutual identity and social space, leading to a collective voice expressed through life stories.

Key Words: life story, ethnography, Canadian elderly, Ismaili Muslims, mutual identity, collective voice

CRITICAL ANTHROPOLOGY AND LIFE STORIES

In the late twentieth century world of postmodernism, the conventional notion of other cultures existing as discrete and self-contained entities can no longer be sustained. In the wake of the realization that societies and cultures are woven together in complex strands of interconnections and asymmetrical power relations, attempts are made to give voice and space to the hitherto alienated and marginalized Other. In response to this challenge, anthropology, together with other neighboring disciplines, has entered into an experimental mode of doing, writing, and reading ethnography.

The new wave of ethnography (critical anthropology) is double-edged. It can either open up uncharted and exploratory avenues, which can further enhance the anthropological endeavor of intercultural dialogue, or alternatively, it can strengthen the discipline's conventional roots in the imperialist complex of West versus the rest (Third World). The either-or scenario is presented for analytical distinction to highlight the complex and problematic issues surrounding critical anthropology within the larger scenario of the contemporary world system. This expanded terrain brings with it the expectation that reconstructed anthropology would engage in "struggles against racist oppression, gender inequality, class disparities and international patterns of exploitation and 'difference' rooted largely in capitalistic world development" (Harrison 1991:2). A major concern here is to show how the closely observed cultural realms (thick description of ethnographic fieldwork) are embedded in the world of larger systems and events. An allied issue is that of granting narrative presence and voice to the subjects of research who are engaged in field (manual) work, in stark contrast to the sedentary work of the metropolitan anthropologist.

173

The most serious charge leveled at critical anthropology is that its claim towards dispersal of authority comes at a time when the Other's voice needs to be acknowledged and heard. More importantly, the dialogical mode included in experimental ethnographies is textual and confined to the situation in the field. Critical anthropology then becomes merely a narrative technique or style geared towards the western educated readership, rather than a means of empowering informants. As a number of critiques have observed (Mascia-Lees, Sharpe, and Cohen 1989:7–33; Crapanzano 1992:97–102), the politics of critical anthropology is that of academia and not the world at large. This is a critical issue in anthropology on account of its preoccupation with human cultural diversity. The discipline's mission has always been to advance multiple cultural perspectives together with deployment of a wider repertoire of communicative strategies. In the process of reconstruction of critical anthropology, I would like to explore the potential of life stories, as distinguished from life histories.[1] In doing so, I would like to stress the way in which life transitions and past experiences are woven in relation to broader historical and cultural contexts. This aspect is succinctly expressed by Ginsburg (1989:60):

> In the life stories, the narrator shows how these events take on new meaning as the self is realigned in relation to some larger collective body and ideology, in this case one of the social movements involved in the abortion issue. Thus, members of each group lay claim to a particular view of American culture and the place of men and women in it, in a way that creates harmonious narrative out of the dissonant experiences of history, both personal and generational.

The viability of this approach lies in its ability to interconnect even the most disparate terrains. Powdermaker's (1966) work is exemplary in showing how her experiences in four vastly different field settings are recounted through her own life story whereby she is able to look inward (towards herself) as well as outward (towards the people she studies). Such an interconnection provides a context for raising questions regarding the relationship between the anthropologist and the field subjects, the choice of field site, experience of fieldwork, and the written text. In life story, we are not looking at the unmediated world of the Other, but the world between ourselves and the others. As this approach bears the impress of the narrator, and at the same time attempts to present the subjects from their own perspectives, it offers considerable leeway for reflexivity.

Recognizing the interrelatedness of life story and autobiography (story of the self) Okely observes (1992:8):

> Whereas in literary studies a concern has been to move the analysis of others' autobiographies into the literary canon, if autobiography were fully incorporated into anthropology, it would be about the construction of both the anthropologists' autobiographies in the field and those of others. An anthropological perspective concerns reflexivity in the field and the process of autobiographical construction, not the critique of others' existing texts. Here social anthropology has characteristics especially apt in relation to any genre of autobiography ... Under pressure to be

'scientifically objective', anthropologists have traditionally compartmentalized their fieldwork experience.

Likewise, in her extensive work on the life history project (used in a general sense to include life stories) in anthropology, Frank (1980:155–171) observes that the life history may be thought of as a process that blends together the consciousness of the investigator and the subjects. This level of consciousness allows the ethnographer to draw upon his or her self through autobiographical reflections. In this context, Myerhoff's (1980) seminal work on *Number Our Days* among elderly Jews in California has been acclaimed to bring anthropology to age. In the preface to this work, Turner (1980: xiii) states: "Barriers between self and other, head and heart, conscious and unconscious, history and autobiography, have been thrown down and new ways have been found to express the vital interdependence of these and other 'mighty opposites'". Using the metaphor "thrice born", Turner further comments that the long term program of the discipline has always included "the movement of return: the purified look at ourselves", emergent from the anthropologist's "journey" from the familiar to a far away place and back to the natal place where engagement in reflexivity through life story and autobiography then becomes inevitable. Myerhoff's work does not merely address the issue of what it is to be Jewish elderly in the form of the Other, but raises the moot anthropological question of what it is to be human.

Drawing upon this tradition of construction of life story/autobiography in anthropology, I wish to show how my own engendered[2] work in the 'field' drew me to exploring the lives of Canadian Ismaili elderly who constitute part of the diaspora community, anchored in the West as well as the Third World. The core concern is not that of disclosing the life stories of the elderly in the ethnographic encounter, but the unfolding dialogue whereby the world of the Ismaili elderly is revealed in relation to my own search for an identity. As an Ismaili Muslim born in Uganda, the 1972 expulsion of Asians from Uganda brought to the forefront the issue of plural identity status. It is important to note that life stories (and the life history project) in anthropology continue to deal with the question of the epistemological relationship between the culturally defined and discrete world of the subjects and the ethnographer from a 'foreign' culture.[3]

THE QUESTION OF PLURAL IDENTITY

The 1972 exodus of Asians from Uganda raised for me the issue of identity. This was the event that triggered the question of: Who was I? What was the status of the Asian community domiciled in East Africa since the end of the nineteenth century? Who were Ismaili Muslims who have natal and cultural links with the diversified Asian community (with origins on the Indo-Pakistan subcontinent) and also religious links with the global Muslim community? Added to this complex was the issue of Asian settlement in the four colonized areas of East Africa: Uganda, Kenya, Tanganyika, and Zanzibar.[4]

In the contemporary world of cultural pluralism, my status as an Ismaili Muslim would be an enviable one. I, like members of other minority groups, have multiple links which are potentially enriching. The word potential is critically significant as, in practice, I ended up having a fragmented and slotted identity. I had access to four languages: Gujerati (mother tongue), Kiswahili (used as a dialect and later on as an official language in Kenya and Tanzania – the post-colonial union of Tanganyika and Zanzibar), English (colonial language), and Arabic (which continued to remain latent and was used only for liturgical purposes). Languages are repositories of cultures and therefore potentially I was in a position to draw from multiple cultural traditions: Asian, African, Muslim, and also European. However this was not to be the case. In retrospect, the scenario which engulfed my life was institutionally and otherwise hierarchical. The colonial message imparted was that the English language, together with its mission of 'civilization', was the language of survival in the rapidly changing world of science and technology. Not only did English become the medium of instruction, but also the school curriculum (from primary to post-secondary level) centered around the colonial British system. British history and that of its 'Empire', geography, literature, and the English language were accorded primary status. A major paradox here was that growing up in East Africa meant knowing next to nothing about African history, geography, literature, tribal cultures, and traditional religions. Only peripheral space was given to these subjects.

As a community, the Ismailis (like other Asian minorities: Sikhs, Hindus, Parsis, Bhoras, Ithna Asharites) were constrained by the colonial system. To begin with, the British confined the Asians (regarded as a homogeneous category) to towns and small trading settlements, where they were channelled into trade. Morris (1956:296) notes that "Any non-African found living or trading outside a gazetted township commits an offence". Likewise Fernando observes that "the Asians were clustered in well-delimited residential districts" (1979: 362). Being sandwiched between the colonized Africans and the colonizers, the status of the Asians became exceedingly precarious without any grounds to stand on. Their engagement in trade and commerce was tenuous as they had no administrative or political voice. Also no sustained provision of social services or education was made by the colonial government for the Asians. Left to their resources and devices, the Asians were compelled to establish their exclusive enclaves. Each of the Asian communities established its own distinctive system. The following historical sketch explicates the formation and development of the Ismaili community in East Africa, followed by the settlement of the community in Canada in the 1970s.[5]

Ismailis are Shia Muslims, whose roots go back to the nascent period of Islam. A group of Muslims pledged their allegiance to Prophet Muhammed's cousin and son-in-law, Ali. These Muslims (referred to as the Shia) believe that the Prophet designated Ali as his successor and claim that this line of succession is continuous and held only by his male descendants. The successor is referred to as the *Imam*, who according to the Ismailis guides his followers materially as well as spiritually, in accordance with changing times and circumstances. The combination of religious and secular authority places the *Imam* in the capacity to influence his followers in all aspects of life. The Ismailis are distinguished from other Shia Muslims (Ithna Asharites and Bhoras) by their belief in the living *(Hadir) Imam*. H.H. The Aga Khan IV is the present *Imam*, whom the Ismailis claim is the direct descendant of the Prophet and Ali. The Sunnis represent the other school of thought. They are in the majority, and they claim that Prophet Muhammed left it to the community of believers *(Umma)* to nominate a successor from among them. There is a sizable Sunni Muslim Community in East Africa, which includes African Muslims. Among these, the *Swahilis* form a distinct group, having come into existence through intermarriage of Arab men and Bantu women from 9th century onwards.

The *Imam* has played a crucial role in the settlement of the Ismaili community in East Africa. The migration of the Ismailis from the Indo-Pakistan subcontinent in the 19th and early part of the 20th centuries took place under the directive of the previous Imam, Aga Khan III (1885–1957). As has been their traditional practice, the Ismailis consolidated their presence through the establishment of *Jamat Khanas* (place of worship). These centers formed the hub around which the religious, social and cultural life of the community was organized. Using the *Jamat Khana* as a base, the *Imam* set up an infrastructure of cosmopolitan health clinics, schools (nursery to secondary), hostels, libraries, trust companies, and also hospitals. These institutions were established to enable the community to participate in the 'modern' era of science and technology. A major and radical change was effected in the status of woman. The *Imam* urged the community to impart formal and the highest possible education to girls; he also directed women to change their attire of long dress and long head scarf and adopt the colonial dress. As he explained it, the traditional Indian dress was cumbersome when it came to attending school or working outside the domestic sphere. This directive was put into practice by *all* the women except for some of the very old who felt uncomfortable wearing the colonial dress. Overall the *Imam's* intention was to strike a judicious balance between tradition and change. While he wished Ismaili women to take their place in the public market sphere, he also made it very clear that he did not wish women to forsake their domestic role of nurturing. On the contrary, the *Imam* explained that 'educated' women would be able to raise their children with greater knowledge of health, nutrition, and conditions of life in their larger environment.

At the time of the 48th *Imam's* death, a strong corporate community had been established with a sound economic and educational base, to the extent that the Ismaili community came to be referred to as the most progressive Muslim community in East Africa. When the present Imam assumed leadership in 1957, the East African countries were in the process of becoming independent nations. In the face of growing Africanization of the economic and market sectors, the Imam's directive to the community was to expand their commercial base to include industries and professions. This meant even greater emphasis on acquisition of formal education, as it pertained to the areas of industry, medicine, science, computers, and engineering. While preparing the community for a competitive African and world markets, the *Imam* directed the Ismailis to take up citizenship of the countries of their adoption.[6]

The Ismaili settlement in East Africa can then be perceived to have taken the form of an enclave, resulting from imposed colonial restraint as well as a response to this restraint. As we have noted, the hallmark of the Ismaili community is an ingenious combination of religious and socio-economic sectors, personified dynamically through the presence of a living *Imam.* While maintaining its distinct religious identity, the community has simultaneously endeavored to take its place in the mainstream life of the various countries (approximately 25) where Ismailis are domiciled. No efforts have been spared to give the community a markedly international presence, as can be observed through numerous Third World projects administered by the Aga Khan Foundation. The latter works closely with Canadian International Development Agency (CIDA) and numerous other national organizations in other parts of the world. The Aga Khan Foundation is especially active in the areas of cosmopolitan health, education, and rural development. Overall, the Ismaili community in East Africa may be characterized as being institutionally complete. A response to colonial constraints together with the *Imam's* vision of ensuring a place for the community in the contemporary world of science and technology led to the formation of a tightly knit administrative infrastructure. Structurally, this infrastructure, geared towards the management of modern institutions, has no central place for the elderly Ismaili population. The latter, nevertheless, enjoyed a supportive environment, sustained through spatial and temporal concentration. Given an integrated spatial environment, which included *Jamat Khanas,* neighbors were kin or provided kin-like ties. Within this space, the elderly continued to perform viable roles within the sphere of the family, kin, and the community. Temporally as well, the lives of the Ismailis continued to remain integrated to the extent that daily attendance at *Jamat Khana* by families remained an integral part of their lives. Occasions did not arise whereby conflicting demands were made on the lives of family members, as is the situation in Canada. Many elderly men as well as women would visit neighborhood families during the day time, and going to *Jamat Khana* for day activities (cleaning for women, reading in the library for men or attending other communal events) was a common occurrence. This form of integration into the family/neighborhood unit and community meant that in spite of the process of modernization, the elderly did not completely lose their status or traditional social roles.

The Ugandan exodus provided greater impetus for the settlement of the Ismailis in Canada and other parts of the West (United States, United Kingdom, Western Europe). Before the exodus of 1972, the total Ismaili population of North America numbered around 600 (Nanji 1983: 94–105). At present the estimated number in Canada is 40,000. A breakdown in relation to gender and age has not been compiled. More than half of the Ismailis live in Ontario, with 70% in metropolitan Toronto. In Western Canada, the largest number is found in

Vancouver, with Edmonton, Calgary, and Winnipeg as important centers. A recurrent theme highlighted in the small body of literature on the Canadian Ismaili community (Fernando 1979: 361–368; Nanji 1983: 94–105; Ross-Sheriff and Nanji 1991: 101–117; Dossa 1985) is that of the entrepreneurial, professional, and organizational skills of the community together with the ability of the community to maintain its distinct religious heritage. The following is a typical observation: "Because of their background in commerce, their middle class values and their considerable adaptability, however, the Ismailis have greater prospects for successful integration than most of the Asian immigrants who have come to Canada" (Fernando 1979: 367). These findings are reiterated in other studies: "On the whole it appears that the Ismailis have addressed the process of integration into North American life successfully. The foresight of young parents, adult children, and community leaders have facilitated the initiation of programs to meet the religious and intercultural needs of children, youth and elderly. The adjustment has benefitted from community support networks and proven traditional coping strategies. Some difficulties have arisen because of intergenerational differences, pressures on both parents to work, and other stresses involved in adapting to a highly industrialized and differentiated society. For most Ismailis, their traditional Muslim heritage remains the critical resource that they turn to when they encounter problems (Ross-Sheriff and Nanji 1991: 115).

While the community is perceived to be well-equipped to adapt to their new home in Canada, the supportive environment of the elderly in East Africa is virtually non-existent. The spatially dispersed and highly differentiated environment of the Ismailis in Canada, together with greater preference for a nuclear family life-style, has led to a situation whereby the elderly are left to their own devices to cope with the exigencies of daily life. The life-style of the elderly has been delineated within a framework that is all too familiar in the literature on ethnic minorities and aging (for example: Bastida 1987; Canadian Ethnic Studies 1983; Gelfand and Kutzik 1979). Ross-Sheriff and Nanji (1991: 106) make the following observation:

> For the elderly, especially those living in isolated areas, stresses arise from such factors as lack of mobility, limited opportunity for socializing, perception that they receive too little attention from their children (especially daughters and daughters-in-law, who might, in their countries of origin, have remained in an extended family), loss of their traditional position of authority in the family, and lack of access to a regular and formal religious environment.

My previous work (1991: 37–43) on Ismaili elderly has dealt with the issue of how this population deals with the paradox of adapting to the mainstream norms of independence and self-reliance, while at the same time sustaining an interdependent world of mutually binding relationships. In East Africa, the elderly lived with their married sons. The alternative option of living away from the family was not regarded as viable. Filial obligation of looking after elderly parents was interpreted as living under one roof, which led to mutual consultations and reciprocal relations. In Canada, a large number of elderly parents live separately from their sons. This is largely because of differing intergenerational life-styles and perceptions, and the adoption of mainstream nuclear family life with its values of individualism and autonomy. This form of living translates into limited intergenerational interactions which take place on special occasions (birthdays, religious festivals, occasional family outings) and weekly visits. Despite its limitations, this form of interaction provides the elderly with some space, however tenuous, to maintain their social and symbolic status. In an environment where the elderly are easily perceived as a burden, the immediate questions that arise are: (a) who should be entrusted with the responsibility of looking after the elderly and (b) what roles can the latter continue to perform so that they do not become a total 'burden' on the family. Responsibility for the elderly is diffused within an extended and dispersed family unit so that daughters (married and single) as well as sons and their wives provide instrumental as well as emotional and expressive support, according to their circumstances. The most common role assigned to the elderly (especially females) is child care. This, in most cases, amounts to baby sitting until the child is of age to join the school system. While most parents find it consoling to think that traditional values are imparted by the elderly to their young children, this is by no means an intense process. The main problem here is that very often the younger children do not speak the native language of the elderly, and they generally end up talking to their grandchildren in English. In a highly structured and positivist education system, there is minimal value accorded to the process of imparting informal education, involving symbolic and emotive mediums of communication. Once the child joins the school system, the amount of time spent with the elderly grandparents is limited and structured. Compounding this state of affairs, the role of the elderly is performed with an increasingly redundant and marginalized status, amounting to a lack of deference from younger family members.

A mitigating factor for elderly Ismailis is the presence of *Jamat Khana* (place of worship and congregation) in their new homeland in Canada. As in East Africa, the community has maintained its practice of setting up *Jamat Khanas* in all the areas where Ismailis have settled. At present, there are nineteen *Jamat Khanas* in British Columbia. While some are situated in leased locations, others have been built to reflect Islamic/Ismaili architectural structure and motifs. Two built *Jamat Khanas* are located in Burnaby and North Vancouver. The *Jamat Khanas* serve as a tangible focus of religious, cultural, and social life of the community. Most of the *Jamat Khanas* are open daily in the early hours of the morning as well as evenings. Attendance varies from day to day, and the largest congregation takes place on Fridays and religious occasions. For elderly Ismailis, *Jamat Khanas* serve a special purpose. This is one place which has allowed the elderly to maintain a sense of continuity with their past in as much as it serves as a locus for opening up of social and symbolic space as indicated in the following account of a female respondent:

Were it not for the *Jamat Khana*, the elderly people would be at a loss. They pass their whole day in isolation with the expectation that they would go to *Jamat Khana*. When they do come to *Jamat Khana*, they have a sense of belonging. Other people (young and old) come up and ask: 'How are you? How is your health'? Even a brief exchange like this means so much. It shows that there are people out there who care. We are not alone. We get special strength. We know that Allah (God) is with us and we get the strength and courage to pass another day. The *Jamat* (congregation) is our family.

Attending *Jamat Khana* for the elderly on a daily basis is so vital that the community has arranged special transportation whereby individual members are picked up and taken to the location nearest to their place of residence.

My fieldwork among the Ismailis in Vancouver (1982–1984) and in Calgary (1987) was prompted by the question of change and adaptation of a distinctive religious minority community to a secularized and industrialized society. Within the framework of conventional ethnography, I engaged in participant-observation, semi-structured interviews, and conversations with a cross-section of the community (men, women, youth, and elderly males and females). Contacts were established primarily through community leaders and personal relations with families. My entry into the community took place through voluntary work with women and families and through participation in rituals and social activities. I presented myself as an indigenous researcher who was interested in exploring the question of tradition and change. Data were collected on socio-economic characteristics, pattern of migration, residential arrangements, status and changing role of women, religious and ritual practices, and intergenerational relationships. During the early stages of fieldwork, I realized that the responses of the elderly participants were markedly different from the younger generation. The former responded by relating to me life stories in the native tongue of *Gujerati*. This pattern continued during the second phase of my research in Calgary. In recounting their life stories, the elderly Ismailis were reaching out to claim their full humanity, having been bypassed by the sweep of rapid change. Furthermore, my encounter with the elderly Ismailis made me depart from conventional anthropological approach. Their social invisibility and muteness touched a nerve within me as I began to realize that their muted condition formed an integral part of my intellectual evolution and understanding of tradition and change.

It was during the process of collecting life histories of elderly Ismailis that I realized that their muted condition was part of my muted plural identity. In relating their life stories, my purpose was not only to make visible, within the limited span of the printed word, their social world of aspirations and daily struggles, but to understand the larger socio-economic forces that lead to suppression of ways of life which are humane and enriching on account of their inclusion of diversity. In endeavoring to conduct collaborative research, my intention was to capture the dilemmas faced by elderly Ismailis in a context that gave some visibility to my role as an indigenous researcher, engaged in a search for a plural identity as opposed to a muted identity.

The beginnings of my muted identity can be traced to the process of coloniza-
tion in East Africa. Within the imposing hegemonic colonial system, other ways
of life had a muted and limited space. The indigenous African way of life was
dismissed as insignificant; the subgroups within the Asian community were
mere enclaves, to the extent that the latter were not able to establish deep roots
in African soil, despite 3rd and 4th generational continuity.

The Ugandan exodus was for me an awakening from the slumber of an
enclaved, exclusive, and segregated way of life. It was at this juncture that I
turned to the discipline of anthropology for insights as to what constitutes
cultural pluralism. My initiation into the discipline in the late 1970s was
exclusively through the medium of conventional and positivist anthropology.
Works that now fall into the category of 'critical anthropology' were regarded as
peripheral to doing real core anthropology. There was also the assumption that
the pursuit of soft anthropology, which included emotional, biographical or
autobiographical components, could be carried out by female anthropologists.
Writings of 'classical' male scholars like Evans-Pritchard, Boas, Malinowski,
Needham, Leach, and Fortes, among others, were taken to represent prime
examples of how the experience of people from another culture could be
interpreted according to the norms of science and positivism, distinct from the
empathetic involvement of the ethnographer. As Callaway (1992: 31) has
expressed it, the issue is that of embodied persons and disembodied texts. In
sum, conventional ethnographic texts, geared towards representing non-western
culture for a western audience, did not address the issue of cultural diversity or
plural identity in the empathetic mode that would also acknowledge the presence
of the ethnographer. Critical anthropology, where life stories are given central
place, recognizes the importance of the emotional resonance of the narrators and
brings to the center the moot question of the relationship of the narrator and the
ethnographer. The context then of the life stories of Ismaili elderly included my
own search for plural identity. This endeavor, far from beaing an individualistic
enterprise, formed part of the process of a conscious communal discourse where
I attempted to capture the collective experiences of the Ismaili elderly. The latter
constitute pioneers and, in some cases, the first generation in East Africa. In
their new homeland in Canada, this was not the case. Their status of being
'pioneers' was taken away from them through intense forms of marginalization
and social invisibility. Their life stories were part of a search for a collective
voice. My involvement with the elderly constituted part of this collective voice.
A common ground that we shared was that of the non-existence of social space
that caused their identity and status to become muted; in this muted condition
my plural identity had not bloomed. The following extracts from life stories then
constitute part of the process whereby forms of mutedness are identified in such
a manner that an emergent collective voice is heard. Such an enterprise constitutes a double frame of reflexivity, leading to a deepening understanding of
their situation as well as that of mine.

My personal narrative as an anthropologist in the 'field' requires some
mention of my engendered role as a woman. The elderly population took me as

a person who could empathize with their changed situation in terms of loosening of family ties and their intense isolation, amounting to their loss of a social arena where they would count as whole persons. Traditionally, Ismaili women have been regarded as the hub around which family and kinship ties have revolved and where primary forms of nurturing take place. As a woman, I was perceived in two roles: the traditional role which was being eroded very rapidly and, more importantly, a new role which encapsulated women's movement into the labor force. The elderly Ismaili narrators believed that younger women had more 'power' and this being the case, the latter were in a position to revive their traditional functions in a modified form. It appears that this was the message they were attempting to convey in relating their life stories. In retrospect, life stories of the Ismaili elderly may be viewed as a continuous dialogue about possible alternative forms of life in their new homeland in Canada. As in other societies, gender as an organizing principle of social life is salient among Ismailis. However, distinct gender roles are not sharply defined in old age. In Ismaili culture the term 'retirement' is used in relation to freeing oneself from material responsibilities and devoting greater time towards nurturance of spiritual life. The traditional gender distinction in terms of roles, division of labor, and images of males and females then becomes blurred during old age. The following extracts from a total of 40 life stories (25 females and 15 males, aged 60 to 86) are selected to identify (1) collective predicaments of the elderly and (2) a process of engagement revealing efforts to recreate a niche where their social worth and status would have some standing.

INTERRELATEDNESS OF MUTED IDENTITIES

The subject population of Ismaili elderly consider themselves to be displaced as their immigration to Canada is an enforced move, all the more complicated as the decision to migrate is at times perceived to be voluntary. Except for the elderly from Uganda, the others made a conscious decision to emigrate, the primary reason being that they wanted to be with their children and grandchildren. The following excerpt from a male narrator illustrates a typical situation:

> I had a good life in Mwanza (Tanzania). It was peaceful and quiet. We had a nice house and we were well off. But I could not continue to live there without my children. My sons and daughters all decided to leave Tanzania because of political circumstances but also for the sake of their children's education. I want to see my grandchildren grow up and when I die, I want to be surrounded by my family.

The elderly informants were well aware of the fact that, unlike their children, their participation in the mainstream sector of life (labor force, recreational activities, and social interactions) would be minimal. However, psychologically, they had prepared themselves for a way of life that would include the continual presence of family members, in spite of their experiential knowledge that familial relationships also include conflict and strife. A proverbial expression of this is: "Where there are dishes, there is bound to be noise." The sense of being displaced was felt to be acute and compounded as it was not merely a matter of making adjustments to the way of life of the host society. More devastating was the paradoxical realization that the most profound adjustment was required in the area of familial relationships. What was familiar suddenly turned out to be strange: ("I raised my son and we lived together for twenty years. I can't believe that he has changed so much"). The taken for granted reality (the presence of the family) has become a special occurrence: ("We don't live with our sons anymore; they visit us"); a once solid ground has become shaky: ("I don't know whether my family will look after me until I die. It is hard to tell. The world has changed").

The response of the elderly Ismailis to this sense of displacement is to work towards a mediation of the difficult and contradictory process of becoming independent (amounting to a loosening of family ties) while maintaining some measure of interdependence (sustaining family ties). The mediating process is partially accomplished through dialectical engagement with the larger order, involving a process of inter-reference.

Foremost is the issue of dealing with feelings of anxiety, related in the life stories of all narrators. This mode of experience begins with the realization that reverence, respect, and care, accorded to them traditionally, are subject to rapid erosion, as manifested in everyday life situations: ("From 9 to 5, I am all alone; when the family comes home in the evening, they do not have much time for me; everyone is busy; I do not think that anyone cares"); times of crisis: ("I was sick, yet I had to get up and make my own lunch"); and last period of their lives: ("I might die alone; this is a horrible thought"). The knowledge that their way of life is not transmitted to the younger generation and that their status within the family has been made redundant has reinforced and accentuated their anxiety further. The silence of family members on the issue of whether they would be in a position to take care of their elderly, if the latter became terminally ill, is another ever-present dimension expressed ambiguously by one respondent:

> I should not expect my family members to look after me; they are pressured them-
> selves; they have their own children to look after; they can't do everything; if I have
> to go to an institution, I will have to learn to accept it – God will always be with me.
>   I am afraid – afraid of dying alone. I have seen 'Canadian' (white) elderly who
> have been living in the institutions for many years. What will happen to them? When
> they die, their family will not be around them. It is not that the family does not care
> but we cannot choose the moment of death, God does. What if I die in my sleep and
> nobody is around. What will happen then? I do not wish to die that way. When my
> father died, and my grandfather too, there were more than 30 people in the room. My
> father always used to tell me that the biggest asset in old age is family members. Our
> family members are our descendants. Look, how our descendants are scattered all
> over. My two sons are in England and the other three are in Toronto. I have only one
> son in Vancouver. Yes, I am sure that they care; they care very much. But the pressure
> of life here is such that they can't be with me. I cannot even expect that. Son,
> daughter-in-law go to work, children go to school and I am all alone in the house. I
> lost my wife five years ago. No, my children don't care, otherwise I would not have to

spend so many hours alone. I am in a 'prison'. But what can they do; it is the circumstances, it is the circumstances. When I die, it will be the end of a long journey. Like all journeys, it contains moments of happiness and difficulties; frustrations and accomplishments. Such is life. Do not mourn for me. I did learn how to live and I shall be free.

The above passage portrays a crisis of identity, a struggle emanating from a core area of social existence. For the Ismailis, the formation of social identity, which in itself is continual and dynamic, is a function of familial and nonfamilial relationships. The mere possibility of reaching old age without a life of social relationships, where one counts as a whole person, is unthinkable and absolutely foreign. A person is not regarded as an isolated individual living independently, but a being who is embedded in a wide range of relationships with a 'social arena'. Here, people move around in networks within which their views, actions, and reputations are taken into account and considered as being significant. For the Ismaili elderly then, the issue does not rest at the level of social loneliness but revolves around generational continuity. Having 30 people around one's death bed is not a sudden occurrence, emerging from a vacuum, but a work of a life time. Perception of the undermining of their social arenas translates into the possibility of dying alone, even in a situation of the elderly living with their families.

One strategy adopted to exorcise this anxiety is finding solace in Allah, but this also contains ambiguities. In the Ismaili tradition, the sustenance of faith is closely linked with the performance of good deeds. One without the other is unthinkable. The relationship between the two is conceived in relation to material and spiritual. Without the material context (involving action in an arena of social relationships) the spiritual remains unmanifested; without the spiritual, the material becomes stasis. A life of isolation and redundance means that the elderly are denied the opportunity to play their traditional action-oriented role such as: containing familial conflicts, being hospitable, offering advice, promoting social ties, offering consolation and solace. It is worth noting that here it is not a matter of help and support being offered to the older generation by the younger (the main focus of the literature on ethnic aged) but the older generation being deprived of the opportunity to engage in reciprocal and mutual relationships in their respective social arenas.

Eventually, there is a process of engagement, a movement outside of the self leading to the recognition of connections between personal dilemmas and those of the collectivity, inclusive of mainstream elderly of Caucasian origins. The predicament of having to grow old in a society which allows social death to precede physical death by many years (Moore 1978: 70) is confronted at many levels. Passages from a male and a female respondent illustrate this point.

Male Respondent

See here, in this country, the basic needs are provided. There is T.V., sometimes my son brings in a video (Indian movie). Then there is the tape recorder, I listen to the 'Ginans' and 'Geets' (religious recitations). In doing this, half the day goes by. One has to kill time, this is part of survival. Yes, I feel lonely, but who does not. For us old people, this is the way of life here. My peer lives on his own; he had made his life; he tries to fill his time just like I do. But, I know there are great moments of sadness in his life. His family members visit him once a week. I am better off; at least I am with my son. At least, I get to see my family everyday. Look at the other mainstream (white) elderly. They are independent. They go out more than we do. They drive or catch a bus; but I don't know whether they are happy. May be they are, may be not. What happens when they fall sick, or they are on their death bed. Who will be around. Will they have a hand to hold or a face to relate to?

Female Respondent:

Us women, we keep busy in the house. I do whatever my health permits. I cut a few vegetables, clean the cupboards, make some pickle, there is always something to do. I also watch T.V. Time passes. Then I talk to my relatives and friends in the city, over the phone. Something or the other needs to be looked after. It is matter of filling time. There are no neighbors to talk to. These people (white elderly) do not talk to us very much. They say 'Hello', 'How are you', 'Nice weather' or something like that. May be they feel they we can't talk to them because we don't know English. I can understand some English. It is a matter of feelings. Here, people don't have time for feelings. Too much hustle and bustle. It is all wrong. One day we will have to leave everything behind. People don't understand. Although 'white' elderly are independent, I don't know how they can live without family. Everyone for himself or herself. That is the way of life here. My peers are in the same situation. We all attempt to fill our time, yes that's what it is – filling your time; empty – What does it all mean? I live with shattered dreams and so do others.

Cathartic breakthrough in the predicaments and dilemmas of Ismaili elderly occurs through a process of inter-reference and inter-connection. A common denominator identified by the respondents is that of filling time. Unlike the younger members, engaged in 'productive' and more validated forms of work in the labor force, Ismaili elderly are acutely aware that each day has to be lived and each hour has to be passed, albeit in the company of a living spouse or alone. Significantly, a crucial aspect here is not filling in hours for themselves individually, but struggling and finding ways to maintain contact with kin and the outside world. A context for social interaction does not exist but requires continual reformulation and recreation. There is also the recognition that establishing such contacts with their cohorts is inadequate. Such a situation does not allow for the transmission of valued cultural traditions. The most difficult and a mammoth task is to penetrate and establish a niche in the space occupied by the younger generation, an opportunity which is structurally taken away from the elderly through redundancy of their roles.

Efforts to Resolve the Dilemma

Through an ingenious usage of electronic paraphernalia (T.V., V.H.S., tape recorder, and radios), commonplace in the majority of Canadian homes, Ismaili elderly are engaged in transmitting some of the cherished values of their heritage. At one level, it appears that the electronic devices are used by elderly

Ismailis to pass their time in a manner that is meaningful and entertaining. But there is another dimension to this. Our observations reveal that the elderly are engaged in a vigorous process of re(formulation) and re(discovery) of their heritage in relation to, and not divorced from, mainstream life. A message that was repeatedly conveyed by the informants was that, unlike the younger generation, the former had time on their hands. The elderly then did not merely watch the programs or listened to the tapes that their children would often borrow for them from Indian stores. They are actively engaged in screening the information. Oftentimes, the elderly would identify familial themes, especially from Indian films. The two contrasting themes for selection were those of nurturing and the importance of family ties and forces that lead to a state of disarray. The latter condition resulted from intense involvement in individualistic material forms of life, divorced from kinship ties and obligations. Elderly Ismaili ensured that the powerful medium of film conveyed the message of family life more effectively, especially in a situation whereby their voices were not heard or taken note of. Likewise, through the usage of professionally recorded religious tapes (available from *Jamat Khanas*) and, occasionally, *Gujerati* bulletins (available from Indian stores), Ismaili elderly were engaged in transmitting cherished values of their tradition in fragments. As one respondent explained it:

> Our children may listen to these tapes in bits and pieces; someday these messages will take root. Little by little these things will enter their minds.

Many times the elderly are engaged in conveying information, which though traditionally commonplace, had become submerged. This information was brought to light by the elderly, based on themes extracted from films, tapes or bulletins. Some of the common sayings related are:

> "Time that will go by will never come back; so if you have to act, do so now".
> "A person always dies with empty hands. Nothing will accompany a dead person."
> "A person never becomes poor by giving".
> "Say kind words. You have nothing to lose".

Taping of the narratives that the elderly Ismailis related to me in their native tongue of *Gujerati*, formed part of the process of conveying messages in bits and pieces, with the hope that someone out there would listen to the life stories of a generation whose ways of life were not otherwise transmitted in any form or shape. While the elderly were striving to create social space to reverse their muted conditions of life, I was, likewise, seeking means through which I could create a space where I could at least talk about my muted identity. Collecting life stories of the elderly within a tentative framework of 'critical anthropology' provided me with the opportunity to centrally locate the collective voice of the elderly and my own voice which form part of their life stories in terms of muted identities.

CONCLUSION

Life story as a genre of expression for participants of field research as well as the ethnographer has the potential to make an innovative contribution to critical anthropology. Despite its claim to have accommodated the voices of the other through the production of multi-genred text, critical anthropology continues to occupy a slippery slope. Grave doubts have been voiced by critics as to whether this new wave of critical anthropology is truly dialogical and whether it constitutes a mask for the perpetuation of asymmetrical power relations between those who do the studying and those who are studied. Crapanzano (1992: 92) refers to this state of affairs as "double indexing". He (ibid.: 92) writes:

> The difference may be masked meta-pragmatically by the dialogue's pretense. Court speech, diplomatic exchange, conventional hypocrisy, and, of particular interest to us, those cross-cultural exchanges 'between equals' in this postcolonial era that just a few years ago, during colonialism, were manifestly hierarchical, are especially revealing of this double indexiality.

A closer scrutiny of the situation reveals that critical anthropology has as yet not questioned the notion of 'fieldwork'. This is a moot issue on account of the fact that the distinctiveness of the discipline of anthropology derives from the ethnographer's personal encounters with the subjects of the field. This encounter (subdued within conventional anthropology) is now receiving increasing recognition within critical anthropology in terms of dynamics of relationships as well as acknowledgement of the ethnographer's location as a positioned subject. This stance, however, continues to view the field as a bounded and discrete unit. Bracketing the field in this manner has serious implications as the colonial demarcation of the West studying the rest of the Other remains unchanged. Most importantly, fieldwork has entailed the suspension of the identity of the ethnographer through its insistence that the latter remain a 'participant observer'. 'Participant' and 'observer' are not compatible when it comes to recognition of the totalizing experience of the ethnographer. The latter is a participant for the purpose of obtaining special access to data, written up in the form of a text. To achieve this goal, the ethnographer is compelled to maintain the status of an observer. In this regard, the life story approach recognizes the ambivalent and suspended position of the ethnographer. Relating one's life story in relation to and as evoked by the field experience (as I have attempted to do in this paper) defies bracketing of field site. This process is all the more vigorous in a situation where life stories are constructed mutually between participants of field research and the ethnographer. Being able to construct my own life story while listening to those of the Ismaili elderly led to mutual attempts to reconstruct our identities in a changed milieu. It is in the realm of mutual learning and search that the life story approach holds its greatest potential.

The life story approach leads to connection of lives. The mutual encounter between elderly Ismailis and myself as an indigenous ethnographer took place in the 'field'. However, the emergent life stories and our continuous search for reconstruction of identities reveal that there is no bounded field. Likewise the dialogue is not located at points of 'field' interaction between Ismaili elderly and myself but at those points where our life stories are interconnected through our mutual search for a plural identity (East African/Canadian), which by its nature is a continuous process. In critical anthropology then, the life story approach is a means for connecting lives. Such an enterprise is not merely dialogical or confined to the text, but goes beyond to embrace mutual aspirations and concerns.

ACKNOWLEDGEMENTS

I would like to acknowledge my gratitude for the valuable comments of the 3 anonymous reviewers and to the President's Research Grant, Simon Fraser University, for its support. The question of plural and muted identities came into sharper focus during my recent trip (May/June, 93) to Lamu, Kenya. For this, my gratitude goes to Social Science Humanities Research Council of Canada for sponsoring this research.

NOTES

[1] The life history approach in anthropology and social science has reached a high level of sophistication in relation to collection of life histories in the field, delineating narrative forms, scrutinizing modes of interpretation, and legitimizing multiple forms of literary expressions. The attempt at reconstructing life experiences of individuals from the 'bottom up' has led to greater sensitivity of the way in which non-western cultures have been represented for a western audience. The life history approach has also illuminated the dynamic and ongoing interaction between social structure and the individual. Return to life history has, by and large, been acclaimed as a return to the individual in the fullness of his/her social and unique humanness. Of special importance to this paper is the exploration of the relationship between the interpreter and the narrator(s). Dwyer's *Moroccan Dialogues* (1982), Dumont's *The Headman and I* (1978), Crapanzano's *Tuhami* (1980), Myerhoff's *Number Our Days* (1980), Okley's *The Traveller-Gypsies* (1983), and Shostak's *Nisa: The Life and Works of a !Kung Woman* are notable examples of works that explicitly and boldly acknowledge the transformative experiences, resulting from an encounter between the self and the other. Given the extensive ground covered, life stories, life histories, autobiography and biography come under the same rubric. In this paper, I use the term life story in a specialized context to include collective voices (as opposed to a full life history) where the author's/interpreter's voice is not excluded.

[2] Personal narratives of women have been explored within the framework of feminist theory. Major themes covered in this context are those of power and the ways in which women both perpetuate as well as undermine hegemonic structures by means of narratives of acceptance as well as rejection. Brodzki's and Schenck ed. (1988), Benstock ed. (1988) *Personal Narratives Group* (1989) and Abu-Lughod (1986; 1990: 41–55) are especially insightful in relation to how the life history approach has led to recovery of women' lives in the context of the reconstruction of history and the dynamics of change. My gender came into play in the context of how I was perceived by the elderly narrators.

[3] The almost unlimited potential of the life history approach is brought out exemplarily by Bertaux ed. (1981).

[4] For background information on Asians in East Africa refer to Bharati (1972); Ghai and Ghai (1965: 35–51); Ghai and Ghai (1970); Morris (1956: 194–211; 1959: 779–789) and

Gregory (1971).

[5] For background information on the Ismaili community in Canada refer to Nanji (1983: 94–105); Ross-Sheriff and Nanji (1991: 101–117); Fernando (1979: 361–368); Hawkins (1973: 268–275); Dossa (1983: 232–239; 1985; 1988: 45–65; 1991: 37–43).

[6] East African Asians were placed in a precarious situation; essentially, they were trapped. In the 1960s when the independent nation states were emerging, the British Parliament restricted the entry of Asian immigrants, inclusive of those who held British passports. In 1976, the Asian population in East Africa numbered around 360,000 (Bharati 1972: 3).

REFERENCES

Abu-Lughod, L. 1986 Veiled Sentiments: Honor and Poetry in a Bedouin Society. Berkeley and Los Angeles: University of California Press.

Abu-Lughod, L. 1990 The Romance of Resistance: Tracing Transformations of Power Through Bedouin Women. American Ethnologist 17: 41–55.

Bastida, E. 1987 Issues of Conceptual Discourse in Ethnic Research and Practice. In Ethnic Dimensions of Aging. D.E. Gelfand and C.M. Barresi, eds. Pp. 51–63. New York: Springer Publishing Company.

Benstock, S., ed. 1988 The Private Self: Theory and Practice of Women's Autobiographical Writings. Chapel Hill & London: The University of California Press.

Bertaux, D., ed. 1981 Biography and Society: The Life History Approach in the Social Sciences. California: Sage Publications Inc.

Bharati, A. 1972 The Asians in East Africa. Chicago: Nelson-Hall Co.

Brodzki, B. and C. Schenck, eds. 1988 Life/Lines: Theorizing Women's Autobiography. Ithaca and London: Cornell University Press.

Canadian Ethnic Studies 1983 Special Issue: Ethnicity and Aging 15 (3).

Callaway, H. 1992 Ethnography and Experience: Gender Implications in Fieldwork and Texts. In Anthropology and Autobiography. J. Okely and H. Callaway, eds. Pp. 30–49. New York: Routledge.

Crapanzano, V. 1980 Tuhami: Portrait of a Moroccan. Chicago and London: The University of Chicago Press.

Crapanzano, V. 1992 The Postmodern Crisis: Discourse, Parody, Memory. In Reading Cultural Anthropology. G.E. Marcus, ed. Pp. 97–102. Durham and London: Duke University Press.

Dossa, P.A. 1983 The Shia-Ismaili Muslim Community in British Columbia. In The Circle of Voices: A History of Religious Communities of British Columbia. C.P. Anderson, T. Bose, and J.I. Richardson, eds. Pp. 232–239. British Columbia: Lantzville

Dossa, P.A. 1985 Ritual and Daily Life: Transmission and Interpretation of the Ismaili Tradition in Vancouver. Unpublished Doctoral Dissertation, The University of British Columbia.

Dossa, P.A. 1988 Women's Space and Time: An Anthropological Perspective on Ismaili Immigrant Women in Calgary and Vancouver. Canadian Ethnic Studies 20 (1); 45–65.

Dossa, P.A. 1991 Time, Age, and Ritual: The Dynamics of Interdependence/Independence Among Canadian Elderly Ismailis. In Immigrants and Refugees in Canada. S.P. Sharma, M. Erwin and D. Meintel, eds. Pp. 37–43. Saskatoon: University of Saskatchewan.

Dumont, J.-P. 1978 The Headman and I: Ambiguity and Ambivalence in the Fieldworking Experience. Austin and London: University of Texas Press.

Dwyer, K. 1982 Moroccan Dialogues: Anthropology in Question. Baltimore: Johns Hopkins University Press.

Fernando, T. 1979 East African Asians in Western Canada: The Ismaili Community. New Community 7(3): 361–368.

Frank, G. 1980 Life Histories in Gerontology: The Subjective Side to Aging. In New Methods for Old Age Research: Anthropological Alternatives. C. Fry and J. Keith, eds. Pp. 155–171. Chicago: Loyola University Center for Urban Policy.

Gelfand, D. and A. Kutzik 1979 Ethnicity and Aging: Theory, Research and Policy. New York: Springer Publishing Co.

Ghai, D.P. and Y.P. Ghai 1965 Asians in East Africa: Problems and Prospects. Journal of Modern African Studies 3: 35–51.

Ghai, D.P. and Y.P. Ghai, eds. 1970 Portrait of a Minority: The Asians in East Africa. London: Oxford University Press.

Ginsburg, F. 1989 Dissonance and Harmony: The Symbolic Function of Abortion in Activists' Life Stories. In Interpreting Women's Lives: Feminist Theory and Personal Narratives. Personal Narratives Group, ed. Pp. 59–84. Bloomington and Indianapolis: Indiana University Press.

Gregory, R.G. 1971 India and East Africa: A History of Race Relations within the British Empire, 1890–1939. Oxford: Clarendon Press.

Harrison, F.V. 1991 Anthropology as an Agent of Transformation: Introductory Comments and Queries. In Decolonizing Anthropology: Moving Further Toward an Anthropology of Liberation. F.V. Harrison, ed. Pp. 1–14. Washington, D.C.: American Anthropological Association.

Hawkins, F. 1973 Ugandan Asians in Canada. New Community 2(3): 268–275.

Marcia-Lees, F.E., P. Sharpe, and C.B. Cohen 1989 The Postmodernist Turn in Anthropology: Cautions from a Feminist Perspective. Signs: Journal of Women in Culture and Society 15(1): 7–33.

Moore, S.F. 1978 Old Age in a Life-Term Social Arena: Some Chagga of Kilimanjaro in 1974. In Life's Career – Aging: Cultural Variations on Growing Old. Myerhoff, B.G. and A. Simic, eds. Pp. 23–76. Sage Publications: Newsbury Park.

Morris, H. 1956 Indians in East Africa. British Journal of Sociology 7: 194–211.

Morris, H. 1959 The Indian Family in Uganda. American Anthropologist 61: 779–789.

Myerhoff, B.G. 1980 Number Our Days. New York: Simon and Schuster.

Nanji, A. 1983 The Nizari Ismaili Muslim Community in North America: Background and Development. In The Muslim Community in North America. E.H. Waugh, B. Abu-Laban, and R. Qureshi, eds. Pp. 94–105. Edmonton: University of Alberta Press.

Okely, J. 1983 The Traveller-Gypsies. Cambridge: Cambridge University Press.

Okely, J. 1992 Anthropology and Autobiography: Participatory Experience and Embodied Knowledge. In Anthropology and Autobiography. J. Okely and H. Callaway, eds. Pp. 1–27. London and New York: Routledge.

Personal Narratives Group, ed. 1989 Interpreting Women's Lives: Feminist Theory and Personal Narratives. Bloomington and Indianapolis: Indiana University Press.

Powdermaker, H. 1966 Stranger and Friend: The Way of an Anthropologist. New York: W.W. Norton & Co.

Ross-Sheriff, F. and A. Nanji 1991 Islamic Identity, Family and Community: The Case of the Nizari Ismaili Muslims. In Muslim Families in North America. E.H. Waugh, S.M. Abu-Laban, and R.B. Qureshi, eds. Pp. 101–117. Edmonton: The University of Alberta Press.

Shostak, M. 1981 Nisa: The Life and Words of a !Kung Woman. Cambridge, Mass.: Harvard University Press.

Turner, V. 1980 Preface. In Number Our Days. B. Myerhoff. Pp. xiii–xvii. New York: Simon and Schuster.

Department of Sociology and Anthropology
Simon Fraser University

Burnaby, British Columbia
V5A 1S6, Canada

BUDDHA AND *OKINA* ("AGED MAN"):
THE EXPRESSION OF DYING AND MATURITY

TETSUO YAMAORI

1

Today, the elderly are considered as the epitome of people who must be protected and cared for. Withdrawing from the arena of actual duties in the world and being elevated – or perhaps relegated – to the margins of society and family life, they have little choice but to find themselves as the weak who must receive nurture and care. The perspective of social policy in general, including social services for the elderly, has contributed to the birth of this view of old people, and such concerns as "protection for the elderly" and "medical care for the elderly" have reinforced, and continue to reinforce, this view of the aged as frail (cf. Ōtō, Shimizu and Toshitani 1990). However, this perspective gives little idea of old people as living people. There is only the image of old people who are the victims of the concept of "social welfare for the elderly," of shriveled old people.

The view of the aged as powerless springs, of course, from an outlook in which human beings are divided into the strong and the weak. The strong who accomplish the work of society and of family life must protect, care for, and finally nurse the old and sick. Underlying this attitude is the assumption that the old are infirm people living out the final stage of life. Such human beings, who undergo sickness, weaken, die, and then are mourned, are to be watched over and surrounded by concern and sympathy. In short, old people are the objects of the activity of the savior-strong; "elderly" is another word for the extremely weak. It is probable that from this paradigm of the weak and the strong, the "problem of the aged" cannot be grasped. The very attempt to wrest an authentic image of the aged from the duality of savior and saved is futile. If this is so, how can we liberate ourselves from this sterile paradigm?

193

Several years ago, the movie *The Whales of August* caused a stir. Two elderly sisters are living on an island surrounded by the sea. The older sister (Bette Davis) is a difficult woman who has lost her sight. She is cared for by the younger sister (Lillian Gish), who is rather child-like, with a beautiful face and a sweet-tempered disposition. As memories of the past are revived and exchanged, the lives of the two women are lightly sketched. At the same time, occasional visitors give rise to complications that are like small ripples in their daily life. The older sister gives open expression to a selfish animosity, while the younger sister delicately copes with awkward situations. One clear summer morning, however, the two sisters, apprehending each other's loneliness, go out to a hill overlooking an inlet, wondering expectantly whether the whales would pass again in their seasonal migration as they had when they were girls . . .

The two sisters in *The Whales of August* appear to be passing an extremely fragile old age, but they do not hold the expectation of being nurtured and cared for. They are overpowered by their solitude in a lonely environment, but they live bravely, without succumbing to it. In this sense, the two sisters are not at all simply weak or vulnerable persons or objects to be saved. Although hemmed about by various kinds of constraints, they seek to perform with all their might the leading role of the lives they have been dealt by circumstance. In this, they are even imbued with a kind of maturity bestowed by their stage in life as elderly people. Of course, beyond that maturity a long darkness opens out. That darkness will completely engulf their silhouettes, which will before long flow out into it. The small brilliance of old age that comes at the very end just before this – this is the message communicated to us by *The Whales of August.*

Let us consider one other movie, *On Golden Pond,* which was also released several years ago. One summer day, an aged college professor and his wife arrive at their summer cottage on a lake surrounded by woods. Here, their daughter, who had left home after a quarrel some time past, appears with her lover. On top of that, the daughter's lover has a son who has accompanied them. As would be expected, difficulties arise in the relationships among the family members. The relationship between the boy Billy and the old professor is also strained. One day, however, the old man offers to take Billy fishing. In the hidden recesses of the lake, there dwells an unusually large fish. The professor has saved it for a special occasion. Billy's eyes come alive, and the two set off on the lake in a boat in order to catch it. A storm comes up, however. Tossed about by the wind and waves, the boat capsizes, and the old professor is thrown into the water. Billy desperately tries to save him. With this incident as a turning point, the boy and the old man suddenly become close, and among the family members a quiet composure arises.

In this movie, the aged professor, at the time of his arrival at the cottage, has come to despair of life, and his face is dominated by a sour expression. His elderly wife, with concern for this difficult man, endeavors to humor him. The movie opens with this gloomy situation, but through the encounter with the mischievous boy, the irascible old man gradually recovers his interest in life. He had felt himself being pushed into a marginal role in human life, but through the joyful exchanges with the boy, gradually he shifts back into the leading role. For the boy also, this involves the discovery of a new and unexpected world. The process of the changes in the old man and the boy unfold amid the beautiful natural world of forest and lake.

As summer ends and the daughter and her lover leave, the old professor and his wife again return to their solitary life together. Just as the two sisters in *The Whales of August* cherish expectations of the distant seas, so, perhaps, the elderly couple also retain some hope. Were they freed of the apprehensions of the deep darkness that was engulfing them? Of course, the movie does not attempt to enter upon this problem. I feel, however, that the ending of *On Golden Pond* is slightly more affirmative than that of the *Whales of August.* Rather than the scene with the two elderly sisters standing together casting their gaze out over the sea, that in which the old professor and the boy reach their final accord conveys a feeling of having found wholeness. Of course, we do not know what lies at the end of the professor's life.

With both *The Whales of August* and *On Golden Pond,* the old people who appear are neither the objects of social welfare nor pitiable actors who are active only at the fringes of human life. In other words, they are not weak people. Here, the paradigm that unconsciously colors the ordinary talk that we hear around us has vanished. This is the first point.

At the same time, however, we should note here that in spite of this, a not insignificant distance separates the world of *The Whales of August* and that of *On Golden Pond.* While in *The Whales of August,* the story revolves around the two elderly sisters, in *On Golden Pond,* the relationship between the old man and the boy forms the axis about which the story unfolds. Further, to my mind, *The Whales of August* closes with the somewhat dark image of the two sisters, while the ending with the old man and the boy lends a somewhat optimistic light. This is the second point.

From these two movies, three images of old age may be delineated. First, there is the figure of the elderly represented by the two sisters in *The*

Whales of August. The movie deftly depicts the atmosphere of two blood relatives growing old and facing their last years together. Second, there is the image of aging seen in the old professor and his wife in *On Golden Pond.* This is a widely seen pattern; most people who marry enter old age in this way. The third pattern is crystallized in the latter half of *On Golden Pond.* It is the figure of aging that arises out of the relationship between the old professor and the boy. This third pattern may also be seen as a variation on the first or second pattern. However, when we focus on the human relationships that occur in old age, that between elderly person and child forms a distinctive image.

In considering the possibilities of the future of old age, I feel that the third pattern is the most important. The life of an aged person as a leading part and not a weak person can be realized most readily through the third pattern. Is not the genuine saving of the old person, who is considered the object of social welfare, in fact the role of the child?

2

We may note here that the ancient Japanese, when they sculpted images of the gods, often based them on figures of old people. They believed that the gods manifested themselves to them as old people. Let us consider why this should have been so.

For some time, I have felt that, among the cultural properties of Japan, Buddhas and old men or *okina* have played particularly important roles. While relatively young, I tended to think of the Buddhas as inhabiting the world of Buddhas and the *okina* as inhabiting their own world, clearly distinguishing them. At some point, however, it suddenly occurred to me that we must consider what problems arise when the images of Buddha and of the "aged man" or *okina* are taken up together. Since then, I have always thought of them in comparison with each other. In this way, problems I had not conceived of up to then have emerged.

Before taking up these issues directly, I would like to turn briefly to a related topic. It concerns the morning of June 26, 1985. A newspaper article reporting on the condition of former Prime Minister Kakuei Tanaka appeared prominently in the newspapers, surprising many people. Tanaka had collapsed with a stroke and entered hospital on February 27, and had not appeared in the media for four months.

The impetus for the report was an article that appeared in a local monthly publication, the *Gekkan Etsuzan.* The article bore the title "The former prime minister has made a remarkable recovery," and included three photographs taken at Tanaka's mansion in the Mejiro district of Tōkyō. The photographs showed Tanaka sitting on a sofa, but at his side was a wheelchair. His right side was paralyzed by the stroke, and he suffered speech impairment as well. The photographs conveyed a sense of his efforts in rehabilitation. In them, he is shown holding papers and letters in his left hand, while his right hand rests powerlessly on the sofa or his body.

The recovery of the former prime minister was indeed a major news story. It could influence even the present government. The newspapers sought the opinions of political analysts and experts who inspected the photographs. As a matter of course, optimistic prognosis and pessimistic predictions were mixed. One comment printed in the *Yomiuri* newspaper caught my attention. It occurred in an interview with a Dr. Kazuo Miwa, a neurosurgeon. In response to questions by a reporter, he is quoted as stating:

"The muscles of the right side of the face show a light paralysis, and the right arm and leg may be assumed also to be paralyzed. The aftereffects of a stroke sometimes include a gentle "Buddha face," and the former prime minister's expression is placid and without vigor, which is a cause for concern. It will probably be impossible for him to carry out strenuous work or demanding activity in the future" (*Yomiuri Shinbun* 1985).

As it turned out, Miwa's prognosis was correct, but what caught my attention in reading the article was the expression "Buddha face" used in this context. Needless to say, the face of the Buddha image is an idealized expression of an awakened human being. Whether Buddhist or not, all Japanese can readily call to mind the features of that calm and profound countenance. How is it that this "Buddha face" can be used to express the placid expression that may result from the effects of a stroke? Is it appropriately used as an adjective to describe a face that has lost vital expression because of physical illness? I felt as though I were swallowing a thorn when I came across the expression, "Buddha face."

I continued to be troubled by it, and some days later, I telephoned Dr. Miwa to ask him about his description. He replied immediately that it was the reporter who implied the expression, asking whether the term "Buddha face" was not normally used in the medical world to describe a condition like Tanaka's. Miwa went on to add that, in Western medical textbooks, the placid expression resulting from illness was sometimes likened to the tranquil expression of the Buddha, but that this was in the past. Current medical textbooks avoid terms that may express discriminatory attitudes or be offensive to Asian Buddhists.

In this way, I learned that the face that for Asian Buddhists represented the idealized visage of the enlightened Buddha appeared, to Western Christians, to be similar to the expressionless face resulting from physical illness. It was a blow. I was struck that the differences in values of Eastern and Western cultures should work such an inversion. The characteristic facial expression of the Buddha did not necessarily appear venerable to Westerners. This puzzled my sense of values.

I will mention one other example. Dean Rusk, who was U.S. Secretary of State under Lyndon Johnson (1908–1973), was known for never expressing facially any personal feelings. Whatever political crisis might be occurring, he never displayed his emotions. Among the American press, his reputation suffered somewhat from this, for he was known as an uncanny man about whom one could never tell what he was thinking. Politicians who openly express their feelings can gain in popularity among the public, but Rusk did not engage in such conduct. Thus, news reporters wrote wryly that his face was like the Buddha's. It was an inscrutable face that did not show what he was thinking.

Here again, the face of Śakyamuni Buddha is negatively appraised. I had thought that Buddhism was a great Eastern religion of which the whole world could be proud and had assumed that Westerners would have no disagreement with this, but I realized that this was not necessarily the case.

It seems, however, that the expression "Buddha face" is no longer used. It has lost its currency as a medical expression. To take the face of the Buddha as corresponding to a typical feature of the expression of an invalid may have been judged inappropriate and therefore to be avoided. I sense in this the self-reflection of Christians with regard to Buddhists.

In the past several years, I have seen three close friends stricken with cancer and die. Each of these three had been extraordinarily energetic in his field of activity, but I noticed that, after coming down with cancer, their faces, as they weakened, quite mysteriously grew to resemble the peaceful expression of the traditional *okina* or old man. I was struck at how human facial expression could, through internal sickness, change in this way.

The pain and suffering of sickness, and the daily effort to endure that pain, may have worked a profound transformation of their facial expressions. It is impossible to grasp any thread of cause and effect here, but my three friends who suffered from cancer and died, in the final stages of their illness, all underwent a transformation of their countenance into the peaceful, gentle face of the *okina*. It can only be called a mystery. I came to think that I would like to approach death with the expression of the *okina* also.

At that time, it occurred to me that, through illness in body and mind, human beings' expression sometimes undergoes a gradual change. That is, in sustaining the illness, the human facial expression ages rapidly, and in the end approaches that of the *okina*. It is by undergoing illness that torments body and mind that for the first time one obtains the gentle expression of the aged that is termed *okina*. This paradoxical human maturation emerges naturally.

Speaking generally, in our ordinary daily lives, we age little by little, adding one year after another. In the steady advance of time, we grow older and mature. People who undergo a serious illness in body and mind, however, through bearing the weight of the disease, age considerably all at once. Moreover, they do not simply age, but in cases, they may experience a rapid maturation occasioned by the sickness. Perhaps they are bestowed with the expression of the *okina* in this way. Of course, this is not the case with all people. In that case, whether or not one is blessed with the *okina* expression must be called a matter of fate; that fate, however, surely holds a profound meaning.

Considered in this way, it seems to me that the expression "Buddha face" that I mentioned before is illuminated by a new context and that it gains new life. To summarize the discussion up to this point, in the thinking in Western medicine in the past, "Buddha face" described the placid facial features that appeared in some people who suffered physical disease; I have mentioned the sense of incongruity I felt on discovering this. Further, in the background of that sense of incongruity lay what may be called a traditional conviction that I held that originally there was no relationship between the Buddha's face and physical illness. I have come to think, however, that such a view may be superficial. The Buddha's face does not simply symbolize the tranquil expression of a person who has attained awakening. Rather, is it not the serene and self-possessed expression attained for the first time through enduring all human pain and suffering and transcending it?

If one shifts one's perspective in this way, then there is no necessity to be concerned about the use of the expression "Buddha face" when a gentle expression happens to appear in a person who has been stricken by sickness. If the facial expression that appeared in Tanaka after he collapsed with a stroke and then recovered resembled the face of the Buddha, why is there need to be surprised? To be sure, he had lost the great energy that had previously propelled his very active life, and he could never return to the world of politics. Nevertheless, in place of these losses he had gained for his own the calm facial features that not everyone can obtain. The term

"Buddha face" even seems a term reserved for precisely such a use. Tanaka, whatever his own awareness, had approached the realm of maturity in his expression.

Here, however, I am caused to pause once more. There is one point that makes me uneasy. When I think of the "aged man" or *okina* face that my three friends who died of cancer had and Tanaka's Buddha face together, I am struck by an inexpressible sense of unlikeness. My friends' *okina* face and Tanaka's Buddha face seem the same, but there is a difference. From the perspective of the calmness and gentleness of the expression, the *okina* face seems to me to surpass the Buddha face. With regard to human maturity also, the *okina* face seems a more appropriate expression than the Buddha face. Further, when I speak of the *okina*, I naturally call to mind the mask used in the *okina* dance in Nō. It is the gentle, kindly, smiling face of an old man.

These days, I am constantly occupied with a certain topic. Put into words, it might be expressed, "Buddha is young, *okina* is old." Buddhist statues and the face of the Buddha are generally youthful in appearance; their bodies, too, are depicted with the radiance of youth. There seems little question that they manifest idealizations of the bodies of youths. What of images of the Japanese gods (*kami*)? Such images began to be made in the Nara period (710–794) under the influence of Buddhist statuary. Until then, it was unthinkable that images depicting the gods should be sculpted or painted. Behind the construction of images of gods the cultural collision brought about by the introduction of Buddhism was clearly at work.

3

Here, let us turn briefly to a historical perspective. Taking up concrete examples of Buddhist images and the figure of the *okina*, I will compare them as they appear in traditional culture. Famous Buddhist statues, whether they represent Buddhas or Bodhisattvas, are all youthful in expression, and it may be said that none show slack or wrinkled faces. As mentioned before, they are idealizations of the facial appearance of youths. Of course, this is not to say that there are no Buddhist statues at all revealing somewhat older figures, but we cannot find Buddhist statues clearly depicting an aged appearance. Since such statues were first made in India from about the first to the second centuries (Takada 1967), we may say that from that time down to the present, statues of Buddhas created and transmitted in Buddhist countries have all had youthful expressions.

By comparison, what are the images of gods like? Originally, the gods of Japan were without form or physical characteristics, and drawing pictures or carving statues of them was not permitted. One will find, at any shrine one may visit, that a mirror is enshrined. The real body of the god is the mountain, hill, or forest behind the shrine. The god hides its form in the mountain, hill, or forest, and at the time of festivals, it appears suddenly and inhabits the mirror. When the festival is over, it vanishes far off into the universe. This is the original character of the Japanese gods. Hence, ancient shrines, when the time of festivals approached, constructed a temporary shrine, and when the festival ended, that temporary shrine was burned.

When Buddhism was transmitted from the Chinese continent, however, it brought with it resplendent statues; moreover, exquisite accessories came to be made and temples were built. It was inevitable that most people were drawn to Buddhism. Japanese Shinto considered this a moment of crisis and moved to cope with the situation. Statues of gods came to be made in the same way as statues of Buddhas; this is thought to have occurred from the 6th to the 7th centuries. That Japanese Shinto at present constructs shrines and enshrines various god images is the result of the influence of Buddhism (Yamaori 1991:89–99).

What kind of facial features, then, did the Shinto statues of the early period have? Records survive indicating that during the Nara period, various kinds of statues of gods were made, but not a single one survives. The oldest statues of gods extant today are the male and female deities enshrined in the Matsuo Shrine in Kyōto, and were made during the Heian period (794–1185). Interestingly, the male figure is of an old man. He is depicted in Chinese-style clothing with a headdress and he holds a ceremonial wooden scepter. Further, a white beard hangs from his chin. The face is wrinkled and the eyes raised into a frightening expression. It is, in other words, an *okina* or old man figure and expression. Why, then, should the oldest extant statue of a god in Japan depict the *okina* figure? Certainly, the images of gods in shrines of the early period depict predominantly aged figures. The statue of the male god at the Kumano Hayatama Shrine (Shingū, Wakayama Prefecture), which is said to have been made about the same time as the male statue at the Matsuo Shrine, also depicts an aged figure (Oka 1966; Yamaori 1991:161–166).

Here, let us turn to the question of how gods are described in ancient documents in Japan, taking up two or three representative examples. First, in *Kojiki* (712) and *Nihon shoki* (720), the myth of the descent of the grandchild of the gods is narrated. The sky god of Takamagahara descends to earth and reigns over the land of Nakatsukuni in Toyoashihara. This sky god is Niniginomikoto, the grandson of goddess Amaterasu ōmikami. He descended to the mountain peak of Takachiho in Hyūga. At that time, he was greeted by an old man known as "the old man Shiotsuchi ('salt-earth')." This old man guides the sky god to the sea coast and goes out together with him in a boat, speaking of the bounty of the sea and the paths through the sea. Finally, he says, "Actually, I am the god of this country. As the god of this country, I have greeted you, a god of the sky, and give you great welcome." (*Nihon Shoki*, vol. 1; NKBT 67:157–167). In this way, at the important scene when the grandson of the goddess of the sky descends and is greeted, the one who welcomes him takes the form of an old man; further, he declares himself to be the god of the country. We see here that at a very early stage in the records of myths, the god of the Japanese land is said to have taken the form of an old man.

Another example are the descriptions in the records of the various regions (*fudoki*) that gradually began to be written throughout the country. In reading such extant records as the *Izumo fudoki* or the *Hitachi fudoki*, we find numerous legends concerning geographical place names. These legends record why a mountain or a river has a certain name, giving its origin. Among these are traditions concerning the visits of gods. On such occasions, the one who greets the gods is the old man or *furu okina* (cf. *Fudoki*, NKBT 2:34–35). The god and the old man speak together, and this is related in the tradition concerning the name of the place. Thus, an important leading figure of the local record is the old man, and this old man sees the god, hears the god's words, and passes them down to his children and grandchildren. In the world of the local records, the figure of the old man is focused on as the one who orally transmits culture.

Next, in the Nara period, the way of thinking in Buddhism gradually surfaces. Under the influence of myths and legends transmitted from the Asian continent, various stories come to be told and recorded throughout the country. For example, in the *Nihon ryōiki* (c. 822), a collection of Buddhist tales complied by the Yakushiji monk Kyōkai in Nara, the following is recorded (*Nihon ryōiki* 1/6; NKBT 70:88). The Nara period monk Gyō-zen goes to the Korean peninsula, where he travels about and performs various practices. Once, because a flood has washed out the bridge, he cannot cross a river. Powerless, he concentrates his thought on the Bodhisattva Kannon, when from upstream a single boat appears. An old man with a white beard is poling the boat, and he waves to beckon Gyōzen. The monk boards the boat as he is told and crosses to the opposite shore. As he turns in order to thank the boatman, he finds that the old man has suddenly vanished. Gyōzen is recorded as saying that the old man in the boat was in fact a manifestation of Kannon Bodhisattva. It is important to note here that Kannon Bodhisattva takes on the form of an old man.

Above, citing examples form the *Kojiki*, *Nihon shoki*, and local records, I stated that the Japanese gods frequently appeared in the form of old men, but here we see that even the Buddhist figure of Kannon Bodhisattva, in a story told in *Nihon ryōiki*, manifests itself in this world as an old man. Here also, we see another example of the close interrelationship and fusion of Buddhism and Shinto. In any case, we see that, already in this early period, the idea was widespread that when gods and Buddhas appear before human beings, they assume the figure of an old man.

4

I would like to consider here the character of representative gods in greater detail. Three gods – Hachiman, Inari, and Kitano Tenjin – account for more than eighty percent of the god population in Japan. There is hardly a village throughout the country where these three gods are not enshrined. In this sense, they cannot be ignored in seeking to clarify the basic characteristic of god worship in Japan.

The Hachiman god descended to earth in the Nara period at Usa in Ōita prefecture, Kyūshū. The Hachiman of Usa was bidden to Iwashimizu in Kyōto during the Heian period, and further to Tsurugaoka in Kamakura, by Yoritomo Minamoto, in the Kamakura period (1185–1333). The original, central shrine is the Hachiman Shrine in Usa, the first branch shrine at Iwashimizu, and the second branch at Tsurugaoka; with these as headquarters, Hachiman shrines were built throughout the country. According to the legend concerning the descent of the Hachiman god to Usa, an old man with awesome features and tattered clothes, known as the "blacksmith *okina*," lived on Ogura mountain behind the present Hachiman Shrine in Usa. The priest who worshipped the mountain was troubled by this. He went to the old man and said, "If you are really a god, please give me some evidence." Some time later, the strange old man suddenly transformed himself into a three-year-old child and identified himself, saying "It is I who am the god Hachiman" (*Fusō ryakki* vol. 3; KT 12:31). With this, the surprised priest realized that the old man was indeed a manifestation of the god. It is important to note here that in the Japanese worship of gods, the gods have the power to transform themselves from old men to children. Old men and children are in a relationship of transformation into each other based on their divine nature. Commonly it is said of the elderly that through aging they return to a condition of childhood, and in the worship of gods, the same kind of thinking is manifested. Through aging, one approaches the gods, and also approaches the world of children. In other words, the possibility of being reborn into another condition becomes nearer.

Next, let us consider the Inari god. The center of Inari faith is the Fushimi Inari Shrine in Kyōto. This shrine was built and developed during the Heian period. The image of the Inari god seen in the *Inari engi* and other documents is generally that of an old man. Depictions show the god with white whiskers, carrying sheaves of rice, and accompanied by two women. In addition, a cooperative relationship between the Inari god and Kūkai is told. When Kūkai built Tōji temple, legend states that he used the cedar trees of Fushimi Inari Mountain. In old versions of the *engi* or legends on the origins of the shrine, it is recorded that Kūkai and the Inari god met at Tanabe in Kii (present Wakayama Prefecture). At that time, the Inari god had the form of an old man. Kūkai, declaring that he would soon built Tōji temple in the capital, invited the god there. When the temple was completed, the Inari god visited it (*Inari daimyōjin ruki*, in Fushimi Inari taisha 1957:39). Exchanging encouragement, Kūkai wished for the prosperity of Shinto and the Inari god wished for the growth of esoteric Buddhism; their relations were very close. In this way, in the early period, faith in Inari and faith in esoteric Buddhism were deeply intertwined. During the movement to separate Shinto and Buddhism, however, they came to be considered completely distinct and that perspective has continued down to the present. Their history has been forgotten.

There are a great many examples of paintings and sculptures of the Inari god. It must not be forgotten, however, that they are not all in the image of old men. We should note that there are also depictions as women. In other words, the Inari god has also been imagined in female form. Furthermore, I believe that this female image is older than the male image. The Inari god, in ancient times, had a female form, and gradually this image was transformed into that of an old man. It is not clear why this should have been so, but I think we must recognize two aspects in the Inari faith – the feminine character and the character of an old man (Yamaori 1989:17–24).

The Kumano Gongen god also appears in the world as an old man. Ippen, the 13th century founder of the Buddhist Ji school, traveled about the country distributing *nenbutsu fuda* (strips of paper block printed with the Name of Amida Buddha) to the ordinary people. Once, on being asked if the *fuda* really could ensure birth in the Pure Land, he lost his confidence. Making a pilgrimage to the main shrine at Kumano, he purified himself at the river and spent the night in prayer. In the middle of the night, the Kumano god appeared, having the form of an old man in white robes. This incident is depicted in the *Ippen hijiri-e*, a biographical handscroll that is considered a masterpiece of the genre. In it, the scene in which the Kumano god appears is vividly painted and splendidly depicts the figure of an old man (*Ippen hijiri-e* 1975:66).

5

As we have seen, the tradition of representing gods as aged men gradually consolidated itself. This religious awareness reached its climax in the world of Nō, which attained its consummation with Zeami in the 15th century. It was Zeami who gave this tradition of representing gods as aged men artistic refinement by developing it as a stage performance. The *okina* dance comes immediately to mind when thinking about Nō. Different traditions of Nō have developed, beginning with the Kanze school, and a variety of works have been created. The *okina* dance is regarded as the most important among them. It is usually performed at New Year's, when it opens the program. The *okina* mask with a white beard growing from the cheeks and white face is worn for one dance and then the actor withdraws. Next, a child named "Senzai" appears. A young boy who does not wear a mask, he performs a dance and withdraws. Finally, the third movement is performed. The actor wears a black *okina* mask and performs a dance that is the same as that performed by the white-faced *okina* earlier, except that the movements are rougher and more animated. Overall, then, the *okina* dance consists of two *okina* performances and the dance of the child.

Zeami wrote a detailed treatise on the rules of performance, the *Fūshi kaden* (commonly referred to as *Kadensho*). According to this work, in the *okina* dance in Zeami's time, three *okina* performers danced (*Fūshi kaden*, NST 24:40). After Zeami's time, the format changed to the present version with two *okina* dances and that of the child. The reason for this change is not clearly accounted for in the academic fields of the history of performing arts and of Nō drama (cf. Nose 1938). It may be that three *okina* dances were felt to be boring, and variation was added by substituting one with the child. This answer is too simple, however. Rather, I think that we may be closer to the truth by conjecturing that there was a cultural tradition in which the aged and children were interrelated, with the possibility of mutual transformation. Of course, this is not in itself a sufficient explanation. But at least we should keep in mind the deep connection between the existence of the *okina* and that of the child.

In the legendary literature of Japan, such as *Konjaku monogatari*, there are many depictions of various monks who perform religious practices on such sacred mountains as Mount Hici and Mount Kōya. Some tales describe how a boy suddenly appears where a monk is diligently performing practices and helps him by preparing meals and gathering firewood. In some versions, the child heats water for the bath. Afterwards, he vanishes. But if the monk becomes lax in practice even once, the child immediately ceases to come with food and firewood, and in the end, the hut of such a monk may even be burned down. This alarming child appears from nowhere like the wind, and then before one knows it, vanishes. There are many such tales (*Konjaku monogatari* 12/34, 13/1, 13/3, NKBT 24:185–186, 207, 211).

The children who appear in such tales and legends are not mere children. They are small, frightening sprites who closely watch the activities of adults. With the slightest opening, these nimble beings can strike a blow. They require constant vigilance. For example, Fudō Myōō is usually accompanied by two children, Seitaka and Kongara. In paintings and sculpture, the two children have severe, terrifying expressions. Behind these figures one senses the vestiges of gods. They are children, but gods often manifest themselves in the form of children. Just as one senses the working of gods in the figures of aged men, so it is with these children (Yamaori 1991:20–21). The ancient Japanese possessed this fundamental sense concerning the aged and children.

The expressions of the two *okina* who appear in the *okina* dance – the white *okina* and the black *okina* – are extremely gentle and mild. In Nō drama, this gentle *okina* appears only in the *okina* dance, and the aged men who appear in other pieces all wear the *jō* mask. This mask representing an old man has various types, but, by and large, they are all frightening. The expression is grave, with eyes somewhat slanted upward and the face as a whole deeply wrinkled. It differs completely in mood from the *okina* who appear in the *okina* dance. It may be said that in the world of Nō in the 15th century, these two types of *okina* – gentle and frightening – coexisted (Yamaori 1986:62–82).

I believe that the frightening *okina* in the world of Nō, represented by the *jō* mask, is connected with the Japanese gods. The figure of the old man of "salt-earth" who, in the myth mentioned before, greets the sky god Niniginomikoto, belongs to this tradition, as does the strange old man who is the manifestation of the Hachiman god and the male god statues

with frightening expressions preserved at the Matsuo Shrine and the Kumano Hayatama Shrine. This tradition was crystallized in the 15th century
in the *jō* mask of Nō. When we compare the male god figure of the Matsuo
Shrine with the expression of the 15th-century *jō* mask, we find that they
closely resemble each other. By contrast, however, the gentle *okina* that
appears in the *okina* dance clearly represents a different lineage. What,
then, is this other tradition? The least that can be said is that the gentle *okina* does not represent a god lineage, but rather the idealization of a farmer.

In the different regions of Japan, a variety of folk performing arts have
been handed down, for example, *dengaku, sarugaku, kagura*, and *sato kagura*. In such performing arts, dancers in the form of aged men inevitably
appear. The *okina* performs an important role. This *okina*, however, in
most cases accompanies a female figure, and the two perform a dance with
lewd gestures (Yamaori 1986:75–77; 1994:91–108). For example, at the
Shinshū Shinno snow festival (at the Izu Shrine, Ana-chō, Shimo Ina-gun,
Nagano Prefecture), two performers – one wearing an *okina* mask with a
festival jacket and a cloth tied over his head, and the other wearing a
woman's mask and robe with hanging sleeves – tumble and turn em-
bracing each other and making the audience laugh with sexual gestures.
Again, in the *sato kagura* dance transmitted at the Suwa Shrine at Shimo-
Akatsuka in the Itabashi ward of Tōkyō, two performers wearing the cos-
tumes of a farming couple, with *okina* and woman's masks, dance with
similar gestures. These performances are enacted as part of festivals cele-
brating the year's harvest or praying for the fertility of the fields; the
sexual gestures in the performance may be understood as spells performed
in expectation of the fruition of the earth.

To return to our original subject, we should note that the *okina* masks
that are used in these performances all have a gentle expression. It is the
same expression as that of the *okina* in the *okina* dance finalized by Zeami.
It is clearly the figure of an aged man born from the world of agriculture.
In other words, Zeami elevated the *okina* that was the idealized face of a
farmer to the world of gods. He established it as an image of an aged man
superior to that of the *jō* mask, which originally stemmed from the lineage
of divine representation. Earlier, I stated that in terms of types, the *okina*
with a frightening expression belonged to the gods, while the *okina* with a
gentle expression had the idealized face of a farmer. Zeami, however,
broke with this tradition, discovering rather in the gentle *okina* the image
of gods with divine refinement and grace. This may seem an attempt by
Zeami at a kind of intentional distortion, but I do not think so. Zeami introduced a new way of thinking about the world of old people. Originally, the

gods were feared as beings who would swiftly punish those who grew lax in their offerings. For this reason, they were depicted with the figure of the frightening *okina*. At the same time, however, this frightening *okina* bestowed a rich harvest and various blessings. Zeami sought to give a bright, gentle expression to the *okina* as a deeply compassionate existence. Furthermore, this gentle figure gradually gained the position of the supreme *okina*.

6

When we reflect on the above, we realize that it is hardly accidental that most images of deities made far back in the past are in the form of an old man (*okina*). On the contrary, it may even be said that the Japanese gods from the very beginning have borne the fate of appearing in the world as *okina*. It is in consideration of this historical condition that I have asserted that Buddhas are young and gods are aged.

Various reasons may be adduced for the fact that gods were depicted as aged. The most important among them – it may be said to be quite obvious – is the Japanese view of death and life. In the past, our ancestors believed that when a person died, the human spirit went up into the mountains; there, it was purified, and with the passage of time, became a deity of the mountain. Those gods of the mountain, during certain limited periods of time, descend to the villages. *Obon* and New Year's were such periods. There were, in addition, cases when, for example at the time of rice planting, the gods descended from the mountain and became the gods of the fields. Then, when the harvest was over, they would return again to the mountains. The dead moved toward the mountains – the other world – and at times returned to this world of the village. This rhythm of circulation was naturally believed in.

If this is the case, then the stage of our human lives in this world that is closest to the gods is that of old age. Human beings grow old and die; then, receiving good fortune, they become gods. In the world where such faith was alive, it was surely naturally believed that existence as an aged person represented the shortest distance to divinity. The process from elderly person to god is settled by prearrangement. Probably because of this, the invisible gods, when they manifested themselves in this world, frequently took the form of *okina*.

Considered in this way, the proposition "Buddhas are youthful, gods are aged," became all the more pressing. Behind the proposition, I find that the difference between Buddhism and Shinto, and the distinction in their views of human life, gradually begin to emerge. Finally, I would like to touch on this problem.

I believe that Buddhas are depicted with youthful facial expressions and physical characteristics because the Mahayana scriptures teach the concept of the "eternal Buddha." The "eternal Buddha" is undying. He transcends the ordinary life of human actuality. When, while transcending human life, he further manifests its eternal dimension in concrete form, the physical characteristics of youth are adopted as an ideal model. When viewed from the perspective of the expression of the physical body, youth was taken to be the absolute age to symbolize the eternal.

Why is it that, by contrast, the Japanese gods are aged like the *okina*? It is because of the underlying idea that human beings can only be transformed into gods at the final stage of human life. In this case, the final stage of human life may be considered the climax of maturation. This climax may manifest itself as a symbol of the decline of the physical body, or a decrease in energy, like the withering of a tree. But at the same time, in the physical body that is moving toward death, the luminance of wisdom quietly dwells.

If this is so, then the *okina* does not necessarily manifest "long and never-aging" human life, for "never-aging long life" means maintaining life. The realm of the *okina* is not a long life. Rather, the point of the existence of the *okina* lies in maintaining long life while aging. It signifies living to the very limit of life while affirmatively accepting aging. In the condition of age maturation is reached, and at the same time the world of the gods approaches. The shift toward the world of the gods has begun without our noticing it.

As we have seen, the face of the Buddhas and the face of the *okina* indicate quite different things. A fundamental qualitative difference in thinking about human life underlies them. It may be said to be the difference between awakening in Buddhism and maturity in Shinto. Of course, as an actual problem, in awakening the element of maturity is included, and in the same way, in the realm of maturation, the world of awakening is putting forth shoots. Even so, ultimately the facial expressions of the Buddha and *okina* make manifest to us ways of thinking that are clearly quite distinct.

LIST OF REFERENCES

FUSHIMI INARI TAISHA, ed. 1957. *Inari taisha yuishoki shūsei, Shinkō cho-saku hen*. Kyōto: Fushimi Inari taisha.
Ippen hijiri-e. 1975. *Shinshū Nihon emakimono zenshū 11*. Tōkyō: Kadokawa shoten.
KT 12. *Fusō ryakki*. Ed. Katsumi Kuroita. Tōkyō: Yoshikawa kōbunkan 1942 (= Shintei zōho kokushi taikei 12).
NKBT 2, 24, 67, 70. *Nihon koten bungaku taikei* 2, 24, 67, 70 {Collected Works of Classical Japanese Literature}. Tōkyō: Iwanami shoten 1970–1971.
NOSE, ASAJI. 1938. *Nōgaku genryū-kō* {Study of the Origin of Nō dramas}. Tōkyō: Iwanami shoten.
NST 24. *Nihon shisō taikei* 24 {Collected Works of Japanese History of Thought}. Tōkyō: Iwanami shoten 1974.
OKA, NAOKI. 1966. *Shinzō chōkoku no kenkyū* {Study of Kami Sculptures}. Tōkyō: Kadokawa shoten.
ŌTŌ, OSAMU, HIROAKI SHIMIZU, and NOBUYOSHI TOSHITANI, eds. 1990. *Oi no hikaku kazokushi* {Comparative Family History of Old Age}. Tōkyō: Sanseidō 1990 (= Shīrizu Kazoku-shi 5).
TAKADA, OSAMU. 1967. *Butsuzō no kigen* {Origin of Buddha-Sculptures}. Tōkyō: Iwanami shoten.
YAMAORI, TETSUO. 1986. *Nihonjin no kao* {Facial Images of the Japanese}. Tōkyō: NHK shuppan kyōkai.
– – – – – . 1989. "Kami – henyō to tenkai {Kami – A History of Change and Development}." In *Nihon shisō 1*, ed. Shunpei Ueyama, 4–41. Tōkyō: Iwanami shoten (= Iwanami kōza: Tōyō shisō 15).
– – – – – . 1991. *Kami to Okina no minzokugaku* {Ethnology of Gods and Okina}. Tōkyō: Kōdansha.
– – – – – . 1994. "Okina to ōna {Old man and Old woman}." In *Jinsei to koi* {Human Life and Love}, eds. Nobutaka Furuhashi, Miura Sukeyuki and Mori Asao, 91–108. Tōkyō: Benseisha (= Kodai bungaku kōza 4).
Yomiuri Shinbun. 1985. 26 June 1985.

HOW CULTURAL VALUES SHAPE LEARNING IN OLDER ADULTHOOD: THE CASE OF MALAYSIA

SHARAN B. MERRIAM
University of Georgia, Athens

MAZANAH MOHAMAD
University Putra Malaysia, Serdang, Selangor, Malaysia

Culture shapes the meaning people make of their life as well as how people experience movement through the life course. Although there is some literature on how one's culture influences the experience of older adulthood, there is little on how culture defines the nature of learning in late life. The purpose of this study was to understand how cultural values shape learning in older adulthood in the Southeast Asian country of Malaysia. A qualitative research design was employed to explore this question. Nineteen men and women between the ages of 60 and 83 were interviewed as to their experience of aging and their learning activities. Using the constant comparative method of data analysis, three themes were inductively derived from the interview data. First, older adult learning in Malaysia is nonformal and experiential. Second, learning is communal. Third, much of the learning is religious or spiritual in orientation.

Although there is no single understanding of culture, most definitions center on the notion of shared beliefs, values, customs, and meanings that distinguish one group of people from another (Hofstede, 1991). Manifest in patterns of language and thought and in forms of activity and behaviors, culture is transmitted through symbols, artifacts, rituals, heroes, and values. The culture of a society is "the glue that holds its members together through a common language, dressing, food, religion, beliefs, aspirations and challenges. It is a set of learned behavior patterns so deeply ingrained" that we act them out in "unconscious and involuntary" ways (Abdullah, 1996, p. 3). Indeed, culture shapes the meaning people make of their lives and defines how people experience movement through the life course: "Social and cultural factors shape the way people make a living, the social units in which

Editors' Note: This article was accepted for publication under the previous editorship.

SHARAN B. MERRIAM is a professor in the Department of Adult Education at the University of Georgia, Athens (smerriam@coe.uga.edu). MAZANAH MOHAMAD is a professor in the Department of Professional Studies and Continuing Education at the University Putra Malaysia, Serdang, Selangor, Malaysia.

ADULT EDUCATION QUARTERLY, Vol. 51 No. 1, November 2000 45-63
© 2000 American Association for Adult and Continuing Education

they live and work, and the meanings they assign to their lives" (Fry, 1990, p. 129). Cultural constructions of the meaning of old age may even determine how well an aging person adapts to changing life circumstances, for a "group's cultural heritage represents the accumulation of its tried and tested methods for adapting to life" (Giordano, 1992, p. 23). It is a premise of this study that the nature of learning engaged in by older adults will also reflect the particular cultural context in which it takes place.

Perhaps because most of the research on aging has been conducted in the West (Bee, 2000), it is not surprising that a Western cultural bias characterizes models of development and learning. For both aging and learning, self-reliance, personal achievement, and autonomy underlie attitudes, behavior, and activities at any particular life stage. In an Eastern context, however, collective and interdependent behavior is valued. The purpose of this study was to understand the nature of learning in older adulthood in a non-Western culture. The Southeast Asian country of Malaysia was deemed a particularly rich setting for this study, as the culture itself is a blend of three Asian cultures—Malay, Chinese, and Indian. It was assumed that participants' learning would reflect, at least partially, if not wholly, the cultural values inherent in this Asian society.

CULTURAL VALUES, AGING, AND LEARNING

The study of culture is indeed a complex undertaking. Competing concepts of culture together with postmodern and/or poststructural critiques "of a commonsensical, usually materialist notion of the social" (Bonnell & Hunt, 1999, p. 8) have made it desirable for researchers to identify their perspective. We align ourselves with the notion of culture as defined by cognitive anthropologists; that is, culture is acquired knowledge, including beliefs, concepts, and standards, organized by cognitive structures that people use to function properly in a cultural context (Quinn & Holland, 1987). Cultural values are emotion-laden, internalized assumptions, beliefs, or standards that shape how we interpret our life experiences. We have chosen to investigate older adult learning in Malaysia through the framework of cultural values.

A number of writers have compared Western and Eastern or Asian cultural values and this seemed like a place to begin. We do recognize that these values are in flux and "do not correspond in any neat way with national or societal [and we would add regional] boundaries" (Sewell, 1999, p. 55). Furthermore, because Malaysia is fast becoming a modern, postindustrial nation with multinational and global interests, we would expect cultural values of *both* the East and the West to be influencing Malaysian society today.

Western cultural values favor controlling nature and focusing on the individual over the group, that is, being task oriented rather than relationship oriented and being independent and competitive. Control of nature or the environment manifests itself in Western media-based narratives of aging that reflect "a battle against the

212

decay of human nature in the form of wrinkles, loss of energy, and memory," whereas political narratives "are dominated by discussions about the costs of care required by the aging society" (Baars, 1997, p. 294). Cultural values of autonomy, control, and production are implicit in Western models of development that focus on "successful" and "productive" aging. Successful aging involves optimizing gains and compensating for losses so that "a given individual continues to perform life tasks that are important to him or her despite decreases in skills, ability, memory, and performance" (VandenBos, 1998, p. 12). Riley and Riley (1994), although they recognize that their orientation is "frankly and perhaps inevitably American," still argue that "all older people, everywhere," want to remain contributing, *productive* members of society and will be able to do so if social norms and structures allow for their participation (p. 19).

For American, if not most Western cultures, remaining independent as one ages is valued above all else. Fry (1990) explains:

> Americans emphasize rugged individualism and self-reliance. As an ideal, it reflects an economic organization that emphasizes the immediacy of reciprocity and participants as mobile, unconnected entities. Individuals are responsible for themselves. Also, affluence has made it possible for many individuals to achieve most of the ideal by maintaining separate households. . . . The value of independence is by no means universal. . . . Where social units are more cohesive and life more collective, the value of interdependence, not independence, is accentuated. (p. 138)

Because the meaning of aging shapes values of productivity, independence, self-sufficiency, and control over the physical manifestations of aging, it follows that what older adults choose to learn and how they go about their learning will also reflect these values. In a recent review of the literature on the learning needs of older adults in the United States, Wolf (1998) offers the following summary. Note how the learning needs reflect Western values associated with aging:

> *Self-sufficiency, the ability to remain in control of one's life,* is a prime motivation for adults of all ages. Interestingly, older individuals who become deprived of this "locus of control" have been found to be especially vulnerable to illness and passive behaviors (Beatty and Wolf, 1996; Langer and Rodin, 1977; Rodin and Langer, 1977). Learning for exercise and health maintenance is essential (Deobil, 1989; Hasselkus, 1983; Peterson, Valliant, and Seligman, 1988; Rowe and Kah, 1987). *Education for continued self-sufficiency,* for community living, for vocational, retirement, health, housing, and for other concerns is ongoing (Reingold and Werby, 1990). Indeed, new ways of approaching aging, known as "successful aging" in medical gerontology and *"productive aging"*in political gerontology, are a part of understanding the changing role of the older adult (Rowe and Kahn, 1987). *Education for autonomy* for older cohorts will be essential. (p. 20, italics added)

In contrast to Western cultural values associated with aging and learning, Eastern or Asian cultural values emphasize being in harmony with nature, relationships, and cooperation rather than competition and interdependence. Spiritual well-being

213

is of more concern than material well-being. Cultural values can shape how something as fundamental as physical aging is viewed. In a youth-oriented culture, every effort is made to slow the aging process, cover it up, or deny it. In other cultures, efforts are made to act and look older to accrue the prestige and authority associated with that stage of life (Fry, 1990). Retirement presents another example. In Western societies, there is "a premium on overt and evident active involvement in life, on doing, going, belonging, making. Passivity, contemplation, withdrawal, introspection or even the giving of sage advice are disvalued as styles of life" (Antonovsky & Sagy, 1990, p. 364). One has to legitimize retirement by maintaining an active, "working" lifestyle. In contrast, Thomas's (1991) study of three religious renunciates in India found these wise men to be socially disengaged, detached from the concerns of life including their own physical welfare, living a life of meditation and reflection. Thomas makes the point that this was totally acceptable to their wives, extended families, and communities: "Unlike the ethos of Western society, which in popular culture and gerontic advice . . . extol[s] the virtues of the active mode of aging, elderly Indians are provided with cultural support to engage in reflection and contemplation in old age" (p. 226).

Studies with Asian older adults suggest that although there are some commonalties in the issues and concerns during this life stage, there are also differences. Most older adults, whether Asian or Western, are concerned with health matters and, to some extent, the security of their living situation. But even issues of health and security can be culturally defined as noted above. Certainly family relationships, the community, and spiritual life appear much more prominently in studies with Eastern elderly, reflecting Eastern cultural values of the collective, harmony, and spirituality. In Japan, for example, intergenerational interaction is based on the traditional belief that "the souls of the elderly and of children were thought to be deeply connected. Thirty-three years after the death of an old person, the soul was thought to be reborn as the soul of a child" (Yamazaki, 1994, p. 454). Likewise, in a comparative study of moral development of American and Japanese adults of all ages, Americans tended "to emphasize the autonomy of individual human life separated from the rest of the world, while Japanese . . . tend[ed] to see human life embedded in a human network" (Iwasa, 1992, p. 8). For the Japanese, "it was more moral . . . to pursue a way to achieve harmony between individual and society" (p. 8).

In another study, native Hawaiian female elders were interviewed to identify life themes and cultural values. Three major themes were found to be central to their lives: (a) relationships with people, (b) relationships with nature, and (c) spiritual and religious beliefs (Mokuau & Browne, 1994). In yet another study, adequate social relationships were found to be the key contributor to successful aging and mental health of elderly Vietnamese refugees (Yee, 1992).

Although no studies could be found that focused specifically on older adult learning in Eastern societies, it can be assumed that just as studies of Western older

214

adult learning reflect Western cultural values, the same will hold true with regard to Eastern societies. The purpose of the study was to understand how culture defined the nature of learning for older adults in Malaysia.

Malaysia and Malaysian Values

The setting of this study is the Southeast Asian country of Malaysia. Two regions make up the country of Malaysia in Southeast Asia. West Malaysia, where the capital city of Kuala Lumpur is located, borders Thailand to the north and Singapore to the south. East Malaysia, made up of two states on either side of Brunei, occupies the northern part of Borneo. This study was conducted in East, or Peninsular, Malaysia. The population is approximately 22 million and of that, 6% are senior citizens. Islam is the official religion, but freedom of worship is guaranteed by the constitution. Peninsular Malaysia has been colonized by the Portuguese, Dutch, and British (from 1854 to 1957), and by the Japanese during World War II.

Perhaps the most striking characteristic of Malaysian society is its cultural diversity. In addition to numerous ethnic minorities, there are three main groups: Malays, constituting about 60% of the population; Chinese, 30%; and Indians, 10%. Malays predominate in rural areas and in government jobs, whereas Chinese are recognized as wielding economic power; Malay Indians often work in large estates and in public works. Each group has maintained its cultural heritage, including language, dress, food, religion, and customs. Following racial strife in the late 1960s, legislative policies enacted beginning in the early 1970s have been aimed at building a unified, multiracial nation. Today, each group retains its own cultural identity while living and working side by side in forging a strong, modern Malaysia.

Although each ethnic group retains its own identity, certain values appear to be common to all Malaysian ethnic groups. Abdullah (1996) has identified the following five values. First, Malaysians are *collectivistic*; identity is determined by the collectivity or group to which one belongs, not by individual characteristics. Second, Malaysians are *hierarchical* in that power and wealth are distributed unequally; this inequality manifests itself in respect for the elders and "is considered normal as manifested in the way homage is paid to those who are senior in age and position" (p. 105). Third, Malaysians *are relationship oriented*. Their lives are embedded in a complex web of ties to family, village, country, and/or social group, where mutual and reciprocal obligations are clearly understood and acted upon. Fourth, *face*, or "maintaining a person's dignity by not embarrassing or humiliating him in front of others" is key to preserving social harmony and personal relationships (p. 106). Fifth, Malaysians are *religious*. Happiness comes "from suppressing selfinterests for the good of others or discovering it from within oneself through prayers and meditations" (p. 106). It was anticipated that these cultural values would, to some extent, be reflected in the learning engaged in by older adults in Malaysia.

215

METHOD

To understand how culture shapes the nature of learning in older adulthood in Malaysia, a qualitative research design was employed. Qualitative research is descriptive and inductive, focusing on uncovering meaning from the perspective of participants (Bogdan & Biklen, 1998; Merriam, 1998; Patton, 1990). As a cross-cultural team conducting the research, we embodied both Western and Eastern values. An American, Sharan B. Merriam has traveled extensively in Asia and lived for 2 years in Afghanistan; she has been to Malaysia four times, most recently as a Fulbright scholar for a 6-month period (during which this research was conducted). Mazanah Mohamad is a Malay Moslem and professor of adult education. She received her doctorate from North Carolina State University and has traveled throughout Asia, Europe, and North America. (For an extensive methodological discussion of our insider and/or outsider statuses in conducting this study, see Merriam & Mohamad, in press.)

The sample consists of 19 Malaysian adults older than age 60. The minimum age of 60 was set as a criterion for inclusion in the sample for several reasons. First, retirement age for civil servants in Malaysia is 55. Second, life expectancy is 72 for women and 69 for men, somewhat lower than that of Western industrial nations. Maximum variation was used in an effort to include men and women from the three major ethnic groups of Malay, Chinese, and Indian in proportion to their presence in the population and to draw from both rural and urban areas of the country. Participants were located through the researchers' professional, academic networks; none were known personally to the researchers.

Of the 19 participants, 10 are Malays, 5 are Chinese Malaysians, and 4 are Indian Malaysians. There are 12 men and 7 women distributed across the three ethnic groups. The youngest participant is 60 years old, and the oldest is 83; the average age of the sample is 68. Level of education ranges from 3 participants with no formal education to 1 who has a Ph.D. Participants also represent a range of work experiences from business, agricultural, and educational settings. Seventeen of the 19 respondents characterized their health as good. Table 1 presents a summary of participant characteristics.

Data were collected through interviews of approximately 1 hour in length. Eleven of the 19 interviews were conducted in English. Six were conducted primarily in Malay and translated simultaneously from Malay to English by the bilingual research team member, Dr. Mazanah. Two interviews were conducted in Tamil and translated into English by a bilingual (English and Tamil) assistant. All interviews were audiotaped and transcribed. The interview schedule consisted of open-ended questions regarding the issues, concerns, and learning activities of this stage in life.

Informal observations of the setting in which the interview was conducted (village, home, workplace) provided confirmatory data. For example, an interview with an Indian barber was held in his shop. While his assistant conducted business as usual, the barber "advised" clients and others who strolled in regarding community

TABLE 1

Demographic Profile of Participants

Name	Ethnic Group	Age	Sex	Work Experience	Education
Manan	Malay	75	Male	Governor and educator	B.A.
Ismail	Malay	65	Male	Farmer	Grade 5
Karimah	Malay	66	Female	Housewife	Grade 2
Ramli	Malay	61	Male	University dean	M.A.
Rokiah	Malay	81	Female	Housewife	No formal education
Shahkan	Malay	62	Male	Teacher and businessman	Grade 6
Shafie	Malay	60	Male	Tobacco farmer	Grade 9
Ali	Malay	67	Male	CEO and consultant	Ph.D.
Jafar	Malay	71	Male	Farmer	Grade 5
Aziza	Malay	61	Female	Businesswoman	Grade 3
Daniel	Chinese	70	Male	Military	Diploma[a]
Yin	Chinese	61	Male	Radio technician	Grade 11
Amy	Chinese	60	Female	Teacher	Diploma[a]
Grady	Chinese	80	Female	Housekeeper	Grade 6
Mary	Chinese	70	Female	Housekeeper	No formal education
William	Indian	69	Male	Military/educator	Diploma[a]
Velu	Indian	83	Male	Rubber tapper	No formal education
Gopal	Indian	68	Male	Barber	Grade 4
Devi	Indian	70	Female	Housewife	Grade 3

a. Two or 3 years study beyond high school.

events and activities, underscoring his view of learning for community service. Interviews, however, were the primary source of data. Data were analyzed by using the constant comparative method as presented by Glaser and Strauss (1967). First, each researcher analyzed the transcripts and coded data that appeared to address the research question, comparing segments of data with each other *within* each interview transcript. Next, themes and concepts were compared *across* interviews. The two researchers then met and compared coding and analyses. From this process, a set of themes was inductively derived that characterized the nature of learning in older adulthood from the perspectives of these participants. These themes were informed by our understanding of Malaysian cultural values as defined above by Malaysian author Abdullah (1996), as well as our knowledge of the largely Western research base on aging and learning.

FINDINGS

Three themes capture the nature of learning for the older Malaysian adults in this study. First, learning is nonformal and embedded in the concerns and activities of everyday life. Second, learning is communal. Third, learning is driven by spiritual and/or religious concerns.

Learning Is Nonformal and Experiential

Malaysia is a young country that gained its independence from England in 1957. Only within the past couple of decades has education been a priority; the first university was established in 1965. Consequently, the older cohort of Malaysians has had minimal formal schooling. In our sample, for example, 3 participants had no formal education, and 7 had less than Grade 6. For this cohort, Grade 6 was considered highly educated; one could become a teacher with a Grade 6 education. The lack of experience with formal education is coupled with the lack of educational programs for older adults. In a country that is concentrating on educating its youth, there are no senior centers, Universities of the Third Age, Elderhostels, or Learning-in-Retirement Institutes. Only a few designated programs for seniors exist sponsored by institutions or community agencies.

Older adult learning in Malaysia is thus characterized by its nonformal and incidental nature. "School" is not seen as a place for learning once one has become an adult, let alone an older adult. Religious classes at the local mosque are the closest thing to a formal learning setting mentioned by the participants. Although these classes are open to all ages, the classes tend to be composed mostly of older adults who have time to attend them. Learning is not only nonformal but is experientially based, embedded in respondents' everyday lives. There appears to be very little learning for leisure activity.

Participants mentioned a number of nonformal mechanisms for learning. Devi, a 70-year-old Indian housewife, listens to a Tamil radio program where she learns songs and poetry; she is also learning English informally from her children and grandchildren. Yin, a Chinese retired radio technician, enjoys cooking and teaches himself new recipes through experimentation.

Although he has only a Grade 4 education, Gopal, a 68-year-old barber, reads widely in Tamil textbooks on medicine, science, and philosophy. Ali, the only participant with a doctoral degree, reads motivational books, has learned to fly an airplane, and stays connected to his grown children through electronic mail. Ramli, who is a trained linguist, is perfecting his Thai since he now lives in northern Malaysia near the border of Thailand. He also plans to learn Japanese in the future. Much of Ramli's learning is through reading and the Internet:

> Before I went to the States I took some courses on speed reading. . . . When you have that skill—speed reading—I can read say one or two books a day and I can finish early in the morning. Before coming to work, I open the Internet, to see all the newspapers in the world—Malaysia, CNN, Short Channel Morning Post, Hindu Media, Indonesian newspapers, the Kopang Post from Timor, Bajo Maskin Post from Suawesi. Open those newspapers and read. . . . Scanning everything about the world.

Shafie, a tobacco farmer, has learned and continues to learn from experience and from community-based agricultural extension classes. He feels he has something to add to these classes:

I have my own experience. . . . The LTN [tobacco training institute] says, "This tobacco died because you use this, this and this." And I say, "No, death is a natural part of
life." So I always kind of argue back because I have experience, they have the book
learning. I always enjoy the dialog.

Even Ari, with both an earned doctorate and an honorary doctorate to his credit,
says he learns the most from "the average farmer" who has worked out basic concepts in commonsense ways.

What the study participants are learning is embedded in their everyday lives. As
a function of normal aging, maintaining health has become a focus of informal
learning for several. Yin walks two miles each day to stay fit and reads about health
and nutrition. Ali has learned about hormone injections in chicken and has stopped
eating it. Daniel and Amy have become vegetarian and are now learning about
organic gardening. They have taken a short course and are experimenting with a
small "kitchen garden" on their property. "We are still learning [with the garden],"
Amy says, "because we are not learning in school, you know. And now we are
learning about herbs." She recounts how their garden of vegetables and indigenous
herbs has become something of a model for the neighborhood children and their
parents.

For the Muslim Malays, religious instruction is also a part of their everyday
lives. From Rokiah, with no formal education, to the most educated, reading the
Qur'an and/or attending religious instruction, usually at the mosque, are daily
activities. Ismail, a rural farmer and village elder, receives religious instruction at
the mosque on a daily basis and also meets once a week with a religious teacher.
Businesswoman Aziza, whose formal education was Grade 3, goes to a religious
center for instruction once a week for 2 hours. She also reports having more time for
learning now that she is semiretired.

Learning is also integrally related to the respondents' work life. Aziza, for example, whose business is batik (hand-drawn wax designs on silk), is a member of an
association that takes trips in the region and abroad to learn about different batik
techniques and patterns. William, retired military but now working as marketing
director for a private college, has had to learn computer skills for his job. Manan, a
respected politician and educator, told us how at the age of 75 he was learning what
he needed to know to start new businesses in Thailand and China. All four farmers,
Shahkan, Safie, Ismail, and Jafar, reported learning new farming techniques to
improve crop yield through a combination of experimentation and advice from
local extension agents. Amy, a retired schoolteacher who now finds herself teaching exercise classes to older adults, had to first learn the exercises herself.

Thus, learning for these Malaysian older adults is nonformal, experiential, a
function of their life circumstances. For those still working, some of their learning
is directly related to what they have been doing, whether it is farming, teaching, or
business. Other learning is also embedded in the concerns and issues of daily living.

There is a seamlessness about their learning, in that the nature of the learning is congruent with past and present life circumstances.

Learning Is Communal

The group or community is a common Eastern cultural value. From this perspective, relationships with one's family, community, and country take precedence over individual needs and interests. The Malaysian older adults in this study expressed this communal orientation to learning in two ways. First, much of the learning was in the context of a community; learning was seen as a social activity that provided a vehicle for interacting with others. Second, informants engaged in learning to be able to better contribute to the well-being of others.

The community context. For most of the adults in the study, learning activities were seen as social activities. Aziza, who owns a batik shop, participates in association functions as much for the social interaction as for learning different batik techniques. She particularly enjoys the association-sponsored trips because of the friends she has made. She has no desire to expand her business as she just does it "to pass the time and not be lonely." Aziza wants to be seen as "a friendly businesswoman" to whose shop you can come, not to buy, but just to visit. Amy and Daniel joined a very educational "environmental walk" recently. "We decided to walk," she says, as

> it was for a fund raising cause, to get funds. And there again . . . we got to meet people of all ages, very young people, and people from all walks of life. And some were really impressive, and they invited us in.

Yin also likes to travel to sightsee and "meet some friends." Sisters Grady and Mary who live in a retirement home spoke of their prized possession, a television set. This private set allows them to watch television away from the men and in the company of their women friends. Asked what makes them happy, Grady replied that it is their friends, "people who talk and love, and tell stories—friends." For Manan, learning and education are synonymous with personal relationships. Ramli observes that in a changing society such as Malaysia's, "the world is getting smaller" and although "mobility may be less when you get older, communication will be more and more." He will be able to keep up with his "wide circle of friends" through the Internet.

For others such as Devi, learning is intertwined with family relationships. For Devi, learning some English has more to do with the accompanying pleasure of interacting with her grandson in particular, than how much English she will actually learn. Shahkan, a retired schoolteacher who currently runs a tobacco-curing business, was motivated to learn to use a computer to communicate with his daughter who is studying in England. William finds his harmonica and piano playing a good means of linking with his 7-year-old granddaughter whom he "seduces" into play-ing the piano when he goes for a visit.

Attending study groups is a socially important activity for those who are learn-ing more about their religion. For some, especially the women, it may be their only social outlet outside family activities. Rokiah, who had no formal schooling, learned to read in religious classes and became a leader of a women's Islamic study group. Until a year ago when she turned 81, Rokiah participated in these classes on a regular basis. Karima, a wife of a rural farmer with a Grade 2 education, attended religious classes at the *surau* (prayer room for women) after all of her eight children had left home; only recently has she been confined to the farm due to a major health problem. For a number of the men in the study, attending religious classes was also a social activity, sometimes involving the discussion of political and community civic issues.

Contributing to others' well-being. Besides the social interaction of much of the participants' learning, learning was also seen as a responsibility or obligation. That is, many spoke of the necessity of learning so that they could be better prepared to help others. Ari echoed several respondents when he observed that "I am what I am today because somebody gave me a break." They in turn want to be prepared to help someone else. As Manan said,

> Some of the things that are seen to come my way are given to me. Some I have created myself and developed myself. So it is a combination of what is given and what is de-velopmental. So I have developed this very . . . beautiful experience that I live, not so much for myself, but for people [who have] trained and educated me. . . . And there-fore I believe I owe . . . those that helped me grow up.

Shafie, a tobacco farmer, studies religious books so he can teach at the mosque. Ramli, a university dean, also recognizes that "in order to teach I have to learn a lot." He speaks of being "challenged" by his students: "The more they challenge me, the more I have to learn, and the better I am. In Malaysia you have the Chinese, the Indi-ans, the Eurasian Malays. Everyone who comes to me I consider as a special case." He feels that because he is continuously learning, he has "something to offer." This something is not just book learning; it's what he has learned from "the big book [of life]." Both Daniel and Amy are learning Tai Chi for their own benefit but also so that they can teach older adults. Amy recounts how in the Home for the Aged where she volunteers, flowers are a luxury that few can afford. She has learned how to make plastic flower arrangements so that the home now has flowers. She even convinced a local florist to teach her free since it was "for the old people and for charity."

The barber Gopal has an extensive learning program going on, not only to satisfy his own curiosity but also to be of help to others. He reads newspapers and books about medicine, politics, physical science; he writes poetry but says most of his learning "comes through meeting people." He wants to be a good example to young people. As a member of the Malaysian Dravidian Association, a social action group dedicated to uplifting the community, he tries to get scholarships for students to attend higher education. He himself speaks to community groups fostering self-help and development of the community. "He likes people to be cooperative," translated our research assistant. "He likes people to be in good situations. . . . He is happy if people are helping each other in good spirit. He has no self-interest." Gopal is particularly concerned about the Malaysian Indians:

> There are three major races in this country—the Malays, the Chinese, and the Indians. Among these three races, the most unprogressive race is the Indian race. The other two races have already gone up—they have progressed, they are involved in business, in politics, and all these things. They are developed. But the Indians, they are progressing but very slow, very slow. This is the reason for the Dravidians . . . to bring the Indian race equal to the other two races.

To summarize this second theme, the communal dimension of learning, older adults in Malaysia see learning as embedded in social interaction, whether it is with their families or with the larger community. Learning is communal in another sense also. Participants felt that their own learning was something to be used for the benefit of others and for improving community. This responsibility was carried out through being good role models, through volunteering, and through engaging in social-action agendas.

Learning Is Spiritually and/or Philosophically Driven

Whether Moslem, Christian, Hindu, or Buddhist, the participants in this study spoke of learning in philosophical and spiritual terms. Personal or material gain did not appear to motivate these older adults. To a person, they are content with their lives as they are. Asked what guides their life and learning at their present age, most spoke about being open to new ideas, being tolerant of other races and religions, helping others, and generally leading a good life.

Yin, a Buddhist, had this to say: "To me, if you got the straight heart, you don't have to worry. . . . Do straight and do no harm to others. Don't hurt anybody and don't be too greedy." He does volunteer work at the temple and says, "I don't care whether he is a Malay, a Chinese or Indian, you know. If they need my help, I help them. That's my policy." He says people should try their best to improve, so they "can do something for the country. . . . Don't be too selfish about life." William, a Christian, says only the fellow "who is lying in the grave has completed his education. Until that time you got to learn. And learning is a focus that goes throughout our life." Health and other things are only possible if "your God is with you. . . . My philosophy is, God, King and country, in that order." Through learning and a belief in God, anything is possible:

> I think God has really been good to me. I cannot thank God enough, you know, be-
> cause I never suffered hardship. The only time I suffered hardship was during the Jap-
> anese occupation. . . . But fortunately, again, two strong hands, healthy body and . . .
> hard work. You know, if you have been used to hard work, nothing is difficult. With
> God, everything is possible.

William sees learning as integral to living. We should be "eager to learn" and that "even in a dark tomb, there's always light." He quotes a proverb that says, "zeal without knowledge is fire without light. I want to learn all things and ideas."

At 83, Velu is our oldest participant. He is Indian Malay, a Hindu, and worked as a rubber tree tapper on a plantation all his life. He has no formal education. His philosophy is to "help others, don't do harm, don't rob, don't rogue, and don't visit others' wives." He works in his garden for exercise because he wants to stay healthy so as not to be a burden on others. He is at peace and comments that unlike Europeans who "would like to live up to 90 or 100," Asians are ready to die, as he is, at 55, 65, or 70.

The Moslem participants spoke of their religious-based responsibility to keep learning for their spiritual health as well as to give back to others as discussed above. Ismail, a farmer and village elder, goes to the mosque for instruction because he is preparing for the afterlife. He has no concern about material things as he did when he was younger. Religious instruction is very important because at age 65, he has already lived 2 years beyond when the prophet Muhammad died; one should begin preparing for the afterlife early (as he did at age 45), because "how do you know when you will leave [this world]?" Likewise, Karimah, the 66-year-old housewife with eight children, says she has no concerns about this life. Rather, she is "making preparation" for when she leaves this world. Shahkan, a rural business-man and former headmaster who has learned how to use a computer for his business and for e-mailing his daughter, is also studying religious books, "because as a Muslim we have to focus ourselves on the next world." He reads the Qur'an "at least 20 or 30 minutes every day . . . and the book of knowledge of our religion." The best thing about this stage of life, he says, is that he is "closer and closer to my God. That is the good thing."

The spiritual dimension to these participants' learning was further underscored when we asked them whether they had a role model for this stage of life. Four identified someone whose philosophy they admired, but these role models were for living a good life in general, rather than a model for aging. Velu, for example, named a politician in the state of Madras, India, who was a philosopher and lecturer. Velu, himself poor and illiterate, admires all that this man did to raise the standard of living— "he built a lot of schools, a lot of roads and houses for the poor." The most important thing this man did was to build schools and provide free education until Grade 6. Jafar, who at 71 feels he is living on bonus years because the Prophet died at 63, seeks out a man in his village for religious education who is older than 80. Gopal mentions an Indian who models the social justice philosophy that he lives by. This man "was known to set the first justice society in India. He is known as the Eastern Socrates." Gopal admires his philosophy and "the truth in his speech. He was an independent thinker."

The older adults in this study are also aware of the role they play as mentors, advisers, and wise elders, a role that inspires them to continue learning. Most respondents agreed that being elderly and experienced brought with them a favored position and status in their family and community. Ismail, a village elder, explains it this way: "Town people have a saying that you go back to the village to the older one, the one who has taken lots of salt [meaning had lots of experience which in Malaysian culture equates to wisdom] to learn." Rokiah, an 81-year-old widow living with her children, recounted how she is consulted when major decisions are made with regard to children and grandchildren. Finally, our contact person for Gopal, who is himself a well-educated engineer, told us how he regularly visits Gopal (who has very little formal education) at his shop to learn the "way of life" from the older man.

In summary, learning in older adulthood is characterized by a spiritual or philosophical overlay that most participants were aware of and could articulate. This quality permeates their view of aging as well as learning.

DISCUSSION

The purpose of this study was to understand how culture shapes the nature of learning in older adulthood. From interviews with 19 Malaysian older adults, it was discovered that learning is nonformal and experiential, that it is communal, and that much of it is spiritual or religious in nature. These findings are discussed in terms of what we know about older adults and learning, and the Malaysian cultural values of collectivism, hierarchy, relationships, face, and religion (Abdullah, 1996).

That older adult learning in Malaysia is nonformal and embedded in the context of everyday life is hardly surprising, given what we know about adult learning in general. Throughout human history, learning has been firmly linked to living; indeed, humans had to learn to survive. The association of learning with formal institutions such as schools is a 20th-century phenomenon. So firmly established is the link between learning and schooling that adults have a difficult time identifying the learning that is a part of their everyday lives. Only through careful probing and attentive listening can this embedded learning be surfaced. Nearly 30 years ago, just such a study by Tough (1971/1979) brought this type of learning to the attention of adult educators. He discovered that 90% of adults are engaged in learning projects, most of which were self-directed. Subsequent studies, including one with older adult learners (Sears, 1989), have substantiated the prevalence of self-directed learning projects among adult learners.

Participants in our study learned through experience and sometimes in combination with nonformal programs such as agricultural extension workshops, association meetings, and religious institutions. They also learned through *informal* adult education activities—those activities that occur naturally within the context of people's lives. Coombs (1985) defines informal learning as "the spontaneous, unstructured learning that goes on daily in the home and neighborhood, behind the school and on the playing field, in the workplace, marketplace, library and museum, and through the various mass media" (p. 92). Coombs also observes that because so much of adult learning takes place this way, nations should attend to enriching their informal learning environments especially through the availability of print materials, radio, television, and computers. Indeed, a number of our participants told us how they used radio, books, newspapers, and the Internet for learning.

Although the majority of adult learning, including learning by older adults, in all cultures is through nonformal and informal means (Merriam & Brockett, 1997), there are also some contextual factors that help explain its prevalence in Malaysia. The country's priority is on formally educating its youth. Even middle-aged adults have little opportunity to pursue formal education; for older adults there are no policies, resources, or support for education. Access to higher education and programs such as Elderhostel, Learning-in-Retirement Institutes, Universities of the Third Age, senior centers, and retirement communities with educational programs are nonexistent in Malaysia. Even if opportunities existed, the level of education of this generation of older adults would mitigate against participation (as the level of previous education is the best predictor of current participation). Nor is participating in formal education later in life a culturally accepted practice as it is in North America. For example, since 1976, when the Department of Professional Development and Continuing Education at University Putra Malaysia was established, only one student older than 60 years has attended (in 1999).

The second finding of our study on the collective nature of older adult learning in Malaysia is congruent with the cultural values (Abdullah, 1996) of this Asian society. Elders talked of learning as a highly social activity where they enjoyed being in a group and relating to other learners as much, if not more, than what they were actually learning. Socialized from birth "to maintain harmonious relationships in a social setting of mutual interdependence as found in the village . . . family, friends and the community take precedence over self-centered interests such as profit and materialism" (Abdullah, 1996, p. 26). This orientation helps to explain why Aziza cares more for making her batik shop a place to socialize than for increasing her profits. For a number of our participants, attending religious study groups was as much for the social interaction as for learning. Even for those who were learning on their own, their projects involved interacting with other people. For example, Devi was learning English from her grandson, and Ramli and Ali were learning computers to be in touch with family members. As Abdullah explains, "The notion of a concept of self as an individual and maintaining privacy or solitude is neither well-known nor desirable. [A Malaysian] is affectively related to the others and gains from them satisfaction and a sense of being" (p. 26).

Malaysian older adults also see learning as a responsibility and a means of giving back to their communities. Several spoke of learning to be better mentors to younger people, and several were learning so that they could be more effective as social activists in their communities. Ann and Daniel, for example, first learned Tai Chi themselves so they could teach it to other elders. They are currently learning about organic gardening and have made their own "kitchen garden" accessible to interested visitors from the community. Triandis (1995) points out that "in collectivist cultures helping is a moral obligation, thus, obligatory, not voluntary [as it is in individualistic cultures]. In many collectivist cultures doing one's duty is realizing one's nature, and individual happiness is not important" (p. 120). In Malaysian culture, a priority is placed on making others happy. Personal happiness is secondary.

Motivational studies of participation in formal adult learning activities in the West have uncovered a complex picture of why adults participate. A number of studies have identified six factors that explain participation. Two of those factors— social relationships and social welfare—appear similar to what we are calling the communal nature of older adult learning in Malaysia. People say at least part of their motivation to participate is to make new friends or because they want to serve others or their community. These motives are in conjunction with motives related to external expectations, professional advancement, escape and/or stimulation, and cognitive interest (Merriam & Caffarella, 1998). Studies focusing just on *older* adults and their reasons for learning have also found social contact to be a major motivator (Fisher, 1998). However, the social dimension of learning in these studies is but one factor among many, whereas in our study it appears to be a major characteristic of older adult learning in Malaysia.

Our third finding, that learning is religiously or philosophically oriented, can be explained from a Malaysian cultural perspective. Malaysia is officially a Muslim country and approximately 60% of the population are Moslems. Other Malaysians are Buddhist, Hindu, Christian, Taoist, and so on. Malaysians are quite conscious of the diversity of religious practices and customs in their country and make an effort to be informed and tolerant of others' religious perspectives. This factor, combined with the service and learning orientation of these religions, shapes much of older adult learning in this setting. Islam, for example, "looks at education as a form of worship. . . . 'To seek knowledge is a sacred duty of every Muslim, male and female'" (Abdullah, 1996, p. 33). According to the Qur'an, learning is an obligation for every Muslim to meet individual needs (e.g., how to pray) and community needs (as in learning to prepare the dead for burial). This focus on learning extends into adulthood; Muslims are reminded that the first word from God to the 40-year-old illiterate prophet Muhammad was, "Read! In the name of your Lord, who has created all that exists" (Al Qur'an, surah 96, verse 1). Furthermore, the companions of the prophet studied despite being old.

This religious-philosophical orientation was further underscored by respondents' answers to our question about role models or mentors for aging. Those who mentioned someone were clear that these role models were not for aging alone but rather for leading a good life, doing good works, and exhibiting high moral authority throughout life. Finally, religious motivations could be seen in their desire to help others and their communities. In Islam, this can be explained by the obligation to learn to meet community or societal needs. Christianity calls for similar attention to the less privileged of society, evidenced in our study by Daniel and Amy's fervor in contributing to the old-folks home run by a Christian missionary. Hindu principles and culture also emphasize education in the service of society. This is evidenced by the exalted position given to the largely learned Brahmin caste. Hindus also believe in a selfless self. It is a duty for a Hindu to help others. This philosophy prompts Hindus like Gopal to be charitable. To be able to make meaningful contributions to society, one needs to continuously learn. Buddhists also see learning contributing toward life happiness for self and others. The close association between religion and learning in Malaysia is reflected in the role of the places of worship. The Muslim mosque, Christian church, and Hindu and Buddhist temples all double as places of learning and as community centers.

The philosophical orientation of several of the participants can also perhaps be linked to the developmental literature on late life. Erikson (1982) in particular has written about this stage of life and how people make meaning when their lives are nearly over. The developmental task for this stage is to be able to achieve a sense of ego integrity through reviewing one's life, through care taking, through feeling at peace with one's life as it has been lived. Of this stage in life, he writes,

> What is the last ritualization built into the style of old age? I think it is philosophical: for in maintaining some order and meaning in the disintegration of body and mind, it can also advocate a durable hope in wisdom. (p. 64)

In summary, Eastern cultural values contributed to shaping the learning of older adults in this ethnically (Malay, Chinese, Indian) and religiously (Islam, Buddhist, Hindu, Taoist) diverse Asian country. But like other countries in the region, Malaysia is changing. And although we found the learning of the *current* generation of older adults in Malaysia to be a function of the cultural context and the values discussed above, we would expect to see a somewhat different scenario with the next generation of elders. For example, the current retirement age of 55 is based on life expectancy rates of the 1950s. Little, if any, attention is given to older, retired persons in terms of formal learning programs. As a result, the nature of learning for older adults in Malaysia is nonformal, experiential, and embedded in their everyday lives. With longer life expectancy and the rising cost of living, many will need to work longer. Improved health and living conditions are creating an experienced resource that would be to the country's advantage to tap. Thus, we would expect to see more attention given to formal learning programs for older adults focusing on both leisure activities and training for continued employment. At the same time, we would expect the collectivist orientation where family, friends, and community are priorities, as well as philosophical and spiritual values, to remain important in shaping older adult learning. This study has underscored the importance of considering cultural context and cultural values in mapping the learning activities of any particular group of adults. In applying a "cultural" lens to future research in adult learning, we might better describe the nature of adult learning, as well as shed light on the field's crucial issues of access and opportunity.

REFERENCES

Abdullah, A. (1996). *Going glocal: Cultural dimensions in Malaysian management.* Kuala Lumpur, Malaysia: Malaysian Institute of Management.

Antonovsky, A., & Sagy, S. (1990). Confronting developmental tasks in the retirement transition. *The Gerontologist, 30*(3), 362-368.

Baars, J. (1997). Concepts of time and narrative temporality in the study of aging. *Journal of Aging Studies, 11*(4), 283-295.

Bee, H. (2000). *The journey of adulthood* (4th ed.). Princeton, NJ: Prentice Hall.

Bogdan, R., & Biklen, S. (1998). *Qualitative research for education.* Needham Heights, MA: Allyn & Bacon.

Bonnell, V. E., & Hunt, L. (1999). Introduction. In V. E. Bonnell & L. Hunt (Eds.), *Beyond the cultural turn* (pp. 1-34). Berkeley: University of California Press.

Coombs, P. H. (1985). *The world crisis in education: The view from the eighties.* New York: Oxford University Press.

Erikson, E. H. (1982). *The life cycle completed* (2nd ed). New York: Norton.

Fisher, J. C. (1998). Major streams of research probing older adult learning. In J. C. Fisher & M. A. Wolf (Eds.), *Using learning to meet the challenges of older adulthood* (pp. 27-40). New Directions for Adult and Continuing Education, No. 77. San Francisco: Jossey-Bass.

Fry, C. L. (1990). Cross-cultural comparisons of aging. In K. F. Ferraro (Ed.), *Gerontology: Perspectives and issues* (pp. 129-146). New York: Springer.

Giordano, J. (1992). Ethnicity and aging. *Journal of Gerontological Social Work, 18,* 23-37.

Glaser, B. G., & Strauss, A. L. (1967). *The discovery of grounded theory.* Chicago: Aldine.

Hofstede, G. (1991). *Culture and organization.* London: McGraw-Hill.

Iwasa, N. (1992). Postconventional reasoning and moral education in Japan. *Journal of Moral Education, 21*(1), 3-16.

Merriam, S. B. (1998). *Qualitative research and case study applications in education.* San Francisco: Jossey-Bass.

Merriam, S. B., & Brockett, R. G. (1997). *The profession and practice of adult education.* San Francisco: Jossey-Bass.

Merriam, S. B., & Caffarella, R. S. (1998). *Learning in adulthood* (2nd ed.). San Francisco: Jossey-Bass.

Merriam, S. B., & Mohamad, M. (in press). Insider/outsider status: Reflections on cross-cultural interviewing. *Inquiry.*

Mokuau, N., & Browne, C. (1994). Life themes of native Hawaiian female elders: Resources for cultural preservation. *Social Work, 39*(1), 43-49.

Patton, M. Q. (1990). *Qualitative evaluation methods.* Newbury Park, CA: Sage.

Quinn, N., & Holland, D. (1987). Culture and cognition. In D. Holland & N. Quinn (Eds.), *Cultural models in language and thought* (pp. 3-40). New York: Cambridge University Press.

Riley, J. W., Jr., & Riley, M. W. (1994). Beyond productive aging. *Aging International, 21* (2), 15-19.

Sears, E.J.B. (1989). *Self-directed learning projects of older adults*. Unpublished doctoral dissertation, University of North Texas.

Sewell, W. H., Jr. (1999). The concept(s) of culture. In V. E. Bonnell & L. Hunt (Eds.), *Beyond the cultural turn* (pp. 35-61). Berkeley: University of California Press.

Thomas, L. E. (1991). Dialogues with three religious renunciates and reflections on wisdom and maturity. *International Journal of Aging and Human Development, 32*(3), 211-227.

Tough, A. (1971/1979). *The adult's learning projects: A fresh approach to theory and practice in adult learning*. Toronto: Ontario Institute for Studies in Education.

Triandis, H. C. (1995). *Individualism & collectivism*. Boulder, CO: Westview.

VandenBos, G. R. (1998). Life-span developmental perspectives on aging: An introductory overview. In I. H. Nordhus, G. R. VandeBos, S. Berg, & P. Fromholt (Eds.), *Clinical geropsychology* (pp. 3-14). Washington, DC: American Psychological Association.

Wolf, M. A. (1998). New approaches to the education of older adults. In J. C. Fisher & M. A. Wolf (Eds.), *Using learning to meet the challenges of older adulthood* (pp. 15-26). New Directions for Adult and Continuing Education, No. 77. San Francisco: Jossey-Bass.

Yamazaki, T. (1994). Intergenerational interaction outside the family. *Educational Gerontology, 20*(5), 453-462.

Yee, B.W.K. (1992). Markers of successful aging among Vietnamese refugee women. *Women and therapy, 13*(3), 221-238.

Journal of Aging and Identity, Vol. 5, No. 4, 2000

Respect for Elders: Myths and Realities in East Asia

Kyu-taik Sung[1,2]

The trend in East Asia from authoritarian and patriarchal relationships to egalitarian and reciprocal patterns of mutual respect between generations is eroding the willingness of younger generations to respect the elderly in traditional ways. Have the Confucian teachings on respect for elders become myths? This article reviews traditional ways of treating parents and elders prescribed in Confucian literature and examines how they are expressed in modern times.

KEY WORDS: aging; elder respect; filial piety; Confucian teachings; East Asian culture.

The issue of declining respect for elders is an age-old concern of human society. History records disrespectful and inhumane treatment of old and burdensome family members in past eras. In the East "obasute" was practiced in Japan where elderly parents were taken to a hilltop and discarded; in Korea "koryojang" was practiced where old parents were sealed off in a cave with some food. In the West the Bactria disposed of their elders by feeding them to dogs and the Sardinians hurled their elders from a high cliff and shouted with laughter when they fell on the rocks (Cox, 1990).

In recent years, concern over declining filial morality has increased (Streib, 1987; Post, 1989; Chipperfield & Haven, 1992; Lew, 1995; Koyano, 1996; Palmore, 1999). Studies have reported the tendency of some adults to mistreat and abandon frail and sick elderly parents, to disrespect older persons by neglecting and disregarding their problems, and to respect only the elderly who possess wealth and social status (Nydegger, 1983; Pillemer & Finkelhor, 1988; Moon & Williams, 1993; Tomita, 1994; Kim, 1998). In recent decades, industrialization and urbanization have been eroding the tradition of family-centered parent care in Korea and other East Asian nations such as Japan and China.

[1]University of Southern California, Los Angeles, California.
[2]Correspondence should be directed to Kyu-taik Sung, School of Social Work and E. P. Andrus Gerontology Center, University of Southern California, Los Angeles, CA 90089-0411.

Are the traditional ideals of respect and care for parents prescribed in Confucian writings now myths? Or, do they still exert cultural influences that shape the ways in which the East Asians treat parents and elderly persons?

This article examines the meanings of traditional teachings of respect for the elderly prescribed in Confucian literature and discusses the practice of these teachings in East Asian culture. Passages from Confucian literature are included that describe ways in which parents and elders are to be treated. A number of rules that children are to follow to fulfill their filial duties including respect for parents and elders are found in *The Book of Rites* (Li Chi: Confucian teachings on rites or propriety), *Analects of Confucius* (Lun Yu: sayings and deeds of Confucius and his disciples on subjects including education and moral cultivation), *Works of Mencius* (Meng Tzu: a collection of Mencius' opinions and conversations), and *The Teachings of Filial Piety* (Hsiao Ching: guidelines for the practice of filial piety).

IDEALS OF ELDER RESPECT

The peoples of East Asia have a notable tradition of elder respect. The Chinese, Japanese, and Koreans have shared this tradition for many generations (Lang, 1946; Silberman, 1962; Park, 1983). The traditional basis for elder respect in East Asia is Confucian teachings of filial piety that essentially direct offspring to recognize the care they received from their parents and, in return, direct the offspring to respect and care for their parents (Kong, 1995; Takahashi, 1995; Lew, 1995). More than 2000 years ago, Confucius and Plato addressed the need for respect for elders. In the East, Confucius stressed the need for young adults to respect their elders: "Filial piety today is taken to mean providing nourishment for parents, but dogs and horses are provided with nourishment. If it is not done with reverence for parents, what is the difference between men and animals?" (*Analects*, bk 2., ch. 7; de Bary, 1995). Plato focused on youth as the impressionable period in a person's life when reverence should be stamped on the mind of the learner. He trusted reverence to check the rise of insolence in the young (Hastings, 1908).

For Confucius (also known as "The Master") being filial to parents meant treating parents with propriety. The Chinese "li" (propriety or rites; rules of proper conduct) refers to formal ritual prescriptions for elder respect and to an inner disposition of the mind and heart for elder respect (de Bary, 1995, pp. 58–59). The Master said: "That parents, when alive, should be served according to propriety; when dead, they should be buried according to propriety; and they should be sacrificed to according to propriety" (*Analects*, bk. 2, ch. 5). The nexus of propriety in Confucian teachings is both deference (respectful submission) and reverence (a feeling of deep respect tinged with awe) toward parents. Confucius said: "If a man is governed by showing deference, what difficulty would there be in performing propriety?" (*Analects*, bk. 4, ch. 13).

The Master outlined specific ways of providing care and services for the elderly: "In caring for parents, filial children should make them feel happy, not act against their will, let them see and hear pleasurable things and provide them with comfortable places to sleep..." (*Book of Rites*, bk. 1, ch. 1; bk. 2, ch. 12). Discouraging anxiety is an important way of caring for parents. The Master said: "When one's parents are alive, one should not go far away. If one goes, one should tell them where one is going" (*Analects*, bk. 4, ch. 19).

Traditionally such care and services were provided by family members, typically co-residing with adult children and their wives (Maeda, 1997; Sung, 1998). Stories of filial children in China, Japan, and Korea invariably describe how devoutly they served foods and drinks of their parents' choice (*Twenty-Four Stories*, 1956).

In old age, receiving food and drink of his/her choice is an elderly person's blessing. If the elder likes the food salty or spicy, it should be salty or spicy. A filial daughter would ask her mother what type of meal she would like for dinner. She then prepares the meal according to her mother's wish as a way of paying respect. The Master said: "When a child is called by parents, he should answer 'Yes' politely and greet them in a courteous manner. In entering and exiting their room, he should keep sincere and respectful posture" (*The Book of Rites*, bk. 2, ch. 12).

Young persons coming in contact with elders are expected to have dressed plainly and neatly, to have their hairdos and makeup neat and moderate, and to maintain a posture that is polite and deferent. Thus, arrogant and indifferent manners, and any type of appearance that would cause displeasure or disapproval of elders is considered not respectful. In East Asian culture, deference and ritualistic mores still take on great importance.

In speaking and addressing parents, the child should always use respectful language (*Teachings of Filial Piety*, ch. 4). "A gentleman should take care to speak the proper words in the proper tone of voice so as to avoid coarseness" (*Analects*, bk. 8, ch. 4). Commonly, the young use honorifics when they salute, have conversation with, and write letters to elders so as to convey a sense of respect. The Chinese, Japanese, and Koreans use a variety of honorific expressions elaborately differentiated to convey the proper degree of respect or deference. The level of respect is reflected not only in different nouns but also verbs, prefixes, and suffixes, and even phrases and sentences when these are used in interaction with parents, teachers, elders or superiors. Elder respect is built into East Asian languages.

However, the use of honorific language is not enough. One must exhibit the proper body language; the level of deference is usually determined by the degree to which one bows, bends the body, or raises the placed hands. Often, such a salutatory movement is repeated to convey one's respect or deference. This form has been the first social behavior that East Asian children learn from their parents and teachers.

The Master also stressed the importance of respectfully complying with parents' wishes and directives (*Book of Rites*, ch. 12). Young children listen to the parents' advice and usually follow it. They tend to patiently accept scolding from parents and do not talk back. In workplaces, informal advice from seniors is often obediently followed. And at school, students obey their teachers almost unreservedly. Such behaviors reflect young persons' deference and reverence toward parents and elders. In the family- and group-oriented East Asian culture, respect for grandparents and parents, elderly relatives, teachers, and neighborhood elders has been a social norm.

Children should offer parents and elders seats or roles which are tied to respect (*Book of Rites*, bk. 1, ch. 1). In a room, one must always leave center seats for parents . . . and the direction of parents' seats or chairs should be arranged according to their wishes (*Book of Rites*, bk. 2, ch. 12). In gatherings, elders are furnished with center or head seats (seats of honor), chairs by the fireplace, or quiet rooms. Elders are often given the role of the master of marriage ceremonies or the president of public meetings. Such seats and roles are tied to respect.

Young persons serve foods and drinks, and give assistance and services to elders first such as allowing them to go through doorways, to get in and out of cars first, and to use a shower or bath first. Such precedential treatments are arranged in order of seniority. In Japan, Korea, and China where elderly persons tend to be highly conscious of age-related prestige, precedential treatment has been considered more important than linguistic or salutatory respect.

The Master advised on the celebration of parents' birthdays: "One must always keep in mind parents' birthdays; on the one hand, one is glad to offer birthday congratulations; on the other hand, one is worried to see they grow one year older" (*Analects*, bk. 4, ch. 21). Parents' sixtieth birthdays have been the most celebrated family event among East Asian peoples (Palmore & Maeda, 1985; Jannelli, 1986). The birthday ceremony signals the entrance into old age marking a crucial event within a parent's life cycle, and it becomes a special occasion for family to honor the aged parent. Throughout the year children frequently visit their parents to celebrate their birthdays and attend other family events. An important purpose of such events is to dramatize the esteem accorded to parents and elders.

Dedicating gifts is a valued expression of respect frequently described in the classics (*Book of Rites*, bk. 2, ch. 12). There are two components of gift respect. The first refers to artifacts, usually gifts including clothes, money, and other things of symbolic value. The second refers to the bestowal of favors and prayers. Presenting gifts, particularly those for elders and seniors, has been endemic to East Asians although material support without reverence could not be called filial piety. Mencius (the principal disciple of Confucius) said: "Honoring and respecting are what exist before any offering of gifts" (*Works of Mencius*, bk. 7, pt. II, ch. 37).

The greatest regret a child could have is an eternally lost opportunity of serving his parents with medicine and soup on their deathbeds or not being present when they die (Lin, 1982). Mencius said: "The nourishment of parents when living is not sufficient to be accounted as the great thing. It is only in the performance of funeral rites when dead that we have what can be considered a great thing" (*Works of Mencius*, bk. 4, pt. II, ch. 12).

In discharging funeral duties, the children wear special attire and express mournfulness by wailing and weeping. For them their parents' deaths and subsequent burials are most emotional and solemn times. They hold respectful funeral ceremonies and follow elaborate formalities to mourn for departed parents. Thus, the respect for parents—whether alive or dead—is concerned with our external behavior as well as our inner disposition. Confucius said: "One should offer sacrifices to one's ancestors as if they were present" (*Analects*, bk. 3, ch. 12). "They served the dead as they would have served them alive; they served the departed as they would have served them had they continued among them. This was the highest exemplification of filial piety" (Doctrine of the Mean, qtd. in Chen, 1986, p. 384).

Ancestors' graves and family shrines where the tablets of ancestors are consecrated are built on well-drained and sunny hillsides. In the East Asian culture, where so much energy is expended to select auspicious sites for houses and graves, spatial consideration has been an important form of respect. Individual ancestors within certain generations are commemorated on their death anniversaries and on major holidays. On the anniversary rite for a deceased ancestor, family members typically gather in a clean hall or room, or a Buddhist temple where their ancestor's tablet and picture are kept, arrange carefully prepared foods and drinks on a table for sacrifice, and make bows to the tablet or picture. After the rite, parents introduce their children to memorable stories about the ancestor. Rebuilding or decorating the family temple and ancestors' graves are also important ways of paying respect. The keeping of genealogy and the maintenance of the clan society, still extensively practiced in most East Asian societies, reinforces ancestor worship.

CHANGING TIMES AND CULTURAL RESISTANCE

Although the forms of showing respect change with time, the expression of respect appears not to be subject to limitations of time. In recent years, the number of three generation families has decreased, the authority of elderly members is declining, and a growing number of adult children live separately from their aged parents. Adult children prefer individualistic lifestyles, value reciprocity between generations, and demand freedom from rigid family rules and obligations. Thus, the family is changing—the very institution in which the elderly have been respected and cared for. Meanwhile, the elderly themselves are changing. Sensible elderly persons interact with members of younger generations on an equal footing and earn respect from them (Chow, 1997). Increasingly, public respect and community care are taken more seriously by voluntary and public organizations (Chow, 1995; Palmore & Maeda, 1985; Sung, 1998).

These shifts largely indicate a new trend, a move from authoritarian and patriarchal relationships to egalitarian and reciprocal patterns of mutual respect between generations. Traditionally Koreans expressed their elder respect—the key dimension of filial piety—by giving care and services, complying with directives, greeting and bowing, using respectful languages, holding courteous appearances, giving precedential treatment, etc. These are behaviors they customarily show in their interaction with parents, teachers, neighborhood elders, and seniors in workplaces (Sung & Kim, 2000).

In recent years, however, the meanings of some of these forms of elder respect appear to be undergoing modification. For instance, listening to what an elder says has emerged as an alternative to the traditional form of obedience. And, consulting an elder over personal matters has emerged as another new form of respect, which involves open communication and mutually beneficial exchanges between generations. Thus, expressions of elder respect appear to be shifting from subservient forms to reciprocal or egalitarian ones.

In response to the challenges from social changes, efforts to promote the status of the elderly is carried out under the joint auspices of public and voluntary agencies in Hong Kong and other Chinese communities, Japan, and South Korea such as the establishment of Respect for Elders Day/Week, the enactment of the Senior Citizens' Welfare Law and the Filial Responsibility Law; the development of community care approach, and the holding of campaigns for elder respect (Leung, 1997; Chow, 1995; Palmore & Maeda, 1985; Sung, 1995; Singapore Ministry of Community Development, 1996). Filial piety prizes awarded to exemplary filial children, programs designed to educate young to treat elders with respect, and television dramas showing cases of elder respect are all for the purpose of promoting the status of the elderly.

CONTINUITY AND CHANGE

The traditional ways of respecting parents and elders examined in this article are still being practiced in East Asia although less intensively than in the past (Chow, 1997; Maeda, 1997; Sung, 1998; Elliott & Campbell, 1993). Filial piety and respect for elders are not really myths but are realities among most East Asian peoples. Gerontologists insist that while expressions of elder respect are changing, cultural influences remain to bind generations together in Japan, Korea, and China as well as in other Chinese communities, such as Hong Kong, Taiwan, and Singapore (Chow, 1995; Parish & White, 1978; Olson, 1993; Meyer, 1988; Park, 1989; Goldstine & Ku, 1993; Ma & Smith, 1991; Harper, 1992; Xie et al., 1996; Singapore Ministry of Community Development, 1996; Sung, 1995).

Despite the change in expressions of elder respect, adult children still pay respect for and support their elderly kin. Over ninety percent of young Koreans feel strongly that parents in their old age must be cared for and supported by grown children (Sung, 1995). Streib (1987) finds in China that elder respect is automatically expressed by Chinese people. Palmore and Maeda (1985) report that elder respect is deeply ingrained in the social system of Japanese people.

These findings are applicable in Korea as well. In Korea, children are taught how to respect their grandparents, parents, teachers, and other elders. This process goes on although less intensively than in the past.

Multigenerational coresidence—a living arrangement in which grandparents, parents, and adult children live together and care for and support each other—exists in Korea. This has been a traditional custom and a cultural norm. Kim (1998) reports that sixty-five percent of the elderly sixty years and over are still living with their children in highly urbanized Seoul. (There are more elderly persons living with adult children in urban areas (sixty-four percent) than in rural areas (forty percent) according to Lee et al. (1994)). A recent study of impaired elderly persons needing long-term care reports that fifty-seven percent of the elderly live with their children. Such coresidence is motivated more by desire for companionship and reciprocal support rather than by housing shortages or financial necessity (Maeda, 1977). This high incidence of coresidence partly reflects the persistence of moral prescriptions about filial piety.

Therefore, as Caudill states: "In the course of modernization, cultural characteristics persist and keep each country unique" (1973, p. 346). Cultural influences must be studied and made explicit, so they can be understood as realities rather than as myths or sources of misunderstanding.

REFERENCES

Analects of Confucius (Lun Yu). (1966). (2nd ed.). Beijing: Sinolingua.

The Book of Rites (Li Chi). (1993). (O. S. Kwon, Trans.). Seoul: Hongshin Moonwha-Sa.

Caudill, W. (1973). The Influence of Social Structure and Culture on Human Behavior in Modern Japan. *Ethos 1*, 343–382.

Chen, L. F. (1986). *The Confucian Way*. London: Routledge & Kegan Paul.

Chipperfield, J.G., & Havens, B. (1992). A Longitudinal Analysis of Perceived Respect among Elders. Changing Perceptions for some Ethnic Groups. *Canadian Journal on Aging 11*, 15–30.

Chow, N. (1995, November). *Filial Piety in Asian Chinese Communities*. Paper presented at 5th Asia/Oceania Regional Congress of Gerontology Symposium on Filial Piety. Hong Kong.

Chow, N. (1997). The Policy Implications of the Changing Role and Status of the Elderly. (*Hong Kong Monograph Series No. 28*). Hong Kong: The University of Hong Kong, Department of Social Work & Social Administration.

Cox, H.G. (1990). Roles for Aged Individuals in Post-Industrial Societies. *International Journal of Aging and Human Development, 30*, 55–62.

deBary, W. T. (1995). Personal Reflections on Confucian Filial Piety. In *Filial Piety and Future Society* [Hyo-wa Mirae-Sahoe] (pp. 19–36). Kyunggido, Korea: The Academy of Korean Studies.

Doctrine of the Mean. (1969). In J. Legge (Ed. & Trans.) *The Chinese Classics* (3rd ed.). Hong Kong: Hong Kong University Press.

Elliott, K. S., & Campbell, R. (1993). Changing Ideas about Family Care for the Elderly in Japan. *Journal of Cross-Cultural Gerontology 8*, 119–135.

Goldstein, M.C., & Ku, Y. (1993). Income and Family Support Among Rural Elderly in Jheziang Province, China. *Journal of Cross-Cultural Gerontology 8*, 197–223.

Harper, S. (1992). Caring for China's Ageing Population: The Residential Option—A Case of Study of Shanghai, *Ageing and Society 12*, 157–184.

Hastings, J.(Ed.). (1908). *Encyclopaedia of Religion and Ethics*. New York: Charles Scribner's Sons.

Jannelli, D.Y. (1986). Ancestors, Women, and the Korean Family. In W. H. Slote (Ed.) *The Psycho-Cultural Dynamics of the Confucian Family: Past and Present*. Seoul: International Cultural Society of Korea.

Kim, H.G. (1998). Public Perceptions of Elder Mistreatment and its Reality in Taegu. *Journal of the Korean Gerontological Society 18*, 184–197.

Kim, K. H. (1998). A Study of Determinants of Elderly People's Living Patterns. *Journal of Korea Gerontological Society, 18 (1)*, 107–122.

Kong, D. C. (1995). The Essence of Filial Piety. In *Filial Piety and Future Society* [Hyo-wa Mirae-Sahoe) (pp. 127–137), Kyunggido, Korea: The Academy of Korean Studies.

Koyano, W. (1996). Filial Piety and Intergenerational Solidarity in Japan. *Australian Journal on Ageing 15*, 51–56.

Lang, O. (1946). *Chinese Family and Society*. New Haven, CT: Yale University Press.

Lee, K. O., Kwon, S.J., Kwon, J.D., & Lee, W. S. (1990). *Study of Support for the Elderly* [Noin-Buyang-ae kwanhan Yunkoo]. Seoul: Korean Institute for Health and Social Affairs.

Legge, J. (1960). *The Chinese Classics* (3rd ed.). Hong Kong: Hong Kong University Press.

Lew, S. K. (1995). Filial Piety and Human Society. In *Filial Piety and Future Society* [Hyo-wa Mirae-Sahoe] (pp. 19–36). Kyunggido, Korea: The Academy of Korean Studies.

Leung, J.C. B. (1997). Family Support for the Elderly in China: Issues and Challenges. *Journal of Aging and Social Policy 9*, 87–101.

Lin, Y. (1982). On Growing Old Gracefully. In P. L. McKee (Ed.) *Philosophical Foundation of Gerontology*. New York: Human Sciences Press.

Ma, L.C., & Smith, K. (1991). Social Correlates of Confucian Ethics in Taiwan. *Journal of Social Psychology 132*, 655–659.

Maeda, D. (1997, August). *Filial Piety and the Care of Aged Parents in Japan*. Paper presented at the 16th World Congress of Gerontology Symposium on Myths, Stereotypes, and Realities of Filial Piety. Singapore.

Meyer, J.F. (1988). Moral Education in Taiwan. *Comparative Education Review, 32*, 20–38.

Moon, A., & Williams, O. (1993). Perceptions of Elder Abuse and Help-Seeking Patterns among African-American, Caucasian American, and Korean-American Elderly Women. *The Gerontologist 33*, 386–395.

Nydegger, C. N. (1983). Family Ties of the Aged in the Cross-Cultural Perspective. *The Gerontologist 23*, 26–32.

Olson, P. (1993). Caregiving and Long-term Health Care in the People's Republic of China. *Journal of Aging and Social Policy 24*, 91–110.

Palmore, E. B. (1999). *Ageism: Negative and Positive*. New York: Springer.

Palmore, E. B., & Maeda, D. (1985). *The Honorable Elders Revisited*. Durham, NC: Duke University Press.

Parish, W. L., & Whyte, M. K. (1978). *Village and Family in Contemporary China*. Chicago: The University of Chicago Press.

Park, J. G. (1989). The Traditional Thought of Filial Piety and its Modern Meaning. In K. H. Chi (Ed.), *Re-illustration of Traditional Ethic* [Junt'ong Yunli-ui Hyundaijuk Chomyung] (pp. 89–116). Kyunggido, Korea: Center for Korean Studies.

Park, C. H. (1983). Historical Review of Korean Confucianism. In *Main Currents of Korean Thoughts*. The Korean National Commission for UNESCO. Seoul: The Si-Sa-Yong-O-Sa.

Pillemer, K. A., & Finkelhor, D. (1988). The Prevalence of Elder Abuse: A Random Sample Survey. *The Gerontologist 28*, 51–57.

Post, S. G. (1962). Filial Morality. *Journal of Religion and Aging 5*, 15–29.

Silberman, B. (1962). *Japanese Character and Culture*. Tucson: University of Arizona Press.

Silverstein, M., Burholt, V., Wenger, G. C., & Bengtson, V. L. (1998). Parent-Child Relations among very Old Parents in Wales and the United States: A Test of Modernization Theory. *Journal of Aging Studies 12*, 387–409.

Singapore Ministry of Community Development. (1996). *Report of the Advisory Council on the Aged*. Singapore: The Author.

Streib, G. F. (1987). Old Age in Sociocultural Context: China and the United States. *Journal of Aging Studies 7*, 95–112.

Sung, K. T. (1995). Measures and Dimensions of Filial Piety in Korea. *The Gerontologist 35*, 240–247.

Sung, K. T. (1998). An Exploration of Actions of Filial Piety. *Journal of Aging Studies 12*, 369–386.

Sung, K. T., & Kim, H. S. (2000). *Respect for the Elderly: Exploring Forms Practiced by Young Adults in South Korea*. Seoul: The Center for Filial Piety Studies.

Takahashi, S. (1995). Historical Transition of Filial Piety and its Modern Transformation. In *Filial Piety and Future Society* [Hyo-wa-Mirae-Sahoe] (pp. 103–115). Kyunggido, Korea: The Academy of Korean Studies.

Teachings of Filial Piety [Hsiao Ching] (1989). In J. Legge (Trans.), *Sacred Books of the East* (Vol. III). London: Oxford. Originally published 1879–1885.

Tomita, S. (1994). The Consideration of Cultural Factors in the Research of Elder Mistreatment with an In-depth Look at the Japanese. *Journal of Cross-Cultural Gerontology 9*, 39–52.

Twenty-Four Stories of Filial Piety. (1956). [Bilingual edition]. Taipei: Cheng Ta Press.

Works of Mencius. (1932). (L. Lyall, Trans.). London: Murray.

Xie, X., Defrain, J., Meredith, W., & Combs, R. (1996). Family Strengths in the People's Republic of China: As Perceived by the University Students and Government. *International Journal of Sociology of the Family 26*, 17–27.

Social Science & Medicine 53 (2001) 1383–1396

SOCIAL
SCIENCE
—&—
MEDICINE
www.elsevier.com/locate/socscimed

"No strength": sex and old age in a rural town in Ghana

Sjaak van der Geest

Department of Anthropology, Medical Anthropology Unit, University of Amsterdam, Oudezijds Achterburgwal 185, 1012 DK Amsterdam, Netherlands

Abstract

This article is part of a larger project on social and cultural meanings of growing old in a rural community of Ghana, the fieldwork for which was carried out between 1994 and 2000. It deals with ideas and practices concerning sex among the elderly. Informal conversations were held with individual elders and with groups of people that were, middle-aged and young. Sex was generally regarded as a matter of "strength", which was diminishing at old age. For men the concept of strength specifically referred to sexual potency, whereas for women "strength" was part of a more general feeling of physical power and the ability to perform the many activities expected from being a man's sexual partner. Sex at old age is looked at with a considerable amount of ambivalence. On the one hand, it is something that the elderly should have left behind them. On the other hand, sex confirms the vitality and status of the elder. If sex is practised at old age, it should be orderly and restrained, "respectful". © 2001 Elsevier Science Ltd. All rights reserved.

Keywords: Sex; Strength; Old age; Kwahu; Ghana

"Your mind gets away from it." (Kwahu man)

"I want strength to get food to eat." (Kwahu woman)

Introduction

Sex and sexuality are universally regarded as the prerogative of young people. Elderly people are viewed as sexually unattractive and not interested in sex. If they *are* interested, there must be something wrong with them. Sexual intercourse between elderly people is typically "considered embarrassing or aesthetically unappealing", writes Levy (1994, p. 291). She continues: "Images in the media and other forms of popular culture, such as cartoons and greeting cards, tend to portray older adults' interest or attempts to be sexual as humorous, ludicrous, scornful or repugnant", even as perverse (see Butler & Lewis, 1986; Gibson, 1993, p. 111). A "normal" elderly person is not or should not be interested in sex.

E-mail address: vandergeest@pscw.uva.nl (S. van der Geest).

Recently, however, that view of the sexually disinterested elderly is being challenged by a stream of publications. These should be viewed against the backdrop of growing criticism of ageism. Levy (1994) points at the contradictory evidence. On the one hand, decline of sexual interest is indeed reported. Quoting a number of authors, she mentions: "mental or physical fatigue, preoccupation with business interests, over indulgence in food or drink, physical illness, fear of sexual failure, etc. Monotony in sexual relationships, related to over-familiarity and the predictability of sex with the same partner" (Levy, 1994, p. 291).

On the other hand, several authors emphasise that sexual desires continue to be felt throughout the life span, although there remains disagreement as to whether this applies solely to men or to men and women alike (Weg, 1983; Nadelson, 1984; Crose & Drake, 1993; Hodson & Skeen, 1994; Minichiello, Plummer, & Seal, 1996). Kellet (1991) concludes that reduction of sexual activity at old age is more cultural than biological in origin. Traupmann (1984) points at the discomfort of children thinking of their parents' sexuality. According to Freud (1918), witnessing one's parents making love could be traumatic for a child. Freud's assumption was tested in a study by Hoyt (1977), which showed that parental sex was the most anxiety-provoking fantasy for young people, men as well as women.

The literature on sex and old age is slowly expanding, showing both consistency and contradiction. Consistent are conclusions about the widespread social and cultural production of the asexual elderly and the recognition that underneath the abnegation of sex, sexual desires may continue to exist until a very advanced age. Contradictory evidence is reported with regard to what extent this applies to what percentage of the elderly and whether there are significant differences between men and women. Virtually, nothing is known about cultural variations in both the acceptability and the actual existence of prolonged sexual interest and activity among elderly people. The studies quoted thus far refer exclusively to North American and Western European populations.

Anthropological studies of sexual behaviour in Africa, for example, are extremely rare if we exclude the avalanche of research on sexual behaviour as risk in the era of HIV/AIDS (Standing, 1991; Standing & Kisekka, 1989; Ahlberg, 1994; Savage & Tchombe, 1994). It is not surprising, therefore, that studies on *sex at old age* in Africa are practically non-existent. Apt's (1996) study of elderly Ghanaians does not contain any reference to the topic of sex, for example. This paper is one of the first attempts to explore the field of sexual desires and practices among elderly people in an African community. The main objective was to record people's views on the topic and to analyse their statements in light of their culture, with a particular focus on gender differences. The result of this attempt is mainly descriptive, which may seem disappointing to some, but it provides a promising start to gaining insight into a topic still surrounded by taboo and embarrassment both among the elderly and younger generations.

Research strategy

The article is based on anthropological fieldwork in Kwahu-Tafo, a rural town on the Kwahu Plateau in the southeastern part of Ghana. The aim of the research was to describe and understand the position of elderly people in a rapidly changing society.

The field research involved open-ended conversations with 35 elderly people, which were taped and later transcribed and translated. Some people were interviewed only once, others twice or more often. Apart from these more formal conversations, this author often went to greet the old people informally and chat with them. These more casual visits enabled me to observe the daily life of elderly people and the attitudes of other people in the same house. Most of these observations were recorded in my diary. In addition, old age was discussed with many other people in the town including opinion leaders such as teachers and church members as

well as with other key informants. Focus group discussions were held with young people and groups of middle-aged men and women. In three schools, students completed a questionnaire expressing their views on old people or completed sentences on the same issue. Some students wrote essays about the old or made drawings of them. The research was almost entirely qualitative, in order to arrive at a deeper understanding of what it means to be old and dependent. That understanding was gradually acquired by the method of participant observation. I joined some of the elderly at their farm, in church and at funerals.

The elderly people in this study form a diverse group. A few of them were well off—socially, psychologically, financially, and in terms of health. They were surrounded by caring relatives and received attention and respect. Others were quite miserable because of poverty and loneliness. The extremes of happiness and misery occurred particularly among men. Those whose lives had been a success enjoyed the fruits of their work and did not have any worries. Those who had been less successful in their active days had often been deserted by the ones they had failed to care for. A strictly applied measure of reciprocity accounted for this difference in well-being at old age. As a result, women usually found themselves more in the middle than in the extremes. Even if they had not been successful in giving their children what they needed to progress in life, the children recognised that their mothers had tried their utmost and now returned their love.

Most of the elderly people were able to walk, only one of the 35 spent the whole day in bed. Five of them were blind, which restricted their movements considerably. Two more were almost blind. Only one old lady suffered from dementia and had to be "watched" throughout the day. The care they received from people in the house or children nearby included cooking food, helping them bathe, washing their clothes, assisting them in visiting the toilet, and doing all kinds of chores such as running errands, buying food, and sweeping the room. Remittance of money becomes increasingly important as a form of indirect care, since many children are earning their living elsewhere. The people who were actually taking care of the elderly varied from wives, daughters, and daughters-in-law to more distant relatives or anyone who happened to live in the same house.

Their condition of life did not remain the same over the period of my research. Some people who had been vigorous when the fieldwork began, fell sick a short time later and died. Others lost their partner or caregiver or became more handicapped and lonely. In 1995, the marital status of 29 elderly was as follows: seven still had their partner (more or less), 11 were divorced or had separated, and 11 were widowed. Of the 35 elderly people who had been involved in this research, only six were still alive in April, 2001.

In this article, six of the elderly play a role: Kwame Opoku who used to be a farmer and a trader and functioned as an ókyeame[1] in the Chief's court; Yaa Amponsaa, formerly a farmer and a trader who is living with her three daughters; Kwaku Nyame, a former cocoa farmer; Kwame Frempong, who used to be a cocoa marketing agent; George Adu Asara, in his active life, secretary to the Paramount Chief; and his friend, Kwaku Martin, a man of many different trades: teacher, trader, pig farmer. The last three men had attended school in their youth.[2]

Reading through field notes and interview transcriptions, the aim was to discover some common underlying theme in the diverse experiences of old age. This essay focuses on one aspect: what people, old as well as young, think about love and sex in old age. It was only after some time and much hesitation that the topic was broached. Initially, this author thought it would not be possible to include questions surrounding sexuality in the research, having been made to understand that sexual desires and sexual practices are secret. Ókyeame Opoku: "How somebody makes love to his wife or girlfriend, he will never tell you unless you are his friend." Why is it bad to talk about it? The answer completed the circle: because it is secret. If people hear about your sexual habits or desires, they will talk about them and may laugh at you. It is shameful. It is a breach of intimacy. Instructions to young people about correct or enjoyable sex were not given in the past or at present. It is "not done."

Taking these warnings into account, there was some pessimism about the possibility of discussing sex with the elderly. Among the young, sex has become a more open thing to do and talk about without "shame", but not among the older generation. I was therefore rather surprised to find many of them open to the subject and willing to share some of their "secrets" with me. I say "some" because I am convinced that the most intimate details were not disclosed. Extensive quotations taken from these conversations reveal people's ambivalence and uncertainty about the topic of sex. What they declined to say was often as significant as what they spoke about.

(The quotations may also enable the reader to interpret for him- or herself the meaning of their statements.)

It cannot be denied that a certain culture of "prudishness" may have affected the conversations. Among women, for instance, it seemed more proper to deny than to admit an interest in sex. It took some time before I realised this. In my own culture, most women would probably be more embarrassed to admit having no interest in sex. That bias towards denying sex was particularly strong when one day we had a discussion with 15 Christian mothers aged between 30 and 65. I was initially doubtful that a *group* discussion of *Christian* women would produce the kind of information I was interested in, but a friend, a woman of 55 helping me with my research, was more optimistic. My scepticism grew when it was made clear that the women wanted to have the meeting in the back of the church.

The discussion that took place under the eyes of Our Lady of Good Counsel was much more fruitful than expected, however. A lively debate occurred during which I realised that some of the women were talking a lot while others were completely quiet. All those who had spoken emphasised that they were no longer interested in sex. Some boasted about this. They applauded one woman who said she had not slept with a man in 30 years. It appears that those who spoke did speak their mind and express their feelings and that their remarks were reliable and useful. However, no access to the views of those women who were still interested in sex and practising it was made. My suspicion was that they were the ones during the meeting who were silent and possibly keeping those views hidden.

If sex is such a delicate and uncomfortable topic for conversation, it is no surprise that one encounters extremely contradictory statements. In answer to the question "Is it good for old people to have sex?" an elderly woman (AM) said:

AM: No. It is not good, you have led this sort of life, so you have to stop (*Yɛabu Ɔbra no bi ara*).[3]
S: Why?
AM: Because I have already finished giving birth. I have given birth to 10 children. One has given birth to seven children, another to eight, another to six. The youngest has given birth to four children. So I don't have to marry again.
S: Is it not good to have sex after you have ceased giving birth to children?
AM: You see, I married my husband and had ten children with him, and he died.
S: If he were still alive, would you continue to have sex with him?
AM: Yes, if he were alive, I couldn't have denied him anything.

---

[1] Ɔkyeame (often translated as "linguist") is an official at the chief's court. Yankah (1995, p. 3) describes the function of the ɔkyeame as "speaking for the chief": "Being a counselor and intermediary to the chief, he is responsible, among other things, for enhancing the rhetoric of the words the chief has spoken. In the absence of an ɔkyeame's editorial art, the royal speech act is considered functionally and artistically incomplete".

[2] The names of people mentioned or quoted in this article have not been changed. When I asked the elderly people I conversed with if I should give them a fictitious name to protect their identity, they indicated that they wanted their names to be "boldly" written in my publications (they wished to be remembered).

[3] All texts preceding a Twi phrase is its English translation.

S: If your husband is dead, is it not good to marry
      again and have sex with your new husband?
AM: If an elderly fellow is willing to marry me, I will agree.
S: At your present age, do you sometimes have the
      desire to have sex?
AM: Yes, if I get an old man, I will marry him.

Another consequence of the secrecy around sex is that
there is very little popular or general knowledge about
sexual ideas and practices. People have to rely on their
own experiences, some "secrets", and on rumours. It is
very likely, therefore, that the information presented
here is of a certain idiosyncratic nature—the Kinsey
Report of Ghana does not exist.

Village setting

Kwahu-Tafo is a rural town of about 5000 inhabitants. Most of them are Kwahu, a subgroup of the
(approximately) six million matrilineal Akan who live in
the south of the country. *Akan* is a collective name for a
number of ethnic groups that share important linguistic
and cultural traits.[4] They have a matrilineal inheritance
system which now is undergoing a process of modernisation and individuation, although it is as yet
impossible to say where this process will lead. Decisions
regarding filiation, kinship adherence, family support
and inheritance, which are the result of heated
arguments and intensive social bargaining, are often
unpredictable. Much depends on the social weight of the
different parties. "Automatic" decisions based on the
application of unambiguous cultural rules—if they ever
existed—are out of the question.

Marriage is an uncertain undertaking. Couples often
do not stay together because one of them has travelled
or is trading or doing other work somewhere else. It is
also possible that the wife prefers to stay in her own
family house if the husband has no place of his own and
the woman is not eager to stay with her in-laws. In most
cases marriage is also a temporary affair. Divorce is
common and both men and women initiate it (Bleek,
1975, 1977). Very few couples put their money together,
which may be the clearest indication that husband and
wife do not perceive each other as having one common
purpose in life. They are likely to have different interests
and they may attach more importance to their family
(*abusua*)[5] ties than to their marriage bond. After all,
marriage is only friendship, it is not *abusua*, as the

----

[4]The main ethnographers of Akan culture are Rattray (1916,
1923, 1927, 1929) (who produced five volumes on the Akan),
Field (1960), Fortes (1969), Warren (1974), Arhin (1979) and
Oppong (1982). Studies focusing on the Kwahu are Bleek (1975,
1976), Bartle (1977) and Miescher (1997).

[5]*Abusua* is the matrilineage. The term can refer to a very
large group of related people (a 'clan'), or to a more restricted
group of matrikin, three to five generations deep.

proverb goes (*awadeè yè òyonkò, ènyè abusua*). As a
result, the relationship of a father with his children is
ambiguous. He bears responsibility for them but strictly
speaking, his children belong to his wife's *abusua*. The
extent to which he bonds with his children and takes
care of them depends very much on the person, his
character but even more his economic position. The one
who is well-off is able to build his own house and have
his wife and children gathered together. He will pay for
his children's upkeep and education, and help his wife
financially with trading or farming. The wife and
children, in return, are likely to stay with him. A poor
man, however, may find it difficult to keep his wife and
children with him. He has little to offer them and they
may therefore seek support from her *abusua*. The
marriage may break down altogether if the wife thinks
there is no longer anything in it for her. Financially and
sexually, she is no longer interested in the marriage and
the man may find himself deserted in his old age.

The shifting loyalty, from the marital partner to the
abusua, is illustrated in an old story that my friend
Kwame Fosu told me to explain how matrilineal
inheritance came to the Akan.[6]

A certain man, Abu, was about to die. He went to the
òbòsom ('fetish') and asked for help. The *òbòsom* said
he would be saved if he sacrificed a child. The man
came home and discussed the matter with his wife
and they decided which one of their children he
would give to the *òbòsom*. When he went to sleep the
wife secretly went to the children and told them to
run away because their father wanted to sacrifice one
of them. The next morning the man looked for his
children but they had disappeared. He then turned to
his sister and asked her to give him one of her
children. The sister felt pity for him and gave him a
child. To thank her, the man decided that he would
let his sister's children inherit from him.

Kwahu-Tafo is a poor town unlike some of the other
towns on the Kwahu Plateau. Its inhabitants were not
very successful in trading and farmers encountered
many difficulties due to land conflicts and lack of rain.
In 1983 and 1984, severe droughts hit a large part of the
country, including Kwahu, and many people lost their
cocoa farms. Kwahu-Tafo has electricity, piped water,
and a clinic but only a minority has access to these
facilities. Erosion and lack of maintenance have caused
the collapse of many houses in the centre of town, which
gives the place a rather gloomy appearance. Few people
have the means to build a new house or repair their old
one. A painting on the wall of the house where I lived
showed a man climbing a tree. In the tree a snake is

----

[6]Fosu, a teacher with a special interest in Akan tradition, was
helping me with the research.

waiting for him, below are a lion and a crocodile. The text below the painting reads: *Òbra yè den* (Life is hard).

Two conversations

One day, I visited *Òpanyin*[7] Edward Yaw Addo, an elder in the nearby town of Abetifi. Kwame Fosu introduced me to him. When we arrived, the *òpanyin* was talking with three friends in front of his house. He invited us inside where we had a long conversation. Apart from *Òpanyin* Addo (A), two of his friends *Òkyeame* Safo (S) and Kwame Tawia (T) also took part in the conversation.

We talked about the different stages in a person's life, about the position of an *òpanyin* (elder), about funerals, and about care. Then the topic turned to sex. The conversation was in Twi. Most of the questions were in English and Kwame Fosu (F) translated them. I expected that the old men would not be very keen to talk about this topic but the discussion was lively and open and everyone seemed to be enjoying it. I asked them if elderly people still had an interest in sex. Below are a few excerpts from the discussion that ensued.

A. When you grow old, you have to leave behind all the work you did and think about what is ahead of you. You may know whether you are progressing or going backward. Going after women is based on love and happiness (*Efisè mmaa-pè no yède òdò ne anigye na èfa*). This time I am not happy because I am not strong. You see I am not strong. But chasing a woman takes more energy than felling trees. It is very tiring (*Èyè den papa, èyè den papaapa*). If you are old like me... now I have sons and daughters... If I go to take someone while my son has not yet been married, it would mean, that I have not thought about my son. If you resort to chasing women it is not good. There is no use in doing that. Even your children will not look after you.

F. Is it you yourself who decides to stop going after women or is it because there is no feeling for it?

A. Listen, it gets to a time that when you try to lift up your penis it is not possible. It is dead (*Tie, èbètò*

---

[7] *Òpanyin* ('elder') is someone past middle age who is considered wise and experienced and behaves in a civilised and exemplary way. According to Rattray (1916, p. 23) the term is derived from *nyin* (to grow) and *apa* (old, long-lived). My co-researcher Anthony Boamah gave a different etymology: *W'apa nyin (ho)*, which means: you have passed (*wapa*) the age of growing (*nyin*). The *òpanyin*, therefore, is someone who has stopped growing (taller). For a more elaborate discussion of the concept of *òpanyin*, see further below in this article (see also Van der Geest, 1998).

bere bi no na wopagya wo kòte koraa a na ònkò baabiara. Na awu). And if your penis is not strong there is nothing you can do with it (*Sè wo kòte yi nso nni ahoòden a biribiara nni hò a, wubetumi de ayè*).

[...]

F. Is it true that men keep their interest in sex longer than women?

A. In fact, you have asked a question. We men are quicker with our mouths (*Mmarima, yèn ano na èyè hare*). A woman feels a man more than a man feels a woman. Men are quicker in asking for it. You go to tap her shoulder. Women won't ask for it. Look, if you leave your wife and stay in Hweehwee [a nearby town] for only four days, she will think you are fornicating over there. By all means she will think that you are going to do something. You see? I conversed with a certain woman as we are doing now. She said that as for us men, we are only quick in speaking about sex. She said I should ask a feather with which we prick our ears: Is it the feather or the ear that feels the sensation (*Takra no na èyè dè anaasè aso no?*)? I could not give any answer. I could not answer. You see what I mean? Therefore, as regards the feeling, it is women who get most of it. Yours is once, that of the woman is thrice.

F. So if a woman grows to be *aberewa*...

A. Every woman...

S. She will never stop?

F. But as for a man his...

A. His is short.

S. That of the woman is everlasting (*Èmmaa deè no deè sè èwò hò ara ne no*).

A. Hers [her vagina] is a path, it always lies there. His [penis] hangs, it bends down and does not lift itself up anymore.

Sj. This morning there was a conversation with ladies, some old, some younger. But they all said they were not interested in sex. They remarked: I have no strength, I have no desire (*Minni ahoòden, me kòn nnò*). I wonder if there is a difference in the enjoyment between men and women.

A. The man's enjoyment is once, but the woman's is three times.

F. Did you say a woman may grow very old before her mind gets away from it?

S. Yes.

F. And that a man does not grow very old before his mind gets away from it?

A. At all! As for a woman, even if she becomes very old... It is a path. A bicycle can ride on it.

[...]

T. It is over a year since I took a woman (*Mefaa èbaa èboro afe*) [looking miserable].

S. Yet, he is there (*Nso òwò hò*).

T.   I am still alive. I have no desire for it (Me kòn
     nnò).
Sj. You have no desire?
T.   Yes.
A.   He has grown old.
T.   I have grown old... Nothing attracts me in sex. I
     sleep. My mind has moved away from it
     (M'adwene afiri so). I am old.
Sj. What about you [to S]?
S.   As for me, I speak the truth. I am old, I am old.
     Sickness disturbs me but as for me I do it small
     small (Me deè meyè no kakra kakra). [laughter] I
     have spoken the truth. If you are doing anything
     with somebody it is nice to speak the truth. I for
     one, I do it a little bit. When I am doing it I tell
     her to take time. I tell her not to rush. I am not all
     that strong (Ahoòden nni hò papa).
[...]
F.   An old man may marry a young woman or an old
     woman may marry a young man. Do people
     approve of that or do they speak against it?
A.   I am old. If my uncle dies and I marry his young
     widow people would mock her.
[...]
F.   (to Sj): They will laugh at her because her
     husband is an old man. Is it because the old
     man is not strong sexually?
S.   Yes.
F.   What about an old man who does not inherit
     nd marry a widow but marries another
     woman? For instance, you have your wife, your
     equal. And then you go to marry another wife in
     addition to your first wife. What will people say
     about it?
A.   They will tell you: Oo hou!
F.   Oh hou means what?
A.   Why? They will ask you: Why? An old man taking
     this young lady. Will she stay? (Akwakora
     woakòfa ahabaawa yi. Òbètena?)
F.   Why won't she stay?
A.   Because even though you can give her anything to
     eat, you cannot sleep with her.
S.   You cannot fuck her (Worentumi nni no). Say it
     plainly to him.
[...]
F.   What, if an old woman marries a young man?
     What will society say about that?
A.   When an old woman marries a young man, people
     will ask her whether she can pound fufu. At your
     age, you want to marry a man. Can you go and
     fetch water, can you pound fufu? Can you go and
     fetch firewood?
F.   They will ask the woman?
A.   Yes. An old woman should not marry a young
     man since she is not strong.
[...]

Two things stand out in this conversation. The first is
that the men were very concerned about respect. Interest
in sex should not damage one's reputation. A good
father diverts his interest from sex to taking care of his
children and avoids competing with his sons for women.
That would be extremely embarrassing for him as well as
for his sons. Public censorship also extends to other
aspects of sex at later age: a young woman who marries
an elderly man will be laughed at, which also affects the
man. The second striking thing is the men's emphasis on
sexual potency and strength in a more general sense.
Chasing a woman, one of them remarked, was harder
than felling a tree. Women, they thought, do not have
that problem. They can continue to have sex much
longer than men.

This conversation and another in the morning of the
same day marked the beginning of several discussions
about sex that took place both with men and women,
elders, middle-aged people and youngsters. Usually,
when I approached women on this topic, I asked
Monica Amoako, a woman of 55, to accompany me. A
year after the above conversation, Monica and I
visited an old lady, Yaa Amponsaa, in Kwahu-Tafo.
The lady showed us a church document, which stated
that she had been born in the year 1905. We
(A = Amponsaa, M = Monica, S = Sjaak) talked about
the way a man and a woman loved one another in the
olden days and how a girl was prepared for marriage.
We then broached the topic of love and sex in old age
and asked what she thought about it.

A.   Now I am old. It is many years ago that I slept
     behind a man (medaa barima akyi). When you
     grow old, you begin to change and when you are
     changing, you also change your character.
S.   Is it because it is difficult when we get to a certain
     age that we don't want to do it [have sex]
     anymore?
A.   Well it is a type of work that you should stop
     when you grow old. There are however some old
     people who still like it.
S.   Did you stop doing it because you lose the
     enjoyment of it or did you stop because people
     will say: This woman is old but she still goes after
     men?
A.   I do not have the taste for it.
M.   I agree with you. When I was a young woman at
     the age of 30 I remember how I enjoyed having
     sex with my lover but now that I am around 50, I
     have lost the sort of feelings I had during my
     youthful days. So I do agree with you if you say
     you don't have interest in it. I do not know what
     will happen if I grow to your present age, but I
     may also dislike it.
S.   Why are you not interested in sex?
A.   It is not something I need like we need food. A

nurse once came to educate us that there is no need for a woman to run after a man. What is important is that you should eat a little in the morning, in the afternoon, and in the evening. That will help you to be healthy. Good health does not remain by meeting a man. That is the advice my granddaughter gave to us in the church. I took that advice and have stayed away from sex and I look healthy every day.

S. Why is it that women always say they do not have the strength to meet a man. Is there any special strength that you need before you meet a man?

A. I do not know that. According to my character I do not like to do it. If you are a woman and you become older, you should not indulge in that act. It is bad to do that work.

M. I believe that the whole reason is that you don't have the feeling or taste for it.

S. If you would marry now and your husband wanted to have sex with you, would you do it?

A. That is different. When an old man is staying with an old woman in marriage, that is different. When one day you are there with your husband and he likes to come to you, you will agree but that is different. Once in a while if the old man wants to do it, you may allow him.

S. If you are there with your husband, and the man loses his sexual power and he wants to play with your sex organ, will you allow that?

A. That is possible because the woman remembers his strength when he was young. You will know how to stay with him and play with him.

S. Which of the two, a man or a woman, keeps the desire for sex longer and which of the two enjoys it most?

A. I can't tell what happens to others. What I know is that a man and woman can marry during their youth and stay together until they become old and are separated by death.

M. I believe it is the men. Because some men who are rich during their old age, may go and marry a young girl. If they did not have the strength or desire, they wouldn't have done so. It never happens that an old lady marries a young man. The old lady who does so is the one who was once a harlot. Men at the age of sixty or even older sometimes marry girls who are eighteen years.

S. This is a difficult question but you must try to answer. Do women have more pleasure during sex or is it the men who enjoy most?

A. It depends on their love for one another....

M. I believe that the woman enjoys most. I remember when I was young how I had the feelings. So if you divide the enjoyment proportionately it will be one for the man and two for the woman. Mother, what is your opinion about it?

A. Well, that is something natural. When you see the man then you have the desire for it. The two of you become happy so if he sleeps with you (*òfa wo*) about once or twice, then you all sleep. That is what I know.

[...]

S. Suppose you grow old and have a husband but you feel you are not strong enough to have sex with him. If the man wants to go and take another woman as his lover (*mpena*), will you agree?

A. When the man wants to take another woman, I can't tell him to go and find a woman. It depends upon his own character.

S. If he secretly takes a woman and it becomes known to you, will you stay unconcerned or will you quarrel with the woman.

A. I will not say anything. If a man has the feeling and goes out, I will not say anything. If you don't mind him it is there that he will pamper you and provide you with your needs.

S. A lot of people believe that it is because of money that young girls or young women marry old men. What is your idea about that?

A. Yes, that is true. When the young girls see that somebody is rich, they may go to him with the intention to collect money.

Nana Amponsaa is honest: she is no longer interested in sex, but she is also pragmatic and tolerant. She would willingly undergo sex out of love for her husband, if she had one. She would even allow him to have sex with another woman, if he wanted. But sex, she emphasises, is not something we really need like we do food. A few times Monica spontaneously joined in, projecting her own feelings: women lose their interest in sex when they become old.

The culture of sex

Sex is not a common topic for discussion. What you feel and how you do it, is a secret you share with a close friend, not just with anyone. Nana Kwaku Nyame (N) was asked if people could speak freely about sex. The following conversation ensued:

N. Yes. When old people who are friends meet, they talk about it. When friends meet, they are able to talk about what may be termed as 'nonsense' on sex (*Sè ayònkofoò hyia a, yètumi di nsèm hunu ho nkòmmò*).

S   Can an old person talk about sex to his own children?

N. No. No one can. Impossible.

S   What about if the child asks him about it?

N. Even the child can't ask such a thing.

Nana Amponsaa also denied that sex was a topic for discussion. Monica asked her if in the olden days

247

parents or elders instructed the young about sex before they married.

A.   No. Once the man has called you to the room, the two of you know that it is a custom that you meet in sleep *(wo ne no hyia nna)*. The proverb goes: *Obi nkyerè akwadaa Nyame* ("Nobody teaches a child who God is."—i.e., there are certain things which do not need to be taught).

Monica agreed with Yaa Amponsaa saying that no mother tells her daughter that when she meets a man to have sex, she should act this way or that way. What mothers instruct their children on are the ways to keep the sex organs and other parts of the body clean:

M.   Is there a rule that after a man and woman have had sex, the woman should clean the man or the man should clean the woman?

A.   We were not taught, but it is common sense that when you go to a man you should take with you a handkerchief. The man too may have his....

M.   Which means one couple may do it this way and another couple may do it that way. No one knows what the other one does.

A.   Yes, because that is not taught.

Moreover, there is the idea that one should not be too interested in sex. Foreplay, "romantic play" as some call it, is probably not practised very much. It is 'bad' because it shows that one "likes the thing too much." A man or woman who is fond of it will be called *òdwamanfoò* (a 'loose' person). A woman should not make sounds during sex nor indulge in unconventional sexual acts. The secrecy surrounding sex is part of a more general culture of modesty.

One person suggested that the paucity of sexual techniques and the absence of romantic foreplay could lead to an early loss of interest in sex among women: "If the man inserts his penis before the woman is sexually aroused, the intercourse may be unpleasant and even painful to her. She may not reach her orgasm before the man has 'finished' his and gradually becomes frustrated and starts to dislike sex."[8] Sex becomes a tiresome thing,

---

[8] Pellow (1977, p. 162), who studied the lives of women in Adabraka, a suburb of Accra with a high concentration of Kwahu, suggests that many women derive little pleasure from sex in their marriage. She then refers to an article by a Ghanaian woman journalist, a 'been-to' [i.e. someone who has lived in Europe or North America]: "In a 1970 article entitled 'Woman, do you lie about 'it'?,' Ms Addo alludes to the past when the woman's role on a marital bed was a simple one. She was expected to be submissive and unresponsive. Her place was not to receive pleasure but to provide it (*The Daily Graphic*, 19 October). Now, she writes, there is a more liberal attitude towards the woman's role in general and sex in particular, yet many women still find the sex act a disappointment."

equated to "work" she has to do in the night while she had hoped that her day's work was finished. Moreover, some women complain of pain in the vagina, a sickness they refer to as *pintayè*.

Sexual problems can be the reason for divorce, but this is rarely disclosed. Here again, the taboo on sex prevents people from mentioning their problems to others. The woman may just say that the love has ended (*òdò asa*). Speaking about it openly could lead to others talking about it, a shame which is very much feared. Opoku, the *òkyeame*, however, stressed that if a man looked after his wife well, she would love him and take care that no one would ever hear about his impotence. Impotence is something a man will try to hide at all costs. When this secret gets into the open, he will be publicly mocked and called names such as *Aban agye ne tuo* (The government has collected his gun) or *Òda Benada* (He sleeps on Tuesday).[9] A man whose impotence is revealed may be so ashamed that he commits suicide. The "impotence" of a woman is not ridiculed and talked about as that of a man. People may just say: she fears man (*òsuro òbarima*).

The question as to who enjoyed sex most and who kept their interest longest, men or women, always engendered a lively discussion. Taking into account that the question is impossible to answer, it is not surprising that the opinions differed. However, it is striking that men often thought that women enjoy sex more than men and that women often held the opposite view.

Love and sex are very much a matter of money and gifts. If a man does not give his wife money and does not provide her with a cloth every year, with sandals, head-gear (*duku*), she will not stay with him. The same applies to lovers. Gifts (money is also considered a gift) prove and measure a man's love. "No self-respecting woman would remain in a 'friendship' without material recompense", Pellow (1977, p. 208) writes. Nana Dedaa described the good quality of her first marriage thus: "He loved me as I loved him. He used to give me a cloth every six months at Christmas and in the middle of the year."

Two basic views of old age, a positive and a negative one, prevailed during discussions. They are contrasting but do not necessarily exclude one another. In both views the idea prevails that sex and old age do not go well together, though for very different reasons.

The *òpanyin*: beautiful old age

The *òpanyin* (elder) represents the beautiful image of old age. He (or she) receives what is most highly regarded in Akan culture: respect. *Òpanyin* is an honorific term. It is the title which elderly people like

---

[9] I have in vain tried to trace the origins of these mockeries.

most for themselves. An òpanyin can be a man or a woman, though most will think of a man when the word is used. Usually, an òpanyin is someone of advanced age: "He has lived in the house much longer than you. You came to meet him. 'Òpanyin' is a big word. He is a person who knows what is going on. He must receive respect and obedience," according to one of the elders. The òpanyin gains this respect by possessing three virtues: wisdom, self-restraint, and dedication to his[10] family.

The fact that one has lived for a long time means that one has seen many things and has begun to understand how they are connected. Life experience, in other words, teaches how events follow one anoth0er. On the basis of that understanding, the òpanyin is able to predict the future and advise people on how to act in order to prevent trouble. The second virtue refers to the good manners of the òpanyin and his overall self-restraint. The òpanyin controls his emotions, does not get angry, and does not shout at people. The ability to keep one's self in check is revealed foremost in the way he deals with information that has been given to him and in his ascetic attitude. The òpanyin's careful dealing with rumours is expressed in many proverbs. Nothing shows so well that one is still a child as when one cannot hold one's tongue. The òpanyin is indeed the opposite of a child. The òpanyin's self-restraint reveals itself also in the attitude toward food and other material pleasures. Greediness does not befit him. One proverb says: Òpanyin mene nsono ("the elder eats his own intestines"), i.e., that he can forego food. If there is not enough food in the house, the òpanyin will give his part to the children. He has eaten enough in his life. The third virtue is love for the family. The òpanyin's gentleness and wisdom are directed first of all to the abusua. It is the abusua that benefits from the òpanyin's life experience and civilised manners. He may have travelled a lot, but in his old age, when he reaches the stage of òpanyin, he will come home and spend his days with the members of the family. He will give them good advice on all kinds of problems and promote peace and unity among them. He will mediate in conflicts. "There is nothing left for him to do than guarding the people in the house", according to one elder. That is why they say Òpanyin ntu kwan ("the elder does not travel").

All three virtues, and the second in particular, point toward a declining interest in sex at old age. The òpanyin sees himself primarily as someone who has left behind the tempestuousness of his youthful days. Sex too is regarded as something from the past. It is a passion that may cause people to act without thinking. Sex often implies loss of self-control, it is selfish and may harm the interests of the abusua or the children. As one

of the Abetifi elders said, "Whatever I am doing, I reserve it for my children. So, I am not going to take a woman."

The idea that the òpanyin has left behind his youthful turbulence was vividly expressed by Nana Frempong (F) when I (S) asked him how he felt, being an old man. He answered:

F.   When you grow old, you loose interest in a lot of things which are of interest to the young.

S.   At this age, do the activities of the young remind you of your own youth?

F.   Yes, but they also set my mind on the saying of Saint Paul in the Bible, which goes: "When I was a child, I spoke like a child and did things like a child." Because of this age you realise that most of the activities of the young are useless and at times I laugh when I see them indulging in them.

S.   Wouldn't you like it, if you were a young man again?

F.   No, because when you are young, you make a lot of mistakes. Now that I have grown old, I have realised it, and I don't want to become young again.

A few minutes later he added:

F.   When you are an òpanyin, money does not have much value to you. You always remember that money is the root of all evil (bòne nyinaa ti ne sika).

S.   Do you value the presence of your children and grandchildren around you more than money in your hands?

F.   Yes, when they are around and they provide me with my food, it is enough for me, because now I have no plans to put up a building or buy a car, so I don't need money for anything.

[...]

S.   Nana, you mentioned women just now and I know your wife died a long time ago. Don't you feel the desire to be with her?

F.   Yes, because there are some things I need which she could do for me, for example providing me with hot water in the morning to have my bath. In fact providing me with such services is the main reason why I wish she were with me. Apart from that I don't need her for any other purpose.

S.   Nana, I know very well that your wife also would have been an old lady if she were still alive, but would you still sleep with her?

F.   No, because at this age it will not do me any good to sleep with a woman. It will reduce my strength and my life span.

Nana Frempong pointed out an important nuance. If it does not befit the òpanyin to be interested in sex, it

---

[10] For the sake of style, the masculine pronoun will be used to refer to the òpanyin throughout.

does not mean he should not be married. On the contrary, a true òpanyin should have a wife to serve him (not to have sex with). As one elder remarked: "People don't respect an òpanyin who does not have a wife. Even if he were impotent, he could still have a wife." At that age, marriage is first of all an institution that brings social esteem. Sex would rather harm the òpanyin. It makes him (her) sick and weak and accelerates old age. It is better to abstain from it. "If you desist from too much sexual activity, you will stay longer," according to another elder. Having no interest in sex is a sign of wisdom, discipline, moderation, and gentleness. It enhances the status of the òpanyin and the beauty of old age.

"No strength": miserable old age

Losing interest in sex was seen a sign of maturity and wisdom, but others saw it as one of the unfortunate consequences of old age. I asked two elderly men, Agya Kwaku Martin (M) and Mr. Asare (A), who were friends, whether it was true that sexual desire diminishes when people grow older.

M. Yes it is true, but not for everyone. Some will be old yet their organs will be strong and effective, while there are also young men whose organs are weak and ineffective. We are all human. Our organs become weak and unable to operate. When you are young, you can go two or three times per night but as it is now, if God doesn't help, you cannot go even one round.
S. Because of what?
M. Because of the pains and lack of interest too. We have done this thing all our life. We become fed up.
S. Can the old man who finds it difficult to have sex with an old woman have sex with a young one?
A. Yes, a beautiful person can generate the machine to erect and do a small job.

The topic of ageing was intensely discussed in the group of Christian mothers mentioned earlier. Monica first asked the women if they would have liked to remain young. During the discussion that followed, one woman said:

At first, when we were young, we were able to do a lot of things that we can't do now. At first I could chase my child, catch him and punish him but now I can't do it anymore. You may start having grey hair and when you dress it does not fit you as when you were young. The strength also decreases. When you see these signs, you know you are ageing and there is nothing you can do about it.

Monica then asked what was more painful in growing old, the loss of strength or the loss of beauty. They all agreed that strength was more important to them. When she asked them what they needed beauty for, three of them answered:

I am now growing old, my face has changed, what do I need beauty for, whom am I going to show beauty to? I don't need it. I need only strength.

When you are ageing the time of beauty is gone, you don't need it. Your husband and you got married when you were both young. When you are ageing he is too, so both of you don't need beauty for anything. Both of you saw the beauty you had when you were young. So we need only strength.

If you have strength, you have beauty because you can work and get money to buy clothes, which will make you beautiful. So we pray for strength. When there is strength there is beauty all the time.

At that moment the discussion turned to sex. Monica asked: "Is it true that when men and women grow old, they lose interest in sex?"

W1. When you are ageing and you see a man, you don't regard him as a person you can sleep with. The strength I need is not for marriage. You are not happy about sex and you don't have any feelings for it. That is what I think about it.
W2. As for me when I see a man, it does not come to my mind that you can do something with him. I am not interested in it. I just don't get any feeling when I see a man. Even now I don't notice that a man is handsome (Sè mehu obarima a ne ho yè fè a, menhu).
M. Must we conclude that ageing people and the old are anti-sex? What we want to know is if they still have a desire for men or not. For example some of you are widows. Do you think that you would be sleeping with your husband in case he were still alive?
W1. As for me, sex does not interest me. I just don't have a feeling for it.
W2. As for men they never grow old but women grow old. No matter how old a man may be, he has the feeling for sex. In case I were to have a husband, I could sleep on the same bed for over one month without inviting him to do anything but a man can't do that. So to me when you are old, you don't have the feeling for it.

The idea that men have more strength and, therefore, more interest in sex is generally accepted among women as well as among men. The following statements were made during a discussion with some "station boys", young men who hang around in the lorry park and help drivers and passengers with odd jobs. Three of their remarks are quoted below:

> There is a stage when an old man or woman won't have the desire for sex. There are cases when old women do not let their husbands sleep with them. It usually happens among the women.

> It is so among the women. The women usually don't have the strength for it when they become old, so they will refuse, especially those who brought forth many children. But as for a man, the desire is always there unless he becomes impotent.

> To me, it is only impotence that can make the desire for sex in a man vanish, nothing else. Because no matter how old you are, when your man gets it up (*wo barima sòre a*), you will by all means have the desire for it.

There is a difference between the "strength" a woman needs and the "strength" men refer to when discussing sex. The women complain about lack of strength in a general sense. They are tired at the end of the day and want to sleep. As for sex itself, the Abetifi elders insisted, women don't need any strength. They don't have to "perform". They can lie down, "as a path; a bicycle can ride over it". They can continue doing so in their old age. Nana Posuo, a blind man who used to be a mason, held the same opinion:

> The desire leaves a man earlier and stays longer in a woman. Even in their old age women have the desire for it and demand it. A man may become weak. At times a man's penis can become weak and without medicines to revive it, it becomes useless.

The terms "desire", "interest", and "strength" tend to merge. *Òkyeame* Opoku (O), in a conversation with my co-researcher Patrick Atuobi (P), described the fusing of interest and strength. In his view, 'no strength' had become a euphemism for 'no desire'.

O.   No matter how old a woman may be, she can sleep with a man. As for their thing, it does not spoil, it only grows old [laughter]. But with a man it can spoil (*Òbaa deè n'ayi no nsèe da. Dada na èyò na nso ènsèe da. Nanso òbarima deè èbetumi asèe.*).

P.   But why do the women complain that they don't have strength?

O.   That is what I always attribute to individual differences. Some people don't like doing it from their youth, so when they grow older, they lose every interest in it. But some like it and will do it to the end. I know a woman who was about one hundred years old and was still interested in sex.

P.   So when a woman says she has no strength it can mean she does not have the desire for it but not that she can't do it?

O.   Yes. It is exactly so.

P.   What is strange to me is that the women always say: "I have no strength." (*Minni ahoòden*). Why don't they say: "I don't enjoy it." (*M'ani nye ho.*)?

O.   They feel shy to speak the truth.

P.   Some women give the excuse that they do a lot of work. They usually say, I went too far, I weeded and I prepared the food so I am tired, when I sleep I don't want a man to disturb me. What do you think about that?

O.   All those excuses mean that she has no interest in it. A woman with interest in it, will agree to do it as soon as she has taken her bath after returning from the farm.

In contrast to women, men need that special type of strength to get "the machine erect and do a small job", as *Òpanyin* Asare called it. Men would like to do it, but may not have that particular type of strength. When women speak about lack of strength, they complain about life in general; about their poverty, about having too many children, about their hard work, and about the way their husbands treat them:[11] Below are three statements of women to illustrate this:

W1.   What I have realised in married life is that if your husband does not shift all the burden on you but helps in caring for the family, this helps you, the woman to have a healthy or peaceful mind. This will go a long way to make you look beautiful, healthy and young.

W2.   What my sister said is true. Before it can be said of a person that she is beautiful, she is strong or healthy, she must be a bit well off. If you have these qualities but you have no money to maintain them, you will soon be like an old lady. But it is different if your husband does his work, if he helps you look after the children and yourself so that the children grow up and are well-off. They will be remitting you money and sending you delicious food, clothes, etc. Then you may never grow old and even if you become old, you can still maintain your beauty, and stay young and healthy because of your high standard of living.

W3.   If you are married and your husband is someone who likes to have sex with you every day, it may weaken your body and make you lose your beauty. Because having sex is hard work. If a day's work on the farm and at home is followed by sex every night, it will not be good for the body. I advise my fellow women to have sex fortnightly. This helps

---

[11] Studies on the heavy workload of women in Ghana, and among the Akan in particular, never discuss the "tiresome work of sex" (Klingshirn, 1971; Bukh, 1979; Fogelberg, 1982; Oppong & Abu, 1987; Dei, 1994; Avotri & Walters, 1999).

them to maintain their beauty as well as to make them strong and healthy.

The women almost seemed to be competing in denying their interest in sex, even those who were middle-aged. No doubt the situation—we were sitting in the back of a church—and the strong views of some of their leaders set the tone for this discussion and for the women's laments about their loss of strength and the uselessness of beauty. However, even if we accept their statements some reserve and take into account the possibly more positive views of those who kept silent, they remain remarkable. Obviously, these women complained about the hard work they had to do and the lack of solidarity they felt with men, a partner or otherwise. Under those conditions, sex had become something of a low priority. That view was succinctly expressed by one of them who remarked that what they really needed was proper food to eat. No doctor had ever told her that she should have sex. On the other hand, many concluded that sex made you more tired and grow old quickly. They not only lacked the strength for sex, they also avoided sex in order to retain the little strength they still possessed.

'Public opinion'

The disapproval or disbelief on the part of younger people that older people do not engage in sexual activity appears to be a near-universal phenomenon. In the Freudian paradigm mentioned earlier, there seems to be some primordial anxiety among children to look upon their parents as sexual beings. I do not know of any research that has explored the inter-cultural variations in the tolerance of children towards their parents' sexual activity.[12] Earlier on I called the Kwahu sexual culture modest, even "prudish"—partners should not make any sound during sex, "romantic play" seems limited. One wonders if that muted style of sexual activity and the accompanying secrecy have anything to do with parents' attempts to hide their sexual activity from children who

---

[12] Some indirect conclusions on the sensitivity of sex between different generations in Africa may be drawn from ethnographies which describe the inappropriateness of a mother getting pregnant after her own daughter has brought forth. The competition between fathers and sons over marriage payment points in the same direction (e.g., Fernandez, 1982, p. 196; Parkin, 1972). This intergenerational conflict seems to imply that the sons expect their fathers to stop being interested in sex and marrying and to make room for them. Fortes (1949) who devoted a whole chapter on "Tensions in the parent-child relationship" among the Tallensi in Northern Ghana, speaks of a "latent antagonism behind their [father and son] mutual identity and comradeship." He continues: "A psychoanalyst might say that the Oedipus complex is built into their social organization ...."

may be sleeping in the same room. Even younger couples, without children, may be handicapped in their love-making because they are worrying about how to keep their love-making hidden from their parents and older relatives. They too cannot afford to make much "noise." Here the elderly have an advantage, according to Òkyeame Opoku:

The elders say, love has reached its sweetest point. When there were children they used to disturb you a lot. After you have stopped having children, there is the time for joy. Whenever you meet you can enjoy freely [laughter] (Bere biara mohyia a, sè moagye mo ani.).

Opoku emphasised the respectfulness of older people's behaviour. As we have seen, an òpanyin should be married, otherwise he is not respected, but he should not lower himself to "chasing women". Opoku further strongly denounced the attempts of children to prevent their father from marrying again:

Children preventing their father whose wife is dead from marrying again. It is a mistake. You will try to give him food and provide many services but can you sleep with him? When you do that to a father it is great mistake. It means you are disturbing him. I have seen exactly such a thing and because of that the children did not like their father's wife. Whenever such a thing happens the man should be bold enough to talk to the children as a man. You should be bold and tell them not to deprive you from eating (Èsè sè wo kyerè wòn sè wònsi wo adidieè ho kwan). If you are not able to stand up in front of them you will be disgraced.

The women's statements quoted earlier suggest that most believe that they had better stop engaging in sexual activity now that their energy is diminishing. Their views were not directed, however, at elderly people in general but were self-reflections of middle-aged women. They did not so much express societal norms but emphasised the uselessness and energy-absorbing nature of sex for themselves. Talking about men too, the discussion did not include moral pronouncements. The women seemed to accept the ongoing interest in sex among elderly men, after their potency had gone, as a fact of nature. "That's how they are."

In the discussion with "station boys", I asked what they thought of older people having sex. One of them answered:

At times when a man and a woman grow to a certain age and have many children, they think that they have achieved what they want so their interest in sex goes away because they see no reason why they should do it.

I (S) asked them if it was good for old women and old men to have sex. One answered:

A. It is good especially for the men because, they have to expel something out of their bodies (*èsè sè woyi biribi fi wòn mu*).

[...]

S. Yesterday, I had discussion with some women and they said it is not good, and now you men here are telling me it is good. How do you explain that?

A. The explanation is that old women don't have the strength to do it. But as for a man, if you are not impotent, you can always do it. Because of their strength, it is not good for women but for me it is good.

In summary, this preliminary exploration suggests that public opinion turns against "unorderly" sex, i.e. sex that takes place outside of a marital relationship. The sexual prowess and secret love affairs of the young are condoned—even admired—but are disapproved of in the elderly. Yet there is nothing wrong with orderly sex between elderly people as long as sexual desires and practices remain unseen and unheard—as if they do not exist.

Conclusion

Nothing has been written about older people's sexuality in Ghana. This article is a first albeit impressionistic exploration of the topic. The ambiguity, which has been reported in the Western literature on sex at old age, is largely born out by my observations and conversations in Kwahu-Tafo. The elderly people— Θ women in particular—reported a decline in "strength", which in most cases appeared to be a euphemism for loss of sexual desire. Men, however, indicated that they still had the desire but were not always able to perform the sexual act. Based on both male and female conversations, it seems that sex was almost exclusively conceived in terms of genital penetration. Erotic alternatives, "romantic play" as some called them, seemed little practised.

By the same token, the conversations revealed that some elderly people continued to be interested in sex "till they died". The younger generation generally accepts that older married people continue to be sexually active provided they do not express this publicly. A public demonstration of love and sexual attraction, one that would be considered acceptable in Western societies, is considered bad taste in Kwahu. As one older woman said: "You may have sex in the room and during the course of it you may kiss one another, but not in public. It is shameful. Your custom [referring to me] is not good. Ours is very good." If public signs of sexual attraction are so strictly censored for everybody (although less for youths living in the cities), they certainly are taboo for the elderly. An elder, an *òpanyin*, shows restraint in all his emotions, he is civilised and "cool". The "heat" of sexual excitement and the wild "foolishness", which characterise the young, do not befit the elder. The decline in sexual interest is as much a social and cultural as a biological phenomenon.

The term "strength" (*ahoòden*) deserves a final remark. It presented itself as the most frequently mentioned word when people discussed old age and sex. Sex is primarily seen as a physical achievement that requires energy. A strenuous, "tiresome work", harder than breaking stones, one woman assured us. Only once was sex described in terms that referred to tenderness. It is no wonder that sex at old age becomes problematic. The term "strength" seemed to have different meanings when used by men or by women. Men were mainly concerned about their sexual potency. Women, according to the men, had nothing to worry about this type of energy—they simply had to lie down. Women used the term "strength" in a more general way. Their strength to work and to earn their living was decreasing and they needed to rest at night. Sex interfered with that need and made them even more tired. "No strength" was the most effective way for them to express their rejection of sex.

Acknowledgements

I dedicate this article to Mr. George Adu Asare, a gentle *òpanyin*, who died a few months before this article was published.

The research was carried out with the help of many people. Most prominent was the assistance given by my Ghanaian co-researchers Kwame Fosu, Samuel Sarkodie, Patrick Atuobi, Anthony Obeng Boamah and Michael Buabeng. Benjamin Buadi and Yaw Darko Ansah typed most of the research material. I am also indebted to Monica Amoako, Martin Asamoah, Abena Ansah, *Abusuapanyin* Daniel Osei Yeboah, Marek Dabrowski, Grzegorz Kubowicz, Lisa Hayes, Kofi Ron Lange, Geertje Amma van der Geest and Kendra McKnight for various kinds of help. Financial help was provided by the University of Amsterdam and the Royal Netherlands Academy of Sciences (KNAW). Last but not least, I should thank the old people for their openness with me.

References

Ahlberg, B. M. (1994). Is there a distinct African sexuality? *Africa*, 64(2), 220–242.

Apt, N. A. (1996). Coping with old age in a changing Africa: Social change and the elderly Ghanaian. Aldershot: Avebury.

Arhin, K. (Ed.) (1979). Brong Kyempim: Essays on the society, history and politics of Brong people. Accra: Afram Publications.

Avotri, J. Y., & Walters, V. (1999). You just look at our work and see if you have any freedom on earth: Ghanaian womens accounts of their work and their health. Social Science & Medicine, 48(9), 1123–1133.

Bartle, P. F. W. (1977). Urban migration and rural identity: An ethnography of a Kwawu community. Ph.D. thesis, Legon, University of Ghana.

Bleek, W. (1975). Marriage, inheritance and witchcraft: A case study of a rural Ghanaian family. Leiden: African Studies Centre.

Bleek, W. (1976). Sexual relationships and birth control in Ghana: A case study of a rural town. Ph.D. thesis, University of Amsterdam.

Bukh, J. (1979). The village woman in Ghana. Uppsala: Scandinavian Institute of African Studies.

Butler, R. N., & Lewis, M. I. (1986). Love and sex after 40. New York: Harper & Row.

Crose, R., & Drake, L. K. (1993). Older womens sexuality. Clinical Gerontologist, 12(4), 51–56.

Dei, H. J. S. (1994). The women of a Ghanaian village: A study of social change. African Studies Review, 37(2), 121–146.

Fernandez, J. W. (1982). Bwiti: An ethnography of the religious imagination in Africa. Princeton: Princeton University Press.

Field, M. J. (1960). Search for security: An ethno-psychiatric study of rural Ghana. London: Faber & Faber.

Fogelberg, T. (1982). Nanumba women: Working bees or idle bums. Sexual division of labour, ideology of work, and power relations between women and men. Leiden: ICCS, ICA Publication 53.

Fortes, M. (1949). The web of kinship among the Tallensi. London: Oxford University Press.

Fortes, M. (1969). Kinship and the social order. London: Routledge & Kegan Paul.

Freud, S. (1918). From the history of infantile neurosis. London: Hogarth Press.

Gibson, H. B. (1993). Emotional and sexual adjustment in later life. In S. Arbar, & M. Evandrou (Eds.), Ageing, independence and the life course (pp. 104–118). London: Jessica Kingsley.

Hodson, D. S., & Skeen, P. (1994). Sexuality and aging: The Hammerlock of myths. Journal of Applied Gerontology, 13(3), 219–235.

Hoyt, M. (1977). Primal scene and self-creation. Voices, 13.

Kellet, J. M. (1991). Sexuality of the elderly. Sexual and Marital Therapy, 6(2), 147–155.

Klingshirn, A. (1971). The changing position of women in Ghana. Inaugural Dissertation, Marburg.

Levy, J. A. (1994). Sex and sexuality in later life stages. In A. S. Rossi (Ed.), Sexuality across the life course (pp. 287–309). Chicago: University of Chicago Press.

Miescher, S. F. (1997). Becoming man in Kwawu: Gender, law, personhood, and the construction of masculinities in colonial Ghana 1875–1957. Ph.D. thesis Anthropology, Northwestern University, Evanston.

Minichiello, V., Plummer, D., & Seal, A. (1996). The 'asexual' older person? Australian evidence. Venereology, 9(3), 180, 181, 184–188.

Nadelson, C. C. (1984). Geriatric sex problems: Discussion. Journal of Geriatric Psychiatry, 17(2), 139–148.

Oppong, Chr. (1982). Middle class African marriage. London: George Allen & Unwin.

Oppong, C., & Abu, K. (1987). Seven roles of women: Impact of education, migration and employment on Ghanaian mothers. Geneva: ILO.

Parkin, D. (1972). Palms, wine and witnesses. London: Intertext Books.

Pellow, D. (1977). Women in Accra: Options for autonomy. Algonac, MI: Reference Publications.

Rattray, R. S. (1916). Ashanti proverbs. Oxford: Clarendon Press.

Rattray, R. S. (1923). Ashanti. Oxford: Clarendon Press.

Rattray, R. S. (1927). Religion and art in Ashanti. Oxford: Clarendon Press.

Rattray, R. S. (1929). Ashanti law and constitution. Oxford: Clarendon Press.

Savage, O. M. N., & Tchombe, T. M. (1994). Anthropological perspectives on sexual behaviour in Africa. Annual Review of Sex Research, 5, 50–72.

Standing, H. (1991). AIDS: Conceptual and methodological issues in researching sexual behaviour in sub-Saharan Africa. Social Science & Medicine, 34(5), 475–483.

Standing, H., & Kisekka, M. N. (1989). Sexual behaviour in Sub-Saharan Africa: A review and annotated bibliography. London: Overseas Development Association.

Traupmann, J. (1984). Does sexuality fade over time? A look at the question and the answer. Journal of Geriatric Psychiatry, 17(2), 149–159.

Van der Geest, S. (1998). Ɔpanyin: The ideal of elder in the Akan culture of Ghana. Canadian Journal of African Studies, 32(3), 449–493.

Warren, D. M. (1974). Disease, medicine and religion among the Techiman-Bono of Ghana: A study in culture change. Dissertation, Indiana University, Microfilms, Ann Arbor.

Weg, R. B. (Ed.) (1983). Sexuality in the later years. New York: Academic Press.

Yankah, K. (1995). Speaking for the chief: Ɔkyeame and the politics of Akan royal oratory. Bloomington & Indianapolis: Indiana University Press.

Indian Elders

Family Traditions in Crisis

DAVID BALDRIDGE
National Indian Council on Aging

Nowhere in the United States do elders enjoy a more revered status than in tribal communities. They are, according to many Indian leaders, our strength, our living heritage, our teachers. They are the keepers of our traditions and the guardians of our way of life. Even the U.S. Congress, in its preamble to Title 6 of the Older Americans Act, describes Indian elders as "a vital resource." If a single common value were to be expressed by the nation's 568 Indian tribes, it might be simply "respect for elders."

ELDERS: THE IMAGE

For many Americans, Indian elders seemingly enjoy a positive, larger-than-life public image. It is shaped in part by movies like *Little Big Man*, *Thunderheart*, and *Dances With Wolves*, all of which portray elders according to sentimental clichés: wise, tolerant, spiritual, brave, taciturn, generous, and humorous. Television commercials, too, have contributed to America's public image of elders: Iron Eyes Cody, an Indian actor, paddles a canoe along a trashy, polluted river. He stops to shed a quiet tear for America.

It should be noted that this process of romanticization extends to Indians in general—not just to elders. In numerous other movies and television shows, Indian males frequently found themselves characterized as noble savages or relentless warriors or caricatured as foolish drunks. Indian women were romanticized as Indian princesses or demeaned as squaws. In any case, the result was the same. These one-dimensional images oversimplified and dehumanized their subjects.

Americans, for the most part, know very little about Indian elders and tend to view them anthropologically, like a daguerreotype photo from the 1860s: a metallic snapshot frozen in time. That image is perhaps more comfortable to see than those of destitute Indian children with uncertain futures. Indian elders are generally perceived as nice and as nonthreatening. They are not activists, and they are not complainers. They are not going to rock America's boat.

255

This view provides a safe, distant way of "understanding" Indian elders. It does not reveal the complexities of their daily lives nor does it contribute to a realistic understanding of them as contemporary Americans who are struggling, often with unusual dignity, to overcome daily problems of poverty, poor health, and minimal access to services.

However, although elders may indeed fulfill, or are perceived as fulfilling, some of the romanticized roles attributed to them, the realities of their daily lives provide a sobering contrast to their public image. In tribal communities, a pertinent question is not whether Indian elders can live up to anyone's image of them but whether Indian Country can cope with its own expectations of how elders should be treated. The fact that elders are so highly regarded in Indian political rhetoric contrasts dramatically with their poor health and socioeconomic status and with tribes' frequent failure to provide adequate senior programs for them.

Indian people are rightfully proud of the role elders have played, and continue to play, in their history. But in an increasingly complex society, with Indian families and communities experiencing the same wrenching stresses and changes as mainstream America, it is becoming more difficult to sustain the traditional familial and community roles that Indian elders play.

> I believe the Pueblo of San Felipe elders would say, "Believe in yourself, respect yourself, love yourself. If you have a religion, consult it, consult your spiritual and be together, be there for other, comfort each other, listen to each other, respect each other because you get strength from your own people, from your own workers, from your own elders, and that's what keeps you going." (Emily Velasquez, senior program director; personal communication, October 8, 1999)

WHO'S AN ELDER?

Traditional Indian concepts of tribal elders as deserving of respect and deference exist without regard for numerical age and are defined more by the significance of elders' roles in society. If one were to ask what is the difference between an Indian elder and an Indian old person, the answers in Indian Country would doubtless be as interesting as they would be varied.

Federal definitions of the elderly begin at age 55, based on eligibility criteria for most Older Americans Act programs. Age 55 is also used for voting membership by the National Indian Council on Aging (NICOA). Age 65 (or soon 67), used to determine eligibility for Medicare and social security, are not as commonly acknowledged.

Statistically, 236,713 American Indian and Alaska Native (AI/AN) elders, aged 55 and older, live in the United States (Data Analysis Services, 1990). Comprising nearly 12% of the Indian population, they speak an estimated 150 different languages. As of 1990, two thirds of Indian elders aged 60 and older lived in 10 states, and approximately half of them lived in 5 states ("Profiles in

Diversity," 1999). These are Oklahoma (18%), California (13%), Arizona (9%), New Mexico (6%), and North Carolina (5%). They live diversely: in desert hogans miles from the nearest paved roads, in reservation housing projects, and in urban apartment complexes. More than 1,700 of them, age 65 and older, live in New York City (U.S. Census, 1990). They live on treaty-based reservations, executive order reservations, state-created reservations, or with bands of Indians who do not have federal recognition. They live scattered throughout America's cities, although seldom in ethnic neighborhoods. A high percentage of both rural and urban elders are not served by the reservation system (Baldridge, 1996).

The 1990 census classifies 62% of Indian elders as "urban," meaning that they live off reservation, in small rural towns and in cities of all sizes. Many were relocated to large cities in the 1950s and 1960s as part of the termination era's unsuccessful attempt to assimilate them into mainstream society. Today, second and third generations of urban Indians are living with only distant (and probably diminishing) contact with their tribes. The extent to which this phenomenon will affect their families remains unknown.

Because urban Indian elders frequently do not access the Indian health care delivery system, are not served by their tribes, and do not tend to live in ethnic neighborhoods, little is known about them statistically. The nation's 35 or so urban Indian health centers are so underfunded that they frequently can provide little more than information and referral services. Some centers report that they serve primarily itinerant, transient populations, and few, if any, provide services for elders.

NICOA's 1996 publication *The NICOA Report: Health and Long-Term Care for Indian Elders* (John & Baldridge, 1996) reports that urban elders enjoy greater income and somewhat better health status than their reservation counterparts. The report also indicates that female Indian elders older than age 60 are much less likely to be married than male elders (38.2% vs. 65.7%) and are nearly three times more likely to be widowed (44.9% vs. 14.6%). Female Indian elders, therefore, are at a higher risk of social isolation and economic hardship with related health consequences as they age (John & Baldridge, 1996, p. 26).

The lives of many Indian elders are most accurately reflected by findings of the 1980 census about their homes: 16% lacked electricity, 17% had no refrigerators, 21% had no indoor toilets, and 50% had no telephones. A 1981 White House Conference on Aging report (U.S. Department of Commerce, 1983) added that 26% of their homes were built prior to 1939, 26.3% had no indoor plumbing at all, and only 50% had complete bathrooms indoors.

Households headed by an Indian elder tend to be larger than Black or non-Hispanic White households, with 15.4% of Indian households having four or more persons, as compared with only 3.8% for non-Hispanic Whites (John & Baldridge, 1996).

The U.S. Department of Commerce (1994) reports that nationally, 5% of all households were crowded (more than one person per room) in 1990, compared with 20% in 1940. "But the national conditions of a half-century ago were nothing compared with what American Indian households on reservations face today. In 1990, an astounding *one-third* of them were crowded" (U.S. Department of Commerce, 1994).

ASSIMILATION

Historically, the roles of elders have composed an important thread in the daily fabric of Indian life. As part of extended families—which often included uncles, aunts, grandchildren, other relatives, and clan members—elders served as mentors and counselors, reinforcing a wide range of mores and folkways. Elders also helped tend crops and gardens, maintained households, and provided day care for young relatives. They continue to do so today:

> We need to spend more time with the kids. Sit down with them . . . explain to them . . . and show them that we love them. We should listen to them at all times, whether they're in trouble or doing good in grades. But we need to listen to them every day. (Joseph "Gabe" Trujillo, Pueblo of Cochiti elder; personal communication, October 7, 1999)

Over the entire past century, however, assimilation—engendered by both federal policy and technology—began to change the primary roles of Indian family members, including elders. On reservations, once-essential hunting or agricultural skills diminished in value as entire communities became reliant on processed foods. Diets changed dramatically with an influx of commodity and fast foods. Reservation lifestyles became sedentary. Urban Indians, removed from their extended families, lost contact with tribal socialization and support mechanisms. They began to integrate into new communities and lifestyles. Given their former status and prominence in traditional Indian society, both rural and urban elders subsequently experienced an evolution—one that is ongoing—into unclear and less meaningful roles.

In some cases,

> traditional medical values were replaced by contemporary (values). Traditional leaders . . . were replaced by appointed or elected tribal officials. Extended, family-based long-term care was sometimes replaced by distant nursing homes. Reservation economics required elders to seek full or part-time employment. Traditionally healthy elders began to experience health problems associated with diabetes and alcoholism. The elder population, once carefully nurtured . . . became instead primary care-givers and, frequently, sole financial providers. (Baldridge, in press)

In Indian extended families, elders served as mentors and counselors, reinforcing a wide range of values. Their authority over Indian children was generally unquestioned. As one Laguna Pueblo Indian woman put it:

Our grandparents taught us that every visitor to our home should be fed. My grandmother always said, "Even if you have nothing, offer them a drink of water." Years later, a salesman knocked on our door and I left him on the porch for a few minutes. My grandmother was upset with me: "What's the matter," she said, "have you forgotten everything?" (Laura Graham, Laguna Pueblo, personal communication, 1993)

Although younger Indian people have not forgotten everything, the pace of their lives was gradually changing. Traditional subsistence lifestyles were giving way to off-reservation jobs. Horseback rides were replaced by commuting, evening storytelling sessions were upstaged by television shows, and the once unquestioned authority of elders was being challenged by a new set of consumer-based, youth-oriented values:

We carried water, we chopped wood, and all of that. It wasn't a hardship for us because that's the way we lived. And it's sad to say that we live in a push-button age and the kids can't even empty our trash cans. They don't get any exercise and they don't eat right. (Betty Thinelk, Rosebud Sioux elder; personal communication, October 21, 1999)

Moreover, although many traditional Indian families exist today, they do so without the geographic and cultural isolation that characterized the lives of their grandparents.

FEDERAL POLICY AND INDIAN FAMILIES

From the inception of the first Congress through the era of the Indian Wars (1776-1880s), the U.S. government's policies toward Indian tribes were driven by the acquisition of tribal lands. At the same time, however, the U.S. government showed little interest in either governing Indian tribes or interfering with the infrastructure of Indian families and communities. If Indians could be removed from conflicts generated by the westward expansion of the republic, there was little to be gained from further interfering with internal tribal activities. Tribes were accorded the formal status of "domestic dependent nations" (*Cherokee Nation v. Georgia*, 1831; cited in DeLoria, 1985), with large measures of sovereign self-governance.

By the end of the 1800s, however, the federal government had expanded its initiatives to assimilate Indians into the larger society. The Dawes Act of 1887, described by Teddy Roosevelt as "a great pulverizing engine, designed to break up the tribal mass" (Roosevelt, n.d.), dissolved tribal governments and institutions.

Under the pretext of assimilation, the Dawes Act dissolved tribal ownership of lands, and 80- or 160-acre parcels were dispersed to individual tribal members, ostensibly to be farmed, even by nonagrarian tribes. "Surplus" tribal lands were appropriated and allotted to non-Indians. As a result, two thirds of Indian lands had passed into White hands by 1943 (O'Brien, 1985).

259

In addition to the devastating loss of the Indians' homelands, the Dawes Act and subsequent attempts to assimilate Indians have effectively resulted in the destruction of their traditional societies. In the 1950s and 1960s, the federal government began the termination era, "with the ultimate goals of assimilating Indian people by breaking down tribal bonds. By 1961, Congress had terminated its relationship with 109 tribes and bands" (O'Brien, 1985, p. 45).

Even enlightened efforts to restore tribal sovereignty brought radical changes to tribal institutions. Commissioner of Indian Affairs John Collier's promotion of the Indian Reorganization Act of 1934 resulted in the reconstitution of tribal governments modeled after mainstream municipal governments. "Many critics charge, however, that rather than allowing the establishment of governments that reflected Indian values and traditions, the Bureau of Indian Affairs drafted tribal constitutions that were tailored to Anglo-American standards" (O'Brien, 1985, p.44).

As a result of these federal initiatives, traditional tribal decision-making procedures, consisting of deliberation, community consultation, and informal consensus building, were discarded in favor of democratic, efficiency-driven models. The roles of elders as key shapers of tribal policies began to erode. Decisions, once driven by the advice of elders, were now made by appointed or elected tribal officials.

Educational patterns and content also changed dramatically. Indian children—once raised by extended families, instructed by elders, and fully integrated into their communities—were removed from their homes to be placed in federal or church-run boarding schools.

And I think Hilary learned it from Indian Country where she said, "It takes a village." Well, you need the elderlies to provide the rest of that. And they're looking forward to it. (John Eagleshield, Rosebud Sioux Community Health Representative; personal communication, October 19, 1999)

BOARDING SCHOOLS

Another federal initiative to assimilate Indians, led in the late 1800s and early 1900s by educator Richard Pratt, involved the establishment of Bureau of Indian Affairs (BIA) boarding schools. "Pratt had urged total assimilation of Indian youth through the expansion of an off-reservation Industrial boarding school system" (Szasz, 1996, pp. 182-183). These off-reservation, English-only industrial boarding schools increasingly provided only the most basic curricula for children "who were forced to spend much of their day in tedious chores that maintained the school itself. Thus Indian pupils sewed the school uniforms, cooked the meals and washed the dishes, and constructed and repaired the buildings" (Szasz, 1996, p. 183). Underfed, frequently ill from contagious diseases, and homesick, many children ran away.

In these schools, an entire generation of Indian children reportedly suffered widespread emotional, physical, and sexual abuse. At best, BIA boarding schools offered inferior educations. At their worst, they succeeded in dampening any pride that many Indian children felt for their culture or hopes they carried of living traditional lives. Indian boarding schools coerced thousands of Indian children into denials of their cultural heritage, presumably to learn the manners and ways of the larger society.

> I had 11 children and I think I got about 50 or 60 grandchildren. I got several great-grandchildren. Every time they come home from school, the grandchildren they come to me and hug me, before they go to school in the morning they kiss me and say, "Grandmother, I'll see you later." And I like that and enjoy taking care of everybody. (Candelaria Valencia, Pueblo of San Felipe elder; personal communication, October 8, 1999)

ELDER ABUSE

Some service providers have speculated that many of today's Indian elders, as survivors of institutional abuse at boarding schools, became abusers themselves. That cycle of abuse, passed from generation to generation, may now mean that these same elders, ironically, are suffering abuse from their own grandchildren. Elder abuse, in fact, has become a topic of growing concern and keen interest among elders throughout the nation. In 1998, Baldridge and Brown concluded that studies on American Indian elder abuse confirm a national pattern that "most elder abuse is related to the many problems of elderly people being cared for on a daily basis at home by informal caregivers" (p. 3).

In a study of Navajo elderly, Brown (1989) found a number of caregiver factors associated with elder abuse, including the suddenness of becoming dependent and families "having caregiving responsibilities thrust upon them for which they were unprepared" (p. 17).

In 1998, the NICOA conducted an informal survey of 189 elders in five states, soliciting comments about the perceived impact of welfare reform legislation. Eighty-six percent of respondents indicated that elders should not be asked to care for young children for extended periods of time, and 77% felt that if it was difficult for an elder to take care of young children, asking them to do so would be "abusive or wrong." More than four out of five elder respondents (81%) thought that "some elders are worried about being abused."

The unpublished final report from NICOA's 1998 national aging conference, "American Voices: Indian Elders Speak," included comments from elders that "violence, gang activity, and undisciplined children are real threats to elders on the reservations." Elders asked for "abused elderly protection teams" and for advocates to alert tribal leaders about upcoming grants designed to reduce youth and gang violence.

261

Elders' concerns about crime appear to be substantiated by statistics. The Department of Justice *1997 Final Report on Indian Country Law Enforcement* (U.S. Department of Justice, 1998) cited the following:

- Violent crime is rising significantly in Indian Country—in sharp contrast to national trends.
- The homicide rate for Indian males is almost three times higher than the rate for White males. In 1996, the Navajo nation's homicide rate would have placed it among the top 20 most violent cities in the nation.

In addition, a 1975 Bureau of Indian Affairs study (U.S. Department of Justice, 1998) showed 375 gangs with some 4,650 gang members in or near Indian Country.

Statistics such as these are particularly distressing for elders, as the concept of intratribal crime or familial abuse is so foreign to their belief system. It is interesting that elders often do not even perceive abuse as crime. Brown's 1989 study found that elder victims of financial exploitation felt that "giving money to family members in need was a cultural duty. They insisted that it was their duty to share financial resources with family members even though they were often severely deprived as a result" (Brown, 1989, p. 7).

> To me life is grand and life is great no matter how difficult. It may be you don't have to live it difficult. You do something about it, you know. The most important thing to me is love. With love you can't lose. (Liza Alery, Turtle Mountain Chippewa elder; personal communication, October 18, 1999)

ELDER HEALTH: IMPLICATIONS FOR FAMILIES

Today, epidemics of communicable diseases no longer devastate Indian populations as they did in past centuries. Where once smallpox and influenza were the scourges of Indian Country, behavioral health issues now dominate morbidity and mortality statistics. This change has significant implications for elders, their families, and for Indian public health care providers. Each of the five leading causes of death for Indians 55 to 64 years relates, directly or indirectly, to behavioral health (U.S. Department of Health and Human Services, 1997):

- Diseases of the heart, the leading cause of death, are closely associated with diabetes.
- Malignant neoplasms are linked, at least to some extent, to Indian Country's high rates of smoking.
- Diabetes mellitus is increasing to epidemic proportions in Indian Country.
- Accidents, with a strong relationship to drinking, are the fourth leading cause of death.
- Chronic liver disease and cirrhosis are obviously related to alcohol abuse.

In any case, health care for Indian elders—particularly in relation to long-term care—remains their foremost concern (NICOA, 1992). Indian elders suffer poorer overall health than any comparable population in America. With a life expectancy of 73.2 years, 3.3 years less than that of Whites, Indians are 4.6 times more likely than Whites to die of alcoholism, 4.2 times more likely to die of tuberculosis, 1.6 times more likely to die of diabetes, and .51 times more likely to die of pneumonia (U.S. Department of Health and Human Services, 1997).

Although Indian health care is provided by law, Indian Health Service (IHS) budgets are discretionary and must be reauthorized every year by Congress. The result is a pattern of chronically insufficient funding, resulting in the IHS being unable to meet even the immediate, primary care needs of its service population. Consequently, long-term care—whether institutional or community-based—has never been available for Indian elders. Not only is institutional care generally absent in Indian Country, few community-based programs are in place. With only 12 tribally operated nursing homes operating in the entire nation, America's 236,000 Indian elders are understandably distressed at the lack of community- or home-based care. Elders requiring nursing home care must either find a way to pay for private care—an impossibility for most—or depend on their families. The Indian health care delivery system does not provide a geriatric focus; it offers no individual case management, and it has not, over the past five decades, created an infrastructure for the provision of long- term care.

Not surprisingly, the burden of long-term care is heaviest for Indian families. "This situation is consistent with tribal values that emphasize familial obligations and interdependence" (Red Horse, 1980, p. 491). However, family members often undertake extremely demanding tasks in caring for and preventing the institutional placement of an elderly relative (Manson, 1989).

Even though elder life expectancy has improved dramatically in recent years, "longevity has been accompanied by relatively high rates of chronic illness" (Johnson & Taylor, 1991) and functional impairments among American Indian elders. For example, a high proportion of older American Indians have self-identified health impairments: 73% of those aged 55 and older report limitations in their ability to carry out the basic activities of daily living (John & Baldridge, 1996).

Indian elders' high rates of disability undoubtedly increase burdens on family caregivers. According to the U.S. Department of Education (1987), the prevalence of disability among American Indians is among the highest of any ethnic group in the nation. Among American Indians between the ages of 65 and 74, a total of 21% of men and 23% of women reported either a mobility or self-care limitation. In the 75-and-older age group, 33% of men and 41% of women reported these limitations (U.S. Department of Justice, 1998).

Hennessy and John (1996) found that Indian family caregivers perceive abnormally high levels of burden and express strong concerns about the effects of caregiving on their own health and family relationships. As John pointed out:

263

It is true that American Indian families continue to provide most of the care elders receive, but American Indian families are not immune to the stresses and strains that can compromise their ability to care for American Indian elders. Indeed there are a variety of threats to the informal support system among American Indians.

DIABETES

Perhaps no health condition in Indian Country has greater implications for Indian families than that of diabetes. Beginning in the 1940s, an epidemic of Type 2 diabetes has swept through Indian Country and today has grown to epidemic proportions. The IHS Diabetes Program reports that more than one out of every five Indian elders has this disease (the highest proportion of any Indian age cohort). In some Indian communities, more than half the residents older than age 50 suffer from diabetes. According to the National Institutes of Health, the Indian diabetes rate is four times the national average, with some Arizona reservations exhibiting the highest known rates in the world. *The Arizona Republic* reported in 1999 that more than 80% of Pima Indians have diabetes (Sevilla, 1999).

Diabetes in Indian elders results in increased demands on family caregivers. Unlike previous epidemics of infectious diseases, diabetes is patient manageable by controlling diet, exercise, and insulin. For untrained and frequently undereducated patients and family care providers, the burden of managing these factors can be enormous.

It's very, very difficult to get an older person to change their habits, especially when they're poor, 'cause they can't go out and buy all the fruits and all the healthy foods they should have. For years they've eaten fatty commodity foods and that's all a lot of people have to eat and live on. But to try to change someone at that level, even if it means impending death, is very difficult because they have to eat. And they have to survive. (Joyce Dugan, former chief, Eastern Band of Cherokee Indians; personal communication, October 12, 1999)

CONCLUSION

Addressing family issues of Indian elders will involve solutions as varied and complex as the issues themselves. Initiatives will necessarily involve a range of political arenas—national, state, and tribal—and solutions must be sought within a broad range of issues: housing, nutrition, education, employment, transportation, and, above all, health. Reservation Indian elders are caught in a vicious cycle of interrelated needs and a lack of services—both for themselves and for their families.

It will be very difficult to improve the health status of reservation elders, for example, when they may be providing most of their social security income to their children and grandchildren who live with them in overcrowded, substandard

BIA housing; when they have no car and no public transportation is available; when reservation roads are poor and dangerous; when they have little education and no prospects for finding work; when their nutrition primarily consists of commodities; and when they put family members' well-being ahead of their own.

There will not be a short-term fix to the economic and social inequities that have arisen in Indian Country over many decades. The lack of adequate health, long-term care, economic, social service, and educational infrastructures in tribal communities will not be easily changed.

If there is a common thread that weaves through the fabric of these concerns, it is poverty. Until tribes can generate sufficient revenues or until federal and state governments provide better funding and access to programs, local improvement of these infrastructures is unlikely. Further, solutions will need to be effective in increasingly complex health care and social service environments. The devolution of Medicaid managed care and welfare reform from federal to state control are recent examples of programs that now pose exceptional problems for Indian families.

In the final analysis, solutions are more likely to come from Indian communities, families, and the elders themselves than from advocates, providers, or politicians. National- and state-designed programs and initiatives do not translate easily into Indian communities. Too often, we have forgotten to listen to the people who know the most about Indian elders: the elders themselves.

MEMORIES OF 1934

The little knot of crew-cut Indian boys stood uneasily in the center of the Bureau of Indian Affairs (BIA) Chemewa Boarding School gymnasium. They were going to be punished. Today, a special assembly had been called to embarrass them for their secret ceremony. They had been caught sneaking down to a little clearing in a nearby forest to dance. They often did this—partly in play, partly serious—wearing their homemade cardboard feathers and singing traditional songs when they danced, using a stick and a discarded wash tub for a makeshift drum.

Now they were going to have to dance again. And look foolish, embarrass themselves in front of the several hundred other Indian kids who, like them, had been taken from their reservation homes and forced to attend Chemewa. The school superintendent told them, "If you want to be Indian so much, you can do your little dance in front of us all."

R.S., age six and the tallest of the five boys, was scared. This was going to be embarrassing. Ever since he came to this school last year—taken against his grandparents' wishes—his life had been miserable. More than anything, he wanted to go home. When he spoke the only language he knew, Tututni, teachers had whipped him with canes, leaving red welts on his back and legs. But they hadn't made him white . . . and they hadn't made him quit. In his coveralls, cardboard feather sticking up behind his right ear, he looked up from the floor with an anger that would follow him for much of his life. He began to sing, in a quavering, adolescent falsetto: "Wi hi yiii . . . ." Every eye in the gym was on him. Silence.

Then, from just behind him, the voice of another young boy. "Wi hi yo, yah . . ." And then another, and another, until five hundred Indian kids were singing the ancient prayer song. Heads high, defiant, eyes shining. They knew they would pay for their insubordination—but for that one afternoon, they didn't care.

R.S. graduated from Chemewa, overcame a drinking problem, and soon earned two Purple Hearts and a Silver Star as a Marine in Korea. His classmates weren't so fortunate. Most of them have died from alcohol-related causes. (Baldridge, 1996)

REFERENCES

Baldridge, D. (1996). Elders. In M. B. Davis (Ed.), *Native America in the 20th century* (Vol. 452, pp. 185-187). New York: Garland Reference Library of Social Science.

Baldridge, D. (in press). The elder population and long-term care. In M. Dixon & Y. Roubideaux (Eds.), *Public health policy for American Indians and Alaska Natives in the 21st century*. American Public Health Association.

Baldridge, D., & Brown, A. (1998). *An American Indian elder abuse monograph*. University of Oklahoma, Center of Child Abuse and Neglect.

Brown, A. (1989). A survey on elder abuse at one Native American tribe. *Journal of Elder Abuse and Neglect, 1*(2).

Cherokee Nation v. Georgia (1831).

Fowler, L., & Dwyer, K., (1996). *American Indian approaches to disability policy—Establishing legal protections for tribal members with disabilities: Five case studies*. University of Montana—Missoula, Research & Training Center on Rural Rehabilitation, Montana Affiliated Rural Institute on Disabilities.

Hennessy, C. H., & John, R. (1996). American Indian family caregivers' perceptions of burden and needed support services. *Journal of Applied Gerontology, 15*, 275-293.

John, R. Defining and meeting the needs of Native American elders: Applied research on their current status, social service needs, and support system network operation. In *Final report to the Administration on Aging*. (Vols. 1-13). Lawrence: University of Kansas.

John, R., & Baldridge, D. (1996). *The National Indian Council on Aging report: Health and long-term care for Indian elders*. Washington, DC: National Indian Policy Center.

Johnson, A., & Taylor, A. (1991). *Prevalence of chronic diseases: A summary of data from the survey of American Indians and Alaska Natives*. Rockville, MD: Agency for Health Care Policy and Research.

Manson, S. M. (1989). Long-term care in American Indian communities: Issues in planning and research. *The Gerontologist, 29*, 43-44.

National Indian Council on Aging. (1992). *National Indian aging agenda for the future*. Albuquerque, NM: Author.

O'Brien, S. (1985). Federal Indian policies and the international protection of human rights. In V. Deloria, Jr. (Ed.), *American Indian policy in the 20th century* (pp. PAGES). Norman: University of Oklahoma Press.

Red Horse, J. G. (1980). American Indian elders: Unifiers of Indian families. *Social Casework, 61*, 490-493.

Roosevelt, T. *Messages and papers of the presidents* (vol. 15, p. 6672).

Sevilla, G. (1999, October-November). A people in peril: People on the front lines of an epidemic. *The Arizona Republic*.

Szasz, M. C. (1996) Educational policy. In M. B. Davis (Ed.), *Native America in the 20th century* (Vol. 452, pp. 182-183). New York: Garland Reference Library of Social Science.

The Construction of Personhood Among The Aged: A Comparative Study of Aging in Israel and England
by Haim Hazan

The Problem

The problem faced by anthropologists in dealing with the aging self is how to identify the characteristics of that self within a social context which by nature does not inform such identification. Whether researchers are mindful of this difficulty or not, the practical solutions offered in the literature are socially telling and intellectually intriguing, for they reflect common attitudes toward the aged as well as mirror the analytic perplexity embedded in the whole subject of aging.

Two diametrically opposite of models for handling the problem could be identified. One is based on the view that the life of elderly people is best understood in terms of their immediate environmental constraints and the exigencies of their functional-economic and social conditions-all of which are unfolded in the form of "adjustment" problems. The other model recognizes the boundaries of the self as extending beyond the present and hence furnishing the conception of the self with content and meaning stemming from past identities and lifelong cumulative experience. In neither case is the process of continuous construction of self vis-a-vis existing interactional and symbolic contexts thrown into relief. Rather, in both approaches the self is viewed through its sociocultural resources rather than via the structure of relationships responsible for its constitution as a pragmatic response to an overall social arena.

This raises a host of important theoretical and methodological issues, some of which will be addressed at a later stage. For the purpose of this introduction, however, suffice it to state that unlike recent trends in sociocultural research, which put a premium on autobiographical narrative as a major source of ethnographic data about the self, the conception guiding this discussion draws mostly on situational-contextual analysis as a basis for establishing a perceived profile of the aged self. This is not to say that matters of life history and its interpretation are to be overlooked, but it does suggest that the independent set of variables for explaining the emergence of the construction of the aged self in question will hinge on the structural arguments rather than biographically slanted discourses.

The two case studies I will present, of a residential home and a day center are interrelated primarily by virtue of the concept under study, the self. While, the two groups studied have some limited cultural commonalities the link between them is not to be sought in similarities of content or meaning, nor in shared cultural universals. It is my assumption that the discovery of the

267

aging self in its manifestation within the context and structure of the varied realities under consideration provides the rationale for juxtaposing the two ethnographic descriptions in this chapter.

Having said that context and structure are at the core of our search for the concept of selfhood among the aged, it is necessary to stress that context and structure are not regarded as "given" or "taken for granted" arenas where action and interaction take place but are indeed viewed as the social product of behavioral patterns. In other words, by locating the idea of selfhood within a contextual-structural frame of reference, a host of cultural, interactional, and biographical factors would be reflected and identified.

This will be handled by addressing three sets of relevant units of information regarding images and construction of selfhood. The first consists of views and ideas concerning humanity, individuality, and the moral order associated with "proper" and desirable conduct. The second evinces emergent systems of categorization and corresponding social relationships delineating boundaries of the self, and the third describes some of the social strategies of exclusion and inclusion employed in maintaining these boundaries. This threefold account of the context wherein conceptions of selfhood are generated, constructed, and sustained constitutes the basis for the final section of this discussion, whose main objective is to arrive at some tentative propositions regarding the study of selfhood among the aged. In this analysis it is suggested that three major analytic categories should be considered as appropriate dimensions of the self. These are the mental-both emotive and intellectual aspects-the sociocultural, and the physiological. Evidently, all three are viewed merely as social constructs and not as objectively ascertained variables.

The Home

The first setting to be discussed is an old age Home in Israel.1 At the time of the research (1972/73) the institution catered to 400 able-bodied residents. It was established and run by the welfare agency of Israel's biggest trades union federation and admission was based on being a union member or a member's parent. However, the location of the Home at the midst of one of the most desirable residential areas in Tel Aviv, and the modern facilities with which it was equipped made demand for accommodation exceed supply. For an applicant to be successful he or she had to display not only mental alertness and functional independence but also to enjoy the backing of some influential figure in the political arena of the trade unions.

This last constraint contributed a great deal to molding the character and the composition of the population of residents. Those whose background and connections furnished them with a position of power and influence within the Home usually upheld an uncompromising socialist ideology combined with strong nationalistic fervor. Having been deeply involved in the core of Israel's nation-building epoch and ethos, some of those residents became nationally famous living legends. This halo followed them to the Home and was reflected in both their status among fellow residents and their own behavior.

Thus articulation and fluency in the use of Hebrew were highly esteemed as linguistic insignia of previous involvement in political and educational scenes. Simple but tidy outfits were regarded as signs of nonostentatious yet respectable appearance and avoidance of jewelry and other means of bodily adornment was almost universal among residents. The values of austere living in the service of national and socialist goals were cherished as the foundation and the justification for the existence of Israel as a state and for the continuity of the Zionist enterprise. Some of the residents whose past seemed to represent such personal sacrifice and patriotic legacy set the indisputable principles for social esteem and moral judgment in the Home.

This came into being by establishing a body of residents whose explicit purpose was to debate various subjects of interest. These discussions evolved into an arena for discussing the affairs of other residents, the administration of the Home, and the desirable code of practice of institutional life. Eventually, the discussion group used outside connections in an attempt to influence the manager and wrest from him the power to regulate the flow of residents into and out of the institution. It was proposed that an executive committee of residents-all of whom were members of the discussion group-would be authorized to determine criteria for admitting new residents and to set up a disciplinary court whose jurisdiction would include decisions concerning the removal of unwanted residents from the Home.

This last issue of conditions for transferring residents to other institutions or back to their families was a crucial one for a number of reasons. To begin with, adequate alternative care facilities for the frail elderly at the time of the research were scarce and, in any case, not within the financial reach of most residents. The pressure of applicants-many of them backed by influential connections-on the Home was enormous (3,000 on the waiting list); hence the increasing vulnerability of residents without outside support. In addition, cases of genuine inability to perform as independent elderly people were in constant jeopardy of having their secret malfunctioning exposed with all the impending consequences incurred by such disclosure. The result was that public display of personal competence and social vigor became not only the order of the day among those whose future residence was at stake but also an imperative which put a whole new, institutionally conditioned, complexion on the concept of a person. We shall see how the components of physical ability, mental agility, and social capacity interplayed to delineate boundaries and to shape relationships and behavior.

If the internal, though externally inspired, pyramid of stratification is to be sketched, the following ladder would emerge. At the top, occupying the revered position almost belonging to a mythical sphere, were those residents whose life histories and present association made them into the epitome of some of the most commonly shared set of values in Israeli society--patriotism, self-sacrifice, and socialism. Immune to removal and assured of future provision, these people advocated the idea of "good functioning" more than those residents who had cause for concern regarding their capacity to maintain the image of competence.

Out of the three dimensions of selfhood--the mental, the sociocultural and the physical--they gave priority to the latter, setting it as the final yardstick for an ascription of human qualities and thus for participation in the Home. Evidently, their social capacity was beyond dispute. Having been the stalwarts of Israeli society at large and of particular institutions in it, and being organized into a hierarchically ordered, well-disciplined group within the Home, each was dependent upon the collectivity.

Their mental alertness was also beyond doubt, since it was constantly displayed in the form of linguistic articulation, heightened awareness of current affairs, and considerable reading. It was all thrown into relief in the course of the discussions where great importance was attached to being fluent, clear, and well informed. The debate procedures were made to safeguard these qualities through rigid agenda, orderly discussion, and lucid presentation.

However, the somatic element of personhood put members of the group on an equal footing with other elderly people and thus endangered the other two dimensions of a seemingly immutable existence. Three social contexts bear on the significance and the extent of the physical image of personhood as embedded in the notion of being old, incapacitated, and unworthy.

The Disciplinary Court

The first was the attempt to remove from the institution all disabled residents through the already mentioned disciplinary court. Although this claim for power was aborted by due agreement among residents goaded by fear of the proposed "court" abusing its authority in internal disputes, there was a broad consensus among members of the group about its main objective: removing physically unsuitable residents from the Home.

This position was explicitly formulated in a series of discussions concerning the desirable mode of institutional care for the aged. Out of the various proposed structures of care facilities on the agenda, one was unequivocally and unanimously favored, that of a functionally homogeneous residential population. The arguments made in support of that view were numerous, the most prominent being the need to avoid any visible reminder of the impending deterioration incurred by old age.

In a group reputed for its extensive intellectual activities and whose social image was one of solidity and viability, it was unexpected to witness the prevalence of the physiological criterion expressed not only in assertions regarding other residents but also reflexively. The outside world--that of nationwide admiration and almost sanctification--was often described in terms of its negative reaction to the appearance and physical faculty of members of the group. Thus, a member whose educational stature was much revered in the country told tearfully how a teenaged youth maliciously and scornfully tripped him over, causing him to fall and calling him "an old man."

Consistency in the categorization of the old into the physically fit and the physically unfit was accomplished and affirmed by applying this dichotomy to members of the group. Thus, a woman member who confessed that she lost control of her bowels while suffering from a stomach complaint was scoffingly laughed at and was made to leave the group for good. Other members expressed their wish to avert such disgrace and indignity by urging their coresidents to make plans for their removal from the Home in case of physical incapacitation, even against their own will. Furthermore, if such eventuality should arise, any form of loyalty or solidarity which could shield, albeit temporarily, the handicapped resident ought to be dissolved. This unmitigated position is rendered even more forceful in view of the fact that the privileged status of members of this group in the Home was a secure safeguard against any possibility of administrative decision taken to their detriment.

Other residents, however, were vulnerable to measures affecting their living conditions in the Home ranging from transfer to another institution to the imposition of an unwanted roommate. Here physical adequacy was not sufficient to guarantee continued residence. Obvious evidence of social involvement and mental capabilities was expected to demonstrate to the management of the Home that the resident in question is "functioning" to the extent of extending his or her sojourn.

This challenge was met variously by different residents. One noted made of reaction was the formation of groups of residents whose joint resources created a basis for negotiating terms with the administrative authorities of the Home. Those who engaged in such efforts relied on their collective presentation rather than on individual achievements. Thus interdependency centered around common interest or in pursuit of a set objective was not just a manifestation of sociability and communication but a means of survival and an invaluable resource in its own right. Furthermore, such social formations, by the structure of their members'

271

interaction and through their activities, generated boundaries and images of personhood based on group distinctions.

Handicrafts Group

Attesting to these generalized principles was, among other clusters of activities, the handicraft group. This group was the result of the initiative of a few women residents whose main objective in setting it up was to provide a stage for displaying good "functioning." The manager of the Home, having realized the potentialities of this enterprise for advancing some of his projects--particularly in promoting the institution's public image--offered extensive resources in aid of the operation of the group. Thus, sewing machines, materials, and paid instructors were provided to enhance and intensify the activities. Other residents who were aware of the manager's interest in the group joined in the activities in pursuit of recognition as well-functioning participants.

Indeed, not only did the recruits perfect a front of accomplished residents, but they also gained a host of benefits and privileges bestowed by the management of those favored by it. Hence, belonging to the group became a self-perpetuating engagement reinforced by constant rewards. Within the sponsored cohesiveness of the group there emerged social markers to define the position of members vis-a-vis other residents.

Being occupied was, for a member of the group, more than a mere badge of acceptable functioning or even an active behavior defying the passive image attributed to old age. It was, in the main, a way of relating to the elite echelon of the Home, whose reputed socialist doctrines and dedication to a public cause were deemed to be faintly emulated in the mode of operation evolved in the handicraft group. Work was regarded as an ultimate value, sharing and equality were cherished as ideal forms of interaction, mutual care was advocated as a prime objective of the relationships within the group, and acting in the service of a collective goal was set as the main target of the activities.

All these characteristics were embedded in the daily meetings of the group. Incessant sewing, knitting, embroidery and weaving constituted the major areas of work activity. The products--baby clothes, soft toys, crochet, decorations and light repairs--were prepared for sale in a grand bazaar annually held at the Home to raise funds for the Soldiers' Welfare Association. The amount of proceeds was considered an indication of the group's success. Furthermore, the event was attended by officials and dignitaries whose presence at the bazaar signified social recognition and endorsed the group's endeavor as a contribution to the public.

Thus, the production activities combined with the distribution proceeding, embodied values of work, nonprofit, charity, and involvement in a national enterprise. The implication of this for the perceived internal stratification in the Home was asserted by a founding member of the group: We are all hardworking people who did not have the chance to prove our dedication to the country and its ideals before we entered the Home. Now we have been given this opportunity, and for this we ought to be thankful to the discussion group and its members. Naturally, we are far from the standards they set, but we try our hardest to follow their example.

Under the aegis of that sheltered arena, a number of handicapped residents found welcoming sanctuary. These were residents whose functioning capacity was in doubt due to physical or mental disability. Yet by virtue of their faithful participation in the group they enjoyed an identification with the most turbulent display ground for active functioning in the Home. The other members, mindful of the real purpose behind this type of participation, treated these joiners as equals, especially during encounters with the management. Hence, group membership provided a protective social cover under which both the able and the disabled could secure continued care and immunize themselves against the consequences of pejorative personal change. Social participation was infused with equivocal meanings spanning the whole gamut of existence in the Home--from the survival prospects in the institutions through the internal status system to the broad cultural arena.

If the physical personhood dominated the activities of the discussion group and social personhood prevailed over the operation of the handicraft group, the mental sphere pervaded the actions of some of the most vulnerable residents whose locus of assembly was the institution's synagogue.

Synagogue Study Group

Religious persuasion and practices were much disdained and almost unanimously maligned in the Home. Rooted in an atheist socialist stance and anchored in the long-established political schism in Israel between religious and nonreligious parties, veteran trade unionists expressed little sympathy for anything remotely associated with religiosity. Moreover, coming from a nonsocialist background, most residents who participated in the activities of the local synagogue did not enjoy the shield of previous connections. Unable to associate themselves with the institutional elite and snubbed at other group activities, the synagogue participants could only construct their conception of personhood on resources other than physical and social. They resorted to some of the religious practices in Judaism which most practically and ritually suggested a high degree of mental alertness.

These practices were the assiduous study of religious lore and mores. Since such activities are often performed collectively in specially designated, communal study forums, this tradition of

273

learning was adopted to justify the formation of a multitude of study groups attended by most members and led by hired tutors. Close observation of members' behavior in the course of such gatherings revealed that, far from following the arduous and mind-boggling lessons, the students were preoccupied in a host of extracurricular activities such as humming, gazing at a fixed spot, chatting, and browsing through other chapters. Having no student feedback whatsoever, the instructors would proceed unabated, getting through an outstanding amount of Talmudic material.

Provisions were made by the members to disseminate knowledge of their activities in the Home and particularly to make the management cognizant of their learning capacity. The manager was often invited to witness the study groups, and his help was sought to enhance the scope of the lessons. In conversations, members took great pride in their participation, never failing to stress the implications of this activity for certifying their mental abilities.

To bolster the image of mental agility and grasp of reality, the members developed an explicitly resentful attitude toward those residents whose behavior suggested disorientation and mental incapacity. Thus during the High Holy Days--the New Year festival and the Day of Atonement--when the majority of residents attend synagogue, the seemingly confused among them were forcibly denied access to the synagogue. This was done by blocking the gangway or by pushing them back to the elevators from which they emerged. It is interesting to note that these residents, negligible minority though they were, featured prominently in the self-definition of the other two groups. They were labeled "exhibition" by members of the discussion group, no doubt in line with the physical criteria applied by them, and "vegetables" or "animals" by members of the handicraft group in accordance with their social yardstick. The former represented the ultimate in physical ossification and inertia, while the latter referred to imputed lack of human communication and relationships. In effect this category served as an appropriate barrier between being a person and a nonperson for all the other residents. Having forfeited their attributes as homo physical, homo social and homo mental in the respective eyes of members of the discussion group, the handicraft group, and the congregants of the synagogue, that category was made into a symbolic vehicle through which the three differently based identities could be forged.

The Day Centre2*

While external and internal boundaries in the old age Home were contingent on isolating physical, social, and mental properties to generate referential frames of a "person," the members of the day Centre in the following case study eliminated all these to allow for a nascent idea of self or, as will be

274

explicated later, a "selfless" self to emerge.

The day care Center catered to elderly Jewish residents of the London borough of Hackney. It was administered by the biggest Jewish charity in England, the Jewish Welfare Board, and registered a total of 400 participants with a daily attendance of 150. The services provided by the Centre's staff--a team of two qualified social workers and eight other workers in various capacities-- included hot lunches, tea, occupational therapy, transport arrangements, and some welfare care. Recruitment was on a broad ground of needs ranging from destitution and loneliness to a general "inability to cope." The population served covered a wide age spectrum from the late forties to early nineties. Daily routine was leniently regulated by staff with ample scope for members' initiative. Indeed, most activities unconnected with the financial running of the Centre were taken up by participants. Thus cooking and serving meals, tea making, light entertainment, and recreational pastimes were all organized and conducted by members.

Most members shared a common background of similar life histories. As a first or second-generation Eastern European Jewish emigrants to Britain, they experienced childhoods of poverty, unemployment, heavy reliance on extended families, and welfare assistance from the Jewish Welfare Board. Adulthood was characterized by unskilled or semiskilled, low-income occupations and by bringing up children of their own who, due to their parents' massive investment in their education, became professionals of a much higher socioeconomic status. Old age was typified by insufficient means, poor housing, malnutrition, and increased dependency. Added to that was almost invariably a disengaged and reluctant family, alienated Jewish establishment, run-down neighborhood with a high crime rate, and a paucity of community institutions.

This common socioeconomic background with its shared cultural heritage and similar existential and living conditions made for a nondifferentiated environment where past could not be used as a valuable resource and future prospects held no hope in store. The social structure created in the Centre reflected this state of affairs but was also a reaction to some of the main scourges encountered by the participants. Its constitution reinforced egalitarian behavior and disassociation from previous affiliations, disregarded physical differences and functional disability, and put participants of different mental capacities on an equal footing. To understand how this was accomplished, it is necessary to describe the main principles upon which relationships in the Centre were based.

Participants, with outstanding unanimity and without any form of external guidance, expressed and practiced a set of values of which the core symbol and the main uniting theme was the idea of unbounded care and unconditional help. This was not an ideology advocating mutual concern and reciprocal assistance. Rather the notion of a noncumulative, nonmutual communal pool of available-to-all resources was the most representative feature of this system. Thus participants were expected to spare any resource at their disposal--be it material possession, a piece of advice, a comforting gesture, or some relevant information--to whomever was in need of it. Inversely, those in need were entitled to lean on such help regardless of past relationships, loyalties and obligations. Even married couples attending the Centre were pressured to stay apart and act with as little mutual acknowledgment as possible.

This structure was unaffected by the high turnover of participants, nor was it modified by changes in staff or services. Furthermore, the nature of other activities held in the Centre seemed to support and furnish its competitive games, and contests were avoided by converting them into no-win "learning situations" or laughing them off as "unreal." Patterns and designs of craftwork were incessantly repeated, and renegade attempts of creativity and ingenuity were suppressed through joking, derision, criticism, and, in extreme cases, ostracism.

The combined effect of these properties on the social context of Centre life resulted in lack of both hierarchical order and recognizable power structure among members. Since care was regarded as an absolute measure by which everybody and everything ought to be valued, and as no limits were set on participants' potential capacity to give and to receive, members found themselves in the simultaneously two-pronged position of helper and helped. Thus those who experienced a disproportion between need and contribution would usually restore the balance by creating mock events when an objectively unfounded plea for assistance was manufactured by a participant. For example, a man who was fit enough to climb the stairs pretended to have difficulties, inducing a prompt reaction from a disabled member who rushed to his aid with alacrity.

The obliteration of differences and the demolition of boundaries took various forms, of which the most persistent was the erasure of the past. Occupational careers were a taboo subject among participants, and so were familial associations and community ties. Children were renounced as "traitors," and the lack of contact and financial support from offspring who lived affluently not far away from their parents were often adduced as evidence of disregard and disengagement on the part of the former. The latter, however, insisted that the breakdown in relationship was mutual and that their interest in their children equalled the children's concern with them. Contrary to common stereotypes, the past was not imbued with nostalgia. Inversely, the hardship of childhood, the injustices of adulthood, and the frustrations of aging were viewed grimly as consequences of lack of economic opportunity, social inequality, cultural deprivation, and "bad luck."

Nevertheless, the Centre offered open opportunities and socioeconomic equality where physical, mental, and social differences were abandoned, participants considered themselves as agents of care and "humanity" rather than project-oriented beings whose predetermined goals are contingent upon past resources and future plans.

I shall restrict the rest of the discussion to the three constituents of self-body, mind, and society as handled and constructed by the Centre people.

Physically heterogenous as it was, the participants did not adopt somatic yardsticks to erect social divisions. This was particularly evident in those activities which apparently, by definition, invoke differences in bodily ability. Noteworthy among them was the most popular pastime in the Centre, dancing. Every afternoon participants would gather in the dining hall and engage in old-time dancing to the accompaniment of a record or a member singer. No one was excluded, dancers aided by sticks and crutches, rolling and roving wheelchairs, and stooped handicapped men and women--all dancing out of time and irrespective of any rhythmical discipline--were a common sight on such occasions.

Illnesses and disabilities, abundant though they were among participants, were ignored as irrelevant to the experience of "living the day" or dismissed as mere annoyances. Even terminal conditions were publicly treated as belonging to another sphere of existence. A man suffering from an incurable cancer of the throat described himself as "always cheerful, no matter what. My throat bothers me only as far as my speech is concerned. I want people to understand what I say." When faced directly and explicitly in discussion groups or interviews with the problem of terminal conditions and physical deterioration, participants insisted on their right to euthanasia or suicide. Some, having experienced periods of institutionalization in old-age homes, geriatric wards, or mental hospitals, depicted such a past as "another life," "a state of vegetation," or "not being human". Leaving the Centre, therefore, was conceived of as a departure to such alternative modes of existence, and deaths occurring shortly after were attributed to such leaves rather than to any other causes.

Although differences in physical ability were considered irrelevant to participation in Centre life, an unavoidable cleavage existed between the severely handicapped and the rest of the members. This was due to the absence of an elevator to facilitate mobility between the first and the second floors. In effect, the ground floor was occupied mostly by disabled members far removed from the bustling hub of activity above them. Yet this territorial division was not recognized by members as a valid one, since the example of a few handicapped participants who struggled valiantly and successfully to make their way upstairs was invoked to demonstrate both the extent of willpower and the effectiveness of

277

the care system.

Although as the notion of care was pervasive, deviant behavior of a mental nature posed an intractable problem for participants. Although accounts of Centre induced "recoveries" from a stroke or getting out of depression were widespread among members, other cases seemed to defy the idea of care as a panacea. Display in public of offensive behavior, idiosyncratic characteristics, and unsolicited allusions to the past and to death were viewed not only as embarrassing and unpleasant, but also challenged the fundamentals of the care system. A number of participants whose presence in the Centre evoked strong reactions were compelled, sometimes forcibly, to leave. Others, particularly those who were themselves a product of the care system, called for handling within and by means of the care principles. One example of such treatment was Sid.

Sid was a manic-depressive who suffered a severe relapse following a car crash involving his son. He arrived at the Centre subdued, withdrawn, and completely unresponsive. Attended by his wife, who acted as a volunteer in the Centre, he retired to a corner and spent his days gazing blankly at the others. A sudden mood swing reversed the whole situation. Sid entered into a state of boundless elation and exhilaration, became extremely talkative, and offered to help far beyond his capabilities. This transformation was welcomed by participants as a response to their incessant efforts and to the influence of the Centre atmosphere. Sid was introduced to outsiders as the "great success," or "miraculous recovery." These descriptions invariably were echoed by Sid himself, who would reassure the listener that he felt fine and that his only concern was to look after people who might have been through similar emotional distress. In discussion groups and informal gatherings, Sid always brought up the subject of helping other participants and preached the teachings of the care system to whomever was ready to listen.

Petty bickering and brawls with participants, coupled with unfounded claims to power "officially" delegated to him by staff, provided the first indications that Sid was diverging from the expected path of participation and might even prove to be a menace, particularly to the care system. In fact, occasional bouts of depression and recurrent defiance made it virtually impossible to handle Sid within the care system rules. The reaction among participants was to convert Sid into the Centre jester—a figure to be ridiculed, not to be taken seriously and yet to be integrated into the light-hearted, joking atmosphere of the place. Thus, everything Sid said, regardless of its logical merits and contextual relevance, aroused laughter. His mere presence seemed to provoke waves of gaiety, and his apparent cooperation in building up this image contributed to establish this status. Gradually Sid sank into a long spell of depression and withdrew completely from

Centre activities. Only then was he recognized by his fellow participants as "mental", "sick," and "a psychiatric case."

This assumption of pseudo-psychiatric labels was apparently borrowed from the extensively used psychologically laden terminology employed by social workers. Yet being a "case" enabled Sid to remain within the domain of the care system and rendered his ascribed mental faculties acceptable, manageable, and inherently reversible. Such incorporation was structurally contingent on total segregation of the Centre reality from the outside world and on phasing out internal divisions within it. It was the maintenance of external boundaries and the lack of inner differentiations which fostered the free flow of resources among participants and the obliteration of somatic and mental factors as regulators of social relationships.

The society of participants, therefore, developed mechanisms through which differentiation processes were averted and threats and challenges could be handled. An attempt by several participants to form a "committee" to represent members' interests was aborted by those who were supposed to benefit from its operation on the ground that the self-nominated candidates were "power-mad" and "status seekers." Disputes and conflicts between participants were confined to short-term altercations taking the form of brief outbursts after which relationship would go back to normal. Those whose unsettling presence could not be contained were ostracized or expelled. This was the fate, for example, of a participant who was exposed as a beggar, thus subjecting his fellow members to shame, questioning by his actions the validity and efficacy of the care system. In another instance a woman who, despite incessant demands, dwelt on her glorified past which stood in direct contradiction to the others and in any event negated the present-bound egalitarian ethos of the Centre's reality, also was forced to leave the Centre for good.

Discussion

At first glance any attempt to ascertain some common ground between these two examples might seem to be a futile exercise. The materials and methods employed in the construction of a concept of personhood appear almost diametrically opposite. The residents of the Home drew heavily on past experiences and cultural continuity, the Centre people endeavored to disengage themselves from their memories and heritages. The Home's residents interrelated the categories of body, mind, and society in a hierarchical fashion, whereas the Centre's members fused them into a unitary immutable collective entity. Internal boundaries were dimmed in the Centre, highlighted in the Home. Conversely, the Centre presented itself as an impervious environment while the Home was an extension of its outside milieu. However, a more careful scrutiny of the data would unveil a different comparative dimension. Beyond the unrelatedness of the commitment to function and the idea of care, beyond the highly stratified society of residents and the egalitarian near-commune of participants, and beyond the differences in background and the organizationally contrasting care facilities looms a core of seemingly similar properties.

The idea of a "person" was built in both institutions on key cultural concepts derived from a common past and infused with nascent context-bound content and proportions. Thus neither "functioning" nor "care" could be placed on an uninterrupted continuum anchored in previous values, nor could they be regarded as realization or fulfillment of lifelong experiences. Rather the unreservedly caring person of the Centre[3] as well as the functioning actor at the Home arena were engaged in adapting themselves to the exigencies of one existential dilemma. This was the problem of uncontrollable deterioration and unarrested adverse change associated with the aging process.

Erecting rigid boundaries based on physiological, social, or mental categories in the Home and blurring these very three categories in the Centre, although apparently contradictory practices, serve the same ultimate objective–facing up to the uncertainties embedded in the futureless, unpredictable world of the inhabitants of either establishment. It would seem that the very idea of continuity[4] is defied by the lack of progress and the loss of social time in old age. Hence the attempt to reconstruct a concept of a person is induced and shaped by selecting and organizing cognitive and social components in a manner amenable to encounter such fundamental problems.

If values and life experiences are to be treated as manipulable resources rather than deterministic impositions, the two cases could illustrate the emergence of a context-bound conception of personhood among the aged without the bind of cultural presuppositions[5] and psychological bias. The key assumption for such an approach, however, must be that control of meanings and identity is accomplished through addressing a major existential predicament rather than through perfunctory reference to one's life history.[6] The process of "deculturation",[7] while divesting the personhood of aged of some of its symbolic anchorage,[8] makes for a reconstitution of cultural classifications based on a newly acquired balance between the desirable and the attainable.[9] If, as Myerhoff (1978a) suggested in her analysis of another Jewish day center, the aged are engaged in fighting their social invisibility and in securing their symbolic survival, then notions of continuity of personhood and preservation of identity should be viewed through the prism of present context rather than life course development.

Notes

1. For an overview of the Home, see Hazan (1980b).
2. For a detailed ethnography of the Centre, see Hazan (1980b).
3. It would seem that the existentialist perspective of "life project" advocated by Sartre and applied to the study of history by Langness and Frank (1981) is not attested to by the case of the Centre people.
4. As Fontana (1976), McCulloch (1980), and many others observe, the idea of continuity does not withstand the scrutiny of extending into a dubious future. Some solution to this dilemma is offered by Myerhoff (1978a), who suggests the presence of a myth-like orientation among the people she studied.
5. Viewing personhood as generated by culture (Geertz 1979) is an approach adopted by many anthropologists to the study of aged self. See, for example, Plath (1980), Bateson (1950), Myerhoff (1978b), and Henry (1963:391-474).
6. A similar approach emphasizing interaction rather than culture is proposed by Gubrium (1975) and Gubruim and Buckholdt (1977).
7. This is a concept proposed by Anderson (1972), whose study with Clark on older Americans (Clark and Anderson 1967) points to the gap between culture and the aged self.
8. For an analysis of some social complications of the growing incongruity between symbolic messages and the self conception of the aged, see Teski (1979, 1987).
9. Some indication to this line of argument could be found in Tornstam (1982) and is reflected in the works of Rosenmayr (1981) and Thomas (1970).

Bibliograph

Anderson, B. 1972. "The Process of Deculturation--Its Dynamics among United States Aged." Anthropological Quarterly 45(4):209-216.

Bateson, G. 1950. "Cultural Ideas About Aging." In Proceedings of a Conference Held in August 7-10, 1950 at University of California, Berkeley, H.E. Jones ed. New York: Pacific Coast Committee on Old Age Research, Social Science Research Council.

Clark, M, and B. G. Anderson. 1967. Culture and Aging: An Anthropological Study of Older Americans. Springfield, IL: Charles Thomas.

Fontana, A. 1976. The Last Frontier. Beverly Hills, CA: Sage.

Geertz, C. 1979. "From the Native's Point of View: On the Nature of Anthropological Understanding." In Interpretive Social Science: A Reader, P. Rabinow and W. N. Sullivan, eds. Berkeley: University of California Press.

Gubrium, J. F. 1975. Living and Dying at Murray Manor. New York: St. Martin's.

Gubrium, J. F. and D. R. Buckholdt. 1977. Toward Maturity: The Social Processing of Human Development. San Francisco, CA: Jossey-Bass.

Hazan, H. 1980a. "Adjustment and Control in an Old Age Home." In A Composite Portrait of Israel, E. Marx ed. London: Academic Press.

—— 1980b. The Limbo People: A Study of the Constitution of the Time Universe Among the Aged. London: Routledge & Kegan Paul.

Henry, J. 1963. Culture Against Man. New York: Random House.

Langness, L. L. and G. Frank. 1981. Lives: An Anthropological Approach to Biography. Novato, CA: Chandler & Sharp.

McCulloch, A. W. 1980. "What do We Mean by 'Development' in Old Age." Aging and Society, 1:230-245.

Myerhoff, B. 1978a. Number Our Days. New York: Dutton.

—— 1978b. "Aging and the Aged in Other Cultures: An Anthropological Perspective." In The Anthropology of Health, E. Bauwers ed. St. Louis, MO: C. V. Mosby.

Plath, D. W. 1980. Long Engagements: Maturity in Modern Japan. Stanford, CA: Stanford University Press.

Rosenmayr, L. 1981. "Age, Lifespan and Biography." Aging and Society, 1:29-49.

Venerable ancestors: strategies of ageing in the Chinese novel *The Story of the Stone*

Dore J Levy

Veneration of the aged (*laonian*, "venerable in years") is a cliché of traditional Chinese culture. Although the association of age and virtue reaches into dim antiquity, this convention was first articulated by Confucius (551–479 BC) with the worship of ancestor spirits mediated by shamans. The spirits of a family's ancestors were aware of human affairs and could be called upon in due season and in times of crisis for protection from harm and mediation in cosmological matters, thereby making the transfer of such veneration to living elders a logical step.[1,2]

Confucius set the model for this authority of elders by his own example, explaining that the accumulation of knowledge and experience was the basis of respect:

> "The Master said, At fifteen, I set my heart upon learning. At thirty, I had planted my feet firm upon the ground. At forty, I no longer suffered from perplexities. At fifty, I knew what were the biddings of Heaven. At sixty, I heard them with a docile ear. At seventy, I could follow the dictates of my own heart, for what I desired no longer overstepped the boundaries of right."[3]

In Confucius' eyes, however, age alone did not automatically confer virtue:

> "The Master said, Respect the young. How do you know that they will not one day be all that you are now? But if a man has reached forty or fifty and nothing has been heard of him, then I grant there is no need to respect him."[4]

According to Confucius, age could not be taken at face value: whereas age implied the chance for the necessary experience, virtue was demonstrated by action.

The strict deference to age in and of itself as a sign of moral authority and virtue was codified by Mencius (372–289 BC), who systematised Confucian thought for home, government, and society two generations after the Master's death. The writings of Mencius are explicitly

Dore J Levy is professor of comparative literature and chair of the department of East Asian studies at Brown University, Providence, Rhode Island, USA. She pursued graduate study at Cambridge University and Princeton University, where she received her PhD in 1982. She has studied the representation of medicine in literature as metaphor and record of contemporary issues. Her article "Why Bao-yu can't concentrate: attention deficit disorder in *The Story of the Stone*" appeared in *Literature and Medicine* in 1994 (vol 13, no 2, pp 255–73). She is the author of *Chinese Narrative Poetry* (Duke University Press, 1989) and *Ideal and Actual in The Story of the Stone* (Columbia University Press, 1999)

Department of Comparative Literature, Box 1850, Brown University, 341 Brook Street, Providence, RI 02912, USA (e-mail: Dore_Levy@brown.edu)

political, and so veneration of parents was a model for the veneration of the king, and essential to the stability and prosperity of the state:

> "Of services which is the greatest? The service of parents is the greatest. . . .The substance of humanity is to serve one's parents; the basis of righteousness is to obey one's elder brothers."[7]

Respect for a hierarchy based on seniority was a natural expression of the essential goodness of human nature, which, when allowed to find its proper expression, ensured the stability of society and the state. In principle, each household was a microcosm of the world, and following correct principles would contribute to the prosperity of all.

It is no surprise, then, that the Chinese family is a frequent model for society as a whole, especially in fiction. *The Story of the Stone* (*Shitou ji*), also known as *The Dream of the Red Chamber* (*Honglou meng*), by Cao Xueqin (1715?–63), is the most esteemed work of prose fiction in the tradition.[5,7] A mammoth narrative in 120 chapters, it is valued as a compendium of Chinese culture, focusing on the life of two branches of a wealthy gentry family, the Jias, who owe their noble rank to the favour won by two glorious ancestors for outstanding service to their Manchu overlords under the Qing dynasty (1644–1911). During the Qing, members of the Chinese aristocracy could attain great wealth and influence, yet they remained subject to the absolute authority of the ruling Manchus. In the novel, the present generation of Jia males are not as talented as their forebears, and the family fortunes are definitely in decline. Tracing the Jias' collapse in the present generation, the narrative describes the inevitable conflict between ideal patterns of social, political, and personal conduct, and the impossibility of implementing them in the actual patterns of everyday life (ref 8, p 7–26).

Even while dominated by foreigners, Qing China was very much a Confucian society, associating successful ageing with moral virtue and the favour of heaven. An elder who survived to the age of 60 in good health was an exemplar, to whom the younger generation had to defer. In *The Story of the Stone*, the Rong-guo branch of the Jia household is ruled by an all-powerful widowed matriarch, the formidable Grandmother Jia. Freed from the domination of her husband, Grandmother Jia overrides the authority of her two sons, who as the eldest males in the household should in fact exercise authority over her. In social terms, then, age is power.[8] This cachet transcends even social status, because the Jias extend the respect for old age and experience not just to members of their own clan but also to the retainers who have grown old in the service of their masters. Such members of the household feel it is their right and duty to arbitrate family standards. One such servant, 80-year-old Big Jiao, saved his master's life in battle when both were young. Although the current generation regards him as an unruly old drunkard, in his own eyes he drinks to escape from the

283

Figure 1: The Buddhist concept of the cycle of rebirth: the soul is born again as a bird, an insect, an animal
One of four images by a Chinese artist who also depicted rebirth as a fruit or vegetable, as many different kinds of inanimate objects, and as shellfish. From *Superstitions en Chine* by Henri Dore (vol I, 1915).

spectacle of their relentless dissolution, he remonstrates with them as a responsible elder ought to do, and when they try to hush him wails that he is going to the ancestral temple to weep before his deceased master's tablet. Big Jiao's age and moral status put him beyond discipline, and the Jias must either suffer his tirades or pension him off to one of the family farms.

The inversion of conventional authority patterns as they relate to the matriarch, Grandmother Jia, illustrates a fundamental contradiction of filial piety: on the one hand, younger family members are expected to respect and defer to their elders; on the other hand, as soon as her husband has died, a mother is supposed to defer to the authority of the new head of household, her eldest son. As the only surviving member of her generation, one who moreover remembers the glory days of the Jias' early ennoblement, Grandmother Jia demands deference from all members of the household. Her age and absolute good health confirm her right to this deference, because her longevity and health are signs of the favour of heaven. Her authority cannot be challenged by anyone, because even her sons are inhibited in exercising their proper authority by the strict rules of respect due to the aged in general and to aged parents in particular.[10]

The nominal head of the family is Grandmother Jia's second son, Jia Zheng. He is torn between two strict Confucian duties: to please his mother and show her respect on the one hand, and the larger duty to prepare his only surviving son, Bao-yu, to meet his social obligations to carry on the family line and bring glory to its name. Jia Zheng's attempts in both endeavours are often frustrated not just by the interference of his mother, who dotes on the boy and shields him from his father's authority, but also by his own scrupulous and literal-minded zeal to adhere to ideal Confucian patterns of personal conduct (ref 8, pp 31–32). Grandmother Jia often exploits these scruples of Jia Zheng's to manipulate his authority and strengthen her own control.

A good deal of the success of Grandmother Jia's ageing seems to come from her power both to indulge her emotional inclinations and to protect her own interests. Rather than become dependent on her sons and their rather feckless wives for her support and daily care, she carefully trains and protects her own staff and favours

a clever granddaughter-in-law, Xi-feng, whom she supports in taking over most of the household management.[11] When her older son, Jia She, casts a lecherous eye on Faithful, Grandmother Jia's most intimate body-servant, the old lady quashes the attempt in no uncertain terms:

"Tell him that if he wants to be a dutiful son, he'll be doing more for me by leaving me my Faithful, to serve me during the few years that yet remain, than if he were to come over and wait on me in person, morning, noon and night" (ref 6, vol 2, p 429).

The chain of implications is both reasonable and ironic: the opportunity and capacity to take care of oneself improves the chances of a healthy and vigorous old age, which brings the assumption that the elder has received the favour of heaven and demands veneration, which allows a strong-minded person like Grandmother Jia to exercise complete control over her own care and to enforce her desires. Although much attention is given to Grandmother Jia's scrupulous personal hygiene, including her belief in the virtues of fasting when she is indisposed, she herself sees her age and health as the result of her personal virtue and self-awareness.[12] Unlike most women of the time, she is not coy about medical matters and refuses to conceal herself behind a curtain when a doctor comes to take her pulse:

"I'm old, too, woman—old enough to be his mother, I shouldn't wonder. What have I got to fear from him at my age?" (ref 6, vol 2, p 328).

Grandmother Jia's good health finally receives a fatal blow when the family is subjected to a raid by the Embroidered Jackets, a terrifying branch of the Manchu secret police. Eschewing all support, she prays to the Buddha:

"The blame for all these misfortunes must rest on my shoulders, for having failed to teach the younger generation the true principles of conduct. . . . May I alone be permitted to carry the whole family's burden of guilt! And may the sons and grandsons be forgiven! Have pity on me, Almighty Heaven, and heed my devout supplication: send me an early death that I may atone for the sins of my children and grandchildren!" (ref 7, vol 5, p 134).

This offer of personal sacrifice, to take responsibility for her descendants' faults and to atone for them by casting away her life, is the matriarch's trump card. Although, objectively speaking, a woman of 82 anywhere in the world in the 18th century would hardly be expected to live much longer, all members of Grandmother Jia's household would have faith that her store of moral capital, manifest by the favour of heaven in granting a healthy old age, could preserve her for years to come. Far from making an empty sacrifice, the matriarch is offering to place all her accumulated virtue and privilege in the balance against her descendants' failings, to provide them with a clean slate and a chance to make a fresh start.[13] Whatever her shortcomings "for having failed to teach the younger generation the true principles of conduct" (ref 7, vol 5, p 134), she now provides them with a model of authority, responsibility, and dedication that cannot fail to inspire them to do honour to her legacy.

Soon after the family's debacle, Grandmother Jia actually slips into her final illness, which starts as a typical

284

indisposition after a birthday party. She and Faithful are the only ones who can imagine her end. Even a Buddhist nun, renowned for her insight, offers the usual platitudes when consulted on the matter:

"A person as charitable and virtuous as yourself, Lady Jia, will surely live to a ripe old age. . . . At your age the important thing is to relax and not worry so much" (ref 7, vol 5, p 187).

Grandmother Jia knows better:

"The last doctor I saw said it was because I was letting myself get too overwrought. But you know perfectly well that no one dares to rub me the wrong way! I don't think that doctor really knew what he was talking about" (ref 7, vol 5, p 187).

She dies peacefully, surrounded by her devoted family, to whom she has been able to deliver her final admonitions. A good death is also a reward for virtue.

Grandmother Jia is prepared for the ultimate sacrifice by both the Confucian rationalist tradition, which respects life while attempting to detach from fear of death, and the Buddhist tradition of exercising compassion to accumulate good karma for a better rebirth. Grandmother Jia's death evokes a favourite *jataka*—a sacred tale of one of the innumerable lives of the Buddha before his final incarnation and enlightenment. In this tale, the prince who is destined to be the Buddha many incarnations later is touched by the plight of a starving tigress and her cubs, and so throws himself from a cliff to provide for her. This act of human self-sacrifice out of pity for an animal illustrates the reach of Buddhist compassion: all living beings—human beings and tigers and beetles and hummingbirds and slimy eels—are bound on the wheel of reincarnation to suffer until they awaken to the vanity of existence and so achieve liberation through enlightenment (figures 1 and 2). In Confucian terms, Grandmother Jia boldly accepts the proper authority and responsibility of an elder; in Buddhist terms, she shows her compassion and can take comfort in the thought that her virtue should aid her to a better rebirth.[16] Although the family is devastated by her death, there is no question that they mourn a heroine.

Not every elder in the Jia family provides such an example. One of the most telling signs of the family's decline is the inability or refusal of the eldest males to take up their necessary positions as heads of the household, leaving the field wide open for a strong personality like that of the matriarch. The proper head of the Ning-guo branch of the family, Jia Jing, is actually a member of the generation below Grandmother Jia. Long before the novel begins, he has abdicated his family responsibilities and obligations in favour of joining a bizarre Taoist sect and devoting his life to the pursuit of physical immortality.

Although philosophical Taoism advocated transcendence of fear of death through acceptance of humanity's place in the organic cycle of nature, throughout Chinese history theorists of alchemy and mystical hygiene borrowed from Taoist rhetoric to legitimise their occult practices.[15] Jia Jing's affiliation is derided by society:

"He spends all his time over retorts and crucibles concocting elixirs, and refuses to be bothered with anything else. . . . He refuses outright to live at home and spends his time fooling around with a pack of Taoists somewhere outside the city walls" (ref 6, vol 1, p 74).

For a person of Jia Jing's family background to descend to the superstitious pursuit of physical immortality puts him literally beyond the pale—he removes himself from family and state to spend his old age trying to cheat death.

Jia Jing comes to a predictably unpleasant end: after years of ingesting cinnabar (mercuric sulphide) and other lethal substances, he ends up cooking his internal organs into a solid mass. The doctors summoned by the family deliver this verdict:

"That death was due to edema and corrosion following ingestion by the deceased of some toxic metallic substance in pursuance of his Taoist researches" (ref 6, vol 3, p 240).

Jia Jing's associates protest:

"It *wasn't* toxic. . . . It was an infallible secret formula, but it needed to be taken in the right conditions. We *told* him that he wasn't ready for it, but he wouldn't believe us. . . . We must rejoice that he has cast off the corrupt garment of flesh and left this sea of misery behind him" (ref 6, vol 3, p 240).

Although these two assessments seem at cross-purposes, metaphorically they are the same: Jia Jing put himself outside of the conventions and authority of his community, and so brought about his own destruction. No school of Chinese thought countenances such behaviour, and Jia Jing's midnight demise is a warning to all.

Figure 2: The Buddhist wheel of rebirth of the soul—the cycle of metempsychosis
By a Chinese artist. Taken from *Superstitions en Chine* by Henri Doré (vol VI, 1914).

In the 20th century, ideologically based social upheavals have dealt a severe blow to the Chinese tradition of veneration for age, but the greatest threat to that tradition is modernisation itself. In traditional Chinese society, beyond the symbolic value of the assumption of the favour of heaven, the experience of the oldest generation had much practical use and application, and its transmission was vital to the success of the community. Modernising societies, however, face unknown futures: knowledge of how things were done in the past may be of no use, and a system which privileges old people on the basis of that knowledge may be a positive impediment to progress.

With this in mind, the fact that China, like so many modernised societies, faces an unprecedented boom in its aged population makes this conflict between old ideals and new realities even stronger. In pre-modern China, Confucian, Taoist, and Buddhist modes of thought placed ultimate responsibility for the individual in the hands of the individual, to live a good life in harmony with the community. This cultural assumption still persists in the modern era, but even the most deep-seated, flexible, and materially beneficial conventions of pre-modern society can be powerless against the unforeseen stresses of modernisation. It remains to be seen whether the traditional Chinese view of ageing can survive this test.

References

1 Mote FW. Intellectual foundations of China. New York: Knopf, 1971: 31–32.
2 Waley A. Three ways of thought in ancient China. London: George Allen and Unwin, 1939: 96.
3 Confucius. Analects II.4. In: Waley A, transl. The analects of Confucius. London: George Allen and Unwin, 1964: 88.
4 Confucius. Analects IX.22. In: Waley A, transl. The analects of Confucius. London: George Allen and Unwin, 1964: 143.
5 Mencius. IV.19, 27. In: de Bary T, transl. Sources of Chinese tradition. Vol. 1. New York: Columbia University Press, 1960: 98.
6 Cao X. Shitou ji. In: Hawkes D, ed. and transl. The story of the stone. Vols 1–3. London: Penguin, 1973, 1977, 1980.
7 Cao X. Shitou ji. In: Minford J, ed. and transl. The story of the stone. Vols 4–5. London: Penguin, 1982, 1986.
8 Levy DJ. Ideal and actual in The Story of the Stone. New York: Columbia University Press, 1999.
9 Levy MJ Jr. The family revolution in modern China. Cambridge: Harvard University Press, 1949: 127–33.
10 Hsiung P. Constructed emotions: the bonds between mothers and sons in late imperial China. Late Imperial China 1994; 15: 87–117.
11 Ebrey P. The inner quarters: marriage and the lives of Chinese women in the Sung period. Berkeley and Los Angeles: University of California Press, 1993: 114–30.
12 Bray F. Technology and gender: fabrics of power in late imperial China. Berkeley and Los Angeles: University of California Press, 1997: 218–23.
13 Mann S. Precious records: China's long eighteenth century. Stanford: Stanford University Press, 1997: 204–07.
14 Tu W. Embodying the universe: a note on Confucian self-realization. In: Ames RT, ed. Self as person in Asian theory and practice. Albany: State University of New York Press, 1994: 177–86.
15 Schipper K. The Taoist body. Duval K, transl. Berkeley and Los Angeles: University of California Press, 1993: 26–32.

286

BETWEEN SEVERAL WORLDS: IMAGES OF YOUTH AND AGE IN TUAREG POPULAR PERFORMANCES

SUSAN J. RASMUSSEN
University of Houston

Youth cannot be understood without examining elderhood, and age more generally. Among the Tuareg, Islamic religious rituals and liturgical music tend to be identified with the "aged" (those with children of marriageable age), and these are symbolically opposed to secular popular musical performances classified as "anti-Islamic," which are identified with "youth." These images comment upon long-standing concerns with marriage, courtship, sexuality, and descent, but they are also increasingly being translated into concerns of cultural autonomy, as local youths struggle for cultural survival in conflict between Tuareg and the central state. I analyze three types of popular musical performance and the instruments featured in them, and show how their age-related imagery, commentary, and interaction express changing intergenerational relationships. These concerns, however, do not fall into a binary of "old" and "new," or align with any one age group; rather, they suggest shifting associations of agentive power and questioning of "tradition" by youth and aged in diverse contexts. These data on age symbolism in Tuareg popular musical performances suggest more dynamic, nuanced formulations of "traditional," "modern," and "global" in anthropological theory. [Africa, Tuareg, aging, performance, globalization]

Youth and Age in Tuareg Imagery

Young people make up a significant segment of the population in Africa. Yet "youth" itself, as well as the apparently opposed category of "elderly," are indexical categories that include people of diverse ages. In this essay I proceed from the premise that youth cannot be understood without examining elderhood and age more generally. Among the Tuareg of northern Niger Republic, West Africa, age groups are not defined according to biological or chronological markers, but rather in terms of one's social and ritual position in the life course. For example, one does not achieve fully adult status until becoming a parent and is not considered "elderly" (in Tamajaq, masc. *amghar*, fem. *tamghart*) until one's children marry (Rasmussen 1997a). Upon attaining this status, men and women alike are expected to practice greater devotion to Islam and distance themselves from youths, who are their potential and actual affines. A child becomes an adolescent or young, marriageable adult (masc., *amawat* or *ekabkab*, fem. *tamawat* or *tekabkab*) when his or her parents determine that he/she is ready for marriage. Around this time, men don the face-veil and women the head-scarf, and these young persons are encouraged to attend and to perform as musicians at these secular musical festivals, where much courtship takes place.

Tuareg social categories have been undergoing rapid transformation, in particular since the recent nationalist/separatist armed conflict and cultural revitalization movement.[1] Local aging imagery displays both continuity and change. On the one hand, in the semi-nomadic rural communities of the Aïr Mountains, much age imagery still identifies Islamic and pre-Islamic religious ritual and its prayer and liturgical music with aged persons. Secular evening festivals featuring non-liturgical music, courtship, and dancing, are classified as "anti-Islamic," and still tend to be identified with youthful, single persons. At a youth's first wedding the evening musical festival following the religious ritual emphasizes loud drumming, according to local residents, "in order to open the couple's ears." By contrast, the earlier phase of the wedding ritual at the mosque emphasizes the role of the parents and the Islamic scholar (*marabout*), who marries the couple. In Tuareg society older persons are supposed to become authority figures. While widowed and divorced persons may re-marry in late life, their weddings are held only at the mosque and lack the evening festival phase.

Striking is an age-related symbolism: for men and women alike, tropes of aging refer to musical performance frames. Performances with the *anzad*, a one-stringed, bowed lute, the *tende*, a mortar drum, and the recently-popular guitar, are all associated with youthful age groups. They are featured at evening festivals where there is much social license, but also much "work" such as critical social commentary, marriage negotiations, and the establishment of economic and political alliances taking place. These festivals often follow the religious phases of rites of passage (Rasmussen 1995, 1997a, 1997b, 2000). They may also occur during holidays and political party rallies, particularly in the towns. The guitar accompanies songs that originated in the Tuareg rebellion, originally called *ichumar*, and now called merely "guitar" music. It provides the third important performance context for age-related imagery. *Guitar* music is performed in "rock-style" bands at dances of youths.

The presence of older persons, while peripheral, suggests more conflict, and more rapprochement between age roles than is the case in the more traditional anzad and tende performances. All these performances—of anzad, tende, and guitar—always feature a relaxing of normally reserved conduct between social categories. Affines, whose conduct is marked by highly formalized reserve, may joke with each other and behave immodestly. Much flirting and courtship may occur between persons of different social origins (nobles, smiths, and descendants of slaves), who ideally do not intermarry. Many Tuareg use the terms tende and increasingly, guitar, as generic terms for all non-liturgical, popular musical performances.

In this article I explore the changing nature of social relations according to age among the Tuareg of the Aïr Mountains. I examine the changes taking place through the lens of different types of musical performance: two "traditional" forms and one "modern" form (electric guitar). I show that the way in which these musical forms are performed and enjoyed by onlookers illustrates complicated changes in age relations in Tuareg society, mixing parts of the "old" with infusions of the "new." I also show that, at a time of tension between Tuareg and the state musical expression has more to do with cultural unity and survival than it did previously, when it spoke primarily to internal issues for Tuareg (honor, social stratum, and kinship).

Youth-elder roles, interaction, and discourse in these festivals thus provide a useful frame for analyzing wider questions about performance of aging (Myerhoff 1977, 1982), and suggest revisions of conceptualizations of "tradition," "modernity," and "globalization" in anthropology (Featherstone 1990; Appadurai 1991). I examine the symbolism and social interaction comparatively in each performance,

in order to illustrate how age-related concerns are played out in these settings. Many Tuareg elders, particularly the devoutly Muslim, tend to be ambivalent toward these performances. In song texts and audience interactions at these performances there is much age-related social criticism. These performances contain much inter-generational dialogue on age issues. These commentaries suggest the agentive power, as opposed to the malleability, of youths. Yet their themes do not always follow binary elder/traditional/authority vs. youth/modern/resistance alignments.

Most audiences and participants at the festivals and dances are persons culturally-defined as "youthful"—single, recently married and childless, or with children not yet of marriageable age. In contrast, those culturally-defined as "old"—persons who have married children or children of marriageable age—do not attend these evening festivals, but play prominent roles in the daytime Islamic ritual phases that precede them.[2] The images they use comment upon sexuality, courtship, marriage, and descent. They show that these long-standing concerns among Tuareg, while still important, are increasingly being translated into concerns of cultural autonomy, as many local youths, uprooted from their communities by migrant labor and guerrilla warfare, return, reflect upon, and sometimes dispute, those values embedded in traditional age imagery. They struggle with cultural survival and sometimes question elders' definitions of what is important in transitions over the life course. There is often conflict between elders and youths about the age imagery of these festivals. However, there is no rigid association of "traditional" or "modern" with any age group or festival frame. For example, even in the songs of the new guitar music, including those from the Tuareg rebellion in which younger groups have been active, there is not complete rejection of the interests of elders or conservative customs of nomadic Tuareg culture. Conversely, many songs and performances of the more traditional anzad and tende do not always promote elders' interests, but sometimes challenge them.

In these contexts what is happening to age roles and relations between elders and youths, and how are these roles commented upon, questioned, reinforced, and re-formulated during musical performances at rituals and festivals? In the anthropology of aging it is now almost a truism that age categories cross-culturally are based upon social, rather than chronological or linear markers. But the Tuareg data show how more nuanced processes are also occurring. Age categories and their associated imagery, as well as "tradition" and "modernity," more generally, are increasingly subject to dispute and redefinition, as Tuareg elders and youths self-consciously reflect on the value of youth and age as they cope with economic hardship and political tensions. Ronald Manheimer observed that

> individuals who belong to the same generation, who share the same year of birth, are endowed, to that extent, with a common location in the historical dimension of the social process (1989: 240).

Often, however, as Myerhoff observes,

> membership in a common cohort is background information, like grammatical rules, more interesting to outside analysts than members. Outsiders find and want explanations where the subjects continue un-selfconsciously in the habits of everyday life (1982: 100).

Sometimes conditions conspire to make a generational cohort acutely self-conscious and then they become active participants in their own history and provide their own sharp, insistent definitions of themselves and explanations for their destiny, past and future. They are knowing actors in a historical drama they script, rather than subjects of someone else's study. They "make" themselves, sometimes even "make themselves up," an activity which is not inevitable or automatic but reserved for special people and special circumstances. This making visible one's own identity in age-related discourse and performance illuminates the nature of what Myerhoff (p. 101) terms the "performed" individual and collective definitions, the uses and kinds of witnesses needed for these performances, and the nature and uses of memory.

Cultures include these moments for self-presentation to their members, also found in such processes and conditions as Turner's (1969, 1974) communitas and liminality, and Handelman's (1990) modeling and mirroring. But the beginning and end of such processes resist pinning-down with specific social categories. Among the Tuareg these musical festival performances, as the major forum in which these processes are played out, offer Tuareg interpretations of themselves. They comment as well as mirror.

The Performinance of Youth to Age Transitions

My attention was first drawn to the cultural imagery

surrounding age during my earlier research on Tuareg rites of passage and life histories. At a rural wedding I sat with other guests in the courtyard of the groom's side of the family, where smith women had just applied henna to the groom's hands and feet. We listened as the smiths began singing their wedding praise-songs. These included many jokes, often very ribald, and much covert sexual imagery. At that moment a prominent Islamic scholar walked by and greeted our party, but remained outside the compound. When I returned his greeting and added that we were enjoying the wedding festivities and songs, he gave me a solemn look and commented, "Prayer is better, isn't it?" Another elderly Islamic scholar elaborated on this idea during an interview when he related how, over his life, he had changed his patterns of public participation:

> When I was young, I attended [evening] songs, I danced, I listened to the anzad and the tende, I did these things until I had children. But then I abandoned these powers to my children. I go now to the mosque and I do my prayers; I am saved, I have forgotten everything that I did during my youth. Now, I know Qur'anic study only, I have abandoned all that, as I am old.

Retreat from secular, youthful festivals also ideally entails ceasing to play specific musical instruments. One woman, formerly a famous player of the anzad in the nearby town of Agadez, said she was now too old to play because she did not want to display herself before young people. Another woman elaborated on this theme: "The anzad is of no use to me now—prayer is better. A young girl prefers the anzad; an old woman prefers prayer." This woman, between 55 and 65 years of age, had two grown sons, both of marriageable age. She now participated only in the Islamic rites of passage—weddings, namedays, mortuary rituals.

The newly popular guitar (locally pronounced GEE'tsr) music attract crowds of diverse ages. However, most persons culturally-defined as "old" do not dance, but remain on the sidelines in age-segregated groups. Islamic scholars do not attend. In the town of Agadez the only older person to approach the main performance space of the guitar music and dancing (beneath a large canopy) is a man called an animateur (Fr.) whose role as "master of ceremonies" consists of making announcements, praising the families hosting the wedding or nameday, encouraging the youths to dance, and also keeping order. He often carries a long livestock whip, although I never saw him use it. Such a person also tends to often be of low or ambiguous social origin in the pre-colonial system: a smith, or one of servile descent.[3]

In the next sections I examine Tuareg meanings of music, song, and festivals in relation to youth and age symbolism. I interweave descriptions of relations between the generations. I conclude with an analysis of age in household dynamics as youths and elders critically reflect on these processes in the performances. Throughout, there is analysis of age roles during social, economic, and political upheavals.[4]

Distraction From Prayer: Music, Youth, and the Orchestrating of Festivals

Anzad and Tende Performances

Music in the Sahara enjoys much prestige; yet there is also an undercurrent of disapproval, which barely tolerates it. To Islamic scholars all music is suspect, and the Devil, called Iblis, is present at musical festivals. He is all the more involved if this music is played or sung by a beautiful young woman. Musical expression, while not in itself illicit, distracts from Islamic duties of prayer and cultural values of dignity and reserve. In the opinion of many older persons certain instruments should be regarded with caution, for they are sufficiently beautiful to "transport one beyond oneself." The anzad (a one-stringed, bowed lute) and the tende (a mortar drum) are two such instruments. The anzad, very ancient and associated with women's praise of men returning from battle, is identified in myth and cosmology with heaven, the nobility in the pre-colonial stratification system, bilateral descent, and endogamous marriage. The *tende*, constructed by stretching a goat-hide across the top of a mortar, is identified with the earth and lower social status (former slaves, smiths, and other client peoples in the pre-colonial system).

Singing exposes the open mouth. In local body symbolism the mouth is analogous to the genitals. A proverb says that "the man's face-veil and the trousers are brothers," and one reason men cover their mouths with the veil is to display respect toward affines and elders, in particular their mothers-in-law. This symbolic association occurs as well in other musical contexts. Singers sometimes leave out words and substitute vocables during the late afternoon, when affines, with whom they practice reserve, are present. After sundown there is less reserve about singing with the mouth wide open, and fewer voca-

bles are used.

At "secular" festivals (in local definition those featuring non-liturgical music) guests put on their best clothing and jewelry, but avoid wearing Islamic amulets. Although spirits are mentioned in the Qur'an, there are also non-Qur'anic spirits in Tuareg cosmology and these latter are believed to be pleased by the music, noise, and jokes pervasive at evening festivals. The pattern of vulnerability to such spirits is in large measure age-based and related to transitions: for example, many of these spirits are believed to threaten adolescents engaged to marry, newly-married couples, mothers who have just given birth, and newborn babies. Loud music and noise, particularly drumming, presided over by smiths, traditionally follow the more Islamic religious rituals, presided over by marabouts, marking these transitions.

Even today many rural Tuareg of all ages feel that it is not appropriate to attend such performances or to listen to non-liturgical music in the presence of someone older than themselves, particularly if there is a close kinship tie. This taboo is reciprocal: an older person avoids listening to music and sexual conversation in the presence of younger relatives. A man who is "truly noble and dignified" ideally withdraws, however gradually, from attending such youth-oriented performances, as more of his children marry over time. There is a subtle reference here to incest and avoidance or reserve, in a analogy between the music of the tende and sexual relations. All secular festivals traditionally take place out of the view of older persons, in particular, Islamic scholars. In rural areas these festivals are held outside villages and camps, on their fringes, in smith neighborhoods, and always far from the mosque. It is young single persons, or young people whose spouses are away, who are active participants.

During these musical festivals youths communicate covertly and circumvent elders' official discourse of authority. Youthful male age-mates use special festival nicknames as forms of address in joking and gossip. Much poetry in the songs is first rehearsed among age-mates, away from elders and other authority figures, outside of villages and camps. Secret hand greetings indicating favor or disfavor toward suitors' overtures often accompany the music and singing.

Yet although musical festivals feature much relaxed conduct and have the purpose of sociability between the sexes, they are not unstructured events. Traditionally, particularly at the anzad performance gathering called *ahal*, there is a counterbalancing force of social control: preference for what is culturally-defined as "gallant" and "dignified" conduct. One way of approaching women, for example, is first discretely to circle the gathering. Some men then beam flashlights on women's faces flirtatiously, but women should pretend not to notice. Physical violence (for example, fights over women) on the spot is considered reprehensible. There is also, ideally, much indirect expression by allusion. Men and women must not openly show preference for any one person at these gatherings. Men intermittently chant a sound—*t-hum-a-hum*—described as "addressing the spirits" and associated with encouragement of love, courtship, and spirits. Poetry in the songs accompanying these performances traditionally was to win the favor of the opposite sex by metaphorical allusion, for example, by commemorating a momentous, heroic deed. Song verses have a similar purpose today, often praising an individual or offering social commentary with a covert message for the audience.

The tende now is predominant over the anzad at national holidays such as Republic Day and Independence, in the evening phases of rites of passage, and at spirit possession rites, but not at Islamic holidays, prayer days, or funerals, when it is forbidden. It is usually played in neighborhoods far from the mosque. Tende music is called "the music of the earth." Until recently nobles did not play it; rather, they left it to tributaries, smiths, and servile peoples and their descendants. Ambivalence toward the tende derives, first, from its functions in pre-colonial times: its handling by non-nobles in manual labor of crushing grain. This stereotype has been breaking down, particularly in the towns since the Tuareg nationalist rebellion of the early 1990s, when leaders attempted to downplay pre-colonial social origins and encouraged wider identification along ethnic and language lines, but it has not altogether disappeared in the countryside. A rural man of noble origin once explained to me that playing the tende was "like work, and therefore only slave and smiths should play this instrument." Ambivalence toward the tende is also related to its continuing association with spirits and Iblis, the Devil, said literally to reside inside the tende. In addition to avoiding mention of specific musical instruments in the presence of elders, there is also a taboo against speaking of non-Qur'anic spirits or Iblis in the elders' and Islamic scholars' presence. Refraining from pronouncing these names indicates respect for these persons, but

also suggests the power these performances have to circumvent their authority. In other words, tende festivals, with their more relaxed etiquette and song texts, provide a forum for public intergenerational disagreement, abandoning of reserve and respect, and open mixing of persons from diverse social origins in pre- and extra-marital flirting and courtship.

Both anzad and tende are potentially subversive, but they are have important cultural memory educational functions, as songs often mention social conduct, moral standards, and ideology. For example, personal qualities based upon individual merit and achievement, such as courage and men's endurance in battle, are praised. Yet while these are officially "noble" attributes, and many elderly parents still seek to arrange marriages within the same social stratum and between close cousins, most local residents now admire anyone who displays these qualities. In one tende song, for example, a noble woman wrote verses praising her lover, a man of servile descent, for such qualities, through the device of lauding his camel. In these verses she also indirectly expressed her resentment toward her lover's father for sending him away from her on caravan expeditions.[5] Many Tuareg men must work far from home to raise sufficient means for bride-wealth and to fulfill groomservice obligations to their parents-in-law: they travel in traditional caravan trade east to Bilma for salt and dates, and south to Kano, Nigeria, for millet and other household items. Nowadays, many go for migrant labor and itinerant trade to Libya, Algeria, Nigeria, and even France and Italy.

Thus the tende is traditionally identified with facilitation of relationships between the social categories, rather than the endogamous marriages arranged by elderly parents of youths, ideally between close cousins. Yet it should be noted that the festivals are nonetheless carefully orchestrated. They are supposed to encourage flirting, courtship and conversation, but not sexual relations between persons of different social origins or before marriage, for illegitimate births among Tuareg are highly shameful. Elders warn youths going to wedding festivals to be careful because "many guests there have no shame (reserve, *takarakit*) . . . . Often there are travelers from distant places and non-kin groups there, and sometimes there are thefts."

Many older persons tend to blame thefts upon guests passing for anzad and tende festivals. This is their way of discouraging youths seeking romance beyond the safe choices guided by close kinship. They lament some of these guests' lack of respect, for example, their insulting hosts by allegedly unruly behavior. During one wedding in June 1998 there was disorderly conduct by normally-honored guests from nearby: the affines from the groom's side, called *imartayen*, when they arrived at the bride's home. These guests were criticized for being too impatient to be served, complaining loudly, and even flashing knives (albeit jokingly). The parents of the bride were poor, having lost many herds in the drought. Friends told me that their difficult position in part accounted for the delay in serving food, and the fact that some guests did not receive an expensive wedding dish, *eghale* (pounded millet, dates, and goat-cheese blended in water). Despite parental warnings, however, unmarried adolescents consider unrelated people from a distance "much more interesting" as matches than nearby, closely-related kin. Furthermore, youths who have traveled as migrant laborers and political exiles now constitute a "lost generation": they have difficulty reintegrating into the community, and experience conflicts with elders, particularly over marriage. Other forces also challenge these elders' carefully circumscribing the freedom of the anzad and tende festivals. The acceleration of colonial and post-colonial economies (for example, mining exploration and tourism in northern Niger) and new political structures such as the new political leaders appointed by the state have sent outsiders (soldiers, functionaries, and other travelers) who have not always respected or understood local customs into the Tuareg regions. Sometimes these outsiders misread the relatively free social interaction between young Tuareg men and women as sexual license, and in a few instances some have introduced notions of prostitution, heretofore unknown, into the rural festival context (Gast 1992: 169).

Elders still try, however, to arrange endogamous close-cousin marriages in order to keep wealth in the family. Traditionally, parents have enjoyed some leverage: for example, a camel acquired in bridewealth in many regions is held in trust by the father of the bride until later in life; and livestock, date palms, and oasis gardens—important inheritance property forms—can be given to children by parents in gradual pre-inheritance gifts called *alkhalal*. However, the droughts in 1969-73 and 1984 have considerably diminished livestock and pastures, thereby weakening some parental, elderly, and chiefly leverage.

Youths, however, do not always benefit from this power vacuum. Most do not enjoy sufficient monetary income to replace these traditional forms of property. Thus they are in a kind of power limbo. The wave of young Tuareg *ichumar* men who received a secular (non-Qur'anic) education in colonial and post-colonial government schools did not receive jobs, due to the uneven development of different regions of Niger. There was massive unemployment, political tensions with the government, and 1969-73 and 1984 droughts. So many youths left Niger in the 1970s and 1980s to find work. Bridewealth (whether in livestock as in rural communities, or in money as in towns) is difficult to accumulate for these intermittently-employed youths. A number of tende songs sung by young women mock young men for returning from migrant labor without bringing back any money or presents.

Thus these anzad and tende musical performances address, and indeed provide a forum for, individual agency and assertion of power in youth-elder conflicts. But they cannot be described as either fully structural or fully anti-structural. They collapse the usual communitas and liminal frames, as well as standard associations of authority with the elderly and resistance with the youthful age roles. Many songs at festivals express love founded on admiration of individual achievement rather than social origins, and hint at defiance of older persons' authority. However, at the same time, qualities praised in many songs are often still based upon values similar to parents' values of the old noble nomadic warrior culture: courage, respect and reserve, and dignity. Many songs encourage respect for parents, as in these lines from a smith's wedding tende performance: "The girl who wishes a good bridewealth must stay close to her mothers' cushion." "May God protect the youths who have camels . . . that elderly one over there raised her daughter well; praise to the young bride and her mother."

The anzad and tende are identified with the aggregation of disparate forces in Tuareg society—cultural unity and social solidarity across kin and class lines—but also with the risks of indeterminacy in freedom of association at these festival events. As observed, these are characterized by relative relaxation and informality—joking, horseplay, and often ribald physical advances made by men toward women. Thus the tende and anzad performance forms, in their textual imagery, performer-audience interaction, and commentary, reveal changing youth-elder relationships as complex and nuanced.

Guitar Performances

Similarly the "new" guitar performances age encapsulate dilemmas and indeterminacies, rather than neat structural oppositions or a unilineal direction from "traditional to change." The guitar was introduced into Tuareg society from the western Saharan Polisario Front and Libyan Arab influences, via the *ichumar* separatist/rebels (derived from the French *chômeur*, "the unemployed" and *chômer*, "to be unemployed"). They were probably exposed to it during their military training or exile, and first began playing it during the separatist rebellion. They sang political songs, also called at that time *ichumar*, and accompanied themselves on the acoustic guitar, often in mountainous battle areas. These songs have now been expanded to address topics beyond the armed conflict (albeit with persisting political themes of Tuareg nationalism and cultural revitalization) and are called simply "guitar." Guitar music as a new genre of Tuareg music resembles "rock music" in the sense that it is now performed by bands with electronic amplification of guitars, bass, and drums, with usually a soloist singing lyrics. In northern Niger towns such as Agadez these bands play as adolescent men and women dance—sometimes together, sometimes separately "solo" style, and occasionally with a same-sex partner. These bands also often perform at political rallies of Tuareg nationalist parties.

Since the songs were originally composed by the Tuareg rebels, they initially contained much political commentary and were officially banned by the government during the early 1990s. Following the 1995 Peace Pact between rebels and the central governments of Mali and Niger, the songs have become popularized. They are freely performed in public in both towns and countryside and are diversified in their subject matter. Many verses, however, continue to praise nationalist leaders and to extol the cultural revitalization movement and its leaders. Many of these leaders and singers are those unmarried youths of the new ichumar generation. Striking here is that praise of youthful rebel leaders often refers to elders and traditional cultural values of the nomadic, aristocratic warrior culture. For example, one song goes,

> When one thinks that we had to attack, one thinks about the old one [*amghar*, also denoting leader of a descent group or camp or head of a household] also . . . those one has left to the camps, the heart becomes bitter and that returns into the soul.

In local exegesis this means that one must control

oneself for the sake of the elders, and one is worried about them). At the same time, however, most guitar songs address "brothers" rather than "fathers" in their lyrics, and they emphasize unity with those fictive kin who, ideally at least, share common goals. In the towns players of the new guitar in rock bands often perform before or following the tende performances at festival dances. The players come from diverse social origins, and their music often includes themes emphasizing the unity of all social categories under the banner of the Tamajaq language and culture. Thus these songs encourage a broadening of ties from kinship, parents, and household toward fellow fighters and age cohorts from other regions.

Yet many guitar songs also contain warrior imagery that lauds values oriented toward the past: for example, the saber sword, the retaliatory raid, and the protection expressed by tropes of shade and shadows, images that also appear in traditional Tuareg battle epic and love of earlier generations of youth. Guitar songs often appeal to traditional values such as courage, endurance, bravery, and toughness. Thus their themes of war and struggle appeal to many of the same values as the older sung poetry of the anzad and tende praising earlier war heroes like Kaousan, Firhun, and Boulkhou.

The symbolic repertoires of the poetic verses in the music of all three youth-oriented festivals draw from older historical memory, and their performances often occur in sequence at the same event. On the other hand, in some other songs at these events singers also occasionally insert satirical jokes mocking important elderly authority figures, even local chiefs: for example, at the wedding of the son of a chief, a smith woman sang of the groom's father being replaced in the future. She also mocked some prominent elderly Islamic scholars for making profits from manufacturing religious amulets. Other song verses clearly delineate the traditional distance between youths and elders in matters of love preferences and courtship; for example: "The elder in his place, the youth in bed . . . I do not want an elder."

The ichumar generation of youths, particularly the youngest, who were active in the 1990-95 armed conflict, tend to oppose some older leadership they identify with the past. Their new concepts of social and political identity were acquired from their schooling and migrant labor. Many fighters were rumored to have resisted older Tuareg leaders during the rebellion, and some traditional chiefs in Azawak and Aïr regions were murdered. In one incident, during a robbery attack on tourists in the Sahara during the armed conflict, a newspaper reported that older leaders in this group appeared to be trying to keep order, whereas the younger men were resisting this, attempting to harass the tourist women.

I noticed mixed reactions from the older generation to actions of these young men, but these were usually stated in private. For example, in an incident I witnessed in 1998, former fighters shot off guns during songs to praise the Prophet at an evening celebration of the Prophet's birthday. Such gunfire had not previously been featured in any celebrations, much less sacred ones. No one protested at the scene, but later an older woman expressed disapproval to me in the privacy of her compound. She lamented the gunfire as "shameless" (disrespectful) behavior. By contrast, her adolescent son referred to the shooters as "elements of the resistance" and praised them. He viewed their actions as appropriate to celebrate their heroic roles in protecting the local residents, including respected elders and Islamic scholars, from a recent incident of violence in which some outside militia had attacked their villages. Thus the gunfire was defined by this youth as in fact promoting traditional Tuareg values that are also important to the older generation. Hence the festival gunfire revealed elder and youth conflict, but not in a clear-cut manner. It revealed a haziness of boundaries between "tradition" and "modern," and the indeterminacy of their association with any one age group.

Guitar performances are not exactly disapproved of by most elders, many of whom sympathize with their appeals to these "traditional" values. I did not ever hear an older adult lament youths' enthusiasm for this music or forbid youths to participate in these dances. One older man and popular *animateur* at many guitar performances, upon observing young men and women dancing together during a guitar performance, commented that they danced well, but that now "we have abandoned reserve" (*takarakit*, reserve, respect, or shame). He said this with neither sadness nor satisfaction, but rather matter-of-factly.

Indeed, guitar concerts are popular with all ages in town and countryside. Almost everyone attends such concerts, except perhaps Islamic scholars. In much guitar music today, singers tend to be either famous adolescent performers, some of whom were former rebels (thus far predominantly male, and a very few non-combatant female singers) or primary-school children, who have learned these songs from

cassette tapes or live performances. The reason children sing the music is interesting. Many older Tuareg adults believe children have no sins (*bakaten*), and that this confers on them a kind of benediction and protection (Rasmussen 1997a). As a consequence, children are often expected to be adults' mouthpieces for political statements that adults cannot make for fear of retaliation. On several occasions I listened to children's performances of ichumar with scathingly mocking political commentary and even insults, both sung and shouted, live and on tapes recorded by friends and field assistants. I was amused by one song in which primary school-aged children hurled insults and reproaches about current events and politicians. When I expressed surprise, these persons indicated that children often sing particularly critical political lyrics "because unlike adults, who may be punished for this, children are not taken seriously and thus are good singers [of this genre]."

Many adults nonetheless recognize the inflammatory potential of these performances, and, even at dances where the lyrics are less overtly political, there is usually an older man present whose role is to organize, introduce, comment, and keep order. The animateur acts as a broker or facilitator between, not solely youths and elders or different families and descent groups as in traditional marriages, but also between the local community and the nation-state, and host family and the guests. This elder's role is broadly instrumental and his position ambiguous. The role of the guitar festival's "master-of-ceremonies" (called animateur at dances and "the ichumar's messenger," or in local slang, "the camel of the ichumar" at political party rallies) reflects the emergent role of guitar musical performances in articulating changing age roles and intergenerational relationships.

As a relatively new instrument and musical genre in Tuareg culture, the guitar's place in traditional cosmology and elder-youth roles and relations is as yet ambiguous. It is not, however, merely an instrument of "globalization." The associations of the guitar are complex. What is clear is that, among Tuareg, it is now the major expressive medium of political nationalism and cultural revitalization movements. Its players and listeners, nonetheless, tend to be less clearly defined in local cultural imagery in terms of their religious devotion, social origins, political views, gender, and age, and its performances are more broad-based and open-ended, allowing for greater negotiability. Its audiences are even more diverse than those at evening tende performances. For example, in the towns they are often multi-ethnic. Even in the countryside many Tuareg who attend guitar performances are relatively youthful outsiders. They come from distant regions as participants in the recent post-rebellion regional reorganization programs (for example, garden and boutique cooperatives and peacekeeping forces. In these contexts, rather than being merely "uninvited guests," these visitors bringing food distributions, projects for new wells, gardens, and livestock replenishment, are welcomed with tende, guitar, and camel-race performances (Rasmussen 1994). Older generations of Tuareg have tended to fear some of these programs as sources of coercion, for example, immunizations from outside health-workers were often accompanied by political speeches (Rasmussen 1994). Thus these new performances are also carefully orchestrated beneath their surface of license and feature important cultural mediators.

Thus the guitar's age-related cultural symbolism is thus far open-ended and ambiguous. Like the more "traditional" anzad and tende, it allows much indeterminacy and agency in age relations and interaction, since its music often seeks to unify disparate elements. But its nationalist performers appeal to wider (though not "global") bases beyond kinship, age, gender, and social stratum: common identity of the Tamajaq language and pride in Tuareg culture. In public, at least, most people want to be seen as supporting revival. Elderly persons may privately hold diverse opinions on these matters, but generally they do not voice as strong opinions about the guitar as they do about the tende and anzad. Early in my field research, for example, marabouts insisted that after attending a *tende n goumaten* (a type of tende performance occurring during spirit possession exorcism rituals), one must remove and wash one's clothes before praying (Rasmussen 1995). I did not hear such disparaging comments concerning the guitar performances. The role of the tende itself may be undergoing transformation toward more indeterminate and ambiguous associations for elders and youths. It is more frequently complemented by the guitar to welcome visitors, narrate the wedding, praise the family, but also to praise the diverse new guests in the audience. All these persons are affected in different ways by the event celebrated by the musical festival performance, and thus audience, as much as author, control these meanings.

Analysis

These descriptions of the anzad, tende, and guitar suggest they have strong cosmological, social, and political resonance to the different age groupings in Tuareg society. They evoke alternately love, praise, and scorn, prestige and shame, reward and punishment, and generalized cultural pride, based on both individual achievement and norms of structural (albeit changing) positions in society. But they also emerge as important stages for the orchestration of dissonant interests, indicating inter-generational, but also intra-generational, unities, on the one hand, and on the other, discontinuity and disjunction of age groupings' experiences in Tuareg society. Their music and its long-standing cultural symbolism, as well as its re-shaping by outside forces, evoke ideal transformations of age roles over the life course, but also agency, in critical reflections on them. Youths and elders alike participate as active agents in both these processes, of old and new, ideal and debated values.

These musical festivals all serve as a forum for public debate on changes that persons of all ages are experiencing, albeit in ways not always predictable in age, expressive performative consequences, or relationship between the "old/traditional authority" to the "new/modern resistance." In particular, the guitar, since it is the most-recently introduced instrument provides a forum for discourse on forces affecting youth-elder relationships. These forces include both long-standing and recent, local and wider, sources of conflict and transformation of youth and elder roles.

The marriage of children is important to elders' autonomy in later years. Thus elders are at once facilitators and innovators; they attempt to secure privileges, security, and autonomy. The household unit, while usually nuclear, consisting of husband, wife, and children, is also in rural areas based on matrifocal ties between mothers and daughters and sisters who prefer to live next-door to each other, even as husbands try to move wives to live near their own kin. Older men have tried to manage these occupations from home, like heads of firms. Nowadays, it is the children of a household and, increasingly also contract labor, who usually do these tasks. My longitudinal and life history data suggest that over the life course many men first work for elders, but this is almost always viewed as hard work with little return, and insufficient nowadays for making a living. Many need to alternate between subsistence gardening, herding, and caravan trading, or to supplement it with migrant labor, particularly to raise bridewealth. This sometimes entails greater freedom from the opinions of parents, at least temporarily. In one case, for example, I heard the opinions of children on older parents' re-marriage powerfully expressed:

One elderly man, whom I will call Moutafa, a successful Islamic scholar, the father of grown and married children, lost his wife in 1992. Several years later Moutafa married a woman many years his junior. His daughters told me they disliked the new wife. By 1995 he had moved with his new wife to a small camp near her own kin outside the village. His sons and daughters occasionally visited him there, and he continued to practice successful Islamic scholarship and Qur'anic healing, but he never came to his childrens' households. This case is interesting because it represents an inversion of ideal postmarital residence in men's late life and also, perhaps more importantly, a reversal of the usual expression of opinion in matters of marriage: here, the children disapprove of the parent's new marriage, rather than vice versa. Garden land is becoming scarce, and many younger men are compelled to start gardens at a distance from their own kin. Despite his children's genuine love and affection for him and his prominence as a respected marabout, this man was somewhat weakened by two factors: the social conflict between his new wife and his daughters, and the intermittent travel and distant work of his own sons. He literally found himself without a tent, except in his new wife's compound.

The presence of older men and women at sacred daytime rituals of birth and marriage, presided over by Islamic scholars, constitutes a symbolic expression of their ideally productive socioeconomic and authority roles in the traditional household (Rasmussen 1997a, 1998, 2000). Older men and women in effect are supposed to guide youths toward their own socioeconomic independence in these staged liminal situations, when youths are viewed as potentially endangered by jealous spirits and humans. They are supposed to provide continuity and security, when these are perceived as threatened. The musical performance forms of anzad, tende, and guitar encapsulate, in different ways, long-standing and recent contradictions, tensions, challenges, and transformations in youth-elder relations.

Conclusions

Images of age in these popular musical perform-ances, not surprisingly, express current negotiations of youth-elder categories in the wake of the Tuareg rebellion and the cultural revitalization in Niger today. They reveal more nuanced processes: not only are age categories culturally, rather than biologically constructed, they are also undergoing transformation. New experiences and conditions confront elders and their vested interests. Youths often question elders' authority, but also respect many traditions. Youths and elders alike listen to appeals from Tuareg nationalist leaders, in festival contexts often superimposed on traditional weddings, sacred ceremonies, and other events, for the unity of all social categories in a wider Tuareg cultural identity.

For many Tuareg the performance contexts of the three musical instruments, so resonant and highly-charged in experiences and preoccupations of aging, stimulate reflection and debates concerning youth and age. More broadly for anthropology, these performances suggest refinements in ways of thinking about categories of "the old" and "the new." As in our own "youth cultures"—in age imagery of rock concerts and popular music, on the one hand, and so-called "high culture," on the other—the Tuareg performances reveal how local residents experience their own idioms of youth and age, convert them into long-standing and changing social roles and experiences, and reflect upon them in dialogues between the generations. These processes, conveyed in age tropes, are played out in these age-marked ritual contexts. These data also challenge some anthropological tendencies to associate rigid structural oppositions such as "traditional/modern" with static age categories, or to identify one age cohort with authority and the other with malleable or rebellious roles. They suggest that "traditional" and "modern" beliefs and practices do not line up so neatly with authority and subordinate roles according to one or another age or generation. Traditional and modern, and indeed "global," are too simplistic terms for characterizing the changes taking place among the different age groups in African societies and elsewhere. Among the Tuareg these are nonetheless salient categories, reflected upon and played out largely through how music is performed and enjoyed. Tuareg elders today remain ideally and officially respected authority figures, particularly in the rural communities. Yet they are also subject to criticism from youths, and their authority has intermittently been challenged by colonial and post-colonial events affecting Tuareg social and political organization. Although youths and elders often stand in conflict, many self-consciously put aside differences to unite under the banner of common concerns. This was shown in the youthful singers' guitar songs that glorified older warrior traditions.

More broadly, the Tuareg data suggest that the "modern" and the "new" are only effects of globalization in very secondary ways. The guitar music style, for example, comes from the Arab and Polisario front influences. The separatist conflict, still sporadically erupting in some regions, has been directed toward the central government to the south.

Age-related themes in these contexts suggest that some anthropological formulations of modernization and globalization are ethnocentric. Traditional and modern are a false dichotomy; there is no sharp line between them, nor are they static qualities of one or another age or generation, regardless of context. Indeed, "youth" and "aged," and what is perceived and promoted as new and old have finer nuances, are attached to diverse agents, and moreover, shift in meaning according to different purposes in diverse contexts.

NOTES

Acknowledgments Data for this essay are based on my residence and research in Niger between 1974 and 1998 on topics of Tuareg spirit possession, aging and the life course, traditional healing systems, and rural and urban smith/artisans. In these projects I am grateful for assistance from Fulbright Hays, Wenner-Gren Foundation, Social Science Research Council, National Geographic Society, Indiana University, and University of Houston.

1. Between approximately 1990 and 1995 there was a separatist Tuareg rebellion in parts of Mali and Niger. The roots of this conflict are beyond the scope of this essay; rather, its consequences for inter- and intra-generational relationships are one focus of interest here. For details of the historical and political background to the Tuareg rebellion, see Claudot-Hawad 1996; Bourgeot 1990, 1994; Dayak 1992; and Decalo 1997.

2. For extensive description and analysis of rituals (divination, possession, and rites of passage) in Tuareg society, in different contexts and from somewhat different theoretical perspectives, see Nicolaisen 1961; Casajus 1987; Claudot-Hawad 1993; Rasmussen 1995, 1997a, 1997b, 1998.

3. Pre-colonial Tuareg society was hierarchically-stratified in specialized occupational groups based upon descent, and in theory these social strata were supposed to marry endogamously, although there was some negotiation of this practice, as well as other attributes of ranking in this system. Nobles, tributary groups, smith/artisans (called "smiths" here), and servile peoples practiced client-patron rights and obligations that have been breaking down for some time. See Murphy 1964, 1967; Nicolaisen and Nicolaisen 1997; Keenan 1977; Bernus 1981; and Claudot-Hawad 1993, 1996 for descriptions of Tuareg social organization, political structure, kinship, and descent, in traditional and recent forms, and for discussions of their transformations and continuities.

Although the smiths still serve as important ritual specialists, go-betweens, general "handy-persons," jewelers, leatherworkers and repairers, and oral historians for noble patron families in the countryside, these relationships and roles have been modified. In the towns, smiths are becoming more specialized and now work predominantly, though not exclusively, for the tourist market in silver and gold work. See Saenz 1991 and Rasmussen 1997b.

4. Niger has been suffering from economic problems of budgetary IMF and World Bank-imposed austerity programs, unemployment, intermittent droughts in the North and West, and social and political tensions in alternations between parliamentary government and several coups-d'etat. The Tuareg separatist rebellion still intermittently emerges in the form of guerrilla warfare, and there has recently emerged a Tubu separatist movement in parts of the East as well.

5. The salt caravan (Nicolaisen and Nicolaisen 1997; Bernus 1981) continues today, particularly among the men of the Kel Ewey confederation of Aïr. It has been in some decline since the advent of trucks that carry more merchandise and also since the 1984 drought, which killed many camels necessary to make the trip. Traditionally, however, caravanning is a point of great masculine pride among the senior generation of Kel Ewey men: they continue to go on caravans for as long as they are able. Caravan expeditions are known to be arduous journeys that test the strength and valor of men (Rasmussen 1997a). Many elderly men eventually cease to go themselves and send younger relatives in their place, managing these trips from home. Some young men in most families continue to make this trip annually, departing in September or October for Bilma to obtain salt and dates, and then go south toward Kano, Nigeria, to trade these goods for millet and household items. They are gone for six or seven months at a time, returning to Aïr in March or April at the beginning of the hot season, followed by the rainy season. This latter is the season most popular for weddings and other festivals, such as the Cure Salée, for which the more nomadic groups assemble around a salt lick near In Gall, an oasis south of Agadez.

REFERENCES CITED

Appadurai, Arjun. 1991. Global ethnoscapes: Notes and queries for a transnational anthropology. In *Recapturing anthropology: Working in the present,* ed. Richard G. Fox. Santa Fe NM: School of American Research Press.

Bernus, Edmond. 1981. *Touaregs Nigeriens: Unité d'un people pasteur.* Paris: Editions de l' Office de la Recherche Scientifique et Technique d'Outre-Mer.

Bourgeot, Andre. 1990. Identité touarègue: De l'aristocratie à la révolution. *Etudes Rurales* 120: 129-62.

———. 1994. Révoltes et rebellions en pays touareg. *Afrique Contemporaine* 170(2): 3-18.

Casajus, Dominique. 1987. *La Tente dans l'Essuf.* London: Cambridge University Press.

Claudot-Hawad, Hélène. 1993. *Touareg: Portrait en fragments.* Aix-en-Provence: Edisud.

Claudot-Hawad, Hélène, ed. 1996. *Touaregs et autres Sahariens entre plusieurs mondes.* CNRS, Aix-en-Provence: Edisud.

Dayak, Mano. 1992. *Touareg: La tragédie.* Avec la collaboration de Michael Stuhrenberg et de Jerome Strazzula, sous la direction de

Jacques Lanzmann. Paris: Editions Jean-Claude Lattes.

Decalo, Samuel. 1997. *Historical dictionary of Niger*, 3ᵈ ed. Lanham MD: Scarecrow Press.

Featherstone, Michael, ed. 1990. *Global culture: Nationalism, globalization, and modernity*. Thousand Oaks CA: Sage Publications.

Gast, Marcel. 1992. Relations amoureuses chez les Kel Ahaggar. In *Amour, phantasmes, et sociétés en Afrique du nord et au Sahara*, ed. Tassadit Yacine. Paris: Harmattan-Awal.

Handelman, Don. 1990. *Models and mirrors*. Cambridge: Cambridge University Press.

Keenan, Jeremy. 1977. *Tuareg: People of Ahaggar*. New York: St. Martins Press.

Manheimer, Ronald. 1989. The narrative quest in humanistic gerontology. *Journal of Aging Studies* 3(3): 231-252.

Murphy, Robert. 1964. Social distance and the veil. *American Anthropologist* 66: 1257-1274.

_____. 1967. Tuareg kinship. *American Anthropologist* 69: 163-170.

Myerhoff, Barbara. 1977. *Number our days*. New York: E.P. Dutton.

_____. 1982. Life history among the elderly: Performance, visibility, and re-membering. In *A crack in the mirror*, ed. Jay Ruby. Philadelphia: University of Pennsylvania Press.

Nicolaisen, Johannes. 1961. Essaie sur la religion et la magie touaregues . *Folk* 3: 113-162.

Nicolaisen, Johannes and Ida Nicolaisen. 1997. *The pastoral Tuareg*. London: Thames and Hudson.

Rasmussen, Susan. 1994. Female sexuality, social reproduction, and medical intervention: Kel Ewey Tuareg perspectives. *Culture, Medicine, and Psychiatry* 18: 433-462.

_____. 1995. *Spirit possession and personhood among the Kel Ewey Tuareg*. Cambridge: Cambridge University Press.

_____. 1997a. *The poetics and politics of Tuareg aging: Life course and personal destiny in Niger*. DeKalb: Northern Illinois University Press.

_____. 1997b. Between ritual, theater, and play: Blacksmith praise at Tuareg marriage. *Journal of American Folklore* 110(435): 3-27.

_____. 1998. Only women know trees: Medicine women and the role of herbal healing in Tuareg culture. *Journal of Anthropological Research* 54(2): 147-171.

_____. 2000 Elders, alms, and ancestors. *Ethnology*. In press.

Saenz, Candelario. 1991. They have eaten our grandfather! The special status of Twareg smiths. Ph.D. Dissertation, Columbia University.

Turner, Victor. 1969. *The ritual process: Structure and anti-structure*. Chicago IL: Aldine.

_____. 1974. *Dramas, fields, and metaphors*. Ithaca NY: Cornell University Press.

MARK R. LUBORSKY
Polisher Research Institute
Philadelphia Geriatric Center

Questioning the Allure of Aging and Health for Medical Anthropology

With the allure of the mythic sirens' call, a new terrain for study beckons anthropologists to explore the culturally entrenched concepts, practices, and biases towards aging that shape the daily lives and health practices of the elderly. The articles in this issue give glimpses of a discipline expanding its view of social life to include aging and the aged. In these brief comments I point to the allures, the contributions, and the associated pitfalls for anthropological studies of aging. I also suggest why readers may find both a sense of familiarity and puzzlement in these articles.

The enticement to study aging springs from old yet familiar roots in our field. The shattering of dearly held but little-examined stereotypes, overgeneralizations, and biases has always been a touchstone of cultural inquiry. Anthropology's ancestors, for example, labored to change the dominant demeaning stereotypes about the natural inferiority of non-European peoples, societies, and women that validated their mistreatment. Fieldwork documented that the sources of such stereotypes were lack of firsthand information, romanticization of simpler lifeways or bygone eras, and power issues.

In a corresponding way, anthropological interest in old age and aging was piqued by a similar discourse about old people, a discourse that resonated with familiar assertions about the elderly's "primitive" mentalities and lifeways. A few decades ago, elderly people were presumed to live healthier, more valued lives in other societies and in earlier eras. Simultaneously, as many anthropologists have noted, the elderly were derided as being intrinsically uninteresting ("simple minded"), helpless, and socially detached. These sentiments linger today in popular thought and biomedical research. Additionally, the elderly are not just objects of study but may romanticize or devalue parts of their own past and present lives, processes that we usually attribute to the outside observer.

The articles in this issue highlight the many enduring system-level barriers to equal care and to basic social validation for the elderly population, conditions that are not tolerated for youths or adults. As illustrated by the articles on stroke, incontinence, bereavement, and interactions with medical staff, these barriers perpetuate inadequate treatment and lead to excess disability, illness, and distress. The resulting disability and distress re-create public images and experiences of elderly as being mentally and physically infirm and unable to demonstrate basic capacities of full adult personhood.

But there are pitfalls to stereotype bashing. Stereotypes are persistently reinvented within the popular and scientific community. While fieldwork findings debunk one set of contemporary ageist stereotypes, the same data are drawn into the production of a next generation of "truths" about aging. We need to remain aware of how our own brand of questions and findings enter into the formulation of new stereotypes. Agenda and data from several sources, including anthropological studies, infuse the new images of aging with new stereotypes. For example, we "know" now that there is nothing natural about being helpless, frail, and dependent in old age. Today, vigorous political, economic, and research agendas endeavor to impose an opposite, but perhaps equally restrictive and uniform, image of positive functioning and well-being in late life. Competing candidates for the new image of later life include "successful aging," "healthy aging," "normal aging," and "productive aging." Each of these images resonate with U.S. social ideals of ambition, self-betterment, and independence.

The problems with such images are threefold. First, they do not adequately allow for individual variability within the elderly community and instead tend to portray aging as being uniformly positive. In addition, they may not be flexible enough to embrace the cultural, ethnic, or personal diversities in ideals or capacities of elderly people, especially in light of individual lifelong inequalities in health, income, and occupational backgrounds. Second, they do not adequately take into account the importance of social interdependency in old age and instead focus on individual competence and effort. Third, the proffering of an image of uniform positive functioning and well-being in old age undermines the larger community's responsibility for providing supportive barrier-free environments and resources that help enable the elderly to remain functional. These purposefully designed positive visions of aging also tend to ignore questions of which segments of populations survive into old age and neglect lifelong differences in the aging process from childhood. In sum, anthropological interest in gerontology must illuminate aging and culture in a broad sense as well as provide humanizing and particularizing perspectives needed to counterweight the generalizing and reductionist view of social life in biomedicine.

The articles presented here reflect the tussle created at the local level by competing and socially contested images of old age and health care. They focus on such contested images as recovery versus life reorganization in bereavement, rehabilitation to regain functioning versus recovery of prior abilities, and bladder control versus dryness management. The outcomes of these debates will have a pervasive impact on the experiences of current and future cohorts of elderly people as well as on the allocation of social and financial resources.

Fundamental anthropological and medical anthropological contributions to social and behavioral science are repeated in these articles. These include the social consequences of disease and the cultural design of illness and disability. Specifically, they examine the social consequences of losses of neurological function for gait (stroke), muscle control (incontinence), mental acuity (dementia), and anchoring social relationships (bereavement). In doing so they shed light on the contents of personal experiences associated with such losses (for example, hope, anxiety, wishes, dreads); in addition, they illuminate the medical practices and institutional policies that foster conditions of helplessness, hopelessness, shame, and stigma among elderly persons—conditions that themselves reinforce negative social stereotypes of old age. The focus on social and personal illness experience in old age is a particularly important one because the occurrence and management of comorbid conditions is a common situation that shapes the subjective reality and consciousness of people in late life.

Critical development of theory is pursued too infrequently in medical anthropology generally, and in research on aging in particular. These articles only indirectly address theoretical concerns about the aging process, the nature of age, or the whole life course. Perhaps, as Himmelfarb (1994) warns, interdisciplinary cultural inquiry does produce coarser rather than more refined theory. This lack of theory development also may be partly understood in terms of the national climate for social, behavioral, and medical research that assigns the highest importance to biomedical and policy studies. We share with all social scientists the need to convincingly demonstrate that behaviors and experiences are not simple and predictable by such traditional factors or measures as race, age, or disease type. Rather, we must strive to demonstrate that actions and experiences differentially vary according to personal and community settings. Thus, one aspect of these articles that may puzzle medical anthropologists derives from this multidisciplinary and political climate (Kaufert and O'Neil 1993). There are silent interlocutors visible that shape both the scope and direction of anthropological work on aging and the style of writing dictated by the gatekeepers who support research and publications.

A final observation is due regarding methods. Tendrils of strain or unease about the credibility and generality of ethnographic insights weave through descriptions and interpretations in these articles. This unease appears in presentations of vague quantifiers (e.g., "some," "many," "most") and unspecified odds-ratios (e.g., "far more likely") to describe results of content analyses, experiences, or themes. Anthropologists have not worked to develop criteria or standards for quantifying terms such as "some" or "many." Nor have we developed standards for determining when and where "some" or "many" are important or how qualitative data can be used to infer risk factors and odds-ratios. Further, such descriptions are offered unsystematically. Negative cases, for example, are inadequately discussed.

Drawing on my own observations while reviewing research grant applications and articles, I see the above issues as being significant in two ways. First, the use of vague quantifiers and unsystematic comparisons undermines reception of valuable anthropological work by nonanthropologists because they read it as vague or intentionally biased. Second, it mires anthropological thought in ambiguity by mixing conflicting epistemologies and insights. While frequency is a marker of significance in quantitative paradigms, in anthropology, where cultural phenomena do not have normative distributions, infrequency is often a guide to significance and meaning.

The use of vague quantifiers and unsystematic comparisons may also derive in part from the discourse of interdisciplinary studies dominated by U.S. behavioral, experimental, and survey science paradigms in which researchers customarily have to address questions about sample size, reliability, generalizability, and validity. At heart, none of these are alien concepts to anthropology, but they receive different emphasis and language in our work. Vague quantifications seem to derive from or are responsive to inquiries posed by other behavioral and social science methodologies. Or perhaps their use is simply a response to the generic U.S. ethos that "more" is better: thus the more people or the more often something is stated, the more important it implicitly becomes. In any case, frequency is a curious marker for a field that argues that cultural values and moral frameworks are primary, and that typically occurring actions are not necessarily morally normative. Certainly, there is room for clarification of this uneasy alliance in medical anthropology.

A last observation concerns the melange of theory and methods in gerontological anthropology. Clearly, such studies are multidisciplinary—issues of history, local values, cultural frameworks, bodies and disease, and personal experiences are all relevant. But borrowing from different sets of knowledge brings with it different approaches to building and exploring knowledge. Reflective of the field as a whole, the projects represented in these articles use a host of epistemologies, including concepts from sociolinguistics, medicine, culture, and psychiatry. A challenge for future work is to conduct more detailed inquiry into the implications and dilemmas posed by piecing together theories, concepts, and methods that span across wide disciplinary divides. Another area for study is the youth- and adult-centrism of anthropology's core questions and concepts. For example, at a symposium in 1987, anthropologists who had fieldwork ongoing in another culture for 20 or more years examined how their personal sense of the core problems for study shifted with age, a shift that reflected their own social and psychological development and the unfolding of their experience of their several selves as they aged within and across multiple cultural settings (Luborsky 1987).

In summary, these articles show that anthropological curiosity is alive in spirit, mind, and body, although these dimensions do no always coalesce smoothly on each occasion when anthropology perspectives are invoked. Collectively, the articles are a challenge to a medical anthropology of the human condition that has yet to fully embrace the whole range of human existence across the life span just as it embraces the whole range of human existence cross-culturally.

Correspondence may be addressed to the author at the Polisher Researcher Institute, Philadelphia Geriatric Center, 5301 Old York Rd., Philadelphia, PA 19141.

REFERENCES CITED

Himmelfarb, Gertrude
    1994   On Looking into the Abyss: Untimely Thoughts on Culture and Society. New
           York: Alfred E. Knopf.
Kaufert, Patricia A., and John O'Neil
    1993   Analysis of a Dialogue on Risks in Childbirth: Clinicians, Epidemiologist and Inuit
           Women. In Knowledge, Power and Practice: The Anthropology of Medicine and
           Everyday Life. Shirley Lindenbaum and Margaret Lock, eds. Pps. 32–76. Berkeley:
           University of California Press.

Luborsky, Mark R.
1987   Two Ages of Self and Other: Anthropologists Aging in Two Cultures. Symposium and paper presented at the 86th annual meeting of the American Anthropological Association, Chicago, IL.

Psychological Medicine, 1996, **26**, 1061–1074. Copyright © 1996 Cambridge University Press

Dementia in old age: an anthropological perspective

P. A. POLLITT[1]

From the NHMRC Social Psychiatry Research Unit, The Australian National University, Canberra, Australia

SYNOPSIS This paper examines the assumption that dementia in old age is a universal phenomenon that will vary in its prevalence and manifestation because of social and cultural factors. It finds that while researchers have been successful in demonstrating the commonality of dementia, they have been less successful in showing whether or not it varies across cultures and between social and ethnic groupings. The inconclusiveness of findings may, in part, be a function of diagnostic differences and the research methodologies employed.

New instruments and measures are being devised to overcome these problems. However, the sociocultural context in which dementia occurs and the meaning of the disorder to those involved (as sufferers and caregivers) are often missing dimensions. In particular, there is little knowledge about how the disorders of old age in non-Western settings are experienced and understood. In this respect anthropology has a special contribution to make to research on dementia.

INTRODUCTION

Among the industrialized nations of the West, dementia is increasingly viewed as a major public health problem. In the United States, for example Alzheimer's disease, the principal form of dementia, is described as 'the disease of the century' and a leading cause of death (Gubrium, 1986; Stafford, 1992). The costs of this disorder are enormous, both economically and in terms of suffering, diminished quality of life and the multiple effects on others involved. Recognition of the special needs of sufferers has led to the earmarking of funds and the targetting of services. It is expected that developing countries, where the rate of population growth for older people is even greater than in the industrial countries (Macfadyen, 1990), will follow suit. This assumption raises questions about the cross-cultural validity of the concept of dementia and the extent to which it is influenced by particular social and cultural circumstances. This paper addresses these questions by examining dementia in the Western context, the evidence for its universality and for social and cultural differences in its manifestations.

Dementia is basically a Western diagnostic category and most of the research findings, as well as the instruments devised to assess the disorder and to measure cognitive loss, are from Western sources. The phenomenon is, nevertheless, thought to be universal. The World Health Organization has endeavoured to standardize the meaning of dementia and to give it universal, cross-cultural application. After 'extensive consultation with experts throughout the world' (Henderson, 1993, p. 2), the following definition has been formulated:

A syndrome due to disease of the brain, usually of a chronic or progressive nature, in which there is disturbance of multiple higher cortical functions, including memory, thinking, orientation, comprehension, calculation, learning capacity, language and judgement. Consciousness is not clouded. Impairments of cognitive function are commonly accompanied, and occasionally preceded, by deterioration in emotional control, social behaviour, or motivation. This syndrome occurs in Alzheimer's disease, in cerebrovascular disease and in other conditions primarily or secondarily affecting the brain. (World Health Organization, 1990)

DEMENTIA IN THE WEST

While such a definition may suggest a relatively unproblematical clinical syndrome, in practice

[1] Address for correspondence: Dr P. Pollitt, NHMRC Social Psychiatry Research Unit, The Australian National University, 3 Liversidge Street, Canberra, ACT 0200, Australia.

dementia is 'a diagnostic category of uncertain boundaries' (Robertson. 1990. p. 430). Ambiguities surround it. Diagnostic problems are presented by the immense variability of the condition. its resemblance to many other conditions. and its frequent co-morbidity. Where should it be located professionally: with psychiatry. neurology or geriatrics. or does it more properly belong to the social domain?[1]† Is it a discrete disease or disease syndrome. or – because it is so strikingly age-dependent – is it part of normal ageing? Huppert & Brayne (1994) suggest two opposing interpretations of the 'uneasy relationship' (Gubrium, 1986) between dementia and normal ageing: 'One is that researchers have not yet identified those changes which are unique to the dementias. because the changes observed are confounded with age-related changes. The other is that normal aging and dementia form a continuum, the changes differing in magnitude but not in kind' (p. 3).

The confusion is most marked in the case of mild dementia, definitions of which (for example. Roth et al. 1986) imply impairment but not necessarily more than might be expected in old age generally. Mild dementia does not fall neatly into the category of abnormal old age. The researcher may have difficulty in fitting it into the 'research paradigm' (Stafford, 1992, p. 174). while for the clinician, 'the reliable diagnosis of mild dementia is technically demanding' (Jorm & Henderson, 1985, p. 395) and from a lay perspective there are no clear boundaries. Relatives of people identified in epidemiological studies as dementing often appear unaware of abnormality (O'Connor et al. 1989a; Pollitt et al., 1989).

Dementia as a psychiatric illness

Although originally classified as a senile psychosis (Burns et al. 1990a), dementia has not been firmly established as a psychiatric illness. Claims to include it among the psychiatric disorders are based on the common occurrence of psychiatric symptoms in clinical samples (see Wragg & Jeste, 1989, for an overview) and on the fact that such symptoms respond similarly to treatment (Mendez et al. 1990; Sultzer et al. 1993). Some researchers have gone so far as to claim that symptoms such as depression and paranoid delusional beliefs 'are virtually ubiqui-

† The notes will be found on pp. 1070–1071.

tous in Alzheimer's disease' (Merriam et al. 1988. p. 10). However. others have found that people shown to be dementing in neuro-psychological tests may not display these or any other psychiatric symptoms (Loewenstein et al. 1994). Such people are much less likely to be referred for assessment or to be known to services (O'Connor et al. 1988) and. therefore. to appear in clinical samples.

Although evidence varies. the relationship between psychopathology and cognitive decline appears not to be straightforward: 'the intellectual disability and psychiatric symptoms may run independent courses' (Merriam et al. 1988. p. 11).[2] Cooper and colleagues (1990) suggest that 'the level of cognitive functioning accounts for a small percentage of variation in...behaviours [symptoms] and implies that other variables are involved' (p. 869). for example. previous personality. current medication. or social and environmental factors.

Whatever its status in relation to psychiatric illness, dementia is often regarded as unique. For example, Cohler and colleagues (1989) suggest that Alzheimer's disease is distinct from all other disorders because of the sufferer's lack of agency: 'Patients with Alzheimer's disease display behaviour that is socially unacceptable and inappropriate, and yet is completely beyond [their] responsibility' (p. 52).

The social definition of dementia

The view of the behaviour of people with dementia as beyond the realm of their responsibility is one that sees the disorder as largely incapable of being influenced by factors other than biological ones. Kitwood (1993), however, has suggested that 'overly deterministic and pessimistic' views of dementia have dominated the field for too long. He criticizes the view of the disease process as having an inexorable course in which 'the person has almost totally disappeared' (p. 541). As the previous section indicates, there is uncertainty as to the extent to which factors additional to physiological and pathological processes contribute to the manifestation and course of dementia (Kitwood, 1988; and see Gilhooly, 1984, for a review of earlier work). Even those who are firmly of the opinion that dementia is distinct from the ageing process (for example Roth, 1994) suspect that the degree to which handicaps express themselves more or less severely may be influenced by such factors as personality, personal history and life situation (Roth, 1977). Clues may also be found in the social settings and relationships in which dementia occurs and which are 'seldom examined in relation to their contribution to dementia' (Lyman, 1989, p. 597) or in psychosocial states involving helplessness and loss of control (Henry, 1986). Kitwood (1987, 1990) sees dementia as 'societal pathology', a consequence of 'pernicious ageism', which has been reduced to individual pathology and dealt with by socio-technical means that leave out the subjective experience of people who are old and confused. Those who are dementing are subject to the highly damaging effects of stigmatization, disempowerment, infantilization, invalidation and banishment. In a later paper, he points to experimental work showing better outcomes for dementing people as a result of care practices 'which are conducive to the maintenance of self-worth, agency and social confidence' (1993, p. 543; see also Robertson, 1990; Bond, 1992; McGregor & Bell, 1993).

However, it has been pointed out that the separation of dementia (especially in the form defined as Alzheimer's disease) from normal ageing usefully serves the purposes of medical research as well as attracting funds to assist sufferers and their families (Fox, 1989; Grimley Evans, 1990; Miller *et al.* 1992). Such a separation can also be seen as a response to the need of those involved to find an explanation for, and a meaning in, the troubles which commonly arise in old age (Gubrium, 1986).

DEMENTIA IN NON-WESTERN SOCIETIES

Questions about the aetiology of dementia and the contribution to it of social and cultural factors might be answered by comparisons with societies which are very different from each other. 'If it could be established that there are differences between countries in the occurrence of Alzheimer's or vascular dementias, this would be an important clue to the aetiology of these disorders' (Jorm, 1991, p. 240). However, data about distribution, aetiology, and risk factors in the non-Western world are sparse (Osuntokun *et al.* 1991; Chandra *et al.* 1994). What data

there are suggest that dementia is widespread, although it may manifest itself differently and at different rates (see Li *et al.* 1989; Maeda *et al.* 1989; White, 1992).[3]

Prevalence studies have been carried out in a number of countries including China (Li *et al.* 1989), Thailand (Kammant *et al.* 1991), India (Rajkumar *et al.* 1993), Korea (Park *et al.* 1994) and Brazil (Veras & Murphy, 1994).[4] These studies have found some differences in respect of gender, education, socio-economic status and rural/urban living, but in no case was it clear whether these were real differences or due to the methods employed.[5] Researchers in Nigeria have stated that there is neither bio-logical nor clinical evidence for the existence of Alzheimer's disease: 'No authentic case of AD has been reported in an indigenous Black African' (Osuntokun *et al.* 1991, p. 346) al-though cases of vascular dementia have been found (and see Ogunniyi *et al.* 1992). Yet, the prevalence of Alzheimer's disease in Black Americans in the USA, who are predominantly of West African origin, has been found to be as high as, or even higher than, in Americans of European origin (Osuntokun *et al.* 1991). A more recent study comparing Nigerians and Americans of 'similar ethnic heritage' succeeded in finding cases of Alzheimer's disease in Nigeria but the prevalence appeared to be significantly lower than in the United States (Hendrie *et al.* 1994).

There is even less information on the disorders of old age in traditional societies and among indigenous groups than for non-Western so-cieties generally. In the few studies that have been done, findings vary. For example, Alzheimer's disease appeared to be rare among Cree Indians, although other forms of dementia were not (Hendrie *et al.* 1993). A survey of Australian Aborigines aged 65 and over found high levels of cognitive impairment, indicative of a high prevalence of dementia (Zann, 1994).[6]

PROBLEMS FOR RESEARCH IN NON-WESTERN SOCIETIES

The work that has been done on the disorders of old age in non-Western countries has been based largely on Western biomedical categories, using Western measures. Incidence, prevalence, clini-cal and neuropathological studies are all needed to establish the universality of dementia as well as differences in distribution, aetiology and risk factors within and across cultures. There are problems with each of these approaches, however: no single approach can meet all the necessary criteria of representativity and diagnostic validity (Jorm, 1991).[7] All these approaches are likely to encounter a lack of standardization in diagnoses (Evans, 1992; White, 1992). And while the internationally accepted diagnostic manuals, ICD-10 and DSM-IV, indicate that there is considerable agreement on diagnostic criteria and methods of assessment (Henderson, 1993) – that is, agreement about what is to be called dementia – the interpretation of such criteria may vary within different cultural contexts.

Researchers undertaking incidence and prevalence studies in non-Western settings, in addition to problems relating to cost and resource restrictions, have encountered problems in collecting data based on interviews: for example, the tendency for informants to give answers that 'they think are "acceptable" to the interviewer, rather than the true response' (Andrews *et al.* 1986, p. 18; Fox, 1994; Kleiner, 1994); the expectation that questions be addressed to the head of the household or tribe (Andrews *et al.* 1986); the reluctance of women to answer questions in front of their husbands (Blakemore, 1990); and, resistance to being questioned 'about private things' (Zann, 1994, p. 16).

Studies based on clinic populations may not be representative of the wider society from which they are drawn or comparable to other societies. Cultural variations in the meaning of abnormality may affect referrals for or decisions to seek medical assistance (Biernoff, 1984; Good & Kleinman, 1985). Thus, people with dementia will not appear in clinics if their relatives do not perceive them as dementing or are fatalistic about decline in old age (Chandra *et al.* 1994). Even where there is agreement that particular signs or symptoms are abnormal there may be differences in the meanings attached to them. If, for example, dementia represents shame and stigma, the problems may be concealed (Maeda *et al.* 1989). Powerful precepts of filial piety may inhibit sons and daughters from taking a parent with dementia to see a psychiatrist (Sung, 1990). Where advanced dementia is seen as psychiatric

illness or 'madness', help-seeking may be inhibited by fear of supernatural influences or of possible detrimental effects on the family (Kiefer, 1987; Lock, 1987; Lien, 1993).

Neuropathological studies are generally considered to have the greatest diagnostic validity (Jorm, 1991) although some research has demonstrated poor correlation between ante-mortem and post-mortem diagnoses (Crystal *et al.* 1988; Kitwood, 1988; White, 1992). This could be because of variations in the methods and criteria adopted by neuropathologists (Brayne, 1993) or because the structural changes in the brain that occur in dementia are also observed in the 'normal aged brain', albeit to a lesser extent (Bayles & Kaszniak, 1987; and see Stafford, 1992). It could also be because of unreliable ante-mortem data. Not all people diagnosed as dementing will have this information recorded at the time of death (Burns *et al.* 1990*b*; Cordner, 1992).[8]

Neuropathological studies are also likely to be based on non-representative samples since not all patients diagnosed with dementia will undergo post-mortem examination (Jorm, 1991). Reasons will vary, but clearly in some societies cultural and religious factors will prevent access to bodies after death. Orthodox Judaism and some Islamic sects forbid autopsy, for example (Geller, 1984).

Few neuropathological studies of dementia have been done in the non-Western world (with the exception of Japan (Jorm, 1991) and the Nigerian autopsy survey referred to above).[9] While the major world religions do not officially object to autopsy procedures, apart from the exceptions cited above (Geller, 1984), there is a paucity of information on the influence of other cultural and social factors on attitudes to post-mortem examination of the brain, especially in traditional societies. The reasons attributed to declining autopsy rates in the Western world (Geller, 1984; Cordner, 1992; RCPA, 1994) – for example, less people dying in hospital; increasing reluctance of health professionals to seek permission for autopsy from bereaved relatives and of bereaved relatives to grant it because of objections to interference with, and mutilation of, the body (Brown, 1984; Wakeford & Stepney, 1989; Murphy, 1990) – may well apply in non-Western cultures, particularly in relation to body mutilation and the implications for the after-life, or where there might be fears of disturbing the soul or angering the spirit. However, dissection of the body for funeral and ritual purposes is or was until recently practised in some societies.[10] While increasing education levels and acceptance of Western medical models will influence local attitudes, many of the factors that act as obstacles – for both relatives and health professionals – to the 'harvesting' of brains and other organs for medical research are likely to apply in non-Western societies. Thus definitive neuropathological evidence may not be easy to acquire.

CULTURAL AND SOCIAL FACTORS WHICH MAY ACT AS IMPEDIMENTS TO TESTING FOR AND ASSESSMENT OF DEMENTIA

In addition to the general problems associated with research on elderly populations, such as illness and sensory loss, there are problems which are likely to be more common in non-Western societies (Andrews *et al.* 1986), particularly in semi-literate or non-literate populations. Apart from the fact that people may not know their chronological age, thus making the delineation of study populations difficult, the process of assessment itself may be resisted. For example, the study of the prevalence of cognitive impairment in older Australian Aboriginal people (cited above) found that the test was considered by many to be 'childish' and 'silly' (Zann, 1994). Questions about personal characteristics and individual qualities used in some informant questionnaires may be meaningless or unacceptable, for example: 'Aboriginal people think about particular instances rather than general qualities [thus] questions should be specific and impersonal ... [They] are reluctant to speak *for* other people; they seem to feel it is presumptuous to make statements about other people. They might give particular instances rather than broad characterizations of personality and behaviour. At most they may make tentative generalizations. They dislike asking other people direct questions, it causes resentment' (Kearins, personal communication, and see Kearins, 1985).[11]

As Kleiner (1994) points out, measurement assumes that individuals think in precise terms and this may not be the case in all cultural contexts. For example 'the value of the data and conclusions will vary considerably', even though procedural operations may be identical, depending on whether these are being collected in a culture where telling the truth is highly valued or in one where 'lying' in order to present a more favourable image is condoned (p. 59).

Cultural bias in Western-designed tests

Both DSM-IV and ICD-10 require impairment to be sufficient to interfere with normal social and occupational activities. Difficulties arise in determining what are culturally appropriate 'activities of daily living' as well as what is considered to be normal performance of such activities. As Loewenstein and colleagues (1994) point out, 'the scarcity of solid normative data for many culturally diverse groups leads to significant problems' (p. 624). In India, for example, limited demands may be made on dependent elderly people living in extended families. If old people are not expected to do intellectually demanding jobs such as banking, or physically demanding jobs such as shopping or housekeeping, they may not be seen, even when markedly demented, to be functionally disabled (Chandra, personal communication). Loeweinstein and colleagues (1992, 1993), in two studies comparing Spanish-speaking (mainly Cuban) and English-speaking Americans with dementia on a range of neuropsychological tests, found that the former were at a disadvantage 'and may produce potentially misleading results unless a subject's performance is compared with adequate data bases that account for age, educational attainment, and cultural background' (1993, p. 148). Such factors as lack of 'task familiarity' (1992, p. 393) and 'different strategies for chunking data' (1993, p. 148) were considered to be possible contributors to lower scores for the Spanish-speaking group.

In the study of cognitive impairment in Australian Aborigines in northern Queensland, the researchers found that questions associated with memory loss and depression were relatively unproblematical but that there were difficulties with questions on language and comprehension as well as with those on general knowledge. On this last point, the researchers had difficulty in selecting suitable local information on geography and in finding generally known names of celebrities to be used in the test. For example, people in the more isolated communities had not heard of the 'country-and-Western' singer who had been chosen because of his popularity with more urbanized Aboriginal people (Zann, personal communication). People living in 'the environmental adversity of the slum' in Thailand 'did not think it relevant to know the name of the prime minister... and were ignorant of the date' (Kammant et al. 1991. p. 644). Twenty-five per cent of Santa Cruz residents did not know the name of the Brazilian President compared with around 5% in the New York and London survey who did not know the names of the US President and the British Prime Minister respectively (Veras & Murphy. 1994). The conclusion of Veras and Murphy is that 'much future development work needs to be carried out among populations with poor educational levels to produce a socially and culturally sensitive screening instrument' (p. 290).

Problems identified by researchers using Western-designed tests included: lack of task familiarity, for example, drawing or copying a diagram for people not used to handling writing instrument (Andrews et al. 1986; Zann, 1994); differences in category meanings. for example 'Western distinctions between "friends". "neighbours" and "relatives" may either have no meaning or carry different meanings in different Asian communities' (Blakemore. 1990, p. 169); and difficulties with abstract or numerical concepts, particularly with the commonly used subtraction task (Kearins, 1989; Chandra et al. 1994).[12] Other commonly included questions require the identification of specific months or seasons according to the Western calendar. But in some cultures seasons are not fixed but variable periods – 'wet', 'dry', 'long', 'short', 'hot', 'cool', with heavy or light rain, etc. (McRoberts, 1990; Ganguli & Ratcliff, 1995). In remote Aboriginal cultures, for example, time may be conceived of in terms of natural events rather than fixed, abstract months: 'the time of frosted grass, the time when native cherries ripen' (Murray, 1985, p. 20), or 'the time when the lizards are sleeping' (Kearins, personal communication).

There may also be difficulties in obtaining an 'informant history', an essential part of many instruments used to identify dementia. Information is usually obtained from a spouse, child or other family member, but as White (1992) points

out 'Their expectations as to what comprises usual activities and relationships are likely to be strongly influenced by cultural factors. their relationship to the subject [a spouse may have different expectations than a child]. and personal characteristics of both the subject and the informant [sex, age. education]. This criterion [that is, of significant interference with work or usual social activity] is very difficult to apply equally across national populations as well as among groups within nations' (p. 461; and see Evans. 1992). In Thailand. for example, researchers found that the informant history, based on the Blessed Behaviour Rating Scale. showed poor sensitivity, missing 'a third of cases of dementia at best' (Kammant et al. 1991. p. 644). The usefulness of informant reports of psychiatric symptoms in Alzheimer's disease has been questioned by Seltzer & Buswell (1994). These authors make the assumption – an assumption that this paper sets out to question – that dementia is separable from the way it is perceived and experienced by others. They state that 'Respondents have no technical expertise so that a variety of social. cultural, and educational factors may influence how they report psychiatric symptoms. Emotional involvement with the patient may also color their responses' (p. 103).

In summary, the evidence from research in non-Western societies does indicate that dementia is a worldwide phenomenon. As White (1992) points out 'When an effort has been made to identify cases, dementia has been found among older persons in all or nearly all populations' (p. 457). It could thus be included among those disorders considered by Kleinman (1988) to be 'significantly constrained by shared psychobiological processes so that their form bears a resemblance in different societies' (p. 51). Researchers looking at dementia have, however, been less successful in demonstrating Kleinman's further point that such disorders are also characterized by 'significant differences... owing to cultural context' (p. 51).

The findings on differences between countries and between the developed and developing worlds are inconclusive. There is a suggestion, for example, that prevalence is 'currently low in many developing countries' (Osuntokun et al. 1991, p. 345; see also Li et al. 1989), but is the variation found due to differences in relative incidence or in relative survival (Jorm, 1991; Evans, 1992)? Several factors are suspected of contributing to the differences that have been found, such as lifestyle, economic deprivation, education, socioeconomic status, and environmental and occupational pollutants (Osuntokun *et al.* 1991; Henderson, 1993; Park *et al.* 1994), but these have not been confirmed. Clarification is needed on how much the differences found are due to the natural variation in the disease and how much to differences in definition and in methods of assessment. The researchers themselves acknowledge the difficulties in separating differences attributable to cultural, social or economic factors from those resulting from the methods used. The problem is clearly stated by Veras & Murphy (1994), who suggest that while 'It may well prove to be the case that there really is significantly more dementia in the elderly [who] have lived their lives in circumstances of exceptional hardship' (p. 291), the findings from their study may be 'almost wholly spurious' because of the way cognitive impairment is 'identified by tests of memory, general knowledge, use of language and comprehension which depend to a large extent on education and cultural values attached to some kinds of information' (p. 290) (see Mortimer, 1990, for problems in comparing existing prevalence studies for cross-cultural purposes).

SOME RECENTLY DEVELOPED INSTRUMENTS FOR CROSS-CULTURAL RESEARCH

In response to the problems arising from the application of Western methods to non-Western societies, some attempts have been made to find neuropsychological tests that are applicable outside the Western world yet are not so locally specific that they cannot be used comparatively. The Fuld Object–Memory Evaluation was an early attempt to minimize cultural bias in mental status tests (Fuld *et al.* 1988). The World Health Organization has a cross-national programme to develop research protocols which have universal application (Osuntokun *et al.* 1991). Other initiatives include the American-designed Cross-Cultural Cognitive Examination which has been validated in Japan (Wolfe *et al.* 1992); the Cognitive Abilities and Screening Instrument

(CASI) used, for example, in Guam (Waring *et al.* 1994) and in a study of Japanese-American men in Honolulu (White *et al.* 1994); and a community screening instrument (CSI 'D') developed for use with the Cree, and subsequently in Indianapolis and Ibadan (Hall *et al.* 1994). Efforts are also being made to develop instruments appropriate to specific cultures. There is a Japanese version of DSM-III (Honda, 1983). In India, a screening instrument for use with illiterate populations has been designed (Ganguli & Ratcliff, 1995) as well as an India-specific Activities of Daily Living Scale (Chandra *et al.* 1994) (see also Beall & Eckert (1986) for strategies for measuring functional status cross-culturally in relation to dementing illness, and also work on 'culture fair' neuropsychological testing for people from diverse language and cultural groups by Loewenstein *et al.* (1994)).

EMIC OR FOLK VIEWS OF DEMENTIA: A MISSING PERSPECTIVE

From an anthropological point of view, a particularly striking aspect of studies using Western categories and research techniques in non-Western societies is the omission of indigenous or lay views of decline in old age. The failure to incorporate 'meaning-centred accounts', either ethnographic or clinical, into survey methods or to relate them to epidemiological findings (Good & Kleinman, 1985) results in there being almost no information on how dementia is popularly perceived or understood. The researchers themselves sometimes indicate an awareness of a discrepancy between their views and those of the local population under study (Leff, 1990; Littlewood, 1990; Chandra *et al.* 1994).

Because of the absence of this perspective, it is difficult to determine the extent to which social and cultural factors shape the ways in which dementia manifests itself or is seen by others. If, as suggested by some writers cited above (see 'The social definition of dementia'), negative experiences of old age influence the manifestation and course of dementing disorders in Western societies, it would be reasonable to suppose that the putatively more positive experiences of and attitudes to old age in non-Western societies (Fortes, 1984; Sankar, 1984; Apt, 1990) would also be reflected in the ways in which decline in old age was treated. The problem is lack of evidence. In non-Western societies where old age is frequently defined in functional terms (that is, if you can still work you are not old), loss of capacity is intrinsic to old age and therefore not seen as abnormal (Holmes, 1983). Alternatively, behaviour associated with advanced dementia may be seen as illness or madness rather than as a consequence of old age. The response of others will vary according to the interpretation of the disorder and of its cause: whether it is seen as externally inflicted – by a malevolent spirit or malicious human being – or as resulting from breach of taboo or moral infringement (Murphy, 1994). If the cause is thought to be of external origin, the disturbed behaviour may be treated with greater tolerance.

There is very little information about disordered old age and the ways it is viewed in traditional societies. Ethnographic accounts suggesting that people who survived into old age may have fared relatively well have sometimes neglected to distinguish between attitudes towards and treatment of old people (Glascock & Feinman, 1986) or between healthy, active old age and physically or mentally impaired old age (Counts & Counts, 1985a; Barker, 1990). Nevertheless, it appears that the distinction between 'intact' and 'decrepit' elderly people is universal (Keith & Kertzer, 1984). In his pioneering work on old people, Simmons (1960) examined a large number of traditional societies and concluded that 'Among all peoples a point is reached in aging at which any further usefulness appears to be over, and the incumbent is regarded as a living liability. "Senility" may be a suitable label for this' (p. 87). It is the 'intact' elderly who are likely to be accorded high status and deference and who have been the subject of most of the work on the anthropology of old age. However, other research has indicated that even in those societies in which old age is honoured, old people may be mistreated or even killed if they enter the decrepit category (Maxwell et al. 1982; Glascock & Feinman, 1986).[13]

The redefinition from intact to decrepit 'does indeed seem to be associated with "usefulness"', that is, whether an old person is symbolically or instrumentally useful to other members of the society (Maxwell et al. 1982, p. 80). It may also depend on individual factors, such as emotional attachment and whether there is a supportive family (Counts & Counts, 1985b; Barker, 1990). It may also be negotiable according to the status, power and influence that the individual holds (Counts & Counts, 1985a). Accounts of mistreatment and death-hastening behaviour have sometimes failed to distinguish between physical weakness and mental impairment (Maxwell et al. 1982), that is, to draw a distinction between geronticide and 'senilicide' (to use a term that has fallen into disuse). The former involves the killing of the physically frail, who themselves may play a part, or so it is suggested, in the decision to end their lives, for example, among the Eskimo (Balikci, 1970), while the latter involves the killing of those who, by virtue of their cognitive decline, have lost the ability to influence their fate. The Marind Amin of South New Guinea, for example, were buried alive by their children when they became 'helpless and senescent' (Van Baal cited in Counts & Counts, 1985a, p. 13). Hart et al. (1988) describe a similar practice among the Tiwi of northern Australia.[14]

It is the mentally impaired who are more likely to be pronounced 'socially dead' (Counts & Counts, 1985a). Throughout Melanesia it is or was common for the decrepit elderly to be classified with the dead and for this classification to be embodied in both language and behaviour: 'loss of the animating spirit, the soul, of the self, occurs while the body is still vital. The person is, however, socially dead and…no apparent significance is attached to the body once it ceases to be a container for the spirit [and it] may be treated as though it were a corpse' (Counts & Counts, 1985a, p. 17).

Barker's (1990) research on the treatment of the decrepit elderly on the island of Niue in Polynesia is a rare example of a study of disordered old age in a traditional society. She found that the people among whom she worked drew a distinction between those who should be cared for and those who should be left. While some elderly people received medical attention and were admitted to hospital, others were less fortunate. Those who were left unattended or received minimal care were those who 'yelled constantly, swearing at neighbours and kin; those who fought all the time, hitting out at all and sundry; those who wandered away at all times of day and night; those who talked only of events in the remote past, who conversed with absent friends and long-dead relatives; those who stared vacantly about them, constantly drooled, or were incontinent' (p. 301). This description matches many Western descriptions of behaviour in advanced dementia.

Other ethnographic evidence suggests that symptoms or behaviour that could be attributable to dementia are regarded neither as disease nor as madness requiring special treatment. For example, Levy (1973) reported for the Tahitians of the Society Islands that senility was 'just something that happens' (p. 405), in contrast to more serious mental disorders, for which supernatural explanations were sought. Among the Iban of Sarawak, 'Dementia is different from madness, more ordinary and familiar'. These people do not employ elaborate explanations in terms of spirit invasion or ritual infringements neither do they carry out ritual activities for disorders in old age as they do for mental abnormality in younger people (Robert Barrett, personal communication). For the people of some Oceanic societies, decline in old age is part of 'the essential tragedy of human existence – senescence and death are preconditions for the perpetuation of life through birth' (Kelly, cited in Counts & Counts, 1985a, p. 18). People of New Britain (the Kabana and the Lusi) lose their mental strength in old age through giving over their knowledge and experience to the younger generation. This condition is termed '*buobuo*' – 'having immature or childlike thought processes' (Scaletta, 1985, p. 228). The Iban of Sarawak have a concept of 'silliness' (Barrett, personal communication) which appears to be similar to the concept of '*bengwar*' that Berndt & Berndt (1951) found in the Aboriginal people they worked among and also to the idea of 'silly in the head' that has been reported for Torres Strait Islanders (Fox, 1994). It is here rather than with madness that many forms of dementia appear to belong.

CONCLUSION

Definitions of mental disorder and abnormality in old age are culturally variable, as are definitions of old age itself. It follows, therefore, that dementia, in overlapping with both psychiatric illness and old age, will also vary with culture. All societies appear to distinguish between normal and abnormal old age, between 'intact' and 'decrepit' elderly people. However, the ways in which the distinctions are drawn vary greatly. A particular complicating factor with dementia arises from the fact that it cuts across these distinctions, that it is coterminous neither with abnormality nor with decrepitude. It is within these shifting and overlapping boundaries that cultural and social factors play a part.

Researchers have been more successful in demonstrating the commonality of dementia than its variations and the manner in which it differs across cultures and between social and ethnic groupings. This is partly because little research has been done as yet, and partly because the differences that have been found might be attributable to diagnostic differences and methodological artefacts. Attempts to remedy these problems are being made through collaborative research and the development of culture-fair instruments for assessment. Such instruments must cope with a condition of immense diversity, unpredictability and similarity to other conditions. Furthermore, the similarity of milder forms of dementia to normal old age makes the consequences inconspicuous and recognition difficult, while the similarity of more advanced forms to psychiatric illness raises other sorts of questions and problems. These depend on whether the disorder is seen as madness or sickness, requiring attention to causality, attribution and treatment, or as an inevitable consequence of old age for which nothing can or should be done. The lack of information about dementia in traditional societies, many of which have been the subject of intensive ethnographic study, suggests both an anthropological failure to look at how frail old people were treated and the absence of concepts of dementia-like disorders within such societies.

What is clear is that there is still much to be learned about the complex interaction between the experience of ageing and the onset of dementia, both in our own society and in others. While many questions remain about the relationship between ageing and dementia, and between dementia and culture, in Western societies, there is even more to discover about non-Western societies. Suggestions that the way in which the treatment and expectations of people with dementia in Western cultures influence the course of the disorder (Bond, 1992; Kitwood, 1993) need to be tested against treatment and expectations in other cultures, especially those where old age carries more prestige, power and security than in the West. Such differences may however be difficult to demonstrate because many non-Western societies are undergoing rapid social and economic transformation, through urbanization, Westernization, and the fragmentation of extended families. In addition, professional Western medicine is becoming increasingly dominant: 'It is thus not surprising that observed patterns of abnormal behaviour together with the beliefs and social responses associated with them tend increasingly to conform to Western examples' (Littlewood, 1990, p. 310). Looking back at the past and at societies that have resisted Westernization, we see that while life may have been or may still be kinder to those who are chronologically rather than functionally old (and therefore perhaps not defined as old), it was or is rather less kind to those who become dependent or 'decrepit'.

Most societies, Western and non-Western, appear able to accommodate mild dementia as part of the ageing process but, in one form or another, to exclude those whose dementia is marked. What varies between cultures are the definitions of mild and marked dementia and the thresholds separating them. These definitions and thresholds do not necessarily correspond to clinical diagnoses. The transition from 'normal' to 'abnormal' will depend on many factors: economic, social, emotional, psychological and cultural.

Cross-cultural research into old age and dementia, in addition to its potential usefulness to the societies in question, helps to develop an awareness of the cultural content of Western assumptions about old age and the disorders of old age as well as a critique of our forms of treatment and response 'through glimpsing ourselves in the mirror of the other' (Good, 1994, p. 27). Anthropology has a special contribution to make in these areas. In the case of dementia, it can help both conceptually and methodologically with questions of universality, cultural shaping, and social influences. It has a unique role in situations where indigenous or 'folk' concepts are important, in the elucidation both of normative or cultural meanings and of the particular meanings or 'explanatory models' for the people most affected. 'The anthropo-

logical vision can...aid the psychiatrist in moving back and forth between the perspectives of the patient, the family, the cultural chorus of onlookers, and his own medical models' (Kleinman, 1988, p. 171). But such an awareness is limited if it remains within the confines of a single society, especially a Western one. Establishing the similarities and, equally importantly, the differences in mental disorders across cultures is essential for disentangling the 'objective' phenomena from subjective experience and for seeing the extent to which such phenomena and experience are influenced by cultural and social factors (Reser, 1991). For a disorder such as dementia this would be of significant assistance in the search for risk factors and aetiological clues.

Finally, an 'anthropological' awareness of dementia as a social and cultural phenomenon adds an important dimension to scientific efforts to understand it in terms of its neuropathology: 'We commit the grossest philosophical errors in attempting to explain phenomena on the scale of culture and society with phenomena on the scale of gene loci or polypeptides. It is like trying to predict the outline of a cloud by analysing the molecular structure of water' (Dumont, 1993, p. 711).

The author would like to thank Professor A. S. Henderson and other colleagues at the NHMRC Social Psychiatry Research Unit at the Australian National University for their helpfulness and support, and Dr R. Barrett, Dr J. McCallum, Professor D. W. O'Connor, Dr N. Peterson and Professor I. R. Wright for comments on earlier drafts of this paper.

NOTES

1 There is considerable variation in this respect within the English-speaking countries. In Australia dementia is generally viewed as a problem for geriatricians, in Britain for psychiatrists, and in the United States for neurologists. In Australia, for example, many service providers draw a distinction between 'people with dementia and 'people with a psychiatric illness'. This distinction is enshrined in the NSW Mental Health Act, which distinguishes between disorders of the mind and diseases of the brain and includes dementia among the latter (Porter & Robinson, 1987).

2 Some studies, for example Sultzer *et al.* (1992) and Becker *et al.* (1994), have found that

psychopathology increased as cognitive function declined.

[3] It is not clear whether the variations that have been found are due to real differences or to 'diagnostic fashion' (Jorm, 1990). And see the review of dementia research by Brayne (1993) for difficulties in case definition and diagnoses in dementia.

[4] In most of the studies, local versions of the MMSE (Folstein *et al.* 1975) were used for screening purposes, and the criteria for dementia were based on DSM-III or DSM-III-R (American Psychiatric Association, 1980, 1988). Other instruments used included CAMDEX (Roth *et al.* 1986), GMS (Copeland *et al.* 1976), the CRBRS (Wilkin *et al.* 1978), the Blessed Dementia Scale (Blessed *et al.* 1968). Instruments used in the Brazilian study were the Brazil Old Age Schedule (BOAS) derived from the OARS (Duke University) and the PAHO (Pan-American Health Organization); and the mental health section from the CARE schedule designed by Gurland and colleagues (see Veras & Murphy, 1994).

[5] It should be noted that social class and education also affect cognitive test scores in Western countries (O'Connor *et al.* 1989*b*).

[6] Hendrie and colleagues used a selection of well-standardized tests drawn from the CAMDEX, the MMSE, the East Boston Memory Test, and the Blessed Activities of Daily Living Scale (see Hendrie *et al.* 1993). Zann used a modified version of the Psychogeriatric Assessment Scale (Jorm & McKinnon, 1994).

[7] In a review of cross-national comparisons of dementia, Jorm (1991) found that only Scandinavia, Britain and North America had data available on all four approaches.

[8] Beardsall *et al.* (1992) have sought to overcome some of the problems impeding neuropathological research by collecting brain tissue from a community sample of elderly people who have been extensively assessed before death. And see Burns *et al.* (1990*c*).

[9] This survey found no neuropathological changes such as senile plaques or neurofibrillary tangles in the brains of people aged over 65 (Osuntokun *et al.* 1991).

[10] The best known example is that of the people of the Highland villages of New Guinea who contracted *kuru* through contact with highly infectious brain tissue as part of their mourning rites (Gajdusek, 1990).

[11] In work unrelated to dementia but relevant to information-seeking in indigenous populations, Blurton-Jones & Konner (1976), writing of a Kalahari hunter-gathering society, found that the ways in which knowledge was transmitted from

person to person and acquired by individuals was markedly different from Western forms. They comment on 'the adverse reaction many people have to direct instruction. Not only can they become intimidated and confused ... [but they] can be irritated by and can disapprove of people who tell other people what to do or in any way set themselves above anyone else' (p. 345). These authors also cite evidence suggesting similar responses among Australian Aborigines.

[12] Ogunniyi *et al.* (1991) found that tasks requiring numerical calculation on their modified version of the MMSE were not influenced by educational levels.

[13] Maxwell *et al.* (1982) identified various forms of mistreatment of old people in the ethnographies of 91 societies analysed in their study of the determinants of status in old age. Acts of mistreatment ranged from grumbling about old people in their presence to denying them all food except scraps. 'Senile deterioration' was listed among the complaints warranting mistreatment (p. 70).

[14] Glascock (1990) makes it clear that death-hastening activities are not confined to traditional societies but also take place in modern Western societies such as the United States. He gives examples of elder abuse and of passive and active euthanasia (see also Dissenbacher, 1989).

REFERENCES

American Psychiatric Association (1980, 1988). *Diagnostic and Statistical Manual of Mental Disorders (revised)*. American Psychiatric Association: Washington, DC.

Andrews, G. R., Esterman, A. J., Braunack-Mayer, A. J. & Rungie, C. M. (1986). *Ageing in the Western Pacific: A Four-country Study*. World Health Organization: Manila.

Apt, N. A. (1990). The role of the family in the care of the elderly in developing countries. In *Improving the Health of Older People* (ed. R. L. Kane, J. Grimley Evans and D. Macfadyen), pp. 361–379. Published on behalf of the World Health Organization by Oxford University Press: Oxford.

Balikci, A. (1970). *The Netsilik Eskimo*. Natural History Press: New York.

Barker, J. C. (1990). Between humans and ghosts: the decrepit elderly in a Polynesian society. In *The Cultural Context of Aging* (ed. J. Sokolovsky), pp. 295–313. J. Bergen & Garvey: New York.

Bayles, K. A. & Kazniak, A. W. (1987). *Communication and Cognition in Normal Aging and Dementia*. Little Brown Co: Boston.

Beall, C. M. & Eckert, J. K. (1986). Measuring functional capacity cross-culturally. In *New Methods for Old-Age Research: Strategies for Studying Diversity* (ed. C. L. Fry and J. K. Keith), pp. 21–55. Bergin & Garvey: Massachusetts.

Beardsall, L., Barkley, C. & Sullivan, A. (1992). The response of elderly community residents to request for brain donation: an interim report. *International Journal of Geriatric Psychiatry* 7, 199–202.

Becker, D., Hershkowitz, M., Maidler, N., Rabinowitz, M. & Floru, S. (1994). Psychopathology and cognitive decline in dementia. *Journal of Nervous and Mental Disease* 182, 701–703.

Berndt, R. M. & Berndt, C. H. (1951). The concept of abnormality in Australian Aboriginal society. In *Psychoanalysis and Culture: Essays in Honour of Geza Roheim* (ed. G. B. Wilbur and W. Muensterbeign), pp. 75–89. International Universities Press: New York.

Biernoff, D. (1984). Psychiatric and anthropological interpretations of 'aberrant' behaviour in an Aboriginal community. In *Body, Land and Spirit: Health and Healing in Aboriginal Society* (ed. J. Reid), pp. 139–153. University of Queensland Press: St Lucia, Queensland.

Blakemore, K. (1990). Does age matter? The case of old age in minority ethnic groups. In *Becoming and Being Old: Sociological Approaches to Later Life* (ed. B. Bytheway, T. Keil, P. Allatt and A. Bryman), pp. 158–175. Sage: London.

Blessed, G., Tomlinson, B. E. & Roth, M. (1968). The association between quantitative measures of dementia and senile changes in the cerebal grey matter of elderly subjects. *British Journal of Psychiatry* **114**, 797–811.

Blurton-Jones, N. & Konner, M. J. (1976). Kung knowledge of animal behaviour. In *Kalahari Hunter-Gatherers: Studies of the !Kung San and their Neighbours* (ed. R. B. Lee and I. DeVore), pp. 326–348. Harvard University Press: Cambridge.

Bond, J. (1992). The medicalisation of dementia. *Journal of Aging Studies* **6**, 397–403.

Brayne, C. (1993). Research and Alzheimer's disease: an epidemiological perspective. *Psychological Medicine* **23**, 287–296.

Brown, H. G. (1984). Lay perceptions of autopsy. *Archives of Pathology and Laboratory Medicine* **108**, 446–448.

Burns, A., Jacoby, R. & Levy, R. (1990 *a*). Psychiatric phenomena in Alzheimer's disease I–IV, *British Journal of Psychiatry* **157**, 72–94.

Burns, A., Jacoby, R., Luthert, P. & Levy, R. (1990 *b*). Cause of death in Alzheimer's disease *Age and Ageing* **19**, 341–344.

Burns, A., Reith, M., Jacoby, R. & Levy, R. (1990 *c*). 'How to do it' – obtaining consent for autopsy in Alzheimer's disease. *International Journal of Geriatric Psychiatry* **5**. 283–286.

Chandra, V., Ganguli, M., Ratcliff, G., Pandav, R., Sharma, S., Gilby, J., Belle, S., Ryan, C., Baker, C., Seaberg, E., DeKosky, S. & Nath, L. (1994). Studies of the epidemiology of dementia: comparisons between developed and developing countries. *Aging: Clinical and Experimental Research* **6**. 307–321.

Cohler, B. J., Groves, L., Borden, W. & Lawrence, L. (1989). Caring for family members with Alzheimer's disease. In *Alzheimer's Disease Treatment and Family Stress: Directions for Research* (ed. E. Light and B. D. Lebowitz), pp. 50–105. US Department of Health and Human Services: Maryland.

Cooper, J. K., Mungas, D. & Weiler. P. G. (1990). Relation of cognitive status and abnormal behaviors in Alzheimer's disease. *Journal of the American Geriatrics Society* **38**, 867–870.

Copeland, J. R. M., Kelleher, M. J., Kellet, J. M., Gourlay, A. J., Gurland, B. J., Fleiss, J. M. & Sharpe, L. (1976). A semi-structured clinical interview for the assessment of diagnosis and mental state in the elderly: the Geriatric Mental State Schedule: development and reliability. *Psychological Medicine* **6**, 439–449.

Cordner, S. M. (1992). The autopsy in decline. *Medical Journal of Australia* **156**, 448.

Counts, D. A. & Counts, D. R. (1985*a*). Introduction: Linking concepts aging and gender, aging and death. In *Aging and its Transformations: Moving toward Death in Pacific Societies* (ed. D. A. Counts and D. R. Counts), pp. 1–24. University Press of America: Lanham.

Counts, D. A. & Counts, D. R. (1985*b*). I'm not dead yet! Aging and death: process and experience in Kaliai. In *Aging and its Transformations: Moving toward Death in Pacific Societies* (ed. D. A. Counts and D. R. Counts), pp. 131–155. University Press of America: Lanham.

Crystal, H., Dickson, D., Fuld, P., Masur, D., Scott, R., Mehler, M., Masdeu, J., Kawas, C., Aronson, M. & Wolfson, L. (1988). Clinico-pathologic studies in dementia: nondemented subjects with pathologically confirmed Alzheimer's disease. *Neurology* **38**, 1682–1687.

Dissenbacher, H. (1989). Neglect, abuse and the taking of life in old people's homes. *Ageing and Society* **9**, 61–71.

Dumont, M. P. (1993). Book review. *Social Science and Medicine* **36**, 711–712.

Evans, D. A. (1992). Alzheimer's disease – where will we find the etiologic clues? Challenges and opportunities in cross-cultural studies. *Ethnicity and Stress* **2**, 321–325.

Folstein, M. F., Folstein, S. E. & McHugh, P. R. (1975). 'Mini-Mental State': a practical method for grading the cognitive state of patients for the clinician. *Journal of Psychiatric Research* **12**, 189–198.

Fortes, M. (1984). Age, generation, and social structure. In *Age and Anthropological Theory* (ed. D. I. Kertzer and J. Keith), pp. 99–122. Cornell University Press: Ithaca.

Fox, D. (1994). How can the family help itself alleviate the crisis in the Aboriginal and Torres Strait community? In *Alzheimer's Association Australia, 4th National Conference – A Family Crisis: The Positive and Negative Sides of Caring*, pp. 243–247. Sydney, Australia 10–13 April 1994.

Fox, P. (1989). From senility to Alzheimer's disease: the rise of the Alzheimer's disease movement. *Milbank Quarterly* **67**, 58–101.

Fuld, P. A., Muramoto, O., Blau, A., Westbrook, L. & Katzman, R. (1988). Cross-cultural and multi-ethnic dementia evaluation by mental status and memory testing. *Cortex* **24**, 511–519.

Gajdusek, D. C. (1990). Subacute spongiform encephalies. In *Virology*, vol. 2 (ed. B. N. Fields and D. M. Knipe), pp. 2289–2324. Raven Press: New York.

Ganguli, M. & Ratcliff, G. (1995). A Hindi version of the MMSE: the development of a cognitive screening instrument for a largely illiterate rural elderly population in India. *International Journal of Geriatric Psychiatry* **10**, 367–377.

Geller, S. A. (1984). Religious attitudes and the autopsy. *Archives of Pathology and Laboratory Medicine* **108**, 494–496.

Gilhooly, M. (1984). The social dimensions of senile dementia. In *Psychological Approaches to the Care of the Elderly* (ed. I. Hanley and J. Hodge), pp. 88–135. Croom Helm: London.

Glascock, A. P. (1990). By any other name, it is still killing: a comparison of the treatment of the elderly in America and other societies. In *The Cultural Context of Aging* (ed. J. Sokolovsky), pp. 43–56. Bergen & Garvey: New York.

Glascock, A. P. & Feinman, S. L. (1986). Treatment of the aged in nonindustrial societies. In *New Methods for Old-Age Research: Strategies for Studying Diversity* (ed. C. L. Fry and J. K. Keith). pp. 281–296. Bergin & Garvey: Massachusetts.

Good, B. J. (1994). *Medicine, Rationality, and Experience: An Anthropological Perspective.* Cambridge University Press: Cambridge.

Good, B. & Kleinman, A. (1985). Epilogue: culture and depression. In *Culture and Depression: Studies in the Anthropology and Cross-Cultural Psychiatry of Affect and Disorder* (ed. A. Kleinman and B. Good), pp. 491–505. University of California Press: Berkeley.

Grimley Evans, J. (1990). How the elderly are different. In *Improving the Health of Older People* (ed. R. L. Kane, J. Grimley Evans and D. Macfadyen), pp. 50–68. Published on behalf of the World Health Organization by Oxford University Press: Oxford.

Gubrium, J. (1986). *Oldtimers and Alzheimer's: The Descriptive Organisation of Senility*. JAI Press Inc: Connecticut.

Hall, K., Ogunnyi, A., Hendrie, H., Osuntokun, B., Hui, S., Unverzagt, F. & Baiyewu, O. (1994). Community screening for dementia in Indianapolis and Ibadan, Nigeria. *Neurobiology of Aging* **15**, suppl. 1, p. S42.

Hart, C. W. M., Pilling, A. R. & Goodale, J. C. (1988). *The Tiwi of North Australia*. Holt, Rinehart and Winston: New York.

Henderson, A. S. (1993). *Dementia: World Mental Health Situation Report*. Prepared for the Division of Mental Health, World Health Organization: Geneva.

Hendrie, H., Hall, K., Pillay, N., Rodgers, D., Prince, C., Norton, J., Brittain, H., Nath, A., Blue, A., Kaufert, J., Shelton. P., Postl, B. & Osuntokun, B. (1993). Alzheimer's disease is rare in Cree. *International Psychogeriatrics* **5**, 5–14.

Hendrie, H., Osuntokun, B., Hall, K., Ogunniyi, A., Farlow, M., Gurege, O., Unverzagt, F., Baiyewu, O., Hui, S. and the Indianapolis/Ibadan Team (1994). A comparison of the prevalence of dementia and Alzheimer's disease in community dwelling residents of Ibadan, Nigeria and Indianapolis, USA. *Neurobiology of Aging* 15, Supplement 1.

Henry, J. P. (1986). Relation of psychosocial factors to the senile dementias. In *The Dementias: Policy and Management* (ed. M. Gilhooly), pp. 38–65. Prentice-Hall: New Jersey.

Holmes, L. D. (1983). *Other Cultures. Elder Years.* Burgess Publishing Company: Minneapolis.

Honda, Y. (1983). DSM-III in Japan. In *International Perspectives on DSM-III* (ed. R. L. Spitzer, B. W. Williams and A. E. Skodol), pp. 185–201. American Psychiatric Press: Washington, DC.

Huppert, F. A. & Brayne, C. (1994). What is the relationship between dementia and normal aging? In *Dementia and Normal Aging.* (ed. F. A. Huppert, C. Brayne & D. W. O'Connor), pp. 3–11. Cambridge University Press: Cambridge.

Jorm, A. F. (1990). *The Epidemiology of Alzheimer's Disease and Related Disorders.* Chapman and Hall: London.

Jorm, A. F. (1991). Cross-national comparisons of the occurrence of Alzheimer's and vascular dementias. *European Archives of Psychiatry and Clinical Neuroscience* 240, 218–222.

Jorm, A. F. & Henderson, A. S. (1985). Possible improvements of the diagnostic criteria for dementia in DSM-III. *British Journal of Psychiatry* 147, 394–399.

Jorm, A. F. & Mackinnon, A. (1994). *Psychogeriatric Assessment Scales.* ANUTECH: Canberra.

Kammant, P., Sutthichai, J., Chitr, S., Srichitra, C. & Shah, E. (1991). Prevalence of dementia in an urban slum population in Thailand: validity of screening methods. *International Journal of Geriatric Psychiatry* 6, 639–646.

Kearins, J. (1985). Cross-cultural misunderstandings in education. In *Cross-cultural Encounters: Communication and Mis-communication* (ed. J. B. Pride), pp. 65–80. River Seine Publications: Melbourne.

Kearins, J. (1989). Measurement and direction knowledge in Aboriginal and non-Aboriginal children of Western Australia. In *Heterogeneity in Cross Cultural Psychology* (ed. D. M. Keots, D. Munro & L. Mann), pp. 274–283. Swets & Zeitlinger: Amsterdam.

Keith, J. & Kertzer, D. I. (1984). Introduction. In *Age and Anthropological Theory* (ed. D. I. Kertzer and J. Keith), pp. 19–61. Cornell University Press: Ithaca.

Kiefer, C. (1987). Care of the aged in Japan. In *Health, Illness and Medical Care in Japan* (ed. E. Norbeck and M. Lock), pp. 89–109. University of Hawaii Press: Honolulu.

Kitwood, T. (1987). Dementia and its pathology: in brain, mind or society? *Free Associations* 8, 81–93.

Kitwood, T. (1988). The technical, the personal, and the framing of dementia. *Social Behaviour* 3, 161–179.

Kitwood, T. (1990). The dialectics of dementia – with particular reference to Alzheimer's disease. *Ageing and Society* 10, 177–196.

Kitwood, T. (1993). Person and process in dementia. *International Journal of Geriatric Psychiatry* 8, 541–545.

Kleiner, J. (1995). Discussion of J. M. Murphy: 'Anthropology and psychiatric epidemiology'. *Acta Psychiatrica Scandinavica* 90, 58–60.

Kleinman, A. (1988). *Rethinking Psychiatry: From Cultural Category to Personal Experience.* The Free Press: New York.

Leff, J. (1990). The 'New Cross-Cultural Psychiatry'. A case of the baby and the bathwater. *British Journal of Psychiatry* 156, 305–307.

Levy, R. I. (1973). *Tahitians: Mind and Experience in the Society Islands.* University of Chicago Press: Chicago.

Li, G., Shen, Y. C., Chen, C. H., Zhao, Y. W., Li, S. R. & Lu, M. (1989). An epidemiological survey of age-related dementia in an urban area of Beijing. *Acta Psychiatrica Scandinavica* 79, 557–563.

Lien, O. (1993). Attitudes of the Vietnamese community towards mental illness. *Australasian Psychiatry* 1, 110–112.

Littlewood, R. (1990). From categories to contexts: a decade of the 'New Cross-Cultural Psychiatry'. *British Journal of Psychiatry* 156, 308–327.

Lock, M. (1987). Protests of a Good Wife and Wise Mother: the medicalisation of distress in Japan. In *Health, Illness and Medical Care in Japan* (ed. E. Norbeck and M. Lock), pp. 130–156. University of Hawaii Press: Honolulu.

Loewenstein, D. A., Ardila, A., Rosselli, M., Hayden, S., Duara, R., Berkowitz, N., Linn-Fuentes, P., Mintzer, J., Norville, M. & Eisdorfer, C. (1992). A comparative analysis of functional status among Spanish- and English-speaking patients with dementia. *Journal of Gerontology* 47, 389–394.

Loewenstein, D. A., Argüelles, T., Barker, W. W. & Duara, R. (1993). A comparative analysis of neuropsychological test performance of Spanish-speaking and English-speaking patients with Alzheimer's disease. *Journal of Gerontology* 48, 142–149.

Loewenstein, D. A., Argüelles, T., Argüelles, S. & Linn-Fuentes, P. (1994). Potential cultural bias in the neuropsychological assessment of the older adult. *Journal of Clinical and Experimental Neuropsychology* 16, 623–629.

Lyman, K. A. (1989). Bringing the social back in: a critique of the biomedicalisation of dementia. *Gerontologist* 29, 597–605.

Macfadyen, D. (1990). International demographic trends. In *Improving the Health of Older People: A World View* (ed. R. L. Kane, J. Grimley Evans and D. Macfadyen), pp. 19–29. Published on behalf of the World Health Organization by Oxford University Press: Oxford.

McGregor, I. & Bell, J. (1993). Voyage of discovery. *Nursing Times* 89, 29–31.

McRoberts, R. (1990). Counting at Pularumpi. *The Aboriginal Child at School: A National Journal for Teachers of Aborigines* 18, 19–43.

Maeda, D., Teshima, K., Sugisawa, H. & Asakura, Y. S. (1989). Ageing and Health in Japan. *Journal of Cross-Cultural Gerontology* 4, 143–162.

Maxwell, R. J., Silverman, P. & Maxwell, E. K. (1982). The movement for gerontocide. *Studies in Third World Societies* 22, 67–84.

Mendez, M. F., Martin, R. J., Smyth, K. A. & Whitehouse, P. J. (1990). Psychiatric symptoms associated with Alzheimer's disease. *Journal of Neuropsychiatry* 2, 28–33.

Merriam, A. E., Aronson, M. K., Gaston, P., Wey, S. L. & Katz, I. (1988). The psychiatric symptoms of Alzheimer's disease. *American Geriatrics Society* 36, 7–12.

Miller, B., Glasser, M. & Rubin, S. (1992). A paradox of medicalization: physicians, families and Alzheimer's disease. *Journal of Aging Studies* 6, 135–148.

Mortimer, J. A. (1990). Epidemiology of Dementia: cross-cultural comparison. In *Advances in Neurology. Alzheimer's Disease, vol 51* (ed. R. J. Wurtman, S. Corkin, J H. Crowdon and E. Ritter-Walker), pp. 27–33. Raven Press: New York.

Murphy, E. (1990). Brains for biochemical research. *International Journal of Geriatric Psychiatry* 5, 281–282.

Murphy, J. M. (1994). Anthropology and psychiatric epidemiology. *Acta Psychiatrica Scandinavica* 90, 48–57.

Murray, L. (1985). *The Australian Year: A Chronicle of our Seasons and Celebrations.* Angus & Robertson: North Ryde, NSW.

O'Connor, D. W., Pollitt, P. A., Hyde, J. B., Brook, C. P. B., Reiss, B. B. & Roth, M. (1988). Do general practitioners miss dementia in elderly patients? *British Medical Journal* 297, 1107–1110.

O'Connor, D. W., Pollitt, P. A., Brook, C. P. B. & Reiss, B. B. (1989a). The validity of informant histories in a community study of dementia. *International Journal of Geriatric Psychiatry* 4, 203–208.

O'Connor, D. W., Pollitt, P. A., Treasure, F. P., Brook, C. P. B. & Reiss, B. B. (1989b). The influence of education, social class and sex on Mini-Mental scores. *Psychological Medicine* 19, 771–776.

Ogunniyi, A. O., Lekwauwa, U. B. & Osuntokun, B. O. (1991). Influence of education and aspects of cognitive functions in non-demented elderly Nigerians. *Neuroepidemiology* 10, 246–250.

Ogunniyi, A. O., Osuntokun, B. O., Lekwauwa, U. B. & Falope, Z. F. (1992). Rarity of dementia (by DSM-III-R) in an urban community in Nigeria. *East African Medical Journal* 69, 64–68.

Osuntokun, B. O., Ogunniyi, A. O., Lekwauwa, G. U. & Oyediran, A. B. O. O. (1991). Epidemiology of age-related dementia in the third world and aetiological clues of Alzheimer's disease. *Tropical Geographical Medicine* 43, 345–351.

Park, J., Ko, H. J., Park, Y. N. & Jung, C-H. (1994). Dementia among the elderly in a rural Korean community. *British Journal of Psychiatry* **164**, 796–801.

Pollitt, P. A., O'Connor D. W. & Anderson, I. (1989). Mild dementia: perceptions and problems. *Ageing and Society* **9**, 261–275.

Porter, B. E. & Robinson, M. B. (1987). *Protected Persons and their Property in New South Wales*. The Law Book Company: Sydney.

Rajkumar, S., Kumar, S. & Thara. R. (1993). Prevalence of dementia in the community: a rural-urban comparison from Madras, India. *World Psychiatric Association. Book of Abstracts. Changing the Course and Outcome of Mental Disorder: The Contribution of Epidemiology*, p. 119. World Psychiatric Association: Groningen, The Netherlands.

Reser, J. (1991). Aboriginal mental health: conflicting cultural perspectives. In *The Health of Aboriginal Australia* (ed. J. Reid and P. Trompf). pp. 218–291. University of Queensland Press: St Lucia, Qld.

Robertson, A. (1990). The politics of Alzheimer's disease. *International Journal of Health Services* **20**, 429–442.

Roth, M. (1977). Recent progress in the psychiatry of old age and its bearing on certain problems of psychiatry in early life. *Biological Psychiatry* **5**, 102–125.

Roth, M. (1994). The relationship between dementia and normal aging of the brain. In *Dementia and Normal Aging* (ed. F. A. Huppert, C. Brayne and D. W. O'Connor). pp. 57–76. Cambridge University Press: Cambridge.

Roth, M., Tym, E., Mountjoy, C. Q., Huppert, F. A., Hendrie, H., Verma, S. & Goddard, R. (1986). CAMDEX: A standardised instrument for the diagnosis of mental disorder in the elderly with special reference to the early detection of dementia. *British Journal of Psychiatry* **149**, 698–709.

Royal College of Pathologists of Australia. (1994). Autopsy and the use of tissues removed at autopsy. *Medical Journal of Australia* **160**, 442–444.

Sankar, A. (1984). 'It's just old age': old age as a diagnosis in American and Chinese medicine. In *Age and Anthropological Theory* (ed. D. I. Kertzer and J. Keith). pp. 250–280. Cornell University Press: Ithaca.

Scaletta, N. M. (1985). Death by sorcery: the social dynamics of dying in Bairiai, West New Britain. In *Aging and its Transformations: Moving toward Death in Pacific Societies* (ed. D. A. Counts and D. R. Counts). pp. 223–247. University Press of America: Lanham.

Seltzer, B. & Buswell, A. (1994). Psychiatric symptoms in Alzheimer's disease: mental status examination versus caregiver report. *Gerontologist* **34**, 103–109.

Simmons, L. (1960). Aging in preindustrial societies. In *Handbook of Social Gerontology* (ed. C. Tibbitts). pp. 62–91. University of Chicago Press: Chicago.

Stafford, P. B. (1992). The nature and culture of Alzheimer's disease. *Semiotica* **92**, 167–176.

Sultzer, D. L., Levin, H. S., Mahler, M. E., High, W. M. & Cummings, J. L. (1992). Assessment of cognitive, psychiatric, and behavioral disturbances in patients with dementia: the neuro-behavioral rating scale. *Journal of the American Geriatrics Society* **40**, 549–555.

Sultzer, D. L., Levin, H. S., Mahler, M. E., High, W. M. & Cummings, J. L. (1993). A comparison of psychiatric symptoms in vascular dementia and Alzheimer's disease. *American Journal of Psychiatry* **150**, 1806–1812.

Sung, K-T. (1990). A new look at filial piety: ideals and practices of family-centered parent care in Korea. *Gerontologist* **30**, 610–617.

Veras, R. P. & Murphy, E. (1994). The mental health of older people in Rio de Janeiro. *International Journal of Geriatric Psychiatry* **9**, 285–295.

Wakeford, R. E. & Stepney, R. (1989). Obstacles to organ donation. *British Journal of Surgery* **76**, 435–439.

Waring, S. C., Esteban-Santillan, C., Teng, E., Petersen, R. C., O'Brien, P. C. & Kurland, L. T. (1994). Evaluation of a modified version of the Cognitive Abilities Screening Instrument (CASI) for assessment of dementia in elderly Chamorros on Guam. Fourth International Conference on Alzheimer's disease. *Neurobiology of Aging* **15**, S43.

White, L. R. (1992). Towards a program of cross-cultural research on the epidemiology of Alzheimer's disease. *Current Science* **63**, 456–469.

White, L. R., Ross, G. W., Petrovitch, H., Masaki, K., Chiu, D. & Teng, E. (1994). Estimation of the sensitivity and specificity of a dementia screening test in a population-based survey. *Neurobiology of Aging* **15**, Suppl. 1, S42.

Wilkin, D., Mashiah, J. & Jolley, D. J. (1978). Changes in behavioural characteristics of elderly population of local authority homes and long-stay hospital wards, 1976–77. *British Medical Journal* **8**, 1274–1276.

Wolfe, N., Imai, Y., Otani, C., Nagatani, H., Hasegawa, K., Sugimoto, K., Tanaka, Y., Kuroda, Y., Glosser, G. & Albert, M. L. (1992). Criterion validity of the cross-cultural cognitive examination in Japan. *Journal of Gerontology: Psychological Sciences* **47**, P289–P291.

World Health Organization (1990). *ICD-10 1990 Draft of Chapter V: Categories F00–F99. Mental and Behavioural Disorders (including disorders of psychological development). Clinical Descriptions and Diagnostic Guidelines*. WHO, Division of Mental Health: Geneva.

Wragg, R. E. & Jeste, D. V. (1989). Overview of depression and psychosis in Alzheimer's disease. *American Journal of Psychiatry* **146**, 577–587.

Zann, S. (1994). *Identification of Support, Education and Training Needs of Rural/Remote Health Care Service Providers Involved in Dementia Care. Rural Health. Support, Education and Training (RHSET)*. Northern Regional Health Authority: Vincent, Queensland.

Aging & Mental Health 1997;1(2):112–120

ORIGINAL ARTICLE

Cultural aspects of aging and psychopathology

S. DEIN[1] & S. HULINE-DICKENS[2]

[1] *Department of Psychiatry and Behavioural Sciences, University College London Medical School, London,*
[2] *Department of Psychiatry, Princess Alexandra Hospital, Harlow, Essex, UK*

Abstract
A knowledge of cultural factors is essential to an understanding of aging and mental health. This paper surveys cultural aspects and folk theories of aging, attitudes to the elderly, death, disengagement and role theory. The cultural aspects of psychopathology are then reviewed and the evidence for differing prevalences of depression and dementia considered, concluding with a comment on the provision of care for this group. It is argued that an understanding of systems of prestige and esteem gained from anthropology is important in understanding how culture influences the development of mental illness, but clearly also patterns of urbanization and industrialization worldwide influence the position of the aged. The importance of studying attitudes to the elderly is that the elderly come to perceive themselves in the same way. The prevalence of depression and dementia in Japan may be lower than in the West, which implies this culture may exert a protective influence. The position in China is less clear. Differences in family structures, attitudes, integration in the community and fulfilment of roles may account for these findings.

Introduction

The elderly population is rapidly growing worldwide, and it is therefore fortunate that research on aging has now been chosen as a global theme issue for over a hundred international medical journals (Rochon & Smith, 1996). Although attention has been traditionally focused on the physical health of people aged over 65, aging clearly affects every dimension of health care, and there is an impression that the mental health of this group has been neglected.

It is a difficult task to separate cultural factors from other social factors which may be influencing the personal environment, particularly when there has been migration to another country and the associated stresses of disrupted family relationships, increased isolation and breakdown of community support. It is within this context that the assumptions held by Western society that the elderly from ethnic minorities are supported by local communities and extended families may be false and indeed discriminatory (Ballard, 1979).

Other stresses for immigrants are transgenerational conflict, racism and often disadvantages in education and language. 'Double jeopardy' is the term recently used to describe the double challenge of racism and agism faced by people from ethnic minorities (Dowd & Bengston, 1978) and 'triple jeopardy' when they also experience socioeconomic deprivation (Norman, 1985).

This paper, which is intended to stimulate discussion, focuses on the cultural aspects of aging. The elderly have the greatest cumulative experience of culture, and through examining different cultures comparisons can be made of the systems of *prestige, esteem, kinship* and *dependency*. Clearly, this task is not an easy one, as cultures are in a constant state of flux. Modernization is a process whereby knowledge of tradition may become less valued, and there is a complex relationship between modernization and the prestige of the aged: although prestige may be depressed in industrializing societies, it may be elevated in more mature systems which can support more provision of care (Fry, 1980).

This paper firstly examines age and aging, folk theories of aging, attitudes and stereotypes and death and grieving and briefly considers the concepts of disengagement and role theory. It then secondly considers the cultural aspects of psychopathology, the evidence for differing prevalences of the major psychiatric conditions and provision of care.

Correspondence to: Dr Simon Dein, Senior Lecturer in Social and Community Psychiatry, Department of Psychiatry and Behavioural Sciences, University College London Medical School, Wolfson Building, Riding House Street, London W1N 8AA, UK.

Received for publication 16th July 1996. Accepted 21st January 1997.

Age and aging

Although anthropologists have noted structural and demographic aspects in many groups, the experience of aging is a largely neglected topic. Age is an essential ingredient of all cultures, since age is an inscribed characteristic of all individuals and all cultures must resolve the question of how to structure age differences. Age boundaries are enforced by means of formal laws and social sanctions. *Age grades* appear to be universal and denote the progression of individuals through the major divisions of the life cycle. For example, among the Tiriki nomads of sub Saharan Africa, each boy born over a 15-year period becomes a member of an *age set*. Members remain together for life, and move through four age grades 'Warrior', 'Elder Warrior', 'Judicial Elders' and 'Ritual Elders', each implying certain duties and responsibilities. (Haviland, 1996). Every known society has a named social category of people who are old and in every case these people have different rights, duties, privileges and burdens from those enjoyed or suffered by their juniors. Public acknowledgement of discontinuities, which punctuate the life cycle, occurs through *rites of passage* (Van Gennep, 1960; Webster, 1908). These are rare in fragmented societies, but the celebrations surrounding retirement from work, and the symbolic act of presenting a gold watch, may be seen as a rite of passage in the West.

Conceptions of what constitutes 'old age' are culturally variable and may be based on chronological age, social performance or work capacity. In many non-Western societies, people are considered young or at least middle aged if they continue to carry out responsibilities required of them. Definitions of old age, then, are said to be *functional* rather than *chronological*. For example, in Samoa there is a term for old age (matua) but it is unclear when precisely this begins. It appears that many societies divide the aged into two classes: people who are no longer fully productive economically but who can still physically and emotionally attend to their own needs and those who are totally dependent and require custodial care and supervision. This is equivalent to the third and fourth ages in Britain. Those who are mentally incompetent are everywhere regarded as a burden, but some groups make more provision for their care than others. At the most extreme they are abandoned to die when the burden of supporting them endangers the existence of the family. Such was the case until fairly recently among the Chipewyan, a group of hunter gatherers in northern Canada. The elderly are sacrificed in favour of the young and fit. But this does not occur in all hunter gatherer societies. For instance, among the Kung San of southern Africa, old men are able to assert political leadership even after hunting skills have deteriorated. Furthermore, in several polygynous Australian cultures (Warner, 1958) and African societies (Goody, 1969), a man's

career and power does not mature until he is old, at which time he marries several young women (Fry, 1980).

Amoss and Harrell (1981) argue that what has been missing has been any attempt to put aging in a cross-cultural or comparative perspective. What is needed is an examination of those aspects of aging that are universal and have to be planned for as inevitable, and those aspects which are culturally specific and can be avoided, modified or strengthened under certain social conditions. An examination of those cultural factors related to aging may help us understand psychopathological processes in old age, such as the high prevalence of depression in the elderly in Western cultures (Blazer *et al.*, 1991).

Those texts which have examined aging from a cross-cultural perspective adopt a number of perspectives emphasizing roles, statuses, treatment and prestige of the elderly. Leo Simmon's monograph (1945), *The role of the aged in primitive society*, remains a cornerstone of anthropological investigations of the aged. It examines factors relating to the status of the elderly in 71 non-Western cultures. Over 100 sociocultural variables were correlated with 112 variables relating to status and treatment of the elderly. For 20 years following the publication of this book, there was little research done into cultural aspects of aging and it was only in the second half of the 1960s that there was a commitment to investigate aging and the aged from an anthropological perspective, beginning in 1967 with Margaret Clark and Barbara Anderson's *Culture and ageing*, which identified five adaptive tasks for the elderly: recognition, redefinition, substitution, reassessment and reintegration. Since then there have been a number of books examining the process of aging in a number of cultures (Amoss & Harrell, 1981; Bond *et al.*, 1993; Clark, 1973; Fry, 1980; Hazan, 1994).

Folk theories of aging

Anthropological methodology employs a number of ethnographic techniques, including participant observation and surveys using standardized procedures such as formal sets of questions or card sorts. The latter two are derived from cognitive anthropology (Conklin, 1955; Frake, 1962; Romney & D'Andrade, 1964) and elicit an 'emic' or 'inside view' through an analysis of native classifications. This type of information was used by Kagan (1980) in her examination of folk theories of aging in a Columbian peasant village, detailed below.

Kagan used a folk taxonomy, which gives information on what the categories are and how they relate to one another from the perspective of the informant. Thus she was able to ask informants to provide vocabulary appropriate to age grades in Bojaca and their responses would become the basis for formulating questions that would map the life-span and age-related behaviour of the community.

In Bojaca, a Columbian peasant village, older adults are referred to as 'vejez'. Being a 'viejo' does not accord prestige, nor is it associated with isolation and abandonment. Older adults are integrated into family and community life, and actively contribute to areas such as religion, food preparation, manual skills, simple curing, the growth of plants, questions of justice and personal counselling. They are sometimes excluded from economic activities, using machinery, village planning and formal education. Old age is seen as a tranquil period with the family. Deference is shown in a quiet manner, with allowance made for the childlike behaviour of the senile.

Attitudes and stereotypes

In Britain, the notion of old age has a number of connotations. On the one hand, it is seen as a time when one is free from the constraints of work to pursue leisure activities and, if one's financial position allows, to follow desired activities one has been unable to do when one is younger. However, for many, old age is associated with a number of negative cultural stereotypes associated with powerlessness, decline, sickness, dependency and ultimately death. Additionally, the elderly are seen as conservative, inflexible and incapable of creativity (Hazan, 1994).

These stereotypes are supported by age-related expectations concerning appearance, clothing, countenance, posture, hair style and other visible features and their associated implications for attitudes and behaviour. Those elderly people who engage in younger activities such as sport or studying at university are seen as exceptional, almost having evaded the aging process by some mysterious means. Similarly, it is not expected that the elderly will be engaging in sexual activity (Hendricks & Hendricks, 1977).

There have been a number of studies examining attitudes towards the elderly in non-Western cultures, such as Hong Kong and Japan. The two most prominent religions in Hong Kong emphasize the positive qualities of old age. Taoism emphasizes acceptance and reverence for the elderly. Similarly, Confucianism is associated with images of the elderly being wise and demanding respect. However, although cultural practices and religious beliefs remain an important consideration, they are in tension with the demands of modern society where there is a demise of the traditional family and its valuing of filial piety. Leung (1987) examines evidence that Hong Kong families are becoming less caring towards the elderly and concluded that this evidence remains controversial. Among Asian families in Britain, a number of authors (Blakemore & Boneheim, 1994; Walker & Ahmed, 1994) point out that

it can no longer be taken for granted that the immediate family is on hand to provide care when needed.

Japan has often been held up as the last repository of traditional family values and Westerners have often idealized the stability of Japanese family life. However, the feelings of younger Japanese people may be less idealistic (Koyamo, 1989) and attitudes and behaviour may be moving away from according greater status for the elderly and not towards it. The elderly population in Japan is estimated to rise by 50% between 1986 and 2000. Japanese life expectancy is now the highest in the world: 81 years for women and 75 years for men. Looking after elderly relatives becomes a heavier burden as more of them last longer and grow sicker. Caring children are fewer and older. It appears that the family life of elderly people is becoming more stressful and there is a rising incidence of suicide among elderly women which may be associated with family conflict (Ineichen, 1996).

Disengagement

One theory which has attempted to account for the apparent 'universal marginality' of the elderly is disengagement theory (Cumming & Henry, 1961), which postulates that successful aging is contingent on the mutual disengagement of the elderly and their social environment. It holds that the aged must accept a decline in status and must relinquish leadership roles if societal equilibrium is to he maintained. However, the evidence that the process of disengagement is universal is unsupported in the cross-cultural literature (Talmon-Gaber, 1962). Disengagement theory is to be contrasted to *activity theory* (Havinghurst, 1954), which argues that successful aging is related to maintaining reasonable levels of activity and substituting new roles for those lost with retirement.

Hazan (1994) argues that ambiguity, alienation and segregation characterize the elderly in Western society. They are forced to retire and leave the working community, which may lead to serious problems of identity since 'in contemporary Western society, work is a central role; intimately associated with our deepest understanding of the value and virtues of a human being and the ethical justification of our very existence; it has significance for identity far beyond the economic sphere'. Beyond this they are often forced to live separately from the rest of society in 'new communities for the aged'. In Britain, the most familiar solution to the 'problem of the aged' is best exemplified by the old age home of which there are a large variety, ranging from those designed for particular categories of the aged—such as the physically impaired—to those whose residents are heterogeneous and arbitrarily lumped together. What characterizes these 'institutions' is the lack of autonomy of their residents. The existence of these institutions reflects the social conception of the elderly as redundant, bothersome and disturbing. For most residents, the old age home is not a transitory stage but the last stage in their lives.

It is interesting to compare the experience of aging in India to that in British society. As outlined in the Vedas, the Hindu scriptures, during the last two stages of one's life, one should withdraw from this worldly activity and interest. The *Varnashrama Dhama*, the 'duties of social position and stage of life', describe four stages of life in the traditional normative scheme: *Brahmacarya*, the period of sacred learning; *Grhastha*, married life and parenthood; *Vanaprastha*, the stage of dwelling as a forest hermit; and the last stage, *Sannyas*, the period of asceticism and renunciation. This outline is familiar to all Hindus, but as Vatuk (1980) states: 'few lives as actually lived correspond in detail to the prescriptions of the Sanskrit texts'. 'Disengagement' is thus seen as an ideal and normative process and does not result in loss of status. Old age is seen as a period of rightful dependency, with security contingent upon the support of an extended family. Traditionally, the elderly were accorded high status, but this is rapidly changing under the impact of modernization. As Subrahmanium (1988) states: 'By tradition, religious and cultural, the elders are given a high status in Indian society.' In the past the joint family was the common pattern that existed, with the head of the family enjoying rights and responsibilities and commanding obedience and respect. Under the impact of the industrial revolution the joint family is fast breaking down; old age is now seen as a 'problem'. He examines the growth of old age homes and old age aid groups throughout India, phenomena which would have been unthinkable several years ago.

Role theory

Parsons (1949) considered the loss of employment as the central feature of aging, which led to loss of purpose in life. In the West, work roles are of enormous significance for self-esteem, social interaction and identity. Thus, on retirement the elderly may face the loss of power, respect and social rewards (Hazan, 1994). The elderly may become volunteers at work to compensate for their eroded social status, and other initiatives, such as the newly established University of the Third Age (Midwinter, 1984), represent attempts to provide new roles. Other roles may also be found as a grandparent, patient, pensioner or other role in the family unit, but as Hazan (1994) points out, the latter is inherently ambivalent, as authority has often passed to the younger generation and many of these roles may represent 'mock inclusions'. In contrast to the above, in many traditional societies where the knowledge and expertise of the elderly are particularly valuable and the society possesses the resources

to support them, their power is ensured and may even be enhanced. The elderly receive high status roles. In some societies—for instance, among the Merina of Madagascar—the attainment of old age is a prerequisite for the position of leader, but any deterioration in the ability to transmit this knowledge may result in excommunication (Keith, 1979). The status of the elderly in more complex societies is extremely variable and is dependent on their control over valuable resources and their possession of knowledge. In many societies which follow traditional religions, the possession of ritual knowledge is deemed as vital to the continuation of that society and it is often the elderly who hold this knowledge. This may result in their higher status. On account of this knowledge, the elderly are often seen to have the ability to heal. However, when these societies undergo a process of modernization, this cultural knowledge is no longer considered important, with the consequent decline in status of the elderly (Cogwill & Holmes, 1972).

Death and grieving

It is impossible to talk of aging in different cultures without taking into account religious views and attitudes towards death:

> The separation of the aged from society, the identification of ageing with ugliness, evil and horror, and the reluctance to engage in physical contact with the aged all indicate that ageing is perceived as a dangerous area located, as it were, between life and death (Hazan, 1994).

It is the old who are associated with death. However, this has not always been the case, as in Medieval Europe, where death was primarily associated with high infant mortality (Aries, 1965).

A distinction is made between *biological death* (the death of the organism) and *social death* (the termination of social life). The two may not be simultaneous and in complex societies social death, i.e. the loss of social role and cultural identity, precedes biological death. Hertz (1960) has said, 'The problem faced by the bereaved was that the deceased was not only a biological individual but a social being grafted upon the physical individual whose destruction is tantamount to a sacrilege against the social order.' Cultural attitudes to biological and social death are manifest in the preparation for death, theories of afterlife, and the links between the living and the dead (Hazan, 1994). In some groups, such as the Alaskan Eskimo, a man or woman may even determine the date of his or her own death; but the fact that elderly Eskimos are permitted to commit suicide does not mean that they are held in low esteem by their families. In other societies, a continuing link between the living and the dead is manifest in the cult of the ancestors. In societies possessing such cults, the status of the elderly may be high on account of their temporal proximity to the ancestors (Bloch & Parry, 1982). This is exemplified in Madagascar and Mexico, where there are strong cults of the ancestors.

Although it is commonly assumed that fear of death increases with age, there is evidence that elderly people are no more afraid of death than younger age groups and this fear may be greatest in middle age (Kalish, 1976). For middle class Americans, death may mean 'loss of self' (Fulton, 1964; Schultz, 1977) and loss of social success and productivity in a value system which emphasizes youth, health and achievement. Death anxiety, then, is a response to this conflict, and the consequence of this is to suppress conscious awareness of death. American culture is considered to be highly successful in minimizing contact with the phenomenon of death (Schultz, 1980).

Following death, culture determines the modes of grieving. Eisenbruch (1984), in a comprehensive review of the grieving process in a number of cultures (including Chinese, South East Asian refugees and North American blacks), found that the mode of expression of grief was culturally determined, as were the ways of dealing with it. This piece of work emphasized the difficulty in trying to determine what constitutes normal and abnormal grief, and raises important questions for those involved in helping the bereaved of different cultures in Britain. Koenig (1996) points out that religion may be an important coping mechanism in the elderly, especially at times of sickness.

Cultural aspects of psychopathology

It has been recognized that existing instruments used to screen for depression and dementia were developed for use in the Western white population, and thus may be of limited use in ethnic groups who use different languages and communicate distress in different ways (Rait et al., 1996). In the field of cross-cultural research of dementia, in particular, there has been much debate about the appropriacy of using cognitive tests developed for Western people (see below). Not only may education affect the scores obtained on cognitive testing, but there may also be specific cultural factors involved in the performance of cognitive tasks (Salmon et al., 1989). It must also be remembered that consultation behaviour and patients' belief systems may lead them to seek the help of traditional healers before presenting to health services.

Although there is a burgeoning literature examining cross-cultural aspects of psychopathology (Dein, 1994), there has been relatively little work done on cultural aspects of old age psychiatry. In many non-western societies, psychiatric services are poorly developed and there are few psychiatrists. For instance, in Tanzania there are six specialist psychiatrists for 30 million people. In those societies with trained psychiatrists, patients of all ages are treated,

including children and the very elderly. There are few trained old age psychiatrists. The work done so far on cross-cultural aspects of old age psychiatry concentrates predominantly on depression and dementia and most of this has been carried out in Japan, China and India.

Depression

Somatization is common in non-Western cultures (Kleinman & Good, 1985), and ethnographic accounts of depression in China and Taiwan suggest that elderly patients present with somatic symptoms. There are parallels with British-born elderly patients where somatization is a common presentation and many elderly subjects complain of physical symptoms or sleep disturbance rather than depressed mood (Brown, 1988). As Katona (1994) says: 'Presentations which minimise depression but focus on somatic complaints are far more frequently found than in the younger age groups.' The reasons for this remain uncertain.

Hasegawa (1985) reviewed the results of several Western and Japanese prevalence studies of late onset depression. The studies utilize different study populations and methods of identifying depressive symptomology. He concludes that rates of depression are higher in Western cultures than in Japanese culture. He speculated that this may be accounted for by differences in family structure between Western and Japanese culture. Komahashi et al. (1994) also found the prevalence of depression among the elderly in Ohira town in Japan to be low, at 0.45% using DSM-III-R criteria.

However, other studies have reported higher prevalences comparable to those in the UK. Nippon and Eisei (1993) examined prevalence rates of depression in a rural village of the Akita perfecture using the Centre for Epidemiological Studies Depression scale (CES-D) and found a prevalence of 5.3%. Horiguchi and Inanmia (1991) using the Zung and self-rating scales, found prevalence of depression in elderly subjects to be 61% (screening level) in nursing homes, compared to 36% in the community. Kashiwase et al. (1991) emphasize that depression is the major functional mental disorder in Japan, occurring in 31% of those over 70. The marked variability in reported prevalence rates are similar to the findings in Western cultures. Although pharmacotherapy and psychotherapy are common treatment modalities, traditional healing methods such as Kampo (using extracts of crude herbs), acupuncture and moxibustion are often used.

Suicide

Cultural and religious views are likely to determine whether or not suicide is an acceptable course of action. Studies in India show that suicide rates are low among the elderly (Adityanjee, 1986; Bhatia et *al.*, 1987) and this may be a consequence of the support and companionship enjoyed by the senior members of an Indian family. However, in contrast, Shimizu (1990) found that suicide rated highly as a cause of death among elderly Japanese. Although suicide rates have fallen for all age groups in Japan, rates are still significantly higher in the elderly than in younger age groups (Tatai, 1991). This may be due to the tradition of honourable suicide in Japanese culture, which is likely to have more influence on the elderly.

A study by Cohen (1993) reveals that, while the rate of suicide in America is greater in older Americans compared to other US population groups, it is less frequent in older blacks than older whites. Cohen speculates that older African Americans, in reaching later life, have surmounted more threats to self esteem (compared with whites) and are thereby better adapted to new challenges associated with aging.

Dementia

There have been a number of cross-cultural epidemiological studies on dementia. Ineichen (1981) emphasizes the difficulty of making reliable diagnoses and the importance of taking into account cultural factors when assessing dementia. Several studies have found that the prevalence of dementia is higher in blacks and Hispanics in New York, compared to the white elderly (Escobar *et al.*, 1986; Folstein *et al.*, 1987; Schoenberg *et al.*, 1985). However, these results have been questioned by Gurland (1994), who is critical of dementia rating scales which value certain types of information and are biased so that people with language difficulties and poor educational background score lower. He argues that there is a need to develop a culture free instrument.

In Japan, there have been several epidemiological studies of the prevalence of dementia. Fukunishi *et al.*, (1991) found a prevalence rate of 4.5% in those over 65 years. Shibayama *et al.* (1986), in a community sample, found a prevalence rate of 5.9% for moderate to severe dementia. Graves *et al.* (1994) reported the prevalence rates of different subtypes of dementia in Japan and the US. They conclude that in Japan and China the prevalence of multi infarct dementia exceeds that of SDAT; whereas in Western cultures the prevalence of SDAT is higher, but that a diagnosis of multi infarct dementia is more likely to be made since there is a perceived association between vascular disease and rich lifestyle. Similar findings have been reported by Jorm (1991). Of special interest is a recent finding by Homma (1994), which provides good evidence that the prevalence of Alzheimer's disease is greater in the West than in Japan, whilst there is no marked difference in the prevalence of vascular dementia.

In China, Zhang *et al.* (1990) reviewed early studies published in Chinese, reporting low rates of dementia which varied between 0.46% and 1.86% of the aged population. The authors concluded, however, that this may have been accounted for by differences in sampling, data collection and age structure of the samples chosen. The Shanghai study reported by Yu *et al.* (1989) and Zhang *et al.* (1990) is the largest performed to date, involving a sample of 5,055 people over the age of 55 (Ineichen, 1996). A modified form of the Mini-Mental State Examination (MMSE) was used as a screening instrument, followed by detailed interviews with low scorers. In the over 65 group 152 cases of dementia were identified, giving a rate of 4.1%. Poor education appeared to increase the likelihood of dementia.

Early research in China, therefore, appears to show low rates of dementia, and later research higher rates, but still below the rates found in Europe. Only the Shanghai study, which is the most rigorous, gives comparable rates to those in Europe (Ineichen, 1996). These findings raise the question of whether the incidence of dementia in China is really increasing, or whether this is a result of improved and more accurate research techniques.

In non-Western cultures, dementia is often seen as a part of the normal process of aging. There is an expected decline in cognitive functioning in old age which is seen as natural and not requiring medical intervention. It is not medicalized until problems become very extreme (such as violence) and it comes to the attention of doctors. Cohen (1995) examined conceptualizations of senility in Banares, Northern India and found that senility was not seen as a medical problem. The local people used the Hindi term *dimag* or 'weak brain' to refer to senility; a term which suggests that the old person received inadequate support from his or her children: 'Those whose "brains were not quite right" point to a bad family'. This is not surprising in a culture which traditionally emphasizes devotion by the children to their parents. Hernandez (1991) points out that cultural factors may influence the perceived burden associated with caring for an elderly demented relative. One study among caregivers (Hines-Martin, 1995) found that African American carers showed reduced strain in caring for their elderly relatives suffering with senile dementia and institutionalized them to a lesser degree than their white counterparts. However, as Ineichen (1996) explains, although dementia is unlikely to be stigmatized in China, this is at the cost of failing to seek help, and presumably therefore increases the burden on relatives.

In the Far East, as with families elsewhere, the effect on the health, morale and life style of carers of those with dementia is immense (Brown, 1988; Maedal *et al.*, 1989). The Japanese government has responded by spending more on elderly care, but most of this money has been used to provide additional nursing home places, which have been rapidly increasing in numbers. There has been relatively little interest in the quality of care (Kobayashi, 1989) or the development of community services. There are few old age psychiatrists concerned with dementia and there is a resistance to consulting them (Maeda *et al.*, 1989).

Provision of care

According to Littlewood and Lipsedge (1989), elderly black people have been widely ignored in the provision of day care facilities and group homes, perhaps because of a comfortable assumption that they are all part of an extended family network which, unlike the individual white family, continues to care for them. A study by Walker and Ahmed (1994) suggests that it cannot be taken for granted that the immediate family is on hand to provide care when needed. The clinical impression is that statutory services are ill equipped to meet the demands of ethnic minority people. A recent text (Yeo & Gallagher-Thompson, 1996) examines some of these issues in relation to dementia.

Although old age psychiatry has been recognized as a specialty within British psychiatry since 1989, this is not so in many countries. Principles of service delivery identified in the UK have found application in other countries when adapted to the characteristics of local populations and historical views on health care and the elderly (Aries, 1992).

The important components for any old age psychiatry service are the team, facilities used by them, and the structures for collaboration with other agencies. Privately run nursing homes have become an important resource since the mid 1980s, yet this development has often taken place in an unplanned way and without attending to local needs. In the public sector, limits on expenditure have encouraged homes to accept less disabled residents, which may lead to multiply disadvantaged people being difficult to place. The voluntary sector has played an important role in providing specialized services (for example Age Concern initiatives for people of Indian origin in parts of south London) and bringing the needs of the elderly to the attention of the public and politicians.

There are a number of initiatives in Britain for the care of the elderly of ethnic minorities (for example Leicestershire social services), but resources are patchy and social services budgets limited. With respect to specific treatments, psychotherapy has not traditionally been offered to the elderly, but family therapy is now well described in this age group (Benbow *et al.*, 1990). Family therapy enables a multidisciplinary team to work using flexible models which can be sensitively adapted to families of ethnic minorities. There is a need for more research into how families cope and the kinds of help they would most appreciate.

Conclusion

Health care professionals need to understand the cultural factors which affect all aspects of their patients' lives. There are inter-cultural differences in the prevention, presentation, detection and management of psychiatric disorders. Culture also influences the development of the personality, concept of self, consultation behaviours, what is perceived as stigma, options of adopting the sick role and the patients' own explanatory models for their illnesses. In a recent review of folk theories of aging, Kaufman (1995) found that the elderly hold negative expectations about their health, which may reflect negative experiences of health care, or negative attitudes of society as a whole. It is known that health perceptions are influenced by socioeconomic class (Mechanic, 1972), cultural norms, roles and activities (Boyer, 1980).

The evidence surveyed in this paper seems to suggest that in Japan, at least, the rates of depression and dementia may be lower than in the West; which may indicate that this culture in some way protects its members from these conditions. If validated, the finding that the prevalence of SDAT is lower in Japan is significant, for this challenges the notions that dementia is an invariant biological process. Whether this is due to differences in some environmental or cultural factor has yet to be elucidated. Mortimer (1988) has proposed that limited education, poor nutrition, smoking, alcohol abuse and exposure to toxic substances lower the threshold at which the plaques, tangles and infarctions become manifest in dementia, and thus sex, social class, area of residence and country of birth could therefore have discernible effects on prevalence patterns.

The evidence reviewed on the prevalence of dementia in China may indicate that there is an increase in this condition and it is tempting to speculate that this may be associated with some aspect of the process of 'modernization'; but no clear conclusions can be drawn as studies cannot easily be compared. These cross-cultural variations in psychiatric disorder may be due to differences in family structures, attitudes to the aged, community integration, fulfilment of roles, or other cultural or environmental factors.

Anthropological methods are clearly useful for psychiatry. It has been seen in this paper, that it is far from the case that non-Western societies accord their elderly high status, as cultures everywhere are undergoing the changes of urbanization and industrialization. The examination of other cultures' value systems yields valuable information on patterns in the esteem of older people, family structures, and how attitudes can be informed. The importance of negative attitudes and stereotypes is that the elderly themselves may come to believe that they will become incapable, lonely and needy (Hazan, 1994). Social networks and cultural values may have crucial effects on self-esteem and group membership, which in turn will influence the development of psychiatric disorder.

It was a salutary finding by Clark and Anderson (1967), that within American culture the very person who had absorbed the cultural values of work and ambition makes the poorest adjustment to old age and is most likely to be stigmatized as mentally ill due to the failure to adjust to changed circumstances. As the elderly are increasingly excluded from the technological age, it seems likely that their experience of alienation will be heightened, segregation increased and opportunities for occupying fulfilling roles reduced. It seems likely also that the suicide rate will continue to rise with these trends.

Social policy is needed to plan for the increasing numbers of elderly, who will include a substantial proportion of people from ethnic minorities, by the establishment perhaps of a special ministry, and increased resources. In psychiatry much could be done to extend research and develop services. Already, instruments are being developed to screen for depression and dementia in elderly people from ethnic minorities, in an attempt to assess need for services (Rait *et al.*, 1996). Further attention to the burden faced by carers is also a priority. What is clear is that the elderly from cultural minorities bear additional social, economic and psychological burdens, and may suffer greater physical and mental ill health. The challenge remains to provide services to the most needy.

References

ADITJANJEE, D.R. (1986). Suicide attempts and suicides in India: cross-cultural aspects. *International Journal of Social Psychiatry, 32*, 64–73.

AMOSS, P.T. & HARRELL, S. (1981). *Other ways of growing old*. Stanford: Stanford University Press.

ARIES, P. (1965). *Centuries of childhood*. New York: Vintage Books.

BALLARD, R. (1979) Ethnic minorities and the social services. In: V.S. KHAN (Ed.), *Minority families in Britain*. London: Macmillan.

BENBOW, S., EGAN, D., MARRIOT, A., TREGAY, K., WALSH, S., WELLS, J. & WOOD, J. (1990). Using the family life cycle with later life families. *Journal of Family Therapy, 12*, 321–340.

BHATIA, S.C., KHAN, M.H. & MEDIRATTA, R.P. (1987). High risk suicide factors across cultures. *International Journal of Social Psychiatry, 33*, 226–236.

BLAKEMORE, K. & BONEHEIM, M. (1994). *Community care in multiracial Britain: a critical review of the literature*. London: HMSO.

BLAZER, D., BIRKETT, B., SERVICE, C. & GEORGE, L.C. (1991). The association of age and depression among the elderly: an epidemiologic exploration. *Journal of Gerontology, 46*, 210–215.

BLOCH, M. & PARRY, J. (1982). *Death and the regeneration of life*. Cambridge: Cambridge University Press.

BOND, J., COLEMAN, P. & PEACE, S. (1993). *An introduction to social gerontology*. London: Sage.

BOYER, E. (1980). Health perceptions in the elderly: its cultural and social aspects. In: C.L. FRY, (Ed.) *Ageing in culture and society: comparative viewpoints and strategies*. New York: J.F. Bergin Publishers.

BROWN, R.P., SWEEN, J. & LOUTSCH, R. (1984).

Involutional melancholia revisited. *American Journal of Psychiatry, 137*, 439–444.

BROWN, T.R. (1984). Long term care for the elderly in Kyoto, Japan. *Journal of Cross-cultural Gerontology, 3*, 349–360.

CLARK, M.M. (1973). Contributions of cultural anthropology to the study of the aged. In: L. NADE & T. MAKELZKI (Eds), *Cultural illness and health: essays in human adaptation*. Washington DC. American Anthropological Association.

CLARK, M. & ANDERSON, B.G. (1967). *Culture and ageing: an anthropological study of older Americans*. Springfield, IL: Charles C. Thomas.

COGWILL, D. & HOLMES, L. (1972). *Age and modernization*. New York: Appleton-Century Books.

COHEN, G.D. (1995). African American issues in geriatric psychiatry: a perspective on research opportunities. *Journal of Geriatric Neurology, 6*, 195–199.

COHEN, L. (1992). No ageing in India: The use of gerontology. *Culture, Medicine and Psychiatry, 16*, 123–161.

CONKLIN, H. (1955). Hanunoo color categories. *Southwestern Journal of Anthropology, 11*, 339–344.

CUMMING, E. & HENRY, W. (1961). *Growing old: the process of disengagement*. New York: Basic Books.

DEIN, S. (1994). Reading about cross cultural psychiatry. *British Journal of Psychiatry, 165*, 561–564.

DONAGHUE, W. (Ed.) (1962). *Ageing around the world* (pp. 426–444). New York: Columbia University Press.

DOWD, J. & BENGSTON, V. (1978). Aging in minority populations. An examination of the double jeopardy hypothesis. *Journal of Gerontology, 33*, 427–436.

EISENBRUCH, R. (1984). Cross cultural aspects of bereavement. *Culture, Medicine and Psychiatry, 8*, 283–314.

ESCOBAR, J.I., BURNAM, A., KARNO, M., FORSYTHE, A. *et al.* (1986). Use of Mini-Mental State Examination (MMSE) in a community population of mixed ethnicity. *Journal of Nervous and Mental Disease, 174*, 607–614.

FOLSTEIN, M., ROMANOSKI, A., NESTADT, C., MERCHANT, A. *et al.* (1987). *Differential diagnosis of dementia in eastern Baltimore*. NINCDS final report. (Mimeo)

FRAKE, C. (1962). The ethnographic study of cognitive systems. In: T. GLADWIN & W.C. STURTEVANT (Eds), *Anthropology and human behavior*. Washington: Anthropological Society of Washington.

FRY, C.L. (1980). *Ageing in culture and society: comparative viewpoints and strategies*. New York: J.F. Bergin Publishers.

FUKUNISHI, I., HAYABARA, I. & HOSOKAWA, K. (1991). Epidemiological surveys of senile dementia in Japan. *International Journal of Social Psychiatry, 37*, 51–56.

FULTON, R.L. (1964). Death and the self. *Journal of Religion and Health, 3*, 359–368.

GOODY, J. (1969). Normative, recollected and actual marriage payments among the LoWiili. *Africa, 39*, 54–61.

GRAVES, A.B., LARSON, E.B. & WHITE, L. (1994). Opportunities for and challenges of international collaborative epidemiologic research of dementia and its subtypes. *International Psychogeriatrics, 6*, 209–223.

GURLAND, B. (1994). Cross cultural aspects of dementia. In: E. MURPHY & G. ALEXPOULOS (Eds), *Geriatric psychiatry. Key research topics for clinicians*. Chichester: John Wiley & Sons.

HAVINGHURST, R.J. (1954). Flexibility and social roles of the aged. *American Journal of Sociology, 98*, 309–313.

HASEGAWA, K. (1985). Epidemiological study of depression in late life. 14th CINP congress: management of depression in late life. *Journal of Affective Disorders, 1*, 3–6.

HAVILAND, W.A. (1996). *Cultural anthropology.* Fortworth: Harcourt Brace College Publishers.

HAZAN, H. (1994). *Old age: constructions and deconstructions.* Tel Aviv: Cambridge University Press.

HENDRICKS, J. & HENDRICKS, C.D. (1977). Sexuality in later life. In: *Ageing in mass society* (pp. 304–311). Cambridge: M.A. Winthrop.

HERNANDEZ, G.G. (1991). Not so benign neglect: researchers ignore ethnicity in defining family care giver burden and recomending services. *Gerontologist, 31,* 272.

HERTZ, R. (1960). In. R. NEEDHAM & C. NEEDHAM (Eds), *Death and the right hand* (translation). Glencoe, IL: Free Press (original publication 1907).

HINES-MARTIN, V.P. (1992). A research review: family caregivers of chronically ill African American elderly. *Journal of Gerontological Nursing, 18,* 25–29.

HOMMA, A. (1994). Mental illness in elderly persons in Japan. In: J. COPELAND *et al.* (Eds), *Geriatric psychiatry.* Chichester: John Wiley & Sons.

HORIGUCHI, A. & INANMIA, S. (1991). A survey of living conditions and psychological states of elderly people admitted to nursing homes in Japan. *Acta Psychiatrica Scandinavica, 83,* 338–341.

INEICHEN, B. (1981). The scale of the problem: the epidemiology of dementia. In: C. CATONA (Ed.), *Dementia disorders.* London: Chapman Hall.

INEICHEN, B. (1996) The prevalence of dementia and cognition impairment in China. *International Journal of Geriatric Psychiatry, 11,* 695–697.

JORM, A.F. (1991). Cross-cultural comparison of the occurrence of Alzheimer's disease and vascular dementia. *European Archives of Psychiatry and Clinical Neurosciences, 240,* 218–222.

KAGAN, D. (1980). Activity and ageing in a Columbian peasant village. In: C. FRY (Ed.), *Ageing in culture and society.* New York: J.F. Bergin Publishers.

KALISH, R.A. (1976). Death and dying in a social context. In: R.H. BINSTOCK & E. SHANAS (Eds), *Handbook of ageing and the social sciences.* New York: Van Nostrand Reinhold.

KASHIWASE, H., WATANABE, M. ET AL. (1991). Geriatric psychiatry in Japan. *Journal of Geriatric Psychiatry, 24,* 47–57.

KATONA, C. (1994). *Depression in old age.* Chichester: John Wiley & Sons.

KAUFMAN, S. (1995). *Medical Anthropology Quarterly.* 9, 165–187.

KEITH, J. (1979). The ethnography of old age. *Anthropology Quarterly, 52,* 100–120.

KLEINMAN, A. & GOOD, B. (1985). *Culture and depression.* Berkeley: University of California Press.

KOENIG, H. (1996). *Ageing and god: spiritual pathways to mental health in mid-life and later years.* Binghampton: Haworth Pastoral Press.

KOMOHASHI, T., OHMORI, K. & NAKANO, T. (1994). Survey of dementia and depression among the aged living in the community in Japan. *Japanese Journal of Psychiatry and Neurology, 48,* 517–528.

KOYAMO, W. (1989). Japanese attitudes towards the elderly: a review of research findings. *Journal of Cross Cultural Gerontology, 4,* 335–345.

LEUNG, B. (1989) Formation of multidisciplinary teams to deal with elderly abuse cases. *Hong Kong Journal of Gerontology, 1,* 43–46.

LITTLEWOOD, R. & LIPSEDGE, M. (1989). *Aliens and alienists* (2nd edition). London: Unwin Hyman.

MAEDA, D. ET AL. (1989). Ageing and health in Japan. *Journal of Cross Cultural Gerontology, 4,* 143–162.

MECHANIC, D. (1972). Sociology and public health: perspectives for application. *American Journal of Public Health, 62,* 146–151.

MIDWINTER, E. (1984). *Mutual aid universities.* London: Croom Helm.

MORTIMER, J.A. (1988). Do psychosocial risk factors contribute to Alzheimer's disease? In: A.S. HENDERSON & J.H. HENDERSON (Eds), *Etiology of dementia of Alzheimer's type.* Chichester: John Wiley & Sons.

NIPPON, K. & EISEI, Z. (1993). Depression in Japan. *Japanese Journal of Public Health, 40,* 85–94.

NORMAN, A. (1985). *Triple jeopardy growing old in a second homeland.* London: Centre for Policy on Ageing.

PARSONS, T. (1949). *Essays in sociological theory: pure and applied.* Glencoe, IL: Free Press.

RAIT, G., BURNS, A. & CHEW, C. (1996). Age, ethnicity and mental illness: a triple whammy. *British Medical Journal, 313,* 1347–1348.

ROCHON, P. & SMITH, R. (1996). Aging: a global theme issue. *British Medical Journal, 313,* 1502.

ROMNAY, A.K. & D'ANDRADE, R.G. (Eds) (1964). Transcultural studies in cognition. *American Anthropologist, 66* (special publication).

SCHOENBERG, B.S., ANDERSON, D.W. & HAERER, A.F. (1985). Severe dementia, prevalence and clinical features in a bi-racial US population. *Archives of Neurology, 42,* 740–743.

SCHULTZ, C.M. (1977). Death, anxiety and the structuring of a death concerns cognitive domain. *Essence, 1,* 371–388.

SCHULTZ, C.M., (1980). Age, sex and death anxiety in a middle class American community. In: C.L. FRY (Ed.) *Ageing in culture and society: comparative viewpoints and strategies.* New York: J.F. Bergin Publishers.

SHIBAYAMA, H., KASKHARA, Y. & KOBAYASHI, H. (1986). Prevalence of senile dementia in a Japanese elderly population. *Acta Psychiatrica Scandinavica, 74,* 144–151.

SHIMIZU, M. (1992). Suicide and depression in late life. In: M. BERGENER *et al.* (Eds), *Aging and mental disorders: international perspectives.* New York: Springer Publishing Company.

SIMMONS, L.W. (1945). *The role of the aged in primitive society.* New Haven: Archon Books.

SUBRAHMANIUM, C. (1988). Foreword. In A.B. BOSE & K.D. GANGRADE K.D. (Eds), *The aging in India: problems and possibilities.* New Delhi: Abttinav.

TALMON-GABER, Y. (1962). Ageing in collective settlements in Israel. In: C. TIBBITS & W. DONAGHUE (Eds) *Aging around the world* (pp. 426–444). New York: Columbia University Press.

TATAI, K. (1991). Suicide in Japan. *Crisis, 12,* 40–43.

VAN GENNEP, A. (1960). *The rites of passage.* Chicago: University of Chicago Press (original publication 1909).

VATUK, S. (1980). Withdrawal and disengagement as a cultural response to aging in India. In: C.L. FRY (Ed.) *Ageing in culture and society: comparative viewpoints and strategies.* New York: J.F. Bergin Publishers.

WALKER & AHMED (1994). *Age, race and ethnicity: a comparative approach.* Bickenham: Open University Press.

WARNER, L. (1958). *A black civilisation: a social study of an Australian tribe.* New York: Harper and Row.

WEBSTER, H. (1908). *Primitive secret societies.* New York: Macmillan.

YEO, G. & GALLAGHER-THOMPSON, D. (1996). *Ethnicity and the dementias.* California: Taylor-Francis.

YU, E.S.H. *et al.* (1989). Cogitive impairment among elderly adults in Shanghai, China. *Journal of Gerontology, 44,* 597–606.

ZHANG, M. ET AL. (1990). The prevalence of dementia and Alzheimer's Disease in Shanghai, China: impact of age, gender and education. *Annals of Neurology, 27,* 428–437.

Quantitative studies on age changes in the teeth and surrounding structures in archaeological material: a review

D Whittaker PhD FDSRCS   *Department of Basic Dental Sciences, Dental School, University of Wales College of Medicine, Heath Park, Cardiff CF4 4XY*

Keywords: aging; teeth; periodontal disease; archaeological specimens

Introduction

Quantitative studies on disease processes or normal age changes in skeletal material have been difficult to interpret because of the problems of accurate age determination. It is generally accepted that wear on the occlusal surfaces of the teeth is to some extent a measure of the age of the individual but in a given population it has to be presumed that dietary wear was similar in all members of that population. If nothing is known of the real diet then studies of occlusal wear will enable the observer to rank the specimens into age groups rather than to reliably indicate what those age groups might be.

Studies on caries prevalence in archaeological material have depended to some extent upon this aging being correct but since caries is not strictly an age related disease, it is not intended to discuss it more fully.

The study of periodontal disease in archaeological material presents several difficult problems. Changes in alveolar bone architecture represent only a part of the disease process and the extent and stage of development of the condition is difficult to assess from skeletal material. Moreover, apparent changes in alveolar crestal bone may be misinterpreted as periodontal changes under certain circumstances. As has been pointed out by Miles[1] periodontal disease cannot be assessed in skeletal material without due attention being paid to the age of the individual since very severe disease in young age is a more serious problem than the same extent of damage seen in an elderly person. If some of the changes that have previously been described as chronic inflammatory periodontal disease can in fact be shown to be due to age changes per se, then we may have to modify our approach to our understanding of the disease process itself. If it can be shown for instance that occlusal attrition of the molar teeth in itself results in an apparent loss of bone at the alveolar margins, then a circular argument may develop in relating these two conditions as measured in skulls from ancient populations. For these reasons methods of aging skeletal material other than those dependant upon attrition and apparent alveolar bone loss should be investigated. This paper reviews the limitations of the classical methods of aging skeletal material and reports on current advances in the development of techniques which provide more objective data.

Not only is age at death of paramount importance to the archaeological investigator but on many occasions estimates of time elapsed since death will be of considerable interest. This is perhaps the most difficult area of investigation but there has been evidence of progress in this field based largely upon changes in organic content of bones as time elapses.

Occlusal attrition

Scholarly contributions to this area of knowledge have been made in this city by Brothwell[2] who developed a simplified method for age grouping based on patterns of dentine islands on the occlusal surfaces of molar teeth. This method was expanded and refined by Miles in his presentation to this Section in 1962[3]. His method was then, and still is, probably the most used technique for estimation of age in skeletal material and has been used in a number of recent studies[4,5]. The method, to some extent gets over the problem of estimation of rate of wear of the teeth by using the juveniles in a sample as a control for the sample as a whole. The rate of wear in the molars of young individuals, who can be aged by other means such as the stages of development of the teeth, is estimated and this rate of wear is then applied to the molar teeth in the adult members of the same population. The assumption has to be made that diets remain similar throughout life and that attrition rates similarly may be extrapolated into later years. In spite of these limitations there is at present no better way of estimating the age at death of elderly skulls without destroying some of the material.

Approximal attrition of teeth

Although quantitative age studies in skeletal material have to the present time relied upon occlusal attrition studies, it has long been recognized that considerable attrition may take place approximally. In a study carried out on Romano-British material from Poundbury[6], it was shown that approximal attrition can be of three types. The first is where the normally convex surface of the tooth has been reduced in dimension but in a convex wear pattern. Another is where the approximal surface has been worn to a flat facet and the third is where concave approximal attrition has resulted, converting the normally convex approximal surface to a concavity. The study has shown that 'concave' attrition is more commonly seen mesially whereas the convex or flat type of attrition is seen more commonly distally. Although these types of approximal attrition have been quantified, their relationship to the age of the individual has yet to be determined. The mechanism of wear appears to be similar to that employed in the grinding of a telescope mirror where two flat blanks of glass are rubbed against each other with a suitable abrasive. The stationary blank becomes convex in character whereas the revolving blank becomes concave and is used as the telescope mirror. It is suggested that similar

Paper read to Section of Odontology, 25 February 1991

0141-0768/92/
020097-05/$02.00/0
© 1992
The Royal
Society of
Medicine

differentials of movement between adjacent teeth may result in these varying patterns of approximal wear.

Periodontal disease and alveolar crestal bone loss

In many studies of chronic infective periodontal disease in ancient skull material it has been assumed that in normal health the distance between the cervical margin of the molar teeth and the alveolar crest should not be more than about 3 mm. This measurement may increase in older skeletal material and it has been assumed to be an indication of resorption of the alveolar crest as a consequence of chronic infective periodontal disease[7,8]. This is based on the finding by Manson[9], that horizontal alveolar crestal bone loss may occur to some extent throughout life, resulting in exposure of the roots of the teeth as epithelial migration occurs at the junction of soft tissue and the tooth. This would be a reasonable assumption if it could be shown that the teeth themselves remain static in the alveolar process but it was suggested by Murphy[10] that teeth may continue to erupt beyond their normal position of adult occlusion. In a situation where there may be relative movement of both bone and tooth, an objective method of measurement from a suitable fixed baseline is needed. Picton[11], drew attention to the fact that attrition may be occurring on the occlusal surfaces of the teeth, and if the teeth continued to erupt in response to this wear then measurements from the neck of the tooth to the alveolar bone would not be a simple measure of chronic infective periodontal disease throughout the life of the individual. This suggestion proved difficult to verify until it was shown[12] that there was strong evidence that the upper border of the inferior alveolar canal was static throughout life. This work was based on standardized radiographs produced longitudinally throughout the period of growth of an individual and also on the finding that implanted materials close to the inferior alveolar canal remained static in their position over an extended period of years. Using this information it was possible to show that in a mixed population of skulls there was no apparent loss of alveolar crestal bone as age progressed and indeed the molar teeth continued to erupt at the rate at which occlusal attrition was occurring in the specimens. Subsequently, Newman and Levers[13], using radiographs of Anglo-Saxon skulls, measured from the fixed line of the IAC to the apex of the molar teeth, to the alveolar crestal bone, to the cervical margin and the occlusal surfaces of the teeth. They were able to show that in their Anglo-Saxon population continuing eruption of the teeth away from the fixed line of the IAC occurred throughout life and more or less exactly compensated for wear of the occlusal surfaces due to attrition. Surprisingly, they showed that there was very little bone loss, suggesting that chronic infective periodontal disease was of minor significance. We have applied their methods to a large series of Romano-British skulls aged using the traditional methods of occlusal attrition, and have shown that a similar situation apparently obtains in a large collection of this nature[14].

Inaccuracies in age determination could either mask or accentuate the disease process at any particular

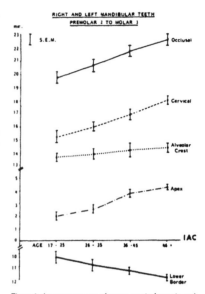

Figure 1. As age progresses, the apex, cervical margin and occlusal surfaces of the teeth move away from the fixed line of the inferior alveolar canal (IAC). The alveolar crest remains static

The material exhumed from the crypt of Christ Church, Spitalfields has provided another large sample of particular interest since the age at death was accurately known from coffin plates and parish registers and also the amount of occlusal attrition of the molars was negligible. It is of considerable interest to repeat these studies on such a sample in order to inquire whether continuing eruption occurs in populations that do not have excessive occlusal attrition. Using standardized radiographs of the mandible measurements were made from the upper border of the inferior alveolar canal to the apices of the teeth, to the alveolar crest, to the cervical margin and to the occlusal surface of the molars. The results (Figure 1) indicate that the teeth are continuing to erupt at about the same rate as in the Romano-British material, even though there was no occlusal wear of the molar teeth[15]. It appears, therefore, that even in populations where little or no occlusal attrition takes place, there is evidence that the molar teeth at least continue to erupt throughout life. There is no comparable evidence from the maxilla, since a fixed point in the maxilla has yet to be determined, but it may be assumed that the maxillary teeth are continuing to erupt in a similar manner. From these data it has been calculated that even in a population such as the 18th century Londoners, where no attrition took place, the molar teeth continued to erupt to an extent of up to 7 mm in the maxilla and the mandible throughout life. This strongly suggests that if the normal freeway space of about 2 mm is maintained then the facial height of these individuals must have increased by about this amount over their life time.

about 0.7 mm over a 40-year period but this increase was not statistically significant. It appears therefore that there is little evidence of alveolar crest bone loss occurring over this time span and there is in fact a non-significant tendency for bone to be added slightly to the alveolar crest. It seems likely therefore that chronic infective periodontal disease was not a major problem in the Spitalfields sample, although in many of the skulls examined there was vertical bone loss due to localized infection around some of the teeth. It is conceivable that the continuing eruption of teeth throughout life in the Spitalfields sample resulted in some deposition of bone at the alveolar crest, and this might compensate for loss of bone due to chronic infective periodontal disease. There is experimental evidence in support of this hypothesis. Anneroth and Erikson[16] showed that bone deposition could be stimulated by continuing eruption of the teeth; and certainly remodelling of alveolar bone is known to be associated with masticatory function resulting in stress applied to the bone[17].

Localized periodontal bone loss around individual teeth would not be statistically evident in a study of this nature so that the data must be interpreted with caution. There is evidence, however, from other sources[18] that the present concepts of variability in susceptibility to chronic periodontitis apply to this population. A new method of assessment of periodontal disease has been developed by Kerr[19] and this is based on changes in architecture and texture of the interdental septae. It would be interesting to apply this method to the Spitalfields material.

It would appear that studies of this type should encourage us to view with some caution previous investigations which indicate high degrees of periodontal bone loss in archaeological specimens. Approximal wear can be considerable in material of this nature and this is commonly thought to be compensated for by mesial drifting of the molar teeth. Since this would change their relationship to the sloping or curved nature of the upper border of the inferior alveolar canal, this factor also has to be taken into consideration when considering apparent continuing eruption of the molars.

Time since death

In forensic practice the time since death is one of the most difficult parameters to determine even when death occurred relatively recently. In archaeological material only vague guesses can be made. Studies[20] using chemical analysis on bones suggested that rough estimates could be made as to the age of skeletal material but there is as yet no accurate method of determination. It was shown[21] that teeth which are known to be of considerable archaeological age may have been infested by fungal hyphae producing channelling in the dentine. Archaeological specimens have been recovered in which only the enamel shell crowns of the teeth have remained and the dentine has been completely removed. This presumably is only explicable on the grounds of collagenase activity of soil organisms removing the collagen base of the dentine and leaving the enamel intact (Figure 2). As yet, no quantification of age since death can be determined from this material since it is in extremely limited supply. In more modern material, time since death may be determined with some degree of accuracy from a study of the degree of woven bone formation in sockets from which teeth are known to have been extracted at a particular time. This phenomenon is only of use where previous dental records are available and therefore is more of forensic importance than archaeological.

We have recently studied bone of known time since death in a number of cases using infrared spectroscopy. This results in a complicated spectrum largely related to the organic component of the bone. Although difficult to quantify, it is interesting to note that the absorption peaks are similar in the three specimens shown in Figure 3, although the extent of absorption varies. The upper line is from modern forensic material, the middle line is from 18th century bone exhumed from the Spitalfields exhumation and the lower line is from known Romano-British material from the 5th century AD. It is interesting to note that the absorption of the various peaks is quite different in these specimens and further work is in progress to determine whether this method might be useful in determining approximate age since death.

Age at death

In those cases where some destruction of tooth material is allowable, the technique of Gustafson[22], which was developed for aging in forensic specimens, may also be applied to archaeological material. In its original form Gustafson used vertical bucco-lingual sections through the teeth and from these estimated the degree of occlusal attrition, the amount of secondary dentine formation, the positioning of the epithelium of attachment, the amount of secondary cementum at the apex, any apical resorption and most importantly, the extent of apical translucency developing in the apical dentine. He awarded points to each of these factors comparing the total with previously produced data from teeth of known age from which a regression line relating these features to age had been produced.

In forensic practice it is now more usual to use one of these factors, namely the extent of apical translucency,

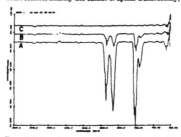

Figure 3. Infra-red absorption lines from modern (A), 19th century (B) and Romano-British (C) bones. The patterns are similar but the extent of absorption varies

Figure 2. The enamel shell is left intact following digestion of crown and root dentine by soil organisms

in order to age the dead from the teeth[23] and it has been shown by subsequent workers[24-26] that in experienced hands ageing may be accurate to within 5-7 years either way of the correct age at death. What is not clear is the extent to which this method may be applied to archaeological material which has lain buried for varying lengths of time.

We have recently applied the method to skeletal material from 18th century Londoners exhumed from the crypt of Christchurch, Spitalfields. This exhumation has provided material of unique interest since in more than 300 of the bodies the time of burial is known from coffin breastplates and contemporary parish records and also the identity and age at death is known in this same number of individuals. This has allowed validity of methods of age determination at death and also time since death to be compared with contemporary records. At this stage the Gustafson technique has been applied to a relatively small number of individuals (Figure 4). This particular specimen was investigated blindly using such a technique and an age of 72 years was predicted from the data. Reference to previous parish records indicated that the age of this individual was 78 years, suggesting that the method may be accurate to within about 5 years of death if applied to archaeological material of this nature.

It has been pointed out by Vasiliadis et al.[27] that apical translucency is not a two dimensional phenomenon but apparently usually forms a butterfly type of distribution when seen in transverse sections of the apices of the teeth. It is important in investigations of this nature therefore to ensure that sections through the teeth are always taken in a particular dimension, preferably bucco-lingually. Using either serial sections or transverse sections along the length of the root a three dimensional image of the degree of translucency may therefore be achieved and this can now be computerized using a plotting device. In this way the volume of translucency may be compared with the age of the individual.

Figure 5. Scanning electron micrograph of sclerotic (A) and non-sclerotic (B) apical dentine. Note the sharp boundary

Scanning electron microscopy of transverse sections through the roots has indicated that there is a very clear delineating line between obliterated and non-obliterated dentinal tubules (Figure 5) and further studies using these high resolution techniques are currently in progress. However useful these methods may prove to be, they are still dependant upon a phenomenon which is poorly understood and which may or may not be directly related to the age of the individual. For this reason the discovery by Masters and Bada[28] has formed the basis for a completely new approach to determinations of age at death.

Their preliminary work carried out on freshly extracted teeth demonstrated a relationship between the ratio of D and L enantiomers of aspartic acid residues in collagen and the time since incorporation of the collagen into the structure of the dentine. The method is based upon the assumption that when amino acids are built into the structure of the collagen during dentine formation the enzymes responsible for the transport of amino acids can only deal with left handed enantiomers. Once the collagen is laid down these enantiomers begin to racemize and change into D enantiomers as time progresses. The rate of racemization is accurately time dependent although other factors such as temperature and the presence of certain trace elements may be important. If the amino acids can be extracted from the dentine and the ratio of L to D enantiomers determined, this should form the basis for an accurate determination of age of the specimen and will of course be dependant upon the age of the individual at which that particular tooth developed. It should be noted that the technique is dependant upon the fact that once collagen has been incorporated and mineralized into adult dentine, it cannot be replaced by new L enantiomers of aspartic acid and for this reason dentine and a few other tissues of the body are unique in providing useful material for age determination using this method. We have collaborated with the Department of Chemistry in University College Cardiff and have measured the ratios of L to D enantiomers of aspartic acid in a series of freshly extracted premolars from modern teeth using high performance liquid chromatography[29]. This has provided a regression line related to the age of these individuals. The line is highly reproducible although for reasons not yet understood, is not linear but follows a shallow curve. Using these data similar premolars from the Spitalfields exhumation and of age unknown to the investigators at the time of the

Figure 4. Ground section of a tooth from Spitalfields

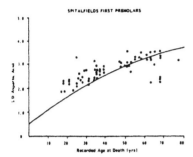

Figure 6. Ratio of D/L aspartic acid residues plotted against known age of exhumed teeth from 18th century burial ground

that of modern teeth but is shifted from the control regression line resulting in inaccuracies of aging in this ancient material. There were discrepancies from the expected regression line of the known ages of the Spitalfields teeth (Figure 6) and in most cases more racemization has occurred than would be expected.

Our conclusion is that at the present time this potentially extremely useful method is providing an accuracy that is no greater than that produced by other standard techniques for aging archaeological, as distinct from fresh material. In more recent studies, we have demonstrated that the shift from the expected regression line appears to occur within a few months of death and further experiments to study this phenomenon are in progress. It is possible that collagenase producing soil organisms are capable of splitting the collagen within dentine, thereby producing fragments of aspartic acid residues which complicate the racemization data. It is hoped that studies now in progress will enable us to correctly interpret age data from archaeological teeth.

In conclusion, a number of techniques have been described which have originated from an interest in forensic investigations but which may provide useful approaches to the quantitative study of archaeological bones and teeth. They have not yet extended our practical abilities much further than the classical methods which have been previously reported to this Society but it is hoped that further studies may reveal more useful data which can be applied to these currently insoluble problems of age at death and time since death.

References

1 Miles AEW. An early Christian chapel and burial ground on the Isle of Ensay, Outer Hebrides, Scotland with a study of the skeletal remains. *BAR Series* 1989:212
2 Brothwell DR. *Digging up bone*. London: British Museum (Natural History), 1965:165
3 Miles AEW. Assessment of the ages of a population of Anglo-Saxons from their dentitions. *Proc R Soc Med* 1962;55:881-6
4 Helm S, Prydso V. Assessment of age-at-death from mandibular molar attrition in medieval Danes. *Scand J Dent Res* 1979;87:79-90
5 Kieser JA, Preston CB, Evans WG. Skeletal age at death: an evaluation of the Miles method of ageing. *J Archaeol Sci* 1983;10:9-12
6 Whittaker DK, Ryan S, Weeks K, Murphy WM. Patterns of approximal wear in cheek teeth of a Romano-British

7 Latcham NL, Powell RN, Jago JD, Seymour GJ, Aitken JF. A radiographic study of chronic periodontitis in 15 year old Queensland children. *J Clin Periodontol* 1983;10:37-45
8 Gjermo P, Bellini H-T, Pereira Santos V, Martins JG, Ferracyoli JR. Prevalence of bone loss in a group of Brazilian teenagers assessed on bite-wing radiographs. *J Clin Periodontol* 1984;11:104-13
9 Manson JD. Bone morphology and bone loss in periodontal disease. *J Clin Periodontol* 1976;3:14-22
10 Murphy TR. Compensatory mechanisms in facial height adjustment to functional tooth attrition. *Aust Dent J* 1959;4:312-23
11 Picton DCA. Calculus, wear and alveolar bone loss in the jaws of sixth-century Jutes. *Dent Practnr* 1957; 7:301-3
12 Darling AI, Levers BGH. The pattern of eruption of some human teeth. *Arch Oral Biol* 1975;20:89-96
13 Newman HN, Levers BGH. Tooth eruption and function in an early Anglo-Saxon population. *J R Soc Med* 1979;72:341-50
14 Whittaker DK, Molleson T, Daniel AT, Williams JT, Rose P, Restighini R. Quantitative assessment of tooth wear, alveolar crest height and continuing eruption in a Romano-British population. *Arch Oral Biol* 1985; 30:493-501
15 Whittaker DK, Griffiths D, Robson A, Roger-Davies P, Thomas G, Molleson T. Continuing eruption and alveolar crest height in an eighteenth century population from Spitalfields, East London. *Arch Oral Biol* 1990; 35:81-5
16 Anneroth G, Ericsson SG. An experimental histological study of monkey teeth without antagonists. *Odontol Rev* 1967;18:345-59
17 Chamay A, Tschantz P. Mechanical influences in bone remodelling. Experimental research on Wolff's law. *J Biomech* 1972;5:173-80
18 Kingsmill V. Chronic periodontitis in an eighteenth century population. *Br Dent J* 1991;170:118-20
19 Kerr NW. A method of assessing periodontal status in archaeological derived skeletal material. *J Palaeopath* 1988;2:67-81
20 Knight BH. Methods of dating skeletal remains. *Hum Biol* 1969;41:322-7
21 Poole DF, Tratman EK. Post-mortem changes in human teeth from late upper palaeolithic/mesolithic occupants of English limestone cave. *Arch Oral Biol* 1976; 23:1115-20
22 Gustafson G. *Forensic odontology*. London: Staples Press, 1966:123
23 Bang G, Ramm E. Determination of age in humans from root dentine transparency. *Acta Odontol Scand* 1970; 28:3-35
24 Johanson G. Age determination from human teeth. *Odontol Rev* 1971;21:40-126
25 Nkhumeleni FS, Raubenheimer EJ, Monteith BD. Gustafson's method for age determination revised. *J Forensic Odontostom* 1989;7:13-16
26 Solheim T, Sundnes PK. Dental age estimation of Norwegian adults - a comparison of different methods. *Forensic Sci Int* 1980;16:7-17
27 Vasiliadis I, Darling AI, Levers BG. The histology of sclerotic human root dentine. *Arch Oral Biol* 1983; 28:693-700
28 Masters PM, Bada JL. Amino acid racemisation dating of bone and shell. In: Carter GF, ed. *Archaeological Chemistry II, Advances in Chemistry Series 171*. Washington DC: American Chemical Society, 1978: 117-38
29 Gillard RD, Pollard AM, Sutton PA, Whittaker DK. An improved method for age at death determination from the measurement of D-aspartic acid in dental collagen. *Archaeom* 1990;32:61-70

INTERNATIONAL JOURNAL OF ANTHROPOLOGY   Vol. 11 - N. 1 (1-9) - 1996

N. Telmon

*Registrar, Forensic Medicine
Department
Rangueil University Hospital
F-31054 Toulouse Cedex, France*

D. Rougé

*Lecturer, Faculty of Medicine
P. Sabatier University, and
Atending Physician
Forensic Medicine Dept.
Rangueil University Hop.
F-31054 Toulouse Cedex, France*

J. F. Brugne

*Anthropology student, Forensic
Medicine Dept.
Rangueil University Hospital
F-31054 Toulouse Cedex, France*

J. Pujol

*Odontologist
3 rue Benjamin Constant
F-31400 Toulouse, France*

G. Larrouy

*Head of Department, Parasitology
Dept.
Purpan University Hospital*

L. Arbus

*Head of Department
Forensic Medicine Dept.
Rangueil University Hospital
F- 31054 Toulouse Cedex, France*

Key words: Physical anthropology,
age determination, auricular surface,
odontology, dental method.

Comparison of a Bone Criterion and a dental Criterion for estimation of age at death in the study of an Ancient Cemetery

Two methods, a visual method based on the appearance of the auricular surface of the ilium and a metric method based on two dental criteria, were used in conjunction for estimation of skeletal age at death in paleodemographic study of an ancient cemetery, and were found to be coherent. However, the paleodemographic profiles differed according to sex, indicating a sexual difference in the evolution of the sacroiliac joint.

Paleodemographic study of ancient cemeteries requires reliable indicators of sex and age. Study of the cemetery at St Bertrand de Comminges, in the Haute-Garonne department of southern France, which dates from the late middle ages (6 th and 7 th centuries) led us to pay particular attention to two methods of age estimation. One was a visual method developed by Lovejoy and based on the appearance of the auricular surface of the ilium (Lovejoy et al., 1985). The other was a metric method, Lamendin's method (Lamendin et al., 1990,1992), based on two dental criteria, periodontosis and root translucency. The burial ground contained sandstone sarcophagi inside the Christian basilica, where the skeletons were well preserved, and earth graves against the wall of the basilica. The results obtained by these two methods in study of this cemetery show the importance and interest of these criteria in paleodemography, as they frequently are found during archaeological excavations (Meindl et al., 1989).

Osteological study of skeletons from St Bertrand de Comminges
A . General Study

Forty-five adult skeletons were studied, whose sex could be determined and in which at least two criteria for age estimation were available. The bone elements selected for sex determination and age estimation were examined by the same observer, each individual criterion separately, to exclude the possibility of bias due to overall estimation of the sex and age of the skeleton.

Sex determination was based on sexual differences of the pelvis. According to availability, the following criteria were used : the pubic criteria of Phenice (1969), the shape of the large sciatic notch, the cotylo-sciatic index of Sauter and Privat (1979), Kelley's acetabulo-sciatic index (1979) the ischio-pubic index of Schultz (1948) and Ferembach's criteria (1979).

Age was estimated by four methods :

-three osteoscopic methods based on observation of the pubis according to Suchey-Brooks (1979, 1986), the extremity of the fourth right rib according to Iscan (1984, 1986), and the auricular surface of the ilium by Lovejoy's method,

- and a dental method based on Lamendin's two metric criteria.

The frequency with which these four criteria were present in this series is given in table 1.

TABLE 1 - Frequency of the four age criteria

	n	%
auricular surface	39	86.7
single-root tooth	25	55.6
Pubis	21	46.7
IVth rib	18	40.0

The posterior part of the pelvis was the best preserved element, followed by the teeth, which were found in over half of cases, whereas the two other components (pubis and rib) had survived in less than half the skeletons.

The auricular surface and a dental element were frequently found in association (25 skeletons) (Table 2) and so could be used to assess the coherence of the two methods.

TABLE 2 - Frequency of association of the four age criteria

	auricular surface	single-root tooth	pubis
single-root tooth	55.5 %		
Pubis	44.4 %	22.2 %	
IVth rib	35.6 %	22.2 %	33.3 %

B. Description of Lovejoy's and Lamendin's methods

The method described by Lovejoy in 1985 is based on changes in the sacroiliac joint and assesses five main criteria : transversal organisation, granulations, retroauricular activity, apical activity and porosity. The appearance of the auricular surface of the ilium is classified in 8 phases. Each phase corresponds to a 5 year age range. The estimations do not overlap. This method excludes subjects aged under 20 years, whose age can be estimated by study of the ossification of the epiphysis of the iliac crest (Mc Kern et al., 1957) (Owing, 1981).

Lamendin's method estimates age by means of two parameters : periodontosis and root translucency measured on single-root teeth : the upper or lower incisives and canines and the lower premolar teeh. The values of the height of periodontosis and transparent dentin increase with ge. If they are expressed as a percentage of root height, age at death can be estimated by the following equation :

$$age \ (years) = 0.18 \ x \ P + 0.42 \ x \ T + 25.53$$

where P = (height of periodontosis x 100) / total root height and T= (height of transparent dentin x 100)/total root height.

This method has two main limits. Firstly, the minimum age that can be estimated by this method is 25.53 years, since young subjects, in principle, have neither periodontosis nor transparent dentin. In such cases, the estimated age can be narrowed down by examining the apical closure of the wisdom teeth if these are available (Guérin, 1971). Periodontal disease, by increasing the P factor, leads to overaging but this is limited by the coefficient of 0.18 given to P. Also, periodontal disease is quite easily detected. No sexual difference has been described in the evolution of these age markers.

C. Results

Estimated ages at death obtained using these two methods in the 25 skeletons are given in table 3. The age estimated from the auricular surface of the ilium corresponds to the age ranges proposed by Lovejoy. With Lamendin's dental method, all single-root teeth available for a given skeleton were examined and the result was expressed as an average estimation and as an age range corresponding to the extremes of age evaluated. A total of 121 teeth were examined, an average of 4.8 (± 3.4) teeth for each subject.

TABLE 3 - Résults of age estimation

N°	Sex	AURICULAR SURFACE		LAMENDIN		
		Phase	Age	number of teeth	mean	Age
2239	M	1	20 - 24	4	25.5	25.5
2243	F	4	35 - 39	5	45.8	42.6 - 49.7
2248	M	3	30 - 34	3	36.8	36.1 - 37.3
2253	F	1	20 - 24	2	28.5	28.3 - 28.7
2256	M	1	20 - 24	11	27.9	27.2 - 28.5
2257	F	2	25 - 29	1	32.9 *	32.9
2258	F	4	35 - 39	9	33.3	31.2 - 35.9
2259	M	3	30 - 34	5	38.1	36.2 - 39.5
2276	F	6	45 - 49	2	51.4	50.5 - 52.2
2280	F	2	25 - 29	6	31.6	28.7 - 34.6
2293	M	6	45 - 49	3	47.2	45.9 - 48.2
2346	M	5	40 - 44	3	38.9	35.3 - 42.4
2374	F	3	30 - 34	2	34.5	33.5 - 35.4
2391	M	5	40 - 44	9	49.7	45.3 - 53.1
2396	M	2	25 - 29	1	30.3 *	30.3
2399	M	2	25 - 29	4	28.1	27.6 - 28.7
2421	F	1	20 - 24	6	25.5	25.5
2440	F	1	20 - 24	2	25.8	25.5 - 26
2441	M	4	35 - 39	2	35.9	35.8 - 36
2458	F	6	45 - 49	3	46.9	44.8 - 50.4
2464	F	4	35 - 39	3	36.9	36.2 - 38.1
2291	F	3	30 - 34	5	28.6	27.9 - 29.2
2245	F	1	20 - 24	12	25.5	25.5
2261	M	1	20 - 24	6	25.5	25.5
2265	M	3	30 - 34	12	35.4	34.4 - 36.3

* only one tooth examined

General paleodemographic study of this cemetery showed that it contained a population of young adults (estimated mean age 32.3 years ± 8.6 by the auricular surface method and 34.7 years ± 8.1 by the dental method) with a small majority of females (12 males and 13 females, a sex ratio of 0.92).

II - Comparison of the two methods
A. General comparison

The age estimations obtained by the two methods were coherent as the age groups were superimposed or overlapped in 10 of 25 cases (40%) and estimated ages differed by less than 5 years in 15 of 25 cases (60%) (Fig 1); thus, differences in estimated age ranges were less than 5 years in 100 % of cases.

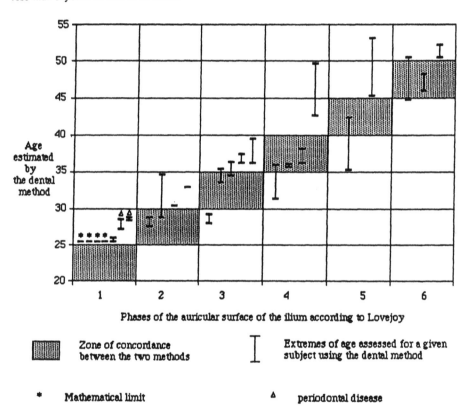

Fig.1. Estimated age obtained using the two methods

In 6 cases, the difference between the estimated ages obtained by the two methods can be explained and leads to reservations as to the estimates made with one of the two methods.

In this population of young adults, the mathematical limit of Lamendin's dental method must be taken into account. It concerns 4 subjects, n° 2239,2421,2245, 2261, shown by an asterisk * in Fig. 1. These are young subjects without periodontosis or transparent dentin, and their minimum age assessable by Lamendin's dental method is 25.53 years. However, their auricular surfaces were estimated as phase I (20-24 years). In three cases n° 2239, 2245 and 2261, age could be confirmed by other criteria, in particular the pubis, which was phase I by

Suchey's method, or the sternal extremity of the ribs, which was phase I or II by Iscan's method. The teeth were poorly preserved and dentition tables could not be used for age estimation.

In two cases, n° 2253 and 2256, overaging by the dental method was due to evident periodontal disease in young subjects without transparent dentin, who had 2 or 3 mm of periodontosis. These two subjects are indicated in Fig. 1 by a D .

In one case, n°2265, age estimation by the bone method (30-34 years) and the dental method (34,4 -36,3 years) was concordant, although the sacrovertebral angle was misshapen with hemo-lumbarization of S1 so that the sacral articular surface of the ilium werre examined, the other having been partially destroyed during the archeological excavations. It would appear that such deformities of the sacrovertebral angle, relatively frequent in paleopathology and causing excessive wear of the superior intervertebral disk, do not affect the evolution of the sacroiliac joint. (Guérin, 1971; Masset, 1971) Fig 2.

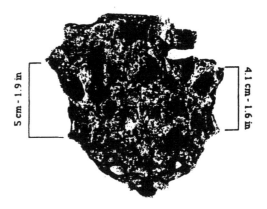

Fig.2 Posterior view of sacrum (n°2265)

B. Paleodemographic comparison

If the age distribution of the population of the cemetery is studied in ten-year spans (Fig. 3), thus eliminating the estimation problems due to the lower limits of the methods, a tendency to overaging is observed with the dental method, particularly in the 30-40 age group. However, this difference in population distribution is not statistically significant (chi-square test x^2 = 1.67, p = 0.64).

340

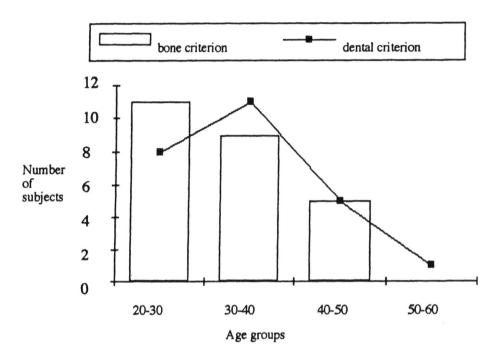

Fig. 3 Distribution by estimated age group

Figures 4 and 5 show the age distribution of the population of the cemetery according to sex. Interestingly, the over-represetation of the 30-40 age group by the dental method only affects males. Althought in theory these two methods of age estimation are not sex-dependent, it should be borne in mind that the sacroiliac joint is part of the pelvis, the bony element of the skeleton in which sexual differences are most marked.

Pathology of the sacroiliac joint related to pregnancy and childbirth: postpartum sacro-iliac joint disease or sacroiliac (Touzet, 1990),could account for aging differences of the auricular surface beteween males and females, with aging occuirng relatively earlier in females. If sex is not taken into account when using Lovejoy's method, this may lead to systematic error, frequant in paleodemography when sex differences are not considered in the evolution of the age marker (Washburn, 1948).

341

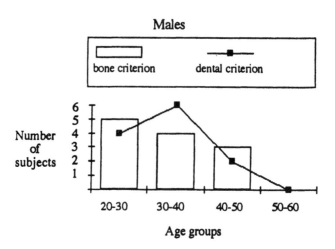

Fig. 4 - Distribution by estimated are group (Males).

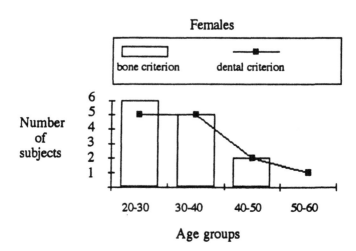

Fig. 5 Distribution by estimated age group (Females)

These two methods, which were developed from modern samples, do not explore the same criteria of aging but they do give relatively concordant results in the estimation of age of historic skeletons. Because the teeth and the auricular surface have both often survived, they are of value in paleodemographic study of a cemetery. The dental criterion appears less affected by sexual differences than the auricular surface, which seems to age relatively earlier in women than in men. Errors of estimation related to the method (5 of 45 cases) are relatively infrequent and can often be explained and therefore corrected by confronting the results of the two methods. Sex-related differences in age distribution according to the method used in paleodemographic study of an ancient cemetery should be taken into account in order to avoid systematic error.

References

Dastugue J., Gervais V., Paléopathologie du squelette, Boubée, Paris, 1992.

Ferembach D., Schiwidetzky I, Stloukal M., Recommandations pour déterminer l'âge et le sexe sur le squelette, Bull. et Mem. Soc. Anthrop. de Paris, 1979; 6: 7-45.

Biggerstaffl R.H., Forensic dentistry and the human dentition in individual age estimations. Dental Clinics of North America - January 1977, 21.

Guerin P., Diagnostic et traitement d'une atteinte sacro-iliaque en dehors de la spondylarthrite ankylosante. Editions techniques. Encycl; Med. Chir (Paris-France) Appareil locomoteur 14370L10 2-1971, 4p.

Iscan M.Y., Loth S.R, Determination of Age Estimation from the Rib by Phase Analysis: White Males, Journal of Forensic Sciences, 1984; 29: 1094-1104.

Iscan M.Y., Loth S.R, Wright R.K., Age Estimation from the Sternal Rib in White Females: A Test of the Phase Method., Journal of Forensic Sciences, 1986; 31: 990-999.

Katz D., Suchey J.M, Age Determination of the Male Os Pubis. Am.J.Phys.Anthropol. 1986; 69: 427-435.

Kelley M.A., Sex determination with fragmented skeletal remains. Journal of Forensic Sciences, 1979; 24: 154 - 158.

Lamendin H., Humbert J.F., Tavernier J.C., Brunel G., Nossintchouk R., Estimation d'âge par une méthode à 2 critères dentaires. Le Chirurgien Dentiste de France , 15 Novembre 1990; 539: 93-96.

Lamendin H., Baccino E., Humbert J.F., Tavernier J.C., Nossintchouk R., Zerilli A., A simple technique for age estimation in adult corpses: the two criteria dental method., Journal of Forensic Sciences, 1992; 37: 1373-1379.

Lovejoy C.O., Meindl R S., Pryzbeck TR., Mensforth RP. Chronological Metamorphosis of the Auricular Surface of the Ilium: A New Method for the Determination of Adult Skeletal Age of Death; Am. J. Phys. Anthropol. 1985; 68: 15-28.

Mc Kern T.W., Stewart T.D, Skeletal Age Changes in young American males Headquarters, quatermaster research and development command, technical report, 1957.

Masset C., Erreurs systématiques dans la détermination de l'âge par les sutures crâniennes. Bull. et Mem. de la Soc. d'Anthr. de Paris, 12, 85-105,1971.

Meindl R.S., Lovejoy C.O, Age changes in the pelvis: implications for paleodemography in Age Markers in the Human Skeleton, Iscan M.Y, 1989.

Owing P.A., Epiphyseal union of anterior crest and medial clavicle in a modern multiracial sample of males and females. University of California State University Fullerton, 1981.

Phenice W., A newly developed visual method of sexing the os pubis. Am.J.Phys.Anthropol. 1969; 30: 297-302.

Sauter M.R., Privat F., Sur un nouveau procédé métrique de détermination sexuelle du bassin osseux. Bull. Soc. Suisse Anthrop. Ethnol. 1955; 31: 60 -84.

Suchey J.M., Problems in the Aging of Females Using Os Pubis, Am.J. Phys.Anthropol. 1979; 51: 467-470.

Touzet P., Rigault P., Malformations congénitales du rachis. Editions techniques. Encycl. Med. Chir (Paris-France) Appareil locomoteur 15880 A 10 12-1990, 26p.

Washburn S.L., Sex differences in the pubic bone. Am.J.Phys.Anthropol. 1948; 6: 199 - 207.

Received August 10, 1994   Accepted October 5, 1995

Acknowledgments

Fry, C. L. (1999). "Anthropological Theories of Age and Aging." In V. L. Bengston and K. W. Schaie (Eds.). *Handbook of Theories of Aging.* NY: Springer, 271–286. Copyright © Springer Publishing Company, Inc., New York 10012. Used by permission.

Holmes, E. R., and L. D. Holmes. (1995). "The Anthropological Perspective." In *Other Cultures, Elder Years.* Second Edition, Thousand Oaks: Sage, 1–17. Copyright © 1995 by Sage Publications, Inc. Reprinted by permission of Sage Publications, Inc.

D'Andrade, R. (2001). "A cognitivist's view of the units debate in cultural anthropology." *Cross-Cultural Research* 35(2): 242–257. Reprinted with the permission of Sage Publications, Inc.

Cohen, L. (1994). "Old age: cultural and critical perspectives." *Annual Review of Anthropology* 23: 137–158. Reprinted with the permission of Annual Reviews, Inc.

Warren, C. A. B. (1998). "Aging and identity in premodern times." *Research on Aging* 20(1): 11–35. Copyright © 1998 by Sage Publications, Inc. Reprinted by permission of Sage Publications, Inc.

Robertson, A. F. (1994) "Evolving, aging, and making culture." *Ethnos* 59(1–2): 57–69. Reprinted with the permission of Folkens Museum-Etnografiska.

Troll, L.E . (1999). "Questions for future studies: social relationships in old age." *International Journal of Aging and Human development* 48(4): 347–51. Reprinted with the permission of Baywood Publishing Co., Inc.

Kaufman, S. R. (1994). "The social construction of frailty: an anthropological perspective." *Journal of Aging Studies* 8:45–58. Reprinted with the permission of Elsevier Science.

Cool, L. and J. McCabe (2001). "The 'Scheming Hag' and the "Dear Old Thing': The anthropology of aging women." *www.stpt.usf.edu/~jsokolov/cool.htm,* 1–15. Reprinted with the permission of University of South Florida St. Petersburg.

Smith, H. L. (2001). "'Age': A problem concept for women." *Journal of Women's History* 12(4): 77–86. Reprinted with the permission of Indiana University Press.

Hawkes, K, J. F. O'Connell, N. G. Jones, et al. (1998) "Grandmothering, menopause, and the evolution of human life histories." *Proceedings of the National Academy of Sciences of the United States of America* 95(3): 1336–9. Copyright © (1998) National Academy of Sciences, U.S.A.

Goldstein, M. C. and C. M. Beall (1981). "Modernization and aging in the Third and Fourth World: views from the rural hinterland in Nepal." *Human Organization* 40(1): 48–55. Reprinted with the permission of Society for Applied Anthropology.

Dossa, P. A. (1994). "Critical anthropology and life stories: case study of elderly Ismaili Canadians." *Journal of Cross-Cultural Gerontology* 9(3): 335–354. Reprinted with permission from Kluwer Academic Publishers.

Yamaori, T. (1997). "Buddha and okina ("aged man"): the expression of dying and maturity. "Aging: Asian concepts and experiences past and present." *Wien*: 79–96. Reprinted with the permission of Verlag der Oesterreichischen Akademie der Wissenschaften.

Merriam, S. B., M. Mohamad (2000). "How cultural values shape learning in older adulthood: the case of Malaysia." *Adult Education Quarterly* 51(1): 45–63. Copyright © 2000 by Sage Publications, Inc.. Reprinted by permission of Sage Publications, Inc.

Sung, Kyu-taik (2000). "Respect for elders: Myths and realities in East Asia." *Journal of Aging and Identity* 5(4): 197–205. Reprinted with the permission of Kluwer Academic-Plenum Publishers.

Van der Geest, S. (2001). "'No Strength': sex and old age in a rural town in Ghana." *Social Science and Medicine* 53(10: 1383–96. Reprinted with the permission of Pergamon.

Baldridge, D. (2001). "Indian Elders: Family Traditions in Crisis." *American Behavioral Scientist* 44(9): 1515–1527. Copyright © 2001 by Sage Publications, Inc. Reprinted by permission of Sage Publications Inc.

Hazan, H. (1990). "The construction of personhood among the aged: a comparative study of aging in Israel and England." *www.stpt.usf.edu/~jsokolov/hazan.htm*, 1–15. Reprinted with the permission of Tel Aviv University.

Levy, D. J. (1999). "Venerable ancestors: strategies of ageing in the Chinese novel—The story of the stone." *Lancet* 354(suppl): SIII13–SIII16. Reprinted with the permission of the Lancet Ltd.

Rasmussen, S. J. (2000). "Between several worlds: images of youth and age in Tuareg popular performances." *Anthropological Quarterly* 73(3): 133–144. Reprinted with the permission of the Anthropological Quarterly.

Luborsky, M. R. (1995). "Questioning the allure of aging and health for

Medical Anthropology." *Medical Anthropology Quarterly* 9(2): 277–81. Reprinted with the permission of American Anthropological Association.

Pollit, P. A. (1996). "Dementia in old age: an anthropological perspective." *Psychological Medicine* 26(5): 1061–74. Reprinted with the permission of Cambridge University Press.

Dein, S. and S. Huline-Dickens (1997). "Cultural aspects of aging and psychopathology." *Aging and Mental Health* 1(2): 112–120. Reprinted with the permission of Carfax Publishing Limited.

Whittaker, D. (1992). "Quantitative studies on age changes in the teeth and surrounding structures in archaeological material: a review." *Journal of the Royal Society of Medicine* 85(2): 97–101. Reprinted with the permission of The Royal Society of Medicine.

Telmon, N. (1996). "Comparison of a bone criterion and a dental criterion for estimation of age at death in the study of an ancient cemetery." *International Journal of Anthropology* 11(1): 1–9. Reprinted with the permission of Angelo Pontecorboli Editore.